THE CAMBRIDGE EDITION OF THE LETTERS AND WORKS OF D. H. LAWRENCE

THE BOY IN THE BUSH

D. H. LAWRENCE
AND
M. L. SKINNER

EDITED BY
PAUL EGGERT

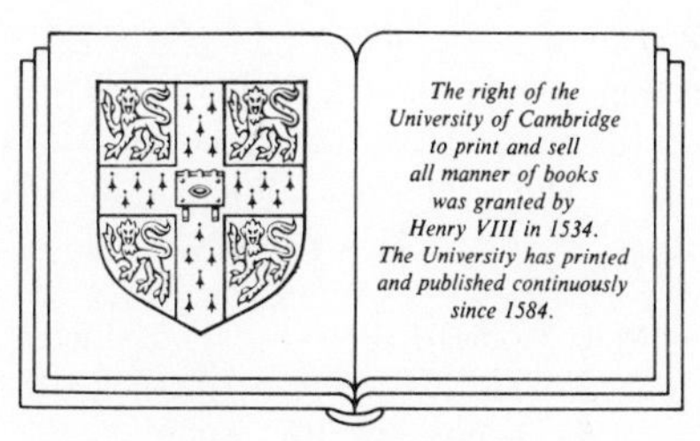

CAMBRIDGE UNIVERSITY PRESS

CAMBRIDGE
NEW YORK PORT CHESTER
MELBOURNE SYDNEY

Published by the Press Syndicate of the University of Cambridge
The Pitt Building, Trumpington Street, Cambridge CB2 1RP
40 West 20th Street, New York, NY 10011, USA
10 Stamford Road, Oakleigh, Melbourne 3166, Australia

Printed in Great Britain at the University Press, Cambridge

British Library cataloguing in publication data

Lawrence, D. H. (David Herbert), *1885–1930*
The boy in the bush.—(The Cambridge edition of the letters and works of D. H. Lawrence).
I. Title II. Skinner, M. L. (Mollie L.) III. Eggert, Paul
823′.912 [F]

Library of Congress cataloguing in publication data

Lawrence, D. H. (David Herbert), 1885–1930.
The boy in the bush / D. H. Lawrence and M. L. Skinner.
p. cm. – (The Cambridge edition of the letters and works of D. H. Lawrence)
ISBN 0-521-30704-X
I. Skinner, M. L. (Mary Louisa), 1876–1955. II. Eggert, Paul. III. Title
IV. Series: Lawrence, D. H. (David Herbert), 1885–1930. Works. 1979.
PR6023.A93B6 1990
823′.912–dc20 89-7348 CIP

ISBN 0 521 30704 X hard covers
ISBN 0 521 37677 7 paperback

CE

CONTENTS

General editors' preface *page* vii

Acknowledgements ix

Chronology xi

Cue-titles xvi

Introduction xix
  Perth and Mollie Skinner xxi
  The writing of *The Boy in the Bush* xxv
  The revision of the typescripts xxxiii
  Publication xxxviii
  Mollie Skinner's and Lawrence's relative responsibilities for the novel xlv
  Reception liii
  Text lvii

THE BOY IN THE BUSH 1

Appendixes
  I Chronology of *The Boy in the Bush* 349
  II Jack Grant's family tree 353
  III Maps 357
  IV A historical background to the setting of *The Boy in the Bush* 363
  V Note on Miss M. L. Skinner 371
  VI Preface to *Black Swans* 375

Explanatory notes 381

Textual apparatus 435

A note on pounds, shillings and pence 498

GENERAL EDITORS' PREFACE

D. H. Lawrence is one of the great writers of the twentieth century – yet the texts of his writings, whether published during his lifetime or since, are, for the most part, textually corrupt. The extent of the corruption is remarkable; it can derive from every stage of composition and publication. We know from study of his MSS that Lawrence was a careful writer, though not rigidly consistent in matters of minor convention. We know also that he revised at every possible stage. Yet he rarely if ever compared one stage with the previous one, and overlooked the errors of typists or copyists. He was forced to accept, as most authors are, the often stringent house-styling of his printers, which overrode his punctuation and even his sentence-structure and paragraphing. He sometimes overlooked plausible printing errors. More important, as a professional author living by his pen, he had to accept, with more or less good will, stringent editing by a publisher's reader in his early days, and at all times the results of his publishers' timidity. So the fear of Grundyish disapproval, or actual legal action, led to bowdlerisation or censorship from the very beginning of his career. Threats of libel suits produced other changes. Sometimes a publisher made more changes than he admitted to Lawrence. On a number of occasions in dealing with American and British publishers Lawrence produced texts for both which were not identical. Then there were extraordinary lapses like the occasion when a compositor turned over two pages of MS at once, and the result happened to make sense. This whole story can be reconstructed from the introductions to the volumes in this edition; cumulatively they will form a history of Lawrence's writing career.

The Cambridge edition aims to provide texts which are as close as can now be determined to those he would have wished to see printed. They have been established by a rigorous collation of extant manuscripts and typescripts, proofs and early printed versions; they restore the words, sentences, even whole pages omitted or falsified by editors or compositors; they are freed from printing-house conventions which were imposed on Lawrence's style; and interference on the part of frightened publishers has been eliminated. Far from doing violence to the texts Lawrence would have wished to see published, editorial intervention is essential to recover them. Though we have to accept that some cannot now be recovered in their entirety because early states have not survived, we must be glad that so much evidence remains. Paradoxical as it may seem, the outcome of this recension will be texts which differ, often radically and certainly frequently, from those seen by the author himself.

Editors have adopted the principle that the most authoritative form of the text is to be followed, even if this leads sometimes to a 'spoken' or a 'manuscript' rather than a 'printed' style. We have not wanted to strip off one house-styling in order to impose another. Editorial discretion may be allowed in order to regularise Lawrence's sometimes wayward spelling and punctuation in accordance with his most frequent practice in a particular text. A detailed record of these and other decisions on textual matters, together with the evidence on which they are based, will be found in the textual apparatus which records variant readings in manuscripts, typescripts and proofs; and printed variants in forms of the text published in Lawrence's lifetime. We do not record posthumous corruptions, except where first publication was posthumous. Significant deleted MS readings may be found in the occasional explanatory note.

In each volume, the editor's introduction relates the contents to Lawrence's life and to his other writings; it gives the history of composition of the text in some detail, for its intrinsic interest, and because this history is essential to the statement of editorial principles followed. It provides an account of publication and reception which will be found to contain a good deal of hitherto unknown information. Where appropriate, appendixes make available extended draft manuscript readings of significance, or important material, sometimes unpublished, associated with a particular work.

Though Lawrence is a twentieth-century writer and in many respects remains our contemporary, the idiom of his day is not invariably intelligible now, especially to the many readers who are not native speakers of British English. His use of dialect is another difficulty, and further barriers to full understanding are created by now obscure literary, historical, political or other references and allusions. On these occasions explanatory notes are supplied by the editor; it is assumed that the reader has access to a good general dictionary and that the editor need not gloss words or expressions that may be found in it. Where Lawrence's letters are quoted in editorial matter, the reader should assume that his manuscript is alone the source of eccentricities of phrase or spelling. An edition of the letters is still in course of publication: for this reason only the date and recipient of a letter will be given if it has not so far been printed in the Cambridge edition.

ACKNOWLEDGEMENTS

An editor of *The Boy in the Bush* can hardly fail to be aware of the collaborative nature of his work, particularly when contemplating a list of contributors as long as the following. The traditional formula nevertheless expresses the limits of the collaboration: though many generous people have given freely of their special knowledge or skills, what errors remain are my responsibility.

The members of the Editorial Board – James Boulton, Michael Black, Lindeth Vasey and John Worthen – all provided, as the project proceeded, a steady supply of shrewd commentary; and Lindeth Vasey's unrelenting devil's advocacy, in matters large and (textually) minute, was of immeasurable benefit to the edition. And Peter Looker has earned special acknowledgement: the Explanatory notes and the appendix on the historical background provided unusually difficult problems which his intensive and prolonged assistance reduced to manageable proportions.

It is a pleasure to acknowledge also the advice and assistance of other people, in particular that of Patricia Barton, Kerry Jackson, Nancy Lutton and Bruce Steele, but also of Bain Atwood, Henry Cruise, Darren Tofts and John Whiter, all of whom gave generously of their time.

For their particular kindnesses it is right I thank, in Western Australia, the relatives of Mollie Skinner (Nancy Dear, Maxwell and Melita Law and Dorothy Muir), and Lorna Barrett-Lennard, Mary Brazier, Barbara Broun, John Burt, James Hammond, Steven Howell, Catherine King, Joan Martin, Margaret Medcalf, Mary Durack Miller, Naomi Segal, Tom Stannage, Tony Templeman, Helen Topliss, Marjorie Young and the Department of Lands Administration. And, elsewhere: the late Barry Andrews, Shirley Andrews, John Barnes, Helen Baron, Gerald E. Bentley Jnr., John Blackwell, Sandra Burchill, Annabel Cooper, Ken Craven, Frank Crowley, Frank Davidson, Frances de Groen, Ellen Dunlap, David Ellis, David Farmer, Brian Finney, Pat Fox, Joanna Gibson, David Heald, Cathy Henderson, Michael Herbert, Harry Heseltine, Kim Knight, Gerald Lacy, the Laurence family, Rose Ann Sherar Lee, John Manchester, Wesley Milgate, the late Harry T. Moore, Arthur Nightall, Iona Opie, Gerald Pollinger, Christopher Pollnitz, Venessa Raison, Bill

Ramson, Charles Rossman, John Ruffles, Faith Sherman, the Shillingsburg family, Frank Singleton, Loes Slattery, Michael Squires, Brian Stevenson, Andrew Underwood, George Wallace, the late Judah Waten, Norah Wilkins and Jake Zeitlin.

I would like to thank the inter-library loans staff at the Australian Defence Force Academy Library; the Borchardt Library, La Trobe University; and the Library, University of Kent at Canterbury. The following libraries and institutions also helped by making unpublished materials available to me: the Bancroft Library, University of California at Berkeley (the manuscript of *The Boy in the Bush*); the J. S. Battye Library of West Australian History (Mollie Skinner's manuscripts, typescripts and letters); the Butler Library, Columbia University (typescript of *The Boy in the Bush*); the Harry Ransom Humanities Research Center, University of Texas at Austin (typescript and marked copy of the novel, and manuscript of 'Preface to *Black Swans*'); the Salisbury House Library, Iowa State Education Association (manuscript of the last chapter); and the University of Illinois (Secker Letter-Books). Also to Frederick Jeffrey (xerox of the manuscript of 'Note on Miss M. L. Skinner'). And I wish to record my gratitude for research grants from: the Australian Academy of the Humanities; the Australian Research Grants Scheme; the Faculty of Military Studies, University of New South Wales, Duntroon; La Trobe University (for a research grant, and study leave in 1983); University College, University of New South Wales, Australian Defence Force Academy (for grants, and study leave in 1988); and also, for appointing me Visiting Scholar in 1988, the University of Kent at Canterbury where this edition was completed.

Acknowledgements of a more personal kind are difficult to specify, but I would like to record my indebtedness to my immediate family, colleagues and friends for their toleration and support over the last seven or eight years.

December 1988 P. E.

CHRONOLOGY

Entries refer to D. H. Lawrence and his works unless otherwise specified.

19 September 1876	Birth of Mary Louisa ('Mollie') Skinner (hereafter MLS) in Perth, Western Australia
11 September 1885	Born in Eastwood, Nottinghamshire
September 1898–July 1901	Pupil at Nottingham High School
1902–1908	Pupil teacher; student at University College, Nottingham
7 December 1907	First publication: 'A Prelude', in *Nottinghamshire Guardian*
October 1908	Appointed as teacher at Davidson Road School, Croydon
November 1909	Publishes five poems in *English Review*
3 December 1910	Engagement to Louie Burrows; broken off on 4 February 1912
9 December 1910	Death of his mother, Lydia Lawrence
19 January 1911	*The White Peacock* published in New York (20 January in London)
19 November 1911	Ill with pneumonia; resigns his teaching post on 28 February 1912
March 1912	Meets Frieda Weekley; they elope to Germany on 3 May
23 May 1912	*The Trespasser*
September 1912–March 1913	At Gargnano, Lago di Garda, Italy
February 1913	*Love Poems and Others*
29 May 1913	*Sons and Lovers*
June–August 1913	In England
August 1913–June 1914	In Germany, Switzerland and Italy
1 April 1914	*The Widowing of Mrs. Holroyd* (New York)
13 July 1914	Marries Frieda Weekley in London
July 1914–December 1915	In London, Buckinghamshire and Sussex
26 November 1914	*The Prussian Officer and Other Stories*
30 September 1915	*The Rainbow*; suppressed by court order on 13 November
June 1916	*Twilight in Italy*
July 1916	*Amores*

15 October 1917	After twenty-one months' residence in Cornwall, ordered to leave by military authorities
October 1917–November 1919	In London, Berkshire and Derbyshire
26 November 1917	*Look! We Have Come Through!*
1918	*Letters of a V.A.D.* by 'R. E. Leake' [MLS]
October 1918	*New Poems*
November 1919–February 1922	In Italy, then Capri and Sicily
20 November 1919	*Bay*
May 1920	*Touch and Go*
9 November 1920	Private publication of *Women in Love* (New York)
25 November 1920	*The Lost Girl*
10 May 1921	*Psychoanalysis and the Unconscious* (New York)
12 December 1921	*Sea and Sardinia* (New York)
26 February 1922	Sails from Naples for Ceylon, meets Annie Jenkins on voyage
13 March–24 April 1922	In Ceylon; works on Verga translations, writes 'Elephant' and 'Apostrophe to a Buddhist Monk'
14 April 1922	*Aaron's Rod* (New York)
4 May 1922	Arrives Fremantle, Western Australia
4–6 May 1922	In Perth
5, 6 May 1922	Meets William Siebenhaar (again on 18 May)
by 6–18 May 1922	At MLS's convalescent home, 'Leithdale', Darlington
13 May 1922	Visits Perth
18 May 1922	Sails for Sydney
?27–8 May 1922	Sydney
29 May–10 August 1922	At Thirroul, New South Wales; writes *Kangaroo*, *c.* 3 June–15 July
September 1922–March 1923	In New Mexico
23 October 1922	*Fantasia of the Unconscious* (New York)
24 October 1922	*England, My England* (New York)
March 1923	*The Ladybird*, *The Fox*, *The Captain's Doll*
23 March–27 April 1923	In Mexico City
29 April–9 July 1923	In Chapala, Mexico
2 July 1923	Receives MLS's letter: 'The House of Ellis' finished and despatched to Robert Mountsier
19 July 1923	Arrives New York City
20 July–21 August 1923	In New Jersey

18 August 1923	Interviewed by *New York Evening Post*
19 August 1923	Receives 'The House of Ellis'
22–30 August 1923	To Los Angeles
27 August 1923	*Studies in Classic American Literature* (New York)
30 August–25 September 1923	In Los Angeles and Santa Monica
September 1923	*Kangaroo*
2 September 1923	Writes to MLS: 'If you like I will take it ['The House of Ellis'] and re-cast it'; begins work on it
24 September 1923	Sends notebooks 1–3 (208 pages) to Thomas Seltzer for typing; first uses novel's published title, *The Boy in the Bush*
25 September–17 October 1923	To Guadalajara, Mexico; probably continues writing en route
9 October 1923	*Birds, Beasts and Flowers* (New York)
17 October–16 November 1923	In Guadalajara
18 October 1923	Writes to Seltzer: '*The Boy* might be popular – unless the ending is a bit startling'; inquires whether notebooks 1–3 received; asks again on *c.* 20 and 28 October
1 November 1923	Writes to MLS: 'I have been busy over your novel, as I travelled' and warns of a 'rather daring development' for her hero Jack
14 November 1923	Finishes *The Boy in the Bush*
15 November 1923	Posts notebooks 4–5 (372 pages) to Curtis Brown, London, for typing
16 November 1923	To England via Mexico City and Veracruz
14 December 1923	In London; writes 'On Coming Home' by 24th
?18 December 1923	Receives typescript (3 copies) of notebooks 4–5 from Curtis Brown (by 24 December at latest)
?19 December 1923	Dorothy Brett and others agree to go with Lawrences to New Mexico
24 December 1923	'Still waiting' for the first part of typescript from Seltzer
by 9 January 1924	Receives *Laughing Horse*, and writes 'Dear Old Horse: A London Letter'
c. 9 January 1924	Writes new last chapter for *The Boy in the Bush*
by 13 January 1924	Receives one copy of the typescript of notebooks 1–3 from Seltzer
c. 13–22 January 1924	Revises 'complete typescript'; has Seltzer

	section re-typed and new last chapter typed; sends copies to Curtis Brown, John Middleton Murry and MLS
23 January–26 February 1924	In Paris and Germany
26 February–5 March 1924	In London
by 3 March 1924	Seltzer receives typescript (TSIa) from Curtis Brown
4 March 1924	Martin Secker receives typescript (TSIb) from Middleton Murry
5 March 1924	Sails for New York
8 March 1924	Seltzer announces *The Boy in the Bush* in *Publishers' Weekly*
11–18 March 1924	In New York
18 March 1924	Writes to Secker: 'Seltzer hasn't sent it to print yet'
by 21 March–19 October 1924	In New Mexico
3 April 1924	Secker sends duplicate proofs together with MLS's 'alterations and suggestions' for correction; proposes 1 September for publication
4 April 1924	Has received MLS's requests for alterations and forwards to Secker and Seltzer
by 18 April 1924	Has received Secker proofs in duplicate; informs Seltzer of Secker's proposed publication date
2 May 1924	Returns corrected proofs to Secker, duplicates to Seltzer with Brett–Lawrence dust-jacket design
10 May 1924	Seltzer announces novel as 'forthcoming'
by 23 May 1924	Secker receives corrected proofs
c. June–December 1924	MLS in London
28 August 1924	*The Boy in the Bush* by D. H. Lawrence and M. L. Skinner published in England by Secker; two impressions printed by publication date
September 1924	Secker, third impression
10 September 1924	Death of his father, John Arthur Lawrence
30 September 1924	*The Boy in the Bush* published in New York by Seltzer
October 1924	Secker, fourth impression
c. October 1924	MLS marks passages by Lawrence in Edward Garnett's copy
20 October 1924–September 1925	In Mexico and New Mexico
22 November 1924	Posts 'Note on Miss M. L. Skinner' for Else Jaffe
?24 December 1924	Writes 'Preface to *Black Swans*'

1925	*Jack im Buschland*, trans. Else Jaffe-Richthofen (Stuttgart), with abridged 'Note on Miss M. L. Skinner' in German
14 May 1925	*St. Mawr together with The Princess*
July 1925	*Black Swans* by MLS
September 1925–June 1928	In England and, mainly, in Italy
7 December 1925	*Reflections on the Death of a Porcupine* (Philadelphia)
12 December 1925	Returns MLS's story, 'The Hand', to *Adelphi* having 'edited' it
21 January 1926	*The Plumed Serpent*
25 March 1926	*David*
June 1927	*Mornings in Mexico*
24 May 1928	*The Woman Who Rode Away and Other Stories*
June 1928–March 1930	In Switzerland and, principally, in France
July 1928	*Lady Chatterley's Lover* privately published (Florence)
August 1928	Secker cheap edition of *The Boy in the Bush*
September 1928	*Collected Poems*
3 December 1928	Returns MLS's novel, 'Eve in the Land of Nod', partly revised
July 1929	Exhibition of paintings in London raided by police; *Pansies* (manuscript earlier seized in the mail)
September 1929	*The Escaped Cock* (Paris)
2 March 1930	Dies at Vence, Alpes Maritimes, France
25 May 1955	Death of MLS at York, Western Australia
January 1968	'Preface to *Black Swans*' published in *Phoenix II*

CUE-TITLES

A. Manuscript locations

Battye	J. S. Battye Library of West Australian History, Perth
ColU	Columbia University
IEduc	Iowa State Education Association
UCB	University of California at Berkeley
UIll	University of Illinois at Urbana-Champaign
UT	University of Texas at Austin

B. Printed works

(The place of publication, here and throughout, is London unless otherwise stated.)

AND	W. S. Ramson, ed. *The Australian National Dictionary: A Dictionary of Australianisms on Historical Principles*. Melbourne: Oxford University Press, 1988.
Fifth Sparrow	Mollie Skinner. *The Fifth Sparrow*. Sydney: Sydney University Press, 1972.
'Fifth Sparrow' Draft	Typescript (1955), signed by Mollie Skinner (Battye).
Letters, ii.	George J. Zytaruk and James T. Boulton, eds. *The Letters of D. H. Lawrence*. Volume II. Cambridge: Cambridge University Press, 1982.
Letters, iv.	Warren Roberts, James T. Boulton and Elizabeth Mansfield, eds. *The Letters of D. H. Lawrence*. Volume IV. Cambridge: Cambridge University Press, 1987.
Letters, v.	James T. Boulton and Lindeth Vasey, eds. *The Letters of D. H. Lawrence*. Volume V. Cambridge: Cambridge University Press, 1989.
OED	Sir James A. Murray and others, eds. *A New English Dictionary on Historical Principles*. 10

volumes. Oxford University Press, 1884–1928. Supplementary volumes 1–4, 1972–86.

Phoenix II	Warren Roberts and Harry T. Moore, eds. *Phoenix II: Uncollected, Unpublished and Other Prose Works by D. H. Lawrence*. Heinemann, 1968.
Roberts	Warren Roberts. *A Bibliography of D. H. Lawrence*. 2nd edn. Cambridge: Cambridge University Press, 1982.
Year-Book	Malcolm A. C. Fraser, ed. *Western Australian Year-Book (Thirteenth Edition) For 1902–1904*. Perth: Government Printer, 1906.

INTRODUCTION

INTRODUCTION

Perth and Mollie Skinner

The genesis of *The Boy in the Bush* may be traced to D. H. Lawrence's visit to Perth, Western Australia in May 1922. He had spent the winter of 1921–2 at Taormina, Sicily. Although it had been a productive period for Lawrence, he was itching to be on the move.[1] The Italy he remembered from before the war had gone, and his pre-war dissatisfaction with modern Western society was hardening into a revulsion. He was tempted by an offer from an American admirer of his writing, Mabel Dodge Sterne (later Luhan), to come to live in Taos, New Mexico where a pre-white culture still subsisted: 'a tribe of 600 free Indians . . . sun-worshippers, rain-makers, and unspoiled' (iv. 123). But he was also sceptical of the USA: 'What is the good . . . of going to [America]', he wrote to Earl Brewster, 'where everything is just *unlearnt* and confused to the utmost' (iv. 171). What then of the East, where Brewster, an American painter friend, was studying Buddhism in Ceylon? At least Ceylon would provide a breathing space before Lawrence tackled America; it would satisfy his need to experiment. But disappointment came almost at once. Stifled by the heat, disillusioned almost immediately with Buddhism, and able to do little but translation,[2] Lawrence left Ceylon for Australia after a stay of only six weeks. Despite his keen sensitivity to spirit of place, the country seems to have offered little stimulation to his imagination.[3] Australia, on the other hand, was to prove a very different case.

Lawrence's decision to go to Australia was initially little more than an accident. Travelling to Ceylon on the *R. M. S. Osterley* which left Naples on 26 February 1922, Lawrence had become friendly with some Australi-

[1] DHL had written 'The Captain's Doll', 'The Ladybird' and his introduction to Maurice Magnus's *Memoirs of the Foreign Legion*, had expanded 'The Fox' to a novella and had revised the *England, My England* stories and *Fantasia of the Unconscious*. See *Letters*, iv. 25–159. (Subsequent references to *Letters*, ii., iv. and v. are given in the text with volume and page number.)

[2] He completed his translation (New York, 1923) of Giovanni Verga's novel, *Mastro-don Gesualdo*, and began Verga's *Novelle Rusticane* (published as *Little Novels of Sicily*, New York, 1925).

[3] Producing only the poems 'Elephant' and 'Apostrophe to a Buddhist Monk'.

ans, among them Annie Louisa Jenkins. Only a fortnight after arriving in Ceylon Lawrence wrote to her, responding to a suggestion she had evidently made on the voyage that he and Frieda should visit Western Australia.[4] They left Ceylon on 24 April 1922, arriving in Fremantle near Perth on 4 May; Annie Jenkins arranged accommodation for them at 'Leithdale', a guesthouse mainly for convalescents, situated in the hills, sixteen miles from Perth. Installed there by 6 May (iv. 236), they were to stay until sailing for Sydney on the 18th. To his surprise Lawrence discovered that one of the nurses at 'Leithdale', Mary Louisa ('Mollie') Skinner, was a writer.

Mollie Skinner had been born in Perth in 1876 but was taken to England at the age of two when her father, a British army officer, was recalled. Not until 1900 did she return to her birthplace. Having completed nursing training before leaving England, she gave herself to demanding years of nursing in country districts in Western Australia. She returned to England for a year to study midwifery and, when World War I broke out, volunteered for medical service in India and Burma – experience which, with the setting transferred to the Western Front, provided the subject matter for her first (epistolary) novel: *Letters of a V.A.D.* Because it sold poorly her writing continued to be a part-time activity, tolerated but not encouraged by family and friends.[5]

Lawrence's interest gave her new hope. He read her novel and then approached her with an idea for another one, prompted by his nocturnal excursions into the nearby bush. Mollie Skinner recounted the conversation in her autobiography, *The Fifth Sparrow*:

[4] *Letters*, iv. 218. Annie Louisa Jenkins (1873–1945; née Burt, a prominent Western Australian family) was a keen musician and frequent traveller to England; widowed in 1917. See ibid., p. 217 n. 2 and her memoir in Edward Nehls, *D. H. Lawrence: A Composite Biography*, 3 vol. (Madison, 1957–9), ii. 115–17.

[5] Before she died at York on 25 May 1955, having spent the rest of her life in Western Australia (hereafter WA), she had published six volumes of fiction – *Letters of a V.A.D.* [Voluntary Aid Detachment nurse], pseud. 'R. E. Leake' (1918), *Black Swans* (1925), *Men Are We* (Perth, 1927), *Tucker Sees India* (1937), *W.X. – Corporal Smith* (Perth, 1941), *Where Skies Are Blue* (Perth, 1946) – as well as short stories, without having achieved much fame.

In her papers at Battye are several unpublished novels (including 'Eve in the Land of Nod': see p. li below); radio scripts on pioneer women of WA, nursing, etc.; an unfinished biography of John Forrest (1847–1918; explorer and first Premier of WA; see also Explanatory note on 226:18); and play scripts. Information about Mollie Skinner (hereafter MLS) is derived from her *Fifth Sparrow*; 'Fifth Sparrow' Draft, 1955, of which *Fifth Sparrow* is an edited abridgement; 'D. H. Lawrence and *The Boy in the Bush*', *Meanjin*, ix (1950), 260–3; 'D. H. Lawrence and M. L. Skinner', typescript, n.d. (Battye; published, in part, in *Australian Observer*, 24 July 1948, p. 110); 'D. H. Lawrence and *The Boy in the Bush*', unpublished typescript, n.d. (Battye); letter to Guy Howarth, *Southerly*, xiii (1952), 233–5.

'It frightens me – all the bush out beyond stretching away over these hills frightens me, as if dark gods possessed the place. My very soul shakes with terror when I wander out there in the moonlight . . . Why don't you write about this strange country?' he said. 'About how it was met by the first settlers? . . . A Mr Siebenhaur brought me his poems[6] to read, and – much more interesting – a little year book, a kind of diary of events from the foundation of the colony till it became a State. You should write of it. I would if I stayed. The settlers – men and women with their children arriving here, dumped on the sand with the surf behind them, a few merchants, a few soldiers, a few packing cases into which they crept for shelter after chucking out the pianos; building camp ovens, burning their hands, looking for fresh water, longing for achievement, hungry for land, their cattle starving, their women scolding, homesick but full of courage, courage carrying them forward. What kept them here?' (pp. 112–13)

The 'little year book' was the *Western Australian Year-Book For 1902–1904* (Perth, 1906), edited by Malcolm A. C. Fraser, Government Statistician and Registrar-General of Western Australia. Siebenhaar's name appears on the title-page; his function is given as 'sub-editor'.[7]

The historical account which makes up the first section of the *Year-Book* is rather dry and matter-of-fact; indeed much of it is simply a year-by-year calendar of events. But Lawrence was as much a creative reader as he was a writer and he may have responded to the pride in colonial achievement never far from the surface in the *Year-Book*. He had long entertained the idea of establishing a colony of his own. Sometimes a whimsical inclination, sometimes a firm utopian intention, Lawrence's 'Rananim' (as he had called the idea ever since 1914; ii. 252 and n. 3) would have faced many practical difficulties – to which Lawrence's 'odd streaks of prudence', as Bertrand Russell put it,[8] could not have failed to alert him. But the hope persisted in the face of them. The *Year-Book*'s determinedly optimistic account of the dispiriting obstacles which the West Australian settlers had doggedly overcome would, accordingly, have had a personal meaning for Lawrence.

[6] Dutch-born William Siebenhaar (1863–1937) – translator, reviewer, poet and anarcho-leftist sympathiser – rose to Deputy Registrar-General of WA (suspended – temporarily – in 1916). By 1922 his principal publications were *Dorothea: A Lyrical Romance in Verse.* (Perth, *c.* 1910) and *Sentinel Sonnets* with Alfred Chandler (Melbourne, 1919). DHL met Siebenhaar in Perth on 5, 6 and 18 May 1922 (Nehls, *Composite Biography*, iii. 104–5, 108). See also N. Segal, *Who and What Was Siebenhaar: A Note on the Life and Persecution of a Western Australian Anarchist* (Studies in Western Australian History Occasional Papers No. 1, Perth, 1988).

[7] MLS stated in 'DHL and *The Boy in the Bush*', p. 2 (Battye) that 'It seemed that he had got hold of Malcolm Fraser's Western Australian Year Book, 1902', which she was to use (see p. xlvi and footnote 104). For its documentation of the colony's (by 1902) success, this volume is the *magnum opus* of the early *Year-Book*s.

[8] *The Autobiography of Bertrand Russell* (1968), ii. 21.

However, with further evidence of Mollie Skinner's literary strengths and shortcomings before him – he had now read 'with despair' her typescript of an early version of a novel, *Black Swans*, set in the early days of the colony[9] – he somewhat changed the nature of his advice:

> 'You are going to write that book about the settlers, eh?' he kept urging. 'Put *Black Swans* aside. Take the new book from the time when you became aware of what went on in this empty country. Know your characters, strip them to the bone. Away with fancy and sentiment, be spiteful.'[10]

Lawrence's suggestion that Mollie Skinner treat not of the first settlers but of the difficulties encountered by a later generation of colonists – 'the time when you became aware of what went on in this empty country' – was probably calculated to make her *record* Western Australian life rather than elevate it. He had good reason to offer this counsel: 'You can splash down what you see', Mollie Skinner reports Lawrence as observing. 'What you don't know is that you can only do that . . . you can't dress with imagination. You have the power of seeing things and making them live, but not the power of flight from your subject.'[11] Evidently Lawrence was attempting to shepherd her away from the self-protective coyness and sentimentalising he had come across in *Letters of a V.A.D.* and away from what Edward Garnett would criticise as the 'soft and dithyrambic' in the manuscript of *Black Swans* which she gave him to read in 1924.[12]

Undoubtedly it was the tougher, more resilient side of Mollie Skinner's writing that Lawrence wished to encourage. In *Letters of a V.A.D.* for instance, when she withholds the emotional embroidery she can tell a story simply, effectively and even memorably.[13] She is at home with the flat ironies, the droll idiom and the shifts and contrivances produced in response to the exigencies of outback life; she is a gifted spinner of yarns. In any case, Lawrence's encouragement was to lead to his rewriting her novel (which she titled 'The House of Ellis') as *The Boy in the Bush*.[14]

This was to be his major literary occupation from September to November 1923 and in January 1924. He did not, as Mollie Skinner

[9] 'Preface to *Black Swans*' (Appendix VI, 377:14). [10] *Fifth Sparrow* 114.

[11] 'DHL and M. L. Skinner', p. 6 (Battye).

[12] From the detailed criticism (Battye) of *Black Swans* by Edward Garnett (1868–1937), reader for Jonathan Cape (see *The Letters of D. H. Lawrence*, ed. James T. Boulton, Cambridge, 1979, i. 297 n. 2); for DHL's reaction, see Appendix VI. On MLS's visit to London in the second half of 1924, see *Fifth Sparrow* 138–51.

[13] DHL must have been impressed by her description of 'counting-out' (p. 98): cf. *Kangaroo*, chap. XVI.

[14] DHL later wrote a preface for MLS's *Black Swans*, revised her story 'The Hand' and her novel 'Eve in the Land of Nod' (see below), and wrote a preface to Siebenhaar's translation of *Max Havelaar* which he also helped to get published (see Roberts B21).

believed, dash off the novel in a fortnight.[15] He devoted at least as much time to it as he did to *Kangaroo* or *The Lost Girl*.[16] As will be shown, a study of all the extant manuscript material, early printed editions and Mollie Skinner's contemporaneous writings leads inevitably to one conclusion: that *The Boy in the Bush* merits the description, a 'Lawrence novel'.

The writing of *The Boy in the Bush*

After arriving in Sydney in late May 1922 Lawrence and Frieda secured accommodation at Thirroul, south of Sydney, where Lawrence wrote his first Australian novel, *Kangaroo*, to be published in 1923. While registering with both fear and admiration the remote primeval nature of the bush, Lawrence reacted with distaste to the egalitarian ethic and unformed rawness (as he felt it to be) of social life.[17] Arriving in the USA in September 1922, he soon found himself entertaining a related response to *that* country: the natural glories were counter-balanced, he sensed, by a human emptiness and a lack of national direction.[18]

Travelling on to Mexico in mid-March 1923, however, he was relieved to find that there the 'great paleface overlay hasn't gone into the soil half an inch . . . And the peon still grins his Indian grin behind the Cross . . . He knows his gods.'[19] The first step towards *The Plumed Serpent* had been taken; indeed Lawrence started writing the first version (titled 'Quetzalcoatl') in early May. It was an ambitious project. Not only had he in mind to offer a diagnosis of the inner sickness of American and generally Western civilisation, but also to imagine a cure inspired by a lost religion set in a country to which he was a virtual stranger. Lawrence realised that he could hope to complete only a 'first rough draft' (iv. 454) of the novel before returning, as he then planned, to England. It was at this stage (2 July 1923) that Mollie Skinner's first letter to him arrived (iv. 466), telling him that she had finished her novel about the settlers and would be sending the typescript to him in New York. Lawrence promised to 'read it carefully, and see what publisher it had best be submitted to', adding: 'If there are a few suggestions to make, you won't mind, will you' (iv. 467).

15 'DHL and *The Boy in the Bush*', *Meanjin*, p. 261.

16 I.e. to the 1920 rewriting of *The Lost Girl*: see Cambridge edition, ed. John Worthen (1981), pp. xxv–xxviii. Apart from some concluding material, *Kangaroo* was written *c.* 3 June–15 July 1922 (*Letters*, iv. 251, 278).

17 *Letters*, iv. 241, 249, 250; and cf. *Kangaroo*, chap. II.

18 See 'Certain Americans and an Englishman', written October 1922 (*Phoenix II* 243).

19 'Au Revoir, U.S.A.', written April 1923 (*Phoenix: The Posthumous Papers of D. H. Lawrence*, ed. Edward D. McDonald, New York, 1936, p. 105).

Lawrence and Frieda left Mexico for New York a week later, but 'The House of Ellis' did not arrive till 19 August,[20] a day before Lawrence set off by himself for the West Coast, Frieda having sailed to England – in what amounted to a temporary separation. In reading Mollie Skinner's novel, the tantalising possibility that he had entertained in Australia – that it was a country large enough, in 'the North West particularly', to 'lose oneself away from the world' (iv. 245) – must have returned to him with a new force and relevance, given the issues he had been addressing in 'Quetzalcoatl'.

In revising *Studies in Classic American Literature* in November 1922, Lawrence had foreshadowed those concerns: 'Men are free when they belong to a living, organic, *believing* community, active in fulfilling some unfulfilled, perhaps unrealized purpose.'[21] In *Kangaroo*, in the character of Somers, Lawrence had explored the possibility of taking active part in political action that would define such a purpose. Worn down by the anxieties of English and Christian culture, democracy and, significantly, politics, Kate Burns, the heroine of 'Quetzalcoatl', is powerfully attracted to Don Ramón Carrasco's attempt to peel off the 'great paleface overlay' in order to restructure Mexican society along revitalised patriarchal lines. To him falls the task of articulating the so far 'unrealized purpose' so that the peons may share in it:

> [he had come] to many conclusions . . . that liberty is an illusion . . . Man is never at liberty to do anything except obey some dictate, some dictate from his own soul, or some dictate from without. The mass of men can never know the dictates of their own soul. It needs a greater man than the ordinary, a man more sensitive and more pure, to be able to listen to the unknown of his own innermost soul. The mass of people . . . hear nothing but the confused roaring of old ideas, old phrases, old injunctions, old habits.[22]

The seer's mantle also descends, gradually, on Jack Grant in *The Boy in the Bush* as he identifies the giver of the dictates as a personal god, nothing like the Christian god of his childhood. His clarity of purpose is achieved only by 'los[ing himself] away from the world': firmly rejecting the old ideas, injunctions and habits of, in his case, Perth society, and acting on that rejection by founding a community in the North-West.[23] By the end of the novel he is fast becoming a latter-day biblical Patriarch, enjoying (as does

[20] Posted by Robert Mountsier (DHL's US agent from mid-1920–February 1923) then in Taos (*Letters*, iv. 489, 477).

[21] 'The Spirit of Place' (vol. published 1923).

[22] Autograph manuscript, Roberts E313a, p. 154; UT.

[23] I.e. the n.w. of Australia: see Explanatory note on 7:29.

Don Ramón) 'the faithful complete attachment of one man . . . a life-and-death fidelity',[24] and entertaining unashamedly polygamous intentions.

Lawrence must have foreseen, at least in dim outline, how Mollie Skinner's novel would enable him to explore his current preoccupations.[25] This helps account for his willingness to take her novel over. On 2 September, a fortnight after having received the typescript, he wrote to her from Los Angeles:

> I have read 'The House of Ellis' carefully: such good stuff in it: but without unity or harmony. I'm afraid as it stands you'd never find a publisher. Yet I hate to think of it all wasted. I like the quality of so much of it. But you have no constructive power. – If you like I will take it and re-cast it, and make a book of it . . . If you give me a free hand, I'll see if I can't make a complete book out of it. If you'd rather your work remained untouched, I will show it to another publisher:[26] but I am afraid there isn't much chance. You have a real gift – there is real quality in these scenes. But without form, like the world before creation. (iv. 495–6)

The fact that Lawrence did not wait to receive her permission to rewrite the novel[27] suggests that he had glimpsed a significantly new direction and new emphases for the novel, and wanted to pursue them immediately.

Most of September Lawrence spent in Los Angeles working on the novel.[28] The pattern of his responses to American life of the previous year was being repeated: the initial attraction of the place ('It's sort of crazy-sensible. Just the moment: hardly as far ahead as *carpe diem*'; iv. 503) gives way to a need to escape to a more sensible clime where the

[24] Roberts E313a, p. 121.

[25] Cf. an interview DHL gave to the *New York Evening Post* (20 August 1923, p. 4) on the day (18 August) Frieda left for London. On the aftermath of an approaching cultural collapse, DHL was quoted: 'There has got to be a thread that carries through from our Western civilization . . . Christianity cannot do it again . . . I think it will hasten the crash . . . A few people make the destinies of the world . . . It is the few people of the world I care for, not the many . . . the people who are living forwards . . . [not the] people who are just sitting and eating their Sunday dinner in their cottages every week . . . They are the stomach of humanity.' Cf. 319:28–31 below.

[26] It is possible that Mountsier and DHL's American publisher, Thomas Seltzer, commented on it before DHL left New York.

[27] MLS's cable giving it ('DHL and *The Boy in the Bush*', *Meanjin*, p. 260) could not have arrived before the end of October: MLS received his letter of 2 September on 25 October (date stamped on the envelope by Darlington Post Office), and her cable would have been sent, as DHL requested, care of Seltzer and re-directed.

[28] He also wrote 'The Proper Study' and a review of *A Second Contemporary Verse Anthology* (*Phoenix*, ed. McDonald, pp. 719–23, 322–6), and began making alterations to an essay by Frederick Carter (*Letters*, iv. 497). Carter, a painter and etcher, was also a writer on astrology and the occult (iv. 365 n. 3).

'consciousness' was not 'pot-bound',[29] where one could regain contact with 'the natural springs of one's soul'. The letter of 24 September to Adele Seltzer, the wife of his American publisher Thomas Seltzer, in which Lawrence uses the last expression is the one in which he reports sending them 'the first part of the *Boy in the Bush*' (iv. 503) – his first use of the title.

He had finished writing out in longhand 'the first part' – notebooks 1 to 3, totalling 208 pages – of his manuscript. The whole manuscript (hereafter MS) consists of five notebooks totalling 580 pages and a separate last chapter on ten sheets of typing paper.[30] No pages from the 'badly typed' version which Mollie Skinner sent Lawrence[31] are interleaved with the manuscript; no trace of any version of 'The House of Ellis' has been found. The rate of composition (approximately 40,000 words in twenty-two days – an average of about 1,800 words per day) indicates that Lawrence did not find rewriting someone else's novel easier than writing his own. Lawrence often wrote quickly: the first 50,000 words of *The Lost Girl* were written in twenty-two days (an average of about 2,250 words per day); with *Kangaroo* he averaged 3,500 words per day.[32]

Lawrence set off for Mexico on 25 September 1923 with a Danish artist, Kai Götzsche whom he had met in Taos in 1922; they travelled by train down the west coast and then, partly by mule, over the mountains to Guadalajara, a city near Lake Chapala (where Lawrence and Frieda had been living earlier in the year), arriving on 17 October. According to Götzsche's account of the trip the heat was sometimes stifling; but, as they broke the trip on three occasions for a few days, Lawrence had the opportunity to work on *The Boy in the Bush* ('I have been busy over your novel, as I travelled', he wrote to Mollie Skinner a fortnight later).[33]

29 Review of *A Second Contemporary Verse Anthology* (*Phoenix*, ed. McDonald, p. 325).

30 Roberts E55a and b: the notebooks (with many pagination errors) are of USA manufacture and are located at UCB; the last chap. is at IEduc. On the front covers of notebooks 4 and 5 is an inscription in DHL's hand: 'To Curtis Brown 6 Henrietta St. London W.C.2.' (DHL's English agent), and Curtis Brown's sticker – he arranged for their typing. Notebook 4 begins mid-sentence, precisely where a new size and grade of paper is introduced in the typescripts (TSIa and b: 20.5×26.7 cm., no watermark, changes to 20.3×25.4 cm., W.M & A/BOND), and where the typed page-numbering ceases (p. 167). Thus it is certain that DHL sent Seltzer notebooks 1 to 3.

31 *Fifth Sparrow* 117.

32 See *The Lost Girl*, ed. Worthen, p. xxviii; information on *Kangaroo* from Bruce Steele, editor of forthcoming Cambridge edition. See also *Mr Noon*, ed. Lindeth Vasey (Cambridge, 1984), p. xxiv.

33 *Letters*, iv. 523. They stopped at Guaymas, 27 September–1 October, Mazatlán, 6–9 October and Tepic, 10–14 October (iv. 505–12). Götzsche gives no indication that DHL did any writing en route (Knud Merrild, *A Poet and Two Painters: A Memoir of D. H. Lawrence*, 1938, pp. 332–9).

As Lawrence had envisaged, Mexico did inspire hope and a qualified optimism in him – which he described in a letter to Adele Seltzer on 28 October: 'The USA and the world shut the flood-gates of my soul tight. And here they begin to open, and the life flows . . . our tough, dry, papier-mâché world recedes' (iv. 522). Perhaps the change gave Lawrence the confidence to rewrite fully the last section of 'The House of Ellis' in a way that would allow him to explore 'a whole new line of emotion',[34] however heterodox.[35]

As early as 18 October he had realised this might present difficulties for Thomas Seltzer ('*The Boy* might be popular – unless the ending is a bit startling'; iv. 517); by 1 November he felt the need to prepare Mollie Skinner for a shock:

> The only thing was to write it all out again, following your MS. [i.e. typescript] almost exactly, but giving a unity, a rhythm, and a little more psychic development than you had done. I have come now to Book IV.[36] The end will have to be different, a good deal different.
>
> Of course I don't know how you feel about this. I hope to hear from you soon. But I think, now, the novel will be a good one. I have a very high regard for it myself. – The title, I thought, might be *The Boy in the Bush*.[37] There have been so many 'Houses' in print . . .
>
> Your hero Jack is not quite so absolutely blameless an angel, according to me. You left the character psychologically at a standstill all the way: same boy at the beginning and the end. I have tried, taking your inner cue, to make a rather daring development, psychologically. You may disapprove. (iv. 523–4)

[34] 'The Future of the Novel', completed 1 February 1923, *Study of Thomas Hardy and Other Essays*, ed. Bruce Steele (Cambridge, 1985), p. 155.

[35] DHL made a list on the inside cover of a notebook (Roberts E55c, privately owned):

Surgeon Capt Reid –
    father of Jack's mother –
    Mrs Grant.
Mary "Stopford."
Aunt Matilda Watson
Mr Ellis – Jacob

(See E. W. Tedlock, *The Frieda Lawrence Collection of D. H. Lawrence Manuscripts: A Descriptive Bibliography*, Albuquerque, 1948, p. 134). 'Watson' and 'Jacob' appear in the post-Los Angeles section of MS, i.e. notebooks 4 and 5 (earlier the names are 'Hawkins' and 'Frank'). If DHL bought the E55c notebook while he was in Mexico City, 16–21 November 1923 (it has a 'Mexico D. F.' stationer's label), then he must have written the list to sort out the confusing family names while revising the typescripts in January 1924; if he got it in Guadalajara, then he could have used it while completing notebooks 4 and 5.

[36] I.e. not notebook 4 of MS, so probably a division in 'The House of Ellis'.

[37] The title had already been used for an Australian novel by Richard Rowe ('Peter Possum'), serialised in 1869 in *Good Words* under the pseudonym 'Edward Howe' and then published anonymously. An illustrated edition of 1885 was subtitled 'A Tale of Australian Life'. DHL could have heard the title in his youth, but there is no evidence.

Lawrence's wave of interest in Jack's 'development' must have held, because only a fortnight after writing the letter to Mollie Skinner he had completed the manuscript (iv. 532) apart from the last chapter. He had written and corrected 372 pages of autograph manuscript in notebooks 4 and 5 (about 84,000 words) in a little over seven weeks,[38] three of which were spent travelling. If it is assumed that he was able to utilise half of those three weeks for writing, then he can be seen to have maintained a higher average rate than in Los Angeles: roughly 2,150 words per day (if a quarter, then 2,500). Surer, evidently, of where the novel was going Lawrence increased his speed of composition by some twenty (to forty) per cent[39] in its last two-thirds – the section which Mollie Skinner was later to claim contained the bulk (on a line count, 86 per cent) of Lawrence's contribution.[40] As Lawrence was not to write the last chapter till after his arrival in England in mid-December (see below), the 'daring development' he refers to is not the plan for Hilda Blessington to join Jack in the North-West the following Christmas. Rather it is Jack's continuing to seek out Monica after having been saved by Mary when lost in the bush and, having married Monica and become a successful gold miner, his making his bigamous proposal to Mary.

Although Lawrence had sent off the first three notebooks to Seltzer for typing on 24 September, a month later he still had not heard whether Seltzer had received them. Having already inquired about them in letters to Seltzer of 18 and *c.* 20 October, Lawrence wrote again on 28 October – a letter which marks the beginning of a train of complications concerning the typescript: 'Have you got *The Boy in the Bush* MS. If the office is busy, have it typed by a hired typist. I will pay it. Very soon I'll send you another booklet of it. It's really good, and I want it out in the spring, before "Quetzalcoatl"' (iv. 523). In his next letter to Seltzer (3 November) Lawrence, still not having had a reply, tells the publisher that he will 'take all this remainder' with him to England and 'have it typed in London' (iv. 527). In the event, however, he posted notebooks 4 and 5 to his English agent, Curtis Brown, in London on 15 November, the day after he had completed the manuscript: 'I am sending you today the chief part of the MS. of a novel *The Boy in the Bush*. Seltzer has the first part: he is having it

38 The corrections are light throughout MS (see Explanatory note on 7:21), except for three pages in chap. XXIV (see notes on 317:17 and 38, 318:11 and 319:5).

39 If DHL did not work en route then his average was 2,950 words per day, and his increase about 65 per cent. While in Guadalajara he also contributed to and helped with the production of the poetry magazine, *Palms*, edited by Idella Purnell: see *Study of Thomas Hardy*, ed. Steele, pp. xlvi–xlvii, 159.

40 See below, p. xlvi.

typed and will send it to you. Please have this MS. typed so that it can be ready when I get to England: and have *two* carbon copies made' (iv. 533).

Lawrence left Guadalajara on 16 November and sailed from Veracruz for England, arriving in London on 14 December. Almost immediately he wrote to Seltzer: 'Shall see Curtis B. tomorrow and get MSS. – I hope he has them all safe: will write you' (iv. 543). Three days later, and having heard disquieting rumours about Seltzer's financial position (iv. 543), a further letter was necessary: 'Have you sent the MSS of *Boy in the Bush* and "Quetzalcoatl": neither is here . . . I feel something's the matter – what is it?' (iv. 544) Lawrence saw Curtis Brown the following day, the 18th (iv. 548); the typescript copies of the 'chief part' of MS (that is, of notebooks 4 and 5) were probably given to him then (or, if not, soon after), for in his next letter to Seltzer on the 24th, he wrote: 'I am still waiting for that MS of *Boy in the Bush*. I have all the typescript from Curtis Brown – am hung up for your part' (iv. 549). The fact that Lawrence was 'hung up for [Seltzer's] part' suggests that, preferring to start at the beginning, he did not immediately commence his checking of the long, second section of typescript. This was to mean a considerable delay and his having to put off for three weeks his plans for travelling to Paris (iv. 544). He did not get Seltzer's typescript until around 13 January.

As he waited, his dislike of England and Europe hardened, and new lines of thought began to develop – which soon had their effects on *The Boy in the Bush*. Images of entrapment, testifying to his depression, are sprinkled through his letters of December 1923 and in his essay 'On Coming Home' (which he had completed by 24 December).[41] Fortunately release soon came, and from an unexpected quarter: Willard Johnson sent him the Christmas 1923 number of the magazine he edited, *Laughing Horse*. It arrived by 9 January 1924.[42] Johnson reprinted the Navajo 'Song of the Horse' as recorded by Natalie Curtis in her recently republished work, *The Indians' Book*.[43] The commentary he included with the translation draws attention to the joyous neigh of the Navajos' mythical turquoise horse as it 'travels across the sky' daily from east to west.

Lawrence's reply, which he sent on the 9th (iv. 555) and which was published in the next number of *Laughing Horse*[44] as 'Dear Old Horse: A

[41] *Letters*, iv. 549; printed in *Reflections on the Death of a Porcupine and Other Essays*, ed. Michael Herbert (Cambridge, 1988), pp. 175–84.

[42] *Letters*, iv. 555; *Laughing Horse*, No. 9; Johnson (1897–1968), a poet from Santa Fe (see *Letters*, iv. 316 n. 5), had travelled with the Lawrences in Mexico in March–July 1923.

[43] New York and London: Harper Brothers, 1923 (originally published 1907), pp. 359–62.

[44] No. 10, May 1924.

London Letter', applies the legend, with a mixture of whimsy and earnestness, to his own situation in Europe:

> It would be a terrible thing if the horse in us died for ever: as he seems to have died in Europe. How awful it would be, if at this present moment I sat in the yellow mummy-swathings of London atmosphere – the snow is melting – inside the dreadful mummy-sarcophagus of Europe, and didn't know that the blue horse was still kicking his heels and making a few sparks fly, across the tops of the Rockies. It would be a truly sad case for me.

In concluding that man must again become like the centaur, Lawrence enumerates its qualities: 'First of all, Sense, Good Sense, Sound Sense, Horse Sense. And then, a laugh, a loud, sensible Horse laugh. After that, these same passions, glossy and dangerous in the flanks. And after these again, hoofs, irresistible, splintering hoofs, that can kick the walls of the world down.' Under the influence both of this newfound stimulus and his inkling that his friend Dorothy Brett *would*, as she had recently promised, come back with Frieda and himself to create the nucleus of a Rananim in New Mexico,[45] Lawrence conceived of a more heartening ending for his novel – an ending it might never have possessed had Seltzer been more efficient.

The new last chapter echoes the 'London Letter' in a number of significant ways, suggesting that it was written at about the same time.[46] Jack finds a oneness with his horse, Adam, as if 'he himself were the breast and arms and head of the ruddy, powerful horse, and it, the flanks and hoofs' (339:31–3). Adam is not only the present means but also a vindication of Jack's escape from the entanglements of Perth society: the horse registers the falseness of Jack's 'affable, rather loving manner' when he is chatting with casual acquaintances, and becomes 'irritable, chafing to go on' (340:7–8). This natural 'horse-sense' culminates dramatically towards the end of the chapter as Adam, having scented Hilda Blessington's

[45] Several friends said they would come, at a drunken dinner party at the Café Royal, inferentially dated as ?19 December 1923: see *Letters*, iv. 546–7, v. 143; Catherine Carswell, *The Savage Pilgrimage: A Narrative of D. H. Lawrence* (1932, reprinted Cambridge, 1981), pp. 199–200, 205–13; John Carswell, *Lives and Letters: A. R. Orage, Beatrice Hastings, Katherine Mansfield, John Middleton Murry, S. S. Koteliansky 1906–1957* (New York, 1978), p. 201. Only one did – the Honourable Dorothy Eugenie Brett (1883–1977), artist and daughter of the 2nd Viscount Esher; see *Letters*, ii. 427 n. 2 and her *Lawrence and Brett: A Friendship* (Philadelphia, 1933; re-issued with 'Epilogue', Santa Fe, 1974).

[46] Parallels between Brett and the Hilda Blessington of the last chap. reinforce the dating. Brett was the daughter of a viscount, and cf. Hilda's 'pure breeding' (345:2); both have seriously impaired hearing. Jack thinks of Hilda as 'the queerest, oddest, most isolated bird he had ever come across' (344:40–345:1); DHL had described Brett to a friend as 'a real odd man out' (Carswell, *Savage Pilgrimage*, p. 200). DHL had, accordingly, to revise nearly all Hilda's earlier appearances (see footnote 50).

'blue-grey mare' (347:21), has to be let out of his stall in the barn lest he smash it to pieces: 'The shut-up stallion sounded like an enclosed thunder-storm' (342:31–2). The idea of enclosure, mentioned in the 'London Letter', is a development of the Chinese boxes image in 'On Coming Home'; the centaur figure[47] offers a symbolic way out.

The physical state of the autograph manuscript of the last chapter confirms a date of *c.* 9 January 1924 for its composition. The paper is of the same kind Lawrence used for the substitution of several pages of typescript at typescript revision stage,[48] a process which was to occupy him virtually until the moment he finally left London for Paris on 23 January.

The revision of the typescripts

Lawrence had received the Seltzer (partial) typescript (i.e. of notebooks 1 to 3; hereafter, the original typescript) by 13 January. As he already had the three typed copies of notebooks 4 and 5 he was able to write on that day to Mollie Skinner:

> I have got the complete typescript of *The Boy in the Bush* now, and am going through it. It's awfully good, I like it immensely. I hope in about four day's time to post you the third of the typed copies. Will you go through it at once, and let me have *by return* any suggestions you can make. Be quick, and you'll be in time for the proofs . . . (iv. 557)

Seltzer had sent Lawrence only one copy of the original typescript (iv. 559), retaining one copy for himself.[49] As Lawrence needed three complete copies – for his English publisher Martin Secker, for Seltzer and for Mollie Skinner – he probably sent off the original typescript for re-typing as soon as he had corrected it, because the re-typing was completed by the time Lawrence and Frieda left for Paris (iv. 560). Further, it is very likely that Lawrence's writing of the last chapter (*c.* 9 January) determined the new emphasis displayed in the revisions of at least the 'chief [second] part' of the typescript (*c.* 13–22 January) – rather than vice versa.[50] Considerable revision was necessary because of the newly optimistic (and polygamous) future in the North-West now envisaged for

47 DHL had foreshadowed the idea when writing chap. VIII (see 121:15).

48 *C.* 21.4×27.4 cm., watermark 'DESPACHO BOND'. DHL used a sheet for the title-page of TSIa (see below).

49 7 pp. of it (the remainder is lost) were later included in TSIa (see below).

50 E.g. Hilda's physical appearance and Jack's self-sufficiency and mastery: see Textual apparatus for 251:21, 313:38, 314:21 and 301:28, 303:38, 335:38.

Jack. His fierce alienation from Perth society had to be carefully prepared for.

Only two of the three typescripts are extant: the setting-copies used by Seltzer (hereafter TSIa) and Secker (hereafter TSIb).[51] Both are a mixture of ribbon-copy and carbon-copy pages: TSIa consists of 326 ribbon-copy pages and 217 carbon-copy; TSIb of 220 ribbon-copy and 323 carbon-copy. (There are three cases of carbon reversal.) The typed page-numbering of TSIa and TSIb extends to p. 166 and continues for the last chapter, type-numbered 167–81. (Evidently Lawrence sent them to the typist together, and they were given sequential pagination.[52]) Autograph corrections of wording in these 181 pages appear to be those of a typist or typists; in almost every case the correction (from the original typescript) restores the manuscript reading. Probably Lawrence decided not to correct this re-typing: he was short of time and, as he had submitted a revised typescript, he may not have anticipated any problems.[53] He did, however, *see* the re-typed section and note its final page number (p. 166), for most of the subsequent page-numbering from p. 167 to the end of the novel (p. 543) is in his hand.[54]

51 TSIa (Roberts E55f) and TSIb (E55e); proof is provided by the marking-up and by variant typescript revisions transmitted to the first editions (e.g. Textual apparatus for 39:37, 163:9 and 159:22, 301:28).

52 For the pagination of chap. XXVI, see Explanatory note on 340:31. It must have been typed in triplicate, to provide a copy for MLS, because DHL referred unproblematically to the last two chapters which she had asked him to delete (*Letters*, v. 22, 24; see below, p. xl). He must have meant chaps. XXV and XXVI, and her description of the novel in typescript (*Fifth Sparrow* 128) includes matter contained in XXVI.

53 He did not revise the re-typing of *Kangaroo* (Roberts E182e) either, even though it is very likely that he saw it (information from Bruce Steele). See Explanatory note on 24:11.

54 DHL must have asked for two copies of the revised original typescript to be made so as to have three. MLS's copy (now unlocated) must have included that original typescript: two of the deletions she subsequently requested (see below, pp. xxxix–xlii) were cited by page numbers, which do not correspond to TSIa and b, and DHL no longer had a copy.

The paginations of the original typescript and TSIa and b were different. The first cancelled pagination of the part of TSIa corresponding to notebooks 4 and 5 commences with '138', and was probably done before the re-typing was returned. After receiving it DHL made an (uncompleted) attempt to re-paginate, starting with '140' and working backwards, which would have led to negative numbers at the beginning of TSIa; evidently he got '138' or '140', or both, wrong. Since p. '137'/'140' in TSIa and b is type-paginated '166', the difference in the number of pages is about 28; thus the re-typing is about 20 per cent longer, and when this is taken into account, the page numbers of both of MLS's requested deletions are redesignated correctly in TSIa and b.

MLS's copy of pp. 167–543 must have been entirely carbon (no ribbon-copy pages are unaccounted for), which suggests that it was not included in DHL's revision and collation (including pagination) of the copies, when the mixing of ribbon and carbon pages in TSIa and b must have occurred. Hence the absence of page numbers for MLS's requested changes after p. 166.

DHL paginated TSIb once, correcting a mistake in his last (of several) attempts in

On the remainder of TSIa and b (i.e. p. 167 to the end of the penultimate chapter at p. 528) the great bulk of the autograph corrections are in Lawrence's hand, and may be readily distinguished from the marking-up for the printers which, on Seltzer's copy TSIa, is heavy.[55] Lawrence's corrections are generally light, many merely of typing errors. However there are approximately 180 substantive emendations, and they tend to come in clusters.[56] They consist of about 100 single word changes, about 65 changes of short phrases, the remainder being longer revisions. Only on four occasions do they extend beyond three lines of his handwriting – in chapters XXIII and XXIV – chapters for which, as explained below, Lawrence was entirely responsible.[57] (These chapters also bear the heaviest of the shorter revisions.[58])

The longest of these revisions (Jack's bigamous proposal to Mary in chapter XXIV) necessitated a new typing of nine pages (pp. 513–21): hereafter, the 'late' typescript pages.[59] Not only do Lawrence's autograph corrections appear on these pages but it is also clear that he typed them himself. The first five are in a larger (Pica) typeface than the Elite typeface employed elsewhere in the typescripts; the next four are in Elite but done on a different typewriter. The typing is of the same amateur standard in both typefaces: 'x's are used to delete words, there is frequent overstriking of letters and the inking is uneven. This tallies with evidence from Lawrence's known typing of *Women in Love*,[60] and the typing has been done on paper which Lawrence had to hand, for he used the same kind for the autograph manuscript of the last chapter (see above). The first two 'late' pages reflect revisions of the MS version that would have rendered interlinear revision very cramped, and from half-way down the third page (p. 515), the 'late' typescript departs entirely from MS. This third page was typed twice because of carbon reversal. The second typing (in TSIa)

TSIa, all in pencil; see also footnote 134. (An unidentified hand subsequently did the final pagination of TSIa.) The title-pages of TSIa and b also appear to be in DHL's hand.

55 Typist's handwritten corrections do not appear in this section. The marking-up is in pencil; DHL used ink: see also Explanatory notes on 113:23 and 24:11.

56 Pp. 1–166 of TSIa and b contain about 90 substantive variants which appear to be authorial.

57 With the exception of a few pages in chap. XXIV which MLS later claimed to have written (see below, p. xlix); for the four longer revisions see Textual apparatus for 301:28–302:4 (and below, pp. lx–lxi), 318:11–26, 320:8, 328:10–330:1 (and Explanatory note on 328:10).

58 On average, two per page in chap. XXIII and two every three pages in XXIV, totalling about 80.

59 The superseded pages are unlocated.

60 *Women in Love*, ed. David Farmer, Lindeth Vasey and John Worthen (Cambridge, 1987), p. xxxii.

has seven accidental and six substantive variants from its counterpart in TSIb. As the substantive variants are clearly deliberate it seems that Lawrence was revising as he typed.[61] Elsewhere in these 'late' pages there is evidence that he was composing as he typed: on p. 513 'explode' has been overscored by 'x's and replaced by 'break'; on p. 520 'old' in 'old Blessington' and 'Stuffed plush furniture!' have been similarly overscored and deleted.[62]

Another of the long revisions is a deletion: a page which is now missing in both TSIa and b (it would have come between pp. 498 and 499) and the passages which immediately preceded and followed the missing page.[63] While at first it appears possible that the typist mislaid the page and its copies and that Lawrence took the easier path of deleting to fit the omission, closer inspection reveals that the deletion is linked to an altered emphasis in the conception of Mr George which Lawrence was incorporating into the typescript revisions;[64] it is therefore almost certainly intentional.

A compulsive reviser of his work, Lawrence seized the opportunity which preparing two typescripts for his publishers afforded him to introduce further stages of revision. Although it is unlikely that he transcribed any typescript revisions to the third copy for Mollie Skinner, it is clear that, in copying revisions between pp. 167–528 of TSIa and b, he frequently altered them. Evidently pleased in some cases with the new reading, he then transferred it back to the first typescript (but not consistently); with some longer revised passages he transferred back only some parts of the new reading. (The process can be established at such points by examining the pattern of deletions and revisions: see 'Text' below.) The inevitable result was that Lawrence's publishers would not receive identical setting-copy.

It was either during the collating or, more likely, after TSIa reached Seltzer that seven pages of TSIa were lost. In their place, seven carbon-copy pages from what can only be the duplicate of the original typescript were subsequently inserted into TSIa (pp. 15, 27, 31–3, 37, 50).[65] Because these seven pages have a number of readings that are at variance

61 See Textual apparatus for 329:25, 35 and 330:1. He had revised when typing *Women in Love*: see the Cambridge edition, p. xxx.

62 Respectively 328:23, 333:28 and 333:36 (after 'furniture').

63 See Textual apparatus and Explanatory note for 320:8.

64 E.g. see Textual apparatus for 318:26 and 325:24.

65 The typist's check of pp. 1–166 would have revealed a discrepancy, but the pages could have gone missing any time afterwards. See Explanatory note on 24:11. All of the substituted pages are carbon copy; the missing pages in TSIa were also carbon.

with their re-typed counterparts in TSIb, it follows that Lawrence cannot have corrected the copy of the original typescript to which these pages belong. They must, therefore, have come from the duplicate copy which Seltzer had retained; thus the insertion was almost certainly done by Seltzer's office at some stage prior to publication. Five of the pages have been partly scored through and two cut and pasted so that the sense would be continuous. In one of the deleted paragraphs (on p. 33), Aunt Matilda is called 'Mrs Hawkins'; on the next (re-typed) page, in the corresponding paragraph, her name is 'Mrs Watson'. Clearly, Lawrence made the change on the copy of the original typescript which he corrected in London, the re-typed version (in TSIb) having only the correction and not the original reading.[66]

Lawrence had squeezed the revision of TSIa and b into a ten-day period: *c.* 13–22 January 1924.[67] Shortly before leaving for Paris on 23 January he decided to retain Curtis Brown as his agent in America and through him to handle his business dealings with Seltzer, an erstwhile friend now in financial and legal difficulties.[68] Lawrence gave Curtis Brown instructions in a letter of 22 January:

> After all I am sending you the Amer. copy of *The Boy in the Bush*. Murry has the copy for England.[69]
>
> This novel might serialise in America. They can cut it as they like for serialisation purposes . . . If it seems unlikely that the thing would serialise, let Seltzer have the MS *at once* for spring publication. (iv. 560)

Lawrence had reassured Seltzer that Curtis Brown's New York office would forward copy 'for book publication at the earliest possible date' (iv. 559). The possibility of serialisation made the despatch of the American typescript even more urgent. Seltzer wished to publish in spring 1924 (iv. 597), and Lawrence was anxious not to upset him unnecessarily.

66 There is a deleted note on (substituted) p. 50 of TSIa written in an unknown hand in ink: 'Lawrence: How could he [Jack] look round the drawing room if, according to first paragraph she [Lady Bewley] led him along a path'. Such a note was apparently also made on the copy sent to DHL since the re-typed version resolves the problem: see Textual apparatus for 40:26 and 40:14.

67 Slightly longer if DHL had started revising before writing to MLS on the 13th (see above).

68 See G. Thomas Tanselle, 'The Thomas Seltzer Imprint', *Papers of the Bibliographical Society of America*, lviii (1964), 394–408.

69 John Middleton Murry, S. S. Koteliansky and DHL were trying (unsuccessfully) to float a publishing venture (*Letters*, iv. 565, 571, 574, 579; v. 16; for biographical details, see ii. 31 n. 6, 205 n. 4); *The Boy in the Bush* was to have been one of the initial publications (iv. 557).

Publication

After their trip to the Continent and return to England (26 February 1924) Lawrence and Frieda sailed for New York, but before leaving he sent Mollie Skinner a full account of publication plans: '*The Boy in the Bush* is in the printer's hands, both here and in New York. After all Martin Secker is publishing it here: and I am signing a contract for it, drawn up by Curtis Brown.' Lawrence proceeds to discuss in detail matters of payment and royalty-division, and he goes on to predict publication dates – Secker, 'early June'; Seltzer, 'May, or even end of April' (iv. 596–7). Both estimates were to prove wrong.

Curtis Brown, through his New York representative Arthur Barmby, either did not attempt or, more likely, failed to sell the serialisation rights.[70] Seltzer, in possession of the typescript by 3 March (iv. 596), announced on 8 March in *Publishers Weekly* his intention to publish the novel, but a fortnight later had still not sent it to the printer: 'Fix a date with Secker', Lawrence wrote to Curtis Brown, 'for *Boy in the Bush*. Seltzer hasn't sent it to print yet. I don't really mind if they hold it over till autumn' (v. 19). It was probably Seltzer's delay in sending TSIa to the printer that prevented the problem of the seven missing pages from coming to light while Lawrence was in New York (11–18 March) – his hand does not appear on the substituted pages. However it is possible that the omission was noticed soon afterwards, and it may help explain why the idea of Seltzer's setting up from Secker's proofs – rather than from TSIa – was raised.

Certainly by early April Secker was under the impression that this would happen. He wrote to Lawrence: 'I have posted to you today [3 April] two sets of proofs of "The Boy in the Bush" . . . When you have corrected this [first set] will you transfer the alterations to the second set, which will do for Seltzer to set up from.'[71] Although Lawrence followed these instructions, he was aware by 2 May that Seltzer, in deepening financial trouble and impatient to publish, had decided not to wait but to set up from TSIa instead. If he had not yet done so, Seltzer now had to make good the seven missing pages in TSIa, using his duplicate of the original typescript; he would be able to check his proofs of those pages against Secker's – where he would find any corrections Lawrence had made in the meantime

70 The Melbourne *Herald* inquired of Secker about serialisation, but nothing came of it (letter from Secker to Maud Drummond at Curtis Brown, 2 September 1924; Secker Letter-Book, UIll).

71 3 April 1924; Secker Letter-Book, UIll.

(v. 37). Moreover, Seltzer's checking the duplicate corrected (Secker) proofs against his own would save the time and trouble of Lawrence's having to check them as well. Lawrence wrote to Seltzer (2 May): 'I am sending . . . the duplicate of Secker's proofs for *The Boy in the Bush*. There are a few alterations – not much. I think I have eliminated to fit the insertions [that is, he had made deletions so as to make space for the new material], so it won't mean any moving of the type.'[72] It appears from this letter that Seltzer's edition was in proof (or at least being typeset) by the end of April, but not printed; it was listed in *Publishers Weekly* of 10 May 1924 as forthcoming.

Seltzer's decision to delay publication till autumn was evidently a last minute affair.[73] It was commercially desirable that Secker and Seltzer publish simultaneously, and Secker was inclined to wait till 1 September.[74] To be sure of securing US copyright Seltzer could not publish *after* Secker so that Secker's change of plans in favour of this later date gave Seltzer the option of also delaying publication. But what tipped the scales for Seltzer may have been his increasing financial difficulties coupled with his reluctance to place himself further in the debt of a former, now disaffected, friend – particularly one less inclined than formerly to wait for his money.[75]

From New York Lawrence and Frieda travelled to Taos, arriving on 22 March. Within a fortnight Lawrence received from Mollie Skinner a list of requested alterations to *The Boy in the Bush*. She had returned her copy of the typescript to Curtis Brown in London at the same time. Her various accounts of her dismay upon reading the typescript tend to conceal the fact that her requests for alterations were, with the important exception of her objection to the last two chapters, very slight. Secker, when sending the proofs to Lawrence, had mentioned the alterations: 'We received from

[72] *Letters*, v. 37; DHL's wording here and at v. 38 suggests that Seltzer and Secker had gone straight to page proofs (for further evidence, see Explanatory note on 42:20). Secker had also bypassed galley proofs with *Women in Love* (see *The Letters of D. H. Lawrence*, ed. James T. Boulton and Andrew Robertson, Cambridge, 1984, iii. 617 and n. 1, 621 and 625), and cf. *The Plumed Serpent* (ed. L. D. Clark, Cambridge, 1987, p. xxxv).

DHL also sent Seltzer a design for a dust-jacket which Brett had drawn and he had coloured (v. 37); it was used for the American first edition (reproduced in *D. H. Lawrence: Letters to Thomas and Adele Seltzer*, ed. Gerald Lacy, Santa Barbara, 1976, p. 125). DHL sent Secker another design (v. 34), but it was not used (reproduced in Keith Sagar, *The Life of D. H. Lawrence: An Illustrated Biography*, 1980, p. 132).

[73] Seltzer's spring publications stopped in mid-May; he resumed in mid-September (see Tanselle, 'Seltzer Imprint', *PBSA*, pp. 438–9).

[74] Letter from Secker to DHL, 3 April 1924; Secker Letter-Book, UIll.

[75] Seltzer had published six DHL titles in 1923; in 1924 he published only two: see Tanselle, 'Seltzer Imprint', *PBSA*, pp. 403, 433–7. Cf. *Letters*, v. 18 and n. 4.

Curtis Brown (but after the book had gone to the printer) a second typescript which contained some small alterations and suggestions, presumably from Mrs Skinner. These have been transferred to the marked set [of proofs], and you will also find among its pages some of the suggestions, which you may like to adopt.' The next day (4 April) Lawrence, not realising that the proofs were already on their way to him, wrote to both Secker and Seltzer, asking both publishers to 'make the alterations she wishes: at least the smaller ones' (v. 22). In his letter to Seltzer, Lawrence enclosed Mollie Skinner's letter containing the list of alterations (now unlocated), and he copied out the list in his letter to Secker (Roberts E55d[76]):

Alterations in *The Boy in the Bush*
(for Miss Skinner).

Omit.

Ch XX. the dog "began to lick the scattered brains."
Ch XI – "At the Sacrament. This is my Body, he knew he never wanted to taste that Body, nor drink that Blood."
Ch IX – "Our Lady and her Blessed Son – "
Ch I. p.4 – his trousers "seemed as if they were slipping down"
p.35. – "in front of"[77]

Miss Skinner would also like the last chapter, & if possible, the last two chapters, omitted. A moi, ça m'est égal. Je m'en fiche de ce monde craintif[78]

D.H.L

Miss Skinner would like worked in at the end of Ch. XXIV, this refrain:

"And the changing, curious truth remained. He didn't want to love the family, but he loved them with an enduring love. He couldn't do without them: would be lost without them: Tom, and Lennie, and Monica. His individuality seemed merged in them, that part of his individuality that was human, and flesh that perisheth. He loathed loving them, their hands gripping and clinging and wringing his heart, but nevertheless, while he lived he would love them. He resented it, but he couldn't help it. He loved them. Even Jane – she was part of the

76 2 pp.; IEduc (*Letters*, v. 24–5 transcribes this list by *Letters* conventions).
77 The two instances in pp. 25–50 of TSIa and b cannot be reasonably deleted; however 'the front of' at 35:1 (TSIa, p. 42) can. Perhaps DHL misread her letter.
78 'To me, it's all the same to me. I don't give a damn about this timid world'.

family. He might ride away for a time. He might philander round other folk. But he would always come back to Monica and Tom and Lennie and Jane. They held him. But he held them: he was their master. They were his. They clung to him, and he could never cut adrift from them – "

Chap. XXIII – Monica should say, after she shook her head: "It seems dreadful, dreadful – but I'm glad, deep down within me I'm glad he's gone. He was frightful to me, leaving me. No one knows the dreadfulness to a girl, facing the world with her trouble – facing it alone – he marrying that Mary Ann, leering at me over his barrier of respectabilities. *I'm glad you killed him.* The thought of him alive, and leering, was unbearable – an unbearable torture"

The two long passages seem to be in Lawrence's own words. Evidently, in writing out the list of omissions, he took the opportunity of rewriting two of Mollie Skinner's suggested alterations. The first passage seems meant to soften Jack's bigamous impulse (voiced earlier in chap. XXIV) by referring to it indirectly as 'philandering'. This, together with the deletion of the last two chapters, would help to 'twist the tail' of the story 'back into place'.[79] The second passage relates to Monica's acceptance of Jack's having murdered Easu. The typescript reads: 'I was always in love with you, really';[80] now, Lawrence seeks to justify the response.

Since the Secker proofs were already on their way to him, Lawrence's efforts were in vain. But, aware that he had invited Mollie Skinner to correct her copy of the typescript, he may have felt (not having a copy of the novel by him) that deletion was the simplest (and a fair) way of responding to five of her objections. Nor would he have kept a copy of the corrections: which helps explain why, when the marked and duplicate sets of proofs arrived, he simply ignored the decisions he had communicated to Secker in the list. He was able to respond to Mollie Skinner's suggested alterations afresh and in context (see below). For the time being, however, he was able, with a clear conscience, to report to his collaborator: 'I have written to Secker and Seltzer to make the alterations you wish, if it is not too late. Also I tell them they may leave out both chapters at the end, if they wish . . . We shall see' (v. 20–1). For his part Secker, replying to Lawrence's letter of 4 April, expressed strong opposition to scrapping the last two chapters.[81] Perhaps Seltzer just ignored

[79] *Fifth Sparrow* 129. [80] TSIa and b (as typed), p. 467 (301:4).
[81] 25 April 1924; Secker Letter-Book, UIll.

the letter to him: no trace of the corrections appears on TSIa or in his edition.

In any case, Lawrence makes plain his opinion in the letters to Secker and Seltzer, and implicit in his letter to Mollie Skinner, that omitting the last two chapters would amount, in his opinion, to a capitulation to the pruderies of a 'timid' world; only out of a sense of duty to his collaborator was he prepared to sanction the cut. When he corrected the Secker proofs (which he had received by 18 April)[82] he had a further opportunity to delete the last two chapters if he so wished. But he did not; the chapters are retained in this edition.

Lawrence had completed his proof corrections by 2 May 1924, and in his letters to Secker and Seltzer of that date he mentions that there are only 'a few alterations' (v. 37–8). However the transcribing of proof corrections from the set for Secker to the duplicate set for Seltzer gave Lawrence latitude to introduce a further revision stage analogous to that generated by his transcription of the typescript revisions. Although the proof sets do not survive it is possible, on the basis of variation between Seltzer's edition (hereafter A1) and TSIa, and Secker's (E1) and TSIb, to see that Lawrence made more than just 'a few' changes and that he is probably responsible for some of the variants where TSIa and b are identical but A1 and E1 differ. Many come in clusters,[83] and four are responses to Mollie Skinner's alterations and suggestions. For example, in response to her third request on the list, 'of Our Lady and her Blessed Son' is changed to 'with very noble subjects' in E1; in A1 it is simply omitted.[84]

Although Secker had indicated that Mollie Skinner's alterations had been marked on the proofs, what he did not tell Lawrence was that he had made two significant deletions from the typescript before sending it to the printer.[85] The first deletion of about 100 words removes descriptions of the barmaid Lucy Snook's 'posterior and perspiration' (233:32). Secker, without informing Lawrence, had also deleted 'objectionable' passages in his editions of *Women in Love*, *The Lost Girl* and *Kangaroo* in order to avoid possible legal action or to satisfy the anticipated scruples of the

[82] *Letters*, v. 35: DHL passed on Secker's suggested publication date of 1 September to Seltzer.

[83] E.g. see Textual apparatus for 67:19, 27 and 28, 67:33 and 35, 68:12, 295:27 and 33, 296:9 and 41. There are about 55 substantive (and related) revisions; six are variant revisions (listed in Explanatory note on 67:30).

[84] See Textual apparatus for 134:20; his other three responses in proof occur at 167:26, 282:7 and 301:4.

[85] The evidence is in the Explanatory note on 233:33.

circulating libraries.[86] In his negotiations with Curtis Brown about his terms for publishing *The Boy in the Bush*, Secker had remarked 'that it is extremely doubtful whether the circulating libraries will admit it to their shelves';[87] he was evidently taking no chances. There is another sentence deleted in E1 (233:38–9) which occurs shortly after the Lucy Snook passage: either Lawrence himself deleted it on the proofs (it had been deprived of its context) or, more likely (for it remains in A1), Secker deleted it after the proofs were returned to him (he had them by 23 May).[88] Half a page after the passage, Secker took it upon himself to delete a further 600 words (234:12–235:28) – a digression which provides the detail that Lucy has most likely committed bigamy, and thus that Tom has little to worry about when he deserts her. What Secker's motives were in this case is less clear: the reference to bigamy occupies only three lines which could have been deleted independently of the rest.

The Dunedin Press, Secker's printers, were a source of further changes[89] – a fairly consistent regularisation of Lawrence's unusual habits of punctuation, over and apart from that which had already been imposed by the typists. A1 was even more carefully regularised – as witnessed by the heavy marking-up of TSIa – and a distinctive house-styling resulted. (This and the other layers of regularising are removed in the present edition.) Because Seltzer's office checked their own proofs against the duplicate corrected Secker proofs, many of the variants introduced by Secker and his printers – including the deletion of the passages Secker had censored – were incorporated, and some variants caused by the seven substituted pages in TSIa were eliminated. The duplicate Secker proofs were evidently assumed to have more authority, so that many TSIb readings were transmitted to the American first edition. The checking was not uniformly careful however, and many variants between the two first editions, not the result of house-styling, remained.

In their imperfect and differing states E1 was published on 28 August 1924[90] and A1 on 30 September.[91] Meanwhile Lawrence's sister-in-law,

[86] See *Women in Love*, ed. Farmer, Vasey and Worthen, p. xlviii; *The Lost Girl*, ed. Worthen, pp. xxxix–xl; information for *Kangaroo* from Bruce Steele.

[87] *C.* 6 March 1924; Secker Letter-Book, UIll.

[88] Letter from Secker to DHL, 23 May 1924; Secker Letter-Book, UIll. A similar thing happened with *The Plumed Serpent* (ed. Clark; see note on 233: 31, p. 468).

[89] Cf. *The Lost Girl*, ed. Worthen, p. xliii.

[90] See Secker's letter to DHL, 13 August 1924: 'I am publishing "The Boy" on August 28' (Secker Letter-Book, UIll), and the first review appeared in *The Times Literary Supplement* on that date.

[91] The novel was republished in USA in 1930 by Albert and Charles Boni to whom Seltzer had sold his business (see Tanselle, 'Seltzer Imprint', *PBSA*, p. 409). While Seltzer's

Else Jaffe, had begun preparing a translation of the novel into German[92] for which Lawrence wrote his prefatory 'Note on Miss M. L. Skinner', sending it on 22 November (v. 178). Deutsche Verlagsanstalt in Stuttgart published the Jaffe translation, under the title *Jack im Buschland*, in 1925;[93] the 'Vorwort' is a shortened translation of Lawrence's 'Note'. It is published in Appendix V for the first time in full (and the first time in English).

It is not known how large Seltzer's first edition was, but it is unlikely that he enjoyed Secker's success. When writing the novel Lawrence had predicted that it might prove popular (iv. 517). In the short run, at least, it did. Perhaps vindicating his censoring, Secker was able to inform Lawrence that 'a substantial cheque for the subscription sales will go to Curtis Brown on publication day'.[94] A fortnight later (26 August 1924) Secker reported that the first impression of 2,000 copies 'was quickly exhausted, and I reprinted 1000 before publication. Now I am on the point of printing another 1000. I think it will do well.'[95] The last mentioned impression – the third – appeared in September and a fourth in October. These four printings were completely sold out by the end of 1928.[96] Secker reprinted the novel three more times (in a cheap 'pocket' edition in August 1928, and again in June 1930 and 1932)[97] before he sold his Lawrence interest to Heinemann in January 1935.[98]

plates were used, the newly set title-page gave DHL as the sole author. An edition by Viking, now with US rights, was advertised in 1933 but did not appear. In 1971 Southern Illinois University Press published an offset facsimile edition of E1, reprinted by Viking Compass in 1972.

92 In a letter of 26 June 1924 to DHL, Secker reported advance copies of E1 being sent to DHL and Else Jaffe (Secker Letter-Book, UIll).

93 For details of the other translations see Roberts D63, D137.21, D212, D246.4. (The Russian, an abridgement, has n.d. but '1927' appears on the dust-jacket.)

94 13 August 1924; Secker Letter-Book, UIll.

95 Secker Letter-Book, UIll. These figures included 1,500 copies sold to Robertson and Mullen in Melbourne – an initial order of 1,000 and a 'repeated 500' (letter to DHL, 9 October 1924; ibid.). In a letter to Maud Drummond (3 September 1924; ibid.), Secker explained his royalty statement: 'The 1000 Colonial copies are a special Australian edition'. 'Colonial' profits were normally less because of the high discount to agents; however no Secker copies inspected in Australia have different bindings, title-pages or other obvious variations.

96 See letter from Laurence Pollinger to DHL, 9 January 1929; UT. The first four impressions must have been printed from standing type because Secker sent 'a [stereotype] moulding order for "The Boy in the Bush"' to his printers on 4 February 1925 (Secker Letter-Book, UIll); see also next note.

97 Optical collation of the first with later impressions to June 1930 reveals only the loss of a comma from the second and subsequent impressions (after 'too' at 333:35, E1, p. 354); some disturbances to the positioning of the type (but without textual variation) also occurred (one in the second impression, and three in the fourth).

98 Heinemann printed a re-set edition in 1936 from Secker's 1928 cheap edition. In 1972 Heinemann's Phoenix edition appeared, identical to the Southern Illinois University Press

Mollie Skinner's and Lawrence's relative responsibilities for the novel

There is no doubt that, even after Lawrence's rewriting of the story, *The Boy in the Bush* still reflects its origins in Mollie Skinner's life and background. Jack Grant's story, in outline at least, is an adaptation of that of her brother, John Russell ('Jack') Skinner.[99] Born in 1881 in Ireland and rebellious as a child, he had been sent to Western Australia at seventeen or eighteen (in advance of the family's remove there from England in 1900) to learn farming at his uncle's farm at Beverley. He remained there for a year and then went to work as a jackeroo on a station in the North-West, returning to Perth to meet his family about two years after they arrived.[100] They were shocked by the changes they saw in him, particularly his disreputable clothing and bushman's language.[101] Unabashed, he was soon off to the goldfields around Kalgoorlie. Then, after a period on a farm at Moora which failed,[102] he went prospecting again, only to join the Australian army when World War I broke out; he was seriously wounded in the face. Returning, he took up farming once again, having been granted a smallholding as a returned soldier. When his sister opened up 'Leithdale' at Darlington, he swapped his farm for a few acres nearby. By late 1924 he was off gold-prospecting again, only to die in penury and squalor on the fields the following July. His was a life of apparently aimless and unsuccessful drifting, yet Lawrence (unlike Mollie Skinner) saw it as an honest and resolute refusal to submit to 'fixed' convention (v. 292). Lawrence had had only a passing acquaintance with Jack Skinner while at 'Leithdale', but it became the stimulus for an extension of what he sensed as the man's instinctive distaste for conventional mores into Jack Grant's conscious revolt against them.

Other characters and happenings in the novel draw on Mollie Skinner's

edition (see footnote 91). Penguin issued a re-set edition of the 1928 Secker in 1963, and reprinted in 1981 (twice) and 1984. The novel was first printed in Australia in 1980 by Macmillan – a re-set edition of the 1972 Heinemann text.

Two passages about Lennie (181:36–183:4 and 188:39–191:11) were included, with DHL's permission (*Letters*, v. 193), in *An Anthology of Youth in Verse and Prose*, ed. Susan Miles [pseud. for Ursula Roberts] (1925), pp. 301–7.

99 *Letters*, v. 114; see also *Fifth Sparrow* 114.

100 Jack Skinner arrived in WA probably in 1899 (see Explanatory note on 37:4). 'Fifth Sparrow' Draft has: 'In 1902 Daddy came home – to die' and 'Jack arrived soon after Daddy was buried' (pp. 39, 42).

101 Cf. Explanatory note on 229:26.

102 He also earned money breaking-in horses; MLS remembered his 'masterly control' of rearing horses (*Fifth Sparrow* 86; cf. 66:28–68:8).

own experiences and reflect aspects of people she knew,[103] and the historical, botanical, legal and geographic information in the novel is very probably her material; in fact, at certain points the novel draws on the *Year-Book* in a detailed way, sometimes echoing its wording.[104] But no conclusion about the collaborators' relative responsibilities for the novel as it was published can be reached on the basis of source material alone. Nor, in the absence of Mollie Skinner's typescript of 'The House of Ellis', can the authorship of more than a small percentage of *The Boy in the Bush* (the typescript revisions and the last chapter) be attributed to Lawrence with absolute certainty. However Mollie Skinner's and Lawrence's accounts of the collaboration, together with Edward Garnett's copy of the novel[105] in which late in 1924 she, at Garnett's request, marked passages written or altered by Lawrence, concur in attributing to him most of chapters XX and XXII–XXVI. On this evidence only one quarter of the novel can thus be attributed to Lawrence alone.

A count of the number of lines in Garnett's marked copy which Mollie Skinner designates as wholly or partly by Lawrence indicates that she was prepared to attribute approximately 37 per cent of the novel to Lawrence. However the markings cannot be trusted. Mollie Skinner had not seen

103 See Explanatory notes on 9:15, 10:25, 11:22, 53:32, 134:21, 195:19 and 234:15. In an unpublished typescript of a novel, '"Noise of Swans." A Saga of the West' (dated in an unknown hand, *c.* 1932–3) MLS used material similar to some in *The Boy in the Bush*. A radical re-working of 'The House of Ellis' (assuming she had retained a copy) is a possibility, but the pronounced remaining dissimilarities more strongly suggest a common source in her family background being drawn upon a second time (see Explanatory note on 9:15). In 'Noise of Swans' a younger Mr George gives advice about opportunities in the colony to a scapegrace recently returned from England (who had been looked after by an Aunt Matilda and who had won first prize for scripture at school: cf. 8:3); the young man dines at Mr George's where he meets the three giggling Miss Georges (cf. 28:23). He and a relative, Steve, drove sheep to Geraldton and then work on a sheep station (cf. 193:4); and Steve seems to have 'a wife in every settlement' (p. 30; cf. 206:30–9 and 233:34). The two are invited to sleep at the encampment, crawling with fleas (cf. 224:7), of a Mr Snook (cf. 232:37); they see a family living in the bole of a huge tree (cf. 220:33–6 and note on 220:40); and later Steve is sought for being a wife-deserter (cf. 235:11–19). After the hero's adventures in the goldfields he returns to Perth whereupon the focus for the rest – the bulk – of the novel moves to his son who becomes a constable.

104 See Explanatory notes on 22:35, 18:36, 45:1, 46:22 and 93:6; these and other notes attempt to distinguish between MLS's original material and that which is likely to be DHL's alone. Attention has been paid to the novel's historical accounts because of the light they may throw on DHL's recasting and because of the conception of the novel implied in his advice to MLS (pp. xxiii–xxiv above). It is very unlikely that DHL would have taken the bulky *Year-Book* with him: MLS specified the edition which DHL read, and some sheets from that edition (each new one was re-set) are among her papers – which suggests that DHL may have left her his copy.

105 A Secker fourth impression (UT; Roberts E55g).

'The House of Ellis' for eighteen months, and in one afternoon or less[106] she could only have scanned Garnett's copy of the published novel. She would presumably have been working by a principle of exclusion, marking only those passages which, as they stood, she knew could not possibly be hers, passages which, for her, had a distinctive (or objectionable) Lawrentian flavour. In the following passage for instance (see 130:23–35 for the full text), she has marked as Lawrence's only the words here italicised: 'Jack's anger *coiled to rest* at the supper . . . He would have liked to hold her again, *close, close; her agile, live body, quick as a cat's. She was mysterious to him as some cat-goddess, and she excited him in a queer electric fashion*'. Mollie Skinner evidently recognised the metaphors of electricity and the Egyptian cat-goddess as Lawrentian and marked them accordingly, not stopping to wonder whether such metaphors could simply be added to her version without the episode itself being re-conceived, re-imagined as a whole. Moreover, although Lawrence's heaviest revisions occur in chapters which she attributes to Lawrence almost in their entirety, she has in fact elsewhere failed to mark many of Lawrence's shorter revisions on TSIa and b.[107]

Interviewed for the *Sunday Times* of 15 February 1925, she is reported as saying: 'All the plot, except the very last little bit is mine, and I provided the local facts and color. I love those people of my creation' (p. 29). In her note on the collaboration published in 1950, she claims to have written 'about three-fourths of the book in question'.[108] While her claims over the years to having written the great bulk of the novel – as it stands – may partly derive from her (erroneous) impression that Lawrence had rewritten her novel in a fortnight, it is nevertheless impossible to overlook the fact that her part-authorship of *The Boy in the Bush* remained her principal claim to literary fame.

Lawrence, on the other hand, was acutely aware of the need to promote *her* cause, especially after her share in the authorship of the novel was scoffed at in some early reviews.[109] The intention of Lawrence's public

106 *Fifth Sparrow* 149.

107 Disregarding chaps. XX and XXII–XXVI MLS marked approximately one-third of DHL's autograph revisions on TSIa and b: one is noted specifically; the rest fall within longer marked passages. While a large proportion of those she missed are adjustments of local effects, many are obvious 'Lawrentian' alterations: e.g., see Textual apparatus for 251:21 (both entries) and 174:9 (second entry). She also failed to signal passages (deriving from MS) related to marked sections, e.g. 135:35–8 ('But Jack . . .'), 136:16–22, 160:8–27 ('Jack began . . . much *time*' – marked as 'very little changed'), 246:37–247:24 (see Explanatory note on 247:22).

108 'DHL and *The Boy in the Bush*', *Meanjin*, p. 262.

109 See Reception below, and *Letters*, v. 121, 123.

pronouncements seems to have been to take the blame, as it were, for the 'objectionable' last chapters and generally to minimise the importance of his role in the collaboration. In his 'Note on Miss M. L. Skinner' he observes: 'I wrote it all out again, altering freely. Some of the chapters, and the whole of the end, after the return to Perth, are mine—the rest is Miss Skinner's material.'[110] In a preface Lawrence wrote for her *Black Swans* in December 1924 he describes a similar process: 'I wrote the whole book over again, from start to finish, putting in and leaving out, yet keeping the main substance of Miss Skinner's work . . . the last chapters and anything in the slightest bit "shocking," are, of course, my fault: not Molly Skinner's.'[111] On first reading, Lawrence seems to be proposing a rough and ready division of authorship ('the rest is Miss Skinner's material') while simultaneously downgrading the creative significance of his rewriting. Yet he is also quietly making a distinction between her 'material' and his rewriting of it.

When not on public record Lawrence may be more reliable: certainly his emphasis is different and underlines the importance of the distinction. In a letter to Curtis Brown written on the day he reports finishing the novel he commented: 'I don't know how she managed to keep it [*Letters of a V.A.D.*] so sane. The later stuff is just muddled and a bit crazy' (iv. 533). He could only be referring to 'The House of Ellis' and *Black Swans*. When the idea of his rewriting *Black Swans* was being canvassed, he commented in a letter to his sister: 'I doubt if I want to re-write another book, and re-create it, as I did *The Boy*.'[112]

Mollie Skinner thanked Lawrence warmly for his services: 'You have been most kind and generous . . . and I've got to forgive you for those end chapters – because they are yours. And I do think you have *brought* it all *out* like a magician.'[113] The last remark suggests that though she felt grateful, and in awe of Lawrence's talent, she neither understood how he had 're-created' her novel nor appreciated the amount of creative effort involved. Her letter was written on 28 August 1924. During the next couple of months many reviews appeared questioning the importance of her contribution; by the time she came to mark Garnett's copy of the novel later in the year she may have been less inclined to acknowledge the full

[110] See 373:19–22 below, and Explanatory note.

[111] P. 377:35–9 below. 'Preface to *Black Swans*' (Appendix VI) was first published in *Phoenix II* 294–6. DHL changed his mind about sending it: 'Critics would only be dragging me in all over everything again' (*Letters*, v. 190).

[112] *Letters*, v. 114. DHL described 'The House of Ellis' to his first bibliographer, Edward McDonald, as 'full of material, but disjointed, disconnected, all wrong: somehow one couldn't read it' (ibid., v. 121).

[113] *Letters*, v. 123 n. 1. MLS underlined 'out' three times.

extent of Lawrence's assistance. Recognising, doubtless, a plot line and a series of situations and characters of her own invention she took the treatment and development of them to be more or less her own, marking Garnett's copy of the novel accordingly.

Thus the markings are probably trustworthy at least in regard to plot. On the last page of chapter XVIII of Garnett's copy there is a note in her hand: 'original now on/from 271 to Ch XXIV/back to XIX/finished at XXII'. Evidently 'The House of Ellis' originally jumped from p. 271 (259:21) to the present chapter XXIV in which Mollie Skinner claims as her own the letter about the inheritance of Mad Jack Grant's farm and a description of the interior of the house. The original resumed in the present chapter XIX (the return to Wandoo), finishing in present chapter XXII (where Jack, lost in the bush, is found). By comparing this note and Mollie Skinner's other markings with Lawrence's account of 'The House of Ellis' in his 'Preface to *Black Swans*', the last section of the original plot can be reconstructed: Jack journeys from Perth to Wandoo via Mad Jack Grant's farm; he subsequently becomes lost in the bush, after having set out to find Monica who has disappeared in disgrace, and is found by Mary, Tom and Lennie; in being nursed back to health by Mary, he finds that she is the one he really loves after all. (And Jack's surprise inheritance of the Grant farm is to provide the suitable venue for future marital happiness.) Lawrence's Jack, on the other hand, becomes lost only after killing Easu but then, after being nursed back to health, sets off again to find Monica, marries her, and goes after gold, nourishing, the meanwhile, his Patriarchal notions.

It is clear both that Lawrence could not simply have re-conceived Jack's story without a reciprocal development being given to most of the characters with whom he comes into contact and that Lawrence would have had to prepare carefully for these developments from the earliest stages of the novel. This centrifugal effect of altering Mollie Skinner's conception of Jack may be a very pronounced form of what is known of Lawrence's habits in correcting his own typescripts. Examination of some of Lawrence's typescripts of the twenties – *Mr Noon*, *Kangaroo*, *The Boy in the Bush* and, though later, *Lady Chatterley's Lover* – reveals that, while Lawrence's emendations are generally light, there are occasional clusters of much more extensive revisions where he has evidently come to a particular scene with a fresh perspective, has had to rewrite most of it (perhaps a page or more), and then to effect corresponding changes in the following pages. It is likely, therefore, that Lawrence's revision of 'The House of Ellis' was much more extensive in some places than others.

(Mollie Skinner's markings, which also tend to come in clusters, reinforce this likelihood.)

Though Lawrence, when rewriting his own work, was sometimes able to incorporate substantial sections of (corrected) autograph from a previous version,[114] he preferred in other cases to rewrite afresh, feeling the need, evidently, to immerse himself more completely in the compositional flow than the superintending role of (however creative) editor would allow. The three separate versions in manuscript of *Lady Chatterley's Lover* provide the most famous example: though containing related situations and characters Lawrence's rewritings produced different works, worthy of independent publication.

With *The Boy in the Bush* the collaborators' physical distance apart meant that co-writing, in the sense of Lawrence's frequent consultation with, and acceptance of correction from, his co-writer, was out of the question. It was the distance, indeed, that helped make the project feasible: Lawrence's imagination was too idiosyncratic, his vision too personal for him to 'co-write'. In other proposed (or part-) collaborations he followed a similar course. With Helen Corke he shied away from submitting the final manuscript of *The Trespasser* to her for approval, as he had said he would: it was based on a tragic episode in her life.[115] Proposing a joint novel to Mabel Luhan about her life, he told her: 'I don't want you to read my stuff till the end'.[116] Although with Catherine Carswell, a good friend and published novelist, he suggested a division of responsibility, the proposed collaboration did not materialise: predictably it was Lawrence himself who went on to write a very different version of her story as 'The Princess'.[117] As Frederick Carter, yet another collaborator, had reason to observe: Lawrence 'had an insistent desire to amend, enhance and colour anything that deeply moved his interest'.[118]

114 E.g. in *The Trespasser*, 'The Daughters of the Vicar', *The Rainbow* and *Sons and Lovers*: see Introductions of the respective Cambridge editions: ed. Elizabeth Mansfield (1981), p. 21; ed. Worthen (*The Prussian Officer and Other Stories*, 1983), pp. xl–xli; ed. Mark Kinkead-Weekes (1989), p. xxvi. For *Sons and Lovers* see: '*Sons and Lovers': a Facsimile of the Manuscript*, ed. Mark Schorer, Berkeley, 1977; and Helen Baron, '*Sons and Lovers*: The Surviving Manuscripts from Three Drafts Dated by Paper Analysis', *Studies in Bibliography*, xxxviii (1985), 289–328.

115 See *The Trespasser*, ed. Mansfield, pp. 8, 22.

116 *Letters*, iv. 318. See *St. Mawr and Other Stories*, ed. Brian Finney (Cambridge, 1983), p. xx.

117 See *St. Mawr*, ed. Finney, pp. xxix–xxxiv. Cf. DHL's unfinished re-working of a translation of a Yiddish fairytale, 'Maimonides and Aristotle' (*London Mercury*, February 1937, 362–70) as 'The Undying Man' (*Phoenix*, ed. McDonald, pp. 808–10).

118 Frederick Carter, *D. H. Lawrence and the Body Mystical* (Denis Archer, 1932), p. 32. Cf. *Apocalypse and the Writings on Revelation*, ed. Mara Kalnins (Cambridge, 1980), pp. 8–9.

It is possible to get a firm, if not quantitative, sense of how that desire might manifest itself by considering Lawrence's other collaborations with Mollie Skinner. When on 3 December 1928 Lawrence returned a later novel of hers ('Eve in the Land of Nod') which she had asked him to help her with, he replied: 'I can't do with it as I did with *Boy in the Bush* – that was a *tour de force* which one can do once, but not twice.' In the letter he goes on to give her advice about restructuring the novel, 'in place', he apologises, 'of more strenuous help'. However, inspection of the 1928 typescript of 'Eve in the Land of Nod'[119] reveals that Lawrence had gone to very considerable trouble, deleting and relocating material to provide clearer causal links and foreshadowing in the triple crime, romance and aboriginal plot lines. Apart from this 'creative editing' where Lawrence is seeking to act as the judicious servant of Mollie Skinner's material, attempting to display it to its best advantage, there are a number of 'novelistic' interventions where Lawrence rewrites passages of passion or introspection, giving them an emotional plausibility and a psychological depth which they had lacked. Linked to this was Lawrence's attempt to convert the fictional autobiography in the first person which Mollie Skinner had sent him into a third person novel with an omniscient narrator.[120] The change was presumably aimed at giving the narrator more room and authority to probe the characters' inner lives. However to follow *that* intention through would mean, he evidently realised, a re-imagining on another plane of the novel's sequence of events and situations. He drew back, instead advising her to return to what he had reason to believe she *could* handle: a simple first person narration and diary form.[121]

There is a clear distinction here between two kinds of collaboration; re-creating Mollie Skinner's work as he had in *The Boy in the Bush* did not mean to Lawrence merely rearranging or restructuring it while accepting her terms of engagement with her subject matter. He evidently did not think of *that* as 'strenuous help', whereas *The Boy in the Bush* he thought of as a '*tour de force*', as a genuine re-creation. This consideration lends weight to the distinction he drew in relation to the novel between her 'material' and his rewriting of it.

For a list of DHL's collaborations and a discussion of one with Carter in 1924 and another with a Mexican friend, Luis Quintanilla, in 1925, see Paul Eggert, 'D. H. Lawrence and Literary Collaboration', *Etudes Lawrenciennes*, iii (1988), 153–62.

119 It has been rearranged, cut and pasted, and parts of it discarded; and there is a later typed version (1934).

120 DHL's alterations are autograph, but included are some pages, in the third person and with a few corrections in his hand, which DHL may have had typed.

121 *Letters of a V.A.D.* is in the first person.

Underestimation of his own contribution is a consistent factor in Lawrence's collaborations. When in 1925 John Middleton Murry asked him to prepare for publication a story ('The Hand') which Mollie Skinner had submitted to the *Adelphi*, Lawrence returned it on 12 December stating that he had rewritten 'the first four pages, and cleared the rest a bit'.[122] Although in printed form the story is only five-and-a-half pages long (and only *c.* 330 words per page), Lawrence refers to his efforts as 'editing', indicating probably that he had no desire to enrich her simple realist tale with a deeper psychological/passional sub-stratum. Instead he would attempt simply to clear its muddle[123] – in a way that he would later with 'Eve in the Land of Nod'. He asked Murry 'just [to] let her think your office did the editing'. The generous impulse is unmistakable.

The fact that the autograph manuscript of *The Boy in the Bush* is entirely in Lawrence's hand is very significant in this context. If he meant that the 'rest' of the novel apart from the last few chapters was basically as Mollie Skinner had written it (and not just that it was loosely based on her 'material'), and if as a result Lawrence's emendations were light and sparing, then he could simply have written in the margins and other white spaces of her typescript (as he was to with 'Eve in the Land of Nod'), interleaving it as necessary with rewritten passages or pages of his own. If his contributions were more significant than this, he had the option of inserting occasional typescript pages of hers into *his* notebooks.[124]

Either alternative would have saved time and effort. But he did neither. The fact that he wrote out instead 580 pages of manuscript argues for a complete imaginative appropriation on his part of the 'material' he found in 'The House of Ellis'. It was only when that material no longer allowed him to pursue his interests – interests reflected in his other writings of the period – that he rejected it entirely and felt the need to prepare his collaborator for the shock. The facts, taken together, that the autograph manuscript is in his hand alone, and that he claimed the novel as a collaboration when he habitually (and modestly) underestimated the extent of his own assistance to other writers' works, are strong evidence that he

122 *Letters*, v. 351. Judging from her silence MLS does not seem to have known of DHL's intervention. (Original manuscript unlocated; Battye has a later, copy-typescript.)

123 But a number of DHL touches are evident, e.g. 'The moon was up, a brilliant white night, white and black, and still. From where I sat I could see the bush, mysterious under the bright moon', and 'Fear smothered me for a moment. He was strong in demented spasmodic desire for water' (*Adelphi*, iii, 1926, pp. 795, 797).

124 Although such interleaving would have been clumsy, while he was travelling, DHL *did* keep the typescript with him for copying (it was intact after he had finished; *Letters*, iv. 533). He promised to show it to Curtis Brown and to return it to MLS (iv. 524), but it is not known whether he did.

had made the novel his own and, importantly, that he had accepted responsibility for it: it would be – it is – a Lawrence novel.

Reception

Mollie Skinner, in England for the second half of 1924, paid a press-cutting agency to send her reviews and other notices of *The Boy in the Bush*;[125] the collection which she gathered in this way testifies to the very widespread attention Lawrence's writings were receiving by 1924. At least 138 reviews and notices of the novel appeared around the world: not only were there a large number in Britain (47), in the USA (19) and in Australia (where editors of review pages had a special reason to give Lawrence space: 49), but there were also some in Canada (5) and New Zealand (4), France (3) and in India, South Africa, Italy and the Netherlands (1 each).[126] The *Standard* in Buenos Aires reviewed the novel on 3 February 1925 as well as having quoted, on the previous 21 October, from the review in *The Times Literary Supplement*. And the *Havana Post* (3 October 1925) mentions the novel in reporting an interview with Lawrence who had left New York for England on 21 September.

The range of newspapers and magazines reviewing or mentioning the novel is also surprising: in Australia, not just the metropolitan dailies but also the *Australian Baptist* (26 August 1924), the Rockhampton *Morning Bulletin* (12 December 1924) and the *Journal of Pharmacy* (which picks up for rebuke an incidental remark in chapter XVII about chemists' overcharging; 20 November 1925); in the USA, the *Medical Journal and Record* noted the novel's publication (1 October 1924); in Great Britain, there were at least twelve notices in non-London papers, and *John O'London's Weekly*'s 'Mr. Curdle', after referring familiarly to 'the amazing hero who wanted more than one wife', goes on to satirise the novel's account of a cricket match (21 February 1925, p. 764).

Sparked off by Secker's (perhaps calculated) failure to specify the sex of Lawrence's collaborator or to provide any details of her background in his advertisement leaflet for the novel[127] (or on the dust-jacket; the title-page

125 'DHL and *The Boy in the Bush*', *Meanjin*, p. 261; they are in a notebook (Battye).

126 Over 90 are listed in the AUSTLIT database, The Library, University College, Australian Defence Force Academy, Canberra. The publication in 1925 of the German translation led to four more reviews – in Germany, Austria and Switzerland.

127 Secker's advertisement (Battye) read: 'In this book Mr. D. H. Lawrence has collaborated with an Australian writer to produce a real masterpiece of the West Australian bush. All the colour and mystery of background which makes *Kangaroo* memorable will be found again, together with a straightforwardness of narrative and a strength of human interest which that novel did not attempt. The book paints a family and a love-story in the setting

gave only her initials), confusion reigned as to the status and sex of the unknown 'M. L. Skinner'. The first review (by Harold Child), in *The Times Literary Supplement* of 28 August 1924, referred to 'Mr. M. L. Skinner' (p. 523); others (although not all) followed suit, making the same mistake. The *Daily Telegraph*'s reviewer commented: 'In every collaboration, perhaps, there is a dominant partner; and it is not surprising that Mr. Lawrence's vivid literary temperament should spread itself over the whole composition' (5 September, p. 4). Some reviewers speculated, with the *New Statesman*'s John Franklin, that 'it is a case of writing over . . . the original being a framework of facts and incidents' (27 September, p. 706). In *Outlook* of 27 September H. C. Harwood, evidently possessed of some inside knowledge, went further: 'The queer genius of Mr. D. H. Lawrence is most queerly harnessed with the mildly pleasurable talent of Miss M. L. Skinner. The story that Miss Skinner was writing might profitably have been contributed to the *Boy's Own Paper* . . . [A]t first tentatively, then with a semblance of impatience, and lastly to Miss Skinner's complete exclusion, Mr. Lawrence intervenes' (p. 227). Finally Humbert Wolfe's declaration in the *Weekly Westminster* of 27 September that 'there is no sich person' (p. 633) must have elicited a response from Mollie Skinner which resulted in a clarification of the circumstances of the collaboration in *TP's and Cassell's Weekly* (8 November), and subsequently in other newspapers.[128]

In Australia the question of authorship was not as generally taken up,[129] although the *West Australian* for 18 October was prepared to advance the notion that 'the more excellent parts are probably the work of Miss Skinner . . . [who] could, with advantage, have dispensed with Mr. Lawrence's literary aid and benediction' (p. 13). American reviewers, served by a slightly more informative dust-jacket on A1 (which referred to 'Miss Skinner, a talented Australian novelist'), were less curious about the authorship; only A. Donald Douglas (in the *New York Evening Post Literary Review* of 8 November) was inclined to speculate that: 'Miss Skinner wrote the novel and Mr. Lawrence then cast it in his own mold' (pp. 3–4).

of hard work and hard play which make up the Australia of to-day. The descriptions of nature, it is certain, could have come from no other pen than Mr. D. H. Lawrence's, and the same may be said of the story's *dénouement*, which is as daring as it is characteristic. 7s. 6d.'

128 *Aberdeen Evening Express*, 19 November 1924; *Birmingham Post*, 31 January 1925. See letters from Wolfe and Sewell Stokes (gossip columnist of *TP's and Cassell's Weekly*) to MLS, 6 and 11 October 1924 (Battye).

129 See Vance Palmer (*Bulletin*, 8 January 1925); Francis Brien (*Triad*, Sydney, 2 February 1925): 'with the possible exception of the opening of the kangaroo hunt, every sentence

Through most of the British reviews runs a common line of observation: whereas, according to Frank Swinnerton in the *Manchester Guardian* (12 September), in the 'first part . . . we glimpse a masterpiece and are conscious of actual contact with life itself' ('His pictures of life in the bush . . . tingle with reality', says the *Scotsman* of 8 September, p. 7), later we see 'the very nearly hysterical bewilderments of an over-sensitive nature . . . Mr. Lawrence's philosophy – the powerless fist-beating of an imprisoned child – comes in where his imagination fails' (p. 250). The novel's espousing of polygamy – 'the old story of Mr. Lawrence debasing a high theme' (*The Times Literary Supplement*, p. 523) – seemed to cause widespread shock among reviewers. In Australia this was expressed directly, sometimes verging on abuse: 'a touch of vulgarity – even beastliness – in almost every chapter' said the *Sydney Mail*, 15 November 1924 (p. 14); the Melbourne *Argus* of 17 October 1924 found the 'coarsening of the Englishman's character . . . rather nauseating' (p. 15); and the *Age* of 18 October found passages 'disgusting' (p. 4). In Britain the shock was more usually rendered in tones of confident knowingness (as in J. B. Priestley's review in the *Daily News*, 9 September 1924) or took the form of psychoanalytic condescension: Lawrence 'is still hag-ridden by sex', the Aberdeen *Press and Journal* told its readers on 1 September 1924 (p. 3). The Auckland *Star* of 25 October 1924 bemoaned the 'unrestrained sex emotionalism' of the last quarter of the novel (p. 18); and Elizabeth McDowell Jacobs in the New York *Literary Digest International Book Review* (June 1925) found the novel's philosophy 'too ridiculous to be taken seriously' (p. 483). A related complaint was that of the novel's portrayal of women: they 'are never given a chance' wrote Colin Gray, in *Eve: The Lady's Pictorial* (10 September 1924, p. 329); they 'have a prescriptive right to nonentity' commented L. P. Hartley in the *Spectator* (13 September 1924, p. 366).

Australian reviewers, some apparently writing out of a spirit of insulted patriotism, were not as willing as their British and American counterparts to grant the verisimilitude of the novel's presentation of Australian life. In the *Onlooker* (Perth) 'L. W. P.' criticised in detail the historical and geographical vaguenesses of the novel and the impression it gives that the morality of colonials is 'simply farmyard morality' (15 January 1925, p. 11). The *New Graphic of Australia* (Melbourne, 6 November 1924) was more generous when it commented that though the 'environment . . . bears little

. . . was written by D. H. Lawrence' (p. 64); and 'W.C.T' (*Bulletin*, 5 February 1925) who rebuked Palmer for failing to credit MLS with co-authorship.

resemblance to Australian actualities . . . nevertheless, in some strange way [the novel] breathes a certain atmosphere of Australianism' (p. 13).

Some reviewers were able to get beyond the shock of Lawrence's dealings with sexuality and marriage, although it is notable how few dealt directly with the themes of power and darkness except as new terms in Lawrence's vocabulary.[130] 'Panurge' in the *Liverpool Courier* denounced 'these foolish attacks, [which] are so many admissions of unreceptiveness, of mental sterility and lack of courage' (30 April 1925, p. 4). There were attempts in some reviews to put the novel in a context of Lawrence's development. Gerald Gould in the *Saturday Review* (6 September 1924) found the novel 'far more intelligible and coherent' than *Kangaroo* (p. 244), a view which Edwin Muir, in the *Nation and Athenæum* (20 September), echoed: 'The ideas of the hero . . . are living, incarnated ideas, and not notions falling to pieces in a general discussion, the discussion which made "Kangaroo" a failure' (p. 752). In similar vein a New York reviewer professed himself glad that Lawrence had 'recovered from his philosophic megrims rather too muddily exhibited in *The Lost Girl* and *Aaron's Rod*'; and he announced his discovery of Count Dionys in 'The Ladybird' (1923) as 'the type and revealment of all the Lawrence characters' including Jack Grant.[131] L. P. Hartley sensed a falling off from *Women in Love* which, 'chaotic and difficult as it was, the persistent anger and sense of isolation under which the characters laboured was unformulated and inseparable from them . . . It was the rich, sombre accompaniment to a theme that dealt with real relationships . . . But Jack Grant is the study of a man whose essential self-sufficiency allowed of no such reactions. He is real; the rest are puppets'.

A very few reviewers hailed the salutary nature of the novel's challenge to conventional mores. Reacting against several Australian reviews which had confused 'morals with [literary] merits' R. S. Ross, in the Sydney *Bulletin* (11 December 1924), hailed Lawrence as 'our one approximation to Dostoievsky . . . There is a cult which thinks it finishes with the gift for disrobing Human Nature by putting its fingers to its nose as it runs for cover. "It smells!" this cult cries, not understanding that a stink, if it is a grand stink, is Letters equally with the primrose by the river's brim. Here [in *The Boy in the Bush*] . . . Lawrence confounds the muck-raking canons' (p. 3). With a different emphasis Grant Madison Hervey (pseudonym of George Henry Cochrane) commented in the Brisbane *Sun* (14 March

[130] E.g. *The Times Literary Supplement* and *Saturday Review*, 6 September 1924.

[131] Douglas, *New York Evening Post Literary Review*, pp. 3–4. Cf. Explanatory notes on 308:5 and 260:11.

1926) that Lawrence is a 'priceless moral executioner' who 'goes to the core of the thing, and fears not' – or, as John Franklin put it in the *New Statesman*, Lawrence is one whose 'mind ... has burnt its ships, with complete courage and complete honesty'.

Text

The five notebooks of MS which Lawrence wrote in California and Mexico from September to November 1923, and the last chapter which he wrote in London in January 1924, represent the only complete state of the text over which he exercised full control; accordingly, it is chosen as base-text for this edition. The copy of original typescript from Seltzer which he corrected in London is no longer extant and was subsequently re-typed as pp. 1–166 of TSIa and b; he did not check the re-typing. Nor did he check, except to glance at, the typing of the last chapter (pp. 529–43 of TSIa and b). Moreover collation confirms that, in the section of TSIa and b which he read and corrected, he held to his habit of not checking typescript against manuscript and thus was unaware of the extent to which typists had miscopied (especially his punctuation: indeed pp. 1–166 have undergone this twice). Only in the case of the longer revisions, and in particular the 'late' pages, was there a total rewriting (or deletion). He did not see the seven surviving pages from Seltzer's copy of original typescript which were inserted in TSIa;[132] they have no authority except as a copy of part of MS. House-styling and Secker's censorship vitiate the authority of both first editions. In addition, in a letter to Secker Lawrence gave his publisher permission to 'alter a word or two' in order to avoid any moving of the type as a result of his proof corrections (v. 38). Choice of MS as base-text allows these accumulations of non-authorial interference to be stripped away. The compositional development of the work from MS to the first printed editions may be traced in the Textual apparatus which records all authorial and non-authorial variants occurring subsequent to the base-text, with the exceptions given in the 'Note on the text'.

In general the base-text is emended wherever Lawrence himself revised a later state.[133] While most substantive variants from MS in the re-typed pages of TSIa and b (pp. 1–166) are accepted, variant punctuation is

[132] In these pages 'Mona' is altered in an unknown hand to 'Monica': while in MS notebooks 1 to 3 DHL used 'Mona', she is 'Monica' in notebooks 4 and 5 (and in the re-typing of the original typescript).

[133] DHL's revisions carried out in response to defective copy (e.g. see Textual apparatus entries for 134:27 (both entries) and 236:16) are accepted only when they fall within a substantially revised passage (e.g. see Textual apparatus for 299:19 and 335:38).

adopted only when closely related to an accepted substantive variant. In the remainder of TSIa (except for the last chapter) Lawrence's autograph revisions are nearly always accepted, but problems arise when the revisions in TSIa and TSIb are not identical (see above). Then the chronological sequence of the revisions becomes significant.

The sequence can be detected readily in some cases: for example, on p. 404 of TSIa (263:33), Len's age is 'not seventeen' which Lawrence changed first to 'not eighteen' and then to 'only seventeen'. TSIb bears only the final revised reading. Again, on p. 361 of TSIa (228:28), 'red sands' has been revised to 'white sands' and then back to 'red sands'; TSIb is not altered. However, such clarity of chronological supersession is exceptional, and considerable difficulty is faced in dealing with the other cases: thirty-seven instances where emendations appear on only one typescript; and twenty-nine variant emendations. Neither TSIa nor TSIb contains in its entirety the later (or, in some cases of multiple revision, last) stage of revision.

That Lawrence would have kept (or tried to keep) the sheets together in chapters as he revised is suggested by the following facts: first, the handwritten pagination of pp. 167–528 was done *after* Lawrence had finished revising, including re-typed pages;[134] second, as in the case of the duplicate corrected typescripts of *Women in Love*, the alteration of ribbon and carbon copy occurs precisely at the end of chapters;[135] and third, the only cancellation of a sequence of pagination in TSIb (see footnote 54) was the result of chapter XI having been temporarily left out of the count. Thus it can be deduced that Lawrence must have been presented with the typescript copies either in one bundle (ribbon copy of a chapter followed by its first carbon and its second carbon, then the ribbon copy of the next chapter, and so on) or in three separate bundles. The fact that Mollie Skinner's copy cannot have contained any ribbon copy (see footnote 54) suggests that the latter is more likely.

Neither possibility offers any assistance in reconstructing the order in which Lawrence revised. Although the evidence suggests that he pulled off the piles (or pile) one chapter and its copy (or copies) at a time, the mixture of ribbon and carbon in both TSIa and b means that he re-collated them pretty much at random. (And he must have known he had done this when

[134] Shown by the pattern of cancelled paginations in TSIa continuing through the 'late' typescript pages which DHL re-typed; see footnote 54.

[135] With the exception of 3 pages (pp. 315, 425, 524 – see footnote 141) and 3 carbon reversals. There were 7 in the *Women in Love* typescripts TSIa and TSIb (ignoring one section, pp. 36–93, which does not conform); information on *Women in Love* from David Farmer.

he subsequently paginated; evidently it did not worry him.) For an editor notionally to re-sort TSIa and b into ribbon and carbon copy would be of no avail, because textual evidence shows that while Lawrence frequently corrected ribbon copy first and transcribed his corrections to the carbon copy, he did not always do so.[136] (Even if he intended to do so he could accidentally have pulled pages off the wrong pile – if there was more than one pile – or he could have shuffled the two copies of the particular chapter in his hands as he laid them down.)

Despite the likelihood that Lawrence revised a chapter at a time, he appears to have stopped to transcribe after each page. The evidence lies in his correction of a great number of misstruck and faint characters – up to ten per page. Where Lawrence corrects such mistyping on any page the proportion he transcribes to the other copy is high. If he had waited till he got to the end of a chapter, it is unlikely that he would have picked up so many by leafing back through. This consideration introduces the possibility – and textual evidence confirms it – that, *within* a chapter Lawrence would occasionally swap from revising say, ribbon copy (and transcribing to carbon) to revising carbon copy (and transcribing to ribbon);[137] he would even move from one copy to the other while working on a particular page. (After making an emendation he could have immediately transcribed, then continued to read down the page on which he had transcribed the emendation.)[138] The result when Lawrence had finished revising the typescripts was that the novel, at the stage of textual development it had reached and with the exception of errors the typists had introduced, was not fully represented by either typescript but by *both*.

Given this situation, the choice for an editor producing a (single) reading text is either to adopt a mechanical principle of emendation, incorporating into MS only those revisions Lawrence inscribed in TSIa (*or* in TSIb – it would not matter which, for there is no evidence that he preferred one over the other) and relegating the others to the Textual apparatus; or to follow so far as possible Lawrence's zig-zag course of revision between the two copies. While Lawrence did not think it of crucial importance that his publishers should receive identical setting-copy, this does not license editorial convenience in favour of the mechanical principle; to adopt it would be to obscure an important distinction between

[136] See Explanatory note on 319:5.

[137] See footnote 140 and Explanatory note on 319:5 for examples.

[138] See footnote 141 for an example ['but I . . . help myself']; p. 2 of TSIa and TSIb of *Women in Love* furnish an earlier example: see facsimile reproduction in Charles L. Ross, *The Composition of 'The Rainbow' and 'Women in Love': A History* (Charlottesville, 1979), pp. 157–8.

Lawrence's responsibility as scribe and collator – a responsibility discharged in this case under a considerable pressure of time – and his responsibility as author. It is indisputable that he took the latter more seriously. As well as correction of obvious error and awkwardness of expression his revising involved a concerted creative effort – a partial re-writing of the novel. He added a new last chapter and needed to revise the typescript copies to take account of the shift in emphasis to which it committed him. That he repeatedly went to the trouble of refining or amplifying his emendations as he transcribed them (i.e. for pp. 167–528) underlines his creative – rather than merely scribal – engagement in the process.

Fortunately there is sufficient evidence in all but one case of variation between authorial revisions in TSIa and TSIb[139] to allow the succession of emendations to be confidently tracked. Lawrence's failure to transcribe substantive emendations, and the existence of transcriptions of words or phrases demonstrating a chronological progression, provide (as instanced above) the sharpest evidence, but frequently the pattern of transcription of his corrections of punctuation and illegible characters reveals the order of emendation for any one page (or, occasionally, part-page). In the light of this evidence the present edition adopts the second alternative mentioned above: the chronologically last reading is normally deemed to have superior authority, and MS is emended accordingly, with all other readings being recorded in the Textual apparatus.

A full list of the variant revisions is provided in the introduction to the Textual apparatus; the following example illustrates the method adopted. In the passage 301:28–302:9 on p. 468 of TSIa and b, successive autograph alterations in TSIa indicate that TSIb witnesses the second stage of revision ('⟨ ⟩' and '⌜ ⌝' indicate deleted and added readings respectively): TSIaR (i.e. TSIa as revised by Lawrence) reads 'so terribly against ⟨him⟩ ⌜the thought of him⌝ . . . ⟨But⟩ ⌜Now⌝ he had arrived'; TSIbR reads 'so dangerously against the thought of him . . . Now he had arrived'. After revising the TSIa passage Lawrence either went back over it making the two further changes which he duly incorporated unaltered into TSIb (along with other compositional development: see Textual apparatus for 301:28–302:4), or he made the further alterations to TSIa *after* transcribing to TSIb, not bothering to insert the others (including 'dangerously') he had just made to TSIb. There is subsequent evidence suggesting that, for several pages at least, he continued reading and revising TSIa – which is ribbon copy throughout the chapter – and transcribing to TSIb. As part of a revision on p. 472 (304:19–20) he crossed out in TSIa the

139 See Explanatory note on 304:2.

(typed) words 'she couldn't' and then rewrote them; in TSIb he saw the shortcut and did neither. Such evidence[140] argues the chronological supersession, and therefore the adoption, of the TSIbR readings whenever they vary from TSIaR in the passage.[141]

There are two exceptions to this policy:

1. Where the revised reading occurs only in one typescript it is normally accepted: Lawrence's revisions were certainly intentional, whereas his failure to transcribe them could be accidental in any particular case, especially as he was often distracted by having to transcribe corrections of typing errors as well. On p. 526 of TSIa for instance, in a page sequence where he had been using TSIa as his correction copy and TSIb as his transcription copy,[142] he added, in TSIa only, a comma after 'Rodrigo' and deleted 'But' (336:29 and 33); however these are only two of a total of nine authorial alterations on the same page: the other seven (five corrections of obvious typing errors, the restoration of a comma after 'lives' at 336:39 and the change of 'in' to 'into' at 336:31) are successfully transcribed. While Lawrence *may* have changed his mind about the two revisions, the obvious chance of (scribal) error renders the explanation less compelling than the alternative one which relies on unambiguous autograph evidence.

140 Earlier in the chap., on TSIa only, he had made good a lacuna (p. 462: see Textual apparatus for 298:16) but must have swapped to using TSIb as his correction copy, at least for p. 467, where he corrected 'an' to 'and' before replacing it with a new reading (see entry for 301:10 – TSIa has just the revision), and corrected 'aid' to 'said', on TSIb only.

141 Another example of variant revisions occurs at 335:35–6. There is strong evidence that DHL was using TSIa (ribbon copy) as his correction copy in this chap. (see following footnote and text) and TSIb (carbon) as transcription copy. But carbon and ribbon copies have been swapped for p. 524 (see footnote 135), and there is a clear difference in the sizes of interlinear writing which suggests two sets of changes. There is the correction of the misspelling 'unciton' at 335:37, that DHL is likely to have noticed at once, and in both TSIa and b DHL's rewriting is quite large, as is the inserted 'h' in 't ink' at 335:30 (first case) and two commas he restored (after 'honour' and 'then' at 335:15, 33). One line above 'unction' is the variant revision ('but I . . . help myself') and, in the line below, a revision which is linked to it and was probably suggested by it, and by the addition of 'and' in the next line (335:40); all three additions are in much smaller writing. Presumably DHL made the spelling and punctuation corrections on the ribbon-copy page (now in TSIb, but which was probably still with the other ribbon-copy pages) and transcribed them on the carbon-copy page (now in TSIa), *then* saw the need for further revision which he made on the carbon-copy page that he had in front of him, and, in transcribing these revisions back to the ribbon-copy page, thought of a phrasing he preferred. It was presumably his having to return to the ribbon-copy page to insert the revisions which, throwing him out of sequence, led to the miscollation. Thus the reading on the ribbon-copy page (TSIbR) is adopted.

142 On p. 525 he deleted the first 'e' in 'judgement' in TSIa only (336:3); on p. 528 he deleted 'in' and then restored it in TSIa (338:4) whereas there is no change in TSIb (for p. 524 evidence see previous footnote).

2. In cases of multiple stages of revision and transcription there are a few occasions where the last revised page either does not incorporate all the intervening stages of emendation which are necessary for it to make sense (so that it is not the 'last' emendation in its entirety),[143] or it contains what is probably a transcriptional error.[144] The penultimate reading is accepted in these cases, and an Explanatory note records each transcriptional step.

Because Lawrence did not see the A1 proofs at any stage and because it is not possible to track the sequence of his revisions between the duplicate sets of Secker proofs (they, and the A1 proofs, do not survive), readings from E1 attributed (conservatively) to Lawrence are given priority on the grounds that E1 is more likely than A1 to transmit correctly the alterations he made to the proofs. It is possible that Lawrence miscollated or altered differently the two sets of proofs he sent to Secker and Seltzer (as he had the typescripts), but, however that may be, A1 was already typeset. Thus each of Lawrence's corrections on the duplicate E1 proofs had to be noticed and entered correctly into the A1 proofs, presumably at the same time as the latter were being checked against the former and the different printed (E1) readings also being entered. Thus where E1 appears to have been authorially altered in proof the added possibility of error in A1 cautions against the acceptance, except in rare cases, of its readings.[145] Where both first editions agree in their variance from TSIa and b (and editorial interference and compositorial error seem unlikely) the base-text is normally emended. This is so even for quite small corrections:[146] a great many differences were missed when the A1 proofs were being checked against the Secker, and small ones were especially liable to be overlooked; those which were not may be attributed to Lawrence's having marked them on the duplicate proofs. And in accepting any suggestions on Secker's 'marked set' of proofs, and transferring them to the set for Seltzer Lawrence gave them authority.

Because Lawrence had the opportunity of reconsidering Mollie Skinner's suggestions, the corrections he sent his publishers on 4 April 1924 were superseded; and because they were formulated or agreed to without a copy of the novel to hand, they do not directly participate in its textual development, and so have been deemed to have no textual significance. In addition, Lawrence's attempts in the proofs to cater to Mollie Skinner's

143 See Explanatory note on 319:5; for the only other instance, see above, p. lx.
144 See Explanatory note on 178:7.
145 See Explanatory notes on 67:30 and 36.
146 Except for punctuation unconnected to a change in wording. See Explanatory note on 123:33 and Textual apparatus for 325:19.

objections have been overruled. Although his changes were not made under commercial pressure, they were made, nevertheless, under moral pressure. He had encouraged her to write her novel and send it to him; he had then made it into something very different and, as his letters to her acknowledge, quite possibly objectionable to her.[147] With her list of corrections she was attempting partially to reverse or soften a daring and intensive textual development which had taken the novel far beyond the version she had written and had done so in ways which her comments and her markings of Garnett's copy show she could only partially recognise. To incorporate her outsider's tinkering would be to perpetuate an artificial situation. 'The House of Ellis' had become *The Boy in the Bush*; the present edition must – and does – recognise and reveal the *fait accompli*.

[147] See *Letters*, iv. 566, and also *Fifth Sparrow* 128.

THE BOY IN THE BUSH

Note on the text

The base-text for this edition is the autograph manuscript (MS) which, with the exception of the last chapter in the possession of IEduc, is located at UCB. Emendations have been adopted from the two typescripts (TSIa at ColU, and TSIb at UT) used as setting-copy for the American and English first editions (respectively A1 and E1), and from E1 (and, rarely, A1) where the typescripts or (unlocated) proofs show evidence of having been corrected by Lawrence.

The apparatus records all textual variants subsequent to MS except for the following categories of emendation which are silent. Instances are recorded only when they form part of another variant (e.g. see Textual apparatus for 318:26, 330:1 and its linked entries).

1. Though DHL in MS sometimes placed commas or other punctuation outside or directly under closing double inverted commas, he usually placed them inside (," or .") – which is the convention followed by A1 and E1 and this edition.

2. DHL often wrote colloquial contractions in MS without joining them up, e.g. 'Are n't'. The typists and typesetters of A1 and E1 normally regularised the contraction, which practice this edition adopts.

With the unconventional contraction 'y'' for 'you', 'your' and 'you're' DHL was attempting to imitate a common Australian pronunciation (see 16:32–3); he always separated 'y' from the adjacent word but placed the apostrophe at varying distances between the two words, and he did not close up the space where 'y'' and the following word may be spoken as one word (e.g. 'y'are') as opposed to cases where the words are spoken as two words ('y' should'). DHL's typists and typesetters dealt with the problem inconsistently. In this edition a spaced 'y'' is employed except where only one word is involved (e.g. 'y'r' for 'your') or where both words are contracted and only one apostrophe supplied by DHL (e.g. 'y've', 'y'll', 'y're' for 'you are', 'y'd'; cf. 'eatin' 'em' 57:16, 'chewin' 'em' 52:16). Contractions involving 'ye' (for 'you') are treated as conventional contractions. The contractions 'an'' for 'and', ''n' ('and', 'in' and 'than'), 't'' ('to'), ''t' ('it'), 'd'' ('do'), ''s' ('as', 'it is' and 'it has'), ''m' ('him' and 'them'), 'm'' ('me' and 'my'), 'wi'' ('with'), 'th'' ('the'), 'f'' ('for'), ''e' ('he'), ''er' ('her') and 'o'' and ''f' ('of') are treated as for 'y''.

3. Errors by typists, copy-editors and typesetters which were corrected to the original reading before publication are not noted, and errors involving the italicising of punctuation are recorded only when the punctuation is part of another variant. (DHL's habit in MS was to underline word by word, indicating that following and enclosing punctuation was to be in roman rather than italics.)

4. Typists and typesetters frequently omitted DHL's dash following terminal punctuation; the dashes are silently restored.

5. Clearly unwitting errors on DHL's part in MS (but corrected by the typists) or on the part of the typesetters have been silently corrected: inadvertent spelling errors; the use of double inverted commas to enclose material itself within double inverted commas; omitted or misplaced apostrophes in possessive cases, 'o'clock' and conventional colloquial contractions; omissions of opening *or* closing inverted commas, and of full stops at the end of sentences when no alternative punctuation

is supplied; DHL's failure in MS to indent a new paragraph after a preceding sentence which ends well before the right hand margin or indenting by inconsistent amounts; and superfluous punctuation (unnecessary closing inverted commas, e.g. where the prose is not direct speech and no inverted commas open it; a redundant full-stop, e.g. immediately after a question mark). DHL's use of single inverted commas at 252:22 and 306:27–311:7 was corrected by typists or typesetters to his majority practice, double inverted commas; these corrections are accepted.

6. While writing MS, DHL changed the name 'Mona' to 'Monica' and occasionally wrote 'Elliott' instead of 'Ellis'; when revising TSIa and b he changed 'Pink-eyed Percy' to 'Pink-eye Percy' and removed inverted commas around 'Wandoo'. All exceptions are corrected to their final form.

7. DHL's usual practice in writing 'Mr', 'Mrs' and 'Dr' without a full stop and in not hyphenating 'tonight', 'tomorrow' and 'today' have been followed. (E1 provided a full stop for 'Dr.', and A1 did for all three titles; the typists, E1 consistently and A1 inconsistently hyphenated 'to-night', 'to-morrow' and 'to-day'.) E1 and A1 always hyphenate 'good-bye' (except for A1 at 347:32 and 34); DHL sometimes did – his forms are followed silently.

8. DHL wrote 'aunt(s)' or 'Aunt(s)' depending on the word's function and (often, apparently) its contexts. TSIb and E1 normally follow MS, but in TSIa 'aunt(s)' was copy-edited to 'Aunt(s)' and so appears in A1; these variants are not noted.

9. Variants resulting from the house-styling of chapter titles, chapter and section numbering, and the opening of the first paragraph in each chapter are not noted. DHL made errors in chapter numbering and frequently neglected to number the first section in a chapter. (His habit, followed by E1, was to use roman lower case section numbers without punctuation; A1 used upper case.) This edition preserves DHL's styling in MS (e.g. 'Chapter XVI./ The Governors Dance./ *P* Three' where A1 prints 'CHAPTER XVIII/ THE GOVERNOR'S DANCE/ *P* THREE' and E1 prints 'CHAP: XVIII. THE GOVERNOR'S DANCE/ THREE') except that chapter and section openings are not indented (MS, A1 and E1 indent the latter).

Differing indentations and type sizes in A1 and E1 in the presentation of letters, songs and biblical quotations are ignored; DHL's practice in MS is followed as closely as possible.

10. DHL did not indicate the continuation of monologues and letters by reminder quotation marks before each paragraph; these have been supplied if not already inserted by the typesetter.

11. These majority usage autograph spellings are adopted silently: ''roo' (which A1 and E1 follow), 'bible' (A1 and E1 have 'Bible'), 'Marm' (A1 and E1 use lower case in pp. 7–145, and upper case in pp. 146–347) and 'for ever' (A1 spells 'forever' except in pp. 290–1; E1 is inconsistent in following MS – variations from majority practice are reported).

12. Where 'Hello', 'Yes' or 'No' is the first word of a sentence and MS has no punctuation A1 and E1 supply a comma (except A1 does not add a comma at 18:8, 29:33 and 36, 37:32, 144:34–5): MS is followed silently – as also in the case of 'Oh' after which E1 supplies a comma (except at 173:20 and 186:21).

CONTENTS

I	Jack Arrives in Australia.	7
II	The Twin Lambs.	24
III	Driving to Wandoo.	37
IV	Wandoo.	51
V	The Lambs Come Home.	59
VI	In the Yard.	84
VII	Out Back, and Some Letters.	92
VIII	Home for Christmas.	108
IX	New Year's Eve.	122
X	Shadows Before.	139
XI	Blows.	156
XII	The Great Passing.	171
XIII	Tom and Jack Ride Together.	192
XIV	Jamboree.	201
XV	Uncle John Grant.	208
XVI	On the Road.	219
XVII	After Two Years.	229
XVIII	The Governor's Dance.	245
XIX	The Welcome at Wandoo.	258
XX	The Last of Easu.	269
XXI	Lost.	283
XXII	The Find.	291
XXIII	Gold.	295
XXIV	The Offer to Mary.	311
XXV	Trot Trot Back Again.	334
XXVI	The Rider on the Red Horse.	339

Chapter I.

Jack Arrives in Australia.

i

He* stepped ashore, looking like a lamb. Far be it from me to say he was the lamb he looked. Else why should he have been sent out of England?—But a good-looking boy he was, with dark-blue eyes and the complexion of a girl and a bearing just a little too lamb-like to be convincing.

He stepped ashore on the newest of new colonies, glancing quickly around, but preserving his lamb-like quietness. Down came his elegant kit, and was dumped on the wharf: a kit that included a bran-new pigskin saddle and bridle, nailed up in a box straight from a smart shop in London. He kept his eye on that also, the tail of his well-bred eye.

Behind him was the wool ship that had brought him from England. This nondescript port was Fremantle,* in West Australia: might have been anywhere or nowhere. In his pocket he had a letter of introduction to a well-known colonial lawyer, in which, as he was aware, was folded also a draft on a West Australian bank. In his purse he had a five-pound note. In his head were a few irritating memories. In his heart he felt a certain excited* flutter at being in a real new land, where a man could be *really* free. Though what he meant by "free," he never stopped to define. He left everything suitably vague.

Meanwhile, he waited for events to develop, as if it were none of his business.

This was forty years ago, when it was still a long long way to Australia, and the land was still full of the lure of promise. There were gold and pearl findings, bush and bush-ranging,* the back of beyond,* and everything desirable. Much misery too, ignored by all except the miserable.

And Jack was not quite eighteen, so he ignored a great deal. He didn't pay much attention even to his surroundings.* Yet from the end of the wharf he saw pure sky above, the pure, unknown, unsullied sea to westward; the ruffled, tumbled sand glistened like fine silver, the air was the air of a new world, unbreathed by man.*

The only prize Jack had ever won at school was for scripture. The bible-language exerted a certain fascination over him, and in the background of his consciousness the bible images always hovered. When he was moved, it was scripture that came to his aid.* So now he stood, silent with the shyness of youth, thinking over and over: "There shall be a new heaven and a new earth."*

Not far off among the sand near the harbour mouth lay the township, a place of strong, ugly, oblong houses of white stone, with unshuttered bottle-glass windows, and a low whitewashed wall going round, like a sort of compound; then there was a huge stone prison with a high whitewashed wall. Nearer the harbour, a few new tall warehouse buildings, and sheds, long sheds, and a little wooden railway-station. Further out again, windmills for milling flour, the mill-sails turning in the transparent breeze from the sea. Right in the middle of the township was a stolid new Victorian church with a turret:* and this was the one thing he knew he disliked in the view.

On the wharf everything was busy. The old wool steamer lay important in dock, people were crowding on deck and crowding the wharf in a very informal manner, porters were running with baggage, a chain was clanking, and little groups of emigrants stood forlorn, looking for their wooden chests, swinging their odd bundles done up in coloured kerchiefs.—The uttermost ends of the earth! All so lost, and yet so familiar. So familiar, and so lost. The people like provincial people at home. The railway running through the sand-hills. And the feeling of remote unreality.

This was his mother's country. She had been born and raised here, and she had told him about it, many a time, like a fable. And this was what it was like! How could she feel she actually *belonged* to it? Nobody could belong to it.

Himself, he belonged to Bedford, England. And Bedford College.*—But his mind turned away from this in repugnance. Suddenly he turned desirously to the unreality of this remote place.

Jack was waiting for Mr George, the lawyer to whom his letter of introduction was addressed. Mr George had shaken hands with him on deck: a stout and breezy gentleman, who had been carried away again on the gusts of his own breeze, among the steamer crowd, and had forgotten his young charge. Jack patiently waited. Adult and responsible people with stout waistcoats had a habit, he knew, of being needed elsewhere.

Mr George! And all his mother's humorous stories about him! This notable character of the Western lonely colony, this rumbustical* old gentleman who had a "terrific memory," who was "full of quotations," and who "never forgot a face"—Jack waited the more calmly, sure of being recognised again by him—was to be seen in the distance with his thumbs hooked in his waistcoat armholes, passively surveying the scene with a quiet, shrewd eye, before hailing another acquaintance and delivering another sally. He had "a tongue like a razor," and frightened the women to death. Seeing him there on the wharf, elderly, stout, and decidedly old-fashioned, Jack had a little difficulty in reconciling him with the hearty colonial hero of his mother's stories.

How he had missed a seat on the bench,* for example. He was to become a judge. But while acting on probation, or whatever it is called, a man came up before him charged with wife-beating and serious maltreatment of his better half. A verdict of "Not Guilty" was returned. "Two years hard labour," said Mr George, who didn't like the looks of the fellow. There was a protest. "Verdict stands!" said Mr George. "Two years hard.* Give it him for *not* beating her and breaking her head. He should have done. He should have done. 'Twas fairly proved!"

So Mr George had remained a lawyer, instead of becoming a judge. A stout, shabby, provincial-looking old man with baggy trousers* that seemed as if they were slipping down.—Jack had still to get used to that sort of trousers.—One of his mother's heroes!

But the whole scene was still outside the boy's vague, almost trancelike state. The commotion of unloading went on—people stood in groups, the lumpers* were already at work with the winches, bringing bales and boxes from the hold. The Jewish gentleman standing just there had a red nose. He swung his cane uneasily. He must be well-off, to judge by his links and watch-chain. But then why did his trousers hang so low and baggy, and why was his waistcoat of yellow cloth—that cloth cost a guinea a yard, Jack knew it from his horsey acquaintances—so dirty and frayed?

Western Australia in the year 1882. Jack had read all about it in the official report* on the steamer. The colony had three years before celebrated its fiftieth anniversary. Many people still remembered the fiasco of the first attempt at the Swan River Settlement. Captain

Stirling brought the first boatload of prospective settlers. The Government promised not to defile the land with convicts. But the promise was broken. The convicts had come: and that stone prison-building must have been the convict station. He knew from his mother's stories.—But he also knew that the convicts were now gone again. The "Establishment"* had been closed down already for ten years or more.

A land must have its ups and downs. And the first thing the old world had to ship to the new world was its sins, and the first shipments were of sinners. That was what his mother said. Jack felt a certain sympathy. He felt a sympathy with the empty "Establishment" and the departed convicts. He himself was mysteriously a "sinner." He felt he was born such: just as he was born with his deceptive handsome look of innocence. He was a sinner, a Cain.* Not that he was aware of having committed anything that seemed to himself particularly sinful. No, he was not aware of having "sinned." He was not aware that he ever would "sin."

But that wasn't the point. Curiously enough, that wasn't the point. The men who commit sins and who know they commit sins usually get on quite well with the world. Jack knew he would never get on well with the world. He was a sinner. He knew that as far as the world went, he was a sinner, born condemned. Perhaps it had come to him from his mother's careless, rich, uncanny Australian blood. Perhaps it was a recoil from his father's military-gentleman nature. His father was an officer in Her Majesty's Army.* An officer in Her Majesty's Army. For some reason, there was always a touch of the fantastic and ridiculous, to Jack, in being an officer in Her Majesty's Army. Quite a high and responsible officer, usually stationed in command in one or other of Her Britannic Majesty's Colonies.

Why did Jack find his father slightly fantastic? Why was that gentleman in uniform who appeared occasionally, very resplendent and somehow very "good," why was he always unreal and fantastic to the little boy left at home in England? Why was he even more fantastic when he wore a black coat and genteel grey trousers? He was handsome, and pleasant, and indisputably "good." Then why oh why should he have appeared fantastic to his own little boy, who was so much like him in appearance?

"The spitten image!" one of his nurses had said. And Jack never forgave it. He thought it meant a spat-upon image, or an image in spit. This he resented and repudiated absolutely, though it remained vague.

"Oh you little sinner!" said the same nurse, half caressingly. And this the boy had accepted as his natural appellation. He was a little sinner. As he grew older, he was a young sinner. Now, as he approached manhood, he was a sinner without modification.

Not, we repeat, that he was ever able to understand wherein his sinfulness lay. He knew his father was a "good man."—"The colonel your father is such a *good man*, so you must be a *good little boy* and grow up like him."—"There is no better example of an English gentleman than your father, the General. All you have to do is to grow up like him."

Jack knew from the start that he wouldn't. And therein lay the sin, presumably. Or the root of the sin.

He did not dislike his father. The General was kind and simple and amiable. How could anyone dislike him?—But to the boy he was always just a little fantastic, like the policeman in a Punch-and-Judy show.

Jack loved his mother with a love that could not but be intermittent, for sometimes she stayed in England and "lived" with him, and more often she left him and went off with his father to Jamaica or some such place—or to India or Khartoum,* names that were in his blood—leaving the boy in the charge of a paternal aunt. He didn't think much of the aunt.

But he liked the warm, flushed, rather muddled delight of his mother. She was a handsome, ripe Australian woman with warm colouring and soft flesh, absolutely kindly in a humorous, off-hand fashion, warm with a jolly sensuousness, and good in a wicked sort of way. She sat in the sun and laughed and refused to quarrel, refused also to weep. When she had to leave her little boy a spasm would contract her face and make her look ugly, so the child was glad if she went quickly. But she was in love with her husband, who was still more in love with her, so off she went laughing sensuously across seven seas, quarreling with nobody, pitching her camp in true colonial fashion wherever she found herself, yet always with a touch of sensuous luxury, persian rugs and silk cushions and dresses of rich material. She was the despair of the true English wives, for you couldn't disapprove of her, she was the dearest thing imaginable, and yet she introduced a pleasant, semi-luxurious sense of—Of what?

Why, almost of sin. Not positive sin. She really was the dearest thing imaginable. But the feeling that there was no fence between sin and virtue. As if sin were, so to speak, the unreclaimed bush, and goodness were only the claims that the settlers had managed to fence in. And there was so much more bush than settlement. And the one was as good as the other, save that they served different ends. And that you always had the wild and endless bush all round your little claim, and coming and going was always through the wild and innocent, but non-moral bush. Which non-moral bush had a devil in it. Oh yes! But a wild and comprehensible devil, like bush-rangers who did brutal and lawless things. Whereas the tame devil of the settlements, drunkenness and greediness and foolish pride, he was more scaring.

"My dear, there's tame innocence and wild innocence, and tame devils and wild devils, and tame morality and wild morality. Let's camp in the bush and be good."

That was her attitude, always. "Let's camp in the bush and be good." She was an Australian from a wild Australian homestead. And she was like a wild, sweet animal. Always the sense of space and lack of restrictions, and it didn't matter *what* you did, so long as you were good inside yourself.

Her husband was in love with her, completely. To him it mattered very much what you did. So perhaps her easy indifference to English rail fences satisfied in him the iconoclast that lies at the bottom of all men.

She was not well-bred. There was a certain "cottage" geniality about her. But also a sense of great, unfenced spaces, that put the ordinary ladylikeness rather at a loss.—A real colonial, from the newest, wildest, remotest colony.

She loved her little boy. But also she loved her husband, and she loved the army life. She preferred, really, to be with her husband. And you can't trail a child about. And she lived in all the world, she couldn't bear to be poked in a village in England. Not for long. And she was used to having men about her. Mostly men. Jolly men.

So her heart smarted for her little boy. But she had to leave him. And he loved her, but did not dream of depending on her. He knew it as a tiny child: he would never have to depend on anybody. His father would pay money for him. But his father was rather jealous of him. Jealous even of his beauty as a tiny child, in spite of the fact that the child was the "spitten" image of the father: dark blue eyes, curly hair, peach-bloom skin. Only the child had the easy way of accommodating himself to life and circumstances, like his mother, and a certain readiness to laugh, even when he was by himself. The easy laugh that made his nurse say: "You little sinner!"

He knew he was a little sinner. It rather amused him.

Jack's mind jolted awake as he made a grab at his hat, nearly knocking it off, realising that he was being introduced to two men: or that two men were being introduced to him. They shook hands very casually, giggling at the same time to one another in a suppressed manner. Jack blushed furiously, embarrassed, not knowing what they were laughing at.

Just beside him, the Jewish gentleman was effusively greeting another Jewish gentleman. In fact they were kissing; which made Jack curl with disgust. But he couldn't move away, because there were bales behind him, people on two sides, and a big dog was dancing and barking in front of him, at something which it saw away below through a crack in the wharf timbers. The dog seemed to be a mixture of wolf and grey-hound. Queer specimen! Later, he knew it was called a kangaroo dog.[*]

"Mr A. Bell and Mr Swallow. Mr Jack Grant from England."—This was Mr George introducing him to the two men, and going on without any change, with a queer puffing of the lips: "Prrh! Bah! Wolf and Hider! Wolf and Hider!"

This left Jack completely mystified. And why were Mr Bell and Mr Swallow laughing so convulsedly? Was it the dog?

"You remember his father, Bell, out here in '59.—Captain Grant. Married Surgeon-Captain Reid's youngest daughter, from Woolamooloo Station."[*]

The gentlemen said: "Pleased to make your acquaintance," which was a phrase that embarrassed Jack because he didn't know what to answer. Should one say "Thank you!"— or "The pleasure is mine!"—or "So am I to make yours!"—He mumbled: "How do you do!"

However, it didn't matter, for the two men kept the laugh between themselves, while Mr George took on a colonial *distrait* look, then blew out his cheeks and ejaculated: "Mercy and truth have met together: righteousness and peace have kissed each other."[*]—This was said in a matter-of-fact way. Jack knew it was a quotation from the Psalms, but not what it was aimed at. The two men were laughing more openly, at the joke.

Was the joke against himself? Was it his own righteousness that was funny?—He blushed furiously once more.

ii

But Mr George ignored the boy's evident embarrassment, and strolled off with one of the gentlemen—whether Bell or Swallow, Jack did not know—towards the train.

The remaining gentleman—either Bell or Swallow—clapped the uncomfortable youth comfortably on the shoulder.

"New chum,* eh?—Not in the know? I'll tell you."

They set off after the other two.

"By gad, 's a funny thing! You've got to laugh if old George is about, though he never moves a muscle. Dry as a ship's biscuit. D' y' see the Jews kissing? They've been at law for two years, those two blossoms. One's name is Wolf, and the other's Hider, and Mr George is Wolf's attorney. Never able to do anything, because you couldn't get Hider into the open.—See the joke? Hider! Sneak Hider! Hider under the rafters! Hider hidden! And the Wolf couldn't unearth him. Though George showed up Wolf for what he is: a mean, grasping, contentious mongrel of a man.—Now they meet to kiss. See them?—The suit ended in a mush.—But that dog there hunting a rat right under their feet—wasn't that beautiful? Old George couldn't miss it.—'Mercy and truth have met together,' ha! ha!—However he finds his text for everything, beats me—"

Jack laughed, and walked in a daze beside his new acquaintance. He felt he had fallen overhead into Australia, instead of arriving naturally.

The wood-eating little engine was gasping in front of a little train of open carriages. Jack remarked on her tender piled high with chunks of wood.

"Yes, we stoke 'er with timber. We carry all we can. And if we're going a long way, to York,* when she's burned up all she can carry she stops in the bush and we all get down, passengers and all, to chop a new supply. See the axe there! She carries half a dozen on a long trip."

The three men, all wearing old-fashioned whiskers, pulled out tobacco pouches the moment they were seated, and started their pipes. They were all stout, and their clothes were slack, and they behaved with such absolute unconcern that it made Jack self-conscious.

He sat rather stiffly, remembering the things his mother had told him. Her father, Surgeon-Captain Reid, had arrived at the Swan River on a man-of-war, on his very first voyage. He had landed with Captain Fremantle from H.M.S. "Challenger," when that[*] officer took formal possession of the country in the name of His Majesty King George IV. He had seen the first transport, the "Parmelia," prevented by heavy gales from landing her goods and passengers on the mainland, disembark all on Garden Island, where the men of the "Challenger" were busy clearing ground and erecting temporary houses. That was in midwinter, June 1827: and Jack's grandfather! Now it was midwinter, June 1882; and mere Jack.

Midwinter! A pure blue sky and a warm, crystal air. The brush outside green, rather dull green, the sandy country dry. It was like English June, English midsummer. Why call it midwinter? Except for a certain dull look of the bushes.[*]

They were passing the convict station. The "Establishment" had not lasted long: from about 1850 to 1870. Not like New South Wales, which had a purely convict origin. Western Australia was more respectable.

He remembered his mother always praised the convicts, said they had been a blessing to the colony. Western Australia had been too big and barren a mouthful for the first pioneers to chew, even though they were gentlemen of pluck and education, and bit off their claims bravely. Came the rush that followed occupation, a rush of estimable and highly respectable British workmen. But even these were unprepared for the hardships that awaited them in W.A. The country was too much for them.

It needed the convicts, to make a real impression: the convicts, with their law, and discipline, and all their governmental outfit: and their forced labour. Soldiers, doctors, lawyers, spiritual pastors and earthly masters . . . and the convicts condemned to obey. This was the beginning of the colony.

Thought speaks. Mr Swallow, identified as the gentleman with the long, lean, ruddy face and large nose and vague brown eye, leaned forward and jerked his pipe-stem towards the open window:

"See that beautiful road running through the sand, sir? That road extends to Perth and over the Causeway and away up country, branching in all directions, like the arteries of the human body. Built by the Sappers and Miners with *Convict Labour*, sir. Yes, with *Convict* Labour. Also the bridge* over which we are crossing."

Jack looked out at the road, but was much more enchanted by the full, soft river of heavenly blue water, on whose surface he looked eagerly for the black swans.* He didn't see any.

"Oh yes! Oh yes! You'll find 'em wild in their native state, a little way up," said Mr Swallow.

Beyond the river were sheets of sand again, white sand stretching around on every side.

"It must have been here that the Carpenter wept—"* Jack said in his unexpected young voice, that was still slightly hoarse, as he poked his face out of the window.

The three gentlemen were silent in passive consternation, till Mr George swelled his cheeks and continued:

"Like anything to see such quantities of sand."

Then he snorted and blew his nose.

Mr Bell at once recognised the Westralian joke, which had been handed on to Jack by his mother.

"Hit it, my son!" he cried, clapping his hands on his knees. "In the first five minutes. Useless! Useless! A gentleman of discernment, that's what you are. Just the sort we want in this colony—a gentleman of discernment. A gentleman without it* planted us here, fifty years ago, in the blank, blank sand. What's the consequence? Clogged, cloyed, cramped, sand-smothered, that's what we are."

"Not a bit of it," said Mr Swallow.

"Sorrow, Sin, and Sand,"* repeated Mr Bell.

Jack was puzzled and amused by their free and easy, confidential way, which was still a little ceremonious. Slightly ceremonious, and in their shirt-sleeves, so to speak. The same with their curious, Cockney pronunciation, their accurate grammar and their slight pomposity. They never said "you"—merely "y'."—"That's what y' are."—And their drawling, almost sneering manner was very odd, contrasting with the shirt-sleeves familiarity, the shabby clothes, and the pleasant way they had of nodding* at you when they talked to you.

"Yes yes, Mr Grant," continued Mr Bell; while Jack wished he wouldn't Mister him.—"A gentleman without discernment induced certain politicians in the British Cabinet to invest in these vast areas. This same gentleman got himself created King of Groperland,* and came out here with a small number of fool followers. These fool followers, for every three-quid's-worth of goods they brought with them, were given forty acres of land apiece—"

"Of sand," said Mr George.

"—and a million acres of fine promises," continued Mr Bell, unmoved. "Therefore the fool followers, mostly younger sons of good family, anxious to own property—"

"In parties of five females to one male—Prrrh!" snorted Mr George.

"—came. They were informed that the soil was well adapted to the cultivation of tobacco! of cotton! of sugar! of flax!—and that cattle could be raised to supply His Majesty's ships with salt beef—and horses could be reared to supply the army in India—"[*]

"With Kangaroos and Wallabies."

"—the cavalry, that is. So they came and were landed in the sand—"

"And told to stick their head in it, so they shouldn't see death staring at 'em."

"—along with the goods they had brought."

"A harp!" cried Mr George. "My mother brought a harp and a paisley shawl, and got five hundred acres for 'em—estimated value of harp being twenty guineas—She'd better have gone straight to heaven with it."

"Yes sir!" continued Mr Bell, unheeding.

"No sir!" broke in Mr George. "Do you wish me unborn?"

Mr Bell paused to smile, then continued:

"Mr Grant, sir, these gentle ladies and gentlemen were dumped in the sand along with their goods. Well, there were a few cattle and sheep and horses. But what else? Harps. Paisley shawls. Ornamental glass cases of wax fruit, for the mantelpiece; family bibles, and a family coach, sir. For that family coach, sir, the bringer got a thousand acres of land. And it ended its days where they landed it, on the beach, for there wasn't an inch of road to drive it over, nor anywhere to drive it to. They took off its wheels and there it lay. I myself have sat in it."

"Ridden in his coach," smiled Mr George.

"My mother," continued Mr Bell, "was a clergyman's daughter. I myself was born in a bush humpy:[*] and my mother died shortly after—"

"Of chagrin! Of chagrin!" muttered Mr George.

"We will draw a veil over the sufferings of those years—"

"Oh, but we made good! We made good!" put in Mr Swallow comfortably. "What are you grousing about? We made good. There you sit, Bell, made of money, and grousing, anybody would think you wanted a loan of two bob."[*]

"By the waters of Babylon there we sat down—"[*] said Mr George.

"Did we! No we didn't. We rowed up the Swan River. That's what my father did. A sturdy British yeoman, Mr Grant."

"Where did he get the boat from?" asked Mr Bell.

"An old ship.—I was a baby, sir, in a tartan frock. Remember it to this day, sitting in my mother's lap.—My father got that boat off a whaler. It had been stove in, and wasn't fit for the sea. But he made it fit for the river, and they rowed up the Swan—my father and a couple of 'indented' servants,[*] as we called them. We landed in the Upper Swan valley. I remember that camp fire, sir, as well as I remember anything."

"Better than most things," put in Mr George.

"We cleared off the scrub, we lifted the stones into heaps, we planted corn and wheat—"

"The babe in the tartan frock steering the plough."

"Yes sir, later on.—Our flocks prospered, our land bore fruit, our family flourished—"

"On milk and honey—"[*]

"Oh, cry off, Swallow!" ejaculated Mr Bell. "Your father fought flood and drought for forty odd years. The floods of '62 broke his heart, and the floods in '72 ruined *you*.[*] And this is '82, so don't talk too loud."

"Ruined! When was I ever ruined?" cried Mr Swallow. "Sheep one-hundred-and-ten per-cent—for some herds, as you know, gentlemen, throw twins and triplets. Cattle ninety per-cent, horses fifty: and a ready market for 'em all."

"Pests," Mr Bell was saying, "one million per-cent. Rust destroys fourteen thousand acres of wheat crop, just as the country is getting on its feet. Dingoes breed 135 per cent, and kill sheep to match. Cattle run wild and are no more seen. Horses[*] cost the eyes out of your head before you can catch 'em, break 'em, train 'em, and ship 'em to the Indian market—"

"Moth and rust![*] Moth and rust!" murmured Mr George absently.

iii

Jack, with the uncomfortable philosophy of youth, sat still and let the verbal waters rage. Until he was startled by a question from Mr George.

"Well sir, what were you sent out for?"

This was a colonial little joke at the "Establishment" identity's expense.* But unfortunately it hit Jack too. He had been sent out, really, because he was too tiresome to keep at home. Too fond of "low" company. Too often a frequenter of the stables. Too indifferent to the higher claims of society. They feared a waster in the bud. So they shipped the bud to the antipodes, to let it blossom there upside down.

But Jack was not going to give himself away.

"To go on the land, sir—" he replied. Which was true.—But what had his father said in the letter? He flushed and looked angry, his dark blue eyes going very dark. "I was expelled from school," he added calmly.* "And I was sent down from the Agricultural College. That's why I have come out a year before my time. But I was coming—to go on the land—anyway."

He ended in a stammer. He rather hated adults; he definitely hated them in tribunal.

Mr George held up his hand deprecatingly.

"Say nothing! Say nothing! Your father made no mention of anything.—Tell us when you know us, if y' like. But you aren't called on to indict yourself.—That was a silly joke of mine. Forget it.—You came to go on the land, as your father informs me.—I knew your father, long before you were born. But I knew your mother better."

"So did I," said Mr Swallow. "And grieved the day that ever a military gentleman carried her away from Western Australia. She was one of our home-grown flowers, was Katie Reid, and I never saw a Rose of England that could touch her."

Jack now flushed deeper than ever.

"Though," said Mr George slyly, "if you've got a prank up y'r sleeve, that you can tell us about—come on with it, my son. We've none of us forgotten being shipped to England for a schooling."

"Oh well!" said Jack. He always said "Oh well!" when he didn't know what to say.

"You mean at the Agricultural College? Oh well!—Well I was the youngest there, stable-boy and harness-cleaner and all that. Oh well!—you see there'd been a chivoo[*] the night before. The lads had a grudge against the council, because they gave us bread and cheese, and no butter, for supper, and cocoa with no milk. And we weren't just little nippers. We were—Oh well!—most of the chaps were men, really—eighteen—nineteen—twenty, as much as twenty three. I was the youngest. I didn't care. But the chaps were different. There were many who had failed at the big entrance exams for the Indian Civil, or the Naval or Military,[*] and they were big hungry chaps, you can bet—"

"I should say so," nodded Mr George approvingly.

"Well, there was a chivoo. They held me on their shoulders and I smashed the Principal's windows."

You could see by Jack's face how he had enjoyed breaking those windows.

"What with?" asked Mr George.

"With a wooden gym club."

"Wanton destruction of property. Prrrh!"

"The boss was frightened. But he raised Old Harry and said he'd go up to town and report us to the council. So he ordered the trap right away, to catch the nine o'clock train. And I had to take the trap round to the front door—"

Here Jack paused. He didn't want to go further.

"And so—" said Mr George.

"And so, when I stepped away from the horse's head, the Principal jerked the reins in the nasty way he had, and the horse bolted."

"Couldn't the fellow pull her up? Man in a position like that ought to know how to drive a horse."

Jack watched their faces closely. On his own face was that subtle look of innocence, which veiled a look of life-and-death defiance.

"The reins weren't buckled into the bit, sir. No man could drive that horse," he said quietly.

A look of amusement tinged with misgiving spread over Mr George's face. But he was a true colonial. He had to hear the end of a story against the powers-that-be.

"And how did it end?" he asked.

"I'm sorry," said Jack. "He broke his leg in the accident."

The three Australians burst into a laugh. Chiefly because, when Jack said "I'm sorry," he really meant it. He was really sorry for the hurt man. But for the hurt Principal he wasn't sorry. As soon as the Principal was on the ground with a broken leg, Jack saw only the hurt man, and none of the office. And his heart was troubled for the hurt man.

But if the mischief was to do again, he would probably do it. He couldn't repent.—And yet his feelings were genuinely touched. Which made him comical.

"You're a corker!" said Mr George, shaking his head with new misgiving.

"So you were sent down," said Mr Bell. "And y'r father thought he'd better ship you straight out here, eh? Best thing for you, I'll be bound. I'll bet you never learned a ha'porth, at that place."

"Oh well!—I think I learned a lot."

"When to sow and when to reap, and a Latin motto attached?"*

"No sir, not that. I learned to vet."

"Vet?"

"Well sir, you see, the head groom was a gentleman veterinary surgeon, and he had a weakness, as he called it. So when he was strong he taught me to vet, and when he had his attacks, I'd go out with the cart and collect him at the pub and bring him home under the straw, in return for kindness shown."

"A nice sort of school! Prrrh! Bah!" snorted Mr George.

"Oh, that wasn't on the curriculum, sir. My mother says there'll be rascals in heaven, if you look for them."

"And you keep on looking, eh?—Well, I wouldn't, if I were you. Especially in this country, I wouldn't. I wouldn't go vetting any more for any drunken groom in the world, if I were you. Nor breaking windows nor leaving reins unbuckled either. And I'll tell you for why. It becomes a habit. You get a habit of going with rascals, and then you're done. Because in this country you'll find plenty of scamps, and plenty of wasters. And the sight of them is enough: nasty, low-down lot.—This is a great big country, where an honest man can go his own way into the back of beyond, if he likes. But the minute he begins to go crooked, or slack, the country breaks him. It breaks him, and he's neither fit for god nor man any more.—You beware of this country, my boy, and don't try to play larks with it. It's all right playing a prank on an old fool of a fossil out there in England. They need a few pranks played on them, they do. But out here—no! Keep all your strength and all your wits to fight the bush. It's a great big country. And it needs men, *men*, not wasters. It's a great big country, and it wants men. You can go your way and do what you want: take up land, go on a sheep station, lumber, or try the gold fields. But whatever you do, live up to your fate like a man. And keep square with yourself. Never mind other people. But keep square with *yourself*."

Jack, staring out of the window, saw miles of dull dark-green scrub spreading away on every side to a bright sky-line. He could hear his mother's voice:

"Earn a good opinion of yourself, and never mind the world's opinion. You know when there's the right glow inside you. That's the spirit of God inside you."

But this "right glow" business puzzled him a little. He was inclined to believe he felt it while he was smashing the Principal's window-glass, and while he was "vetting" with the drunken groom. Yet the words fascinated him: "the right glow inside you—the spirit of God inside you."

He sat motionless on his seat, while the Australians kept on talking about the colony.—"Have y' patience? Perseverance? Have ye that?—She wants y', and y' offspring, and the bones y'll leave behind y'. All of y' interests, y' hopes, y' life, and the same of y' sons and son's sons. An' she doesn't care if y' go nor stay, neither. Makes no difference to her. She's waiting, drowsy. No hurry. Wants millions of yer. But she's waited endless ages and can wait endless more. Only she must have *men*—understand? If they're lazy derelicts and ne'er-do-wells she'll eat 'em up. But she's waiting for real men—British to the bone—"

"The lad's no more than a boy, yet, George. Dry up a bit with your *men—British to the bone*."

"Don't toll at *me*, Bell.—I've been here since '31, so let me speak. Came in old sailing-ship 'Rockingham'—wrecked on coast—left nothing but her name, township of Rockingham. Nice place to fish.—Was sent back to London to school, '41—in another sailing-vessel, and wasn't wrecked this time. 'Shepherd,' laden colonial produce.—The first steam vessel didn't come till '45—the 'Driver.' Wonderful advancement.—Wonderful advancement in the colony too, when I came back. Came back a notary.—Couple of churches, Mill Street Jetty, Grammar School* opened, Causeway built, lot of exploration done. Eyre had legged it from Adelaide*—all in my time, all in my time—"

iv

Jack felt it might go on for ever. He was becoming stupefied. Mercifully, the train jerked to a standstill beside a wooden platform that was separated from a sandy space by a picket fence. A porter put his hand to his mouth and yelled "Perth," just for the look of the thing—because where else could it be? They all burst out of the train. The town stood up in the sand: wooden houses with wooden platforms* blown over with sand.

And Mr George was still at it.—"Yes, Bell, wait for the salty sand to mature. Wait for a few of *us* to die—and decay! Mature—manure—that's what's wanted. Dead men in the sand, dead men's bones in the gravel. That's what'll mature this country. The people you bury in it. Only good fertiliser. Dead men are like seed in the ground.* When a few more like you and me, Bell, are worked in—"

Chapter II.

The Twin Lambs.

i

Jack was tired and a little land-sick, after the long voyage. He felt dazed and rather unhappy, and saw as through a glass, darkly.* For he could not yet get used to the fixed land under his feet, after the long weeks on the steamer. And these people went on as if they were wound up, curiously oblivious of him and his feelings. A dream world, with a dark glass between his eyes and it. An uneasy dream.

He waited on the platform. Mr George had again disappeared somewhere. The train was already backing* away.

It was evening, and the setting sun from the west, where the great empty sea spread unseen, cast a radiance in the etherealised air, melting the brick shops and the wooden houses and the sandy places in a sort of amethyst glow. And again, Jack saw the magic clarity of this new world, as through a glass, darkly. He felt the cool snap of night in the air, coming strange and crude out of the jewel sky. And it seemed to him he was looking through the wrong end of a field-glass, at a far, far country.

Where was Mr George? Had he gone off to read the letter again, or to inquire about the draft on the bank? Everyone had left the station, the wagonette cabs had driven away. What was to be done? Ought he to have mentioned an hotel? He'd better say something. He'd better say——

But here was Mr George, with a serious face, coming straight up to say something.

"That vet," he said, "did he think you had a natural gift for veterinary work?"

"He said so, sir. My mother's father was a naval surgeon—if that has anything to do with it."

"Nothing at all.—I knew the old gentleman—and another silly old cuckoo he was, too. But he's dead, so we'll make the best of him.—No, it was your character I wanted to get at.—Your father wants you to go on a farm or a station for twelve months, and sends a pound a week for your board.* Suppose you know—?"

"Yes.—I hope it's enough."

"Oh, it's enough, if you're all right yourself.—I was thinking of Ellis' place. I've got the twins here now. They're kinsmen of yours, the Ellises—and of mine too. We're all related, in clans and cliques and gangs, out here in this colony.* Your mother belongs to the Ellis clan.—Well now, Ellis' place is a fine home farm, and not too far. Only he's got a family of fine young lambs, my step-sister's children into the bargain. And y' see, if y're a wolf in sheep's clothing—for you *look* mild enough—why, I oughtn't to be sending you among them. Young lasses and boys bred and reared out there in the bush, why—Come now, son—y' father protected you by silence—But you're not in court, and you needn't heed me. Tell me straight out what you were expelled from your Bedford school for."

Jack was silent for a moment, rather pale about the nose.

"I was nabbed," he said in a colourless voice, "at a fight with fists for a purse of sovereigns, laid either side. Plenty of others were there. But they got away, and the police nabbed me for the school colours on my cap. My father was just back from Ceylon, and he stood by me. But the Head said for the sake of example and for the name of the school I'd better be chucked out. They were talking about the school in the newspapers. The Head said he was sorry to expel me."

Mr George blew his nose into a large yellow red-spotted handkerchief, and looked for a few moments into the distance.

"Seems to me you let yourself be made a bit of a cat's-paw of," he said dubiously.

"I suppose it's because I don't care," said Jack.

"But you ought to care.—Why don't y'?"

There was no answer.

"You'll have to care some day or other," the old man continued.

"Do you know, sir, which hotel I shall go to?" asked Jack.

"You'll go to no hotel. You'll come home with me.—But mind y'. I've got my two young nieces, Ellis' twins, couple of girls, Ellis' daughters, where I'm going to send you. They're at my house. And there's my other niece Mary, who I'm very fond of. She's not an Ellis, she's a Rath,* and an orphan, lives with her Aunt Matilda, my sister. They don't live with me. None of 'em live with me. I live alone, except for a Good Plain Cook, since my wife died.—But I tell you, they're visiting me. And I shall look to you to behave yourself, now:

both here and at Wandoo,* which is Ellis' station. I'll take you there in the morning.—But y' see now where I'm taking you: among a pack of innocent sheep that's probably never seen a goat to say Boh! to—or Baa! if you like—makes no difference. We don't raise goats in Western Australia, as I'm aware of.—But I'm telling you, if you're a wolf in sheep's clothing—No, you needn't say anything. You probably don't know what you are, anyhow.—So come on. I'll tell somebody to bring your bags—looks a rare jorum* to me—and we'll walk."

ii

They walked off the timber platform into the sand, and Jack had his first experience of "sand-groping." The sand was thick and fine and soft, so he was glad to reach the oyster-shell path running up Wellington Street, in front of the shops. They passed along the street of brick cottages and two-storied houses, to Barrack Street, where Jack looked with some surprise on the pretentious buildings that stood up in the dusk: the handsome square red brick tower of the Town Hall, and on the sandy hill to the left, the fine white edifice of the Roman Catholic Church, which building was already older than Jack himself. Beyond the Town Hall was the Church of England. "See it!" said Mr George. "That's where your father and mother were married.* Slap-dash military wedding, more muslin and red jackets than would stock a shop."

Mr George spoke to everybody he met, ladies and gentlemen alike. The ladies seemed a bit old-fashioned, the gentlemen all wore nether garments at least four sizes too large for them. Jack was much piqued by this pioneering habit. And they all seemed very friendly and easy-going, like men in a pub at home.

"What did the Bedford Headmaster say he was sorry to lose you for? Smart at your books, were you?"

"I was good at scripture and Shakspeare, but not at the other things.—I expect he was sorry to lose me from the football eleven.* I was the cock there."

Mr George blew his nose loudly, gasped, prrrhed, and said:

"You'd better say *rooster*, my son, here in Australia—especially in polite society. We're a trifle more particular than they are in England, I suppose.—Well, and what else have you got to crow about?"

If Jack had been the sulky sort, he would now have begun to get sulky. As it was, he was tired of being continually pulled up. But he fell back on his own peculiar callous indifference.

"I was captain of the first football eleven," he said, in his indifferent voice. "And not bad in front of the sticks. And I took the long distance running cup a year under age. I tell you because you ask me."

Then Mr George astonished Jack again by turning and planting himself in front of him like Balaam's ass,* in the middle of the path, standing with feet apart in his big elephant trousers, snorting behind a walrus moustache, glaring, and extending a large and powerful hand. He shook hands vigorously, saying:

"You'll do, my son. You'll do for me."

Then he resumed his walk.

iii

"Yes sir, you'll do for me," resumed the old man. "For I can see you're a gentleman."

Jack was rather taken aback. He had come to Australia to be a Man, a wild, bushy man among men. His father was a gentleman.

"I think I'd rather be a man than a gentleman," he said.

Mr George stood still, feet apart, as if he had been shot.

"What's the difference?" he cried in a falsetto, sarcastic tone. "What's the difference?—Can't be a man unless you *are* a gentleman. Take that from me. You might say, I'm not a gentleman. Sense of the ridiculous runs away with me, for one thing. But, in order to be the best man I could, I've tried to be all the gentleman I could. No hanky-pankying about it.—You're a gentleman born—I'm not, not *altogether*.—Don't you go trying to upset what you are. But whether you're a bush-whacker* or a lumper you can be a gentleman. A gentleman's a man who never laughs to wound, who's honest with himself, and his own judge in the sight of the Almighty.—That's the Government House down there among the trees, river just beyond. —That's my house, there, see. I'm going to hand you over to the girls, once we get there. So I shan't see you again, not to talk to. I want to tell you, then, that I put my confidence in you, and you're going to play up like a gentleman. And I want you to know, as between gentlemen, not merely between an old man and a boy: but as between gentlemen, if you ever need any help, or a word of advice, come to me. Come to me, and I'll do my best."

He once more shook hands, this time in a conclusive manner.

Jack had looked to left and right as they walked, half listening to the endless old man. He saw sandy blocks of land beside the road, and scattered, ugly buildings, most of them new. He made out the turrets and gables of the Government House, in the dusk among trees, and he imagined the wide clear river below those trees.

Turning down an unmade road, they approached a two-storied brick house with narrow verandahs, whose wooden supports rested nakedly on the sand below. There was no garden, fence, or anything: just an oyster-shell path across the sand, a pipe-clayed doorstep, a brass knocker, a narrow wooden verandah, a few flower-pots.

Mr George opened the door and showed the boy into the narrow wooden hall. There was a delicious smell of cooking. Jack climbed the thin, flimsy stairs, and was shown into his bedroom. A four-poster bed with a crochet quilt and frilled pillows, a mahogany chest of drawers with swivel looking-glass, a washstand with china set complete. England all over again.—Even his bag was there, and his brushes were set out for him.

He had landed!

iv

As he made his toilet, he heard a certain fluttering outside his door. He waited for it to subside, and when all seemed still, opened to go downstairs. There stood two girls, giggling and blushing, waiting arm in arm to pounce on him.

"Oh isn't he *beau*!"* exclaimed one of the girls, in a sort of aside. And the other broke into a high laugh.

Jack remained dumbfounded, reddening to the roots of his hair. But his dark-blue eyes lingered for a moment on the two girlish faces. They were evidently the twins. They had the same thin, soft, slightly-tanned, warm-looking faces, a little wild, and the same marked features. But the brows of one were level, and her fair hair, darkish fair, was all crisp-curly round her temples, and she looked up at you from under her level brows with queer yellow-grey eyes, shy, wild, and yet with a queer effrontery, like a wild-cat under a bush. The other had blue eyes and a bigger nose, and it was she who said: "Oh, isn't he *beau*!"

The one with the yellow eyes stuck out her slim hand awkwardly, gazing at him and saying:

"I suppose you're cousin Jack, Beau."

He shook hands first with one then with the other, and could not find a word to say. The one with the yellow eyes was evidently the leader of the two.

"Tea is ready," she said, "if you're coming down."

She spoke this over her shoulder. There was the same colour in her tawny eyes as in her crisp tawny hair, but her brows were darker. She had a forehead, Jack decided, like the plaster-cast of Minerva. And she had the queerest way of looking at you under her brows,* and over her shoulder. Funny pair of lambs, these.*

The two girls went downstairs arm in arm, at a run. This is quite a feat, but evidently they were used to it.

Jack looked on life, social life inside a house, as something to be borne in silence. These two girls were certainly a desperate addition. He heard them burst into the parlour, the other one repeating:

"He's coming. Here comes Beau."

"I thought his name was Jack. *Bow* is it!" exclaimed a voice.

He entered the parlour with his elbows at his side, his starched collar feeling very stiff. He was aware of the usual hideous room, rather barer than at home: plush cushions on a horse-hair sofa, and a green carpet: a large stout woman with reddish hair in a silk frock and gold chains, and Mr George introducing her as Mrs Watson, otherwise Aunt Matilda. She put diamond-ringed hands on Jack's shoulders, and looked into his face, which he thought a repellant procedure.

"So like your father, dear boy; how's your dear mother?"

And in spite of his inward fury of resistance, she kissed him. For she was but a woman of forty-two.

"Quite well thank you," said Jack; though considering he had been at sea for six weeks, he knew as little about his mother's health as did Aunt Matilda herself.

"Did y' blow y' candle out?" asked Mr George.

"No he didn't," answered the tawny girl. "*I'll* go and do it."

And she flashed away upstairs like a panther.

"I suppose the twins introduced themselves," said Mr George.

"No they didn't," said the other one.

"Only christened you Bow.—You'll be somebody or other's beau before very long, I'll warrant.—This is Grace, Grace Ellis, you know, where you're going to live. And her sister who's gone upstairs to blow your candle out, is Monica.—Can't be too careful of fire in these dry places.—Most folks say they can't tell 'em apart, but I call it nonsense."

"Ancien, beau, bon, cher, adjectives which precede,"* said the one called Monica, jerking herself into the room, after blowing out the candle.

"There's your father," said Mr George. And Aunt Matilda fluttered into the hall, while the twins betrayed no interest at all. The tawny one stared at Jack, and kept slinking about like a lean young panther to get a different view of him. For all the world as if she was going to pounce on him, like a cat on a bird. He, permanently flushed, kept his self-possession in a boyish and rather handsome, if stiff, manner.

Mr Ellis was stout, clean-shaven, red-faced, and shabby, and baggy, and good-natured in appearance.

"This is the young gentleman—Mr Grant—called in Westralia Bow, so named by Miss Monica Ellis."

"By Miss Grace, if you please," snapped Monica.

"Tea's ready. Tea's ready."

They trooped into the dining room, where a large table was spread. Aunt Matilda seated herself behind the tea-kettle, Mr George sat at the other end, before the pile of plates and the carvers, and the others took their places where they would. Jack modestly sat on Aunt Matilda's left hand, so the tawny Monica at once pounced on the chair opposite.

Entered the Good Plain Cook with a dish covered with a pewter cover, and followed by a small, dark, ugly, quiet girl carrying the vegetable dishes.

"That's my niece Mary, Jack. Lives with Aunt Matilda here, who won't spare her or I'd have her to live here with me. Now you know everybody. What's for tea?"

He was dangerously clashing the knife on the steel. Then lifting the cover, he disclosed a young pig roasted in all its glory of gravy. Mary meanwhile had nodded her head at Jack and looked at him with her big, queer, very black eyes. You might have thought she had native blood. She sat down to serve the vegetables.

"Grace, there's a fly in the milk," said Aunt Matilda, who was already pouring large cups of tea. Grace seized the milk jug and jerked from the room.

"Do you take milk and sugar, as your dear father used to, John?" asked Aunt Matilda of the youth on her left.

"Call him Bow. Bow's his name out here—John's too stiff and Jack's too common!" exclaimed Mr George, elbows deep in carving.

"Bow'll do for me," put in Mr* Ellis, who said little.

"Mary, is there any mustard?" said Aunt Matilda.

Jack rose vaguely to go and get it, but Aunt Matilda seized him by the arm and pushed him back.

"Sit still. She knows where it is."

"Monica, come and carry the cups, there's a good girl."

"Now which end of the pig do you like, Jack?" asked Mr George. "Matilda, will this do for you?"—He held up a piece on the fork. Mary arrived with a ponderous gyrating cruet-stand, which she made place for in the middle of the table.

"What about bread?" said Aunt Matilda. "I'm sure John eats bread with his meat. Fetch some bread, Grace, for your cousin John."

"Everybody did it," thought Jack in despair, as he tried to eat amid the hustle. "No servants, nothing ever still. On the go all the time."

"Girls going to the concert tonight?" asked Mr George.

"If anybody will go with us," replied Monica, with a tawny look at Jack.

"There's Bow," said Mr George. "Bow'll like to go."

Under the she-lion peering of Monica, Jack was incapable of answer.

"Let the poor boy rest," said Aunt Matilda. "Just landed after a six-thousand-mile voyage,* and you rush him out next minute to a concert. Let him stop at home quietly with me, and have a quiet chat about the dear ones he's left behind.—Aren't *you* going to the concert with the girls, Jacob?"

This was addressed to Mr Ellis, who took a gulp of tea and shook his head mutely.

"I'd rather go to the concert, I think," said Jack, under the queer yellow glower of Monica's eyes, and the full black gaze of Mary's.

"Good for you, my boy," said Mr George. "Bow by name and Bow by nature. And well set up, with three strings to his Bow already."

Monica once more peered tawnily, and Mary glanced a black, furtive glance. Aunt Matilda looked down on him, and Grace, at his side, peered up.

For the first time since childhood, Jack found himself in a really female setting. Instinctively he had avoided women: but particularly he avoided girls. With girls and women he felt exposed to some sort of danger—as if something were going to seize him by the neck, from behind, when he wasn't looking. He relied on men for safety. But curiously enough, these two elderly men gave him no shelter whatever. They seemed to throw him a victim to these frightful "lambs." In England, there was an *esprit de corps* among men. Man for man was a tower of strength against the females. Here in this place men deserted one another as soon as the women put in an appearance. They left the field entirely to the females.

In the first half-hour Jack realised he was thrown a victim to these tawny and black young cats. And there was nothing to do but bear up.

"Have you got an evening suit?" asked Grace, who was always the one to ponder things out.

"Yes—a sort of a one," said Jack.

"Oh good! Oh put it on! Do put it on."

"Leave the lad alone," said Mr George. "Let him go as he is."

"No," said Aunt Matilda. "He has his father's handsome presence. Let him make the best of himself. I think I'll go to the concert after all."

After dinner there was a bustle. Monica flew up to light his candle for him, and stood there peering behind the flame when he came upstairs.

"You haven't much time," she said, as if she were going to spear him.

"All right," he answered, in his hoarse young voice. And he stood in torment till she left his room.

He was just tying his tie when there came a flutter and a tapping. Aunt Matilda's voice saying: "Nearly time! Are you almost ready?"

"Half a minute!" he crowed hoarsely, like an unhappy young cock.

But the door stealthily opened, and Aunt Matilda peeped in.

"Oh, tying his tie!" she said, satisfactorily,* when she perceived that he was dressed as far as discretion demanded. And she entered in full blow. Behind her hovered Grace—then Monica—and in the doorway Mary. It seemed to Jack that Aunt Matilda was the most objectionable of the lot, Monica the brazenest, Grace the most ill-mannered, and Mary the most repulsive, with her dark face. He struggled in discomfort with his tie.

"Let Mary do it," said Aunt Matilda.

"No no!" he barked. "I can do it."

"Come on, Mary. Come and tie John's tie."

Mary came quietly forward.

"Let me do it for you, Bow," she said in her quiet, insinuating voice, looking at him with her inky eyes and standing in front of him till his knees felt weak and his throat strangled. He was purple in the face, struggling with his tie in the presence of the lambs.

"He'll never get it done," said Monica, from behind her yellow glare.

"Let me do it," said Mary, and lifting her hands decisively she took the two ends of the tie from him.

He held his breath and lifted his eyes to the ceiling and felt as if the front of his body were being roasted. Mary, the devil-puss, seemed endless ages fastening the tie. Then she twitched it at his throat and it was done, just as he was on the point of suffocation.

"Are those your best braces?" said Grace. "They're awfully pretty, with rose-buds." And she fingered the band.

"I suppose you put on evening dress for the last dinner on board," said Aunt Matilda. "Nothing makes me cry like *Auld Lang Syne*, that last night, before you land next day. But it's fifteen years since I went over to England."

"I don't suppose we shall any of us ever go," said Grace longingly.

"Unless you marry Bow," said Monica abruptly.

"I can't marry him unless he asks me," said Grace.

"He'll ask nobody, for a good many years to come," said Aunt Matilda with satisfaction.

"Hasn't he got lovely eyelashes," said Grace impersonally.

"He'd almost do for a girl," said Monica.

"Not if you look at his ears," said Mary, with odd decision. He felt that Mary was bent on saving his manhood.

He breathed as if the air around him were red-hot. He would have to get out, or die. He plunged into his coat, pulling down his shirt-cuffs with a jerk.

"What funny green cuff-links!" said Grace. "Are they pot?"

"Malachite,"[*] said Jack.

"What's malachite?"

There was no answer. He put a white silk muffler round his neck to protect his collar.

"Oh look at his initials in lavender silk!"

At last he was in his overcoat, and in the street with the bevy.

"Leave your overcoat open, so it shows your shirt-front as you walk," said Grace, forcibly unbuttoning the said coat. "I think that looks so lovely. Doesn't he look lovely, Monica? Everybody will be asking who he is."

"Tell them he's the son of General Grant," said Aunt Matilda, with complete satisfaction, as she sailed at his side.

Life is principally a matter of endurance.—This was the sum of Jack's philosophy. He put it into practice this evening.

It was a benefit concert in the Town Hall,[*] with the episcopalian choir singing: "Angels Ever Bright And Fair," and a violinist from Germany playing violin solos, and a lady vocalist from Melbourne singing "home" solos,[*] while local stars variously coruscated. Aunt Matilda filled up the end of the seat—like a massive book-end: and the others like slender volumes of romance were squeezed in between her and another stout book-end. Jack had the heaving warmth of Aunt Matilda on his right, the electric wriggle of Monica on his left, and he continued to breathe red-hot air.

The concert was a ludicrous continuation of shameful and ridiculous noise to him. Each item seemed inordinately long, and he hoped for the next. Which, when it came, seemed worse than the last. The people who performed seemed to him in a ghastly humiliating position. One stout mother-of-thousands leaned forward and simply gurgled about riding over the brow of a hill and seeing a fair city beyond, and a young knight in silver armour riding towards her with shining face, to greet her on the spot as his lady fair and lady dear.[*] Jack looked at her in pained amazement. And yet when the songstress from Melbourne, in a rich contralto, began to moan in a Scotch accent:

> "And it's O-O-O-h! that I'm longing for my ain folk,
> Though the-e-e-ey be but lowly, puir and plain folk—
> I am far across the sea
> But my heart will ever beee-e-e
> At home in dear old Scotland with my ain folk."[*]

Jack suddenly wanted to howl. He had never been to Scotland. And his father, General Grant, with his mother, was at present in Malta. And he hadn't got any "ain folk," and he didn't want any. Yet it was all he could do to keep the tears from showing in his eyes, as his heart fairly broke in him. And Aunt Matilda crowded him a little more suffocatingly on the right, and Monica wriggled more hatefully than ever on the left, and that beastly Mary leaned forward to glance appreciatively at him, with her low-down black eyes. And he felt as if the front of his body was scorched. And a smouldering desire for revenge awoke deep down in him.[*]

People were always trying to "do things" to you. Why couldn't they leave you alone? Dirty cads, to sing "My Ain Folk," and then stare in your face to see how it got you.[*]

But life was a matter of endurance, with possible revenge later on.

When at last he got home and could go to bed, he felt he had gained a brief respite. There was no lock to the door—so he put the arm-chair against it, for a barricade.

And he felt he had been once more sold. He had thought he was coming to a wild and woolly world. But all the way out, he had been forced to play the gentlemanly son of his father. And here it was hell on earth, with these women let loose all over you, and these ghastly concerts and these hideous meals, and these awful flimsy, choky houses. Far better the Agricultural College. Far better England.

He was sick with home-sickness as he flung himself into bed. And it seemed to him he was always homesick for some place which he had never known and perhaps never would know. He was always homesick for somewhere else. He always hated where he was, silently but deeply.[*]

Different people. The place would be all right, but for the people.

He hated women. He hated the kind of nausea he felt after they had crowded on him. The yellow cat-eyes of that deadly Monica! The inky eyes of that low-down Mary! The big nose of that Grace: she was the most tolerable. And the indecency of the red-haired Aunt Matilda, with her gold chains.

He flung his trousers in one direction, and the loathsome starched shirt in another, and his underwear in another. When he was quite clear of all his clothing he clenched his fists and reached them up, and stretched hard, hard, as if to stretch himself clear of it all. Then he did a few thoughtless exercises, to shake off the world. He wanted the muscles of his body to move, to shake off the contact of the world. As a dog coming out of the water shakes himself, so Jack stood there slowly, intensely going through his exercises, slowly sloughing the contact of the world from his young, resistant white body. And his hair fell loose into curl, and the alert defiance came into his eyes as he threw apart his arms and opened his young chest. Anything, anything to forget the world and to throw the contact of people off his limbs and his chest. Keen and savage as a Greek gymnast he struck the air with his arms, with his legs.

Till at last he felt he had broken through the mesh. His blood was running free, he had shattered the film that other people put over him, as if snails had crawled over him. His skin was free and alive. He glowered at the door, and made the barricade more safe.

Then he dived into his night-shirt, and felt the world was his own again. At least in his own immediate vicinity. Which was all he cared about, for the moment.

Chapter III.

Driving to Wandoo.

i

Jack started before dawn next morning, for Wandoo.* Mr George had business which took him south, so he decided to carry the boy along on the coach. Mr Ellis also was returning home in the coach, but the twins, those lambs, were staying behind.* In the chilly dark, Jack climbed the front of the buggy to sit on the seat beside the driver. He was huddled in his overcoat, the happiest boy alive. For now at last he was "getting away"—he always wanted to "get away." From what, he didn't stop to consider: and still less did he realise *towards* what. Because however far you may get away from one thing, by so much do you draw near to another.

And this is the Fata Morgana of Liberty, or Freedom. She may lead you very definitely away from today's prison.* But she also very definitely leads you towards some other prison. Liberty is a changing of prisons, to people who seek *only* liberty.

Away went the buggy at a spanking trot, the driver pointing out the phosphoric glow of the river, as they descended to the Causeway. Stars still shone overhead, but the sky was beginning to open inland. The buggy ran softly over the damp sand, the two horses were full of life. There was an aroma of damp sand, and a fresh breeze from the river as they crossed.

Jack didn't want to talk. But the driver couldn't miss the opportunity.

"I drives this coach back'ards and forrards to Albany week in week out, years without end amen, and a good two hundred miles o' land to cover, taking six days clear with two 'osses, and them in relays fifteen or twenty miles,* sometimes over, as on the outland reach past Wagin."

"Ever get held up?"

"No sir, can't say as I do. Who'd there be to hold me up in Western Australia? And if there was, the mounted police'd soon settle 'em. There's nobody to hold me up but my old woman, and she drives the coach for me up Middle Swan way."

"Can she drive?"

"You back your life she can. Bred and born to it. Drive, an' swear at th'osses like a trooper, when she's a mind. Swear! I'd never ha' thought it of 'er, when I rode behind 'er as a groom."

"How?"

"Oh, she took me in, she did, pretty. But after all, what's a lady but a woman! Though far be it from me to say: 'what's a woman but a lady?'—If I'd gone down on my hands an' knees to her, in them days, I should have expected her to kick me. And what does she do! Rode out of the park gates and stopped. So she did. Turns to me. 'Grey,' she says, 'here's money. You go to London and buy yourself clothes like what a grocer would buy. Avoid looking like a butler or a groom. And when you've got an outfit, dress and make yourself look like a grocer'—she said, though I never had any connections with grocery in my life—'and go to the office in Victoria Street and take two passages to Australia.'* That was what she said. Just Australia. When the man in the office asked me, where to in Australia, I didn't know what to say. 'Oh, we'll go in at the first gate,' I said. And so it was Fremantle. 'Yes,' she said. 'We're going to elope.' 'Nice thing for me,' thinks I. But I says: 'All right, Miss.' She was a pearl beyond price,* was Miss Ethel. So she seemed to me then. Now she's a termagant as ever was: in double 'arness collar-proud."*

The coachman flicked the horses. Jack looked at him in amazement. He was a man with a whitish-looking beard, in the dim light.

"And did she have any children?"

"She's got five."

"And does she regret it?"

"At times, I suppose.—But as I say to her, if anybody was took in, it was me. *I* always thought her a perfect lady. So when she lets fly at me: 'Call yourself a man!' I just say to her: 'Call yourself a lady?'—And she comes round all right."

Jack's consciousness began to go dim. He was aware of a strange dim booming almost like guns in the distance, and the driver's voice saying:

"Frogs sir. Way back in the days before ever a British ship came here, they say the Dutchmen came, and was frightened off by the croaking of the bull frogs: couldn't make it out a-nohow!"—The horses' hoofs were echoing on the boarded Causeway, and from the little islands alongside, came the amazing croaking, barking, booing and booming of the frogs.[*]

ii

When Jack looked round again it was day. And the driver's beard was black. He was a man with a thin red face and black beard and queer grey eyes that had a mocking sort of secret in them.

"I thought your beard was white," said Jack.

"Ay, with rime. With frost. Not with anything else."

"I didn't expect hoar-frost here."

"Well—It's not so *very* common. Not like the Old Country."

Jack realised they always spoke patronisingly of the Old Country. Poor old place, it couldn't help being what it was.

The man's grey eyes with the amused secret glanced quickly at Jack.

"Not quite awake yet?" he said.

"Oh yes," said Jack.

"Coming out to settle, I hope," said the driver. "We can do with a few spruce young lads. I've got five daughters to contend with. Why there's six A.1. families in Perth, maybe you've heard, and six in the country, and possibly six round Fremantle, and nary one of 'em but's got seven daughters.[*] Seven daughters— — —"

Jack did not hear. He seemed to be saying, in reply to some question:

"I'm Jack Hector Grant."

"Contrairy," the servants had called him, and "naughty little boy," his aunts. Insubordinate. Untrustworthy. Such things they said of him. His soul prickled from all the things, but he guessed they were not far wrong.

What did his mother think of him? And his father? He didn't know them very well. They only came home sometimes, and then they seemed to him reasonable and delightful people. The Wandering Grants, Lady Bewley had called them.

Was he a liar? When they called him a liar, was it true? It was. And yet he never really *felt* a liar. "Don't ask, and you'll get no lies told you." It was a phrase from his nurse, and he always wanted to use it to his hateful Aunts. "Say you're sorry! Say you're sorry!" Wasn't that *forcing* him to tell lies, when he *wasn't* sorry. His Aunts always seemed to him despicable liars. He himself was just an ordinary liar.

He lied because he *didn't* want them to know what he'd done, even when he'd done right.

So they threatened him with that loathsome "policeman." Or they dropped him over the garden fence into the field beyond. There he sat in a sort of Crusoe solitary confinement. A vast row of back fences, and a vast, vast field. Himself squatting immovable, and an Aunt coming to demand sharply through the fence: "Say you're sorry. Say you want to be a good little boy. Say it, or you won't come in to dinner. You'll stay there all night."

He wasn't sorry, he didn't want to be a good little boy, therefore he wouldn't "say it"; so he got a piece of bread and butter pushed through the fence. And then he faced the emptiness of the field, and set off.

To find himself somehow in the kitchen-garden of the manor-house. A servant had seen him, and brought him before her ladyship, who was herself walking in the garden.

"Who are you, little boy?"

"I'm Jack Hector Grant"—a pause. "Who are you?"

"I'm Lady Bewley."

They eyed one another.

"And where were you wandering to, in my garden?"

"I wasn't wand'rin'. I was walkin'."

"Were you?—Come then, and walk with me, will you."

She took his hand and led him along a path. He didn't quite know if he was a prisoner. But her hand was gentle, and she seemed a quiet, sad lady. She stepped with him through wide-open window-doors. He looked uneasily round the drawing-room, then at the quiet lady.

"Where was *you* born?" he asked her.

"Why, you funny boy, I was born in this house."

"My mother wasn't. She was born in Australia. And my father was born in India. And I can't remember where I was born."

A servant had brought in the tea-tray. The child was sitting on a foot-stool. The lady seemed not to be listening. There was a dark cake.

"My mother said I wasn't never to ask for cake, but if somebody was to offer me some, I needn't say no fank you."*

"Yes, you shall have some cake," said the lady. "So you are one of the wandering Grants, and you don't know where you were born?"

"But I think I was born in my mother's bed."

"I suppose you were.—And how old are you?"

"I'm four. How old are you?"

"A great deal older than that.—But tell me, what *were* you doing in my garden?"

"I don't know. Well, I comed by mistake."

"How was that?"

"'Cause I wouldn't say I was sorry I told a lie. Well I wasn't sorry. But I wasn't wandrin' in your garden. I was only walkin'. I was walkin' out of the meadow where they put me—"

—"And as I says, she may have been born in a 'all, but she'll die in a wooden shack—"

"Who? Who will?"

"I was tellin' you about my old woman.—Look! there's a joey runnin' there along the track."

Jack looked, and saw a funny little animal half leaping, half running along.

"We call them baby 'roos joeys,* you understand, and they make the cutest little pets you ever did imagine."

They were still in sandy country, on a good road not far from the river, and Jack saw the little chap jump to cover. The tall gum trees with their brownish-pale smooth stems and loose strips of bark stood tall and straight and still, scattered like a thin forest that spread unending, rising from a low, heath-like undergrowth. It seemed open, and yet weird, enclosing you in its vast emptiness. This bush, that he had heard so much of! The sun had climbed out of the mist, and was becoming gold and powerful in a limpid sky. The leaves of the gum-trees hung like heavy narrow blades, inert and colourless, in a weight of silence. Save when they came to a more open place, and a flock of green parrots flew shrieking "Twenty-eight!* Twenty-eight!" At least that was what the driver said they cried.—The lower air was still somewhat chilly from the mist. A number of black-and-white handsome birds, that they call magpies,* flew alongside in the bush, keeping pace for a time with the buggy. And once a wallaby ran alongside for a while on the path, a bigger 'roo than the joey, and very funny, leaping persistently alongside with his little hands dangling.

It *was* a new country after all. It *was* different. A small exultance grew inside the youth. After all, he *had* got away, into a country that men had not yet clutched into their grip. Where you could do as you liked, without being stifled by people. He still had a secret intention of doing as he liked, though what it was he would do when he could do as he liked, he did not know. Nothing very definite. And yet something stirred in his bowels as he saw the endless bush, and the noisy green parrots, and the queer, tame kangaroos: and no man.

"It's dingy country down here," the coachman was saying: "Not good for much. No good for nothing except cemetery, though Mr George says he believes in it. And there's nothing you *can* do with it, seeing as how many gents what come in the first place has gone away for ever lock stock and barrel, leaving nothing but their 'claims' on the land itself, so nobody else can touch it."* Here he shook the reins on the horses' backs. "But I hopes you settles, and makes good, and marries and has children, like me and my old woman, sir. She've put five daughters into the total, born in a shack, though their mother was born in Pontesbeach Hall—"

But Jack's mind drifted away from the driver. He was in that third state, not uncommon to youth, which seems to intervene between reality and dream. The bush, the coach, the wallabies, the coach driver were not very real to him. Neither was his own self and his own past very real to him. There seemed to him to be another, mute world,* another mute core to himself, apart from the known Jack Grant, and apart from the world as he had known it. Even apart from this Australia, which was so unknown to him.

As a matter of fact, he had not yet come-to in Australia. He had not yet extricated himself from England and the ship. Half of himself was left behind, and the other half was gone ahead. So there he sat, mute and stupid.

He only knew he wanted something, and he resented something. He resented having been so much found fault with. They had hated him because he preferred to make friends among "good-for-nothings." But as he saw it, "good-for-nothings" were the only ones that had any daring. Not altogether tamed. He loathed the thought of harness. He hated tameness, hated it, hated it. The thought of it made his innocent face take on a really devilish look. And because of his hatred of harness, he hated answering the questions that people put to him. Neither did he *ask* many, for his own part. But now one popped out.

"There *are* policemen here, are there?"

"Yes sir, a good force of mounted police,* a smart body of men. And they're needed. Western Australia is full of old prisoners, black fellers, and white ones too. The whites, born here, is called 'gropers,' if you take me sir. Sand-gropers. And they all need protection one from the other. And there's half-pay officers, civil and military, and clergy, scattered through the bush—"

"Need protecting from one another, and yet he says there's nobody to hold up the coach,"[*] thought Jack to himself, cynically.

The bush had alternated with patches of wild scrub. But now came clearings: a little wooden house, and an orchard of trees planted in rows, with a grazing field beyond. Then more flat meadows, and ploughed spaces, and a humpy or a shack here and there: children playing around, and hens: then a regular homestead, with verandah on either side, and creepers climbing up, and fences about.

"The soil is red!" said Jack.

"Clay! That's clay! No more sand, except in patches, all the way to Albany. This is Guildford where the roses grow."[*]

They clattered across a narrow wooden bridge with a white railing, and up to a wooden inn where the horses were to be changed. Jack got down in the road, and saw Mr George and Mr Ellis both sleepily emerge and pass without a word into the place marked BAR.

"I think I'll walk on a bit," said Jack, "if you'll pick me up."

But at that moment a fleecy white head peering out of the back of the coach cried:

"Oh Mr Gwey! Mr Gwey! They've frowed away a perfeckly good cat."

The driver went over with Jack to where the chubby arm was pointing, and saw the body of a cat stretched by the trodden grass. It was quite dead. They stood looking at it, Grey explaining that it was a good skin and it certainly was a pity to waste it, and he hoped someone would find it who would tan it before it went too far, for, as for him, he could not take it along in the coach, the passengers might object before they reached Albany, though the weather was cooling up a bit.

Jack laughed and went back to the coach to throw off his overcoat. He loved the crazy inconsequence of everything. He stepped along the road feeling his legs thrilling with new life. The thrill and exultance of new life. And yet somewhere in his breast and throat tears were heaving. Why? Why? He didn't know. Only he wanted to cry till he died. And at the same time, he felt such a strength and a new power of life in his legs as he strode the Australian way, that he threw back his head in a sort of exultance.

Let the exultance conquer. Let the tears go to blazes.

When the coach came alongside, there was the old danger-look in his eyes, a defiance, and something of the cat-look of a young lion. He did not mount, but walked on up the hill.* They were climbing the steep Darling Ranges, and soon he had a wonderful view. There was the wonderful clean new country spread out below him, so big, so soft, so ancient in its virginity. And far beyond, the gleam of that strange empty sea. He saw the grey-green bush ribboned with blue rivers, winding to an unknown sea.* And in his heart he was *determining* to get what he wanted. Even though he did not know what it was he wanted. In his heart he clinched his determination to get it. To get it out of this ancient country's virginity.

He waited at the top of the hill. The horses came clop-clopping up. Morning was warm and full of sun. They had rolled up the flaps of the wagonette, and there was the beaming face of Mr George, and the purple face of Mr Ellis, and the back of the head of the floss-haired child.

Jack looked back again, when he had climbed to his seat and the horses were breathing, to where the foot of the grey-bush hills rested in a valley ribboned with rivers and patched with cultivation, all frail and delicate in a dim ethereal light.

"A land of promise! A land of promise!" said Mr George. "When I was young I bid £1080 for 2,700 acres of it. But Hammersley* bid twenty pounds more, and got it.—Take up land, Jack Grant, take up land. Buy, beg, borrow or steal land, but get it, sir, get it."

"He'll have to go farther back to find it," said Mr Ellis, from his blue face. "He'll get none of what he sees there."

"Oh, if he means to stay, he can jump it.—The law is always bendin' and breakin', bendin' and breakin'."

"Well, if he's going to live with me, Mr George, don't put him on to land-snatching," said Mr Ellis. And the two men fell to a discussion of Land Acts, Grants, Holdings, Claims,* and Jack soon ceased to listen. He thought the land looked lovely. But he had no desire to own any of it. He never felt the possibility of "owning" land. There the land was, for eternity. How could he own it.—Anyhow, it made no appeal to him along those lines.

But Mr Ellis loved "timber," and broke the spell by pointing and saying:

"See them trees, Jack my boy? Jarrah! Hills run one into the other way to the Blackwood River. Hundreds of miles of beautiful Jarrah timber. The trees likes this barren ironstone formation.* It's well they do, for nothing else does."

"There's one o' the mud-brick buildings* the convicts lived in, while they were building the road," said the driver, not to be done out of his say. "One of the convicts broke and got away. Mostly when they went off they was driven in by the bush. But this one never. They say he's wanderin' yet.* I say, dead."

Mr George was explaining the landscape.

"Down there—Darlington.* Governor Darling went down and never came back. Went home the quick way.—Boya, native word for rock.—Mahogany Creek just above there. They'll see us coming. Kids watch from the rise, run back and holloa. Pa catches rooster, black girl blows fire, Ma mixes paste, yardman peels spuds,—dinner when we get there."

"And, sir, Sam has a good brew, none better. Also, sir, though it looks lonesome, he's mostly got company."

"How's that?"

"Well sir, everyone comes for miles round to hear his missus play the harmonium. Got it out from England, and if it doesn't break your heart to hear it! The voice of the past! You'd love to hear it, Mr Grant, being new from home."

"I'm sure I should," said Jack, thinking of the concert.

The dinner at Mahogany Creek was as Mr George had said. Afterwards, on again through the bush.

Towards the end of the afternoon the coach pulled up at a little by-road,* where stood a basket-work shay, and a tall young fellow in very old clothes lounging with loose legs.

"'Ere y' are!" said Grey, and walking the horses to the side of the road, he scrambled down to pull water from a well.

"Here we are!" said Mr Ellis from the back of the coach, where the tall youth was just receiving the floss-haired baby between his big red hands. Fat Mr Ellis got down. The youth began pulling out Jack's bags and boxes, and Jack hurried round to help him.

"This is Tom," said Mr Ellis.

"Pleased to meet you," said Tom, holding out a big hand and clasping Jack's hand hard for a moment. Then they went on piling the luggage on the wicker shay.

"That's the lot!" called Mr Ellis.

"Goodbye Jack!" said Mr George, leaning his grey head out of the coach. "Be good and you'll be happy."

Over which speech Jack puzzled mutely. But the floss-haired baby girl was embracing his trouser-legs.

"I never knew you were an Ellis,"* he said to her.

"Ay, she's another of 'em," said Mr Ellis.

The coach was going. Jack went over awkwardly and offered the driver a two-shilling piece.

"Put it back in y'r pocket, lad, y'll want it more than I shall," said Grey unceremoniously. "The best o' luck to you, an' I mean it."

They all packed into the shay, Jack sitting with his back to the horses, the little girl tied in beside him, his smaller luggage bundled where it could be stowed; and in absolute silence they drove through the silence of the standing, motionless gum-trees. Jack had never felt such silence. At last they pulled up. Tom jumped down and drew a slip-rail,* and they passed a log fence, inside which there were many sheep, though it was still bush. Tom got in again and they drove through bush with occasional sheep. Then Tom got down again—Jack could not see for what purpose. The youth fetched an axe out of the cart, and started chopping. A tree was across the road: he was chopping at the broken part. There came a sweet scent.

"Raspberry jam!" said Mr Ellis. "That's *acacia acuminata*, a beautiful wood, good for fences, posts, pipes, walking-sticks—And they're burning it off by the million acres."*

Tom pulled the trunk aside, and drove on again till he came to another gate. Then they saw ahead a great clearing in the bush, and in the midst of the clearing a "ginger-bread" house,* made of wood slabs, with a shingle roof running low all round to the verandahs. A woman in dark homespun cloth with an apron and sunbonnet, and a young bearded man in moleskins and blue shirt, came out with a cheery shout.

"You get along inside and have some tea," said the young bearded man. "I'll change the horses."

The woman lifted down the baby, after having untied her.

There was a door in the front of the house, a window on each side. But they all went round under the eaves to the mud-brick kitchen behind, and had tea. The woman hardly spoke, but she smiled and passed the tea and nursed Ellie. When the young bearded man came in he smiled and said:

"I've got the mail out of the shay, Mr Ellis."

"That's all right," said Mr Ellis.

After which no one spoke again.

When they set off once more, there was a splendid pair of greys on either side the pole.

"Bill and Lil," said Mr Ellis. "My own breed. Angus lends us his for the twenty miles to the cross roads. We've just changed them and got our own. There's another twenty miles yet."*

It now began to rain, and gradually grew dark and cold. The bush was dree,* the dreest thing Jack had ever known. Rugs and mackintoshes were fetched out, the baby was fastened snug in a corner out of the wet, and the horses kept up a steady pace. And then, as Nature went to roost, Mr Ellis woke up and pulled out his pipe, to begin a conversation:

"How's Ma?"

"Great!"

"How's Gran?"

"Same."

"All well?"

"Yes."

"He's come twenty miles," thought Jack, "and he only asks now!"

"See the doctor in town, Dad?" asked Tom.

"I did."

"What'd he say?"

"Oh, heart's wrong alright just what Rackett said. But might live to be older than he is. So I might too, lad."

"So you will an' all, Dad."

And then Mr Ellis, as if desperate to change the conversation, pulling hard at his pipe:

"Jersey cow calved?"

"Yes."

"Bull again?"

"No, heifer. Beauty."

They both smiled silently. Then Tom's tongue suddenly was loose.

"Little beauty she is. And the Berkshire* has farrowed nine little prize-winners. Cowslip come on with 'er butter since she come on to the barley. I cot them twins Og an' Magog peltin' the dogs with eggs, an' them so scarce, so I wopped* 'em both. That black spaniel bitch I had to kill her for she worried one o' the last batch o' sucking pigs, though I don't know how she come to do such a thing. I've finished fallowin' in the bottom meadow, an' I'm glad you're back to tell us what to get on wif."

"How's clearing in th' Long Mile Paddock?"

"Only bin down there once. Sam's doin' all right."

"Hear anything of the Gum Tree Gully clearing gang?"

"Message from Spencer, an' y' t' go down sometime—as soon 's y' can."

"Well I want the land reclaimed this year, an' I want it gone on with. Never know what'll happen, Tom. I'd like for you to go down there, Tom. You c'n take th' young feller behind here with you, soon 's the girls come home."

"What's he like?"

"Seems a likely enough young chap. Old George put in a good word for 'm."

"Bit of a toff."

"Never you mind, 's long 's his head's not toffy."

"Know anything?"

"Shouldn't say so."

"Some fool."

"Don't know. You find out for y'self."

Silence.

Jack heard it all. But if he hadn't heard it, he could easily have imagined it.

"Yes, you find out," he thought to himself, going dazed with fatigue and indifference as he huddled under the blanket, hearing the horses' hoofs clop-clop! and the rain splash on his shoulders. Sometimes the horses pulled slow and hard in the dark, sometimes they bowled along. He could see nothing. Sometimes there was a snort and jingle of harness, and the wheels resounding hollow. "Bridging something," thought Jack. And he wondered how they found their way in the utter dark, for there were no lamps. The trees dripped heavily.

And then, at the end of all things, Tom jumped down and opened a gate. Hope! But on and on and on. Stop—hope—another gate. On and on. Same again. And so interminably.

Till at last some intuition seemed to communicate to Jack the presence of home.—The rain had stopped, the moon was out. Ghostly and weird the bush, with white trunks spreading like skeletons.* There opened a clearing, and a dog barked. A horse neighed near at hand, there were no trees, a herd of animals was moving in the dusk. And then a dark house loomed ahead, unlighted. The shay drove on, and round to the back. A door opened, a woman's figure stood in the candle-light and firelight.

"Alright Ma!" called Tom.

"All right dear!" called Mr Ellis.

"All right!" shrilled a little voice....

Well here they were, in the kitchen. Mrs Ellis was a brown-haired woman with a tired look in her eyes. She looked a long time at Jack, holding his hand in her one hand, and feeling his wet coat with the other.

"You're wet. But you can go to bed when you've had your supper. I hope you'll be all right. Tom'll look after you."

She was hoping that he would only bring good with him. She was all mother: and mother of her own children first. She felt kindly towards him. But he was another woman's son.

When they had eaten, Tom led the newcomer away out of the house, across a little yard, threw open a door in the dark, and lit a candle stuck in the neck of a bottle. Jack looked round at the mud floor, the windowless window, the unlined wooden walls, the calico ceiling, and he was glad. He was to share this cubby-hole, as they called it, with the other Ellis boys. His truckle bed was fresh and clean. He was content. It wasn't stuffy, it was rough and remote.

When he opened his portmanteau to get out his nightshirt he asked Tom where he was to put his clothes. For there was no cupboard or chest of drawers or anything.

"On your back or under your bed," said Tom. "Or I might find y' an old packing case, if y're decent.—But say, ol' bloke, lemme give y' a hint. Don't y' get sidey or nosey up here, puttin' on jam an' suchlike, f'r if y' do y'll shame me in front of strangers, an' I won't stand it."

"Jam did you say?"

"Yes jam. Macaroni. Cockadoodle. We're plain people out here-aways, not mantel-ornaments nor dickey-toffs, an' we want no flash sparks* round, see."

"*I'm* no flash spark," said Jack. "Not enough for 'em at home. It's too much fist and too little toff that's the matter with me."*

"C'n y' use y'r fists?"

"Like to try me?"

Jack shaped up to him.

"Oh for the love o' Mike," laughed Tom, "stow the haw-haw gab!*—You'll do me though, I think."

"I'll try to oblige," said Jack, rolling into bed.

"Here!" said Tom sharply. "Out y' get an' say y' prayers. What sortta example for them kids of ours, gettin' inter bed an' forgettin' y'r prayers?"

Jack eyed the youth.

"You say yours?" he asked.

"Should say I do. Gran is on ter me right cruel if I don't see to it, *whoever* sleeps in this cubby. They has ter say their prayers, see?"

"All right!" said Jack laconically.

And he obediently got up, kneeled on the mud floor, and gabbled through his quota. Somewhere in his heart he was touched by the simple honesty of the boy. And somewhere else he was writhing with slow, contemptuous repugnance at the vulgar tyranny.

But he called again to his aid that natural indifference of his, grounded on contempt. And also a natural boyish tolerance, because he saw that Tom had a naïve, if rather vulgar, good-will.

He gabbled through his prayers wearily but scrupulously, to the last Amen! Then rolled again into bed to sleep till morning, and forget, forget, forget! He depended on his power of absolute forgetting.

Chapter IV.

Wandoo.

i

Two things struggled in Jack's mind when he awoke in the morning. The first was the brave idea that he had left everything behind, that he had done with his boyhood and was going to enter into his own. The second was a noise of somebody quoting Latin and clicking wooden dumb-bells.

Jack opened his eyes. There were four beds in the cubby-hole. Between two beds stood a thin boy of about thirteen, swinging dumb-bells, and facing two small urchins who were faithfully imitating him, except that they did not repeat the Latin tags. They were all dressed in short breeches loosely held up by braces, and undervests.

O veni, up went their arms smartly,—*vidi*, down came the clubs to horizontal;—*vici*,* the clubs were down by their sides.

Jack smiled to himself and dozed again. It was scarcely dawn. He was dimly aware of the rain pattering on the shingle roof.

"Ain't ye gettin' up this morning?"

It was Tom standing contemplating him. The children had run out barefoot and bare-armed in the rain.

"Is it morning?" asked Jack stretching.

"Not half. We've fed th'osses. Come on."

"Where do I wash?"

"At the pump. Look slippy* and get your clothes on. Our men live over at Red's, we have to look sharp in the morning."

Jack looked slippy, and went out to wash in the tin dish by the pump. The rain was abating, but it seemed a damp performance.

By the time he was really awake, the day had come clear. It was a fine morning, the air fresh with the smell of flowering shrubs: silver wattle, spirea, daphne and syringa* which Ellis grew in his garden. Already the sun was coming warm.

The house was a low stone building with a few trees round it. But all the life went on here at the back, here where the pump was, and the various yards and wooden out-buildings. There was a vista of open clearing, and a few huge gum-trees. The sky was already blue, a certain mist lay below the great isolated trees.

In the yard a score of motherless lambs were penned, bleating, their silly faces looking up at Jack confidently, expecting the milk-bottle. He walked with his hands in the pockets of his old English tweeds, feeling over-dressed and a bit out of place. Cows were tethered to posts or standing loose about the fenced yard, and the half-caste Tim, and Lennie, the dumb-bells boy, and a girl, were silently milking. The heavy, pure silence of the Australian morning.

Jack stood at a little distance. A cat whisked across the yard and ran up a queer-looking pine-tree, a dissipated old cow moved about at random.

"Hey you!" shouted Tom impatiently. "Take hoult of that cart-'oss nosin' his way inter th' chaff-house, and bring him here. An' see to that grey's ropes: she's chewin' 'em free. Look slippy, make yourself useful."

There was a tone of amiability and intimacy mixed with this bossy shouting. Jack ran to the cart-'oss. He couldn't help liking Tom and the rest. They were so queer and naïve, and they seemed oddly forlorn, like waifs lost in this new country. Jack had always had a leaning towards waifs and lost people. They were the only people whose bossing he didn't mind.

The children at their various tasks were singing in shrill, clear voices, with a sort of street-arab abandon. Lennie, the boy, would break the shrilling of the twin urchins with a sudden musical yell, from the side of the cow he was milking. And they seemed to sing anything, songs, poetry, nonsense, anything that came into their heads, like birds singing variously and at random.

> "The blue, the fresh, the ever free
> I am where I would ever be
> With the blue above, and the blue below—"[*]

Then a yell from Lennie by the cows:

> "And wherever thus in childhood's *'our*"

The twins: "I never was on the dull tame shore
But I loved the great sea more and more—"

Again a sudden and commanding yell from Lennie.

"I never loved a dear gazelle
To glad me with its soft black eye,
But, when it came to know me well
And love me—"

Here the twins, as if hypnotised, howled out—"it was sure to die."*

They kept up this ragged yelling in the new, soft morning, like lost wild things. Jack laughed to himself. But they were quite serious. The elders were dumb-silent. Only the youngsters made all this noise. Was it a sort of protest against the great silence of the country? Was it their young, lost effort in the noiseless antipodes, whose noiselessness seems like a doom at last? They yelled away like wild little lost things, with an uncanny abandon. It pleased Jack.

ii

They had all gone silent again, and collected under the peppermint tree* at the back door, where Ma ladled out tea into mugs for everybody. Ma was Mrs Ellis. She still had the tired, distant look in her eyes, and a tired bearing, and she seemed to take no notice of anybody, either when she was in the kitchen or when she came out with pie to the group squatting under the tree. When anyone said: "Some more tea, Ma!" she silently ladled out the brew. Jack was not a very intent observer. But he was struck by Mrs Ellis' silence and her "drawn" look.

Tom came and hitched himself up against the trunk of the tree. Lennie was sitting opposite on a log, holding his tin mug and eyeing the stranger in silence. On another log sat the two urchins, sturdy, wild little brats, barefooted, barelegged, bare-armed, as Jack had first seen them, their dress still consisting of a little pair of pants and a cotton undervest: and a pair of braces. The last seemed by far the most important garment. Lennie was clothed, or unclothed, the same, while Tom had added a pair of boots. The bare arms out of the cotton vests were brown and smooth, and they gave the boys and the youth a curiously naked look.* A girl of about twelve, in a dark-blue spotted pinafore and a rag of red hair-ribbon, sat on a little stump near the twins. She was silent like her mother—but not yet "drawn."

"What d' ye think of Og an' Magog?" said Tom, pointing with his mug at the twins. "Called for giants cos they're so small."

Jack did not know what to think. He tried to smile benevolently.

"An' that's Katie," continued Tom, indicating the girl, who at once looked foolish. "She's younger 'n Lennie, but she's pretty near his size. He's another little un. Little an' cheeky, that's what he is. Too much cheek for his age—which is fourteen. You'll have to keep him in his place, I tell you straight."

"Ef ye *ken*!" murmured Len with a sour face.

Then, chirping up with a real street-arab pertness, he seemed to ignore Jack as he asked brightly of Tom:

"An' who's My Lord Duke of Early Risin', if I might be told?—For before Gosh he sports a tidy raiment."

"Now Len, none o' yer lingo!" warned Tom.

"Who is he, anyway, as you should go tellin' him to keep me in my place?"

"No offence intended, I'm sure," said Jack pleasantly.

"*Taken* though!" said Lennie, with such a black look that Jack's colour rose in spite of himself.

"You keep a civil tongue in your head, or I s'll punch it for you," he said. He and Lennie stared each other in the eye.

Lennie had a beautiful little face, with an odd pathos like some lonely girl, and grey eyes that could change to black. Jack felt a certain pang of love for him, and in the same instant remembered that she-lioness cub of a Monica. Perhaps she too had the same odd lonely pathos: like a young animal that runs alert and alone in the wood. Why did these children seem so motherless and fatherless, so much on their own?—It was very much how Jack felt himself. Yet he was not pathetic.

Lennie suddenly smiled whimsically, and Jack knew he was let into the boy's heart. Queer! Up till now they had all kept a door shut against him. Now Len had opened the door. Jack saw the winsomeness and pathos of the boy vividly, and loved him too. But it was still remote. And still mixed up in it was the long stare of that Monica.

"That's right, you tell 'im," said Tom. "What I say here, goes—no back chat, an' no tales told. That's what's the motto on this station."

"Obey an' please my Lord Tom Noddy
So God shall love and angels aid ye—"* said Lennie,

standing tip-toe on his log and balancing his bare feet, and repeating his rhyme with an abstract impudence, as if the fiends of air* could hear him.

"Aw shut up, you!" said Tom. "You've got ter get them 'osses down to Red's. Take Jack an' show him."

"I'll show him," said Len, munching a large piece of pie as he set off.

"Ken ye ride, Jack?"

Jack didn't answer, because his riding didn't amount to much.

iii

Len unhitched four heavy horses, led them into the yard, and put the ropes into Jack's hands. The child marched so confidently under the noses of the great creatures, as they planted their shaggy feet. And he was such a midget, and with his brown bare arms and bare legs and feet, and his vivid face, he looked so "tender." Jack's heart moved with tenderness.

"Don't you ever wear boots?" he asked.

"Not if I k'n help it. Them kids now, they won't neither, 'n I don't blame 'em. Last boots Ma sent for was found all over the manure heap so the old man said he'd buy no more boots an' a good job too. The only thing as scares me is double-gees:* spikes all roads and Satan's face on three sides. Ever see double-gees?"

Len was leading three ponderous horses. He started peering on the road, the horses marching just behind his quick little figure. Then he found a burr with three queer sides and a sort of face on each side with sticking-out hair.

He was a funny kid, with his scraps of Latin and tags of poetry. Jack wondered that he wasn't self-conscious and ashamed to quote poetry. But he wasn't. He chirped them off, the bits of verse, as if they were a natural form of expression.

They had led the horses to another stable. Len again gave the ropes to Jack, disappeared, and returned leading a saddled stock horse. Holding the reins of the saddle-horse, the boy scrambled up the neck of one of the big draught horses like a monkey.

"Which are you goin' to ride?" he asked Jack from the height. "I'm taking three an' leading Lucy. You take the other three."

So he received the three halter-ropes.

"I think I'll walk," said Jack.

"Please y'self. You k'n open the gates easy walkin', an' comin' back I'll do it, 'n you k'n ride Lucy an' I'll ride behind pillion so 's I can slip down easy."

Yes, Lennie was a joy. On the return journey, when Jack was in the saddle riding Lucy, Len flew up behind him and stood on the horse's crupper, his hands on Jack's shoulders, crying: "Let 'er go!" at the first gate he slid down like a drop of water, then up again, this time sitting back to back with Jack, facing the horse's tail, and whistling briskly.

Suddenly he stopped whistling, and said:

"Y've seen everybody but Gran an' Doc. Rackett, haven't you? He teaches me—a rum sortta doc he is too, never there when he's wanted. But he's a real doctor all right: signs death certificates an' no questions asked. Y' c'd do a murder, 'n if you was on the right side of him, y'd never be hung. He'd say the corpse died of natural causes."

"I didn't know a corpse died," said Jack laughing.

"Didn't yer? Well yer know now!—Gran's as good as a corpse—an' she don't want ter die. She put on Granfer's grave: 'Left desolate, but not without hope.' So they all thought she'd get married again. But she never.—Did y' go to one of them English schools?"

"Yes."

"Ever wear a bell-topper?"*

"Once or twice."

"Gosh!—May I never go to school, God help me. I should die of shame and disgrace. Arrayed like a little black pea in a pod, learnin' to be useless. Look at Rackett. School, an' Cambridge, an' comes inter money. Wastes it. Wastes his life. Now he's teachin' me, an' th' only useful thing he ever did."

After a pause, Jack ventured:

"Who is Doctor Rackett?"

"A waster. Down and out waster. He's got a sin. I don't know what it is, but it's wastin' his soul away."

iv

It was no use Jack's trying to thread it all together. It was a bewilderment, so he let it remain so. It seemed to him, that right at the very core of all of them was the same bewildered vagueness: Mr Ellis, Mrs Ellis, Tom, the men—they all had that empty bewildered vagueness at the middle of them. Perhaps Lennie was most on the spot. The others just could attend to their jobs, no more.

Jack still had no acquaintance with anyone but Tom and Len. He never got an answer from Og and Magog. They just grinned and wriggled. Then there was Katie. Then Harry, a fat, blue-eyed small boy. And then that floss-haired Ellie who had come from Perth. And smaller even* than her, the baby. All very confusing.

The second morning, when they were at the proper breakfast, Dad suddenly said:

"Ma! D' ye know where the new narcissus bulbs are gone? I was waiting to plant 'em till I got back."

"I've not seen them since ye put them in the shed at the end of the verandah, dear."

"Well, they're gone."

Dead silence.

"Is 'em like onions?" asked Og, pricking up intelligently.

"Yes. They are! Have you seen them?" asked Dad sternly.

"I see baby eatin' 'em, Dad," replied Og calmly.

"What my bulbs, as I got out from England! Why what the Dickens, Ma, d' you let that mischievous monkey loose for? My precious narcissus bulbs, the first I've ever had. An' besides—Ma! I'm not sure but what they're poison."

The parents look* at one another, then at the gay baby. There is a general consternation. Ma gets the long, evil blue bottle of castor oil and forcibly administers a spoonful to the screaming baby. Dad hurries away, unable to look on the torture of the baby—the last of his name. He goes to hunt for the bulbs in the verandah shed. Tom says "By gosh!", and sits stupefied. Katie jumps up and smacks Og for telling tales, and Magog flies at Katie for touching Og. Jack, as a visitor, unused to family life, is a little puzzled.

Lennie meanwhile calmly continues to eat his large mutton chop. The floss-haired Ellie toddles off talking to herself. She comes back just as intent, wriggles on her chair on her stomach, manages to mount, and puts her two fists on the table, clutching various nibbled, onion-like roots.

"Vem's vem, ain't they Dad? She never ate 'em. She got 'em out vis mornin' and was suckin' 'em, so I took 'em from her an' hid 'em for you."

"Should Dad have said Narcissi or Narcissuses?" asked Len from over his coffee mug, in the hollow voice of one who speaks out of his cups.

Nobody answered. The baby was shining with castor oil. Jack sat in a kind of stupefaction. Everybody ate mutton chops in noisy silence, oppressively, and chewed huge doorsteps of bread.

Then there entered a melancholy, well-dressed young fellow who looked like a daguerreotype of a melancholy young gentleman. He sauntered in in silence, and pulling out his chair, sat down at table without a word. Katie ran to bring his breakfast, which was on a plate on the hearth, keeping warm. Then she sat down again. The meal was even more oppressive. Everybody was eating quickly, to get away.

And then Gran opened the door leading from the parlour, and stood there like the portrait of an old old lady, stood there immovable just looking on, like some ghost. Jack's blood ran cold. The boys, pushing back their empty plates, went quietly out to the verandah, to the air. Jack followed, clutching his cap, that he had held all the time on his knee.

Len was pulling off his shirt. The boys had to wear shirts at meal-times.

This was the wild new country! Jack's sense of bewilderment deepened. Also he felt a sort of passionate love for the family—as a savage must feel for his tribe. He felt he would never leave the family. He must always be near them, always in close physical contact with them. And yet he was just a trifle horrified by it all.

Chapter V.

The Lambs Come Home.

i

A month later Tom and Lennie went off with the greys, Bill and Lil, to fetch the girls. It had been wet, so Jack had spent most of his day in the sheds mending corn sacks. He was dressed now in thick cotton trousers, coloured shirt, and grey woolen socks, and copper-toed boots. When he went ploughing, by Tom's advice he wore "lasting" socks—none.

His tweed coat hung on a nail on the wall of the cubby, his good trousers and vest were under the mattress of his bed. The only useful garment he had brought had been the old riding-breeches of the Agricultural College days.

On the back of his Tom-clipped hair was an ant-heap of an old felt hat, and so he sat, hour after hour, sewing the sacks with a big needle. He was certainly not unhappy. He had a sort of passion for the family. The family was almost his vice. He felt he *must* be there with the family, and then nothing else mattered. Dad and Ma were the silent, unobtrusive pillars of the house.[*] Tom was the important young person. Lennie was the soul of the place. Og and Magog were the mischievous life. Then there was Harry, whom Jack didn't like, and the little girls, to be looked after. Dr Rackett hovered round like an uneasy ghost, and Gran was there in her room. Now the girls were coming home.

Jack felt he had sunk into the family, merged his individuality, and he would never get out. His own father and mother, England, or the future, meant nothing to him. He loved this family. He loved Tom, and Lennie, and he wanted always to be with all of them. This was how it had taken him: as a real passion.

He loved, too, the ugly stone house, especially the south side, the shady side, which was the back where the peppermint tree stood. If you entered the front door—which nobody did—you were in a tiny passage from which opened the parlour on one side, and the dying room on the other. Tom called it the dying room because it had never been used for any other purpose, by the family. Old Mr Ellis had been carried down there to die. So had his brother Willie. As Tom explained: "The staircase is too narrow to handle a coffin."

Through the passage you dropped a step into the living room. On the right from this you stepped up a step into the kitchen, and on the left, up a step into Gran's room. Gran's room had once been the whole house: the rest had been added on. It is often so in Australia.

From the sitting-room you went straight on to the back verandah, and there were the four trees, and a fenced-in garden, and the yards. The garden had gay flowers, because Mr Ellis loved them, and a round, stone-walled well. Alongside was the yard, marked off by the four trees into a square: a mulberry one side the kitchen door, a pepper the other, a pittosporum with a seat under it a little way off, and across, a Norfolk pine* and half a fir tree.

Tom would talk to Jack about the family: a terrible tangle, they both thought. Why there was Gran, endless years old! Dad was fifty, and he and Uncle Easu (dead) were her twins and her only sons. However, she had seven daughters and, it seemed to Jack, hundreds of grandchildren, most of them grown up with more children of their own.

"I could never remember all their names," he declared.*

"I don't try" said Tom. "Neither does Gran. And I don't believe she cares a tuppenny* for 'em—for any of 'em, except Dad and us."

Gran was a delicate old lady with a lace cap, and white curly hair, and an ivory face. She made a great impression on Jack, as if she were the presiding deity of the family. Over her head as she sat by the sitting-room fire an old clock tick-tocked. That impressed Jack too. There was something weird in her age, her pallor, her white hair and white cap, her remoteness. She was very important in the house, but mostly invisible.

Lennie, Katie, Og and Magog, Harry, Ellie with the floss hair, and the baby: these counted as "the children." Tom, who had had another mother, not Ma, was different. And now the other twins, Monica and Grace, were coming. These were the lambs. Jack, as he sat mending the sacks, passionately in love with the family and happy doing any sort of work there, thought of himself as a wolf in sheep's clothing, and laughed.

He wondered why he didn't like Harry. Harry was six, rather fat and handsome, and strong as a baby bull. But he was always tormenting baby. Or was it baby tormenting Harry?

Harry had got a picture book, and was finding out letters. Baby crawled over and fell on the book. Harry snatched it away. Baby began to scream. Ma interfered.

"Let baby have it, dear."

"She'll tear it, Ma."

"Let her, dear! I'll get you another."

"When?"

"Some day, Harry. When I go to Perth."

"Ya—some day! Will ye get it Monday?"

"Oh Harry, do be quiet do———"

Then baby and Harry tore the book between them in their shrieking struggles, while Harry battered the cover on the baby's head. And a hot, dangerous, bullying look would come into his eyes, the look of a bully. Jack knew that look already. He would know it better before he had done with Australia.

And yet baby adored Harry. He was her one god.

Jack always marvelled over that baby. To him it was a little monster. It had not lived twelve months, yet God alone knew the things it knew. The ecstasy with which it smacked its red lips and showed its toothless gums over sweet, sloppy food. The diabolic screams if it was thwarted. The way it spat out "lumps" from the porridge! How on earth, at that age, had it come to have such a mortal hatred for lumps in porridge? The way its nose had to be held when it was given castor oil! And again, though it protested so violently against lumps in porridge, how it loved such abominations as plaster, earth, or the scrapings of the pig's bucket.

When you found it cramming dirt into its mouth, and scolded it, it would hold up its hands wistfully to have them cleaned. And it didn't mind a bit, then, if you swabbed its mouth out with a lump of rag.

It was a girl. It loved having a new clean frock on. Would sit gurgling and patting its stomach, in a new smart frock, so pleased with itself. Astounding!

It loved bulls and stallions and great pigs, running between their legs. And yet it yelled in unholy terror if fowls or dogs came near. Went into convulsions over the friendly old dog, or a quiet hen pecking near its feet.

It was always trying to scuttle into the stable where the horses stood. And it had an imbecile desire to put its hand in the fire. And it adored that blue-eyed bully of a Harry, and didn't care a straw for the mother that slaved for it. Harry, who treated it with scorn and hate, pinching it, cuffing it, shoving it out of its favourite positions—off the grass patch, off the hearth-rug, off the sofa-end. But it knew exactly the moment to retaliate, to claw his cap from his head and clutch his fair curls, or to sweep his bread and jam on to the floor, into the dust if possible...

To Jack it was all just incredible.

ii

But it was part of the family, and so he loved it.

He dearly loved the cheeky Len.

"What d' y' want ter say 'feece' for? Why can't yer say 'fyce' like any other bloke?—And why d' y' wash y' fyce before y' wash y' hands?"

"I like the water clean for my face."

"What about your dirty hands, smarmin' them over it?"

"You use a flannel or a sponge."

"If y've got one. Y' don't find 'em growin' in th' bush. Why can't y' learn offa me now, an' be proper. Ye'll be such an awful sukey* when y' goes out campin', y'll shame y'self.—Y' should wash y' hands first. Frow away th' water if y' not short, but y' will be. Then when y've got y' hands all soapy, sop y' fyce up an' down, not round an' round like a cat does. Then pop y' nut under th' pump, an' wring it dry. Don't never waste y' huckaback* on it. Y'll want that f' somefin' else."

"What else shall I want my towel for?"

"Wroppin' up things in, meat an' damper,* an' t' lay down for y' meal, against th' ants, or to put over it against th' insex."

Then from Tom:

"Hey, nipper knowall, dry up! I've taught you the way you should behave, haven't I? Well I can teach Jack Grant, without any help from you. Skedaddle!"

"Hope y' can! Sorry for y', havin' to try," said Len as he skedaddled.

Tom was the head of the clan, and the others gave him leal obedience and a genuine, if impudent homage.

"What a funny kid!" said Jack. "He's different from the rest of you, and his lingo's rotten."

"He's not dif!" said Tom. "Xactly same. Same 's all of us—same 's all the nips* round here. He went t' same school as Monica and

Grace an' me, to Aunt's school in th' settlement, till Dr Rackett came.* If he's any different, he got it from *him*: he's English."

Jack noticed they always spoke of Dr Rackett as if he were a species of rattle-snake that they kept tame about the place.

"But Ma got Dad to get the Doc, cos she can't bear to part with Len even for a day—to give 'm lessons at home.—I suppose he's her eldest son.—Doc needn't, he's well-to-do. But he likes it, when he's here. When he's not Lennie slopes off and reads what he pleases. But it makes no difference to Len, he's real clever. And—" Tom added grinning—"he wouldn't speak like you do neither, not for all the tin in a cow's bucket."

To Jack, fresh from an English public school, Len was amazing. If he hurt himself sharply, he sat and cried for a minute or two. Tears came straight out, as if smitten from a rock.* If he read a piece of sorrowful poetry, he just sat and cried, wiping his eyes on his arm without heeding anybody. He was greedy, and when he wanted to, he ate enormously, in front of grown-up people. And yet you never minded. He talked poetry, or raggy bits of Latin, with great sententiousness and in the most awful accent, and without a qualm. Everything he did was right in his own eyes. Perfectly right in his own eyes.

His mother was fascinated by him.

Three things he did well: he rode, bare-back, standing up, lying down, anyhow. He rode like a circus rider. Also he boasted—heavens high. And thirdly, he could laugh. There was something so sudden, so blithe, so impish, so daring, and so wistful in his lit-up face when he laughed, that your heart melted in you like a drop of water.

Jack loved him passionately: as one of the family.

And yet even to Lennie, Tom was the hero. Tom, the slow Tom, the rather stupid Tom. To Lennie Tom's very stupidity was manly. Tom was so dependable, so manly, such a capable director. He never gave trouble to anyone, he was so complacent and self-reliant. Lennie was the love-child, the elf. But Tom was the good, ordinary Man, and therefore the hero.

Jack also loved Tom. But he did not accept his manliness so absolutely. And it hurt him a little, that the strange, sensitive Len should put himself so absolutely in obedience and second place to the good plain fellow. But it was so. Tom was the chief. Even to Jack.

iii

When Tom was away, Jack felt as if the pivot of all activity was missing. Mr Ellis was not the real pivot. It was the plain, red-faced Tom.

Tom had talked a good deal, in snatches, to Jack. It was the family that bothered him, as usual. He always talked the family.

"My grandfather came out here in the early days. He was a merchant, and lost all his money in some East India business.* He married Gran in Melbourne, then they came out here. They had a bit of a struggle, but they made good. Then Granpa died without leaving a will; which complicated things for Gran. Dad and Easu was twins, but Dad was the oldest. But Dad had wandered: he was gone for years, and no-one knows what he did all the time.

"But Gran liked him best, and he was the eldest son, so she had this place all fixed up for him when he came back. She'd a deal of trouble getting the Reds out. All the A'nts* were on their side—on the Reds' side. We always call Uncle Easu's family the Reds. And Aunt Emmie says she's sure Uncle Easu was born first, and not Dad. And that Gran took a fancy to Dad from the first, so she said he was the eldest.* Anyhow it's neither here nor there.—I hope to goodness I never get twins—It runs in the family, and of all the awful things! Though the Easus have got no twins. Seven sons and no girls, and no twins. Uncle Easu's dead, so young Red runs their place.

"Uncle Easu was a nasty scrub, anyway. He married the servant girl, and a servant girl no better than she should be, they say.

"He didn't make no will, either. Making no wills runs in the family as well as twins. Dad won't. His Dad wouldn't, and he won't neither."

Which meant, Jack knew, that by the law of the colony the property would come to Tom.

"Oh, Gran's crafty alright! She never got herself talked about, turning the Reds out! She saved up a stocking—Gran always has a stocking. And she saved up an' bought 'em out. She persuaded them that the land beyond this was better 'n this. She worked in with 'em while Dad was away, like the fingers on your hand: and bought that old barn of a place over yonder for 'em, and bounced 'em into it. Gran's crafty, when it's anyone she cares about. Now it's Len.

"Anyhow there it was when Dad came back, 'Wandoo' all ready for him. He brought me wrapped in a blanket. Old Tim, our half-caste man, was his servant, and[*] there was my old nurse. That's all we know about me. I know no more, neither who I am nor where I sprung from. And Dad never lets on.

"He came back with a bit of money, and Gran made him marry Ma to mind me. She said I was such a squalling little grub, and she wanted me brought up decent. So Ma did it. But Gran never quite fancied me.

"It's a funny thing, seeing how I come, that I should be so steady and ordinary, and Len should be so clever and unsteady. You'd ha' thought I should be Len and him me.

"Who was my mother? That's what I want to know. Who was she? And Dad won't never say.

"Anyhow she wasn't black, so what does it matter, anyhow?

"But it *does* matter!"—Tom brought his fist down with a smack in the palm of his other hand. "Nobody is ordinary to their mother, and I'm ordinary to everybody, and I wish I wasn't."

Funny of Tom. Everybody depended on him so, he was the hero of the establishment, because he *was* so steady and ordinary and dependable. And now even he was wishing himself different. You never knew how folks would take themselves.

iv

As for the Reds, Jack had been over to their place once or twice. They were a rough crowd of men and youths, father and mother both dead. A bachelor establishment. When there was any extra work to be done, the Wandoos went over there to help. And the Reds came over to Wandoo the same. In fact they came more often to Wandoo than the Ellises went to them.

Jack felt the Reds didn't like him. So he didn't care for them. Red Ellis, the eldest son, was about thirty years old, a tall, sinewy, red-faced man with reddish hair and reddish beard[*] and staring blue eyes. One morning when Tom and Mr Ellis were out mustering and tallying, Jack was sent over to the Red house. This was during Jack's first fortnight at Wandoo.

Red the eldest met him in the yard.

"Where's y'oss?"

"I haven't one. Mr Ellis said you'd lend me one."

"Can y' ride?"

"More or less."

"What d' ye want wearin' that Hyde Park costume* out here for?"

"I've nothing else to ride in," said Jack, who was in his old riding breeches.

"Can't y' ride in trousers."

"Can't keep 'em over my knees, yet."

"Better learn then, smart n' lively. Keep them down, n' y' socks up. Come on then, blast ye, an' I'll see about a horse."

They went to the stockyard, an immense place. But it was an empty desert now, save for a couple of black-boys holding a wild-looking bay. Red called out to them:

"Caught Stampede, have y'? Well let 'im go again afore y' break y' necks. Y'r not to ride him, d' y' hear.—What's in the stables, Ned?"

"Your mare, master. Waiting for you."

"What y' got besides, ye grinning jackasses.* Find something for Mr Grant here, an' look slippy."

"Oh master, no horse in, no knowin' stranger come."

Red turned to Jack. Easu was a coarse, swivel-eyed, loose-jointed tall fellow.

"Y' hear that. Th' only thing left in this yard is Stampede. Ye k'n take him or leave him, if y'r frightened of him. I'm goin' tallyin' sheep, an' goin' now. If ye stop around idlin' all day, y' needn't tell Uncle 'twas my fault."

Jack hesitated. From a colonial point of view, he couldn't ride well, and he knew it. Yet he hated Easu's insulting way. Easu went grinning to the stable to fetch his mare, pleased with himself. He didn't want the young Jackeroo planted on *him*, to teach any blankey thing to.*

Jack went slowly over to the quivering Stampede, and asked the blacks if they had ever ridden him. One answered:

"Me only fella ride 'im some time master not tomorrow. Me an' Ned catch him in mob longa time—Try break him—no good. He come back paddock one day. Ned wantta break him. No good. Master tell 'im let 'im go now."

Red Easu came walking out of the stables, chewing a stalk.

"Put the saddle on him," said Jack to the blacks. "I'll try."

The boys grinned and scuffled round. They rather liked the job. By being very quick and light, Jack got into the saddle, and gripped. The boys stood back, the horse stood up, and then whirled around on his hind legs, and round and down. Then up and away like a squib round the yard. The boys scattered, so did Easu. But Jack, because it was natural for his legs to grip and stick, stuck on. His bones rattled, his hat flew off, his heart beat high. But unless the horse came down backwards on top of him, he could stay on. And he was not really afraid. He thought: "If he doesn't go down backward on top of me, I shall be all right." And to the boys he called: "Open the gate." Meanwhile he tried to quiet the horse. "Steady now, steady!" he said, in a low, intimate voice. "Steady boy!" And all the time he held on with his thighs and knees, like iron.

He did not believe in the innate viciousness of the horse. He never believed in the innate viciousness of anything, except a man. And he did not want to fight the horse for simple mastery. He wanted just to hold it hard with his legs until it soothed down a little, and he and it could come to an understanding. But he must never relax the hold of his hard legs, or he was dead.

Stampede was not ready for the gate. He sprang fiercely at it as if it had been guarded by fire. Once in the open, he ran, and bucked, and bucked, and ran, and kicked, and bucked, and ran. Jack stuck on with the lower half of his body like a vise, feeling as if his head would be jerked off his shoulders. It was becoming hard work. But he knew, unless he stuck on, he was a dead man.

Then he was aware that Stampede was bolting, and Easu was coming along on a grey mare.

Now they reached the far gate, and a miracle happened. Stampede stood still whilst Red came up and opened the gate. Jack was conscious of a body of live muscle and palpitating fire between his legs, of a furious head tossing hair like hot wire, and bits of white foam. Also he was aware of the trembling in his own thighs, and the sensual exertion of gripping that hot wild body in the power of his own legs. Gripping the hot horse in a grip of sensual mastery that made him tremble* with a curious quivering. Yet he dared not relax.

"Go!" said Red. And away they went. Stampede bolted like the wind, and Jack held on with his knees and by balance. He was thrilled, really: frightened externally, but internally keyed up. And never for a moment did he relax his mind's attention, nor the attention of his own tossed body. The worst was the corkscrew bucks,* when he nearly went over the brute's head. And the moments of vindictive hate, when he would kill the beast and be killed a thousand times, rather than be beaten. Up he went, off the saddle, and down he came again, with a shattering jerk, down on the front of the saddle. The balance he kept was a mystery even to himself, his body was so flung about by the volcano of furious life beneath him. He felt himself shaken to pieces, his bones rattled all out of socket. But they got there, out to the sheep paddock where a group of Reds and black-boys stood staring in silence.

Jack jumped off, though his knees were weak and his hands trembling. The horse stood dark with sweat. Quickly he unbuckled the saddle and bridle and pulled them off, and gave the horse a clap on its wet neck. Away it went, wild again, and free.

Jack glanced at the Reds, and then at Easu. Red Easu met his eyes, and the two stared at one another. It was the defiance of the hostile colonial, brutal and retrogressive, against the old mastery of the old country. Jack was barely conscious. Yet he was not afraid, inside himself, of the swivel-eyed brute of a fellow. He knew that Easu was not a better man than himself, though he was bigger, older, and on his own ground. But Jack had the pride of his own old, well-bred country behind him, and he would never go back on his breeding. He was not going to yield his manliness before the colonial way of life: the brutishness, the commonness. Inwardly he would not give in to it. But the best of it, the colonial honesty and simplicity, that he loved. There are two sides to colonials, as to everything. One side he loved. The other he refused and defied.*

These decisions are not mental, but they are critical in the soul of a boy of eighteen. And the destiny of nations hangs on such silent, almost unconscious decisions.

Esau—they called him Easu, but the name was Esau—turned to a black and bellowed:

"Give master your horse, and carry that bally saddle home."

Then silently they all turned to the sheep-tallying.

V

Jack was still sewing sacks. It was afternoon. He listened for the sound of the shay, though he did not expect it until nightfall at least.

His ear, training to the Australian alertness, began to detect unusual sounds. Or perhaps it was not his ear. The old bushman seems to have developed a further faculty, a psychic faculty of "sensing" some unusual disturbance in the atmosphere, and reading it. Jack was a very new Australian. Yet he had become aware of this faculty in Tom, and he wanted it for himself. He wanted to be able to hear the inaudible, like a sort of clair-audience.

All he could hear was the audible: and all he could see was the visible. The children were playing in the yard: he could see them in the dust. Mrs Ellis was still at the wash-tub: he saw the steam. Katie was upstairs: he had seen her catching a hornet in the window. The men were out ploughing, the horses were away. The pigs were walking round grunting, the cows and poultry were all in the paddock. Gran never made a sound, unless she suddenly appeared on the scene like the Lord in Judgment.* And Dr Rackett was always quiet: often uncannily so.

It was still rainy season,* but a warm, mellow, sleepy afternoon, with no real sound at all. He got up and stood on the threshold to stretch himself. And there, coming by the grain-shed, he saw a little cortège in which the first individual he distinguished was Red Easu.

"Go in," shouted Red, "and tell A'nt as Herbert's had an accident, and we're bringin' him in."

Sure enough, they were carrying a man on a gate.

Mrs Ellis clicked:

"Tt-tt-tt-tt-tt!—They run to us when they're in trouble." But she went at once to the linen closet, and on into the living room.

Gran was sitting in a corner by a little fire.

"Who's hurt?" she inquired testily. "Not one of the family, I hope and pray."—

"Jack says it's Red Herbert," replied Mrs Ellis.

"Put him in the cubby with the boys, then."

But Mrs Ellis thought of her beloved boys, and hesitated.

"Do you think it's much, Jack?" she asked.

"They're carrying him on a gate," said Jack. "It looks bad."

"Dear O' me!" snapped Gran, in her brittle fashion. "Why couldn't you say so!—Well then—if you don't want to put him in the cubby, there's a bed in my room. Put him there.—But I should have thought he could have had Tom's bed, and Tom could have slept here on the sofa."

"Poor Tom!" thought Jack.*

"Don't—!" Gran banged her stick on the floor—"stand there like a pair of sawneys!* Get to work! Get to work!"

Jack was staring at the ground and twirling his hat. Gran hobbled forward. He noticed to his surprise that she had a wooden leg. And she stamped it at him:

"Go and fetch that rascal of a doctor," she cried, in a startling loud voice.

Jack went. Dr Rackett was not in his room, for Jack Halloed! and knocked at every door. He peeped into the rooms, whose doors were slightly opened. This must be the girls' room—two beds, neat white quilts, blue bow at the window. When would they be home? Here was the family bed, with two cots in the room as well. He came to a shut door. This must be it. He knocked and Halloed! again. No sound. Jack felt as if he were bound to come upon a Bluebeard's chamber.* He hated looking in these bedrooms.

He knocked again, and opened the door. A queer smell, like chemicals. A dark room, with the blind down: a few books, a feeling of dark dreariness. But no Doctor. "So that's that!" thought Jack.

In spite of himself his boots clattered going down, and made him nervous. Why did the inside of the house, where he never went, seem so secret, and rather horrible? He peeped into the dismal little drawing-room. Not there of course! Opposite was the dying-room, the door wide open. Nobody ever was there.

Rackett was not in the house, that was certain. Jack slunk out, went to the paddock, caught Lucy the saddle-horse; saddled her and cantered aimlessly around, within hearing of the homestead. The afternoon was passing. Not a soul was in sight. The gum-trees hung their sharp leaves like obvious ghosts, with the hateful motionlessness of gum-trees. And though flowers were out, they were queer, scentless, unspeaking sort of flowers, even the red ones that were ragged like fire. Nothing spoke. The distances were clear and mellow and beautiful, but soulless, and nobody alive in the world. The silent, lonely gruesomeness of Australia gave Jack the blues.

It surely was milking time. Jack returned quietly to the yard. Still nobody alive in the world. As if everyone had died.—Yes, there was the half-caste Tim in the distance, bringing up the slow, unwilling cows, slowly, like slow dreams.

And there was Dad coming out of the back door, in his shirt sleeves: bluer and puffier than ever, with his usual serene expression, and his look of boss, which came from his waistcoat and watchchain. Dad always wore his waistcoat and watch-chain, and seemed almost over-dressed in it.

Came Og and Magog running with quick little steps, and Len slinking round the doorpost, and Harry marching alone, and Katie dragging her feet, and baby crawling. Jack was glad to see them. They had all been indoors to look at the accident. And it had been a dull, dead, empty afternoon, with all the life emptied out of it.

Even now the family, the beloved family, seemed a trifle gruesome to Jack.

He helped to milk: a job he was not good at. Dad even took a stool and milked also. As usual Dad did nothing but supervise. It was a good thing to have a real large family, that made supervising worth while. So Tom said.—"It's a good thing to have nine children, you can clear some work with 'em, if you're their Dad."—That's why Jack was by no means one too many.* Dad supervised him too.

They got the milking done somehow. Jack changed his boots, washed himself, and put on his coat. He nearly trod on the baby as he walked across to the kitchen in the dying light. He lifted her and carried her in.

Usually "tea"*—which meant mutton chops and eggs and steaks as well—was ready when they came in from milking. Today Mr Ellis was putting eucalyptus sticks under the kettle, making the eternally familiar scent of the kitchen, and Mrs Ellis was setting the table there. Usually, they lived in the living room from breakfast on. But today, tea was to be in the kitchen, with a silence and a cloud in the air like a funeral. But there was plenty of noise coming from Gran's room.

Jack had to have baby beside him for the meal. And she put sticky hands in his hair and leaned over and chewed and sputtered crumbs, wet crumbs in his ear. Then she tried to wriggle down, but the evening was chill and her hands and feet were cold and Mrs Ellis said to keep her up. Jack felt he couldn't stand it any longer, when suddenly she fell asleep, the most unexpected thing in the world, and Mrs Ellis carried off her and Harry, to bed.

Ah the family! the family! Jack still loved it. It seemed to fill the whole of life for him. He did not want to be alone, save at moments. And yet, on an afternoon like today, he somehow realised that even the family wouldn't last for ever. What then? What then?

He couldn't bear the thought of getting married to *one* woman and coming home to a house with only himself and this one woman in it. Then the slow and lonely process of babies coming. The thought of such a future was dreadful to him. He didn't want it. He didn't want his own children. He wanted this family: always this family. And yet there was something gruesome to him about the empty bedrooms and the uncanny privacies even of this family. He didn't want to think of their privacies.

vi

Three of the Reds trooped out through the sitting-room, lean, red-faced, hairy, heavy-footed, uncouth figures, for their tea. The Wandoo Ellises were aristocratic in comparison. They asked Jack to go and help hold Herbert down, because he was fractious. "He's that fractious!"

Jack didn't in the least want to have to handle any of the Reds, but he had to go. He found himself taking the two steps down into the dark living-room, and the two steps up into Gran's room beyond.

Why need the family be so quiet in the kitchen, when there was such a hubbub in here. Alan Ellis was holding one leg of the injured party, and Ross Ellis the other, and they both addressed the recumbent figure as if it were an injured horse, with a *Whoa there*! *Steady on, now*! *Steady*, *boy*, *steady*! Whilst Easu, bending terribly over the prostrate figure, clutched both its arms in a vise, and cursed Jack for not coming sooner to take one arm.

Herbert had hurt his head, and turned fractious. Jack took the one arm. Easu was on the other side of the bed, his reddish fair beard glowing. There was a queer power in Easu, which fascinated Jack a little. Beyond, Gran was sitting up in bed, among many white pillows, like Red Riding Hood's grandmother. A bright fire of wood logs was burning in the open hearth, and four or five tallow candles smoked duskily. But a screen was put between Gran's four-poster and Herbert's bed, a screen made of a wooden clothes-horse covered with sheets. Jack, however, from his position by Herbert's pillow, could see beyond the screen to Gran's section.

His attention was drawn by the patient. Herbert's movements were sudden and convulsive, and always in a sudden jerking towards the right side of the bed. Easu had given Jack the left arm to hold, and as soon as Herbert became violent, Jack couldn't hold him. The left arm, lean and hard as iron, broke free, and Easu jumped up and cursed Jack.

Here was a pretty scene! With Gran mumbling to herself on the other side the hideous sheeted screen!

There was nothing for it but to use cool intelligence—a thing the Reds did not possess. Jack had lost his hold again, and Easu like a reddish, glistening demon was gripping the sick man's two arms and arching over him. Jack called up his old veterinary experience, and proceeded to detach himself.

He noticed first: that Herbert was far less fierce when they didn't resist him. Second, that he stopped groaning when his eyes fell away from the men around him. Third, that all the convulsive jerky movements, which had thrown him out of the bed several times, were towards the right side of the bed. Every time, he had fallen out on the right side of the bed.

Then why not bind him to the left?

The left arm had again escaped his grasp, and Easu's exasperated fury was only held in check by Gran's presence. Jack went out of the room and found Katie.

"Hunt me out an old sheet," he said.

"What for?" she said; but went off to do his bidding.

When she came back she said:

"Mother says they don't want to bandage Herbert, do they?"

"I'm going to try and bind him. I shan't hurt him," he replied.

"Oh Jack, don't let them send for me to sit with him—I hate sickness."

"You give us a hand then with this sheet."

Between them they prepared strong bands. Jack noosed one with sailor's knots round Katie's hands, and fastened it to the table leg.

"Pull!" he ordered. "Pull as hard as you can."—And as she pulled: "Does it hurt, now?"

"Not a bit," she said.

Jack went back to the sick room. Herbert was quiet, the three brothers were sulky and silent. They wanted above all things to get out, to get away. You could see that. Easu glanced at Jack's hands. There was something tense and alert about Easu, like a great wiry bird with enormous power in its lean, red neck and its lean limbs.

"I thought we'd best bind him so as not to hurt him," said Jack. "I know how to do it, I think."

The brothers said not a word, but let him go ahead. And Jack bound the left arm and the left leg, and put a band round the body of the patient. They looked on, rather distantly interested. Easu released the convulsive left arm of his brother. Jack took the sick man's hand soothingly, held it soothingly, then slipped his hand up the hairy fore-arm and got the band attached just above the elbow. Then he fastened the ends to the bed-head. He felt quite certain he was doing right. While he was busy Mrs Ellis came in. She watched in silence too. When it was done, Jack looked at her.

"I believe it'll do," she said with a nod of approval. And then, to the cowed, hulking brothers: "You might as well go and get your tea."

They bumped into one another trying to get through the door. Jack noticed they were in their stocking feet. They stooped outside the door to pick up their boots.

"Good idea!" he thought. And he took off his own boots. It made him feel more on the job.

Mrs Ellis went round the white bed-sheet screen to sit with Gran. Jack went blowing out the reeking candles on the sick man's side of the same screen. Then he sat on a hard chair facing the staring, grimacing patient. He felt sorry for him, but repelled by him. Yet as Herbert tossed his wiry, hairy free arm and jerked his hairy, sharp-featured face, Jack wanted to help him.

He remembered the vet's advice: "Get the creature's confidence, lad, and you can do anything with 'em. Horse or man, cat or canary, get the creature's confidence, and if anything can be done, you can do it."

Jack wanted now to proceed to get the creature's confidence. He knew it was a matter of will: of holding the other creature's will with his own will. But gently, and in a kindly spirit.

He held Herbert's hard fingers softly in his own hand, and said softly: "Keep quiet, old man, keep quiet. I'm here. I'll take care of you. You rest. You go to sleep. I won't leave you. I'll take care of you."

Herbert lay still as if listening. His muscles relaxed. He seemed dreadfully tired—Jack could feel it. He was dreadfully, dreadfully tired. Perhaps the womanless, brutal life of the Reds had made him so tired. He seemed to go to sleep. Then he jerked awake, and the convulsive struggling began again, with the frightful rolling of the eyes.

But the steady bonds that held him seemed to comfort him, and Jack quietly took the clutching fingers again. And the sick man's eyes, in their rolling, rested on the quiet, abstract face of the youth, with strange watching. Jack did not move. And again Herbert's tension seemed to relax. He seemed in an agony of desire to sleep, but the agony of desire was so great, that the very fear of it jerked the sick man into horrible wakefulness.

Jack was saying silently, with his will: "Don't worry! Don't worry old man! Don't worry! You go to sleep. I'll look after you."

And as he sat in dead silence, saying these things, he felt as if the fluid of his life ran out of his fingers into the fingers of the hurt man. He was left weak and limp. And Herbert began to go to sleep, really to sleep.

Jack sat in a daze, with the virtue gone out of him.* And Herbert's fingers were soft and childlike again in their relaxation.

The boy started a little, feeling some one pat him on the shoulder. It was Mrs Ellis, patting him in commendation, because the patient was sunk deep in sleep. Then she went out.

Following her with his eyes, Jack saw another figure in the doorway. It was Red Easu, like a wolf out of the shadow, looking in. And Jack quietly let slip the heavy, sleeping fingers of the sick man. But he did not move his posture.

Then he was aware that Easu had gone again—

vii

It was late, and the noise of rain outside, and weird wind blowing. Mrs Ellis had been in and whispered that Dr Rackett was not home yet—that he had probably waited somewhere for the shay. And that she had told the Reds to keep away.

There was dead silence save for the weather outside, and a noise of the fire. The candles were all blown out.

He was startled by hearing Gran's voice:

"Out of the mouths of babes and sucklings— —"*

"She's reading," thought Jack, though there was no light to read by. And he wondered why the old lady wasn't asleep.

"I knew y'r mother's father, Jack Grant," came the thin, petulant voice. "He cut off my leg.* Devil of a fella wouldn't let me die when I wanted to. Cut it off without a murmur, and no chloroform."

The thin voice was so devilishly awake, in the darkness of the night, like a voice out of the past piercing the inert present.

"What did he care! What did he care! Not a bit," Gran went on. "And y're another. You take after him. You're such another. You're a throw-back, to your mother's father.—I was wondering what I was going to do with those great galoots in my room all night. I'm glad it's you."

Jack thought: "Lord, have I got to sit here all night!"

"You've got the night before you," said Gran's demonishly wakeful voice, uncanny in its thin alertness, in the deep night. "So come round here to the fireside an' make y'self comfortable."

Jack rose obediently and went round the screen. After all, an arm-chair would be welcome.

"Well, say something," said Gran.

The boy peered at her in the dusk, in a kind of fear.

"Then light me a candle, for the land's sake," she said pettishly.

He took a tin candle-stick with a tallow candle, blew the fire and made a yellow light.—She looked like a carved ivory Chinese figure, almost grotesque, among her pillows.

"Yes, y're like y'r grandfather: a stocky stubborn man as didn't say much, but dare do anything. And never had a son.—Hard as nails the man was."

"More family!" thought Jack wearily, disapproving of Gran's language* thoroughly.

"Had two daughters* though, and disowned the eldest. Your mother was the youngest. The eldest got herself into trouble and he turned her out. Regular obstinate fool, and no bowels of compassion.* That's how men are when y' let 'em. You're the same."

Jack was so sleepy, so sleepy, and the words of the old woman seemed like something pricking him.

"I'd have stood by her—but I was her age, and what could I do? I'd have married her father if I could, for he was a widower. But he married another woman for his second, and I went by ship to Melbourne, and then I took poor old Ellis."

What on earth made her say these things he didn't know, for he was dead sleepy, and if he'd been wide awake he wouldn't have wanted her to unload this sort of stuff on him. But she went on, like the old demon she was:

"Men are fools, and women make 'em what they are. I followed your Aunt Lizzie up, years after. She married a man in the mounted police, and he sent the boy off. The boy was a bit weak-minded, and the man wouldn't have him. So the lad disappeared into the bush. They say he was canny enough about business and farming, but a bit off about people.—Anyway he was Mary's half-brother: you met Mary in Perth. Her scamp of a father was father of that illegitimate boy. But she's an orphan now, poor child: like that illegitimate half-brother of hers."

Jack looked up pathetically. He *didn't* want to hear. And Gran suddenly laughed at him, with the sudden daring, winsome laugh, like Lennie.

"Y're a bundle of conventions, like y'r grandfather," she said tenderly. "But y've got a kinder heart. I suppose that's from y'r English father. Folks are tough in Australia: tough as whit-leather.—Y'll be tempted to sin, but y' won't be tempted to condemn. And never you mind. Trust yourself, Jack Grant. *Earn a good opinion of yourself*, and never mind other folks. You've only got to live once. You know when your spirit glows—trust that. That's *you*! That's the spirit of God in you. Trust in that, and you'll never grow old. If you knuckle under, you'll grow old."

She paused for a time.

"Though I don't know that I've much room to talk," she ruminated on. "There was my son Esau, he never knuckled under, and though he's dead, I've not much good to say of him. But then he never had a kind heart: never. Never a woman loved Esau, though some feared him. I was not among 'em. Not I. I feared no man, not even your grandfather: except a little.—But look at Dad here now. He's got a kind heart: as kind a heart as ever beat. And he's gone old. And he's got heart-disease. And he knuckled under. Ay, he knuckled under to me, he did, poor lad. And he'll go off sudden, when his heart gives way. That's how it is with kind-hearted men. They knuckle under, and they die young. Like Dad here. He'll never make old bones. Poor lad!"

She mused again in silence.

"There's nothing to win in life, when all's said and done, but a good opinion of yourself. I've watched and I know. God is y'rself. Or put it the other way if you like: y'rself is God. So win a good opinion of yourself, and watch the glow inside you."[*]

Queer, thought Jack, that this should be an old woman's philosophy. Yourself is God! Partly he believed it, partly he didn't. He didn't know what he believed.—Watch the glow inside you. That he understood.

He liked Gran. She was so alone in life, amid all her children. He himself was a lone wolf too: among the lambs of the family. And perhaps Red Easu was a lone wolf.

"But what was I telling you?" Gran resumed. "About your illegitimate cousin. I followed him up too. He went back, beyond Atherton, and took up land. He's got a tidy place now, and he's never married. He's wrong in his head about people, but all right about the farm.—I'm hoping that place'll come to Mary one day, for the child's got nothing. She's a good child—a good child. Her mother was a niece of mine."

She seemed to be going to sleep. But like Herbert, she roused again.

"Y'd better marry Mary. Make up your mind to it," she said.

And instantly he rebelled against the thought. Never.

"Perhaps I'd ought to have said: 'The best in yourself is God,'" she mused. "Perhaps that's more it. The best in yourself is God.—But then who's going to say what *is* the best in yourself. A kind man knuckles under, and thinks it's the best in himself. And a hard man holds out, and thinks that's the best in himself. And it's *not* good for a kind man to knuckle under, and it's *not* good for a hard-hearted man to hold out. What's to be done, deary-me, what's to be done?—And no matter what we say, people will be as they are.—You can but watch the glow."

She really did doze off. And Jack stole away to the other side of the screen to escape her, leaving the candle burning.

viii

He sat down thankfully on the hard chair by Herbert's side, glad to get away from women. Glad to be with men, if it was only Herbert. Glad to doze and feel alone: to feel alone.

He awoke with a jerk and a cramped neck, and there was Tom peeping in. Tom? They must be back. Jack's chair creaked as he made a movement to get up. But Tom only waved his hand and disappeared. Mean of Tom.

They must be back. The twins must be back. The family was replenished.—He stared with sleepy eyes, and a heavy, sleepy, sleepy head.

And the next thing he heard was a soft, alert voice saying:

"Hello Bow!"

Queer how it echoed in his dark consciousness as he slept, the soft:

"Hello Bow!"

There they were, both laughing, fresh with the wind and rain, Grace standing just behind Monica, Monica's hair all tight-crisp with rain, blond at the temples, darker on the head, and her fresh face laughing, and her yellow eyes looking with that long, meaningful look that had no meaning, peering into his sleepy eyes. He felt something stir inside him.

"Hello Bow!" she said again, putting her fingers on his sleeve. "We've got back."

And still in his sleep-stupor he stared without answering a word.

"You aren't awake!" she whispered, putting her cold hand suddenly on his face,[*] and laughing as he started back. A new look came into his eyes as he stared startled at her, and she bent her head, turning aside.

"Poo! smells of stinking candles in here!" whispered Grace.

Someone else was there. It was Red Easu in the doorway, saying in a hoarse voice:

"Want me to take a spell with Herbert?"

Monica glanced back at him with a strange look. He loomed weird and tall, with his rather long, red neck and glistening beard and quick blue eyes. A certain sense of power came with him.

"Hello girls, got back!" he added to the twins, who watched him without speaking.

"Who's there?" said Gran's voice from the other side of the screen. "Is it the girls back? Has Mary come with you?"

As if in answer to the summons, Mary appeared in the doorway, wearing a white apron. She glanced first at Jack, with her black eyes, and then at Gran. Monica was watching her with a sideways lynx look, and Grace was looking at everybody with big blue eyes, while Easu looked down from his uncouth ostrich height.

"Hello Gran!" said Mary, going to the other side the screen to kiss the old lady. The twins followed suit.

"Want me to take a spell in here?" said Easu, jerking his thumb at the sleeping Herbert. Easu wore black trousers hitched up high with braces over a dark-grey flannel shirt, and leather leggings, but no boots. His shirt-sleeves were rolled up from his sinewy brown arms. His reddish fair hair was thick and rather long. He spoke in a deep gruff voice, that he made as quiet as possible, and he seemed to show a gruff sort of submissiveness to Jack, at the moment.

"No Easu," replied Gran. "I can't do with you. Jack Grant will manage."

The sick man was sleeping through it all like the dead.

"I can take a turn," said Mary's soft, low, insidious voice.

"No, not you either, Mary. You go to sleep after that drive. Go, all of you, go to bed. I can't do with you all in here. Has Dr Rackett come?"

"No," said Easu.

"Then go away, all of you. I can't do with you," said Gran.

Mary came round the screen and shook hands with Jack, looking him full in the eyes with her black eyes, so that he was uncomfortable. She made him more uncomfortable than Monica did. Monica had slunk also round the screen, and was standing with one foot trailing, watching. She watched just as closely when Mary shook hands with the embarrassed Easu.

They all retreated silently to the door. Grace went first. And with her big, dark-blue eyes she glanced back inquisitively at Jack. Mary went next—she too turning in the door to give him a look and an intimate, furtive-seeming smile. Then came Monica, and like a wolf she lingered in the door looking back with a long, meaningful, meaningless sidelong look before she took her departure. Then on her heels went Easu, and he did not look back. He seemed to loom over the girls.

"Blow the light out," said Gran.

He went round to blow out the candle. Gran lay there like an old angel. Queer old soul!—framed by pillow-frills.

"Yourself is God!"

Jack thought of that with a certain exultance.

He went over and made up the fire. Then he sat in the arm-chair. Herbert was moving. He went over to soothe him. The sick man moaned steadily for some time, for a long time, then went still again. Jack slept in the hard chair.

He woke up cramped and cold, and went round to the arm-chair by the fire. Gran was sleeping like an inert bit of ivory. He softly attended to the fire, and sat down in the arm chair.

He was riding a horse a long, long way, on a journey that would never end. He couldn't stop the horse till it stopped of itself, and it would never stop. A voice said: "What has he done?" And a voice answered: "Conquered the world."—But the horse did not stop. And he woke and saw shadows on the wall, and slept again. Things had all turned to dough—his hands were heavy with dough. He woke and looked at his hands to see if it were so. How loudly and fiercely the clock ticked!

Not dough, but boxing-gloves. He was fighting inside a ring, fighting with somebody who was and who wasn't Easu. He couldn't beat Easu—he couldn't beat Easu. Easu had knocked him down, he was lying writhing with pain and couldn't rise, while they were counting him out. In three more seconds he would be counted out! Horror!

He woke, it was midnight and Herbert was writhing.

"Did I sleep a minute Herbert?" he whispered.

"My head! My head! It jerks so!"

"Does it old man! Never mind."

And the next thought was: "There must have been gunpowder in that piece of wood, in the fire."

ix

It was half past one, and Mary unexpectedly appeared with tray and lighted candle, and cocoa-milk for Jack and arrowroot for Herbert. She fed Herbert with a spoon, and he swallowed, but made no sign that he understood.

"How did he get the accident?" Jack whispered.

"His horse threw him against a tree."

"Wish Rackett would come," whispered Jack.

Mary shook her head and they were silent.

"How old are you, Mary?" Jack asked.

"Nineteen."

"I'm eighteen at the end of this month."

"I know.—But I'm much older than you."

Jack looked at her queer dark muzzle. She seemed to have a queer, humble complacency of her own.

"She—" Jack nodded his head towards Gran—"says that knuckling under makes you old."

Mary laughed suddenly.

"Then I'm a thousand," she said.

"What do you knuckle under for?" he asked.

She looked up at him slowly, and again something quick and hot stirred in him, from her dark, queer, humble, yet assured face.

"It's my way," she said, with an odd smile.

"Funny way to have," he replied, and suddenly he was embarrassed. And he thought of Monica's dare-devil way.

He felt embarrassed.

"I must have my own way," said Mary, with another odd, beseeching, and yet darkly confident smile.

"Yourself is God," thought Jack.—But he said nothing, because he felt uncomfortable.

And Mary went away with the tray and the light, and he was glad when she was gone.

x

The worst part of the night. Nothing happened—and that was perhaps the worst part of it. Fortified by the powers of darkness, the slightest sounds took on momentous importance, but nothing happened. He expected something—but nothing came.

Gran asleep there, in all the fixed motionlessness of her years, a queer white clot. And young Herbert asleep or unconscious, sending wild vibrations from his brain.

The thought of Monica seemed to flutter subjectively in Jack's soul, the thought of Mary objectively. That is, Monica was somehow inside him, in his blood, like a sister. And Mary was outside him, like a black-boy. Both of them engaging his soul. And yet he was alone, all alone in the universe. These two only beset him. Or did he beset them?

The opossums made a furious bombilation* as they ran up and down, back and forth between the roof and ceiling, like an army moving. And suddenly, shatteringly a nut would come down on the old shingle roof from the Moreton Bay fig* outside, with a crash like a gun, while the branches dangled and clanked against the timber walls. An immense, uncanny strider! And him alone in the lonely, uncanny, timeless core of the night.

Slowly the night went by. And weird things awoke in the boy's soul, things he could never quite put to sleep again. He felt as if this night he had entered into a dense, impenetrable thicket. As if he would never get out—He knew he would never get out.

He awoke again with a start. Was it the first light? Herbert was stirring. Jack went quickly to him.

Herbert opened dazed eyes, and mutely looked at Jack. A look of intelligence came, and as quickly passed. He groaned, and the torment came over him once more. Whatever was the matter with him? He writhed and struggled, groaning—then relapsed into a cold, inert silence. It was as if he were dying. As if he, or something in him, had decided to die.

Jack was terribly startled. In terror, he mixed a little brandy and milk, and tried to pour spoonfuls down the unresisting throat. He quickly fetched a hot stone from the fire, wrapped it in a piece of blanket, and put it in the bed.

Then he sat down and took the young man's hand softly in his own, and whispered intensely: "Come back, Herbert! Come back! Come back!"

With all his will he summoned the inert spirit. He was terribly afraid the other would die. He sat and watched with a fixed, intent will. And Herbert relaxed again, the life came round his eyes again.

"Oh God!" thought Jack. "I shall die. I shall die myself. What sort of a life have I got to live before I die? Oh God, what sort of a life have I got between me and when I die."

And it all seemed a mystery to him. The God he called on was a dark, almost fearful mystery. The life he had to live was a kind of doom. The choice he had was no choice. "Yourself is God." It wasn't true. There was a terrible God somewhere else. And nothing else than this.

Because, inside himself, he was alone, without father or mother or place or people.* Just a separate living thing. And he could not choose his doom of living nor his dying. Somewhere outside himself was a terrible God who decreed.

He was afraid of the thicket of life in which he found himself like a solitary, strange animal. He would have to find his way through: all the way to death. But what sort of way? What sort of life? What sort of life between him and death?

He didn't know. He only knew that something must be. That he was in a strange bush, and by himself. And that he must find his way through.

Chapter VI.

In the Yard.

i

Ah, good to be out in the open air again! Beyond all telling, good! Those indoor rooms were like coffins. To be dead, and to writhe unreleased in the coffin, that was what those indoor rooms were like.

"God, when I die, let me pass right away," prayed Jack. "Lord, I promise to live my life right out, so that when I die I pass over and don't lie wriggling in the coffin!"

Mary had come as soon as it was light, and found Herbert asleep and Jack staring at him in a stupor.

"You go to sleep now, Bow," said Mary softly, laying her hand on his arm.

He looked at her in a kind of horror, as if she were part of the dark interior. He didn't want to go to sleep. He wanted to wake. He stood in the yard and stared around stupefied at the early morning. Then he went and hauled Lennie and the twins out of their bunks. Tom was already up.—Then he went, stripped to the waist, to the pump.

"Pump over my nut, Lennie," he shouted, holding his head at the pump-spout. Oh 'twas so good to shout at somebody. He must shout.

And Lennie pumped away like a little imp.

When Jack looked out of the towel at the day, he saw the sky fresh with yellow light, and some red still on the horizon above the grey gum-trees. It all seemed crisp and snappy. It was life.

"Ain't yer goin' ter do any of yer monkey trickin' this morning?" shouted Lennie at him.

Jack shook his head, and rubbed his white young shoulders with the towel. Lennie, standing by the wash-tin in his little undervest and loose little breeches, was watching closely.

"Can you answer me a riddle Lennie?" asked Jack.

"I'll try," said Len briskly, and Og and Magog jumped up in gay expectation.

"What *is* God, anyhow?" asked Jack.

"Y'd better [not][*] let my father hear y'," replied Lennie, with a dangerous nod of the head.

"No, but I mean it. Suppose Herbert had died.—I want to know what God is."

Jack still had the inner darkness of that room in his eyes.

"I'll tell y'," said Len briskly. "God is a Higher Law than the Constitution."[*]

Jack thought about it. A higher law than the law of the land. Maybe!—The answer left him cold.

"And what is self?" he asked.

"Crikey! stop up another night! It 'ud make ye sawney.—But I'll tell y' what self is. 'Self is a wilderness of sweets. And selves

They eat, they drink, and in communion sweet
Quaff immortality and joy.' "[*]

Len was pleased with this. But Jack heard only words.

"Ask *me* one, Jack! Ask *me* one!" pleaded Og.

"All right. What's success, Og?" asked Jack, smiling.

"Success! Success! Why success—"

"Success is t' grow a big bingy[*] like a bloke from town, 'n a watch-chain acrost it with a gold dial in y' fob, and ter be allowed ter spout as much gab as y've got bref left over from y' indigest," cut in Lennie, with delight.

"That was *my* riddle," yelled Og, rushing at him.

"Ask me one. Ask me one Jack. Ask me one," yelled Magog.

"What's failure?" asked Jack, laughing.

"T' be down on y' uppers an' hev no visible means of supportin' y' pants up whilst y' slog t' th' nearest pub t' cadge a beer spot,"[*] crowed Lennie in delight, while he fenced off Og.

Both twins made an assault and battery upon him.

"D' ye know y'r own answers?" yelled Len at Jack.

"No."

The brazenness of the admission flabbergasted the twins. They stalked off. Len drew up a three-legged stool, and sat down to milk, explaining impatiently that success comes to those that work and don't drink.[*]

"But—" and he reverted to his original thought—"y've gotta work, not go wastin' y'r time as you generally do of a morning—boundin' about makin' a kangaroo of y'self; tippin' y' elbows and holding back y' nut as if y' had a woppin' fine drink in both hands, and gone screwed with joy afore you drained it; lyin' flat on y' hands an' toes, an' heavin' up an' down, up an' down, like a race-horse iguana frightened by a cat; an' stalkin' an' stoopin' as if y' wanted ter catch a bird round a corner; or roundin' up on imaginary things, makin' out t' hit 'em slap-bang-whizz on the mitts they ain't got; whippin' round an' bobbin' like a cornered billy-goat; skippin' up an' down like sis wif a rope, an' makin' a general high falutin' ass of y'self."

"I see you and the twins with clubs," said Jack.

"Oh that! That's more for music an' one-two-three-four," said Len.

"You see I'm in training," said Jack.

"What for? Want ter teach the old sows to start dancin' on th' corn-bin floor."

"No, I want to keep in training, for if I ever have a big fight."

"Who with?"

"Oh I don't know. But I love a round with the fists. I'll teach you."

"All right.—But why don't y' chuck farmin' an' go in f' prize-fightin'?"

"I wish I could. But my father said no. An' perhaps he's right. But the best thing I know is to fight a fair round.—I'll teach you, Len."

"Huh! What's the sense. If y' want exercise, y' c'n rub that horse down a bit cleaner than y' are doin'."

"Stop y' sauce, nipper, or I'll be after y' with a strap!" called Tom. "Come on, Jack. Tea! Timothy's bangin' the billy-can.* And just you land that nipper a clout."

"Let him 'it me! Garn, let him!" cried Len, scooting up with his milk-stool and pail and looking like David skirmishing before Goliath.* He wasn't laughing. There was a demonish little street-arab hostility in his face.

"Don't you like me, Len?" Jack asked, a bit soft this morning.

Len's face at once suffused with a delightful roguishness.

"Aw, yes,—if y' like!—I'll be dressin' up in Katie's skirts n' spoonin'* y' one of these bright nights—"

He whipped away with his milk-pail, like a young lizard.

ii

"Look at Bow, he looks like an owl," said Grace at breakfast.

"What d' y' call 'im Bow for?" asked Len.

"Like a girl, with his eyes double size," said Monica.

"You'd better go to sleep, Jack," said Mrs Ellis.

"Take a nap, lad," said Mr Ellis. "There's nothin' for y' to do this morning."

Jack was going stupefied again, as the sun grew warm. He didn't hear half that was said. But the girls were very attentive to him. Mary was not there: she was sitting with Herbert. But Monica and Grace waited on him as if he had been their lord. It was a new experience for him: Monica jumping up and whipping away his cup with her slim hand, to bring it back filled: and Grace insisting on opening a special jar of jam for him. Drowsy as he was, their attention made his blood stir. It was so new to him.

Mary came in from the sitting-room: they were still in the kitchen.

"Herbert is awake," she said. "He wants to be untied, Bow. Do you think he ought to?"

Jack rose in silence and went through to Gran's room. Herbert lay quite still, but he was himself. Only shattered and wordless. He looked at Jack and murmured:

"Can't y' untie me?"

Jack went at once to unfasten the linen bands. The twins, Monica and Grace, stood watching from the doorway. Mary was at his side to help.

"Don't let 'em come in," said Herbert, looking into Jack's face.

Jack nodded, and went to the door.

"He wants to be left alone," he said.

"Mustn't we come, Bow?" said Monica, making queer yellow eyes at him.

"Best not," he said. "Don't let anybody come. He wants absolute quiet."

"All right."—She looked at him with a heavy look of obedience, as if making him an offering. They were not going to question his authority. She drew Grace away: both the girls humble. Jack slowly and unconsciously flushed. Then he went back to the bed.

"I want something," murmured Herbert wanly. "Send that other away."

"Go away, Mary. He wants a man to attend to him," said Jack.

Mary looked a long, dark look at Jack. Then she, too, submitted.

"All right," she said, turning darkly away.

And it came into his mind, with utter absurdity, that he ought to kiss her for this submission. And he hated the thought.

Herbert was a boy of nineteen, uncouth, and savagely shy. Jack had to do the menial offices for him.

The sick man went to sleep again almost immediately, and Jack returned to the kitchen. He heard voices from outside.

Ma and Grace were washing up at the slab. Dad was sitting under the pittosporum tree, with Ellie on one knee, cutting up tobacco in the palm of his hand. Tom was leaning against the tree, the children sat about. Lennie skipped up and offered a seat on a stump.

"Sit yourself down, Bow," he said, using the nickname. "I'd be a knot instead of a bow,* if I had to nurse Red Herbert."

Monica came slinking up from the shade, and stood with her skirt touching Jack's arm. Mary was carrying away the dishes.

"I've been telling Tom," said Mr Ellis, "that he can take the clearing gang* over to his A'nt Greenlow's for the shearing, an' then get back an' clear for all he's worth, till Christmas. Y' might as well go along with him, Jack. We can get along all right here without y', now th' girls are back. Till Christmas, that is. We s'll want y' back for the harvest."

There was a dead silence. Jack didn't want to go.

"Then y' can go back to the clearing, and burn off. I need that land reclaimed, over against the little chaps grows up and wants to be farmers. Besides—" and he looked round at Ma—"we're a bit overstocked in the house just now, an' we'll be glad of the cubby for Herbert, if he's on the mend."

Dad resumed cutting up his tobacco in the palm of his hand.

"Jack can't leave Herbert, Uncle," said Mary quietly. "He won't let anybody else do for him."

"Eh?" said Mr Ellis, looking up.

"Herbert won't let me do for him," said Mary. "He'll only let Bow."

Mr Ellis dropped his head in silence.

"In that case," he said slowly; "in that case, we must wait a bit.—Where's that darned Rackett put himself? This is his job."

There was still silence.

"Somebody had best go an' look for him," said Tom.

"Ay," said Mr Ellis.

There was more silence. Monica, standing close to Jack, seemed to be fiercely sheltering him from this eviction. And Mary, at a distance, was like Moses' sister watching over events.* It made Jack feel queer and thrilled, the girls all concentrating on him. It was as if it put power in his chest, and made a man of him.

Someone was riding up. It was Red Easu. He slung himself off his horse, and stalked slowly up.

"Herbert dead?" he asked humorously.

"Doing nicely," said Dad, very brief.

"I'll go an' have a look at 'm," said Easu, sitting on the step and pulling off his boots.

"Don't wake him if he's asleep. Don't frighten him, whatever you do," said Jack, anxious for his charge.

Easu looked at Jack with an insolent stare: a curious stare.

"Frighten him?" he said. "What with?"

"Jack's been up with him all night," put in Monica fiercely.

"He nearly died in the night," said Jack.

There was dead silence. Easu stared, poised like some menacing bird. Then he went indoors in his stocking feet.

"Did he nearly die, Jack?" asked Tom.

Jack nodded. His soul was feeling bleached.

"If Doctor Rackett isn't coming—see if you can trail him up, Tom.—And Len, can you go on Lucy and fetch Doctor Mallett."

"Course I can," said Len, jumping up.

"You go and get a nap in the cubby, son," said Mr Ellis.

They were now all in motion. Jack followed vaguely into the kitchen. Lennie was the centre of excitement for the moment.

"Well Ma, I has no socks fitta wear. If y'll fix me some, I'll go." For he was determined to go to York in decent raiment, as he said.

"Find me a decent shirt, Ma; *decent*! None o' your creases down th' front for me. 'N a starch collar, real starch."

And so on. He was late. Lennie was always late.

"Ma, weer's my tie—th' blue one wif gold horse-shoes?—Grace—there's an angel—me boots. Clean 'em up a bit, go on—Monica! Oh Monica! there y' are. Fix this collar on fer me, proper, do, y're a bloke at it, so y' are, an' I'm no good.— —Git outta th' way, you nips—how k'n I get dressed with you buzzin' round me feet?—Ma! Ma! come an' brush me 'air with that dinkey[*] nice-smellin' stuff.— —There Ma, don't your Lennie look a dream now?—Ocha, Ma, don' kiss me, Ma, I 'ate it."

"Lennie love, don't drop your aitches."

"I never, Ma—I said I 'ate it. Y' kissed me, didn't y',—or *didn't* y'?—Well, I *'ate* it."

He was gone on Lucy, like a little demon. Jack, sitting stupid on a chair, felt part of his soul go with him.

"Come on, Bow!" said Monica, taking him by the arm. "Come and go to sleep. Mary will wake you if Herbert wants you."

And she led him off to the door of the cubby, while he submitted, and Easu stood in his stocking-feet on the verandah watching.

"He saved Herbert's life," said Monica, looking up at Easu with a kind of defiance, when she came back.

"Who asked him," said Easu.

iii

Tom and Jack were to leave the next day. The girls brought out a lot of stores from the cupboard, and blankets and billies and a lantern. They packed the sacks standing there.

"Get y' swag* f' y'selves," said Dad. "The men have everything for themselves.—Take an axe an' a gun apiece."

"Gun!—Gee!—K'n I go, Dad?"

"Shut up, Len.—Destroy all the dingoes y' can. I'll give y' sixpence a head, an' the Government gives another. Haven't y' a saddle, Jack Grant, somewhere in a box. Because I'd be short of one off the place, if you took one from here."

"It must be somewhere," said Jack.

"Get it unpacked. An' you can have Lucy to put it across. It's forty mile from here to virgin forest: real forest. If you get strayed, ever, all you have to do is to drop th' reins on Lucy's neck, 'n she'll bring y' in."

The saddle came out of the dusty box. All were there in a circle to look on. Jack expected deep admiration. But he was hurt to feel Monica laughing derisively. Everybody was laughing, but he minded Monica most. She could jeer cruelly.

"Jolly good saddle," said Jack.

"Mighty little of it," said Len.

"What's wrong with it, Tom?" asked Jack.

"Slithery. No knee-pads, saddle-bags, strap-holder, scooped seat, or any sortta comfort.—It's a whale, on the wrong side."*

Lennie closely examined the London ticket. The unpacking continued in silence, under Tom's majestic eye. Whip, yellow horse-rug, bridle, leathers, a heavy bar bit with double rings and curb, saddle-cloths, reins, extra special blue-and-gold girths wrapped in tissue-paper, nickel cross rowell jockey spurs, and glittering steel stirrup-irons. Cord breeches, assam silk* coat, white water-proof linen stocks, leather gaiters, and a pair of leather gauntlets completed the amazing disclosure.—It was all a mighty gift from one of the unforgiven aunts.

Half way through the unpacking Tom gave a groan and walked away; but walked back. Og and Magog stole the saddle, slung it across a bar, and slid off and on rapturously. Monica was laughing at him disagreeably: strange and brutal, as if she hated him; rather like Easu. And Lennie was tittering with joy.

"Oh Og! Here! Y're missin' it. Leave that hog's back saddle, No. 1. grade—picked material—hand forged—'tree mounted* guaranteed—a topper off; see this princess palfrey bridle for you, rosettes ornamented periwinkle an' all. An' oh look you! a canary belly-band f'r Dada t' strap round th' heifer's neck when she gets first prize at the Royal York show. Look at that crush-bone cage to put round Stampede's mouth when the niggers catches him again. Oh Lor' oh My—"

"Shut up!" said Tom abruptly, catching the boy by the back of his pants and tossing him out of the barn.

"Now roll up y'r bluey"—meaning the new rug, which was yellow. "Fix them stirrup-leathers, take the bridle off that bit an' we'll find you something decent to put the reins on. An' kick th' rest t'gether. What a gear. Glad it's you, not me, as has got to ride that leather, me boy. But ride on 't y'll have to, for there's nought else. Now Monica, close down that mirth of yours, you're not asked for it."

"Let brotherly love continue," said Monica spitefully. "Wonder if it will, even unto Camp."

She went, leaving Jack feeling suddenly tired.

Chapter VII.

Out Back, and Some Letters.

i

Jack was absolutely happy, in camp with Tom. Perhaps the most completely happy time in his life. He had escaped the strange new complications that life was weaving round him. Yet he had not left the beloved family. He was with Tom: who, after all, was the one that mattered most. Tom was the growing trunk of the tree.*

All real living hurts as well as fulfils. Happiness comes when we have lived and have a respite for sheer forgetting. Happiness, in the vulgar sense, is just a holiday experience. The life-long happiness lies in being used by life; hurt by life, driven and goaded by life, replenished and overjoyed with life, fighting for life's sake. That is real happiness. In the undergoing, a large part of it is pain. But the end is like Jack's Camping expedition, a time of real happiness.

Perhaps death, after a life of real courage, is like a happy camping expedition in the unknown, before a new start.

It was spring in Western Australia, and a wonder of delicate blueness, of frail, unearthly beauty. The earth was full of weird flowers, star-shaped, needle-pointed, fringed, scarlet, white, blue, a whole world of strange flowers. Like being in a new paradise, from which man had not been cast out.

The trees in the dawn, so ghostly still. The scent of blossoming eucalyptus trees: the scent of burning eucalyptus leaves and sticks, in the camp fire. Trailing blossoms wet with dew; the scrub after rain; the bitter-sweet fragrance of fresh-cut timber—

And the sounds! Magpies calling, parrots chattering, strange birds flitting in the renewed stillness. Then kangaroos calling to one another* out of the frail, paradisal distance. And the birr! of crickets in the heat of the day. And the sound of axes, the voices of men, the crash of falling timber. The strange slobbering talk of the blacks! The mysterious night coming round the camp fire.

Red gum everywhere! Fringed leaves dappling, the glowing new sun coming through, the large, feathery, honey-sweet blossoms flowering in clumps, the hard, rough-marked, red-bronze trunks rising like pillars of burnt copper, or lying sadly felled, giving up the ghost. Everywhere scattered the red gum, making leaves and herbage underneath seem bestrewed with blood.

And it was spring: the short, swift, fierce, flower-strange spring of Western Australia, in the month of August.[*]

Then evening came, and the small aromatic fire was burning amid the felled trees. Tom stood hands on hips, giving directions, while the blackened billy-can hung suspended from a cross-bar over the fire. The water bubbling, a handful of tea is thrown in. It sinks. It rises. "Bring it off!" yells Tom. Jack balances the cross-stick, holding the wobbling can, until it rests safely on the ground. Then snatching the handle holds the can aloft. Tea is made.

The clearing gang had a hut with one side for the horses, the other for the men's sleeping place. Inside were stakes driven into the ground, bearing cross-bars with sacks fastened across, for beds. On the partition poles hung the wardrobes, and in a couple of boxes lay the treasures, in the shape of watches, knives, razors, looking glasses, etc.—safe from the stray thief. But the men were always tormenting one another, hiding away a razor, or a strop, or a beloved watch.

Just in front of this shelter the camp oven had been built,[*] for baking damper and roasting meat, and to one side was the well: a very important necessity, built by contract, timbered, and provided with winch, rope and bucket.

All around the bush was dense like a forest, much denser than usual. The slim-girthed trees grew in silent array, all alike and all asleep, with undergrowth of scrub and fern and flowers, banksia short and sturdy with its cone-shaped red-yellow flowers like fairy lamps, and here and there a perfect wattle, or mimosa tree, with its pale-gold flowers like little balls of sun-dust, and here and there sandal-wood trees. Jack never forgot the beauty of the first bushes and trees of mimosa,[*] in a damp place in the wild bush. Occasionally there was still an immense karri tree, or a jarrah slightly smaller, though this was not the region for these giants.[*]

And far away, unending, upslope and downslope and rock-face one far unending dimness of these changeless trees, going on and on without variation, open enough to let one see ahead and all around, yet dense enough to form a monotony and a sense of helplessness in the mind, a sense of timelessness. Strongly the gang impressed on Jack that he must not go even for five minutes' walk out of sight of the clearing. The weird silent timelessness of the bush impressed him as nothing else ever did, in its motionless aloofness.* "What would my father mean, out here?" he said to himself. And it seemed as if his father and his father's world and his father's gods withered and went to dust at the thought of this bush. And when he saw one of the men on a red sorrel horse galloping like a phantom away through the dim, red-trunked, silent trees, followed by another man on a black horse: and when he heard their far, far-off yelping Coo—ee!, or a shot as they fired at a dingo or a kangaroo, he felt as if the old world had given him up from the womb, and put him into a new weird grey-blue paradise, where man has to begin all over again. That was his feeling: that the human way of life was all to be begun over again.

The home that he and Tom made for themselves seemed to be a matter of forked sticks. If you wanted an upright of any sort, drive a forked stick into the ground, or dig it in, fork-end up. If you wanted a cross-bar, lay a stick or a pole across two forks. Down the sides of your house you wove brush-wood. For the roof you plaited the long stringy strips of gum-bark. With a couple of axes and a jack-knife they built a house fit for a—savage—king. Then they went out and made a kitchen, with pegs hammered into the bole of a tree, for the frying pans, the sawn surface of a large stump for a table, and logs to lie back against.

North of the clearing lay the nucleus of a settlement, with pub, saw-mill, store, one or two homes, and a farm or two outlying. And as they cleared the land, the teamsters carried the best of the timber on jinkers,* or dragged it with chains hitched to bullock or horse teams, to the mill. But milling was expensive, and most of the wood was hand-split. Jack learned to cut palings and poles, and then to split slabs that would serve to build slab houses, or sheds.—In the spare time they would have little hunts of wallabies or bandicoots or bungarras, or boodie rats;* or they would snare opossums or stalk dingoes.

But because he was really away in the wild, Jack felt he must write letters home. So it is. The letters from home hardly interested him at all. The thin sheets with their interminable writing were almost repulsive to him. He would stow them in the barn and leave them for days without reading them: he was "busy." And sometimes the mice nibbled them, and in that way read them for him.—He was a little ashamed of this indifference. But he noticed other men were the same. When they got these endless thin sheets from home, covered with ink of words, they stowed them away in a kind of nausea, without reading more than a few lines. And the people at home had such a pitying-admonishing tone: like the young naval lieutenant who made friends with the black aborigines by promptly shaving them.—And then letters were not profitable. A stamp home cost sixpence. And the letter took about two months on the way. It was always four months before you got an answer. And after you'd written to your mother about something really important—like money—and waited impatiently several months,* for her answer, when it came it never mentioned the money and made a mountain of a cold in your head which you couldn't remember having had. What was the good of people at home writing: "We are having true November weather, very cold, with fog and sleet," when you were grilling under a fierce sun and the rush of the intense antipodal summer. What was the good of it all?—All dull as ditchwater, and no use to anybody. He had promised his mother he would write once a week. And his mother was his mother, he wanted to keep his promise. Which he did for a month.—But in camp, he didn't even know what day it was, hardly what month: though the mail did come once a fortnight, via the Saw-mill.—He took out his mother's letter—"You said in your letter from Colombo that you were sneezing. Do take care in Australia in the rainy season. Ask not to be sent out in the rain. I recollect the climate, always sunny and bright between showers. That is what we miss so much now we are back in England, the sunny skies. Of course I do not want you to be a molly coddle, but I know the climate of Western Australia, it is very trying, particularly so in the rainy season. I do hope and pray you are on a good station with a good woman who will see you are not out getting drenched in those cold downpours—"

Jack groaned aloud, astonished that his mother had got so far from her own early days. How in the name of heaven had he come to mention sneezing? Never again. He would not even say he was camping.

"Dear Mother,

"I am quite well and like farming out here all right. Old Mrs Ellis knew your father. She says he cut off her leg. I hope Father has got rid of his Liver, you said he was taking variolettes for it. I hope they have done him good. Mr Ellis says a cockles pill* and a ten-mile walk will cure anything. He says it would cure a pig's liver. But when old Tim the half-caste tried to swallow the pill it came out of the gap where his front tooth used to be, so Mrs Ellis gave him a teaspoonful of sulphur, which he said would make him blow up. But it didn't. I think I was more likely to blow up because she gave me a big teaspoon of paraffin which they call kerosene out here. She is a fine doctor, far better than the medical man who lodges here, whose name is Rackett.

"I hope you are quite well. Give my love to all my aunts and sisters and father. I hope they are all quite well—"

Jack hurried this letter in confusion into its envelope, and spent sixpence on it, knowing perfectly well it was all nonsense.

ii

There was a pause in the clearing work, after the early hot spell, and word from Lennie that there was to be a kangaroo hunt, and they were to come down. An old-man kangaroo, a king of boomers,* had been seen around, hoof-marks and paw-pad trails near the pool.

They met at dawn, by the well: Easu with two kangaroo hounds, like greyhounds on leash; Lennie peacocking on an enormous hairy-heeled roadster; a "superior" young Queenslander who had been sent west because his father found him unmanageable, and who wasn't a bad sort, though his nickname was Pink-eye Percy; Lennie's "Cornseed"* friend, Joe Low; Alec Rice, the young fellow who was courting Grace; Ross Ellis, and Herbert, who was well again; then Tom on a grey stallion, and Jack, in riding-breeches and gaiters and clean shirt, astride the famous Lucy.

Easu was born in the saddle, he rode easy on his big roan. He waved his hat excitedly at the group, and led off into the scrub, through the slender, white-barked trees of the open bush. The others rode fast in ragged order, among the thin, open trees. Jack let Lucy pick her way, sometimes ahead, sometimes in sight of the others. They rode in silence.

Then they came out unexpectedly into low, grey-green scrub without trees, and crisp grey-white soil that crumbled under the hoofs of the horses. There they were, all out in the blue and gold light, with billows of blue-green scrub running away to right and left, towards a rise in front.

"Hold hard there!" sang out* Easu, holding up the whip in his right hand. He held the reins loosely in his left, and with the reins, the leash on which the dogs were pulling. Dogs and horse he held in that left hand.

"I want y' t' divide. Tom, y' lead on a zig-zag course down north. Ross, you work south.—And this—this fox-hunting gentleman—" He paused, and Jack felt himself going scarlet.

"Says thank ye, an' hopes he's a gentleman, since y've mentioned it," put in Lennie, in his mild, inconsequential way.

There was a laugh against Red: for there was no mistaking *him* for a gentleman, in any sense of the word. However he was too much excited by the hunt to persevere.

The fellows were stowing away their pipes in their pockets, and buttoning their coats, ready for the dash. Easu, thrilled by his own unquestioned leadership, gave the orders. All listened closely.

"Call up! Call up! Follow my leader and find the trail.—Biggest boomer ever ye—"

"Come!" cried Tom.

"And I'm here!" cried Lennie.

Away they went into the gully and through the scrub, riding light but swift, in different directions.

"Let go th' mare's head," yelled Tom over his shoulder. "We're coming to timber, an' she'd best pilot herself."

"Right!" cried Jack.

"Don't ye kill Lucy," shrieked Lennie, "because me heart's set on her. Keep y' hands an' y' heel off y' horse, an' y' head on y' shoulders."

The bolt of horsemen through the bush sent parrots screaming savagely over the feathery tree-tops. Jack let Lucy have her way. She was light and swift and sure-footed, old steeple-chaser that she was. The slim straight trees slipped past, the motion of the horse surging her own way was exhilarating to a degree.

But Tom had heard something: not the parrots, not the soft thud of the following horses. He must have heard with his sixth sense: perhaps the warning call of the boomer. With face set and eyes burning, he swung and urged his horse in a new direction. And like men coming in to supper, from different directions the handful of horsemen came swish-swish through the scrub, towards a centre.

Lucy pricked one ear. Perhaps she too had heard something. Then she gathers herself together and goes like the wind after the twinkling grey quarters[*] of Tom's stallion. Her excitement mounts to Jack's head, and he rides like a projectile on the wind.

Again Tom was reining in, pulling his horse almost on to its haunches. And Jack must hold like a vise with his knees, for Lucy was pawing the air, frantic at being held up.

"Coo—ee!" came Tom's clean tenor, ringing through the bush. "Coo—ee! Coo—ee! Coo—ee!" A marvellous sound, and Lucy pawing and dancing among the scrub.

"Coo—ee! Coo—ee! Coo—ee!"

It seemed to Jack, this sound in the bush was like God. Like the call of the heroic soul seeking its body. Like the call of the bodiless soul, sounding through the immense dead spaces of the dim, open bush, strange and heroic and inhuman. The deep long "coo," mastering the silence, then the high summons of the long "eee!" The "coo" rising more imperious, and the "eee!" thrilling and holding aloft. Then the swift lift and fall: "Coo—eee! Coo—eee! Coo—eee!" till the air rocks with the fierce pulse, as if a new heart were in motion, and the shriek and scream of the "eee!" rips in strange flashes into the far-off, far-off consciousness.

Much stranger than the weird yelp of the Red Indian's war-cry was this rocking, ripping noise in the vast grey bush.

The others are coming in from right and left, like silent phantoms through the sunny evanescence of the bush, riding hard. Tom is displaced by Red. A few quick words given and taken, Easu has unleashed the dogs, slashed the long lash with a resounding crack in the air. The long lean dogs stretch out—uncannily long, from tip to tip. Tom lets go and away. Jack lets go and away, and unconsciously his hand goes down for the bow of the slippery saddle.

Lucy had the situation well in hand, which was more than Jack had. Thud-thud. Thud-thud. Thud-thud! Up, fly, crash!—— Hello?—all right. A beauty! a dream of a jumper, this Lucy. But Jack wished his seat weren't so slippery.

They were turning into bigger timber: trees further apart, but much bigger, and with hanging limbs. "Look out! Look out f' y' head." Jack kept all his eyes open, till he knew by second sight when to duck. He watched the twinkling hind-quarters of Tom's grey, among the trees.

There was a short yapping of the dogs. Lucy was going like the wind, Jack was riding light, but she was beginning to breathe heavily. No longer so young as she was. How hot the sun was, in the almost shadeless bush. And what was leading, where was the 'roo? Jack strained his eyes almost out of his head, but could see nothing.

They were on the edge of the hills, and the country changed continually. No sooner were you used to Scrub, than it was thin trees. No sooner did you know that Lucy could manipulate thin trees, than you were among big timber, with more space and dangerous boughs. Then it was salty paper-bark country*—and back to forest again: close trees, fallen logs, boodie rat holes, and sudden outcropping of dark-brown, ancient-looking rocks, with little flat crags, to be avoided. But the other men are going full speed, and full speed you must follow, watching with all your eyes, and riding light, and swept along in the run.

Up! That was over an elephant log, and down went a man at Tom's heels. It was Grace's young man. No matter. Jack was going to look over his shoulder when Tom again shouted "Up!", and Jack and Lennie followed over the fallen timber.

Suddenly they were in a great black blanket of burnt country, clear of undergrowth or shrub,* with skeletons of black, charred trees standing gruesome. And there, right under their noses, leapt three kangaroos, swerving across. The baby one, Joey, was first, lithe, light, apparently not a bit afraid, but wildly excited; then the mother-doe, all out, panting, anxious-eyed, stiffly jumping; and behind, a long way, with the dogs like needles coming after, ran the Old Man boomer; a great big chap making mighty springs—and in varying directions. Yes, he was making a rear-guard action for the safety of his mate and spawn. Leaping with great leaps, as if to the end of the world, leaning forward, his little hands curled in, his immense massive tail straight out behind him like some immense living rudder. And seeming perfectly calm, almost indifferent. With steady, easy, enormous springs he went this way, that way, detouring, but making for the same ridge his doe and Joey had passed.

The charred ground proved treacherous, holes, smouldering trunks of trees, smouldering hollows where trunks had been. Soon two horses were running loose, with men limping after them. But on went the rest. Thud and crackle went the hoofs of the galloping horses in the charcoal, as after the dogs, after the 'roos they followed, kicking up clouds of grey ash-mounds and red-burnt earth, jumping suddenly over the still-glowing logs.

The chase paused on the ridge, for the drop was sudden and steep, with rocks and boulders cropping out. Down slid the dogs in a cloud, yelping hard, making Easu at all costs turn to try the right, Tom to try the left.

They dropped awkwardly and joltingly down, between rocks, in loose charcoal powder and loose earth.

"Ain't that ole mare a marvel, Jack!" said Tom. "This nag is rode stiff, all-under my knees."

Jack's face was full of wild joy. The stones rattled, the men stood back from the stirrups, the horses seemed to be diving. But Lucy was light and sure.

Down they jolted into the gully. Easu came up swearing—lost the quarry and dogs. Jack pulled Lucy over a boulder, to get out of Easu's way: a thing he shouldn't have done. Crack! went his head against a branch, and Jack was bruising himself on the ground before he knew where he was.

But he was on his feet again, intently chasing Lucy.

"Here y' are!"—It was Herbert who leaned down, picked up the reins of the scampering mare, and threw them to Jack. Jack's face was bleeding. Lennie came up and opened his mouth in dismay. But somebody Coo-eed, and the chase was too good to lose. They are all gone.

Jack stiffly mounted, to find himself blinded by trickling blood. Lucy once more was stirring between his knees, stretching herself out, and he had to let her go, fumbling meanwhile for a handkerchief which he pushed under his hat-brim, and pulled down the old felt firmly. Wiping his eyes with his sleeve, he found the wound stanched by the impromptu dressing.

The scene had completely changed. Lucy was whisking him around the side of a huge dark boulder. They were in the dry bed of the gully, on stones.

Lucy stopped dead, practically on her haunches, but her impetus carried her over, and she was slithering down into a loose gravelly hole. Jack jumped off, to find himself face to face with the biggest boomer kangaroo he had ever imagined. It was the Old Man, sitting there at the bottom of the gravel-hole, in the hollow of a barren she-oak, his absurd paws drooping dejectedly before him and his silly dribbling under-jaw working miserably.

"He's trying to get the wind up for another fly," thought Jack, standing there as dazed as the 'roo itself, and feeling himself very much in the same condition. Then he wondered where the doe and Joey were, and where were all the other hunters. He hoped they wouldn't come. Lucy stood by, as calm as a cucumber.

Jack took a step nearer the Old Man 'roo, and instantly brought up his fists as the animal doubled its queer front paws and hit out wildly at him. He wanted to hit back.

"Mind the claws!" called somebody, with a quiet chuckle, from above.

Jack looked round, and there was Lennie and the heavy horse, the horse head-down, tail up, feet spread, like a salamander lizard on a wall, slithering down the grade into the hole, Lennie erect in the stirrups. Jack gave a loud laugh.

And the Old Man, either possessed of a sense of humour or terrified to death, seized the nearest thing at hand—which happened to be Jack; grabbed him, gripped him, hugged him in desperate fury, and tried to get up his huge, flail-like hind leg, to rip up the enemy with the toe claw.[*] One stroke of that claw, and Jack was done.

In terror, anger, surprise, Jack jumped at the kangaroo's throat, as far as the animal's grip would let him. The 'roo, trying all the time to use his hind legs, upset, so that the two went rolling on the gravel together. Jack was in horrid proximity to the weird grey fur, clutched by the weird-smelling, violent animal, in a sort of living earthquake, as the kangaroo writhed and bounced to use his great, oar-like hind legs, and Jack clung close and hit at the creature's body, hit, hit, hit. It was like hitting living wire bands. Somebody was roaring, or else it was his own consciousness shouting: "Don't let the hind claw get to work."—How horrible a wild thing was, when you were mixed up with it! The terrible nausea of its powerful, furry, violent-blooded contact. Its unnatural, almost obscene power! Its different consciousness! Its overpowering smell!

The others were coming back up the stream-bed,[*] jumping the rocks, towards this place where Jack had fallen and Lennie had come down after him. Easu was calling off the dogs, ferociously. Tom rushed in and got the 'roo by the head.

Lennie was lying on the gravel laughing so hard he couldn't stand on his legs.

iii

Jack wrote a letter to his old friend, the vet with the "weakness," in England.

"We are out at a place back of beyond, at a place called Gum Tree Valley, so I take up my pen to write as I have time.—Tom Ellis is here bossing the clearing gang, and he has a lot of aunts, whom he rightly calls ants. One of them has a place near here, and we go to dinner on Sundays, and to help when wanted. We stayed all last week and helped muster in the sheep for the shearing. We rode all round their paddock boundaries and rounded in the sheep that had strayed and got lost. They had run off from the main—about a score of flocks—and were feeding in little herds and groups miles apart. It's a grand sight to see them all running before you, their woolly backs bobbing up and down like brown water. I can tell you I know now the meaning of the Lost Sheep, and the sort of joy you have in cursing him when you find him.*

"You told me to let you know if I heard any first hand news of gold finding. Well, I haven't heard much. But a man rode into Greenlow's—that's Tom's aunt—place on Sunday, and he said to Tom: 'Are those the Stirling Ranges?' Tom said: 'No, they're not. They're the Darling Ranges.' He said: 'Are you sure?'—and got very excited. The black-fellows came and stood by, and they were vastly amused, grinning and looking away. He got out a compass and said: 'You are wrong, Mr Ellis, they are the Stirling Ranges.' Tom said: 'Call 'em what you choose, chum. We call 'em Darling.—And them others forty mile south-west we call the Stirling.'—The man groaned. Minnie Greenlow called us to come in to tea, and he came along as well. His manners were awful. He fidgetted and pushed his hat back on his head and leant forward and spat in the fire at a long shot, and tipped his cup so that his tea swobbed* in his saucer, then drank it out of the saucer. Then he pushed the cake back when handed to him, and leaned his head on his arms on the table and groaned. You'd have thought he was drunk, but he wasn't, because he said to Tom, 'Are you sure them's not the Stirling Ranges? I can't drink my tea for thinkin' about it.' And Tom said: 'Sure.' And then he seemed more distracted than ever, and blew through his teeth and mopped his head, and was upset to a degree.

"When we had finished tea and we all went outside he said: 'Well, I think I'll get back now. It's no use when the compass turns you down. I'll never find it.' We didn't know what he was talking about, but when he'd got into his buggy and drove away the blacks told us: 'Master lookin' for big lump yellow dirt—He think that very big fish, an' he bury him longa time. Comin' back no finda him—' While the boys were talking who should shout to have the slip rail let down but this same stranger, and he drove right past us and away down the long paddock. When he got to the gate there he turned round and came back and drew up by us muttering, and said: 'Where did you tell me the Stirling Ranges were?'—Tom pointed it out, and he said 'So long,' and drove off. We didn't see him again. We didn't want to. But Tom is almost sure he found a lump of gold some time back and buried it for safety's sake and now can't find it.

"That's all the gold I've heard about out here.

"Now for news. One day I went out with tucker to old Jack Moss. He's keeping a bit of land warm* for the Greenlows, shepherds sheep down there, about forty miles from everywhere. He talked and talked, and when he didn't talk he didn't listen to me. He looked away over the scrub and sucked his cutty. They say he's hoarded wealth but I didn't see any signs. He was in tatters and wore rags round his feet for boots, which were like a gorilla's. Another day we had a kangaroo hunt. We all chased an Old Man for miles, and at last he turned and faced us. I was so close I had no time to think and was on him before I had time to pull up. I jumped to the ground and grappled, and we rolled over and over down the gully. They couldn't shoot him because of me, but they fought him off and killed him. And then we saw his mate standing near among the stones, on her hind legs, with her front paws hanging like a helpless woman. Then Tom, who was tying up my cuts, called out: 'Look at her pouch! It's plum full of little nippers!' and so it was. You never saw such a trick. So we let her go. But we got the Old Man.

"Another day we rode round the surveyed area here, which Mr Ellis is taking up for the twins Og and Magog. I asked Tom a lot of questions about taking up land. I think I should like to try. Perhaps if I do you will come out. You would like the horses. There are quite a lot wild. We hunt them in and pick out the best and use them. That's how lots of people raise their horse-flesh. They are called brumbies. Excuse me for not ending properly, the mailman is coming along, he comes once a fortnight. We are lucky.

Jack."

iv

To his friend the pugilist, he wrote

"Dear Pug

"You asked me what I think about sending Ned out here. Well, there's no opening that I can see for a gym. But work, that's another question, there's more than enough. I am at work at a place called Gum Tree Valley, clearing, but we came up to Tom's aunt's place last week, to help, and we've been shearing. At least I haven't. I've been the chap who tars. You splash tar on like paint when the shearers make a misfire and gash the poor brute and curse *you*. Lord, don't they curse, if the boss isn't round. He's got a grey beard and dribbles on it, and the flies get caught in it and buzz as if it was a spider's web. He makes everyone work from morn till night like the devil. Gosh, if it wasn't that it is only for a short spell, I'd *get*. Don't you worry, up-country folk know how to get your tucker's-worth out of you all right. Today the Sabbath we had a rest.—I don't think! We washed our clothes. Talk about a goodly pile!—Only a rumour. For the old man fetches along his vests and pants, and greasy overalls and aprons, his socks, his slimy hanks and night-shirt. Imagine our horror! He's Tom's aunt's husband, and has no sons only herds of daughters, so we had to do it. We scrubbed 'em with horse-brushes on the stones. Jinks,* but I rubbed some holes in 'em!

"But cheer up, I'm not grumbling. I like getting experience as it is called.

"I mean to take up land and have a place of my own some day, then you and Ned could visit me and we could have some fun with the gloves. Lennie says I'm like a kangaroo shaping and punching at nothing, so I got a cow's bladder and blew it up and tied it to a branch, and I batter on it. Must have something to hit. You know kangaroos shape up and make to punch. They are pretty doing that. We have a baby one, Joey, and it takes a cup in its little hands and drinks. Honest to God it's got *hands*, you never saw such a thing.

"Kindest regards to your old woman and Ned. Lord only knows how I've missed you, and pray some day I will be fortunate enough to meet you again. Until then

"Farewell.

"A Merry Xmas and a Glad New Year, by the time you get this. Think of me in the broiling heat battling with sheep, their Boss, and the flies, and you'll think of me true.

"Ever your sincere friend
Jack."

V

As the time for returning from camp drew near, Jack dwelt more and more on this question of the future—of taking up land. He wished so often that life could always be a matter of camping, land-clearing, kangaroo hunting, shearing, and generally messing about. But deep underneath himself he knew it couldn't: not for him at least. Plenty of fellows lived all their life messing from camp to camp and station to station. But himself—sooner or later he would have to bite on to something. He'd have to plunge into that cold water of responsible living, some time or other.

He asked Tom about it.

"You must make up y' mind what you want to go in for, cattle, sheep, horses, wheat, or mixed farming like us," said Tom. "Then you can go out to select.* But it's no good before you know what you want."

Jack was surprised to find how little information he got from the men he mixed with. They knew their jobs: teamsters knew about teams, and jobs on the mill; the timber workers knew hauling and sawing; township people knew trading; the general hands knew about hunting and bush-craft and axe-handling; and farmers knew what was under their nose, but nothing of the laws of the land, or how he himself was to get a start.

At last he found a small holder who went out as a hired man after he had put in the seed on his own land. And this, apparently, was how Jack would have to start. The man brought out various grubby Government papers, and handed them over.

Jack had a bad time with them: Government reports, blue books, narratives of operations. But he swotted grimly. And he made out so much:

1. Any reputable immigrant over 21 years could procure 50 acres of unimproved rural Crown land open for selection; if between the ages of 14 and 21, 25 acres.

2. Such land must be held by "occupation certificate," deemed transferable only in case of death etc.

3. The occupation certificate would be exchanged for a grant at the end of five years, or before that time, providing the land had been enclosed with a substantial fence and at least a quarter cultivated. But if at the end of the five years the above conditions, or any of them, had not been observed, the lots should revert to the Crown.

4. Country land was sub-divided into agricultural and pastoral, either purchasable at the sum of 10/– an acre, or leased: the former for eight years at the nominal sum of 1/– an acre, with the right of purchase, the latter for one year at annual rental of 2/– per hundred

acres, with presumptive renewal; or five pounds per 1000 acres with rights.[*]

Jack got all this into his mind, and at once loathed it. He loathed the thought of an "occupation certificate." He loathed the thought of being responsible to the Government for a piece of land. He almost loathed the thought of being tied to land at all. He didn't want to *own* things: especially land, that is like a grave to you as soon as you do own it. He didn't want to own anything. He simply couldn't bear the thought of being tied down. Even his own unpacked luggage he had detested.

But he had started in with this taking-up-land business, so he thought he'd try an easy way to get through with it.

"Dear Father,

"I could take up land on my own account now if you sent a few hundred pounds for that purpose per Mr George. He would pay the deposit and arrange it for me. I have my eye on one or two improved farms falling idle shortly down this Gum Valley district, which is very flourishing. When they fall vacant on account of settlers dropping them, they can be picked up very cheap.

"I hope you are quite well, as I am at present.

"Your affec son

Jack."

Jack spent his sixpence on this important document, and forgot all about it. And in the dead end of the hot summer, just in the nick of time, he got this answer.

Sea View Terrace
Bournemouth
2. 2. '83.

"Dear Jack,

"Thank you for your most comprehensive letter of 30/11/82. It is quite impossible for me to raise several hundreds of pounds, or for the matter of that, one hundred pounds, in this offhand manner. I don't want to be hard on you, but we want you to be independent as soon as possible. We have so many expenses, and I have no intention of sinking funds in the virgin Australian wild, at any rate until I see a way clear to getting some return for my money, in some form of safe interest accruing to you at my death—You must not expect to run before you can walk. Stay where you are and learn what you can till your year is up, and then we will see about a jackeroo's job, at which your mother tells me you will earn £1. a week, instead of our having to pay it for you.

"We all send felicitations

Your affectionate father

G. B. Grant."

But this is running ahead.—It is not yet Christmas, 1882.

Chapter VIII.

Home for Christmas.

i

It was a red hot Christmas that year—'ot, 'ot, 'ot, all day long. Good Lord, how hot it was!—till blessed evening. Sundown brought blessings in its trail. After six o'clock you would sense the breeze coming from the sea. Whispering, sighing, hesitating. Then puff! there it was. Delicious, sweet, it seemed to save one's life.

It had been splendid out back, but it was nice to get home again and sit down to regular meals, have clean clothes and sheets to one's bed. To have your ironing and cooking done for you, and sit down to dinner at a big table with a fresh, hailstorm-patterned tablecloth on it. There was a sense almost of glory in a big, white, glossy, hailstorm table-cloth. It lifted you up.

Mr Ellis had taken Gran away for the time, so the place seemed freer, noisier. There was nothing to keep quiet for. It was holiday—*pinki*,* the natives called it; the fierce midsummer Christmas. Everybody was allowed to "spell" a great deal.

Tom and Jack were roasted like Red Indians, rather uncouth, and more manly. At first they seemed rather bumptious, thinking themselves very much men. Jack could now ride his slippery saddle in fine style, and handle a rope or an axe, and shoot straight. He knew jarrah, karri, eucalyptus, sandal, wattle, peppermint, banksia, she-oaks, pines, paper-bark and gum-trees; he had learned to tan a kangaroo hide, pegging it on to a tree; he had looked far into the wilderness, and seen the beyond, and been seized with a desire to explore it; he had made excursions over "likely places," with hammer and pick, looking for gold. He had hunted and brought home meat, had trapped and destroyed many native cats* and dingoes. He had lain awake at night and listened to the more-porks, and in the early morning had heard with delight the warbling of the timeline and thickhead thrushes that abounded round the camp, mingled with the noise of magpies, tits, and wrens. He had watched the manœuvres of willy-wagtails, and of a brilliant variety of birds:

weavers, finches, parrots, honey-eaters, and pigeons. But the banded wrens and blue-birds* were his favourites in the bush world.

Well, on such a hero as this, the young home-hussies Monica and Grace had better not look too lightly. He was so grand they could hardly reach him with a long pole.

"An' how many emus did y' see?" asked Og. For lately at Wandoo they had had a plague of emus, which got into the paddocks and ate down the sheep's food-stuff, and then got out again by running at the fences and bashing a way through.

Jack had never seen one.

"Never seen an emu!"—Even little Ellie shrilled in derisive amazement. "Monica, he's *never seen an emu*!"

Already they had snipped the tip off the high feather he had in his cap.

But he was still a hero, and Lennie followed him round like a satellite, while the girls were obviously *thrilled* at having Tom and him back again. They would giggle and whisper behind Bow's back, and wherever he was, they were always sauntering out to stand not far off from him. So that of course their thrill entered also into Jack's veins, he felt a cocky young lord, a young life-master. This suited him very well.

But there was no love-making, of course. They all laughed and joked together over the milking and pail-carrying and feeding and butter-making and cheese-making and everything, and life was a happy delirium.

They had waited for Tom to come home, to rob the bees. Tom hated the bees and they hated him, but he was staunch. Veils, bonnets, gloves, gaiters were produced, and off they all set, in great joy at their own appearance, with gong, fire, and endless laughter. Tom was to direct from a distance: he stood afar, "smoking them off." Grace and Monica worked merrily among the hives, manipulating the boxes which held the comb, lifting them on to the milk pans to save the honey, and handing the pans to the boys to carry in.

"OOh!" yelled Tom suddenly. "Ooh!"

A cloud of angry bees was round his head. Down went his fire-protector—a tin full of smouldering chips—, down went flappers and bellows as with a shriek he beat the air. The more he beat the darker the venomous cloud. Crippled with terror, he ran on shaking legs. The girls and youngsters were paralysed with joy. They swarmed after him shrieking with laughter. His head was completely hidden by bees, but his arms like windmills waved wildly to and fro. He dashed into the cubby, but the bees went with him. He appeared at the window for a moment, showing a demented face, then he jumped out, and the bees with him. Leaping the drain gap and yelling in terror, he made for the house. The bees swung with him and the children after. Jack and the girls stood speechless, looking at one another. Monica had on man's trousers with an old uniform buttoned close to her neck, workmen's socks over her shoes and trouser-ends, and a chinaman's hat with a veil over it, netted round her head like a meat-safe. Jack never noticed that she was funny. Suddenly, somehow, she looked mysterious to him, and not just the ordinary image of a girl. Suddenly a new cavern seemed to open before his eyes: the mysterious, fascinating cavern of the female unknown. He was not definitely conscious of this. But seeing Monica there in the long white flannel trousers and the chinaman's-hat meatsafe over her face, something else awoke in him, a new awareness of a new wonder. He had but lately stood on the inward ranges and looked inland into the blue, vast mystery of the Australian interior. And now, with another opposite vision he saw an opposite mystery opposing him: the mystery of the female, the young female there in her grotesque garb.

A new awareness of Monica began to trouble him.

"Oooh! Oooh! Ma! Ma! Ma!" Out rushed Tom straight from the kitchen door, the bees still with him. Straight he dashed to the garden, and to the well in the middle. He loosed the windlass and stood on the coping screaming while the bucket clanged and clashed to the bottom. Then Tom seized the rope, and turning his legs round it, slid silently into the hidden, cool dark depths.

The children shrieked with bliss. Jack and the girls rocked with helpless laughter, convulsed by this last exit.

The bees were puzzled. They poised buzzbee fashion above the well-head, explored the mouth of the shaft, and rose again and hovered. Then they began to straggle away. They melted into the hot air.

And now the girls and Jack drew up from the well a raging and soaking Tom. Drew him up uncertainly, wobblingly, a terrible weight on the straining, creaking windlass. Ma and Ellie took him in hand and daubed him a sublime blue: like an ancient Briton,[*] Grace said. Then they gave him bread and jam and a cup of tea.

Then occurred another honey-bee tragedy. Ellie, who had done nothing at all to the bees, suddenly shrieked loudly and ran pelting round screaming: "I've got a bee in my head! I've got a bee in my head!"

Monica caught and held her, while Jack took the bee, a big drone, out of the silky meshes of her honey hair. And as he lifted his eyes he met the yellow eyes of Monica. And the two exchanged a moment's look of intimacy and communication and secret shame, so that they both went away avoiding one another.

ii

On New Year's Eve there was always a foregathering of the settlers at the Wandoo homestead. They must foregather somewhere, and Wandoo was the oldest and most flourishing place. It occupied the banks of the so-called Avon river,* which was mostly just a great dry bed of stones. But it had plenty of fresh water in the soaks and wells, among the scorched rocks, and these wells were fed by underground springs, not brackish, as is so often the case. Wandoo was therefore a favoured place.

"What am I to wear?" said Jack, aghast, when he heard of the affair.

"Anything," said Tom.

"Nothing," said Len.

"Your new riding suit," said Monica, who had begun to assume airs of proprietorship over him.—"And you needn't say anything, young Len," she continued venomously. "Because you've got to wear that new holland suit Ma got you from England, *and* boots and socks as well."

"It's awful. Oo—er! It's awful!" groaned Lennie.

It was. A tight-fitting brown holland suit with pants half-way down the shin and many pearl-buttons across the stomach, the coat with a stiff stand-up collar and rigid seams. Harry had a similar rig, but the twins outdid Solomon in sailor suits with gold braid and floppy legs. At least they started in glory.*

Tom, in his father's old tennis-flannels and a neat linen jacket looked quite handsome. But when he saw Jack in his real pukka riding rig, he exclaimed:

"God Almighty, but you've got the goods!"

"A bit too dashing?" asked Jack anxiously.

"Not on your life! You'll do fine. Reds all go in for riding breeks and coats as near sporting dog's yank* as they k'n get 'em. There's a couple o' white washing suits o' Dad's as he's grown out of, as I'll plank up in the loft to change into tonight. We can't come in this here cubby again. Once we leave it it'll be jumped by all the women and children from round the country to put their things in."

"Won't they go into the house?"

"Hallelujah no! Only relations go upstairs. Quality into the dyin'-room. Yahoos anywhere, and the ladies always bag our cubby!"

"Lor!"

But it had to be so. For the New Year's shivoo the settlers all saved up, and they all dressed up. By ten o'clock the place was like a fair ground. Horses of all sorts nosing their feed bags; conveyances of all sorts unhitched; girls all muslin and ribbon; boys with hats on at an angle, and boots on; men in clean shirts and brilliant ties, mothers in frill and furbelow, with stiffly-starched little children half hidden under sunbonnets; old dames and ancient patriarchs, young bearded farmers, and shaven civilians ridden over from York. Children rushing relentlessly in the heat, amid paper bags, orange peel, concertina-playing, baskets of victuals and fruit, canvas, rubbish and nuts all over the scorched grass. Christmas!

Tom had asked Jack to organise a cricket eleven to play against the Reds. The Reds were dangerous opponents, and the dandies of the day. In riding breeches made India fashion,* with cotton gaiters, and rubber-soled shoes, white shirts, and broad-brimmed hats, they looked a handsome colonial set—And they had a complete eleven.

Tom was sitting on a bat bemoaning his fate. He had only five reliable men.

"Aw shut up!" said Lennie. "Somebody'll turn up.—Who's comin' in at the gate now? Ain't it the parson from York, and five gents what can handle a bat.* Hell!—ain't my name cockadoodle!"

In top hats and white linen suits these gentlemen had ridden their twenty five miles for a game. What price the Reds now!

Tom's side was in first, Easu and Rossy Ellis bowling. Easu, big, loose, easy, looked strange and *native*, as if he belonged to the natural salt of the earth there. He seemed at home, like an emu or a yellow mimosa tree. He was a bowler of repute. But somehow Jack could not bear to see him palm the ball before he bowled: could not bear to watch it. Whereas fat Ross Ellis, the other bowler, spitting on his hand and rolling the ball in elation after getting the wicket of the best man from York,* Jack didn't mind him.—But unable to watch Easu, he walked away across the paddock,* among the squatting mothers whose terror was the flying leather ball.

"Your turn at the wickets, Mr Grant," called the excited, red-faced parson, who, Lennie declared, "couldn't preach less or act more."

"We're eight men out for twenty-six rounds, so smack at 'em. If ye can get the loose end on Ross, do it. I'll be in t' other end next and stop 'em off Easu. I come in right there as the useful block."

Jack was excited. And when he was excited, phrases always came up in his mind. He had the sun in his eyes. But the bat felt good.

"If a gentleman sees bad, he ignores it. He— —"

"Here comes the ball from that devil Easu!"

"How's that!"

"Finds good and fans it to flame*—fans it to—"

Joe Low, that stripling had the other wicket.

Smack! Jack scored the first run off Easu, running for his life.

"You can be a gentleman even if you are a bush-whacker."

Nine wickets had fallen to Easu for twenty-seven runs, and Easu was elated. Then the parson came forth and stood opposite Jack. He at once whacked Ross' ball successfully, for three. Jack hitched his belt after the run, and hit out for another three,* and got 'em.

Smack!—no need to run that time. It was a boundary.

Lennie's voice outside yelling admiration roused his soul, as did Easu's yelling angrily to Ross: "You give that ball to Sam, this over.—You blanky idjut!"

Ross picked up the returning leather, and sent down a sulky grubber which Jack naturally skied. Herbert, placed at a point in the shade, came out to catch it, and missed—.

Somehow the parson had steadied Jack's spirit. And when, in a crisis, Jack got his spirit steadied, it seemed to him he could get a semi-magical grip over a situation. Almost as if he could alter the swerve of the ball by his pure, clairvoyant *will*. So it seemed. And keyed up against the weird, handsome, native Easu, as if by a magic of will Jack held the wicket and got the runs. It was one of those subtle battles which are beyond our understanding. And Jack won.

But Easu got him out in the end. In the first innings, a terrific full pitch came down crash over his head on to the middle wicket, when he had made his first half century; that was Easu; and Easu stumped him out in the second innings, for twenty.

Nevertheless the Reds were beaten by a margin of sixteen runs, before the parson and the gentlemen in top hats set off for their long and dusty ride to York.

iii

Jack hated the Reds with all the wholesale hatred of eighteen. There they were, all of them, swaggering round as if the place belonged to them, taking everything and giving nothing. Their peculiar air of assertion was particularly maddening, in contrast with the complete lack of assumption on the part of the other Australians. It was as if the Reds had made up their minds, all of them, to leave a bruise on everything they touched. They were all big men, and all older than Jack. Easu must have been over thirty, and unmarried, with a bad reputation among the women of the colony. Yet, apparently, he could always find a girl. That slow, laconic assurance of his, his peculiar, meaning smile as he drifted up loose-jointed to a girl, seemed nearly always to get through. The women watched him out of the corner of their eye. They didn't *like* him. But they felt his power. And that was perhaps even more effective.

For he had power. And this was what Jack felt lacking in himself. Jack had quick intuitive understanding, and a quick facility. But he had not Easu's power. Sometimes Easu could look really handsome, strolling slowly across to some girl with the peculiar rolling gait that distinguished him, and smiling that little, meaningful, evil smile. Then he looked handsome, and as if he belonged to another race of men, men who were like small-headed demons out to destroy the world.

"I'm fighting him," thought Jack. "I wouldn't have a good opinion of myself if I didn't."

For he saw in Easu a malevolent principle, a kind of venom.

Ross Ellis, the youngest of the Reds, was old enough to be joining the mounted police force in a few days, and Mr Ellis had sent up a strong chestnut mount for him, from the coast. Easu, tall, broad, sinewy, with sinewy powerful legs and small buttocks, was sitting close on the prancing chestnut, showing off, his malevolence seeming to smile under his blonde beard, and his blue, rivet eyes taking in everything. All the time he went fooling the simple farmers who had come to the sports, raising a laugh where he could, and always a laugh of derision.

"Tom," said Jack at last, "couldn't you boss it a bit over those Reds? It's *your* place, it's *your* house, not theirs. Go on, put them down a bit, do."

"Aw," said Tom. "They're older 'n me, and the place by rights belongs to them: leastways they think so. And they *are* crack sportsmen—"

"Why they're not! Look at Easu parading on that police horse your father sent up from the coast! And look at all the other cockeys* getting ready to compete against him in the riding events. They haven't a chance, and he knows it."

"He won't risk taking that police horse over jumps, don't you fret."

"No, but he has the pick of your stable, and he'll beat all the others while you stand idling by. Why should *he* be cock of the walk?"

"Why," cried Lennie breaking in, "I could beat anyfin on Lucy. But Tom won't let me go in against the other chaps, will you Tom?"

Tom smiled. He had a plain brick-red face, patient and unchanging, with white teeth and brown, sensitive eyes. When he smiled he had a great charm. But he did not often smile, and his mouth was marred by the look so many men develop in Australia, facing the bush: that lipless look, which Jack, as he grew more used to it, came to call the suffering look. As if they had bitten and been bitten hard, perhaps too hard.

"Well nipper," he said after a moment's hesitation; "if you finds them Waybacks* has it between 'em, you stand out. But y' c'n have Lucy if you like, an' if y' beat the *Reds*—y' c'n beat 'em."

"That's what *I* mean all right!" cried Lennie, capering. "I savvy O. K. I'll give 'em googlies and sneaks an' leg-breaks,* y' see if I don't, an' even up for 'em."

iv

Monica came up and took Jack's arm with sudden impulsive affection, on this very public day. Drawing him away, she said:

"Come and sit down a bit under the Bay Fig, Jack. I want a rest. All these people tearing us in two from morning till night."

Jack found himself thrilling to the girl's touch, to his own surprise and disgust. He flushed slowly, and went on stiff legs, hoping nobody was looking at him. Nobody was looking *specially*, of course. But Monica kept hold of his arm, with her light, tense, girlish hand, and he found it difficult to walk naturally. And again the queer electric thrills went through him, from that light blade of her hand.

She was very lovely today, with a sort of winsomeness, a sort of fierce appeal. As a matter of fact, she had been flirting dangerously with Red Easu, till she was a bit scared. And she had been laughing and fooling with Hal Stockley—otherwise Pink-eye Percy—whom all the girls were mad about, but who didn't affect her seriously. Easu affected her, though. And she didn't really like him. That was why she had come for Jack, whom she liked very much indeed. She felt so safe and happy with him. And she loved his delicate, English, virgin quality, his shyness and his natural purity. He was purer than she was. So she wanted to make him in love with her. She was sure he *was* in love with her. But it was such a shy, unwilling love, she was half annoyed.

So she leaned forward to him, with her fierce young face and her queer, yellow, glowering eyes not far from his, and she seemed to yearn to him with a yearning like a young leopard. Sometimes she touched his hand, and sometimes, laughing and showing her small, pointed teeth winsomely, she would look straight into his eyes, as if searching for something. And he flushed with a dazed sort of delight, unwilling to be overpowered by the new delight, yet dazed by it, even to the point of forgetting the other people and the party, and Easu on the chestnut horse.

But he made no move. When she touched his hand, though his eyes shone with a queer suffused light, he would not take her hand in his. He would not touch her. He would not make any definite response. To all she said, he answered in simple monosyllables. And there he sat, suffused with delight, yet making no move whatsoever.

Till at last Monica, who was used to defending herself, was miffed. She thought him a muff.* So she suddenly rose and left him. Went right away. And he was very much surprised and chagrined, feeling that somehow it wasn't possible, and feeling as if the sun had gone out of the sky.

V

The sun really was low in the heavens. The breeze came at last from the sea and freshened the air and lifted the sweet crushed scent of the trampled dry grass. It was time for the last events of the sports. Everybody was eager, revived by the approach of evening, and Jack felt the drunkenness of new delight upon him. He was still vague, however, and unwilling even to think of Monica, much less seek her out.

The black-boys' event, with unbroken buckjumpers, was finishing down by the river. Joe Low, with a serious face but sparkling eyes, went riding by on a brumby colt he had caught and broken himself. Jack sat alone under a tree, waiting for the flat race, in which he was entered, and feeling sure of himself.

Easu came dancing up on the raw chestnut that had been sent up from the Coast along with the police horse. He wore spurs, and had a long parrot-feather in his hat.

"Here you young Pommy Grant,"* he said to Jack. "Ketch hold of me bit while I fix me girths a bit tighter, and then you c'n hold your breath while I show them Cornseeds what."

He had a peculiarly insolent manner towards Jack. The latter nevertheless held the frothy chestnut while Easu swung out of the saddle and hitched up the girth. As he bent there beside the horse, Jack noticed his broad shoulders and narrow waist and small, hard, tense hips. Yes, he was a man. But ugh! what an objectionable one! Especially the slight hateful smile of derision on the red face and in the light-blue, small-pupilled eyes.

But he clipped into the saddle again, and once more it was impossible not to admire his seat, his close, fine, clean, small seat in the saddle. There was no spread about him there. And the power of the long, muscular thighs.—Then once more he dismounted, leaving Jack to hold the bridle of the chestnut whilst he himself strolled away.

The other farmers were waiting on their horses, so serious and quiet: in their patience and unobtrusiveness, so gentlemanly, Jack thought. So unlike the assertive, jeering Easu.

Lennie came up and whipped the pin out of Jack's favour. It was a rosette of yellow ribbon, shiny as a butter-cup, that Monica had made him.

"Here, what're you doing!" he cried.

"Aw, shut it. Keep still!" said Lennie.

And slipping round, he pushed the pin, point downward, into the back saddle-pad of the chestnut Jack was holding. That wasn't fair. But Jack let be.

The judge called his warning, the Cornseeds lined up, along with Joe Low and a young yellow-faced dairyman and a slender skin-hunter, and a woolly old stockman. Easu came and took his chafing horse, but did not mount.

"One!"—Easu swung up, standing in his stirrups, scarce touching the saddle-seat.

"Two! Three!"—and the sharp crack of a pistol.

Away went the scraggy brumby and Joe, and like a torrent, the dairyman and the skin-hunter and the stockman. But the chestnut had never heard a pistol-shot before, and was jumping round wildly.

"Blood and pace, mark you!" said the judge, waving towards the chestnut. "Them cockeys does their best on what they got, but watch that chestnut under Red Ellis. It's a pleasure to see good horse-flesh like them Ellises brings up to these parts..."

Easu, seeing the field running well and far ahead, wheeled his mount on to the track at that minute, and sat down.

The chestnut sat up, stopped, bucked, threw Easu, and then galloped madly away. It was all so sudden and somehow unnatural, that everybody was stunned. Easu rose and stared, with hell in his face, after the running chestnut. People began to laugh aloud.

"Oh Gawd my fathers!" murmured Tom in Jack's ear. "Think of Easu getting a toss! Easu letting *any* horse get the soft side of him! Oh my Gawd, if I'm not sorry for Easu when that crowd o' Reds sets on to him with their tongues tomorrow."

"I'm jolly glad," said Jack complacently.

"So am I!" said Lennie. "An' I did it, an' I wish it had killed him. I put a pin under the saddle-crease, Tom. Don't look at me, y' needn't. I've had one up again 'im for a long time, for Jack's sake. D' y' know what he did? He put Jack on that Stampede stallion, when Jack hadn't been on our place a fortnight. So he did. An' if Jack had been killed, who'd ha' called him a murderer?—Yah, one o' the blacks told *me*. And nobody durst tell you, cos they durstn't—."

"On Stampede!" exclaimed Tom, going yellow, and hell coming into his brown eyes. "An' a new chum my father trusted to him to show him round—"

"Oh well—" said Jack.

"The sod!"* said Tom: and that was final.

Then after a moment:

"If the Reds is going over the jumps, you go and get Lucy, Len."

"I likes your sperrit, Tom. I was goin' to anyway, case they get that dark 'oss." Lennie threw off his coat, hat, and tie, then sat on the trodden brown grass to take off his boots and stockings. Thus stripped, he stood up and hitched his braces looser, remarking:

"Jack Grant said he'd bash Easu's head for 'im if he said anything to me after I beat 'im over them jumps, so I was goin' to risk it anyway."

Jack had said no such thing, but was prepared to take the hint.

The chestnut had been caught and tied up. Down the field they could see Easu persuading Sept to ride a smart piebald filly that had been brought in. Sept was the thinnest of the Reds. The jumping events continued away on the left, the sun was almost setting.

"Hurry up there for the final!" called the judge.

Sept came up on the delicate piebald filly which they had brought over from their own place. She was dark chestnut, and with flames of pure white, she seemed dazzling.

"That's the dark 'oss I mentioned!" said Len. "Gosh, but me heart is beatin'! It'll be a real match between me an' him, for that there filly can jump like a 'roo, I've watched 'er."

Joe Low rode up to the jumping yard, and lifted his brumby over. The filly danced down and followed. Lennie was in the saddle like a cat and Lucy went over the rail without effort.

When the rail was at five feet two, Joe Low's brumby was done. Lucy clipped the rail and the filly cleared it. Sept brought his creature round to the judge, with raised eyebrows.

"No y' don't!" yelled Lennie, riding down the track hell for leather, and Lucy went over like a swallow. Sept laughed, and came down to the rail that was raised an inch. The filly sailed it, but hit the bar. Lucy baulked. Len swung her round and came again. A perfect over.

Next! The filly, snorting and frothing, tore down, jibbed, and was sworn at loudly by Easu standing near. Sept whipped and spurred her over.

But at that rail, raised to five feet nine, she would not be persuaded, though Lucy cleared it with a curious casual ease. The filly would not take it.

"Say Mister!" called Lennie when he knew he was winner. "Raise that barrier five inches and see us bound it."

He made his detour, brought Lucy along on twinkling feet, and cleared it prettily.

The roar of delight from the crowd sent Easu mad. Jack kept an eye on him, in case he meant mischief. But Easu only went away to where the niggers were still trying out the buckjumpers. Taking hold of a huge rogue of a mare, he sprang on her back and came bucking all along the track, apparently to give a specimen of horsemanship. The crowd watched the queer massive pulsing up and down of the man and the powerful bucking horse, all in a whirl of long hair, like some queer fountain of life. And there was Monica watching Easu's cruel, changeless face, that seemed to have something fixed and eternal in it, amid all that heaving.

Jack felt he had a volcano inside him. He knew that Stampede had been caught again, and was being led about down there, securely roped, as part of the show. Down there among the outlaws.

Away ran Jack. Anything rather than be beaten by Easu. But as he ran, he kept inside him that queer little flame of white-hot calm which was his invincibility.

He patted Stampede's arching neck, and told Sam to saddle him. Sam showed the whites of his eyes, but obeyed, and Stampede took it. Jack stood by, intense in his own cool calmness. He didn't care what happened to him. If he was to be killed he would be killed. But at the same time, he was not reckless. He watched the horse with mystical closeness, and glanced over the saddle and bridle to see they were all right.

Then, swift and light, he mounted and knew the joy of being a horseman, the thrill of being a real horseman. He had the gift, and he knew it. If not the gift of sheer power, like Easu, who seemed to overpower his horse as he rode it; Jack had the gift of adjustment. He adjusted himself to his horse. Intuitively, he yielded to Stampede, up to a certain point. Beyond that certain flexible point, there would be no yielding, none, and never.

Jack came bucking along in Easu's wake, on a much wilder horse. But though Stampede was wild and wicked, he never exerted his last efforts. He bucked like the devil. But he never let himself altogether go. And Jack seemed to be listening with an inward ear to the animal, listening to its passion. After all, it was a live creature, to be mastered, but not to be overborne. Intuitively, the boy gave way to it as much as possible. But he never for one moment doubted his own mastery over it. In his mastery there must be a living* tolerance. This his instinct told him. And the stallion, bucking and sitting up, seemed somehow to accept it.

For after all, if the horse had gone really wicked, absolutely wicked, it would have been too much for master Jack. What he depended on was the bit of response the animal was capable of. And this he knew.

He found he could sit the stallion with much greater ease than before. And that strange powerful life beneath him and between his thighs, heaving and breaking like some enormous alive wave, exhilarated him with great exultance, the exultance in the power of life.

Monica's eyes turned from the red, fixed, overbearing face of Easu, to the queer, abstract, radiant male face of Jack, and a great pang went through her heart, and a cloud came over her brow. The boy balanced on the trembling, spurting stallion, looking down at it with dark-blue, wide, dark-looking eyes, and thinking of nothing, yet feeling so much; his face looking soft and warm with a certain masterfulness that was more animal than human, like a centaur, as if he were one blood with the horse, and had the centaur's superlative horse-sense, its non-human power, and wisdom of hot blood-knowledge. She watched the boy, and her brow darkened and her face was fretted as if she were denied something. She wanted to look again at Easu, with his fixed hard will that excited her. But she couldn't. The queer soft power of the boy was too much for her, she could not save herself.

So they rode, the two men, and all the people watched them, as the sun went down in the wild empty sea westward from hot Australia.

Chapter IX.

New Year's Eve.

i

New Year's Eve was celebrated Scotch style, at Wandoo. It was already night, and Jack and Tom had been round seeing if the visitors had everything they wanted. Ma and a few select guests were still in the kitchen. The cold collation in the parlour still waited majestically. The twins and Harry were no longer visible: they had subsided on their stomachs by the wood-pile, in the hot evening, and found refuge in sleep; for all the world like sailors sunk delapidated and demoralised after a high old spree. But Ellie and baby were at their zenith. Having been kept out of the ruck most carefully upstairs, they were now produced at their best. Mr Ellis was again away in Perth, seeing the doctor.

Tom and Jack went into the loft and changed into clean white duck. They came forth like new men, jerking their arms in the stiff starched sleeves. And they proceeded to light the many chinese lanterns hung in the barn, till the great place was mellow with soft light. Already in the forenoon they had scraped candle-ends on to the floor, and rubbed them in. Now they rubbed in the wax a little more, to get the proper slipperiness.

The light brought the people, like moths. Of course the Reds were there, brazen as brass. They too had changed into white suits, tight round the calf and hollow at the waist, and, for the moment, with high collars rising to their ears above the black cravats. Also they sported elastic-sided boots of patent leather, whereas most of the other fellows were in their heavy hob-nailed boots, nicely blacked, indeed, but destitute of grace. With their hair brushed down in a curl over their foreheads, and their beards brushed apart, their strong sinewy bodies filling out the white duck, they felt absolutely invincible, and almost they looked it. For Jack was growing blind to the rustic absurdities, blinded by the animal force* of these Australians.

Jack sat down by Herbert, who was pleasant and mild after his illness, always a little shy with the English boy. But the other Reds had taken possession of the place. Their bounce and their brass were astounding. Jack watched them in wonder at their aggressive self-assertion. They were real bounders, more crude and more bouncy than ever the Old Country could produce. But that also was Australian. The bulk of the people, perhaps, were dumb and unassuming. But there was always a proportion of real brassy bounders, ready to walk over you and jump in your stomach,* if you'd let them.

Easu had constituted himself Master of the Ceremonies: and we know what an important post that is, in a country bean-feast.* Wherever he was, he must be in the front, bossing and hectoring other people. He had appointed his brothers "stewards." The Reds were to run the show. There was to be but one will: the will of the big, loose-jointed, domineering Easu, with his reddish blonde beard brushed apart and his keen eyes spying everything with a slight jeer.

Most of the guests, of course, were as they had been all day, in their Sunday suits or new dungarees. Joe Low, trim in a clean cotton jacket, sat by the great open doors very seriously blowing notes out of an old brass cornet, that had belonged to his father, a retired sergeant of the Foot. Near him, a half-caste Huck* was sliding a bow up and down a yellow-looking fiddle, while other musicians stood with their instruments under their arms. Outside in the warm night bearded farmers smoked and talked. Mamas sat on the forms round the barn, and the girls, most of them fresh and gay in billowy cotton frocks, clustered around in excitement. It was the great day of all the year.

For the rest, most of the young men were leaning holding up the big timber supports of the barn, or framing the great opening of the sliding doors, which showed the enormous dark gap of the naked night.

Fire-eating Easu waved energetically to Joe, who blew a blast on the cornet. This done, the strong but "common" Australian voice of Easu, shouted* effectively:

"Take partners. Get ready for the Grand March."*

For of course he plumed himself on doing everything in "style," everything grand and correct, this Australian who so despised the effete Old Country. The rest of the Reds straight away marched to the sheepish and awkward fellows who stood propped up against any available prop, seized them by the arm, and rushed them up to some equally sheepish maiden. And instead of resenting it, the poor clowns were glad at being forced into company. They grinned and blushed and the girls giggled and bridled as they coupled and arranged themselves, two by two, close behind one another.

A blast of music. Easu seized Monica, who was self-consciously waiting on the arm of another young fellow. He just flung his arm round her waist and heaved her to the head of the column. Then the procession set off, Easu in front with his arm round Monica's waist, he shining with his own brass and self-esteem, she looking falsely demure. After them came the other couples, self-conscious but extremely pleased with themselves, slowly marching round the barn.

Jack, who had precipitated himself into the night rather than be hauled into action by one of the Red stewards, stood and looked on from afar, feeling out of it. He felt out in the cold. He hated Easu's common, gloating self-satisfaction, there at the head with Monica. Red cared nothing about Monica, really. Only she was the star of the evening, the chief girl, so he had got her. She was the chief girl for miles around. And that was enough for Easu. He was determined to leave his mark on her.

After the March, the girls went back to their Mamas, the youths to their shoulder-supports; and following a pause, Easu again came into the middle of the floor, and began bellowing instructions. He was so pleased with the sound of his own voice, when it was lifted in authority. Everybody listened with all their ears, afraid of disobeying Easu.

When the oration was over, the boldest of the young men made a bee-line for the prettiest girls, and there was a hubbub. In a twinkling any girl whom Jack would have deigned to dance with, was monopolised, only the poorest remained. Meanwhile the stewards were busy sorting the couples into groups.

Jack could not dance. He had not intended to dance. But he didn't at all like being left out entirely, in oblivion as if he did not exist. Not at all. So he drifted towards the group of youths in the doorway. But he slid away again as Ross Ellis plunged in, seized whom he could by the arm, and led them off to the crude and unprepossessing maidens left still unchosen. He felt he would resent intensely being grabbed by the arm and hustled into a partner by one of the Reds.

What was to be done. He seemed to be marooned in his own isolation like some shipwrecked mariner: and he was becoming aware of the size of his own hands and feet. He looked for Tom.

Tom was steering a stout but willing mother into the swim, and Lennie, like a faithful little tug, was following in his wake with a gentle but squint-eyed girl.

Jack became desperate. He looked round quickly. Mrs Ellis was sitting alone on a packing-case. At the same moment he saw Ross Ellis bearing down on him with sardonic satisfaction.

Action was quicker than thought. Jack stood bowing awkwardly before his hostess.

"Won't you do me the honour, Mrs Ellis?"

"Oh dear me!—Oh dear, Jack Grant!—But I believe I will. I never thought of such a thing. But why not? Yes, I will, it will give me great pleasure. We shall have to lead off, you know. And I was supposed to lead with Easu, seeing my husband isn't here. But never mind, we'll lead off, you and I, just as well."

She rose to her feet briskly, seeming young again. Lately Jack thought she seemed always to have some trouble on her mind. For the moment she shook it off.

As for him, he was panic-stricken. He wished he could ascend into heaven; or at least as high as the loft.

"You'll help me through, Marm, won't you?" he said. "This dance is new to me."

And he bowed to her, and she bowed to him, and it was horrible. The horrible things people did for enjoyment!

"This dance is new to him," Mrs Ellis passed over his shoulder to a pretty girl in pink. "Help him through, Alice."

Feeling a fool, Jack turned and met a wide smile and a nod. He bowed confusedly.

"I'm your corner," said the girl. "I'll pass it on to Monica, she'll be your vis-a-vis."

"Pick up partners," Easu was yelling with his domineering voice. "All in place, please!—One more couple! One more couple!"—He was at the other end of the barn, coming forward now, looking around like a general. He was coming for his aunt.

"Ah!" he said, when he saw Mrs Ellis and Jack. "You dancing with Jack Grant, Aunt Alice?[*] Thought he couldn't dance."

And he straightway turned his back on them, looking for Monica. Monica was standing with a young man from York.

"Monica, I want you," said Easu. "You can find a girl there—" he said, nodding from the young fellow to a half-caste girl with fuzzy hair. The young fellow went white. But Monica crossed over to

Easu, for she was a wicked little thing, and this evening she was hating Jack Grant, the booby.

"One more couple not needed," bawled Easu. "Top centre—Where are you, Aunt Alice? Couple from here, lower centre, go to third set on left—"

Easu was standing near the top. He stepped backward, and down came his heel on Jack's foot. Jack got away, but an angry light came into his eyes. His face, however, still kept that cherubic expression characteristic of it, and so ill-fitting his feelings. Easu was staring over the room, and never even looked round.

"All in place?—*Music*!" cried the M.C.

The music started with a crash and a bang, Mrs Ellis had seized Jack's arm and was leading him into the middle of the set.

"Catch hands, Monica," she said.

He loved Monica's thin, nervous, impulsive hands. His heart went hot as he held them. But Monica wouldn't look at him. She looked demurely sideways. But he felt the electric thrill that came to him from her hands, and he didn't want to let go.

She loosed his grasp and pushed him from her.

"Get back to Ma," she whispered. "Corner with Alice."

"Oh Lor!" thought Jack. For he was cornered and grabbed and twisted by the girl with the wide smile, before he was let go, to fall into place beside Ma, panting with a sort of exasperation.

So it continued, grabbing and twisting and twirling, all perfectly ridiculous and undignified. Why oh why did human beings do it!—Yet it was better than being left out. He was half pleased with himself.

Something hard and vicious dug him in the ribs. It was the elbow of Easu, who passed skipping like a goat.

Was Easu making a dead set at him? Was Easu trying to bully him? The devil's own anger began to rise in the boy's heart, bringing up with it all the sullen dare-devil that was in him. When he was roused, he cared for nothing in earth or heaven. But his face remained cherubic.

"Follow!" said a gentle voice. Perhaps it was all a mistake. He found himself back by Mrs Ellis, watching other folks prance. There he stood and mopped his brow, in the hot, hot night. He was wet with sweat all over. But before he could wipe his face the pink Alice had caught and twirled him, taking him unawares. He waited alert. Nothing happened. Actually peace for a few seconds.

The music stopped. Perhaps it was over. Oh enjoyment! Why did people do such things to enjoy themselves?—Only he would have liked to hold Monica's thin, keen hands again. The thin, keen, wild, wistful Monica. He would like to be near her.

Easu was bawling something. Figure Number Two. He could not listen to instructions in Easu's voice.

They were dancing again, and he knew no more than at first what he was doing. All a maze. A natural diffidence and a dislike of being touched by any casual stranger made dancing unpleasant to him. But he kept up. And suddenly he found himself with Monica folded in his arms, and she clinging to him with sudden fierce young abandon. His heart stood still, as he realised that not only did he want to hold her hands—he had thought it was just that; but he wanted to hold her altogether in his arms. Terrible and embarrassing thought! He wished himself on the moon, to escape his new emotions. At the same time there was the instantaneous pang of disappointment as she broke away from him. Why could she not have stayed! And why oh why were they both doing this beastly dancing!

He received a clean clear kick on the shin as he passed Easu. Dazed with a confusion of feelings, keenest among which perhaps was anger, he pulled up again beside Ma. And there was Monica suddenly in his arms again.

"You always go again," he said to her in a vague murmur.

"What did you say?" she answered archly, as she floated from him, just at the moment when Easu jolted him roughly. Across the little distance she was watching the hot anger in the boy's confused, dark-blue eyes.

Another pause. More beastly instructions. Different music. Different evolutions.

"Steady now!" he said to himself, trying to make his way in the new figure. But what work it was! He tried to keep his brain steady. But Ma on his arm was heavy as lead.

And then, with great ease and perfect abandon, in spite of her years, Ma threw herself on his left bosom and reclined in peace there. He was overcome. She seemed absolutely to like resting on his bosom.

"Throw out your right hand, dear boy—" she whispered, and before he knew he had done it, Easu had seized his hand in a big, brutal, bullying grasp, and was grinding his knuckles. And then sixteen people began to spin.

The startled agony of it made a different man of him. For Ma was heavy as a log on his left side, clinging to him as if she liked to cling to his body. He never quite forgave her. And Easu had his unprotected right hand gripped in a vise and was torturing him on purpose with the weight and the grind. Jack's hands were naturally small, and Easu's were big. And to be gripped by that great malicious paw was horrible. Oh the tension, the pain and rage of that giddy-go-rounding, first forward, then abruptly backwards. It broke some of his innocence for ever.

But although paralytic with rage when released, Jack's face still looked innocent and cherubic.* He had that sort of face, and that diabolic sort of stoicism. Mrs Ellis thought: "What a nice kind boy!—but late waking up to the facts of life!" She thought he had not even noticed Easu's behaviour. And again she thought to herself, her husband would be jealous if he saw her. Poor old Jacob! Aloud she said:

"The next is the last figure. You've done very well, Jack. You go off round the ring now, handing the ladies first your right and then your left hand."

He felt no desire to hand anybody his hand. But in the middle of the ring he met Monica, and her slim grasp took his hurt right hand, and seemed to heal it for a moment.

Easu grabbed his arm, and he saw three others, suffering fools gladly, locked arm in arm, playing soldiers, as they called it. Oh God!—Easu, much taller than Jack, was twisting his arm abominably, almost pulling it out of the socket. And Jack was saving up his anger.

It was over. "That was very kind of you, my dear boy," Mrs Ellis was saying. "I haven't enjoyed a dance so much for years."

Enjoyed! That ghastly word! Why would people insist on enjoying themselves in these awful ways! Why "enjoy" oneself at all? He didn't see it. He decided he didn't care for enjoyment, it wasn't natural to him. Too humiliating, for one thing.

Twenty steps involved in the black skirts of Mrs Ellis, and he was politely rid of her. She was very nice. And by some mystery she had really enjoyed herself in this awful mêlée. He gave it up. She was too distant in years and experience for him to try to understand her. Did these people never have living anger, like a bright black snake with unclosing eyes, at the bottom of their souls? Apparently not.

ii

There was an interval in the dancing, and they were having "games." Red was of course still bawling out instructions and directions, being the colonel of the feast. He was in his element, playing top sawyer.*

The next game was to be "Modern Proposals." It sounded rotten to Jack. Each young man was to make an "original" proposal to an appointed girl. Great giggling and squirming even at the mention of it.

Easu still held the middle of the floor. Jack thought it was time to butt in. With his hands in his pockets he walked coolly into the middle of the room.

"You people don't know me and I don't know you," he found himself announcing in his clear English voice. "Supposing I call this game."

Carried Unanimously!

The young men lined up, and Easu, after standing loose on his legs for some time just behind Jack, went and sat down somewhat discomfited.

Jack pushed Tom on to his knees before the prettiest girl in the room—the prettiest strange girl, anyhow. Tom, furiously embarrassed on his knees, stammered:

"I say! There's a considerable pile o' socks wantin' darning in my ol' camp. I'd go so far as to face the parson, if you'd do 'em for me."

It was beautifully non-committal. For all the Bushies were at heart terrified lest they might by accident contract a Scotch marriage,* and be held accountable for it.

Jack was amused by the odd, humorous expressions of the young bush-farmers. Joe Low, scratching his head funnily, said: "I'll put the pot on, if you'll cook the stew." But the most approved proposal was that of a well-to-do young farmer who is now a J. P. and head of a prosperous family.

"Me ol' dad an' me ol' lady, they never had no daughters. They gettin' on well in years, and they kind o' fancy one. I've gotter get 'em one, quick an' lively. I've got fifteen head o' cattle an' seventy-six sheep, eighteen pigs an' a fallowin' sow. I've got one hundred an' ninety-nine acres o' cleared land, and ten improved with fruit trees. I've got forty ducks an' hens an' a flock o' geese, an' no-one home to feed 'em. Meet me Sunday mornin' eight-forty sharp at the cross roads, an' I'll be there in me old sulky to drive y' out an' show y'."

And the girl in pink, with the wide smile, answered seriously:

"I will if mother'll let me, Mr Burton."

The next girl had been looming up like a big coal barge. She was a half-caste, of course named Lily, and she sat aggressively forwards, her bony elbows and wrists much in evidence, and her pleasant swarthy face alight and eager with anticipation. Oh these Missioner half-castes!*

Jack ordered Easu forward.

But Easu was not to be baited. He strode over, put his hand on the fuzzy head, and said in his strong voice:

"Hump* y'r bluey and come home."

The laugh was with him, he had won again.

iii

They went down to the cold collation. There Jack found other arrivals: Mary come in via York with Gran's spinster daughters. Also the Greenlow girls from away back, and they made a great fuss of him. The doctor too turned up. He had been missing all day, but now he strolled back and forth, chatting politely first to one and then another, but vague and washed-out to a degree.

Jack's anger coiled to rest at the supper, for Monica was very attentive to him. She sat next to him, found him the best pieces, and shared her glass with him, in her quick, dangerous, generous fashion, looking up at him with strange wide looks of offering, so that he felt very manly and very shy at the same time. But very glad to be near her. He felt that it was his spell that was upon her, after all, and though he didn't really like flirting with her there in the public supper-room, he loved her hand finding his under the cover of her sash, and her fingers twining into his as if she were entering into his body. Safely under the cover of her silk sash.—He would have liked to hold her again close, close: her agile, live body, quick as a cat's. She was mysterious to him as some cat-goddess, and she excited him in a queer, electric fashion.

But soon she was gone again, elusive as a cat. And of course she was in great request. So Jack found himself talking to the little elderly Mary, with her dark animal's *museau*.* Mary was like another kind of cat: not the panther sort, but the quiet, dark, knowing sort. She was comfortable to talk to, also, soft and stimulating.

Jack and Mary sat on the edge of the barn, in the hot night, looking at the trees against the strange, ragged southern sky, hearing the frogs occasionally, and fighting the mosquitoes. Mrs Ellis also sat on the ledge not far off. And presently Jack and Mary were joined by the doctor. Then came Grace and Alec Rice, sitting a little further down, and talking in low tones. The night seemed full of low, half-mysterious talking, in a starry darkness that seemed pregnant with the scent and presence of the black people. Jack often wondered why, in the night, the country still seemed to belong to the black people, with their strange, big liquid eyes.

Where was Easu? Was he talking to Monica? Or to the black half-caste Lily? It might as well be the one as the other. The odd way he had placed his hand on Lily's black fuzzy head, as if he were master, and she a sort of concubine. She would give him all the submission he wanted.

But then, why Monica? Monica in her white, full-skirted frock with its moulded bodice, her slender, golden-white arms and throat! Why Monica in the same class with the half-caste Lily?

Anger against Easu was sharpening Jack's wits, and curiously detaching him from his surroundings. He listened to the Australian voices and the Australian accent around him. The careless, slovenly speech in the uncontrolled, slack, caressive voices. At first he had thought the accent awful. And it *was* awful. But gradually, as he got into the rhythm of the people, he began even to sympathise with "Kytie" instead of "Katie." There was an abandon in it all—an abandon of restrictions and confining control. Why have control? Why have authority? Why not let everybody do as they liked? Why not?

That was what Australia was for—a careless freedom. An easy, unrestricted freedom. At least out in the bush. Every man to do as he liked. Easu to run round with Monica, or with the black Lily, or to kick Jack's shins in the dance.

Yes, even this. But Jack had scored it up. He was going to have his own back on Easu.—He thought of Easu with his hand on the black girl's fuzzy head. That would be just like Easu. And afterwards to want Monica. And Monica wouldn't really mind about the black girl. Since Easu was Easu.

Sitting there on the barn ledge, Jack in a vague way understood it all. And in a vague way tolerated it all. But with a dim, yet fecund germ of revenge in his heart. He was not morally shocked. But he was going to be revenged. He did not mind Easu's running with a black girl, and afterwards with Monica. Morally he did not mind it. But physically—perhaps pride of race—he minded. Physically he could never go so far as to lay his hand on the darky's fuzzy head. His pride of blood was too intense. He had no objection at all to Lily, until it came to actual physical contact. And then his blood recoiled with old haughtiness and pride of race. It was bad enough to have to come into contact with a woman* of his own race: to have to give himself away even so far. The other was impossible.

And yet he wanted Monica. But he knew she was fooling round with Easu. So deep in his soul formed the motive of revenge.

There are times when a flood of realisation and purpose sweeps through a man. This was one of Jack's times. He was not definitely conscious of what he realised and of what he purposed. Yet there it was, resolved in him.

He was trying not to hear Dr Rackett's voice talking to Mary. Even Dr Rackett was losing his Oxford drawl, and taking on some of the Australian ding-dong. But Rackett, like Jack, was absolutely fixed in his pride of race, no matter what extraneous vice he might have. Jack had a vague idea it was opium. Some chemical stuff.

"—free run of old George's books? I should say it was a doubtful privilege for a young lady. But you hardly seem to belong to West Australia. I think England is really your place. Do you actually *want* to belong, may I ask?"

"To Western Australia?—To the *country*, yes, very much. I love the land, the country life, Dr Rackett. I don't care for the social life of a town like Perth.—But I should like to live all my life on a farm—in the bush."

"Would you now!" said Rackett. "I wonder where you get that idea from. You are the grand-daughter of an earl—"

"Oh, my grandfather is further away from me than the moon. You would never know *how* far!" laughed Mary. "No, I am colonial born and bred. Though of course there is a fascination about the English. But I hardly knew Papa. He was a tenth child, so there wasn't much of the earldom left to him. And then he was a busy A. D. C. to the Governor General.* And he married quite late in life. And then mother died when I was little, and I got passed on to Aunt Matilda.

Mother was Australian born. I don't think there is much English in me."

Mary said it in a queer complacent way, as if there were some peculiar, subtle antagonism between England and the colonial, and she was ranged on the colonial side. As if she were subtle enemy of the father, the English father in her.

"Queer! Queer thing to me!" said Rackett, as if he half felt the antagonism. For he would never be colonial, not if he lived another hundred years in Australia. "I suppose," he added, pointing his pipe-stem upwards, "it comes from those unnatural stars up there. I always feel they are doing something to me."

"I don't think it's the stars," laughed Mary. "I am just Australian, in the biggest part of me, that's all."

Jack could feel in the statement some of the antagonism that burned in his own heart, against his own country, his own father, his own empty fate at home.

"If I'd been born in this country, I'd stick to it," he broke in.

"But since you weren't born in it, what will you do, Grant?" asked the doctor ironically.

"Stick to myself," said Jack stubbornly, rather sulkily.

"You won't stick to Old England, then?" asked Rackett.

"Seems I'm a misfit in Old England," said Jack. "And I'm not going to squeeze my feet into tight boots."

Rackett laughed.

"Rather go barefoot, like Lennie?" he laughed.

Jack relapsed into silence, and turned a deaf ear, looking into the alien night of the southern hemisphere. And having turned a deaf ear to Rackett and Mary, he heard, as if by divination, the low voice of Alec Rice proposing in real earnest to Grace: proposing in a low, urgent voice that sounded like a conspiracy.

He rose to go away. But Mary laid a detaining hand on his arm, as if she wished to include him in the conversation, and did not wish to be left alone with Dr Rackett.

"Don't you sympathise with me Jack, for wishing I had been a boy, to make my own way in the world, and have my own friends, and size things up for myself."

"Seems to me you do size things up for yourself," said Jack rather crossly. "A great deal more than most *men* do."

"Yes, but I can't *do* things as I could if I were a man."

"What *can* man do, then, more than a woman—that's worth doing?" asked Rackett.

"He can see the world, and love as he wishes to love, and work."

"No man can love as he wishes to love," said Rackett. "He's nearly always stumped, in the love game."

"But he can *choose*," persisted Mary.

And Jack, with his other ear, was hearing Alec Rice's low voice persisting:

"Go on, Grace, you're not too young. You're just right. You're just the ticket[*] now. Go on, let's be engaged and tell your Dad and fix it up. We're meant for one another, you know we are. Don't you think we're meant for one another?"

"I never thought about it that way, truly."

"But don't you think so now? Yes you do."

Silence—the sort that gives consent. And the silence of a young, spontaneous embrace.

Jack was on tenterhooks. He wanted to be gone. But Mary was persisting, in her obstinate voice—he wished she'd shut up too:

"I wanted to be a sailor at ten, and an explorer at twelve. At thirteen I wanted to become a painter of wonderful pictures of Our Lady and her Blessed Son."[*]—Jack wished she wouldn't say all this.—"And then I had a streak of humility, and wanted to be a gardener. Yet—" she laughed—"not a sort of gardener such as Aunt Matilda hires. I wanted to grow things and see them come up out of the earth. And see baby chicks hatched, and calves and lambs born."

She had lifted her hand from Jack's sleeve, to his relief.

"Best marry a farmer like Tom," he said roughly. But Mary received this with dead silence.

"And drudge your soul away like Mrs Ellis," said Rackett. "Worn out before your time, between babies and heavy house-work. Groping on the earth all your life, grinding yourself into ugliness at work which some animal of a servant-lass would do with half the effort.—Don't you think of it, Miss Mary. Let the servant-lasses marry the farmers. You've got too much in you. Don't go and have what you've got in you trampled out of you by marrying some cocky farmer. Tom's as good as gold, but he wants a brawny lass of his own sort for a wife. You be careful, Miss Mary. Women can find themselves in ugly harness,[*] out here in these god-forsaken colonies. Worse harness than any you've ever kicked against."

Monica seemed to have scented the tense atmosphere under the barn, for she appeared like a young witch, in a whirlwind.[*]

"Hello Mary! Hello Dr Rackett! It's just on midnight." She had flitted over to Grace. "Just on midnight, Grace and Alec. Are you coming? You seem as if you were fixed here."

"We're not fixed on the spot, but we're fixed up all right otherwise," said Alec, in a slight tone of resentment, as he rose from Grace's side.

"Oh have you and Grace fixed it up!" exclaimed Monica, with a false vagueness and innocence. "I'm awfully glad. I'm awfully glad, Grace."

"I am," said Grace, with a faint touch of resentment, and she rose and took Alec's arm.

They were already like a married couple armed against that witch. Had she been flirting with Alec, and then pushed him over on to Grace?—Jack sensed it with the sixth sense which divines these matters.

Monica appeared at his side.

"It's just twelve. Come and hold my hand in the ring—Mary can hold your other hand—and Doctor Rackett can take Mary's other hand. Come on! Come on, Alec, as well. I don't want any strangers next to me tonight."

Jack smiled sardonically to himself as she impulsively caught hold of his hand. Monica was "a circumstance over which we have no control," Lennie said. Jack felt that he had a certain control.

They all took hands as she directed, and moved into the barn to link up with the rest of the chain. There in the soft light of the big chamber, Easu suddenly appeared, without collar or cravat, his hair ruffled, his white suit considerably creased. But he lurched up in his usual aggressive way, with his assertive good humour, demanding to break in between Jack and Monica. Jack held on, and Monica said:

"You mustn't break in, you know it makes enemies."

"Does it!" grinned Easu. And with sardonic good-humour he lurched away to an unjoined part of the ring. He carried about with him a sense of hostile power. But Jack was learning to keep within himself another sort of power, small and concentrated and fixed like a stone, the sort of power that ultimately would break through the bulk of Easu's domineering.

The ring complete at last, they all began to sing: "Cheer Boys

Cheer!" and "God Bless the Prince of Wales," "John Brown's Body," and "Britons Never Never Never."*

Then Easu bawled: "Midnight!" There was a moment's frightened pause. Joe Low blasted on the cornet, his toe beating time madly all the while. Fiddles, whistles, concertinas, jew's harps raggedly began to try out the tune. The clasped hands began to rock, and taking Easu's shouting lead, they all began to sing, in the ring:

"Should auld acquaintance be forgot
An' never brought to min'?
Should auld acquaintance be forgot,
And the days of auld lang syne?

For auld lang syne, my dear
For auld lang syne,
We'll tak' a cup o' kindness yet
For the days of auld lang syne."

They all sang heartily and with feeling. There was a queer Scottish tang in the colony, that made the Scottish emotion dominant. Jack disliked it. There was no auld acquaintance or auld lang syne, at least for him. And he didn't care for these particular cups of kindness, in one ring with Easu, black Lily, Dr Rackett, Monica, and all. He didn't like the chain of emotion and supposed pathetic clanship. It was worse here even than on shipboard.

Why start the New Year like this? As a matter of fact, he *wanted* to forget most of his own Auld Acquaintance, and start something a little different. And any rate, the emotion was spurious, the chain was artificial, the flow was false.

Monica seemed to take a wicked pleasure in it, and sang more emotionally than anybody, in a sweet but smallish voice. And poor little Mary, with her half-audible murmur, had her eyes full of tears and seemed so moved.

Auld Lang Syne!

Old Long Since.

Why not put it in plain English?

iv

The celebration did not end with Auld Lang Syne. By half past two most of the ladies had retired, though some ardent dancers still footed the floor, and a chaperone or two, like crumpled rag-bags, slept on their boxes. A good number of young men and boys were asleep with Herbert on the sacks, handkerchiefs knotted round their throats in place of collars. The concertina, the cornet, the fiddles and the rest of the band had gone down to demolish the remains of the cold collation, whilst Tom, Ross, and Ned sat on the barn step singing as uproariously as they could, though a little hoarse, for the last dancers to dance to. Someone was whistling very sweetly.

Where was Easu? Jack wondered as he wandered aimlessly out into the night. Where was Easu? For Jack had it on his mind that he ought to fight him. Felt he would be a coward if he didn't tackle him this very night.

But it was three o'clock, the night was very still and rich, still warm, rather close, but not oppressive. The strange heaviness of the hot summer night, with the stars thick in clouds and clusters overhead, the moon being gone. Jack strayed aimlessly through the motionless, dark, warm air, till he came to the paddock gate, and there he leaned with his chin on his arms, half asleep. It seemed to be growing cooler, and a dampness was bringing out the scent of the scorched grass, the essence of the earth, like incense. There was a half-wild bush with a few pale-pink roses near the gate. He could just get their fragrance. If it were as it should be, Monica would be here, in one of her wistful, her fiercely wistful moments! When she looked at him with her yellow eyes and her fierce, naïve look of yearning, he was ready to give all his blood to her. If things were as they should be, she would be clinging to him now like that, and nestling against his breast. If things were as they should be!

He didn't want to go to sleep. He wanted what he wanted. He wanted the night, and young, changeable, yearning Monica, and an answer to his own awake young blood. He insisted on it. He would not go to sleep, he would insist on an answer.—And he wanted to fight Easu. He ought to fight Easu. His manhood depended on it.

He could hear the cattle stirring down the meadow. Soon it would begin to be day. What was it now? It was night, dark night towards morning, with a faint breathing of air from the sea. And where was he? He was in Australia, leaning on the paddock gate and seeing the stars and the dim shape of a gum tree. There was a faint scent of eucalyptus in the night. His mother was far away—England was far away. He was alone there leaning on the paddock gate, in Australia.

After all, perhaps the very best thing was to be alone. Better even than having Monica or fighting Easu. Because when you are alone you are at one with your own God. The spirit in you is God in you.

And when you are alone you are one with the spirit of God inside you. Other people are chiefly an interruption.

And moreover, he could never say he was lonely while he was at Wandoo, while there were Tom, and Lennie, and Monica, and all the rest. He hoped he would have them all his life. He hoped he would never, in all his life, say goodbye to them.

No, he would take up land as near this homestead as possible, and build a brick house on it. And he would have a number of fine horses, better than anyone else's, and some sheep that would pay, and a few cows. Always milk and butter with the wheat-meal damper.

What was that?—Only a morepork. He laid his head on his arms again, on the gate. He wanted a place of his own, *now*. He would have it now if he had any money. And marry Monica. Would he marry Monica? Would he marry anybody?—He much preferred the whole family, to any one of the family. But he wanted a place of his own. If he could hurry up his father. And old Mr George. He might persuade Mr George to be on his side. Why was there never any money? No money! A father ought to have some money for a son.

What was that. He saw a dim white figure stealing across the near distance. Pah! must have been a girl sitting out under the pittosporum tree. When he had thought he was quite alone.

The thought upset him. And he ought to find Easu. Obstinately he insisted to himself that he ought to find Easu.

He drifted towards the shed near the cubby, where Mr Ellis kept the tools. Somebody unknown and unauthorised had put a barrel of beer inside the shed. Men were there drinking, as he knew they would be.

"Have a pot, youngster?"

"Thanks."

He sat down on a case beside the door, and drank the rather warm beer. His head began to drop. He knew he was almost asleep.

Easu loomed up from the dark, coatless, hatless, with his shirt front open, asking for a drink. He was thirsty. Easu was thirsty. How could you be angry with a thirsty man! And he wasn't so bad, after all. No, Easu wasn't so bad after all! What did it matter! What did it all matter, anyhow?

Jack slipped to the ground and lay there fast asleep.

Chapter X.

Shadows Before.

i

But in the morning, memory was back, and the unquenched smouldering of passion. Easu had insulted him. Easu had insulted him, and that should never be forgiven. And he had this new, half painful, more than half painful desire to see Monica, to be near her, to touch her hand; a sort of necessity upon him all the while, which he was not used to. It made him restless, uneasy, and for the first time in his life, a little melancholy. He was used to feeling angry: a steady, almost blithe sort of anger. And beyond that, he had always been able to summon up an indifference to things, cover them with oblivion: to retreat upon himself and insulate himself from contact.

Now he could no longer do this, and it fretted him, made him accessible to melancholy. The hot hot January days, all dry flaming heat, and flies, and mosquitoes, passed over him leaving him strange even to himself. There was work, the drudging work of the farm, all the while. And one just sweated. He learned to submit to it, to the sweating all the time during the day, and the mosquitoes at night. It was like a narcotic. The old, English alertness grew darker and darker. He seemed to be moving, a dim consciousness and an unyielding will, in a dark cloud of heat, in a perspiring, dissolving body. He could feel his body, the English cool body of his being, slowly melting down and being invaded by a new tropical quality. Sometimes, he said to himself, he was sweating his soul away. That was how it felt: as if he were sweating his soul away. And he let his soul go, let it slowly melt away out of his wet, hot body.

Any man who has been in the tropics,* unless he has kept all his mind and consciousness focussed homewards, fixed towards the old poles of home, will know how this feels. Now Jack did not turn homewards, back to England. He never wanted to go back. There was in him a slow, abiding anger against this same "home." Therefore he let himself go down the dark tide of the heat. He did not cling on to his old English soul, the soul of an English gentleman.

He let that dissolve out of him, leaving what residuum of a man it might leave. But out of very obstinacy he hung on to his own integrity: a small, dark, obscure integrity.

Usually he was too busy perspiring, panting, and working, to think about anything. His mind also seemed dissolving away in perspiration and in the curious eucalyptus solvent of the Australian air. He was too busy and too much heat-preoccupied even to think of Monica or of Easu, though Monica was a live wire in his body. Only on Sundays he seemed to come half out of his trance. And then everything went queer and strange, a little uncanny.

Dad was back again for the harvest, but his heart was no better, and a queer frightening cloud seemed over him. And Gran, they said, was failing. Somehow Gran was the presiding deity of the house. Her queer spirit controlled, even now. And she was failing. She adored Lennie, but he was afraid of her.

"Gran's the limit!" he asserted. "She's that wilful. Always the same with them women when they gets well on in years. I clear out from her if I can, she's that obstropulous[*]—tells y' t' wipe y' nose, pull up y' pants, brush y' teeth, not sniff; golly, I can't stand it!"

Sunday was the day when you really came into contact with the family. The rule was, that each one took it in turns to get up and make breakfast, while everybody else stayed on in bed, for a much-needed rest. If it was your turn, you rolled out of bed at dawn when Timothy banged on the wall, you slipped on your shirt and pants and went to the "everlasting" fire. Raking the ashes together with a handful of sticks, you blew a blaze and once more smelt the burning eucalyptus leaves. You filled the black iron kettle at the pump, and set it over the flame. Then you washed yourself. After which you carved bread and butter: tiny bits for Gran, moderate pieces for upstairs, and doorsteps for the cubby. After which you made the tea, and *holloa'd!* while you poured it out. One of the girls, with a coat over her nighty and her hair in a chignon, would come barefoot to carry the trays, to Gran and to the upstairs. This was just the preliminary breakfast: the Sunday morning luxury. Just tea in bed.

Later the boys were shouting for clean shirts and towels, and the women were up. Proceeded the hair-cutting, nail-paring, button-sewing, and general murmur, all under the supervision of Ma. Then down to the sand-bagged pool for a dip. After which, clean and in clean raiment, you went to the parlour to hear Dad read the lessons.

The family bible was carefully kept warm in the parlour, during the week, under a woolen crochet mat. A crochet mat above, and a crochet mat below. Nothing else must ever stand on that book, nothing whatever. The children were quite superstitious about it.

Lennie, the Benjamin of his father Jacob, each Sunday went importantly into the drawing-room, in a semi-religious silence, and fetched the ponderous brass-bound book. He put it on the table in front of Dad. Gran came in with her stick and her lace cap, and sat in the arm-chair near the window. Mrs Ellis and the children folded their hands like saints. Mr Ellis wiped his spectacles, cleared his throat, looked again at the little Church calendar of the lessons, found the place, and proceeded in a droning voice. Nobody looked at him, except Mrs Ellis. Everybody looked another way. Gran usually gazed sideways at the floor. Tick-tock! went the clock. It was a little eternity.

Jack knew the bible pretty well, as a well-brought-up nephew of his aunts. He had no objection to the bible. On the contrary, it supplied his imagination with a chief stock of images, his ear with the greatest solemn pleasure of words, and his soul with a queer heterogeneous ethic. He never really connected the bible with christianity proper, the christianity of aunts and clergymen. He had no use for christianity proper: just dismissed it. But the bible was perhaps the foundation of his consciousness. Do what seems good to you in the sight of the Lord. This was the moral he always drew from bible lore. And since the Lord, for him, was always the Lord Almighty, Almighty God, Maker of Heaven and Earth, Jesus being only a side issue; since the Lord was always Jehovah the great and dark, for him, one might do as David did, in the sight of the Lord, or as Jacob, or as Abraham or Moses or Joshua or Isaiah,* in the sight of the Lord. The sight of the Lord was a vast strange scope of vision, in the semi-dark.

Gran always listened the same, leaning on her stick and looking sideways to the ground, as if she did not quite see the stout and purple-faced Jacob, her son, as the mouthpiece of the Word. As a matter of fact, the way he read scripture irritated her. She wished Lennie could have read the lessons. But Dad was head of the house, and she was fond of him, poor old Jacob.

And Jack always furtively watched Gran. She frightened him, and he had a little horror of her, but she fascinated him too. She was like Monica, at the great distance of her years. Her lace cap was snowy white, with little lavender ribbons. Her face was pure ivory, with fine sharpened features, that subtly-arched nose, like Monica's. Her silver hair came over her dead-looking ears. And her dry, shiny, blue-veined hand remained fixed over the pommel of her black stick. How awful, how unspeakably awful, Jack felt, to be so old! No longer human. And she seemed so little inside her clothes. And one never knew what she was thinking. But surely some strange, uncanny, dim, non-human thoughts.

Sunday was full of strange, half-painful impressions of death and of life. After lessons the boys would escape to the yards and the stables, and lounge about. Or they would try the horses, or take a gun into the uncleared bush. Then came the enormous Sunday dinner, when everyone ate himself stupid.

In the afternoon Tom and Jack wandered to the loft, to the old concertina. Up there among the hay, they squeezed and pulled the old instrument, till at last, after much practice, they could draw forth tortured hymnal sounds from its protesting internals.

"Ha-a-appy Ho-ome! Ha-appy Ho-ome!
O Haa-py Ho-me! O Haa-py Ho-me!
In Paradise with Thee!"*

Over and over again the same tune, till Tom would drop off to sleep, and Jack would have a go at it. And these yearning sort of hymns always sent a chill to his bowels. They were like Gran, on the brink of the grave. In fact the word *Paradise* made him shudder worse than the word *coffin*. Yet he would grind away at the tune. Till he too fell asleep.

And then they would wake in the heat to the silence of the suspended, fiercely hot afternoon. Only to feel their own sweat trickling, and to hear the horses, the draught-horses which were in stable for the day, chop-chopping underneath. So, in spite of sweat and heat, another go at the fascinating concertina.

ii

One Sunday Jack strolled in an hour early for tea. He had made a mistake, as one does sometimes when one sleeps in the afternoon. Gran was sitting by a little fire in the dark living room. She had to have a little fire to look at. It was like life to her.

"Come here, Jack Grant," she said in her thin, imperious voice.

He went on reluctant feet, for he had a dread of her years and her strange femaleness. What did she want of him?

"Did y' hear Mr George get my son to promise to make a will, when y' were in Perth?"

"No Marm," said Jack promptly.

"Well take it from me, if he promised, he hasn't done it. He never signed a paper in his life, unless it was his marriage register. And but for my driving, he'd never have signed that.—Sit down!"

Jack sat on the edge of a chair, his heart in his boots.

"I told you before I'd ha' married your grandfather if he hadn't been married already. I wonder where you'd ha' been then!—Just as well I didn't, for he wouldn't look at me after he took my leg off. Just come here a minute."

Jack got up and went to her side. She put her soft, dry, dead old hand on his face and stroked it, pressing on the cheek-bones.

"Ay," she said. "I suppose those are his bones again. And my bones are in Monica. Don't stand up, lad, take your seat."

Jack sat down in extreme discomfort.

"Well," she resumed, "I was very well off with old Ellis, so I won't complain.—But you've got your English father's eyes. You'd have been better with mine. Those bones, those beautiful bones, and my sort of eyes."

Gran's eyes were queer and remote now. But they had been perhaps like Monica's, only a darker grey, and with a darker, subtler cat-look in them.

"I suppose it'll be in the children's children," she resumed, her eyes going out like a candle. "For I married old Ellis—though to this day I never quite believe it.—And one thing I won't do. I won't die in the dying-room of his house. I won't do it, not if it was the custom of a hundred families. Not if he was here himself to see me do it, I wouldn't. Though he was kindness itself. But not if he was here himself and had the satisfaction of seeing me do it! A dreadful room! I'd be frightened to death to die in it. I like me sheets sun-kissed, heat or no heat, and no sun ever gets into that room.—But it's better for a woman to marry, even if she marries the wrong man. I allus* said so. An old maid, especially a decayed gentlewoman, is a blight on the face of the earth."

"Why?" said Jack suddenly. The old woman was too authoritative.

"That's why! What do you know about it," she said contemptuously.

"I knew a nice old lady, in England, who'd never been married," he said, thinking of a really beautiful, gentle woman who had kept all her perfume and her charm in spite of her fifty-odd years of single blessedness. But then she had a naturally deep and religious nature, not like this pagan old cat of a Gran.

"*Did* you!" said Gran, eyeing him severely. "What do *you* know, at your age?—I've got three unmarried daughters, and I'm ashamed of them. If I'd married your grandfather I never should have had them.—Self-centred, and old as old boots, they are. I'd rather they'd gone wrong and died in the bush, like your aunt who had a child by Mary's father."

Jack made round, English eyes of amazement at this speech. He disapproved thoroughly.

"You've got too much of your English father in you," she said, "and not enough of your hard-hearted grandfather.* Look at Lennie, what a beautiful boy he is."

There was a pause. Jack sat in torment while she baited him. He was full of antagonism towards her and her years.

"But I tell you, you never realise you're old till you see your friends slipping away. One by one they go—over the border. *That's* what makes you feel old, I tell you. Nothing else.—Annie Brockman died the other day.* I was at school with her. She wasn't old, though *you'd* have thought so."

The way Gran said this, was quite spiteful. And Jack thought to himself: What nonsense, she *was* old if she was at school with Gran. If she was as old as Gran, she was awfully old.

"No, she wasn't old—school girls and fellows laughing in the ball-room, or breathing fast after a hard ride. You didn't know Sydney in those days. And men grown old behind their beards, for want of understanding; because they're too dense to understand what living means. Men are dense.—Are ye listening?"

The question came with such queer aged force that Jack started almost out of his chair.

"Yes Marm!" he said.

"'Yes Marm!' he says!" she repeated, with a queer little grin of amusement. "Listen to this grandfather's chit saying 'Yes Marm!' to me!—Well, they'll have their way. My friends are nearly all gone, so I suppose I shall soon be going. Not but what there's plenty of amusement here—"

She looked round in an odd way, as if she saw ghosts. Jack would have given his skin to escape her.

"Listen!" she said, with sudden secrecy. "I want ye to do something for me. You love Lennie, don't ye?"

Jack nodded.

"So do I! And I'm going to help him." Her voice became sharp with secrecy. "I've put by a stocking for him," she hissed. "At least it's not a stocking, it's a tin box, but it's the same thing. It's up there!" She pointed with her stick at the wide black chimney. "D' ye understand?"

She eyed Jack with aged keenness, and he nodded, though his understanding was rather vague. Truth to tell, nothing she said seemed to him quite real. As if, poor Gran, her age put her outside of reason.

"That stocking is for Lennie. Tom's mother was nobody knows who, though *I'm* not going to say Jacob never married her, if Jacob says he did. But Tom'll get everything. The same as Jacob did. That's how it hits back at me. I wanted Jacob to have the place, and now it goes to Tom, and my little Lennie gets nothing.—Alice has been a good woman and a good wife to Jacob: better than he deserved. I'm going to stand by her. That stocking in there is for Lennie, because he's her eldest son. In a tin box. Y' understand?"

And she pointed again at the chimney.

Jack nodded, though he didn't really take it in. He had a little horror of Gran at all times; but when she took on this witch-like portentousness, and whispered at him in a sharp, aged whisper, about money, hidden money, it all seemed so abnormal to him that he refused to take it for real. The queer aged female spirit that had schemed with money for the men-folk she chose, scheming to oust those she had not elected, was so strange and half ghoulish, that he merely shrank from taking it in. When she pointed with her white-headed stick at the wide black mouth of the chimney, he glanced and looked quickly away again. He did not want to think of a hoard of sovereigns in a stocking—or a tin box—secreted in there. He did not want to think of the subtle, scheming, vindictive old woman reaching up into the soot to add more gold to the hoard. It was all unnatural to him and to his generation.

But Gran despised him and his generation. It was as unreal to her as hers to him.

"Old George couldn't even persuade that Jacob of mine to sign a marriage settlement," she continued. "And I wasn't going to force him. Would you believe a man could be such an obstinate fool?"

"Yes Marm!" said Jack automatically.

And Gran stamped her stick at him in sudden vicious rage. The stamping of the stick brought Grace, and he fled.

iii

That evening they were all sitting in the garden. The drawing-room was thrown open, as usual on Sunday, but nobody ever went in except to strum the piano. Monica was strumming hymns now. Grace came along calling Mary. Mary was staying on at Wandoo.

"Mary! Gran wants you. She feels faint. Come and see to her, will you."

Ellie came and slipped her fat little hand into Jack's, hanging on to him. Katie and Lennie sat surreptitiously playing cat's-cradle, on the steps: forbidden act, on the Sabbath. The twin boys wriggled their backs against the gate-posts and their toes into the earth, asking each other riddles. Harry as usual aimed stones at birds. It was a close evening, the wind had not come. And they all were uneasy, with that uncanny uneasiness that attacks families, because Gran was not well.

Harry was singing profanely, profaning the Sabbath.

"A blue jay sat on a hickory limb
He wink at me, I wink at him.
I up with a stone an' hit him on the shin.
Says he, Little nigger, don' do that agin!
Clar de kitchen, ol' folk, young folk!
Clar de kitchen, ol' folk, young folk!
An' let us dance till dawn O'."*

Harry shouted out these wicked words half loud, to a tune of his own that was no tune.

Jack did not speak. The sense of evening, Sunday evening, far away from any church or bell, was strong upon him. The sun was low in the sky, and the light intensely strong, all fine gold. He went out to look. The sunlight flooded the dry, dry earth till it glowed again, and the gum trees that stood up hung tresses of liquid shadow from trunks of gold, and the buildings seemed to melt blue in the vision of light. Someone was riding in from westward, and a cloud of pure gold-dust rose fuming from the earth about the horse and the horseman, with the vast, overwhelming gold glow of the void heavens above. The whole west was so powerful with pure gold light, coming from immense space and the sea, that it seemed like a transfiguration, and another horseman rode fuming in a dust of light as if he were coming, small and Daniel-like,* out of the vast furnace-mouth of creation. Jack looked west, into the welter of yellow light, in fear. He knew again, as he had known before, that his day was not the day of all the world, there was a huger sunset than the sunset of his race. There were vaster, more unspeakable gods than the gods of his fathers. The god in this yellow fire was huger than the white men could understand, and seemed to proclaim their doom.

Out of this immense power of the glory seemed to come a proclamation of doom. Lesser glories must crumble to powder in this greater glow, as the horsemen rode trotting in the glorified cloud of the earth, spuming a glory all round them. They seemed like messengers out of the great west, coming with a proclamation of doom, the small, trotting, aureoled figures kicking up dust like sun-dust, and gradually growing larger, hardening out of the sea of light. Like sun-arrivals.

Though after all it was only Alec Rice and Tom. But they were gilded men, dusty and sun-luminous, as they came into the yard, with their brown faces strangely vague in shadow, unreal.

The sun was setting, huge and liquid and sliding down at immense speed behind the far-off molten, wavering long ridge towards the coast. Fearsome the great liquid sun was, stooping fiercely down like an enemy stooping to hide his glory, leaving the sky hovering and pulsing above, with a sense of wings, and a sense of proclamation, and of doom. It seemed to say to Jack: I and my race are doomed. But even the doom is a splendour.

Shadow lay very thin on the earth, pale as day, though the sun was gone. Jack turned back to the house. The tiny twins were swaggering home to find their supper, their hands in the pockets of their Sunday breeches. The pockets of everyday breeches were, for some mysterious reason, always sewn up, so Sunday alone knew this swagger. Harry was being called in to bed. And Len and Katie, rarely far off at meal-times, were converging towards supper too.

Monica was still drumming listlessly on the piano, and singing in a little voice. She had a very sweet voice, but she usually sang "small." She was not singing a hymn. Jack became aware of this. She was singing, rather nervously, or irritably, and with her own queer yearning pathos:

> "Oh Jane, Oh Jane my pretty Jane, Oh Jane
> Ah never, never look so shy.

But meet me, meet me in the moon-light,
When the dew is on the rye—"[*]

Someone had lighted the piano candles, and she sat there strumming and singing in a little voice, and looking queer and lonely. His heart went hot in his breast, and then started pounding. He crossed silently, and stood just behind her. For some moments she would not notice him, but went on singing the same. And he stood perfectly still close behind her. Then at last she glanced upward at him, and his heart stood still again with the same sense of doom the sun had given him. She still went on singing for a few moments. Then she stopped abruptly, and jerked her hands from the piano.

"Don't you want to sing?" she asked sharply.

"Not particularly."

"What do you want then?"

"Let us go out."

She looked at him strangely, then rose in her abrupt fashion. She followed him across the yard in silence, while he felt the curious sense of doom settling down on him.

He sat down on the step of the back door of the barn, outside, looking southward into the vast, rapidly darkening country, and glanced up at her. She, rather petulantly, sat down beside him. He felt for her cool slip of a hand, and she let it lie in his hot one. But she averted her face.

"Why don't you like me?" she asked petulantly.

"But I love you," he said thickly, with shame, and the sense of doom piercing his heart.

She turned swiftly and stared him in the face with a brilliant, oddly triumphant look.

"Sure?" she said.

His heart seemed to go black with doom. But he turned away his face from her glowing eyes, and put his arm round her waist, and drew her to him. His whole body was trembling like a taut string, and she could feel the painful plunging of his heart as he pressed her fast against him, pressed the breath out of her.

"Monica!" he murmured blindly, in pain, like a man who is in the dark.

"What?" she said softly.

He hid his face against her shoulder, in the shame and anguish of desire. He would have given anything, if this need never have come upon him. But the strange fine quivering of his body thrilled her. She put her cheek down caressingly against his hair. She could be very tender, very, very tender and caressive. And he grew quieter.

He looked up at the night again, hot with pain and doom and necessity. It had grown quite dark, the stars were out.

"I suppose we shall have to be married," he said in a dismal voice.

"Why?" she laughed. It seemed a very sudden and long stride to her. He had not even kissed her.

But he did not answer, did not even hear her question. She watched his fine young face in the dark, looking sullen and doomed at the stars.

"Kiss me!" she whispered, in the most secret whisper he had ever heard. "Kiss me!"

He turned, in the same battle of unwillingness. But as if magnetised he put forward his face and kissed her on the mouth: the first kiss of his life. And she seemed to hold him. And the fierce, fiery pain of pleasure which came with that kiss sent his soul rebelling in torment to hell. He had never wanted to be given up, to be broken by the black hands of this doom. But broken he was, and his soul seemed to be leaving him, in the pain and obsession of this desire, against which he struggled so fiercely.

She seemed to be pleased, to be laughing. And she was exquisitely sweet to him. How could he be otherwise than caught, and broken.

After an hour of this love-making, she blackened him again by saying they must go in to supper. But she meant it, so in he had to go.

Only when he was alone again in the cubby did he resume the fight to recover himself from her again. To be free as he had been before. Not to be under the torment of the spell of this desire. To preserve himself intact. To preserve himself from her.

He lay awake in his bed in the cubby and thanked God he was away from her. Thanked God he was alone, with a sufficient space of loneliness around him. Thanked God he was immune from her, that he could sleep in the sanctity of his own isolation. He didn't want even to think about her.

iv

Gran did not leave her room that week, and Tom talked of fetching the relations.

"What for?" asked Jack.

"They'd like to be present," said Tom.

Jack felt incredulous.

Lennie came out of her room sniffing and wiping his eyes with his knuckles.

"Poor ol' girl!" he sniffed. "She do look frail. She's almost like a little girl again."

"You don't think she's dying, do you Len?" asked Jack.

"I don't *think*, I knows," replied Len, with utmost scorn. "Sooner or later she's bound to go hence and be no more seen.* But she'll be missed, for many a day, she will."

"But Tom," said Jack. "Do you think Gran will like to have all the relations sniffling round her when she gets worse?"

"I should think so," replied Tom. "Anyway *I* should like to die respectable, whether you would or not."

Jack gave it up. Some things were beyond him, and dying respectable was one of them.

"Like they do in books," said Len, seeing that Jack disapproved, and trying to justify Tom's position. "Even ol' Nelson died proper. 'Kiss me 'Ardy' he said, an' 'Ardy kissed him,* grimy grubby and filthy as he was. He could do no less, though it was beastly."

Still the boys were not sent for the relations until the following Sunday, which was a rest day. Jack went to the Gum Valley Homestead, because he knew the way. He set off before dawn. The terrific heat of the New Year had already passed, and the dawn came fresh and lovely. He was happy on that ride, Gran or no Gran. And that's what he thought would be the happiest: always to ride on at dawn, in a nearly virgin country. Always to be riding away.

The Greenlows seemed to expect him. They had been "warned." After he had been refreshed with a good breakfast, they were ready to start, in the buggy. Jack rode in the buggy with them, his saddle under the seat and the neck rope of his horse in his hand. The hack ran behind, and nearly jerked Jack's arms out of their sockets, with its halts and its disinclination to trot. Almost it hauled him out of the buggy sometimes. He would much rather have ridden the animal, but he had been requested to take the buggy, to spare it.

Mr and Mrs Greenlow scarcely spoke on the journey; it would not have been "showing sorrow." But Jack felt they were enjoying themselves immensely, driving in the morning air instead of being cooped up in the house, she cooking and he with the Holy Book.

The sun grew furiously hot. But Gum Valley Croft was seven miles nearer to Wandoo than the Ellis' Gum Tree selection, so they drove into the yard, wet with perspiration, just before the midday meal was put on to the table. Mrs Ellis, aproned and bare-armed, greeted them as they drove up, calling out that they should go right in, and Jack should take the horses out of the buggy.

Quite a number of strange hacks were tethered here and there in the yard, near odd empty vehicles, sulkies* dejectedly leaning forward on empty shafts, or buggies and wagonettes sturdily important on four wheels. Yet the place seemed strangely quiet.

Jack came back to the narrow verandah outside the parlour door, where Mrs Ellis had her fuchsias, ferns, cyclamen and musk growing in pots. A table had been set there, and dinner was in progress, the girls coming round from the kitchen with the dishes. Grace saw Jack hesitate, so she nodded to him. He went to the kitchen, and asked doubtfully:

"How is she?"

"Oh bad! poor old dear. They're all in there to say good-bye."

Lennie, who was sitting on a form under the kitchen window, put his head down on his arms and sobbed from a sort of nervousness, wailing:

"Oh my poor ol' Gran! Oh poor ol' dear!"

Jack, though upset, almost grinned. Poor Gran indeed, with that ghastly swarm of relations. He sat there on a chair, his nerves all on edge, noticing little things acutely, as he always did when he was strung up: the flies standing motionless on the chopping-block just outside the window, the smooth-tramped gravel walk, the curious surface of the mud floor in the kitchen, the smoky rafters overhead, the oven set in brick below the "everlasting" fire, the blackness of the pots and kettles above the horizontal bars....

"Do you mind sitting in the parlour, Jack, in case they want anything?" Mrs Ellis asked him.

Jack minded, but he went and sat in the parlour, like a chief lackey, or a buffer between all the relations and the outer world.

The house had become more quiet. Monica had gone over to the Reds with clean overalls for the little boys, who had been bundled off there. Jack got this piece of news from Grace, who was constantly washing more dishes and serving more relations. A certain anger burned in him as he heard, but he took no notice.—Mary was lying down upstairs: she had been up all night with Gran. Tom was attending to the horses. Katie and Mrs Ellis had gone upstairs with baby and Ellie, and Mr Ellis was also upstairs. Lennie had slipped away again. So Jack had track of all the family. He was always like that, wanting to know where they all were.

Mrs Greenlow came in from Gran's inner room.

"Mary? Where's Mary?" she asked hurriedly.

Jack shook his head, and she passed on. She had left the door of Gran's room open, so Jack could see in. All the relations were there, horrible, the women weeping and perspiring, and wiping tears and perspiration away together, the men in their waistcoats and shirt-sleeves, perspiring and looking ugly. A methodist parson son-in-law was saying prayers in an important monotone.

At last Mary came, looking anxious.

"Yes Gran? Did you want me?" Jack heard her voice, and saw her by the bed.

"I felt so overcome with all these people," said Gran, in a curiously strong, yet frightened voice. "What do they all want."

"They've come to see you. Come—" Mary hesitated—"to see if they can do anything for you."

"To frighten the bit of life out of me, that I've got. But they're not going to. Get me some beef tea, Mary, and don't leave me alone with them."

Mary went out for the beef tea. Then Jack saw Gran's white hand feebly beckon.

"Ruth!" she said. "Ruth!"

The eldest daughter went over and took the hand, mopping her eyes. She was the parson's wife.

"Well Ruth, how are you?" said Gran's high, quavering voice, in a conversational tone.

"*I'm* well, mother. It's how are you?" replied Ruth dismally.

But Gran was again totally oblivious of her. So at length Ruth dropped away embarrassed from the bedside, shaking her head.

Again Gran lifted her head on the pillow.

"Where's Jacob?"

"Upstairs mother."

"The only one that has the decency to leave me alone." And she subsided again. Then after a while she asked, without lifting her head from the pillow, in a distant voice:

"And are the foolish virgins* here?"

"Who, mother?"

"The foolish virgins. You know who I mean."

Gran lay with her eyes shut as she spoke.

There was an agitation among the family. It was the brother-in-laws who pushed the three Miss Ellises forward. They, poor things, wept audibly.

Gran opened her eyes at the sound, and said, with the ghost of a smile on her yellow, transparent old face:

"I hope virginity is its own reward."

Then she remained unmoved till Mary came with the soup, which she took and slowly sipped, as Mary administered it in a spoon. It seemed to revive her.

"Where's Lennie and his mother?" she asked, in a firmer tone.

These also were sent for. Mrs Ellis sat by the bed and gently patted Gran's arm; but Lennie, "skeered* stiff," shivered at the door. His mother held out her hand to him, and he came in, inch by inch, watching the fragile old Gran, who looked transparent and absolutely unreal, with a fascination of horror.

"Kiss me, Lennie," said Gran grimly: exactly like Nelson.

Lennie shrank away. Then, yielding to his mother's pressure, he laid his dark smooth head and his brown face on the pillow next to Gran's face, but he did not kiss her.

"There's my precious!" said Gran softly, with all the soft, cajoling gentleness that had made her so lovely, at moments, to her men.

"Alice, you've been good to my Jacob," she said, as if remembering something. "There's the stocking. It's for you—and Lennie." She still managed to say the last word with a caress, though she was fading from consciousness again.

Lennie drew away and hid behind his mother. Gran lay still, exactly as if dead. But the laces of her eternal cap still stirred softly, to show she breathed. The silence was almost unbearable.

To break it, the methodist son-in-law sunk to his knees, the others followed his example, and he prayed in a low, solemn, extinguished voice. When he had said Amen! the others whispered it, and rose from their knees. And by one consent they glided from the room. They had had enough deathbed for the moment.

Mary closed the inner door when they had gone, and remained alone in the room with Gran.

V

The son-in-laws all melted through the parlour and out on to the verandah, where they helped themselves from the decanter on the table, filling up from the canvas water-bag that swung in the draught to keep cool. The daughters sat down by the table and wept, lugubriously and rather angrily. The son-in-laws drank and looked afflicted. Jack remained on duty in the parlour, though he would dearly have liked to decamp.

But he was now interested in the relations. They began to weep less, and to talk in low, suppressed, vehement voices. He could only catch bits.—"It's a question if he ever married Tom's mother.—I doubt if Tom's legitimate.—I don't even doubt it, I'm sure.—We've suffered from that before.—Where's the stocking?—Stocking!—Stocking—saved up—bought Easu out.—Mother should know better.—If she's made a will.—Jacob's first marriage.—Children to educate and provide for.—Unmarried daughters—first claim—Stocking—" And then quite plainly, from Ruth: "It's hard on our husbands if *they* have to support mother's unmarried daughters." This said with dignity.

Jack glanced at the three Miss Ellises, to see if they minded: and inwardly he vowed that if he ever married Monica, for example, and Grace was an unmarried sister, he'd find some suitable way of supporting her, without making her feel ashamed.—But the three Miss Ellises did not seem to mind. They were busy diving into secret pockets among their clothing, and fetching out secret little packages. Someone dropped the glass stopper out of a bottle of smelling salts, and spilled the contents on the floor. The pungent odour penetrated throughout the house. Jack never again smelt lavender salts without having a foreboding of death, and seeing mysterious little packets. The three Miss Ellises were surreptitiously laying out bits and tags of black braid, crape, beading, black cloth, black lace; all black, wickedly black, on the table edge. Smoothing them out.—For as a matter of fact they kept a little shop.—And everybody was looking with interest. Jack felt quite nauseated at the sight of these black blotches, the row of black patches.

Mary came out of Gran's room, going to the kitchen with the cup. She did not pass the verandah, so nobody noticed her. They were all intent in the muttering gloom of their investigation of those scraps of mourning patterns.

Jack felt the door of Gran's room slowly open: Mary had left it just ajar. He looked round, and his hair rose on his head. There stood Gran, all white save for her eyes, like a yellow figure of aged female Time,* standing with her hand on the door, looking across the parlour at the afternoon and the preoccupied party on the verandah. Her face was absolutely expressionless, timeless and awful. It frightened him very much. The inexorable female!

He uttered an exclamation, and they all looked up, caught.

Chapter XI.

Blows.

i

Jack managed to escape. When the rooks were fluttered by the sight of that ghostly white starling, he just ran. He ran in disgust from the smell of lavender salts, the tags of mourning patterns, respectable dying, and these awful people. Surely there was something rotten at the bottom of people, he thought, to make them behave as they did. And again came over him the feeling he had often had, that he was a changeling, that he didn't belong to the so-called "normal" human race. Nor, by Jupiter, did he want to. The "normal" human race filled him with unspeakable repulsion. And he knew they would kill him if they found out what he really was. Hence that unconscious dissembling of his innocent face.

He ran, glad to get into a sweat, glad to sweat it all out of himself. Glad to feel the sun hot on his damp hands, and then the afternoon breeze, just starting, cool on his wet skin. When he reached the sand-bagged pool he took off his clothes and spread them in the sun, while he wallowed in the luke-warm water. Ay! if one could wash off one's associations! If one could but be alone in the world.

After bathing, he sat in the sun awhile to dry, then dressed and walked off to look at the lower dam pump. Tom had said it needed attending to. And anyway it led him away from the house.

The pump was all right. There had been a March shower that had put water in the dam. So after looking round at the sheep, he turned away.

Which way? Not back home. Not yet.

The land breeze had lifted and the sea breeze had come, clearing the hot dry atmosphere as if by magic, and replacing the furnace breath by tender air. Which way?

At the back of his mind was the thought of Monica not home yet from the Reds' place, and evening coming on, another of those full, golden evenings when the light seemed fierce with declaration of another eternity, a different eternity from ours.

Last Sunday, on such an evening, he had kissed her. And much as he wanted to avoid her, the desire to kiss her again drove him as if the great yellowing light were a wind that blew him, as a butterfly is blown twinkling out to sea. He drifted towards the trail from the Reds' place. He walked slowly, listening to the queer evening noise of the magpies,* and the more distant screeching of flying parrots. Someone had disturbed the parrots beyond the Black Barn gums. So as if by intuition he walked that way, slightly off the trail.

And suddenly he heard the sound his spirit expected to hear: Monica crying out in expostulation, anger, and fear. It was the fear in her voice that made his face set. His first instinct was not to intrude on their privacy. Then again came the queer, magpie noise of Monica, this time with an edge of real hatred to her fear. Jack pushed through the bushes. He could smell the warm horses already.

Yes, there was Lucy standing by a tree. And Monica, in a long skirt of pink-sprigged cotton, with a frill at the bottom, trying to get up into the side-saddle. While Easu, in his Sunday black reach-me-downs and white shirt and white rubber-soled cricketing boots,* every time she set her foot in the stirrup, put his hand round her waist and spread his fingers on her body, and lifted her down again, lifted her on one hand in a childish and ridiculous fashion, and held her in a moment's embrace. She, in her long cotton riding-dress with the close-fitting bodice, did indeed look absurd hung like a child on Easu's hand, as he lifted her down and held her struggling against him, then let her go once more, to mount her horse. Lucy was shifting uneasily, and Easu's big black horse, tethered to a tree, was jerking its head with a jingle of the bit. The girth hung loose. Easu had evidently dismounted to adjust it.

Monica was becoming really angry, really afraid, and really blind with dismay, feeling for the first time her absolute powerlessness. To be powerless drove her mad, and she would have killed Easu, if she could, without a qualm. But her hate seemed to rouse the big Easu to a passion of desire for her. He put his two big hands round her slender body and compassed her entirely. She gave a loud, strange, uncanny scream. And Jack came out of the bushes, making the black horse plunge. Easu glanced round at the horse, and saw Jack. And at the same time our hero planted a straight, vicious blow on the bearded chin. Easu, unprepared, staggered up against Lucy, who began to jump, while Monica, tangled in her long skirts, fell to her knees on the ground.

"Quite a picture!" Jack said it himself. Even he saw himself standing calmly there, like Jack the Giant-killer.[*] And of course he saw Monica on her knees, with tumbled hair and scarlet cheeks, unspeakably furious at being caught, angrily hitching herself out of her long cotton riding-skirt and pressing her cheeks to make them less red. She was silent, with averted face, and she seemed small. He saw Easu, in the Sunday white shirt and rather tight black Sunday breeches, facing round in unspeakable disgust and fury. He saw himself, in a ready-made cotton suit and cheap brown canvas shoes, bought at the local store, standing awaiting an onslaught.

The onslaught did not come. Instead, Easu said, in a tone of unutterable contempt:

"Why what's up with you, you little sod!"

Jack turned to Monica. She had got on to her feet and was pushing her hair under her hat.

"Monica," he said, "you'd better get home. Gran's dying."

She looked at him, and a slow, wicked smile of amusement came over her face. Then she broke into a queer hollow laugh, at the bottom of which was rage and frustration. Then her laugh rose higher.

"Ha! Ha! Ha!" she laughed. "Ah ha-ha-ha-ha-ha! Ah! ha-ha-ha-ha!—ha! ha! ha! Ah!! ha-ha-ha-ha! ha-ha-ha! Ah!!! ha-ha-ha-ha-ha-ha-ha! Ah!—ha-ha! Ha! Ah! Gran's dying! Ha-ha-ha! Is she really? Oh, ha-ha-ha-ha-ha! No, I don't mean it. But it seems so funny! Ah! ha-ha-ha-ha-ha! Ah! ha-ha-ha!"

She smothered herself into a confused bubbling. The two men stood aghast, shuddering at the strange hysterical woman's laughter that went shrilling through the bush. They were horrified lest someone else should hear.

Monica, in her cotton frock and long sweeping skirt, stood pushing her handkerchief in her mouth and trying in vain to stifle the hysterical laughter that still shook her slender body. Occasionally a queer peal, like mad bells, would break out. And then she ended with a passionate sobbing.

"I know! I know!" she sobbed, like a child. "Gran's dying, and you won't let me go home."

"You can go home," Jack said. "You can go home. But don't go with your face all puffed up with crying."

She gradually gained control of herself, and turned away to her horse. Jack went to help her mount. She got into the saddle, and he gave her the reins. She kept her face averted, and Lucy began to move away slowly, towards the home trail.

Easu still stood there, planted with his feet apart, his head a little dropped, and a furious, contemptuous, revengeful hate of the other two in his light-blue eyes. He had his head down, ready for an attack. Jack saw this, and waited.

"Going to take your punishment?" said Easu, in a nasty voice.

"Ready when you are," said Jack.

Ugh! how he hated Easu's ugly, jeering, evil eyes, how he would love to smash them out of his head. In the long run, hate was an even keener ecstasy than love, and the battle of hate, the fight with blood in the eyes, an orgasm of deadly gratification keener than any passionate orgasm of love.

Easu slowly threw his hat on the ground. Jack did the same, and started to pull off his coat. Easu glanced round to see if Monica was going. She was. Her back was already turned, and Lucy was stepping gingerly through the bushes. He lifted his chin, unknotted his tie, and threw it in his hat. Then he unbuttoned his shirt cuffs, and pulled off his shirt, and hitched his belt. He was now naked to the waist. He had a very white skin with reddish hair at the breast, and an angular kind of force. His reddish-haired, brawny arms were burnt brown-red, as was his neck. For the rest his skin was pure white, with the dazzle of absolute health. Yet he was ugly rather than beautiful. The queer angularity of his brawn, the sense of hostile mechanical power. The sense of the mechanism of power in him made him like some devil fallen into a lower grade.

Jack's torso was rather absurdly marked by the sun-burnt scallops of his vest-lines, for he worked a good deal in a vest. Easu always wore a shirt and no vest. And Jack, in spite of the thinness of youth, seemed to have softer lines and a more human proportion, more grace. And there was a warmth in his white skin, making it much less conspicuous than the really dazzling brilliance of Easu. Easu was a good deal bigger, but Jack was more concentrated, and a born fighter. He fought with all his soul.

He shaped up to Easu, and Easu made ready, when they were interrupted by a cry from Monica, in a high, hysterical voice. They looked up. She had reined in her horse among the bushes, and was looking round at them with a queer, sharp, terrified face, from the distance. Her shrill voice cried:

"Don't forget he saved Herbert's life."

Both men faced round, and looked at her as if she had committed an indecency. She quailed in her saddle. Easu, with a queer jerk of the head, motioned to her to go. She sank a little forward in her saddle, and hurriedly urged her horse through the bush, out of sight, without ever looking round, leaving the men, as she knew, to their hearts' desire.

They waited for a while. Then they lifted their fists again, and drew near. Jack began the light, subtle, harmonious dancing which preceded his attack. He always attacked, no matter whom he fought. He could not fight unless he took the initiative. So now he danced warily, subtly before Easu, and Easu stood ready to side-step. Easu was bigger, harder, much more powerful than Jack, and built in hard mechanical lines: the kind that is difficult to knock out, if you have not much weight behind your blow.

"Are y' insured?" sneered Easu.

But Jack did not listen. He had always fought with people bigger and older than himself. But he had never before had this strange lust dancing in his blood, the lust of rage dancing for its consummation in blows. He had known it before, as a sort of game. But now the lust bit into his very soul, and he was quivering with accumulated desire, the desire to hit Easu hard, hit him till he knocked him out. He wanted to hit him till he knocked him out.

And he knew himself deficient in brute power. So he must make up in quickness and skill and concentration. When he did strike, it must be a fine keen blow that went deep. He had confidence in his power to do it. Only—and this was the disturbing element—he knew there was not much *time.* And he would rather be knocked out himself than have the fight spoiled in the middle.

He moved lightly and led Easu on, ducked, bobbed up again, and began to be consummately happy. Easu could not get at him.

"Come on!" said Easu thickly.

So suddenly he came on, and bang! bang! went his knuckles against that insulting chin. And he felt joy spring in his bowels.

But he did not escape without punishment. Pat!—butt! Pat!—butt! went Easu's swinging blows down over his back. But Jack got in two more: Bang! Bang! He knew by the exquisite pain in his knuckles that he had struck deep, pierced the marrow of the other with pain of defeat.

Pat—butt! Pat—butt! came the punishment.

But Jack was out again, dancing softly, electric joy in his bowels.

Then suddenly he sprang back at Ellis, his arms swinging in strange, vindictive sideways swoops. Ping!—pong! Ping! pong! rapid as lightning. Easu fell back a little dazed before this sudden rain of white blows, but Jack followed, followed, followed, nimbly, warily, but with deadly flickering intent.

Crash! Ellis went down, but caught Jack a heavy smash in the face with his right fist as he fell. Jack reeled away.

And then, posed, waiting, watching, with blood running from bruised cuts on his swelling face, one eye rapidly closing, he stood well forward, fists in true boxing trim, and a deep gratification of joy in his dark belly.

Ellis rose slowly, foaming at the mouth; then getting to his feet rushed head down, in a convulsion, at his adversary. Jack stepped aside, but not quite quick enough. He caught Easu a blow with his left under the ear, but not in time to stop the impact. Easu's head butted right where he wanted it to—into his enemy's stomach; though not full in the pit. Jack fell back winded, and Red also fell again, giving Jack time to throw back his head and whoop for a few mouthfuls of air. So that when Red rushed in again, he was able feebly to fence and stall him off, stepping aside and hitting again, but wofully clipping, smacking only. . .

"Foul! He's winded! Foul!" yelled someone from the bushes. "Time!"

"Not for mine," roared Easu.

He sprang and dashed at his gasping, gulping adversary, whirling his arms like iron piston-rods. Jack dodged the propelled whirl, but stumbled over one of the big feet stuck out to trip him. Easu hit as he fell, and swung a crashing left-right about the sinking, unprotected head. And when Jack was down, kicked the prostrate body in an orgasm of fury.

"Foul, you swine!" screamed Rackett, springing in like a tiger. Easu, absolutely blind with rage and hate, stared hellish and unseeing. Jack lay crumpled on the floor.* Dr Rackett stooped down to him, as Tom and Lennie and Alec Rice ran in. Easu went and dropped on a fallen log, sitting blowing to get his wind and his consciousness back. He was unconscious with fury, like some awful Thing, not like a man.

"My God, Ellis!" screamed Rackett, who had lifted the dead head of Jack on to his knees. "If you've done for him I'll have you indicted."

And Easu, slowly, heavily coming back to consciousness, lifted his head, and the blue pupils of his red eyes went ugly with evil fear, his bruised face seemed to have dropped with fear. He waited, vacant, empty with fear.

At length Jack stirred. There was life in him. And at once the bully Easu began to talk wide.*

"Bloody little sod came at me bashing me jaw when I'd never touched him. Had to fight to defend meself. Bloody little sod!"

Jack opened his eyes and struggled to rise.

"Anybody counting?" he said stupidly. But he could not get up.

"It was a foul," said Rackett.

"Foul be blithered!" shouted Easu. "It was a free fight and no blasted umpires asked for. If that bloody bastard wants some more, let him get up. I'm goin' to teach him to come crowin' over an Australian."

But Jack was on his unsteady feet. He would fight now if he died for it.

"Teach me!" he said vaguely, and sprang like a cat out of a bag on the astonished and rather frightened Easu.

But something was very wrong. When his left fist rang home it caused such an agony that a sheer scream of pain tore from him, clearing the mists from his brain in a strange* white light. He was now fully conscious again, super-conscious. He knew he must hit with his right, and hit hard. He heard nothing, and saw nothing. But with a kind of trance vision he was super-awake.

Man is like this. He has various levels of consciousness. When he is broken, killed at one level of consciousness, his very death leaves him on a higher level.* And this is the soul in its entirety being conscious, super-conscious, far beyond mentality. It hardly needs eyes or ears. It is clairvoyant and clair-audient. And man's divinity, and his ultimate power, is in this super-consciousness of the whole soul. Not in brute force, not in skill or intelligence alone. But in the soul's extreme power of knowing and then willing. On this alone hangs the destiny of all mankind.*

Jack, uncertain on his feet, incorporate, wounded to horrible pain in his left hand, was now in the second state of consciousness and of power. Meanwhile the doctor was warning Easu to play fair. Jack heard absolutely without hearing. But Easu was bothered by it.

He was flustered by Jack's unexpected uprising. He was weary and wavering, the paroxysm of his ungovernable fury had left him, and he had a desire to escape. His rage was dull and sullen.

Jack was softly swaying. Easu shaped up and waited. And suddenly Jack sprang, with all the weight of his nine stone behind him, and all the mystery of his soul's deadly will; and planted a blow on Easu's astonished chin with his granite right fist. Before there was any recovery he got in a second blow, and it was a knockout. Easu crashed, and Jack crashed after him, and both lay still.

Doctor Rackett, watch in hand, counted. Easu stared at the darkening blue, and sat up. An oath came out of his disfigured mouth. Dr Rackett put the watch in his pocket as Easu got to his feet. But Jack did not move. He lay in a dead faint.

Lennie, the emotional, began to cry when he saw Jack's bruised, greenish-looking face. Dr Rackett was feeling the pulse and the heart.

"Take the horse and fetch some whiskey and some water, Tom," he said.

Tom turned to Easu, who stood with his head down and his mouth all cut, watching, waiting to depart, undecided.

"I'll borrow your horse a minute, Easu," he said.

And Easu did not answer. He was getting into his shirt again, and for the moment none of him was visible save a belt of white skin round the waist. Tom pulled up the girth of the black horse, and jumped into the saddle. Lennie slipped up behind him, face still wet with tears. Easu's face emerged, disfigured, out of his white shirt, and watched them go. Rackett attended to Jack, who still gave no signs of life. Alec Rice stood beside the kneeling doctor, silent and impassive.

Easu slowly buttoned his shirt-cuffs and shirt-collar, with numb fingers. The pain was just beginning to come out, and he made queer slight grimaces with his distorted face. Slowly he got his black tie, and holding up his chin, fastened it round his throat, clumsily. He was not the same Easu that had set off so large and assertive, with Monica.

Lennie came running with a tin of water. He had slipped off the horse at the lower dam, and found the tin which he kept secreted there. Dr Rackett put a wet handkerchief on Jack's still dead face. Under the livid skin, the bruises and the blood showed terrifying, one eye already swollen up. The queer mask of a face looked as if the soul, or the life, had retreated from it in weariness or disgust. It looked like somebody else altogether.

"He ain't dead, is he?" whimpered Lennie, terrified most of all because Jack, with his swollen face and puffed eye, looked like somebody else.

"No! But I wish Tom would come with that whiskey."

As he spoke, they heard the crashing sound of the horse through the bushes, and Tom's red, anxious face appeared. He swung out of the saddle and dropped the reins on the ground.

Dr Rackett pressed the bruised chin, pressed the mouth open, and poured a little liquor down Jack's throat. There was no response. He poured a little more whiskey. There came a slight choking sound, and then the one dark-blue eye opened vacant. It stared in vacancy for some moments, while everybody stood with held breath. Then the whiskey began to have effect. Life seemed to give a movement of itself, in the boy's body, and the wide-open eye took a conscious direction. It stared straight into the eyes of Easu, who stood there looking down, detached, in humiliation, derision, and uneasiness. It stared with a queer, natural recognition, and a faint jeering, uneasy grin was the reflex on Easu's disfigured mask.

"Guess he's had enough for once," said Easu, and turning, he picked up his horse's reins, dropped into the saddle, and rode straight away.

"Feel bad?" Dr Rackett asked.

"Rotten!" said Jack.

And at last Lennie recognised the voice. He could not recognise the face, especially with that bunged-up eye peering gruesomely through a gradually diminishing slit, Hun-like.*

Dr Rackett smiled slightly.

"Where's your pain?" he asked.

Jack thought about it. Then he looked into Rackett's eyes without answering.

"Think you can stand?" said Rackett.

"Try me."

They got him to his feet. Everything began to swim again. Rackett's arm came round him.

"Did he knock me out?" Jack asked. The question came from his half-consciousness: from a feeling that the battle with Easu was not yet finished.

"No, you knocked him out.—Let's get your coat on."

But as he shoved his arm into his coat he knew he was fainting again, and he almost wept, feeling his consciousness and his control going. He thought it was just his stiff, swollen, unnatural face that caused it.

"Can y' walk?" asked Tom anxiously.

"Don't walk on my face, do I?" came the words. But as they came, so did the reeling, nauseous oblivion. He fainted again, and was carried home like a sack over Tom's back.

When he came to, he was on his bed, Lennie was feverishly pulling off his shoes, and Dr Rackett was feeling him all over. Dr Rackett smelt of drugs. But now Rackett's face was earnest and attentive, he looked a nice man, only weak.

Jack thought at once of Gran.

"How's Gran?" he asked.

"She's picked up again. The relations put her in a wax, so she came to life again."

"You're the one now.* You look an awful sight," said Len.

"Did anybody see me?" asked Jack, dim and anxious.

"Only Grace so far."

Rackett, who was busy bandaging, saw the fever of anxiety coming into the one live eye.

"Don't talk," he said. "Len, he mustn't talk at all. He's got to go to sleep."

After they had got his nightshirt on, they gave him something to drink, and he went to sleep.

ii

When he awoke, it was dark. His head felt enormous. It was getting bigger and bigger, till soon it would fill the room. Soon his head would be so big, it would fill all the room, and the room would be too small for it. Oh horror! He was so frightened, he cried out.

"What's amiss?" a quick voice was asking.

"Make a light! Make a light!" cried Jack.

Lennie quickly lit a candle, and to Jack's agonized relief there was the cubby, the bed, the walls, all of natural dimensions, and Tom and Lennie in their nightshirts standing by his bed.

"What's a-matter ol' dear?" Lennie asked caressively.

"My head! I thought it was getting so big the room couldn't hold it."

"Aw, go on now!" said Lennie. "Y' face is a bit puffy, but y' head's same as ever it was."

Jack couldn't believe it. He was so sensually convinced that his head had grown enormous, enormous, enormous. He stared at Lennie and Tom in dismay. Lennie stroked his hair softly.

"There's y' ol' nut!" he said. "Tain't no bigger 'n it ever was. Just exactly same life-size."

Gradually Jack let himself be convinced. And at last he let them blow the candle out. He went to sleep.

He woke again with a frenzy working in him. He had pain, too. But far worse than the pain was the tearing of the raging discomfort, the frenzy of dislocation. And in his stiff, swollen head, there was something he remembered but could not drag into light. What was it? What was it? In the frenzy of struggle to know, he went vague.

Then it came to him, words as plain as knives.

"And when I die
In hell I shall lie
With fire and chains
And awful pains."*

The aunts had repeated this at him, as a child, when he was naughty. And it had always struck a vague terror into his soul. He had forgotten it. Now it came again.

"In hell I shall lie
With fire and chains
And awful pains."

He had a vivid realisation of this hell. That was where he lay at that very moment.

"You must be a good, loving little boy."

He had never wanted to be a good, loving little boy. Something in his bowels revolted from being a good, loving little boy, revolted in nausea. "But if you're not a good, loving little boy,

Then when you die
In hell you will lie–" etc.

"Let me lie in hell, then," the bad and unloving little boy had answered, to the shocked horror of the aunts. And the answer had scared even himself.

And now the hell was on him. And still he was not a good, loving little boy.

He remembered his lessons: Love your enemies.*

"Do I love Easu?" he asked himself. And he writhed over in bed in disgust. He loathed Easu. If he could crush him absolutely to powder, he would crush him to powder. Make him extinct.

"Lord! Lord!" he groaned. "I loathe Easu. I loathe him."

What was amiss with him? Did he want to leave off loathing Easu? Was that the root of his sickness and fever?

But when he thought of Easu's figure and face, he knew he didn't want to leave off loathing him. He *did* loathe him, whether he wanted to or not, and the fact to him was sacred. It went right through the core of him.

"Lord! Lord!" he groaned, writhing in fever. "Lord, help me to loathe him properly. Lord, I'll kill him if you want me to; and if you don't want me to, I won't. I'll kill him if you want me to. But if you don't want me to, I won't care any more."

The pledge seemed to soothe him. At the back of Jack's consciousness was always this mysterious Lord, to whom he cried in the night. And this Lord put commands upon him, but so darkly, Jack couldn't easily find out what the commands were. The aunts had always said, the command was to be a good, loving little boy. But when he tried being a good, loving little boy, his soul seemed to lose his Lord, and turn wicked. That was what made him fear hell. When he seemed to lose his connection with his great, mysterious Lord, with whom he communed absolutely alone, he became aware of hell. And he couldn't share with his aunts that Jesus whom they always commended. At the sacrament: *This is my Body*,* he knew he never wanted to taste that Body, nor drink that Blood.*

He had his own Lord. And when he could get into communication, or communion, with his own Lord, he always felt well and right again.

Now, in his pain and battered fever, he was fighting for his Lord again.

"Lord, I don't love Easu, and I'll kill him if you want me to. But if you don't want me to, I won't, I won't bother any more."

This pledge, and this submission, soothed him strangely. He felt he was coming back to his own Lord. It was a pledge, and he would keep it. He gave no pledge to love Easu. Only not to kill him, if the Lord didn't want it; and to kill him, if the Lord did.

"Lord, I don't love Monica. I don't love her. But if she'd give up to me, I'd love her if you wanted me to."

He thought about this. Somewhere, his soul burned against Monica. And somewhere, his soul burned for her.

But she must give up to him. She must give herself up. He demanded this submission, as if it were a submission to his mysterious Lord. She would never submit to the mysterious Lord direct. Like that old demon of a Gran, who knew the Lord, and played with Him, spited Him even. Monica would have first to submit to himself, Jack, in person, before she would really yield before the immense Lord. And yield before the immense Lord she must. Through him.

"Lord!" he said, invoking the supreme power; "I love Lennie and Tom, and I want always to love them, and I want you to back them."

Then the prickles of pain entered his soul again.

"Lord, I don't love my father, but I don't want to hurt him. Only I don't love him, Lord. And it's not my fault, though he's a good man, because I wasn't born with love for him in me."

This had been a thorn in his consciousness since he was a child. Best get it out now. Because the fear of *not* loving his father had almost made him hate him. If he ought to love him, and he couldn't love him, then there was nothing to do but hate him, because of the hopeless obligation. But if he *needn't* love him, then he needn't hate him, and they could both be in peace. He would leave it to his Lord.

"Perhaps I ought to love Mary," he continued. "But I don't *really* love her, because she doesn't realise about the Lord. She doesn't realise there is any Lord. She thinks there's only me, and herself. But there is the Lord. And Monica knows. But Monica is spiteful against the Lord. Lord! Lord!—"

He ended on the old human cry of invocation: a cry which is answered, when it comes from the extreme, passionate soul. The strange, dark comfort and power came back to him again, and he could go to sleep once more, with his Lord.

When he woke in the morning, the fever had left him. Lennie was there at dawn, to see if he wanted anything. The quick little Lennie, who always came straight from the Lord, unless his emotions of pity got the better of him. Then he lost his connection, and became maudlin.

Jack wanted the family not to know. But the twins saw his disfigured face, with horror. And Monica knew: it was she who had sent Dr Rackett and Tom and Alec. And Grace knew. And soon Ma came, and said: "Dear o' me, Jack Grant, what d' y' mean by going and getting messed up like this!"—And Dad came, slow and heavy, and said nothing, but looked dark and angry. They all knew.

But Jack wanted to be left alone. He told Tom and Dr Rackett, and Tom and Dr Rackett ordered the family to leave him alone.

It was Grace who brought his meals. Poor old Grace, with her big eyes and rather big nose, she had a gentle heart, and more real sense than that Monica. Jack only got to know her while he was sick, and she really touched his heart, she was so kind, and thought so little of herself, and had such a sad wisdom at the bottom of her. Who would have thought it, of the pert, cheeky, nosy Grace?

Monica slipped in, and stood staring down at him with her queer, brooding eyes, that shone with widened pupils. Heaven knows what she was thinking about.

"I was awfully afraid he'd kill you," she said. "I was so frightened, that's what made me laugh."

"Why should I let him kill me?" said Jack.

"How could you help it! He's much stronger and crueler than you."

"He may be stronger, but I can match him in other ways."

She looked at him incredulously. She did not believe him. He could see she did not believe in that other, inward power of his, upon which he himself depended. She thought him in every way weaker, frailer than Easu. Only, of course, nicer.

This made Jack very angry.

"I think I punished him as much as he punished me," he said.

"*He's* not laid up in bed," she replied.

Then, with her quivering, exquisite gentleness, she touched his bandaged hand.

"I'm awfully sorry he hurt you so," she said. "I know you'll hate *me* for it."

"Why should I?" he replied coldly.

She took up his bandaged hand and kissed it quickly, then she looked him long and beseechingly in the eyes: or the one eye. Somehow, she didn't seem to see his caricature of a face.

"Don't hate me for it," she pleaded, still watching him with that strange, pleading, watchful look.

The flame leapt in his bowels, and came into his eyes. And another flame as she, catching the change in his eyes, softened her look and smiled subtly, suddenly taking his wrist in a passionate, secret grasp. He felt the hot blood suffusing him like new life.

"Goodbye!" she said, looking back at him as she disappeared.

And when she had gone, he remembered the watchfulness in her eyes, the cat-like watchfulness at the back of all her winsome tenderness. There it was, like the devil. And he turned his face to the wall, to his Lord, and two smarting tears came under his eyes, as if they were acid.

The next day, Mary came bringing his pap. She was not going to be kept away any longer. And she would come as a ministering angel.

He saw on her face that she was startled, shocked, and a little repelled by his appearance. She hardly knew him. But she overcame her repulsion at once, and became the more protective.

"Why how awful it must be for you!" she said.

"Not so bad now," he said, manfully swallowing his pap.

He could see she longed for him to have his own good-looking face again. She could not bear this strange horror. She refused to believe this was he.

"I shall *never* forgive that cruel Easu!" she said, and the colour came to her dark cheek. "I hope I never have to speak to him again."

"Oh, I began it. It was my fault."

"How could it be!" cried Mary. "That great hulking brute. How dare he lay a finger on you!"

Jack couldn't smile, his face was of the fixed sort. But his one good eye had a gleam.

"He dare, you see," he answered.

But she turned away in smarting indignation.

"It makes one understand why such creatures had their hands cut off, in the old days,"* she said, with cold fierceness. "How dare he disfigure your beautiful face! How dare he!"

And tears of anger came to her eyes.

A strangled grin caused considerable pain to Jack's beautiful face.

"I suppose he didn't rightly appreciate my sort of looks," he said.

"The jealous brute!" said Mary. "But I hope he'll pay for it. I hope he will.—I do hope he hasn't really disfigured you," she ended on a note of agitation.

"No no! Besides *that* doesn't matter all the world."

"It matters all the world," she cried, with strange fierceness, "to me."

Chapter XII.

The Great Passing.*

i

Jack soon got better. Soon he was sitting in the old arm-chair by the parlour fire. There was a little fire, against the damp. This was Gran's place. But Gran did not leave her bed.

He had been in to see her, and she frightened him. The grey, dusky skin round the sunken mouth and sharpened nose, the eyes that were mostly shut, and never really open, the harsh breathing, the hands lying like old translucent stone on the bed-cover: it frightened him, and gave him a horror of dissolution and decay. He wanted terribly to be out again with the healthy Tom, among the horses. But not yet—he must wait yet awhile. So he took his turn sitting by Gran, to relieve Mary, who got little rest. And he became nervous, fanciful, frightened as he had never been before in his life. The family seemed to abandon him as they abandoned Gran. The cold isolation and horror of death.

The first rains had set in. All night the water had thundered down on the slab roof of the cubby, as if the bottom had fallen out of some well above. Outside was cloudy still, and a little chill. A wind was hush-sh-shing round the house. Mary was sitting with Gran, and he was in the parlour, listening to that clock—Tick-tock! Tick-tock! He sat in the arm-chair with a shawl over his shoulders, trying to read. Curiously enough, in Australia he could not read. The words somehow meant nothing to him.

It was Sunday afternoon, and the smell of roast beef, Yorkshire pudding, cabbage, apple pie and cinnamon custard still seemed to taint the house. Jack had come to loathe Sunday dinners. They seemed to him degrading. They hung so heavy afterwards. And now he was sick, it seemed to him particularly repulsive. The peculiar Sundayness* of it. The one thing that took him in revulsion back to England: Sunday dinner. The England he didn't want to be taken back to.—But it had been a quiet meal. Monica and Grace and the little boy-twins had all been invited to York, by Alec Rice's parents, and they had gone away from the shadowed house, leaving a great emptiness. It seemed to Jack they should all have stayed, so that their young life could have united against this slow dissolution.

Everything felt very strange. Tom and Lennie were out, Mrs Ellis and the children were upstairs, Mr Ellis had gone to look at some sheep that had got into trouble in the rain. There seemed a darkness, a chill, a deathliness in the air. It is like that in Australia: usually so sunny and absolutely forgetful. Then comes a dark day, and the place seems like an immemorial grave. More gruesome than ever England was, on her dark days. Mankind for ever entombed in dissolution, in an endless grave.

"Who shall ascend into the hill of the Lord; or who shall
stand in His holy place?
He that hath clean hands and a pure heart,
Who hath not yielded up himself unto vanity, nor
sworn deceitfully."[*]

Jack was thinking over the words Mr Ellis had read in the morning, as near as he remembered them. He looked at his own hands: already they seemed pale and soft and very clean. What had the Lord intended hands for? So many things hands must do, and still they remain clean. Clean hands! His left was still discoloured and out of shape. Was it unclean?

No, it was not unclean. Not unclean like the great paw of Easu's, hiking Monica out of the saddle.

Clean hands and a pure heart! A pure heart! Jack thought of his own, with two heavy new desires in it: the sudden, shattering desire for Monica, that would rip through him sometimes like a flame. And the slow, smouldering desire to kill Easu. He had to be responsible for them both.

And he was not going to try to pluck them out.[*] They both belonged to his heart, they were sacred even while they were shocking in his blood. Only, driven back on himself, he gave the old pledge: *Lord, if you don't want me to have Monica and kill Easu, I won't. But if you want me to, I will.*—Somewhere he was inclined to cry out to be delivered from the cup.[*] But that would be cowardice towards his own blood. It would be yielding himself up to vanity, if he pretended he hadn't got the desires. And if he swore to eradicate them, it would be swearing deceitfully.—Sometimes the hands must move in the darkest acts, if they are to remain really clean, not deathly like Gran's now. And the heart must beat hard in the storm of darkest desires, if it is to keep pure, and not go pale-corrupt.

But always subject to the will of the Lord.

"Who shall ascend into the hill of the Lord; or who shall
stand in his holy place."

The Seraphim and the Cherubim knew strange, awful secrets of the Lord. That was why they covered their faces with their wings, for the wings of glory also had a dark side.[*]

The fire was burning low. Jack stooped and put on more wood. Then he blew the red coals, to make the wood catch. A yellow flame came, and he was glad.

"Forsake me not Oh God in mine old age; when I am grey-headed; until I have shown my strength to this generation, and thy power to all them that are yet to come."[*]

Jack was always afraid of those times when the mysterious sayings of the bible invaded him. He seemed to have no power against them. And his soul was always a little afraid, as if the walls of life grew thin, and he could hear the great everlasting wind of the mysterious going of the Lord,[*] on the other side.

"Forsake me not Oh God in mine old age; when I am grey-headed."

Jack wished Gran would say this, so that the Lord would stay with her, and she would not look so awful. How could Mary *stand* it, sitting with her day after day.

"Until I have shown my strength to this generation, and thy power to all them that are yet to come."

And again his own stubborn strength of life arose. What was he for, but to show his strength to the generation, and a sign of the power of the Lord for all them that were yet to come.

The clock was ticking steadily in the room. But the yellow flames were bunching up in the grate. He wondered where Gran's "stocking" really was? But the thought of stockings, of concealed money, of people hankering for money, always made him feel sick.

"There is one glory of the sun, and another glory of the moon, and another glory of the stars———There is a natural body and a spiritual body——"[*]

"There is one glory of the sun—" But men don't realise all the same glory. In England the sun had seemed to him to move with a domestic familiarity. It wasn't till he was out here that he had been struck to the soul with the immense assertive vigour and sacred handsomeness of the sun. He knew it now: the wild, immense, fierce, untamed sun, fiercer than a glowing-eyed lion with a vast mane of fire, crouching on the western horizon, staring at the earth as if to pounce on it, the mouse-like earth. He had seen this immense sun, fierce and powerful beyond all human consideration, glaring across the southern sea, as all men may see it if they go there.

"There is one glory of the sun ..." And it is a glory vast and fierce, of a Lord who is more than our small lives.

"And another glory of the moon—" That too he knew. And he had not known, till the full moon had followed him through the empty bush, in Australia, in the night. The immense liquid gleam of the far-south moon, following, following with a great, miraculous, liquid smile. That vast white liquid smile, so vindictive! And himself, hurrying back to camp on Lucy, had known a terrible fear. The fear that the broad liquid fire of the cold moon would capture him, capture him and destroy him,* like some white demon that slowly and coldly tastes and devours its prey. The moon had that power, he knew, to destroy him, tissue, heart, body and soul, consume* him away. The immense, liquid, gleaming, lusting white moon, following inexorably, and the bush like white charred moon-embers.

"There is another glory of the moon——" And he was afraid of it. "The sun is thy right hand, and the moon is thy left hand—" The two gleaming, immense living orbs, moving like weapons in the two hands of the Lord.*

"And there is another glory of the stars—" The strange stars of the southern night, all in unfamiliar crowds and tufts and drooping clusters, with strange black wells in the sky. He never got used to the southern stars. Whenever he stood and looked up at them he felt as if his soul were leaving him, as if he belonged to another species of life, not to man as he knew man. As if there were a metamorphosis, a terrible metamorphosis to take place.

"There is a natural body, and there is a spiritual body—" This phrase had haunted his mind from the earliest days. And he had always had a sort of hatred of the thing his aunts, and the parson, and the poets, called The Spirit, with a capital S. It had always, with him, been connected with his Sunday clothes and best behaviour, and a certain exalted falseness. Part of his natural naughtiness had arisen from his vindictive dislike and contempt of The Spirit, and things of The Spirit.

Now it began to seem different to him. He knew, he always *had* known, that the bible really meant something absolutely different from what the aunts and the parsons and even the poets meant by Spirit, or the spiritual body.

Since he had seen the power of the roaring yellow sun, and the frightening vast smile in the gleaming full moon following him,[*] the new moon like a delicate weapon-threat in the western sky, and the stars in disarray, like a scattered flock of sheep bunching and communing together in a strange bush, in the vast heavens, he had gradually come to know the difference between the natural body and the spiritual body. The natural body was like in England, where the sun rises naturally to make day, and passes naturally at sunset, owing to the earth's revolving; where the moon "raises her lamp above," on a clear night, and the stars are "candles" in heaven.[*] That is the natural body: all the cosmos just a natural fact. And a man loves a woman so that they can propagate their species. The natural body.

And the spiritual body is supposed to be something thin and immaterial, that can float through a brick wall and subsist on mere thought. Jack had always hated this thin, wafting object. He preferred his body solid. He loved the beautiful weight and transfigured solidity of living limbs. He had no use whatsoever for the gossamer stuff of the supposed "ethereal," or "pure" spirit: like evaporated alcohol. He had a natural dislike of Shelley and vegetarians and socialists and all advocates of "Spirit." He hated Blake's pictures, with people waving like the wrong sort of sea-weed in the sky, instead of underwater.[*]

Hated it all. Till hating it had almost made him wicked.

Now he had a new understanding. He had always *known* that the Old Testament never meant any of this Shelley stuff, this Hindu Nirvana business.[*] "There is a natural body, and there is a spiritual body."—And his natural body got up in the morning to eat food and tend sheep and earn money and prepare for having a family; to see the sun usefully making day and setting owing to the earth's revolution: the new moon so shapen because the earth's shadow fell on her; the stars being other worlds, other lumps in space, shining according to their various distances, coloured according to their chemical composition. Well and good.

That is man very cleverly finding out all about it, like a little boy pulling his toy to pieces.

But, willy-nilly, in this country he had seen another sun and another moon. He had seen the glory of the sun and the glory of the moon, and both these glories had had a powerful sensual effect on him. There had been a great passional reaction in himself, in his own body. And as the strange new passion of fear and the sense of gloriousness burned through him, like a new intoxication, he knew that this was his real spiritual body. This glowing, intoxicated body, drunk with the sun and the moon, drunk from the cup in the hand of the Lord, *this* was his spiritual body.

And when the flame came up in him, tearing from his bowels, in the sudden new desire for Monica, this was his spiritual body, the body transfigured with fire. And that steady dark vibration which made him want to kill Easu—Easu seemed to him like the Anti-christ—that was his own spiritual body. And when he had hit Easu with his broken left hand, and the white sheet of flame going through him had made him scream aloud, leaving him strange and distant but super-conscious and powerful, this too was his spiritual body. The sun in his right hand and the moon in his left hand. When he drank from the burning right hand of the Lord, and wanted Monica in the same fire, it was his body spiritual burning from the right hand of the Lord. And when he knew he must destroy Easu, in the sheet of white pain, it was his body spiritual transfigured from the left hand of the Lord. And when he ate and drank and the food tasted good, it was the dark cup of life he was drinking, drinking the life of the dead ox from the meat. And this was the body spiritual communing with the sacrificed body of natural life: like a tiger glowing at evening and lapping blood. And when he rode after the sheep through the bush, and the horse between his knees went quick and delicate, it was the Lord tossing him in his spiritual body down the maze of living.

But when Easu ground down his horse and shoved it after the sheep, it was the natural body fiendishly subjugating the spiritual body. For the horse too is a spiritual body and a natural body, and may be ridden as the one or as the other. And when Easu wanted Monica, it was the natural body malignantly degrading the spiritual body. Monica also half wanted it.

For Easu knew the spiritual body. And like a fallen angel, he hated it, he wanted always to overthrow it more, in this day when it is so abjectly overthrown. Monica too knew the spiritual body: the body of straight fire.* And she too seemed to have a grudge against it. It thwarted her "natural" will; which "natural" will is the barren devil of today.

Gran, that old witch, she also knew the spiritual body. But she loved spiting it. And she was dying like clay.

Mary, who was so spiritual and so self-sacrificing, she didn't know the body of straight fire at all. Her spirit was all natural. She was so "good," and so heavily "natural," she would put out any fire of the glory of the burning Lord. She was more "natural" even than Easu.

And Jack's father was the same. So good! So nice! So kind! So absolutely well-meaning! And he would bank out the fire of the burning Lord with shovelfuls of kindness.

They would none of them, none of them let the fire burn straight. None of them. There were no people at all who dared have the fire of the Lord, and drink from the cup of the fierce glory of the Lord, the sun in one hand and the moon in the other.

Only this strange, wild, ash-coloured country with its undiminished sun and its unblemished moon, would allow it. There was a great death between the two hands of the Lord; between the sun and the moon. But let there be a great death. Jack gave himself to it.

He was almost asleep, in the half-trance of inner consciousness, when Dad came in. Jack opened his eyes and made to rise, but Dad waved him to sit still, while he took the chair on the other side of the fire, and sat down inert. He seemed queer. Dad seemed queer. The same dusky look over his face as over Gran's. And a queer, pinched, far-away look. Jack wondered over it. But he could see Dad didn't want to be spoken to. The clock tick-tocked. Jack went into a kind of sleep.

He opened his eyes. Dad was very slowly, very slowly fingering the bowl of his pipe. How quiet it was!

Jack dozed again, and wakened to a queer noise. It was Dad's breathing: and perhaps the falling of his pipe. He had dropped his pipe. And his body had dropped over sideways, very heavy and uncomfortable, and he was breathing hoarsely, unnaturally in his sleep. Save for the breathing it was dreadfully quiet. Jack picked up the pipe and sat down again. He felt tired: awfully tired, for no reason at all.

He woke with a start. The afternoon was passing, there was a shower, the room seemed dark. The firelight flickered on Mr Ellis' watchguard. He wore his unbuttoned waistcoat, as ever, with the gold watch-chain showing. He was very stout, and very still. Terribly still and sagging sideways, the hoarse breathing had ceased. Jack would have liked to wake him from that queer position.

How quiet it was!* Upstairs someone had dragged a chair, and that had made him realise. Far away, very far away, he could hear Harry and Ellie and baby playing. "There is a quiet of the sun, and another quiet of the moon, and another quiet of the stars; for one star differs from another in quiet. So also is the resurrection of the dead. It is sown a natural body; it is raised a spiritual body.— —"

Was that scripture?* Or wasn't it?—There is a quiet of the sun. This was the quiet of the sun. He was sitting in the cold dead quiet of the sun. For one star differs from another in quiet. The sun had abstained from radiating, this was the quiet of the sun, and the strange shadowy crowding of the stars' differing quietnesses seemed to infest the weak daylight.

It is sown a natural body!—Oh bother the words! He didn't want them. He wanted the sun to shine, and everything to be normal. If he didn't feel so weak, and if it weren't raining, he'd go out to the stable to the horses. To the hot-blooded animals.

Mr Ellis' head hung sagging on his chest. Jack wished he would wake up and change his position, it looked horrible.

The inner door suddenly opened, and Mary came swiftly out. She started seeing Mr Ellis asleep in the chair. Then she went to Jack's side and took his arm, and leaned whispering in his ear. Jack did not like her leaning whispering in his ear.

"Jack! She's gone! I think she's gone. I think she passed in her sleep. We shall have to wake Uncle."

Jack stood up trembling. There was a queer smell in the room. He walked across and touched the sleeping man on the sleeve.

"Dad!" he said. "Dad! Mr Ellis."

There was no response. They both waited. Then Jack shook the arm more vigorously. It felt very inert. Mary came across and put her hand on her uncle's sunken forehead, to lift his head. She gave a little scream.

"Something's the matter with him," she said whimpering.

ii

Thank goodness Dr Rackett was upstairs. They fetched him and Timothy and Tom, and carried Mr Ellis into the dying-room.

"Better leave me alone with him now," said Rackett.

After ten minutes he came out of the dying-room and closed the door behind him. Tom was standing there. He looked at Rackett inquiringly. Rackett shook his head.

"Dad's not dead?" said Tom.

Rackett nodded.

Tom's face went to pieces for a moment. Then he composed it, and that Australian mouth of his, almost like a scar, shut close. He went into the dying-room.

Someone had to fetch the methodist son-in-law from York. Jack went in the sulky. Better die in the cart than stop in that house. And he could drive the sulky quietly.

The methodist son-in-law, though he was stout and wore black and Jack objected to him on principle, wasn't really so bad, in his own home. His wife Ruth of course burst into tears and ran upstairs. The husband kept his face straight, brought out the whiskey tantalus,[*] and poured some for Jack and himself. This they both drank with befitting gravity.

"I must be in chapel in fifteen minutes: that will be five minutes late," said the parson. "But they can't complain, under the circumstances. Mrs Blagg of course will stay at home.—Er—is anyone making arrangements out at Wandoo?"

"What arrangements?"

"Oh, seeing to things... the personal property too—"

"I was sent for you," said Jack. "I suppose they thought you'd see to things."

"Yes! Certainly! Certainly! I'll be out with Mrs Blagg directly after Meeting. Let me see—"

He went to a table and laboriously wrote two notes. Twisting them into cocked hats, he handed them one after the other to Jack, saying:

"This is to the Church of England parson. Leave it at his house. I've made it Toosday, Toosday at half-past ten. I suppose that'll do.—And this—this is to the joiner."

He looked at Jack meaningly, and Jack looked vague.

"Joshua Jenkins, at the joiner's shop. Third house from the end of the road. And you'll find him in the loft over the stable, Sunday or not, if he isn't in the house."

It was sunset, and the single bells of the church and chapel were sounding their last, cracked ping-ping! ping-ping! as Jack drove slowly down the straggling street of York. People were going to church, the women in their best shawls and bonnets, hurrying a little along the muddy road, where already the cows were lying down to sleep, and the loose horses straggled uncomfortably. Ocasionally a muddy buggy rattled up to the brick Church of England, people passed shadow-shape into the wooden Presbyterian Church, or waited outside the slab Meeting House of the Methodists.* The choir band was already scraping fiddles and tooting cornets in the church. Lamps were lighted within, and one feeble lamp at the church gate. It was a cloudy evening. Odd horsemen went trotting through the mud, going out into the country again as night fell, rather forlorn.

Jack always felt queer, in York on Sundays. The attempt at Sunday seemed to him like children's make-belief. The churches weren't real churches, the parsons weren't real parsons, the people weren't real worshippers. It was a sort of earnest make-belief, where people felt important like actors. And the pub, with its extra number of lamps, seemed to feel extra wicked. And the men riding home, often tipsy, seemed vague as to what was real, this York acting Sunday, or their dark, rather dreary farms away out, or some other third unknown thing. Was anything quite real? That was what the shadows, the people, the buildings seemed all to be asking. It was like children's games, real and not real, actual and yet unsubstantial, and the people seemed to feel as children feel, very earnest, very sure that they were *very* real, but having to struggle all the time to keep up the conviction. If they didn't keep up the conviction, the dark, strange Australian night might clear them and their little town all away into some final cupboard, and leave the aboriginal bush again.*

Joshua Jenkins the godless, was in the loft with a chisel, working by lantern light. He peered at the twisted note, and his face brightened.

"Two of 'em!" he exclaimed, with a certain gusto. "Well think o' that, think o' that! And I've not had a job o' this sort for over a month. Well I never, t' be sure! 'T never rains but it comes down cats an' dogs, seemingly. Toosday! Toosday! Toosday! Let's see—" and he scratched his head behind the ear. "Pretty quick work that, pretty quick work. But can be done, oh yes, can be done. I s'll have t' send somebody t' measure the Boss. How deep should you say he was in the barrel?—Never mind though, I'll send Sam over with the measure, come morning. But I can start right away on the old lady. Let's see! Let's see! Let's see! She wouldn't be-e-e—she wouldn't be over five foot two or three now, would she?"

"I don't know," said Jack hoarsely. "Do you mean for her coffin?" He was filled with horror.

"Well, I should say I do. I should say so. You don't see no sewing-machine here, do you, for sewing her shroud. I suppose I do mean her coffin, being joiner and carpenter, and J.P. and coroner as well when required."

Jack fled, horrified. But as he lit his sulky candles, and set off at a slow trot out of the town, he laughed a bit to himself. He felt it was rather funny. Why shouldn't it be rather funny? He hoped it would be a bit funny when he was dead too, to relieve matters. He sat in the easy sulky driving slowly down the washed-out road, in the dark, alien night. The night was dark and strange. An animal ran along the road in front of him, just discernible, at the far edge of the dim yellow candle glow. It was a wild, grey thing, running ahead into the dark. On in to the dark.

Why should one care? Beyond a certain point, one didn't care about anything, life or death. One just left it all. Up to a certain point, one had to go through the mill, caring and feeling bad. One had to cry out to the Lord, and fight the ugly brutes of life. And then for a time it was over, and one didn't care, good or bad, Lord or no Lord. One paid one's whack of caring, and then one was let off for a time. When one was dead, one didn't care any more. And that was death. But life too had its own indifference, its own deep, strong indifference: as the ocean is calm way down, under the most violent storm.

When he got home, Tom came out to the sulky. Tom's face was set with that queer Australian look, as if he were caught in a trap, and it wasn't any use complaining about it. He unharnessed the horse in a rough, flinging fashion. Jack didn't know what to say to him. The strange relief and indifference to things had come over Jack, so he thought he'd better keep quiet.

Lennie came riding in on Lucy. He slid to the ground and dragged the mare's bridle roughly.

"Come on, yer blasted old idjut, can't ye!" he blubbed, dragging her to the stable door. "Blasted idjut, my Uncle Joe!" he continued, between the sniffs and gulps of his blubbing. "Questions! Questions! How c'n I answer questions when I don't know myself!" A loud blub as he dragged the saddle down on top of himself, in his frenzy of untackling Lucy. "Rackett says to me, Len, he says"—blub and a loud sniff—"y' father's took bad and pore ol' Gran's gone, he says"—blub! blub! blub! "Be off an' fetch y' Uncle Joe an' tell him to come at onst—an' he can go to *hell*." Lennie ended on a shout of defiance as he staggered into the stable with the saddle. And from the dark his voice came: "An' when I ask our Tom what's amiss wi' m' Dad," blub! blub! "blasted idjut looks at me like a blasted owl—like a blasted owl!"—And Lennie sobbed before he sniffed and came out for the bridle.

"Don't y' cry, Lennie," said Jack, who was himself crying for all he was worth, under the cover of the dark.

"I'm *not* crying, y' bloomin' fool, you!" shouted Len. "I'm goin' in to see Ma, I am. Get some sense outta *her*—"

He walked off towards the house, then came back.

"Why don' *you* go in, Tom, an' see?" he cried. "What d' yer stan' there like that for, what *do* yer?"

There was a dead and horrible silence, outside the stable door in the dark. A silence that went to the core of the night, having no word to say.

The lights of a buggy were seen at the gate. The three waited. It was the unmarried Aunts. One of them ran and took Len in her arms.

"Oh you poor little lamb!" she cried. "Oh your poor Ma! Your Ma, your poor Ma!"

"Ma's not bad! She's all right," yelped Len in a new fear. Then there was a pause, and he became super-conscious. Then he drew away from the Aunt.

"Is Dad dead?" he asked, in a queer, quizzical little voice, looking from Tom to Jack, in the dim buggy-light. Tom stood as if paralysed.

Lennie at last gave a queer, animal "Whooo!", like a dog dazed with pain, and flung himself into Tom's arms. The only sounds in the night were Tom's short, dry sobs, as he held Lennie, and the whimpering of the aunts.

"Come in to your poor mother, come to comfort her," said one of the Aunts gently.

"Tom! Tom!" cried Lennie. "I'm skeered! I'm skeered, Tom, o' them two corpses! I'm skeered of 'em, Tom."

Tom, who was a little skeered too, gave a short dry bark of a sob.

"They won't hurt you, precious!" said the Aunt. "They won't hurt you. Come to your poor mother."

"No-o-o!" wailed Lennie in terror, and he flung away to Timothy's cabin, where he slept all night.

When the horses were fixed up, Tom and Jack went to the cubby. Tom flung himself on the bed without undressing, and lay there in silence. Jack did the same. He didn't know what else to do. At last he managed to say:

"Don't take it too hard, Tom! Dad's lived his life, and he's got all you children. We have to live. We all have to live. An' then we've got to die."

There was unresponsive silence for some time.

"What's the blasted use of it all, anyhow?" said Tom.

"There's no such thing as *use*," said Jack. "Dad lived, and he had his life. He had his life. You'll have yours. And I shall have mine. It's just your life, and you live it."

"What's the *good* of it," persisted Tom heavily.

"Neither good nor bad. You live your life because it's your own, and nobody can live it for you."

"What good is it to me!" said Tom dully, drearily. "I don't care if people live their lives or not."

Jack felt for the figure on the bed.

"Shake hands though, Tom," he said. "You *are* alive—and so am I. Shake hands on it."

He found the hand, and got a faint response, sulky, heavy. But for very shame Tom could not withhold all response.

Tim came in the morning with tea and bread and butter, saying Tom was wanted inside, and would Jack go with him to attend to the grave. Poor Tim was very much upset, and wept and wailed unrestrained. Which perhaps was good, because it spared the others the necessity to weep and wail.

They hitched up the old buggy, and set off with a pick and a couple of spades. Old black Timothy on the driving-box occasionally startled Jack by breaking forth into a new sudden wail, like a dog suddenly remembering again. It was a fine day. The earth had already dried up, and a hot, dry, gritty wind was blowing from inland, from the east. They drove out of the paddocks and along an overgrown trail, then they crossed the river, heaving and floundering through the slough, for at this season it was no more. The excitement of the driving here made Timothy forget to wail.

Rounding a steep little bluff, they came to a lonely, forlorn little enclosed graveyard, which Jack had never seen. Tim wailed, then asked where the grave should be. The sun grew very hot. They nosed around the little, lonely, parched acre.

Jack could not dig, so he unharnessed the outfit and put a box of chaff before the horses. Tim flung his spade over against a little grey headstone, and climbed in with the pick. Even then they weren't quite sure how big to make the grave, so Jack lay on the ground while Tim picked out a line around him. They got a straight line with a rope.

The soil was as hard as cement. Tim toiled and moiled, and forgot all wailing. But he made little impression on the cement-like earth.

"What we goin' t' do?" he asked, scratching his sweating head. "What 'n hell's name we goin' t' do, sir? Gotta bury 'm Toosday, gotta"—and he looked at the blazing sun. "Gotta dig him hole sevenfut deep grave, gotta do 't."

He set to again. Then two of the Reds came, sent to help. But the work was killing. The day became so hot, you forgot it, you passed into a kind of spell. But that work was heart-breaking.

Jack went off for dynamite, and Rackett came along, with Lennie, who would never miss a dynamiting show. Tim wrung his wet hair like a mop. The Reds, in their vests, were scarlet, and the vests were wet and grimy.

Much more fun with dynamite. Boom! Bang! Then somebody throwing out the dirt. Somebody going for a ladder. Boom! Bang! The explosions seemed enormous.

"Oh, for the love o' Mike!" cried the excited Lennie. "Ye'll blow me ol' Granfather sky high, if y' don't mind. For the love of Mike, don't let me see his bones."

But the Grandfather Ellis was safe in the next grave. Rackett laid another fuse. They all stood back. Bang! Boom! Pouf! went the dust.

iii

Jack would have done anything to escape the funeral, but Timothy, for some reason, kept hold of him. He wanted him to help replace the turf: moral support rather than physical assistance.

The two of them hid behind the pinch.* At last they saw the cortège approaching. Easu Ellis held the reins of the first team, and chewed the end of the whip. Beside him sat Joshua Jenkins, as a mute, fearful in black and like a scarecrow with loose danglings of crape. In the buggy behind them, on the floor-boards, was Gran's coffin, shaking wofully, covered with a black cloth. Joe Low drove the second buggy, which was the second hearse, and he looked strained and anxious as the heavy coffin bumped when the buggy dropped into holes on the track. Then came the family shay with the chief male mourners. Then a little crowd on foot.

The horses were behaving badly, not liking the road. It was hot, the vile east wind was blowing. Easu's horses jibbed at the slough of the stream: would not take it. He was afraid they* would jump, and toss the coffin out of the buggy. He had to get bearers to carry Gran's poor remains across the mud and up the pinch to their last house. The bearers sunk almost to their knees in mud. The whole cortège was at a standstill.

Joe Low's horses, mortally frightened, were jumping round till they were almost facing the horses in the mourners' shay. Easu ran to their heads. More bearers, strong men, came forward to lift out Dad's heavy coffin. Everybody watched in terror as they staggered through the slough of the stream with that unnatural burden. Was it going to fall?

No, they were through. Men were putting branches and big stones for the foot-mourners to cross, everybody sweating and sweltering. The sporting parson, his white surplice waving in the hateful, gritty hot wind, came striding over, holding his book. Then Tom, with a wooden, stupid face. Then Lennie, cracking nuts between his teeth and spitting out the shells, in an agony of nervousness. Then the other mourners, some carrying a few late, weird bush-flowers, picking their way over like a train of gruesome fowls, staggering and clutching on the stones and boughs, landing safe on the other bank. Jack watched from a safe distance above.

There were two coffins, one on either side the grave. Some of the uncles had top hats with dangling crape. Nearly everybody was black. Poor Len, what a black little crow he looked! The sporting parson read the service manfully. Then he announced Hymn Number 225.

Jack could feel the hollow place below, with the black mourners, simmer with panic, when the parson in cold blood asked them to sing a hymn. But he read the first verse solemnly, like an overture.

> "Oh sweet and blessed country
> The home of God's elect!

Oh sweet and blessed country
That eager hearts expect— —"*

There was a deadly pause. There was going to be no answer from the uncomfortable congregation, under that hot sun.

But Uncle Blagg* was not to be daunted. He struck up in a rather fat, wheezy, methodist voice, and Aunt Ruth piped feebly. The maiden aunts, who had insisted on following their mother, though women were not expected to attend, listened to this for an awful minute or two, then they waveringly "tried" to join in. It was really only funny. And Tom, in all his misery, suddenly started to laugh. Lennie looked up at him with wide eyes, but Tom's shoulders shook, shook harder, especially when Aunt Minnie "tried" to sing alto. That alto he could not bear.

The Reds were beginning to grin sheepishly and to turn their heads over their shoulders, as if the open country would not object to their grins. It was becoming a scandal.

Lennie saved the situation. His voice came clear and pure, like a chorister's, rising above the melancholy "trying" of the relations, a clear, pure singing, that seemed to dominate the whole wild bush.

"—Oh sweet and blessed country
That eager hearts expect.

Jesu in mercy bring us
To that dear land of rest;
Who art with God the Father,
And Spirit ever blest."

At the sound of Lennie's voice Tom turned white as a sheet, and looked as if he were going to die too. But the boy's voice soared on, with that pure quality of innocence that was sheer agony to the elder brother.

iv

Jack, who was looking sick again, was sent away to the Greenlows' next day. And he was glad to go, thankful to be out of it. He loathed death, he loathed death, and Wandoo had suddenly become full of death.

The first cool days of the year, golden and blue, were at hand. The Greenlow girls made much of him. He rode with them after sheep, inspecting fences, examining far-off wells. They were not bad girls at all. They taught him to play solitaire at evening, to hold worsted, even to spin. Real companionable girls, thankful to have a young man in the house, spoiling him completely. Pa was home after the first day, and acted as a sort of hairy chimpanzee chaperone, but looking over his spectacles and hissing through his teeth was his severest form of reproof. He didn't set Jack to wash that Sunday, but even gave him tit-bits from the joint, so that our young hero almost knew what it was to have a prospective father-in-law.

Jack left Gum Tree Croft with regret. For he knew his life at Wandoo was over. Now Dad was dead, everything was going to break up. This was bitter to him, for it was the first place he had ever loved, ever wanted to stay in, for ever and ever. He loved the family. He couldn't bear to go away from them.

"Never mind!" he said to himself. "I shall always have them in some way or other, all my life."

Things seemed different when he got back. There wasn't much real difference, except a bit of raking and clearing-up had been done for the funeral. But Wandoo itself seemed to have died. For the meantime, the homestead was as if dead.

Grace and Monica looked unnatural in black frocks. They felt unnatural.

Jack was told that Mr George was having a conclave in the parlour, and that he was to go in.

Tom, Mrs Ellis, and Mr George and Dr Rackett were there, seated round the table, on which were some papers. Jack shook hands, and sat uneasily in an empty chair on Dr Rackett's side of the table. Mr George was explaining things simply.

Mr Ellis had left no will. But the first marriage certificate had been found. Tom was to inherit Wandoo, but not till he came legally of age, in a year and a half's time. Meanwhile Mrs Ellis could continue on the place, and carry on as best she might, on behalf of herself and all the children. For a year and a half.

She heard in silence. After a year and a half she would be homeless: or at least dependent on Tom, who was not her son. She sat silent in her black dress.

Tom cleared his throat and stared at the table. Then he looked up at Jack, and, scarlet in the face, said:

"I've been thinking, Ma, I don't want the place. You have it, for Len. I don't want it. You have it, for Len an' the kids. I'd rather go away.—Best if that certificate hadn't never been found, if you're going to feel you're turned out."

He dropped his head in confusion. Mr George held up his hand.

"No more of that heroic talk," he said. "When Jacob Ellis stored up that marriage certificate at the bottom of that box, he showed what he meant. And you may feel as you say today, but two years hence you might regret it."

Tom looked up angrily.

"I don't believe Tom would ever regret it," put in Mrs Ellis. "But I couldn't think of it. Len wouldn't let me, even if I wanted to."

"Of course not," said Mr George. "We've got to be sensible, and the law's the law. You *can't* alter it yet, my boy, even if you want to. You're not of age yet.

"So you listen to me. My plan is for you and Jack to go out into the colony and get some experience. Sow your wild oats if you've any to sow, or else pick up a bit of *good* oat-seed. One or the other.

"My idea is for you and Jack to go up for a year to Lang's Well-Well station, out Roeburne way. Lang'll give you your keep and a pound a week each, and your fare refunded if you stay your year. The Rob-Roy sails from Geraldton about a month from now;[*] you can get passages on her. And I thought it would be just as well, Tom, if you and Jack rode up through that Midland country.[*] You've a hundred connections to see, who'll change y'r horses for y'. And you'll see the country. And y'll be men of travel. We want men of experience, men of a wide outlook. Somebody's got to be the head-piece of this colony when men like me and the rest of us are gone. It'll be a three hundred mile ride, but ye've nigh on a month to do it.

"Now what do you say, my boy? Your mother will stop on here with the children. I'll see she gets a good man to run the place. And meanwhile she'll be able to fix something up for herself. Oh, we shall settle all right. I'll see your mother through all right. No fear of that. And no fear of any deterioration to the place. I'll watch that. You bet I will—"

Tom twisted his fingers, white at the gills, and mumbled his thanks vaguely.

"Jack," said Mr George. "I know you're game. And you will look after Tom."

Dr Rackett said he thought it a wise plan: and further, that if Mrs Ellis would consent, he would like to bear the expenses of sending Lennie to school in England for the next three years.

Mrs Ellis woke from her dream, to say quickly:

"Although I thank you kindly, Dr Rackett, I think you'll understand if I say No."

Her decision startled everybody.

"Prrrh! Bah!" snorted Mr George. "There's one thing. I doubt if we could make Lennie go. But, with your permission Alice, we'll ask him. Jack, find Lennie for us."

"I'll not say a word," said Mrs Ellis, nervously clutching the edge of the table. "I won't influence him. But if he goes it'll be the death of me. Poor old Lennie! Poor old Lennie!"

"Prrrh! Bah! That's nonsense! Nonsense!" said Mr George angrily. "Give the boy his chance, leave your fool emotions out, d' y' hear, Alice Ellis."

Mrs Ellis sat like a martyr stubborn at the stake. Jack brought the mistrustful Len, who stood like a prisoner at the bar. Mr George put the case as attractively as possible.

Len slowly shook his head, with a grimace of distaste.

"No I *don't* think!" he remarked. "Not fer mine, you bet! I stays alongside my pore ol' Ma, here in Western Austrylia."

Mr George adjusted his eye-glasses severely.

"Your mother is neither poor nor old," he said coldly.

"I never—!" broke out Lennie.

"And this country, thank God, is called Australia, not Austrylia.—When you open your mouth you give proof enough of your need for education. I should like to hear different language in your mouth, my son, and see different ideas working in your head."

Lennie, rather pale and nervous, stared with wide eyes at him.

"You never—" he said. "You never ketch me talkin' like Jack Grant, not if y' skin me alive." And he shifted from one foot to the other.

"I wouldn't take the trouble to skin you, alive or dead, your skin wouldn't be worth it.—But come. You're an intelligent boy. You *need* education. You *need* it. Your nature needs it, child. Your mother ought to see that. Your nature needs you to be educated, well educated. You'll be wasted afterwards—you will. And you'll repent it. Mark me, you'll repent it, when you're older, and your spirit, which should be trained and equipped, is as clumsy and half-baked as any other Cornseed's. You'll be a fretful, uneasy, wasted man, you will. Your mother ought to see that. You'll be a half-baked, quarter-educated bush-whacker, instead of a well-equipped man."

Len looked wonderingly at his mother. But she still sat like an obstinate martyr at the stake, and gave him no sign.

"Don't *he* educate me?" asked Len, pointing to Rackett.

"As much as you'll let him," said Mr George. "But—"

Lennie's face crumpled up with irritation.

"Oh, what for do you *want* me to be educated!" he cried testily. "I don't want to be like Uncle Blagg. I don' wantta be like Dr Rackett even—" He wrinkled his nose in distaste. "'N I don' wantta be like Jack Grant neither. I don' wantta. I don' wantta. I tell y' I don' wantta."

"Do you think they want to be like *you*?" asked Mr George.

Lennie looked from him to Rackett, and then to Jack.

"Jack's not so *very* diff'rent," he said slowly. And he shook his head. "But can't y' b'lieve me," he cried. "I don' wantta go to England.* I don' wantta talk fine an' be like them. Can't ye see I don't? I don' wantta. What's the good! What's the mortal use of it, anyhow? Aren't I right as I am?"

"What *do* you want to do?"

"I wants to work. I wants to milk an' feed, and plough and reap and lay out irrigation, like Dad. An' I wants to look after Ma an' th' kids. An' then I'll git married and be on a place of me own with kids of me own, an' die, like Dad, an' be done for. That's what I wants. It is."

He looked desperately at his mother.

Mr George slowly shook his head, staring at the keen, beautiful, but reluctant boy.

"I suppose that's what we've come to," said Rackett.

"Didn't you learn me!" cried Lennie defiantly. And striking a little attitude, like a naïve, earnest actor he repeated:

"'Here rests, his head upon the lap of earth,
A youth to fortune and to fame unknown.
Fair science frowned not on his humble birth,
And melancholy marked him for her own.

Large was his bounty, and his soul sincere,
Heaven did a recompense as largely send.
He gave to misery all he had, a tear,
He gained from heaven, 'twas all he wished, a friend.'*

There!" he continued. "That's me! An' I've got a friend already."

"You're a little fool!" said Mr George. "Much mark of melancholy there is on you! And do you think Misery is going to thank you for your idiotic tear? As for your friend, he's going away. And you're a fool, putting up a headstone to yourself while you're alive still. Damn you, you little fool, and be damned to you."

Mr George was really cross. He flounced his spectacles off his nose. Len was frightened. Then he said, rather waveringly, turning to his mother:

"We're all right, Ma, ain't we?"

Mrs Ellis looked at him with her subtlest, tenderest smile. And in Lennie's eyes burned a light of youthful indignation against these old men.

Chapter XIII.

Tom and Jack Ride Together.

These days Monica was fascinating in Jack's eyes. She wore a black dress, and her slimness, her impulsive girlishness under this cloud were wistful, exquisite. He would have liked to love her, soothingly, protectively, passionately. He would have liked to cherish her, with passion. Always he looked to her for a glance of intimacy, looked to see if she wouldn't accept his passion and his cherishing. He wanted to touch her, to kiss her, to feel the eternal lightning of her slim body through the cloud of that black dress. He wanted to declare to her that he loved her, as Alec Rice had declared to Grace; and he wanted to ask her to marry him. To ask her to marry him at once.

But mostly he wanted to touch her and hold her in his arms. He watched her all the time, hoping to get one of the old, long looks from her yellow eyes, from under her bended brows. Her long, deep, enigmatic looks, that used to worry him so. Now he longed for her to look at him like that.

Or better still, if she would let him see her trouble and her grief, and love her so, with a passionate cherishing.

But she would do neither. She kept her grief and her provocation both out of sight, as if neither existed. Her little face remained mute and closed, like a shut-up bud. She only spoke to him with a vague distant voice, and she never really looked at him. Or if she did glance at him, it was in a kind of anger, and pain, as if she did not want to be interfered with; didn't want to be pulled down.

He was completely puzzled. Her present state was quite incomprehensible to him. She had nothing to reproach him with, surely. And if she had loved him, even a little, she could surely love him that little still. If she had so often taken his hand and clutched it, surely she could now let him take *her* hand, in real sympathy.

It was as if she were angry with *him* because Dad had died. Jack hadn't wanted Dad to die. Indeed no. He was cut up by it as if he had been one of the family. And it was as bad a blow to *his* destiny as to hers. He was as sore and sorry as anybody. Yet she kept her face shut against him, and avoided him, as if *he* were to blame.

Completely puzzled, Jack went on with his preparations for departure. He had no choice. He was under orders from Mr George, and with Mrs Ellis' approval, to quit Wandoo, to ride with Tom up to Geraldton, and to spend at least a year on the sheep station up north. It had to be. It was the wheel of fate. So let it be.

And as the last day drew near, the strange volcano of anger which slumbered at the bottom of his soul—a queer, quiescent crater of anger which churned its deep hot lava invisible—threw up jets of silent rage, which hardened rapidly into a black, rocky indifference. And this was characteristic of him: an indifference which was really congealed anger, and which gave him a kind of innocent, remote, childlike quietness.

This was his nature. He was himself vaguely aware of the unplumbed crater of silent anger which lay at the bottom of his soul. It was not anger against any particular thing, or because of anything in particular. It was just generic, inherent in him. It was himself. It did not make him hate people, individually, unless they were hateful. It did not make him hard or cruel. Indeed he was too yielding rather than otherwise, too gentle and mindful of the horses and cattle, for example, unmindful of himself. Tom often laughed at him for it. If Lucy had a will of her own, and a caprice she wanted to execute, he always let her go ahead, take her way, as far as was reasonable. If she exceeded her limits his anger roused and there was no doing any more with him. But he very rarely, very rarely got really angry. Only then in the long, slow accumulation of hostility, as with Easu.

But anger! A deep, fathomless well-head of slowly-moving, invisible fire. Somewhere in his consciousness he was aware of it. And in this awareness it was as if he belonged to a race apart. He never felt identified with the great humanity. He belonged to a race apart, like the race of Cain. This he had always known.

Sometimes he met eyes which were the eyes of his own outcast race. As a tiny boy it had been so. Fairs had always fascinated him, because at the fairs in England he met the eyes of gipsies who, in a glance, understood him. His own people *could* not understand. But in the black eyes of a young gipsy-woman he had seen the answer, even as a boy of ten. And he had thought: I ought to go away with her, run away with her.

It was the anger, the deep, burning *life-anger* which was the kinship. Not a deathly, pale, nervous anger. But an anger of the old blood. And it was this which had attracted him to grooms, horsey surroundings, and to pugilists. In them was some of this same deep, generous anger of the blood. And now in Australia too, he saw it like a secret away at the bottom of the black, full, strangely shining eyes of the aborigines. There it lay, the secret, like an eternal, brilliant snake. And it established at once a kind of free-masonry between him and the blacks. They were curiously *aware* of him, when he came: aware of his coming, aware of his going. As if in him were the same Great Serpent[*] of their anger. And they were downcast now he was going away, as if their strength were being taken from them. Old Tim, who had taken a great fancy to Jack, relapsed into a sort of glumness as if he too, now, were preparing to die.

Since Jack had come back from the Greenlows' farm, Monica had withdrawn to a distance, a kind of luminous distance, and put a chasm between herself and Jack. She moved mute and remote on the shining side of the chasm. He stood on the dark side, looking across the blackness of the gulf at her as if she were some kind of star. Surely the gulf would close up. Surely they would both be on natural ground again.

But no! Always that incomprehensible little face with fringed lashes, and mouth that opened with a little smile, a vulnerable little smile, as if asking them all to be kind to her, to be pitiful towards her, and not try to touch her.

"Well goodbye Monica, for the present," he said, as he sat in the saddle in the yard, and Tom started away riding towards the gate, leading the bulky-looking pack-horse.

"Goodbye! Come back!" said Monica, looking up with a queer, hard little question come into her eyes, but her face remote as ever.

Jack kicked his horse and started.

"I'll come back," he said over his shoulder. But he didn't look round at her. His heart had gone hard and hot in his breast. He was glad to be going.

Lennie had opened the gate. He stood there as Jack rode through.

"Why can't *I* never come?" he cried.

Jack laughed and rode on, after the faithful Tom. He was glad to go. He was glad to leave Wandoo. He was glad to say no more goodbyes, and to feel no more pain. He was glad to be gone, since he was going, from the unlucky place. He was glad to be gone from its doom. There was a doom over it, a doom. And he was glad to be gone.

The morning was still orange and green. Winter had set in at last, the rains had begun to be heavy. They might have trouble with drenchings and boggings, but that, Tom said, was better than drought and sunstrokes. And anyhow the weather this morning was perfect.

The dark forest of karri that ran to the left of Wandoo, away on the distant horizon, cut a dark pattern on the egg-green sky. Goodbye! Goodbye to it! The sown fields they were riding through glittered with tender blades of wheat. Goodbye! Goodbye! Somebody else would reap it. The bush was now full of sparks of the beautiful, uncanny flowers of Western Australia, and bright birds started and flew. Sombre the bush was in itself, but out of the heavy dullness came sharp, scarlet, flame-spark flowers, and flowers as lambent gold as sunset, and wan white flowers, and flowers of a strange, darkish rich blue, like the vault of heaven just after sundown. The scent of rain, of eucalyptus, and of the strange brown-green shrubs of the bush!

They rode in silence, Tom ahead with the pack-horse, and they did not draw near, but rode apart. They were travelling due west from York, along a bush track towards Paddy's Crossing.[*] And as they went, they drew nearer and nearer to the dark, low fringe of hills behind which, for the last twelve months, Jack had seen the sun setting with its great golden glow. Trees grew along the ridge of the hills, scroll-like and mysterious. They had always seemed to Jack like the bar of heaven.

By noon the riders reached the ridge, and the bar of heaven was the huge karri trees which went up aloft so magnificently. But the karri forest ended here with a jerk.[*] Beyond, the earth ran away down long, long slopes covered with scrub, down the greyness and undulation of Australia, towards the great dimness where was the coast. The sun was hot at noon. Jack was glad when Tom called a halt under the last trees, facing the great, soft, open swaying of the land seaward, and they began to make tea.

They had hardly sat down to drink their tea, when they heard a buggy approaching. It was the mysterious Dr Rackett, driven by the grinning Sam. Rackett said nothing, just greeted the youths, pulled his tin mug and tucker from under the buggy seat, and joined in, chatting casually as if it had all been pre-arranged.

Tom was none too pleased, but he showed nothing. And when the tea was finished, he made good by handing over the beast of a pack-horse to Sam. Poor Sam sat in the back of the vehicle lugging the animal along, jerking its reluctant neck. Rackett drove in lonely state on the driving-seat. Tom and Jack trotted quickly ahead, on the down-slope, and were soon out of sight. They were thankful to ride free.

Over the ridge, they felt Wandoo was left behind, and they were in the open world again, away from care. Whenever man drives his tent-pegs deep, to stay, he drives them into underlying waters of sorrow.* Best ride tent-less. So thought the boys.

They were going to a place called Paddy's Crossing, a settlement new to Jack, but well known to Tom as the place-where-men-went-when-they-wanted-a-private-jamboree. What a jamboree was, Jack, being a gentleman, that is, not a lady, would learn in due course.

As the ground came to a rolling hollow, Tom set off at a good pace, and away they went, galloping beautifully along the soft earth trail, galloping, galloping, putting the miles between them and Wandoo and women and care. They both rode in a kind of passion for riding, for hurling themselves ahead down the new road. To be men out alone in the world, away from the women and the dead stone of trouble.

They reached the river hours before Rackett's turn-out. Fording, they rode into the mushroom settlement, a string of slab cabins with shingle roofs and calico window-panes—or else shuttered-up windows. The stoves were outside the chimneyless cabins, under brush shelters. One such "kitchen," a fore-runner, had already a roof of flattened-out, rusty tin cans.

But it was a cosy, canny nook, homely, nestling down in a golden corner of the earth, the mimosa in bloom by the river. And it was beautifully ephemeral. As transient, as casual as the bushes themselves.

Jack for the moment had a dread of solid houses of brick and stone and permanence. There was always horror somewhere inside them.

He wanted the empty, timeless Australia, with nooks like this, of flimsy wooden cabins by a river with wattle bush.

There was one older, whitewashed cabin with vine trellises.

"That's Paddy's," said Tom. "He grows grapes, and makes wine* out of the little black ones. But the muscats is best. I'm not keen on wine anyhow. Something a drop more warming."

Jack was amazed at the good Tom. He had never known him to drink.

"There's nobody about," said Jack, as they rode up the incline between the straggling cabins.

"All asleep," said Tom.

It was not so, however, because as they crested the slope and looked into the little hollow beyond, they saw a central wooden building, hall or mission or church, and people crowding like flies.

But Tom turned up to Paddy's white inn, up the side slope. He was remorseful about having galloped the horses at the beginning of such a long trip. The inn seemed deserted. Tom Coo-eed!* but there was no answer.

"All shut up!" he said. "What's that paper on the door?"

Jack got down, and walked stiffly to the door, for the ride had been long and hard and downhill, and his knees were hurting.—"Gone to the wedin be ome soon P. O. T" he read. "What is P. O. T.?"* he asked.

"What I stand in need of," said the amazing Tom.

They were just turning their horses towards the stable when, with a racket and a clatter, an urchin drove round from the yard in a pitch-black wicker chaise, a bone-white, careworn horse slopping between the shafts.

"You two blokes," yelled the urchin, " 'd better get ontta th' trail for th' church, elst Father Prendy'll be on y' tail, I tell y'."

"What's up?" shouted Tom.

"I'm jist off fer th' bride. Ol' Nick 'ere 'eld me up runnin' away from me in th' paddock."

Tom grinned, the outfit swept past. Our heroes took their horses to the stable and settled them down conscientiously. Then they set off, glad to be on foot, down to the church.

The crowd was buzzing. It was half past three. Father Prendy, the old mission priest, who looked like a dusty old piece of furniture from a loft, was peering up the road. The black wicker buggy still made no appearance, with the bride.

"Two o'clock's the legal limit for marriages," said Father Prendy. "But praise God, we've half an hour yet."

And he showed his huge watch, which said half-past-one, since he had slipped away for a moment to put back the fingers.

The slab building—hall, school, and church—was now a church, though the oleographs of the Queen and the Prince Consort in Robes still glowed on the walls, and a black-board stood with its face to the wall, and one of those wire things with coloured beads* poked out from behind, and the globe of the world could not be hidden entirely by the eucalyptus boughs.

But it was a church. A table with a white cloth and a crucifix was the altar. Crimson-flowering gum-blossom embowered the walls, the blackboard, the windows, but left the Queen and Prince Consort in full isolation. Forms were ranked on the mud floor, and these forms were densely packed with settlers dressed in all kinds of clothes. It was not only a church, it was a wedding. Just inside the door, like a figure at Madame Tussaud's, sat an elderly figure in greenish evening suit with white waist-coat, and copper-toed boots, waiting, apparently, for the Last Trump.* On the other side was a brown-whiskered man in frock-coat, a grey bell-topper in his hand, leaning balanced on a stick. He was shod in white socks and carpet slippers. Later on this gentleman explained to Jack: "I suffer from corns, and shouldn't be happy in boots."

There was a great murmuring and staring and shuffling and shifting as Jack and Tom came up, as though one of them was the bride in disguise. The wooden church buzzed like a cocoanut shell. A red-faced man seized Tom's arm as if Tom were a long-lost brother, and Jack was being introduced, shaking the damp, hot, trembling hand of the red-faced man, who was called Paddy.

"It's fair come over me, so ut has!—praise be to the saints, an' may the devil run away wi' them two young turmagants!—Father Prendy making them come to this pass all at onst! For mark my words, in his own mind he's thinkin' the wrong they've done, neither of them speakin' to confess, till he was driven to remark on the girl's unnatural figure. And not a soul in the world, mark you, has seen 'em speak a word to one another for the last year in or out. But she says it's he, an' Denny Mackinnon, he payin', I'll be bound, that black priest of a Father Prendy to come over me an' make me render up my poor innocent Pat to the hussy, in holy matrimony, may the saints fly away with 'em."

He wiped away his sweat, speechless. And Denny Mackinnon, the hussy's father—it could be no other than he—in moth-eaten scarlet coat and overall trousers, and top-boots slashed for his bunions, and forage-cap slashed for his increased head, stood bulging on the other side the door, compressed in his youthful uniform, and scarlet in the face with the compression. He was a stout man with a black beard and a fixed, fierce, solemn expression. Creator of this agitated occasion, he was almost bursting with wrathful agitation as that hussy of a daughter of his still failed to appear. By his side stood an ancient man with a long grey beard, anciently clad.

Patrick, the bridegroom to be, lurked near his father. He was a thin, pale, freckled, small-faced youth with broad brittle shoulders and brittle limbs, who would no doubt, in time, fill out into a burly fellow. As it was, he was agitated and unlovely in a new ready-made suit and a black bomb of a hard hat that wouldn't stay on, and new boots that stank to heaven of improperly-dressed kangaroo hide: one of the filthiest of stinks.

Poor Paddy, the father of this bridegroom, was a tall, thin, well-set-up man with trembling hands and a face like beetroot, garbed in a blue coat with brass buttons, mole trousers,* leggings, and a sideways-leaning top hat. His tie was a flowing red with white spots. His eyes were light blue and wickedly twinkling behind their slight wateriness.

"What's that ye're sayin' about me?" said Father Prendy, coming up rubbing his hands, bowing to the strangers, beaming with a cheerfulness that could outlast any delay under the sun.

" 'Twas black I was callin' ye, Father Prendy," said Paddy. "For the fine pair o' black eyes ye carry, why not? Isn't it a good drink ye'll be havin' on me afore the day is out, eh? Isn't it a pretty penny ye're costin' me, with your marryin' an' givin' in marriage? An' why isn't it Denny what pays the wedding-breakfast, eh?"

"Hold your peace, Paddy my dear. I see a wagon comin', don't I?"

Sure enough, the black wicker buggy rattling down hill, the white horse seeming to swim, the urchin standing up, feet wide apart, elbows high up, bending forward and urging the bone-white steed with curses unnameable.

"What now! What now!" murmured the priest, feeling in his pocket for his stole. "What now!"

"Wheer's Dad?" yelled the urchin, pulling the bone-white steed on to its bony haunches, in front of the church.

Dad had gone round the corner. But he came bustling and puffing and bursting in his skin-tight scarlet coat, that almost cut his arms off, his own ancient father, with a long grey beard, pushing him irritably, propelling him towards the slippery boy. As if this family, generation by generation, got more and more behind-hand in its engagements.

"Gawd's sakes!" blowed the scarlet Dad, as the old grey Granddad shoved him.

"Hold y' breath, Dad, 'n come 'ome!" said the urchin, subsiding comfortably on to the seat and speaking as if he enjoyed utmost privacy. "Sis can't get away. She's had a baby. An' Ma says I was to tell Mr O'Burk as it's a foine* boy, an' would Father Prendy step up, an' Pat O'Burk can come 'n see with his own eyes."

Chapter XIV.

Jamboree.

"Let's get along," said Jack uncomfortably in Tom's ear.

"Get! Not for mine! We're in luck's way, if ever we were."

"There's no fun, under the circumstances."

"Oh Lord my, ain't there! What's wrong? They're all packing into the buggy. Father Prendy's putting his watch back a few more minutes. He'll have 'em married before you can betcher life. It's a wedding this is, boy!"

The people now came crowding, nudging, whispering, giggling, stumbling out of the church. The gentleman in the carpet slippers rakishly adjusted his grey bell-topper over his left brow, and came swaggering forward.

"Major Brownlee—Mr Jack Grant," Tom introduced them.

"Retired and happy in the country," the major explained, and he continued garrulously to explain, his circumstances, his history and his family history. This continued all the way to the inn: a good half-hour, for the major walked insecurely on his tender feet.

When they arrived at Paddy's white, trellised house, all was festivity. Paddy had thrown open the doors, disclosing the banquet spread in the bar parlour. Large joints of baked meat, ham, tongue, fowls, cakes, and bottles and bunches of grapes and piles of apples: these Jack saw in splendid confusion.

"Come along in! Come along in!" cried Paddy, as the major and his young companions hesitated under the vine-trellis. "I guess ye're the last. Come along in—all welcome!—an' wet the baby's eye.* Sure she's a clever girl to get a man an' a baby the same fine afternoon. A fine child, let me tell you. Father Prendy named him for me, Paddy O'Burk Tracy, on the spot, the minute the wedding was tied up. So ye can please yerselves whether it's a christening ye're coming to, or a wedding. I offer ye the choice. Come in."

"P.O.T," thought Jack. He still did not feel at ease. Perhaps Paddy noticed it. He came over and slapped him on the back.

"It's yourself has brought good luck to the house, sir. Sit ye down an' help y'self. Sit ye down an' make y'self at home."

Jack sat down, along with the rest of the heterogeneous company. Paddy went round pouring red wine into the glasses.

"Gentlemen!" he announced from the head of the table. "We are all here, for the table's full up. The first toast is: *The Stranger within our gates!*"

Everybody drank but Jack. He was uncomfortably uncertain whether the baby was meant, or himself.[*] At the last minute, he hastily drank, to transfer the honour to the baby.

Then came "The Bride!": then "The Groom!": then "The Priest, Father Prendy, that black limb o' salvation!"[*] Dozens of toasts, it didn't seem to matter to whom. And everybody drank and laughed and made clumsy jokes. There were no women present: at least, no women seated. Only the women who went round the table, waiting.

One! Two! Three! Four! Five! Six! Seven!—Westminster chimes[*] from the grandfather's clock behind Jack. Seven o'clock! He had not even noticed them bring in the lamps. Father Prendy was on his feet blessing the bride: "at the moment absent on the high mission of motherhood." He then blessed the bridegroom, at the moment asleep with his head on the table.

The table had been cleared, save for bottles, fruit, and terrible cigars. The air was dense with smoke, bitter in the eyes, thick in the head. Everything seemed to be turning thick and swimmy, and the people seemed to move like living oysters in a natural, live liquor. A girl was sitting on Jack's chair, putting her arm surreptitiously round his waist, sipping out of his glass. But he pushed her a little aside, because he wanted to watch four men who had started playing euchre.

"There's a bright moon, gentlemen. Let's go out and have a bit o' sparrin'," said Paddy swimmingly from the head of the table.

That pleased Jack a lot. He was beginning to feel shut in. He rose, and the girl—he had never really looked at her—followed him out. Why did she follow him? She ought to stay and clear away dishes.

The yard, it seemed to Jack, was clear as daylight: or clearer, with a big, flat white moon. Someone was sizing up to a little square man with long thick arms, and the little man was probing them off expertly. Hello! here was a master, in his way.

The girl was leaning up against Jack, with her hand on his shoulder. This was a bore, but he supposed it was also a kind of tribute. He had still never looked at her.

"That's Jake," she said. "He's champion of these parts. Oh my, if he sees me leanin' on y' arm like this, he'll be after ye!"

"Well, don't lean on me then," said Jack complacently.

"Go on, he won't see me. We're in the dark right here."

"I don't care if he sees you," said Jack.

"You *do* contradict yourself," said the girl.

"Oh no I don't!" said Jack.

And he watched the long-armed man, and never once looked at the girl. So she leaned heavier on him. He disapproved, really, but felt rather manly under the burden.

The little, square long-armed man was oldish, with a grey beard. Jack saw this as he danced round, like a queer old satyr, half gorilla, half satyr, roaring, booing, fencing with a big yahoo of a young bushman, holding him off with his unnatural long arms. Over went the big young fellow sprawling on the ground, causing such a splother* that everyone shifted a bit out of his way. They all roared delightedly.

The long-armed man, looking round for his girl, saw her in the shadow leaning heavily and languishingly on Jack's young shoulder. Up he sprang, snarling like a gorilla, his long hairy arms in front of him. The girl retreated, and Jack, in a state of semi-intoxicated readiness, opened his arms and locked them round the little gorilla of a man. Locked together, they rolled and twirled round the yard under the moon, scattering the delighted onlookers like a wild cow: Jack was laughing to himself, because he had got the grip of the powerful long-armed old man. And there was no real anger in the tussle. The gorilla was an old sport.

Jack was sitting in a chair under the vine, with his head in his hands and his elbows on his knees, getting his wind. Paddy was fanning him with a branch of gum-leaves, and congratulating him heartily.

"First chap as ever laid out Long-armed Jake."

"What'd he jump on me for?" said Jack. "I said nothing to him."

"What y' sayin'!" ejaculated Paddy coaxingly. "Didn't ye take his girl, now?"

"His girl! I? No! She leaned on *me*, I didn't take her."

"Arrah! Look at that now! The brazenness of it! Well, be it on ye! Take another drink. Will ye come an' show the boys some o' ye tricks, belike?"

Jack was in the yard again, shaking hands with Long-armed Jake.

"Good on y'!* Good on y'!" cried old Jake. "Ye're a cock bird in fine feather! What's a wench between two gentlemen! Shake, my lad, shake! I'm Long-armed Jake, I am, an' I set a cock bird before any whure* of a hen."

They rounded up, sparred, staved off, showed off like two amiable fighting-cocks, before the admiring cockeys. Then they had good-natured turns with the young farmers, and mild wrestling bouts with the old veterans. Having another drink, playing, gassing, swaggering— — —

Tom came bawling as if he were deaf:

"What about them 'osses!"

"What about 'em!" said Jack.

"See to 'm!" said Tom. And he went back to where he came from.

"All right, Mister, we'll see to 'm!" yelled the admiring youngsters. "We'll water 'm an' feed 'm."

"Water?" said Jack.

"Yes.—Show us how to double up, Mister, will y'?"

"A' right!" said Jack, who was considerably tipsy. "When—when I've—fed—th'osses."

He set off to the stables. The admiring youngsters ran yelling ahead. They brought out the horses and led them down to the trough. Jack followed, feeling the moonlit earth sway a little.

He shoved his head in between the noses of the horses, into the cool trough of water. When he lifted it and wrung out the shower from his hair, which curled when it was wet, he saw the girl standing near him.

"Y' need a towel, Mister," she said.

"I could do with one," said he.

"Come an' I'll get ye one," she said.

He followed meekly. She led him to an outside room, somewhere near the stable. He stood in the doorway.

"Here y' are!" she said, from the darkness inside.

"Bring it me," he said from the moon outside.

"Come in an' I'll dry your hair for yer."—Her voice sounded like the voice of a wild creature in a black cave. He ventured unseeing, uncertain, into the den, half reluctant. But there was a certain coaxing imperiousness in her wild-animal's voice, out of that black darkness.

He walked straight into her arms. He started and stiffened as if attacked. But her full, soft body was moulded against him. Still he drew fiercely back. Then feeling her yield to draw away and leave him, the old flame flew over him, and he drew her close again.

"Dearie!" she murmured. "Dearie!" and her hand went stroking the back of his wet head.

"Come!" she said. "And let me dry your hair."

She led him and sat him on a pallet bed. Then she closed the door, through which the moonlight was streaming. The room had no window. It was pitch dark, and he was trapped. So he felt as he sat there on the hard pallet. But she came instantly and sat by him and began softly, caressingly to rub his hair with a towel. Softly, slowly, caressingly she rubbed his hair with the towel. And in spite of himself, his arms, alive with a power of their own, went out and clasped her, drew her to him.

"I'm supposed to be in love with a girl," he said, really not speaking to her.

"Are you, dearie?" she said softly. And she left off rubbing his hair and softly put her mouth to his.

Later—he had no idea what time of night it was—he went round looking for Tom. The place was mostly dark. The inn was half* dark. Nobody seemed alive.—But there was music somewhere. There was music.

As he went looking for it, he came face to face with Dr Rackett.

"Where's Tom?" he asked.

"Best look in the barn."

The dim-lighted barn was a cloud of half-illuminated dust, in which figures moved.* But the music was still martial and British. Jack, always tipsy, for he had drunk a good deal and it took effect slowly, deeply, felt something in him stir to this music. They were dancing a jig or a horn-pipe. The air was all old and dusty in the barn. There were four crosses of wooden swords on the floor. Young Patrick, in his shirt and trousers, had already left off dancing for Ireland, but the Scotchman, in a red flannel shirt and a reddish kilt, was still lustily springing and knocking his heels in a haze of dust. The Welshman was a little poor fellow in old shirt and trousers. But the Englishman, in costermonger outfit, black bell-bottom trousers and lots of pearl buttons,* was going well. He was thin and wiry and very neat about the feet. Then he left off dancing, and stood to watch the last two.

Everybody was drunk, everybody was arguing, according to his nationality, as to who danced best. The Englishman in the bell-bottom trousers *knew* he danced best, but spent his last efforts deciding between Sandy and Taffy. The music jigged on. But whether it was *British Grenadiers* or *Campbells Are Comin'** Jack didn't know. Only he suddenly felt intensely patriotic.

"I am an Englishman," he thought, with savage pride. "I am an Englishman. That is the best on earth. Australia is English, English, English, she'd collapse like a balloon but for the English in her. British means English first. I'm a Britisher, but I'm an Englishman. God! God! I'm an Englishman. It means the best on earth. The best on earth. What are women to me, when I'm an Englishman! God! I could crumple the universe in my fist, I could. I'm an Englishman, and I could crush everything in my hand. And the women are left behind. I'm an Englishman."

Voices had begun to snarl and roar, fists were lifted.

"Mussen quarrel!—my weddin'! Mussen quarrel!" Pat was drunkenly saying, sitting on a box shaking his head.

Then suddenly he sprang to his feet, and quick and sharp as a stag, rushed to the wooden swords and stood with arms uplifted, smartly showing the steps. The fellow had spirit, a queer, staccato spirit.

Somebody laughed, and cheered, and then they all began to laugh and cheer, and Pat pranced faster, in a cloud of dust, and the quarrel was forgotten.

Jack went to look for Tom. "I'm an Englishman," he thought. "I'd better look after him."

He wasn't in the barn. Jack looked and looked.

He found Tom in the kitchen, sitting in a corner, a glass at his side, quite drunk.

"It's time to go to bed Tom."

"G' on, ol' duck. I'm waitin' for me girl."

"You won't get any girl tonight. Let's go to bed."

"Shan't I get—? Yes shall! Yes shall!"

"Where shall I find a bed?"

"Plenty 'r flore space—"*

And he staggered to his feet as a short, stout, red-faced, black-eyed, untidy girl slipped across the kitchen and out of the door, casting a black-eyed, meaningful look at the red-faced Tom, over her shoulder as she disappeared. Tom swayed to his feet and sloped after her with amazing quickness. Jack stood staring out of the open door, dazed. They both seemed to have melted.

Himself, he wanted to sleep—only to sleep. "Plenty of floor-space," Tom had said. He looked at the floor. Cockroaches running by the dozen, in all directions; those brown, barge-like cockroaches of the south, that trail their huge bellies and sheer off in automatic straight lines and make a faint creaking noise, if you listen. Jack looked at the table: an old man already lay on it. He opened a cupboard: babies sleeping there.

He swayed, drunk with sleep and alcohol, out of the kitchen in some direction: pushed a swing door: the powerful smell of beer and sawdust made him know it was the bar. He could sleep on the seat. He could sleep in peace.

He lurched forward, and touched cloth. Something snored, started, and reared up.

"What y' at?"

Jack stood back breathless—the figure subsided—he could beat a retreat.

Hopeless, he looked in on the remains of the beanfeast. Table and every bench occupied. He boldly opened another door. A small lamp burning, and what looked like dozens of dishevelled elderly women's awful figures heaped cross-wise on the hugest double bed he had ever seen.

He escaped into the open air. The moon was low. Someone was singing.

Chapter XV.

Uncle John Grant.

It was day. The lie was hard. He didn't want to wake. He turned over and was sleeping again, though the lie was very hard.

Someone pushing him. Tom, with a red blank face, saying:

"Wake up! Let's go b'fore Rackett starts."

And the rough hands pushing him crudely. He hated it.

He sat up. He had been lying on the bottom of the buggy, with a sack over him. No idea how he got there. It was full day.

"Old woman's got some tea made. If y' want t' change y' bags, hop over 'n take a dip in the pool. Down th' paddock. Here's th' bag. I've left soap 'n comb on th' splash-board, an' I've seen to th'osses. I'm goin' f'r a drink while you get ready."

Tom had got a false dawn on him. He had wakened with that false energy which sometimes follows a "drunk," and which fades all too quickly. For he had hardly slept at all.

So when Jack was ready, Tom was not. His stupor was overcoming him. He was cross—and half-way through his second pewter mug of beer.

"I'm not coming," said Tom.

"You *are*," said Jack. For the first time he felt that old call in the blood which made him master of Tom. Somewhere, in the night, the old spirit of a master had aroused in him.

Tom finished his mug of beer slowly, sullenly. He put down the empty pot.

"Get up!" said Jack. And Tom got slowly to his feet.

They set off, Jack leading the pack-horse. But the beer and the "night before" had got Tom down. He rode like a sack in the saddle, sometimes semi-conscious, sometimes really asleep. Jack followed just behind, with the beast of a pack-horse dragging his arm out. And Tom ahead, like a sot, with no life in him.

Jack himself felt hot inside, and dreary, and riding was a cruel effort, and the pack-horse, dragging his arm from its socket, was hell. He wished he had enough saddle-tree to turn the rope round: but he was in his English saddle.

Nevertheless, he had decided something, in that jamboree. He belonged to the blood of masters, not of servants. He belonged to the class of those that are sought, not those that seek. He was no seeker. He was not desirous. He would never be desirous. Desire should not lead him humbly by the nose. Not desire for anything. He was of the few who are masters. He was to be desired. He was master. He was real Englishman.

So he jogged along, in the hot, muggy day of early winter. Heavy clouds hung over the sky, lightning flashed beyond the purple hills. His body was a burden and a weariness to him, riding was a burden and a weariness, the pack-horse was hell. And Tom, asleep on his nag, like a dead thing, was hateful to have ahead. The road seemed endless.

Yet he had in him his new, half-savage pride to keep him up, and an isolate sort of resoluteness.

At mid-day they got down, drank water, camped, and slept without eating. Thank God the rain hadn't come. Jack slept like the dead till four o'clock.

He woke sharp, wondering where he was. The clouds looked threatening. He got up. Yes, the horses were there. He still felt bruised, and hot and dry inside, from the jamboree. Why in heaven did men want jamborees?

He made a fire, boiled the billy, prepared tea, and set out some food, though he didn't want any.

"Get up there!" he shouted to Tom, who lay like a beast.

"Get up!" he shouted. But the beast slept.

"Get up, you beast!" he said, viciously kicking him. And he was horrified because Tom got up, without any show of retaliation at all, and obediently drank his tea.

They ate a little food, in silence. Saddled in silence, each finding the thought of speech repulsive. Watched one another to see if they were ready. Mounted, and rode in repulsive silence away.—But Jack had left the pack-horse to Tom this time.—And it began to rain softly, seepily.

And Tom was cheering up. The rain seemed to revive him wonderfully. He was one who was soon bowled over by a drink. Consequently he didn't absorb much, and so he recovered sooner. Jack absorbed more, and it acted much more slowly, deeply, and lastingly on him. On they went, in the rain.

Tom began to show signs of new life. He swore at the pack-horse. He kicked his nag to a little trot, and the packs flap-flapped like shut wings, on the rear pony. Presently he reined up, and sat quite still for a minute. Then he broke into a laugh, lifting his face to the rain.

"Seems to me we're off the road," he said. "We haven't passed a fence all day, have we?"

"No," said Jack. "But you were asleep all morning."

"We're off the road. Listen!"

The rain was seeping down on the grey bush, in the grey evening, the warm horses smelt of their own steam. Jack could hear nothing except the wind and the increasing rain.

"This track must lead somewhere. Let's get to shelter for the night," said Jack.

"Agreed!" replied Tom magnanimously. "We'll follow on, and see what we shall see."

They walked slowly, pulling at the pack-horse, which was dragging at the rope, tired with the burden that grew every minute heavier with the rain.

Tom reined in suddenly.

"There *is* somebody behind," he said. "It's *not* the wind."

They sat there on their horses in the rain, and waited. Twilight was falling. Then Jack could distinguish the sound of a cart behind. It was Rackett in the old shay rolling along in the lonely dusk and rain, through the trees, approaching. Black Sam grinned mightily as he pulled up.

"Thought I'd follow, though you *are* on the wrong road," said Rackett from beneath his black waterproof. "Sam showed me the turning two miles back. You missed it.—Anyhow we'd better camp in on these people ahead here."

"Is there a place ahead?" asked Jack.

"Yes," replied Rackett. "Even a sort of relation of yours, that I promised Gran I would come and see. Hence my following on your heels."

"Didn't know I'd any relation hereabouts," said Tom sulkily. He couldn't bear Rackett's interfering in the family in any way.

"You haven't. I meant Jack.—But we'll get along, shall we?"

"We're a big flood," remarked Tom. "But if they'll give us the barn, we'll manage. It's getting wet to sleep out."

They pressed ahead, the pack-horse trotting, but lifting up his head like a venomous snake, in unwillingness. They had come into the open fields. At last, in the falling dark they saw a house and buildings. A man hove in sight, but lurked away from them. Rackett hailed him. The man seemed to oppose their coming further. He was a hairy, queer figure, with his untrimmed beard.

"Master never takes no strangers," he said.

Rackett slipped a shilling in his hand, and would he ask his master if they might camp in the barn out of the rain.

"Y' ain't the police, now, by any manner of means?" asked the man.

"God love you, no," said Rackett.

"We're no police," said Tom. "I'm Tom Ellis, from Wandoo, over York way."

"Ellis! I've heered th' name.—Well, master's sick, an' skeered to death o' th' police. They're ready to drop in on the place, that they are, rot 'em, the minute he breathes his last.* And he's skeered he's dyin' this time. Oh he's skeered o't. So I have me doubts of all strangers. I have me doubts, no matter what they be. Master he've sent a letter to his only relation upon earth, to his nephew, which thank the Lord he's writ for to come an' lay hold on the place, against he dies. If there's no one to lay hold, the police steps in, without a word. That's how they do it. They lets the places in grants like—lets a man have a grant—and when the poor man dies, his place is locked up by the govenment. They takes it all."

"Gawd's sakes!" murmured Tom aside. "The man's potty!"

"Bush mad!"* supplemented Rackett, who was sitting in the buggy with his chin in his hand, intently listening to the queer, furtive, garrulous individual.

"Say, friend," he added aloud. "Go and ask your master if we harmless strangers can camp in the barn out of the wet."

"What might your names be, Mister?" asked the man.

"Mine's Doctor Rackett. This is Tom Ellis. And this is Jack Grant. And no harm in any of us."

"D' y' say Jack Grant? Would that be Mr John Grant?" asked the man, galvanised by sudden excitement.

"None other," said Rackett.

"Then he's come!" cried the man.

"He certainly has," replied Rackett.

"Oh Glory-Glory! Why didn't ye say so afore? Come in, come in all of ye, come in! Come in, Mr Grant! Come in!"

They got down, gave the reins to Sam, and were ready to follow the bearded man, looking one another in the face in amazement, and shaking their heads.

"Gawd Almighty, I'd rather keep out o' this!" murmured Tom, standing by his horse and keeping the rope of the pack-horse.

"Case of mistaken identity," said Rackett coolly. "Hang on, boys. We'll get a night's shelter."

A woman came out of the delapidated, low stone house, clutching her hands in distress and agitation.

"Missus! Missus! Here he is at last, God be praised!" cried the bearded man. She ran up in sudden effusion of welcome, but he ordered her into the house to brighten up the fire, while he waved the way to the stables, knowing that horse comes before man, in the bush.

When they had shaken down in the stable, they left Sam to sleep there, while the three went across to the house. Tom was most unwilling.

The man was at the door, to usher them in.

"I've broke the news to him, sir!" he said in a mysterious voice to Jack, as he showed them into the parlour.

"What's your master's name?" asked Rackett.

"Don't y' know y're at your destination?" whispered the man. "This is Mr John Grant's. This is the place y're lookin' for."

A melancholy room! The calico ceiling drooped, the window and front door were hermetically sealed, an ornate glass lamp shone in murky, lonely splendour upon a wool mat on a ricketty round table. Six chairs stood against the papered walls. Nothing more.

Tom wanted to beat it back to the kitchen, through which they had passed to get to this sarcophagus, and where a fire was burning and a woman was busy. But the man was tapping at another door, and listening anxiously before entering.

He went into the dark room beyond, where a candle shone feebly, and they heard him say:

"Your nephew's come, Mr Grant, and brought a doctor and another gentleman, the Lord be praised."

"The Lord don't need to be praised on my behalf, Amos," came a querulous voice. "And I ain't got no nephew, if I *did* send him a letter. I've got nobody. And I want no doctor, because I died when I left my mother's husband's house."[*]

"They're in the parlour."

"Tell 'em to walk up."

The man appeared in the doorway. Rackett walked up, Jack followed, and Tom hung nervously and disgustedly in the rear.

"Here they are! Here's the gentry," said Amos.

In the candle-light they saw a thin man in a red flannel night-cap with a blanket round his shoulders, sitting up in bed under an old green cart-umbrella. He was not old, but his face was thin and wasted, and his long colourless beard seemed papery. He had cunning shifty eyes with red rims, and looked as mad as his setting.

Rackett had shoved Jack forward. The sick man stared at him and seemed suddenly pleased. He held out a thin hand. Rackett nudged Jack, and Jack had to shake. The hand seemed wet and icy, and Jack shuddered.

"How d' you do!" he mumbled. "I'm sorry, you know; I'm not your nephew."

"I know y're not. But are y' Jack Grant?"

"Yes," said Jack.

The man under the umbrella seemed hideously pleased.

Jack heard Tom's ill-suppressed, awful chuckle from behind.

The sick man peered irritably at the other two. Then he nodded slowly, under the green baldachino* of the old cart umbrella.

"Jack Grant! Jack Grant! Jack Grant!" he murmured to himself. He was surely mad, obviously mad.

"I'm right glad you've come, Cousin," he said suddenly, looking again very pleased. "I'm surely glad you've come in time. I've a nice tidy place put together for you, Jack, a small proposition of three thousand acres, five hundred cleared and cropped, fifty fenced—dog-leg fences,* broke MacCullen's back putting 'em in. But I'll willingly put in five hundred more, for a gentleman like young master. Meaning old master will soon be underground. Well who cares, now young master's come to light, and the place doesn't go out of the family! I am *determined* the place shall not go out of the family, Cousin Jack. Aren't you pleased?"

"Very," said Jack soothingly.

"Call me Cousin John. Or Uncle John if you like. I'm more like your uncle, I should think. Shake hands, and say Right-you-are, Uncle John. Call me Uncle John."

Jack shook hands once more, and dutifully, as to a crazy person, he said:

"Right you are, Uncle John."

Tom, in the background, was going into convulsions. But Rackett remained quite serious.

Uncle John closed his eyes, muttering, and fell back under the cart-umbrella.

"Mr Grant," said Rackett. "I think Jack would like to eat something after his ride."

"All right. Let him go to the kitchen with yon buck wallaby as can't keep a straight face. Stop with me a minute yourself, Mister, if you will."

The two boys bundled away into the kitchen. The woman had a meal ready, and they sat down at the table.

"I thank my stars," said Tom impressively, "he's not *my* Uncle John."

"Shut up," said Jack, because the woman was there.

They ate heartily, the effects of the jamboree having passed. After the meal they strolled to the door to look out, away from that lugubrious parlour and bedroom. They found a stiff wind blowing, the sky clear with running clouds and vivid stars in the spaces.

"Let's get!" urged Tom. It was his constant craving.

"We can't leave Rackett."

"We can. He pushed us in. Let's get. Why can't we?"

"Oh well, we can't," said Jack.

Rackett had entered the kitchen, and was eating his meal. He asked the woman for ink.

"There's no ink," she said.

"Must be somewhere," said Amos her husband. "Jack Grant's letter was written in ink."

"I never got a letter," said Jack, turning.

"Eh, hark ye! How like old master over again! Ye've come, haven't ye?"

"By accident," said Jack. "I'm not Mr Grant's nephew."

"Hark ye! Hark ye! It runs in the family, father to son, uncle to nephew. All right! All right! Have it your own way," cried Amos. He had been struggling with crazy contradictions too long.

Tom was in convulsions. Rackett put his hand on Jack's shoulder.

"It's all right," he said. "Don't worry him. Leave it to me." And to the woman he said, if there was no ink, she was to kill a fowl and bring it him, and he'd make ink with lamp-black and gall.*

"You two boys had better be off to bed," he said. "You have to be off in good time in the morning."

"Oh, not going, not going so soon, surely! The young master's not going so soon! Surely! Surely! Master's so weak in the head and stomach, we can't cope with him all by ourselves," cried the old man and woman.

"Perhaps I'll stay," said Rackett. "And Jack will come back one day, don't you worry. Now let me make that ink."

The boys were shown into a large, low room—the fourth room of the house—that opened off the kitchen. It contained a big bed with clean sheets and white crochet quilt. Jack surmised it was the old couple's bed, and wanted to go to the barn. But Tom said, since they offered it, there was nothing to do but take it.

Tom was soon snoring. Jack lay in the great feather bed feeling that life was all going crazy. Tom was already snoring. He cared about nothing. Out of sight out of mind. But Jack had a fit of remembering. His head was hot, and he could not sleep. The wind was blowing, it was raining again. He could not sleep, he had to remember.

It was always so with him. He could go on careless and unheeding, like Tom, for a while. Then came these fits of reckoning and remembering. Life seemed unhinged in Australia. In England there was a strong central pivot to all the living. But here the centre-pin was gone, and the lives seemed to spin in a weird confusion.

He felt that for himself. His life was all unhinged. What was he driving at? What was he making for? Where was he going? What was his life, anyhow?

In England, you knew. You had your purpose. You had your profession and your family and your country. But out here? You had no profession. You didn't do anything for your country except boast of it to strangers and leave it to get along as best it might. And as for your family, you cared for that, but in a queer, centreless fashion.

You didn't really care for anything. The old impetus of civilisation kept you still going, but you were just rolling to rest. As Mr Ellis had rolled to rest, leaving everything stranded. There was no grip, no hold.

And yet, what Jack had rebelled against in England was the tight grip, the fixed hold over everything. He liked this looseness and carelessness of Australia. Till it seemed to him crazy. And then it scared him.

Tonight everything seemed to him crazy. He didn't pay any serious attention to Uncle John Grant: he was obviously out of his mind. But then everything seemed crazy. Mr Ellis' death, and Gran's death, and Monica, and Easu Ellis—it all seemed crazy as crazy. And the jamboree, and that girl who called him Dearie! And the journey, and this mad house in the rain. What did it all mean? What did it all stand for?

Everything seemed to be spinning to a darkness of death. Everybody seemed to be dancing a crazy dance of death. He could understand that the blacks painted themselves like white bone skeletons, and danced in the night like skeletons dancing, in their corroborees.* That was how it was. The night, dark and fleshly, and skeletons dancing a clicketty dry dance in it.

Tom, so awfully upset at his father's death! And now as careless as a lark, just spinning his way along the road, in a sort of weird dance, dancing humorously to the black verge of oblivion. That was how it was. To dance humorously to the black verge of oblivion. The children of death. With a sort of horror of death around them. Wandoo suddenly grim and grisly with the horror of death.

Death, the great end and goal. Death the black, void, pulsating reality which would swallow them all up, like a black lover finally possessing them. The great black fleshliness of the end, the huge body of death reeling to swallow them all. And for this they danced, and for this they loved and reared families and made farms: to provide good meat and white, pure bones for the black, avid horror of death.

Something of the black aboriginal horror came over him. He realised, to his amazement, the actuality of the great, grinning black demon of death. The vast infinite demon that eats our flesh and cracks our bones in the last black potency of the end. And for this, for this demon one seeks for a woman, to lie with her and get children for the Moloch.* Children for the Moloch! Lennie, Monica, the twins Og and Magog! Children for the Moloch.

One God or the other must take them at the end. Either the dim white god of the heavenly infinite. Or else the great black Moloch of the living death. Devoured and digested in the living death.

Satan, Moloch, Death itself, all had been unreal to him before. But now, suddenly, he seemed to see the black Moloch grinning huge in the sky, while human beings danced towards his grip, and he gripped and swallowed them into the black belly of death. That was their end.

Dance! Dance! Death has its deep delights! And ever-recurring. Be careless, ironical, stoical and reckless. And go your way to death with a will. With a dark handsomeness and a dark lustre of fatality and a splendour of recklessness. Oh God, the Lords of Death! The big, darkly-smiling, heroic men who are Lords of Death! And they too go on splendidly into death, the great goal of unutterable satisfaction, and consummated fear.

"I am going my way the same," Jack thought to himself. "I am travelling in a reckless, slow dance, darker and darker, into the black, hot belly of death, where is my end. Oh, let me go gallantly, let me have the black joy of the road. Let[*] me go with courage and a bit of splendour and dark lustre, down to the great depths of death, that I am so frightened of, but which I long for in the last consummation. Let death take me in a last black embrace. Let me go on as the niggers go, with the last convulsion into the last black embrace. Since I am travelling the dark road, let me go in pride. Let me be a Lord of Death, since the reign of the white Lords of Life, like my father, has become sterile and a futility. Let me be a Lord of Death. Let me go that other great road, that the blacks go.—"

The bed was soft and hot, and he stretched his arms fiercely. If he had Monica! Oh, if he had Monica! If that girl last night had been Monica!

That girl last night! He didn't even know her name. She had stroked his head—like—like Mary! The association flashed into his mind. Yes, like Mary. And Mary would be humble and caressive and protective like that. So she would. And dark! It would be dark like that if one loved Mary. And brief! Brief. But sharp and good in the briefness. Mary! Mary!

He realised with amazement it was Mary he was now wanting. Not Monica. Or was it Monica? Her slim keen hand. Her slim body like a slim cat, so full of life. Oh, it was Monica! First and foremost, most intensely, it was Monica, because she was really his, and she was his destiny. He dared not think of her.

He rolled in the bed in misery. Tom slept unmoving. Oh, why couldn't he be like Tom, slow and untormented. Why couldn't he? Why was his body tortured? Why was he travelling this road? Why wasn't Monica there like a gipsy with him. Why wasn't Monica there?

Or Mary! Why wasn't Mary in the house? She would be so soft and understanding, so yielding. Like the girl of the long-armed man. The long-armed man didn't mind that he'd taken his girl, for once.

Why was he himself rolling there in torment? Pug had advised him to "punch the ball," when he was taken with ideas he wanted to get rid of. There was no ball to punch. "Train the body hard, but train the mind hard too." Yes, all very well. He could think, now, for example, of fighting Easu, or of building up a place and raising fine horses. But the moment his mind relaxed for sleep, back came the other black flame. The women! The women! The women! Even the girl of last night.

What was a man born for? To find a mate, a woman, isn't it? Then why try to think of something else? To have a woman—to make a home for her—to have children—And other women in the background, down the long, dusky, strange years towards death. So it seemed to him. And to fight the men that stand in one's way. To fight them. Always a new one cropping up, along the strange dusky road of the years, where you go with your head up and your eyes open and your spine sharp and electric, ready to fight your man and take your woman, on and on down the years, into the last black embrace of death. Death that stands grinning with arms open and black breast ready. Death, like the last woman you embrace. Death, like the last man you die fighting with. And he beats you. But somehow you are not beaten, if you are a Lord of Death.

Jack hoped he would die a violent death. He hoped he would live a defiant, unsubmissive life, and die a violent death. A bullet, or a knife piercing home. And the women he left behind—his women, enveloped in him as in a dark net. And the children he left, laughing already at death.

And himself! He hoped never to be downcast, never to be melancholy, never to yield. Never to yield. To be a Lord of Death, and go on to the black arms of death, still laughing. To laugh, and bide one's time, and leap at the right moment.

Chapter XVI.

On the Road.

i

"My dear Nephew, I haven't sent you a letter since the last one which I never wrote, yet you have come in answer to the one you never got. I wrote because I wanted you to come and receive the property, and I never posted it because I didn't know your address, and you couldn't come if I did, because you don't exist. Yet here you are and I think you look very pleased to receive the property which you haven't got yet. I was so afraid I would die sudden after this long lingering illness, but it's you who has come suddenly and the illness hasn't begun yet. So here am I speechless, but you are doing a lot of talking to your dear uncle who never had a nephew. What does it matter to me if you are Jack Grant because I am not, but took the name into the grant of land given me on the land grant system at a shilling an acre. So like a bad shilling the name turns up again on the register, so that the land goes back to the grant and the Grant to the land. But a better-looking nephew I never wish to see, being as much like me as an ape is like meat. So when I'm dead I won't be alive to trouble you, and I'll trouble no further about you since you might as well be dead for all I care— —"

In this vein Tom ranted on the next morning, when they had set out in the glorious early dawn. Tom never wearied of the uncle under the umbrella. He told the tale to everybody who would listen, and wore out Jack's ears with these long and facile pleasantries.

They were both glad to get away from the crazy lugubrious place. Jack refused to give it a thought further, though he felt vaguely, at the back of his mind, that he knew something about it already. Something somebody had told him.*

Rackett had stayed behind, so they made no very good pace, leading the pack-horse. But they pushed on, being already overdue at the homestead of one of Tom's aunts, who was expecting them.

Once on horseback and in the open morning, Jack wished for

nothing more. Women, death, skeletons, the dance into the darkness; the future, the past, love, home, and sorrow, all disappeared in the bright well of the daylight, as if they'd dropped into a pool. He wanted nothing more than to ride, to jog along the track on the rather wet road, through bush and scrub still wet with rain, in a pure Westralian air that was like a clean beginning of everything, seeing the tiny bushman's flowers sparking* and gilding eerily in the dunness of the world.

By midday they reached the highway to Geraldton, via Gingin, and camped at the Three-mile Government well in perfect good spirits. Everything was gone, everything was forgotten except the insouciance of the moment. They knew the uselessness of thinking and remembering and worrying. When worry starts biting like mosquitoes, then, if it bites hard enough, you've *got* to attend. But it's like illness, avoid it, beat it back if you can.

They found the high road merely a bush-track* after all. If it was near a settlement, or allotments or improved lands, it might run well for miles. But for the most part, it was exceedingly bad, full of holes of water, and beginning in places to be a bog.

Tom was now at his best, out in the bush again. All his bush lore came back to him, and he was like an animal in its native surroundings. His charm came back too, and his confidence. He went ahead looking keenly about, like a travelling animal, pointing out to Jack first this thing and then the other, initiating him into bush wisdom, teaching him the big cipher-book of the bush. And Jack learned gladly. It was so good, so good to be away from homesteads, and women, and money, watching the trees and the land and the marks of wild life. And Tom, a talker once he was wound up, told the histories of settlers, their failures and successes, and their peculiarities. It seemed to Jack there was a surplus of weird people out there. But then, Tom said, the weird ones usually came first, and they got weirder in the wild.

They passed an enormous hollow tree, from which issued an old man with a grey beard that came to his waist, dressed in rags. A grey-haired, very ragged woman also came out, carrying a baby. Other children crawled around. The travellers called Good-day! as they passed.

Tom said the woman's baby was the youngest of seventeen children. The eldest son was already grown up, a prosperous young man trading in sandal wood.* But Dad and Mum liked the bush, and would accept nothing for their supposed welfare, either from their sons or anyone else.

In the middle of the afternoon they passed a sundowner* trekking with a cartful of produce down to Middle Swan. At four o'clock they camped for half an hour, to drink a billy of tea. Before the water boiled they saw two tramps coming down the road. The slouchers came straight up and greeted the boys, eyeing them curiously up and down.

"Wot cheer, mate!" said one, a ruffianly mongrel.

"Good-O! How's the goin' Gingin way?" said Tom.

"Plenty grass an' water this time o' the year. But look out for the settlers this side. They ain't over hopeful—" He turned to stare at Jack. Then he continued, to Tom: "How's it y' got y'r baby out?"

"New chum," explained Tom. He spoke quietly, but his mouth had hardened. "You blokes want anything of us?"

"Yessir," said the spokesman, coming in close. "We wants bacca!"

"Do you!" said Tom pleasantly. And he pulled out his pouch. "I've only got three plugs. That's one apiece for me an' the baby, an' you can have the other to do as you likes with. But chum here doesn't keer much for smokin', so he might gi'e you his."

There was a tone of finality in Tom's voice.

"You've surely got more blasted cheek than most kids," said the fellow. "What've ye got planted away in y' swags?" He glanced at his mate. "We don't want to use no bally persuasion, does we Bill?"

Bill was of villainous, but not very imposing appearance. He had weak eyes, a dirty hairy face, and a purple mouth showing unbecomingly through his whiskers.

Tom calmly filled his pipe, and waving to the first tramp, gave him sufficient to fill his cutty. The fellow took it, ignoring his mate, and began to fill up eagerly. He sat down by the fire, and taking a hot ember, lit up, puffing avidly.

"The other can have my share, if he wants it," said Jack.

"Thank ye kindly," said the other with a sneer. And as he stuffed it in his pipe: "It'll do for a start." But he was puffing almost before he could finish his words.

They smoked in silence round the fire for some time. Then Tom rose and went over to the pack, as if he were going to give in to the ruffians. One swaggy rose and followed him.

The other tramp, taking not the slightest notice of the boy sitting there, reached out his filthy hand and began to fill his pockets with everything that lay near the fire: the packet of tea, a spoon, a knife.

He had got as far as the spoon when the astonished Jack said: "Drop it!" as if he were speaking to a dog.

The man turned with a snarl, and made to cuff him. Jack seized his wrist and twisted it cruelly, making him drop the spoon and shout with pain. The other swaggy at once ran on Jack from the rear, and fell over him. Tom rushed on the second swaggy and fell too. Over they all went in a heap. Jack laughed aloud in the scrimmage, as he gripped the swaggy's wrist with one hand and with the other emptied out the contents of the pocket again. He brought out two knives, one which didn't belong to him. Dropping the lot for safety, he got to his feet. Tom and the second swaggy were rolling and unlocking. That villain spied the open knife, seized it and sprang to his feet, snarling and brandishing.

"Come on, ye pair of— — — —."

Jack gave another twist to the arm of his prisoner, who howled, and then he kicked him three yards away. But his heart smote him, for the kick was so bony, the tramp was thin and frail. Then, full of the black joy of scattering such wastrels, he sprang unexpectedly on the other tramp. The swaggy gave a yell, and fled. For a minute or two the couple of ragged, wretched, despicable figures could be seen bolting like running vermin down the trail. Then they were out of sight.

Tom and Jack sat by the fire and roared with laughter, roared and roared till the bush was startled.

They were just packing up when someone else came down the road. It was a young woman in a very wide skirt on a very small pony, riding as if she were used to it. This was not the figure they expected to see.

"Why!" cried Tom, staring. "I do believe it's Ma's niece grown up."

It was. She was quite pleasant, but her hands were stub-fingered and work-hardened, and her voice was common.

"Y' didn't come along yesterday, as Ma expected," she explained; "so I just took Tubby to see if y' was coming today. How's the twins? How's Monica and Grace? I do wish they'd come."

"They're all right," said Tom.

"We heard about your Dad and your Gran. Fancy!—But I wish

Monica had come with you. She was such a little demon at school, I'm fair longing to see her."

"She's not the only one of you that's a demon!" said Tom, in the correct tone of banter, putting over his horse and drawing to the girl's side* and becoming very manly for her benefit. "An' what's wrong with us, that you aren't glad to see us?"

"Oh you're all right," said the cousin. "But a girl of your own age is more fun, you know."

"Well, I don't happen to be a girl of your own age," said Tom. "Just by accident, I'm a man.—But come on. There's some roughs about. We might just as well get out of their way."

He trotted alongside the damsel, leaving Jack to bring the pack-horse. Jack didn't mind.

ii

So they went on, receiving a rough and generous hospitality from one or another of Tom's or Jack's relations, of whom there were astonishingly many, along the grand bush track to Geraldton. If they weren't direct relations they were relations by marriage, and it served just as well. There were the Brockmans, there were the Browns, and Gales, and Davises, Edgars, and Conollys, Burgesses, Cooks, Logues, Cradles, Morrises, Fitzgeralds and Glasses. Families united by some fine-drawn connection or other: and very often much more divided than united, by some very plain-drawn feud. Their names like brooks trickled across the land, and you crossed and re-crossed. You would lose a name entirely: like the Brockman name. Then suddenly it reappeared as *Brackman*, and "Oh yes, we're cousins!"

"Who isn't cousin!" thought Jack.

Some of them had huge tracts of land* fenced in. Some had little bits of poor farms. Sometimes there were deserted farms.

"And to think," said Tom, "that none of them is my *own* mother's relations. All Dad's, or else Ma's. Mostly Ma's."

It was queer, the way he hankered after his own real mother. Jack, for his part, didn't care a straw who was his mother's relation and who wasn't. But you would have thought Tom lived under a matriarchy, and derived everything from a lost mother.

It was not wet enough yet to be really boggy, though camping out was damp. However, they mostly got a roof. If it wasn't a relation's, it was a barn, or the "Bull and Horns" by Gingin. And to the boys, all that mattered was whether they were on the right road: often a very puzzling question; or if the heavy rain would hold off; if there was plenty of grub; if the horses seemed tired or not quite fit; if they were going to get through a boggy place all right; if the packs were fast; if they made good going. The inns were "low" in every sense of the word, including the low-pitched roof. And full of bugs, however new the country. With red-nosed, greasy-whiskered landlords who thumbed the glasses, when there were any glasses to thumb. And there were always men at these inns, almost always the same kind of brutal, empty roughs.

"Look here," said Jack. "Wherever we go there are these roughs, and more roughs, and more. Where the devil do they come from, and how do they make a living?—Apart from the farm labourers, I mean."

"A lot of them are shearers," said Tom, "drifting from job to job, according to the climate. When shearing season's over here, they work on to the south-west, where it's cooler.—And then there are kangaroo and 'possum snarers. That young fellow we saw rooked of all his sugar last night was a skin-hunter. They get half-a-crown apiece for good 'roo skins, and it's quite a trade. The others last night were mostly sandal-wood getters. There's quite a lot of men make money collecting bark for export, and manna-gum.[*] That rowdy lot playing fifty-three were a gang of well-sinkers. Then what with timber-workers, haulers, teamsters, jinkers—oh, there's all sorts.—But they're mostly one sort, swabs,[*] rough and rowdy, an' can't keep their pants hitched up enough to be decent. You've seen 'em. They're mostly like the dirty old braces they wear. All the snap gone out of 'em, all the elastic perished. They just work and booze and loaf and work and booze. I hope I'll never get so that I don't keep myself spruce. I hope I never will. But that's the worst o' the life out here. Nobody hardly keeps spruce."

Jack kept this well in mind. He too hated a man slouching along with a discoloured face and trousers slopping down his insignificant legs. He loathed that look which tramps and ne'er-do-wells usually have, as if their legs weren't there, inside their beastly bags. Despicable about the rear and the legs.—The best of the farmers, on the contrary, had strong, sinewy legs, full of life. Easu was like that, his powerful legs holding his horse. And Tom had good, live legs. But poor Dad had not been very alive, inside his pants.

"Whatever I do, I'll never go despicable and humiliated about the legs and seat," said Jack to himself, as he pressed the stirrups with his toes and felt the powerful elasticity of his thighs, holding the live body of the horse between his muscles in permanent grip. And it seemed as if the powerful animal life of the horse entered into him, through his legs and seat, and made him strong.

"What's a jinker, Tom?"

"A low four-wheeled log-hauler, with a long pole."

"I thought it was a man. A swab is a man?"

"Yes. He's any old drunk."

"But a swaggy is a tramp?"

"It is. It is one who humps it. If he's got a pack, it's his swag. If he's only got a blanket and a billy, it's his bluey and his drum. And if he's got nothing, it's Waltzing Matilda."*

"I suppose so," said Jack. "And his money is his sugar?"

"Right-O! son!"

"And Clink is Chinaman?"

"No sir. That's Chow. Clink means prison. An' a lag is a ticketer: one who's out on lease.—Now what more Child's Guide to Knowledge* do you want?"

"I'm only getting it straight. Jam and dog both mean 'side'?"

"Verily. Only dog is sometimes same as bully—tinned meat."

"And what's *stouch*?"*

"Landin' him one."

Jack rode on, thinking about it.

"What's a remittance man, really, Tom?"

"A waster. A useless bird shipped out here to be kept south o' the line,* because he's a disgrace on England. And his family soothes their conscience by sending him so much a month, which they call his remittance, stead o' letting him starve, or work. Like Rackett. Plenty o' money sent out to him to stink on."

"Why don't you like Rackett?"

"I fairly despise him, an' his money. He's absolutely useless baggage, rotting life away. I can't abear to see him about. Old George gave me the tip he was leaving our place, else I'd never have gone an' left him loose there."

"He is no harm."

"How do you know? If he hasn't got a disease of the body, he's got a disease of the soul."

"What disease?"

"I dunno."

"Does he take drugs?"

"I reckon that's about his figure.—But he's an eyesore to me, loafin', loafin'. An' he's an eyesore to Ma, save for the bit he teaches Lennie. An' when he starts talkin' on the high fiddle,* like he does to Mary the minute she comes down, makes you want to walk on his face."

Poor Rackett! Jack marvelled that Tom had always been so civil.

The two jogged along very amicably together. Tom was hail-fellow-well-met with everybody. At the same time, he was in his own estimation a gentleman, and a person of consideration. It was "thus far—!" with him.

But whoever came along, they all drew up.

"Hello mate! How's goin'?———Well, so long!"

One youth was walking to Fremantle to take a job offered by his uncle, serving in a grocery shop. The lad was in tatters. His blanket was tied with twine, his battered billy hung on to it. But he was jubilant.—And now he is one of Australia's leading lights.* Even it is said of him that he never forgot the kindness he received on the road.

But most of the trailers were sundowners, sloping along anyhow, subsisting anyhow, but ready with the ingenious explanation that they "chopped a bit," or "fenced a bit," or "trapped a bit." Perhaps they never realised how much bigger was the bit they loafed.

They were not bad. The bad ones were the scoundrels down from the Never-Never,* emerging in their rags and moral degeneration after years on the sheep runs or cattle stations, years of earnings spent in drink and squalid, beastly debauchery. Some were hoarding their cheques for coast-town* consumption, like the first two rogues, and cadging and stealing their way.

But then there were families driving to the nearest settlement to do a bit of shopping, or visit their relations, or fetch the doctor to "fix up Teddy's little leg." Once there was a posse of mounted police, very important and gallant, with horses champing and chains clinking. They were out after a criminal supposed to have been landed on the coast by a dago boat "from the other side."* Then there was an occasional minister of the gospel, on a pony, dressed in black. Jack's heart always sank when he saw that black. He decided that priests should be white, or in orange robes, like the Buddhist priests he had seen in Colombo,* or in a good blue, like some nuns.

Gradually the road became a home: more a home than any homestead.

"Let's get!" was Tom's perpetual cry, when they were fixed up in the house of some relation, or in some inn. He only felt happy on the road. Sometimes they went utterly lonely for many miles. Sometimes they passed a deserted habitation. But there were always signs of life near a well. And often there were milestones.

"Fifty-seven miles to where?"

"I don't know. We're leagues from Gingin. Certainly fifty-seven miles to nowhere of any importance on the face of this earth."

"Wonder what Gingin means?"*

"Better not ask. You never know what these natives'll be naming places after. Usually something vile.—But *gin* means a woman, whatever Gingin is."

Gradually they got further and further, geographically, mentally, and emotionally, from Wandoo and all permanent associations. Jack was glad. He loved the earth, the wild country, the bush, the scent. He wanted to go on for ever. Beyond the settlements—beyond the ploughed land—beyond all fences. That was it, beyond all fences. Beyond all fences, where a man was alone with himself and the untouched earth.

Man escaping from man! That's how it is all the time. The passion men have to escape from mankind. What do they expect in the beyond? God?

They'll never find the same God! Never again. They are trying to escape from the God men acknowledge, as well as from mankind, the acknowledger.

The land untouched by man. The call of the mysterious, vast, unoccupied land. The strange, inaudible calling, like the far-off call of a kangaroo. The strange, still, pure air. The strange shadows. The strange scent of wild, brown, aboriginal honey.*

Being early for the boat, the boys camped for twenty-four hours in a perfectly lonely place. And in the utterly lonely evening, Jack began craving again: for Monica, for a woman, for some object for his passion to settle on. And he knew again, as he had always known, that nowhere is free, so long as man is passionate, desirous, yearning. His only freedom is to find the object of his passion, and fulfil his desire, and satisfy his yearning, as far as his life can succeed. Or else, which is more difficult, to harden himself away from all desire and craving, to harden himself into pride, and refer himself to that other God.

Yes, in the wild bush, God seemed another god. God seemed absolutely another god, vaster, more calm and more deeply, sensually potent. And this was a profound satisfaction. To find another, more terrible, but also more deeply-fulfilling god stirring subtly in the uncontaminated air about one. A dread god. But a great god, greater than any known. The sense of greatness, vastness, and newness, in the air. And the strange, dusky-grey, eucalyptus-smelling sense of depth, strange depth in the air, as of a great deep well of potency which life had not yet tapped. Something which lay in a man's blood as well—and in a woman's blood—in Monica's—in Mary's—in the Australian blood. A strange dusky, gum-smelling depth of potency that had never been tapped by experience. As if life still held great wells of reserve vitality,[*] strange unknown wells of secret life-source, dusky, of a strange, dim aromatic sap which had never stirred in the veins of man, to consciousness and effect. And if he could take Monica and set the dusky, secret, unknown sap flowing in himself and her, to some unopened life consciousness—that was what he wanted. Dimly, uneasily, painfully he realised it.

And then the bush began to frighten him, as if it would kill him, as it had killed so much man-life before, killed it before the life in man had had time to come to realisation.

He was glad when the road came down to the sea. There, the great, pale-blue, strange, empty sea, on new shores, with new strange sea-birds flying, and strange rocks sticking up, and strange blue distances up the bending coast. The sea that is always the same, always a relief, a vastness and a soothing. Coming out of the bush, and being a little afraid of the bush, he loved the sea, with an English passion. It made him feel at home, in the same known infinite of space.

Especially on a windy day, when the track would curve down to a greeny-grey opalescent sea that beat slowly on the red sands, like a dying grey bird with white wing-feathers. And the reddish cliffs with sage-green growth of herbs, stood almost like flesh.

Then the road went inland again, through a swamp, and to the bush. To emerge next morning in sun, upon a massive deep indigo ocean, infinite, with pearl-clear horizon; and in the nearness, emerald-green and white flashing unspeakably bright on a pinkish shore, perfectly world-new.

They were nearing the journey's end. Nearing the little port, and the ship, and the world of men.

Chapter XVII.

After Two Years.

i

A sky with clouds of white and grey, and patches of blue. A green sea flecked with white, and shadowed golden brown. On the horizon, the sense of a great open void, like an open valve, as if the bivalve oyster of the world, sea and sky, were open away westward, open into another infinity, and the people on land, inside the oyster of the world, could look far out to the opening.

They could see the bulk of near islands. Further off, a tiny white sail coming down fast on the fresh great sea-wind, emanating out of the North-West. She seemed to be coming from the beyond, slipping into the slightly-open, living oyster of our world.

The men on the wharf at Fremantle, watching her black hull emerge from the flecked sea, as she sailed magically nearer, knew she would be a cattle-boat coming in from the great Nor' West. They watched her none the less.

As she hesitated, turning into the harbour, she was recognised as the old fore-and-aft schooner "Venus";* though if Venus ever smelled like that, we pity her lovers. Smell or not, she balanced nicely, and with a bit of manœuvring ebbed her delicate way up to the wharf.

There they are! There they are, Tom and Jack, though their own mothers wouldn't know them! Looking terribly like their fellow-passengers: stubbly beards, long hair, greasy dirty dungarees, and a general air of disreputable outcasts.* But, no doubt, with cheques of some sort in their pockets.

Two years, nearer three years have gone by, since they set out from Wandoo. It is more than four years since Jack landed* fresh from England, in this very Fremantle. And he is so changed, he doesn't even trouble to remember.

They don't trouble to remember anything: not yet. Back in the Never-Never, one by one the ties break, the emotional connections snap, memory gives out, and you come undone. Then, when you have come undone from the great past, you drift in an unkempt nonchalance here and there, great distances across the great hinterland country, and there is nothing but the moment, the instantaneous moment. If you are working your guts out, you are working your guts out. If you are rolling across for a drink, you are rolling across for a drink. If you are just getting into a fight with some lump of a brute, you are just getting into a fight with some lump of a brute. If you are going to sleep in some low hole, you are going to sleep in some low hole. And if you wake feeling dry and hot and hellish, why, you feel dry and hot and hellish till you leave off feeling dry and hot and hellish. There's no more to it. The same if you're sick. You're just sick, and stubborn as hell, till your stubbornness gets the better of your sickness.

There are words like home, Wandoo, England, mother, father, sister—but they don't carry very well. It's like a radio message that's so faint, so far off, it makes no impression on you; even if you can hear it in a shadowy way. Such a faint, unreal thing in the broadcast air.

You have moved outside the pale, the pale of civilisation, the pale of the general human consciousness. The human consciousness is a definitely limited thing, even on the face of the earth. You can move into regions outside of it. As in Australia. The broadcasting of the vast human consciousness can't get you. You are beyond. And since the call can't get you, the answer begins to die down inside yourself, you don't respond any more. You don't respond, and you don't correspond.

There is no past: or if there is, it is so remote and ineffectual it can't work on you at all. And there is no future. Why saddle yourself with such a spectre as the future? There is the moment. You sweat, you rest, the bugs bite you, you thirst, you drink, you think you're going to die, you don't care, and you know you won't die, because a certain stubbornness inside you keeps the upper hand.

So you go on. If you've got no work, you either get a horse or you tramp it off somewhere else. You keep your eyes open that you don't get lost, or stranded for water. When you're damned, infernally and absolutely sick of everything, you go to sleep. And then if the bugs bite you you are beyond that too.

But at the bottom of yourself, somewhere, like a tiny seed, lies the knowledge that you're going back in a while. That all the unreal will become real again, and this real will become unreal. That all that stuff, home, mother, responsibility, family, duty, etc., it all will loom up again into actuality, and this, this heat, this parchedness, this dirt, this mutton, these dying sheep, these roving cattle that take the flies by the million, these burning tin gold-camps—all this will recede into the unreal, it will cease to be actual.

Some men decide never to go back. And they are the derelicts, the scarecrows and the warning. "Going back" was a problem in Jack's soul. He didn't really want to go back. All that which lay behind, society, homes, families, he felt a deep hostility towards. He didn't want to go back. He was like an enemy lurking outside the great Camp of civilisation. And he didn't want to go into Camp again.

Yet neither did he want to be a derelict. A mere derelict he would never be, though temporary derelicts both he and Tom were. But he saw enough of the real waster, the real out-and-out derelict, to know that this he would never be.

No, in the end he would go back to civilisation. But the thought of becoming a part of the civilised outfit was deeply repugnant to him. Some other queer hard resolve had formed in his soul. Something gradually went hard in the centre of him. He couldn't yield himself any more. The hard core remained impregnable.

They had dutifully spent their year on the sheep-run Mr George had sent them to. But after that, it was shift for yourself. They had stuck at nothing. Only they had stuck together.

They had cashed their cheques in many a well-known wooden "hotel" of the far-away coast. Oh those wooden hotels, with their uneasy verandahs, flies, flies, flies, flies, flies, their rum, or whiskey, their dirty glasses, their flimsy partitions, their foul language, their bugs and dirt and desolation. The brutal, foul-mouthed desolation of them, with the horses switching their tails at the hitching posts, the riders slowly soaking, staring at the blue heat and the silent world of dust, too far gone even to speak. Gone under the heat, the drought, the Never-Neverness of it, the unspeakable hot desolation. And evening coming, with men already drunk, already ripe for brawling, obscenity, and swindling gambling.

They had gone away chequeless, mourning their chequelessness, back on their horses to the cattle station. Then following the droves miles and miles through the tropical, or semi-tropical bush, and over the open country, camping by water for a week at a time, then going on.

Then they had chucked cattle, wasted their cheques, footed it for weary, weary miles, like the swaggies they had so despised. Clothes in rags, boots in holes, another job; away in out-back camps with horsemen prospectors, with well-contractors; shepherding again, with utter wastrels of shepherds camping along with them; chucking the job, chucking the blasted rich aristocratic squatters[*] with all their millions of acres and sheep and fence and blasted outfit, all so dead bent on making money as quick as possible, all the machinery of civilisation, as far as possible, starting to grind and squeak there in the beyond. They had gone off with well-sinkers, and laboured like navvies. Chucked that, taken the road, spent the night at mission-stations, watched the blacks being saved, and got to the mining-camps.

Poor old Tom had got into deep waters. Even now he more than feared that he was legally married to a barmaid, far away back in the sublimest town you can imagine, back there in the blasting heat which so often burns a man's soul away even before it burns up his body. It had burned a hole in Tom's soul, in that town away back in the blasting heat, a town consisting of a score or so of ready-made tin houses got up from the coast in pieces, and put together by anybody that liked to try. There they stood, or staggered, the tin ovens that men and women lived in; houses leaning like drunken men against stark tree-trunks, others looking strange and forlorn with some of their parts missing, said parts being under the seas, or elsewhere mislaid. But the absence of one section of a wall did not spoil the house for habitation. It merely gave you a better view of the inside happenings. Many of the tin shacks were windowless, and even shutterless: square holes in the raw corrugated erection. One was entirely wall-less. And this was the pub. It was just a tin roof reared on saplings against an old tree, with a sacking screen around the bar; through which sacking screen you saw the ghost of the landlady and her clients, if you approached from the back. The front view was open.

Here sat the motionless landlady, in her cooking hot shade, dispensing her indispensable grog, while her boss, or husband, rolled the barrels in. He had a team, with which he hauled up the indispensable from the coast.

The nice-mannered Miss Snook took turns with her mamma in this palace of Circe.[*] She was extremely "nice" in her manners, for the "boss" owned the team, the pub, and the boarding-house at which you stayed so long as you could pay the outrageous prices. So

Miss Snook, never familiarised into Lucy, for she wouldn't allow it, oscillated between the closed oven of the boarding-house, and the open oven of the pub.

Father—or the "boss"—had been a barber in Sydney. Now he cooked in the boarding-house and drove the team. "Mother" had been the high-born daughter of a chemist; she had ruined all her prospects of continuing in the eastern "swim"* by running away with the barber, now called "boss." However, she took her decline in the social scale with dignity, and allowed no familiarities. Her previous station helped her to keep up her prices.

"We're not, y' understand Mr Grant, a Provident concern,* as some foot-sloggers seem to think us. We doing our best to provide for Lucy, against she wants to get married, or in case she doesn't."

She and Lucy did the washing and cleaning between them, but their efforts were nominal. Boss' cooking left everything to be desired. The place was a perfect paradise.

"We know a gentleman when we see one, Mr Grant, and we're not going to throw our only child away on a penniless waster."

Jack wanted loudly to proclaim himself a penniless waster. But Tom and he had a pact, not to say *anything* about themselves, or where they came from. They were just "looking round."

And in that heat, the plump, perspiring, cotton-clad Lucy thought that Tom seemed more amenable than Jack. She was of the short, plump, shrewd, rather flattering sort, but Jack couldn't stand her sort of perspiration. Poor Tom seemed to fall for it, and Jack had to look on in silent disgust. Because when the said Lucy rose from her chair, in Sunday elegance, she would walk across the room with her white muslin frock sticking tight between her legs as if it had been pasted on her posterior, whose more-than-plump movement, as she walked, Jack again could not stand. But Tom seemed to fall even for this. His faculty for being Circied was strange. He went into a queer, stupefied trance, entranced by the posterior and perspiration of this way-back Circe.*

There was even a ghastly, gruesome wedding. Neither of the boys could bear to think of it. Even in the stupefaction of that heat, when the brain seems to melt, and the will degenerates, and nothing but the most rudimentary functions of the organism called man, continue to function, even then a sense of shame overpowered them. But Tom was in a trance, pig-headed as any of Circe's swine. He continued in the trance for about a week after his so-called marriage.

Then he woke up from the welter of perspiration, rum, and Lucy in an amazed horror, and the boys escaped.

The nightmare of this town—it was called "Honeysuckle"*—was able to penetrate Tom's most nonchalant mood, even when he was hundreds of trackless miles away. The young men covered their tracks carefully. The Snooks knew nothing but their names. But a name, alas, is a potent entity in the wilds.

They covered their tracks, and disappeared again. But even so, an ancient letter from Wandoo followed them to a well-digging camp. It was from Monica to Tom, but it didn't seem to mean much to either boy.

By* the same mail came a letter to one of the sinkers in the camp, named Harry Smith. It was from England, and was addressed:

"Mr Harry Smith
West Australia"*

as if West Australia were a village in Surrey. But "try this" and "try that" was pencilled all over the envelope, like a patent-medicine advertisement. And they had struck it at last.

This letter was almost worn out with travel. It had been from the Swan River to Cape Leeuwin, from the Leeuwin to Eucla, and from there to King River; then round all that division of the Swan River, opened and read by dozens of Harry Smiths, each of whom would scratch his head and soliloquise: "This ain't for me. Suppose I'm not the only 'Arry in the colony. Might be for 'Appy 'Arry wot went to Cossack." And off to Cossack it had gone.

But it came to its journey's end at last, and Jack read it with curious emotion.

18 Orset Ter.
Hyde Park.
London.

"Dear Brother Hary,

"This comes hopping to find you well as it leaves me at present thank god but not the futre King of England who has passed away at his palace with all pomp and cerremony as so he should being but a por mortal like us and them Royalty more easy to catch them fevvers of which hes dead and broke his por mother's heart once more.* As all the Nashun is now in Court morning I thinks to myself what about por Arry buried away so young in the back wood so i take up the pen to tell you being the head of the family so far away and I would not have you not morn so I hopes to send a fine wide crape for your hat band by the Packet. This was the masters after buying a new one for the Event and the butler having spint his wage by arrangement with his Uncle let me by this off him for the honor of the fambly which you being the only sin—here the writing changed to a more battered hand still—I relinquish. The gentleman who wrote this for me for a penny as got tired so I close with fond love and kisses

"From your loving sister
Clara Smith"

This letter touched Jack, made him feel cynical about crape again, and bothered him. But Tom went pale, and the snake of fear bit at his vitals. If this letter found out Harry Smith, could not the deadly Snook family much more easily find Tom Ellis? They had only to put an advertisement in the Perth paper.

Horrors! But forget it. Tom decided, if the worst came to the worst, he would be like Pink-eye Percy, and swap sides of the Continent.—The other hope, which Jack insisted on, was that the fair Lucy had been married before, and had committed nothing more serious than bigamy with our Tom.

But Tom felt rather like the convict who asserted: "I never said an untrue word in my life, and I here solemnly declare that I was sent out under false representation."—While Jack was like the soothing Australian who replied: "Forget it son! You've got every chance to redeem your name in this grand new land. Copy the ways of your betters, and you'll do. Don't bear any ill-will against them that sent ye. They did their best according to their lights, and the Queen of England don't have any grudge against ye. We are free-born Britons even if ye've served your time, and free-born Britons we remain."

For almost a year Tom and Jack had never written home. There didn't seem any reason. In his last letter Tom, suddenly having some sort of qualms, had sent his cheque to his maiden aunts in York, because he knew, now Gran and Dad were gone, they'd be in shallow water. This off his conscience, he let Wandoo go out of his mind and spirit.

But now wandered in a letter from Aunt Lucy—dreaded name! It was a "thank you my dear nephew," and went on to say that though she would be the last to repeat things she hoped trouble was not hanging over Mrs Ellis' head.

Tom looked at Jack.

"We'd best go back," said Jack, reading his eyes.

"Seems like it."

So—the time had come. The "freedom" was over. They were going back.—They caught the old ship "Venus," going south with cattle.

To come back in body is not always to come back in mind and spirit. When Jack saw the white buildings of Fremantle he knew his soul was far from Fremantle. But nothing to be done. The old ship bumped against the wharf, and was tied up. Nothing to do but to step ashore.

They loafed off that ship with a gang of similar unkempt, unshaved, greasy, scoundrelly returners.

"Come an' 'ave a spot!"

"What about it, Tom?"

"Y' know I haven't a bean above the couple o' dollars to take me to Perth."

"Oh, dry it up," cried the mates. "What y' come ashore for? You're not goin' without a spot. It's on me. My shout."

"Shout it back* in Perth, then."

"Wot'll y'ave?"

And through the swing doors they went.

"Best an' bitter's mine."*

ii

Jack had not let himself be cleaned out entirely, as Tom had. Tom seemed to *want* to be absolutely stumped. But Jack, with a deeper sense of the world's enmity, and his own need to hold his own against it, had posted a* couple of cheques to Lennie to hold for him. Save for this, he too was cleaned out.

The same little engine of the same little train of four years ago shrieked her whistle. The North-West crowd drifted noisily out of the Hotel and down the platform,* packing into the third class compartment, in such positions as happily to negotiate the spittoons.

"Let's go forward," said Jack. "We might as well have cushions, if we're not smoking."

And he drew Tom forward along the train. They were going to get in another compartment, but seeing the looks of terror on the face of the woman and little girl already there, they refrained, and went further.

Aggressively they entered another smoking compartment. A

couple of fat tradesmen and a clergyman glowered at them. One of the tradesmen pulled out a handkerchief, shook it, and pretended to wipe his nose. There was musk perfume in the air.

"Oh my ant!" said Tom, putting his hand on his stomach. "Turns me right over."*

"What?" asked Jack.

"All this smell o' scent."

Jack grinned to himself. But he was back in civilisation, and he involuntarily stiffened.

"Hello! There's Sam Ellis!" Tom leaned out of the door. "Hello Sam! How's things, eh?"

The young fellow addressed looked at Tom, grinned sicklily, and turned away. He didn't know Tom from Adam.

"Let's have another drink!" said Tom, flabbergasted, getting out of the train.

Jack followed, and they started down the platform, when the train jogged, jerked, and began to pull away. Instantly they ran for it, caught the rail of the guard's van, and swung themselves in. The interior was empty, so they sat down on the little boxes let in at the side. Then the two eyed each other self-consciously, uncomfortably. They felt uncomfortable and aware of themselves all at once.

"Of all the ol' sweeps!"* said Tom. "Tell you what, you look like a lumper, absolutely nothing but a lumper."

"And what do you think you look like, you distorted scavenger!"

Tom grinned uncomfortably.

They got out of the station at Perth without having paid any railway fare.

The first place they went to was Mr George's office. Jack pushed Tom through the door, and stood himself in the doorway fingering his greasy felt hat. Tom dropped his, picked it up, hit it against his knee.

Mr George, neat in pale grey suit and white waistcoat, glanced at them briefly.

"Now then my men, what can I do f' ye?"

"Why—" began Tom, grinning sheepishly—

"Trouble about a mining right?—mate stolen half y' gold dust?—want stake a claim on somebody else's reserve?—Come, out with it. What d' you want me to do for ye, man?"

"Why—" Tom began, more foolishly grinning than ever. Mr George looked shrewdly at him, then at Jack. Then he sat back smiling.

"Well if you're not a pair!" he said. "So it was mines for the last outfit? How'd it go?"

"About as slow as it could," said Tom.

"So you've not come back millionaires?" said Mr George, a *little* bit disappointed.

"Come to ask for a fiver," said Tom.

"You outcast!" said Mr George. "You had me, completely. But look here, lads, I'll stand y' a fiver apiece* if y'll stop around Perth like that all morning, an' nobody spots ye."

"Easy!" said Tom.

"A bigger pair o' blackguards I've seldom set eyes on.—But you have dinner with me at the club tonight, I'll hear all about y' then. Six-thirty sharp. An' then I'll take ye to the Government House. Y' can wear that evening suit in the closet at my house, Jack, that you've left there all this time. See you six thirty then."

iii

Dismissed, they bundled into the street.

"Outcasts on the face value of us!" said Jack.

Tom stopped to roar with laughter, and bumped into a pedestrian.

"Hold hard! Keep a hand on the reins, can't you?" exclaimed the individual, pushing Tom off.

Tom looked at him. It was Jimmie Short, another sort of cousin.

"Stow it,* Jimmie. Don't y' know me."

Jimmie took him firmly by the coat lappels and pulled him into the gutter.

" 'F course I know ye," said Jimmie in a conciliatory tone, as to a drunk. "Meet me in half an hour at the Miners Refuge,* eh? Three steps and a lurch and there y' are!—Come matey—" this to Jack—"take hold of y' pal's arm. See ye later."

Tom was weak with laughter at Jimmie's benevolent attitude. They were not recognised at all, as they lurched across the road.

They had a drink, and strolled down the long principal street* of Perth, looking in at the windows of all the shops, and in spite of the fact that they had no money, buying each a silk handkerchief and a cake of scented soap. The excitement of this over, they rolled away to the river-side, to the ferry. Then again back into the town.

At the corner of the Freemasons' Hotel they saw Aunt Matilda and Mary; Aunt Matilda huge in a tight-fitting, ruched dress of dark purple stuff, and Mary in a black-and-white striped dress with tight bodice and tight sleeves with a little puff at the top, and long skirt very full behind. She wore also a little black hat with a wing. And Jack, with a wickedness brought with him out of the North-West, would have liked to rip these stereotyped clothes and corsets off her, and make her walk down Hay Street *in puris naturalibus*.* She went so trim and exact behind the huge Mrs Watson. It would have been good to unsheathe her.

"Hello!" cried Tom. "There's Aunt Matilda. We've struck it rich."

The two young blackguards followed slowly after the two women, close behind them. Mary carried a book, and was evidently making for the little bookshop that had a lending library of newish books.

"Well Mary, while you go in there I'll go and see if the chemist can't give me something for my breathing, for it's awful!" said Mrs Watson, standing and puffing before the book-shop.

"Shall I come for you or you for me?" asked Mary.

"I'll sit and wait for you in Mr Pusey's," panted Aunt Matilda, and she sailed forward again, after having glanced suspiciously backward at the two ne'er-do-wells who were hesitating a few yards away.

Mary, with her black hair in a huge bun, her hat with a wing held on by steel pins, was gazing contemplatively into the window of the book-shop, at the newest book. *The Booklovers Latest*!* said a card-board announcement.

"Can you help a poor chap, Miss?" said Tom, dropping his head and edging near.

Mary started, looked frightened, glanced at the first tramp and then at the second, in agitation, began to fumble for her purse, and dropped her book, spilling the loose leaves.

Jack at once began to gather up the scattered pages of the book: an Anthony Trollope novel. Mary, with black-kid-gloved fingers, was fumbling in her purse for a penny. Tom peeped into the purse.

"Lend us the half a quid, Mary," he said.

She looked at his face, and a slow smile of amusement dawned in her eyes.

"I should never have known you!" she said.

Then as Jack rose, shoving the leaves together in the book, she looked into his blue eyes with her brown, queer shining eyes.

She held out her hand to him without saying a word, only looked into his eyes with a look of shining meaning. Which made him grin sardonically inside himself. He shook hands with her silently.

"You look something like you did after you'd been fighting with Easu Ellis," she said. "When are you going to Wandoo?"

"Tomorrow I should think," said Tom. "Everybody O. K. down there?"

"Oh I think so!" said Mary nervously.

"What do you men want?" came a loud, panting voice. Aunt Matilda sailing up, purple in the face.

"Lend us the half-a-quid, Mary," murmured Tom, and hastily she handed it over. Jack had already commenced to beat a retreat. Tom sloped away as the large lady loomed near.

"Beggars!" she panted. "Are they begging?—How much—how much did you give him? The disgraceful—!"

"He made me give him half-a-sovereign, Aunt."

Mrs Watson had to stagger into the shop for a chair.

The boys had a drink, and set off to the warehouse to look up Jack's box, in which were his white shirts and other forgotten garments.

Back in town, Jack felt a slow, sinister sense of oppression coming over him, a sort of fear, as if he were not really free, as if something bad were going to happen to him.

"How am I going to get dressed to dine with old George tonight," grumbled the still-careless Tom, who was again becoming tipsy. "Wherever am I goin' ter get a suit to sport."

"Oh, some of yer relations'll fix you up."

Jack had an undefinable, uncomfortable feeling lest he might suddenly come upon Monica, and she might see him in this state. He wouldn't like the way she'd look at him. No, he wouldn't be looked at like that, not for a hundred ponies.*

They turned their backs on the beautiful River, with its Mount Eliza headland and wide sweeps and curves twinkling in the sun, and they walked up William St. looking for an adventure.

A man whom they knew from the north, in filthy denims, came out of a boot-shop and hailed them.

"Come an' stop one on me,* maties."

"Right-O! But where's Lukey? He stood us one this morning. Seen him?"

"Yes, I seen him.—But 'arf a mo'!"*

Scottie turned into the pawnbrokers, under the three balls, and the boys followed.

"If y' sees what y' didn't oughta see, keep y' mouth shut."

"As a dead crab," assented Jack.

"Now then Uncle! What'll y' advance on that pair o' bran new boots I've just bought?"

"Two bob."

"Glory be. An' I just give twenty for 'em. Ne' mind, gimme th' ticket."

This transaction concluded, Jack wondered what he could pawn. He pulled out a front tooth, beautifully set in a gold plate. It had been a parting finish to his colonial outfit, the original tooth having been lost in a football scrum.

"Father Abraham," he said, holding up the tooth, "I'm a gentleman, whether I look it or not. So is my friend, this gentleman. He needs a dress suit for tonight, though you wouldn't believe it. He needs a first-class well-fitting dress suit for this evening."

"I have first-class latest fashion gents clothes upstairs.—But a suit like that is worth five pound to me."

"Let him try the jacket on."

Abraham was doubtful. But at length Tom was hustled shamefacedly into a rather large tail-coat. It looked awful, but Jack said it would do. The man wouldn't take a cent less than two quid deposit: and ten bob for the loan of the suit. The boys said they'd call later.

"What'll you give me on this tooth?" asked Jack. "There's not a more expensive tooth in Western Australia."

"I'll lend y' five bob on that, pecos y' amuth me."*

"And we'll come in later for the dress suit. Alright Aaron. Hang on to that tooth, it's irreplaceable. Treat it like a jewel. Give me the five bob and the ticket."

In the Miners Refuge Jack flung himself down on a bench beside an individual who looked tidy but smelt strongly of rum, and asked:

"Say mate, where can y' get a wash an' a brush-up for two?—local?"

The fellow got up and lurched surlily to the counter, refusing to answer.

Jack sat on, while Tom drank beer, and a heavy depression crept over his spirit. He had been hobnobbing with riff-raff so long, it had almost become second nature. But now a sense of disgust and impending disaster came over him. He would soon have to make an angry effort, and get out. He was becoming angry with Tom, for sitting there so sloppily soaking beer, when he knew his head was weak.

They began to eat sandwiches, hungrily standing at the bar. Another slipshod waster, eyeing the denim man as if he were a fish, sidled over to him and muttered.

"Sorry," said Scottie with a mournful expression, pulling out the pawn-ticket, "I've just had to pawn me boots. Can't be done."

Jack grinned. The waster then came sloping over to him.

"Y' axed me mate a civil question just now, lad, an' I'd 'ave answered it for 'im, but I just spotted a racin' pal o' mine an' was onter him ter get a tip he'd promised—a dead cert f' Belmont* tomorrer."—He leaned nearer, breathing onions and rum in Jack's face.

"Y' might ha' seen him lettin' me inter th' know,"* he breathed. "Hev' a drink, lad!"

"Thanks!" said Jack. "This is my mate.—I'll take the shout, an' one back, an' then we must be off. Going up country tomorrer morning."

This seemed to push the man's mind on quicker.

"Just from up north, aren't ye? Easy place to knock up a cheque. How'd y' like to double a fiver."

"O. K." said Tom.

"Well here's a dead cert. Take it from me, and don't let it past yer. I got it from a racin' pal wot's in the know. Not straight for the punters, maybe—but straight as a die f'r me 'n my pals. Double y' money? Not 'arf! Multiply it by ten. 'S a dead cert."

"Name?"

"Not so quick. Not in 'ere. Come outside, 'n I'll whisper it to y'."

Jack paid for the drinks, and winking warningly to Tom, followed the man outside.

"The name o' th'oss," the fellow said—"But tell yer wot, I'll put ye on the divvy with a book* I know—or y' c'n come wi' me. He keeps a paper-shop in Hay Street."

"We don't know the name of the horse yet."

"Comin' from up north you don't know the name o' none of 'em, do yer? He's a rank outsider. Y' oughter get twenties on 'im."

"We've only got about a quid atween us," said Tom.

"Well, that means a safe forty—after th' race."

"Bob on!"* said Tom. "Where's the book-shop?"

"How can we go in an' back a hoss without knowin' his name?" said Jack.

"Oh I'll tip it y'* in 'ere."

They entered a small paper-shop, and the man said to the fellow behind the counter:

"These two gents 's pals o' mine.—How much did y' say y'd lay, mates?"

"Out with the name o' th' hoss first," said Tom confidentially.

"This shop's changed hands lately," said the fat fellow behind the counter. "I don't make books. Got no licence."

Didn't that look straight? But the boys were no greenhorns. They walked out of the shop again.

In the road the stranger said:

"The name o' th' 'oss is Double Bee. If y'll give me th' money I'll run upstairs 'ere t' old Josh—everyone knows him for a sound book."

"The name o' th' hoss," said Jack, "is Boots-two-Bob. An' a more cramblin'* set o' lies I never heard. Get outter this, or I'll knock y' head off."

The fellow went off with a yellow look.

"Gosh!" said Tom. "We're back home right enough, what?"

"Bon soir, as Frenchy used to say?"*

Rolling a little drearily along, they saw Jimmie Short standing on the pavement watching them.

"Hello mates!" he said. "Still going strong?"

"Fireproof!"* said Tom.

"Remember barging into me this morning? And my best girl was just coming round the corner with her Ma! Had to mind my company, eh, boys. But come an' have a drink now.—I seem to have seen you before today, haven't I? Where was it?"

"Don't try and think," said Tom. "Y' might do us out of a pony."

"Right-O! old Gold dust! Step over on to the Bar-parlour mat."

"I'm stepping," said Tom. " 'N I'm not drunk."

"No he's not," said Jack.

"You bet he's not," said Jimmie. He was eyeing them curiously, as if his memory pricked him.

"My name," said Tom, "is Ned Kelly.* And if yours isn't Jimmy Miller, what is it?"

"Why it's Short.—Well, I give it up. I can't seem to lay my finger on you, Kelly."

Tom roared with laughter.

"What time is it?" he asked.

"Ten past twelve."

"We've won a pony off old George!" said the delighted Tom. "I'm Tom Ellis and he's Jack Grant. *Now* do you know us, Jimmie?"

Jack was glad to get washed and barbered and dressed. After all, he was sick of wasters and roughs. They were stupider than respectable people, and much more offensive physically and morally. To hell with them all. He wouldn't care if some tyrant would up and extirpate the breed.

Anyhow he stepped clean out of their company.

Chapter XVIII.

The Governor's Dance.

Three gentlemen in evening dress passing along by the low brick wall skirting the Government House. One of the gentlemen portly and correct, two of the gentlemen young, with burnt brown faces that showed a little less tan below the shaving line, and limbs too strong and too rough to fit the evening clothes. Jack's suit was on the small side, though he'd scarcely grown in height. But it showed a big piece of white shirt-cuff at the wrists, and seemed to reveal the muscles of his shoulders unduly. As for Tom's quite good and quite expensive suit from the pawn-shop, it was a little large for him. If he hadn't been so bursting with life it would have been sloppy. But the crude animal life came so forcibly through the black cloth, that you had to overlook the anomaly of the clothes.—Both boys wore socks of fine scarlet wool, and the new handkerchiefs of magenta silk inside their waistcoats. The scarlet, magenta, and red-brown of their faces made a gallant pizzicato of colour against the black and white. Anyhow they fancied themselves, and walked conceitedly.

Jack's face was a little amusing. It had the kind of innocence and half-smile you can see on the face of a young fox, which will snap holes in your hand if you touch it. He was annoyed by his father's letter to him for his twenty-first birthday. The General had retired, and hadn't saved a sou. How could he, given his happy, thriftless lady. So it was a case of: My dear boy, I'm thankful you are at last twenty-one, because now you must look out for yourself. I have bled myself to send you this cheque for a hundred pounds, but I know you think I ought to send you something, so take it, but don't expect any more, for you won't get it if you do.

This was not really the text of the General's letter, but this was how Jack read it. As for his mother, she sent him six terrible neckties and awful silver-backed brushes which he hated the sight of, much love, a few tears, a bit of absurd fond counsel, and a general wind-up of tender doting which Jack felt was really meant, like the Harry Smith letter, "for 'Appy Jack wot went up Cossack way."

He was annoyed, because he had expected some sort of real

assistance in setting out like a gentleman on his life's career, now he had attained his majority. But the hundred quid was still a substantial sop.

Mr George had done them proud at the Weld Club, and got them invitations to the ball from the Private Secretary.* Oh yes, he was proud of them, handsome upstanding young fellows. So they were proud of themselves. It was a fine, hot evening, and nearly everybody was walking to the function, showing off their splendour. For few people possessed private carriages, and the town boasted very few cabs indeed.

Mr George waited in the porch of the Government House for Aunt Matilda and Mary. They had not long to wait, before they saw the ladies, in their shawls, and carrying each a little holland bag with scarlet initials, containing their dancing slippers, slowly and self-consciously mounting the steps.

The boys braced themselves to face the introduction to the Representative.* They were uneasy. Also they wanted to grin. In Jack's mind a picture of Honeysuckle, that tin town in the heat, danced as on heat-waves, as he made his bows and his murmurs. He wanted to whisper to Tom: "Ain't we in Honeysuckle?" But it would have been too cruel.

Clutching their programmes as drowning men clutch straws, they passed on. The primary ordeal was over.

"Oh Lord, I'm sweating already," said Tom with a red-faced grin. "I'm off to get me bill-head crammed."

"Take me with you, for the Lord's sake," said Jack.

"Y're such an owl of a dancer.* An' y' have to do it proper here. You go to Mr George."

"Don't desert me, you swine."*

"Go-on! Want me to take you back to Auntie?—Go-on! I'm goin' ter dance an' sit out an' hold their little white hands."

Tom pulled a droll face as he took his place in the line of glove-buttoning youths who made a queue on the Governor's left hand, where his daughter stood booking up duty dances. Jack, galvanised by the advent of the A. D. C., ducked through the crowd to Aunt Matilda's side.

He was always angry that he couldn't dance. The fact was, he would never learn. He could never bring himself to go hugging promiscuous girls round the waist and twiddling through dances with them. Underneath all his carelessness and his appearance of "mixing," there was a savage physical reserve which prevented his mixing at all. He could not bear the least physical intimacy. Something inside him recoiled and stood savagely at a distance even from the prettiest girl, the moment she seemed to be "coming on." To take the dear young things in his arms was repugnant to him, it offended a certain aloof pride and a subtle arrogance in him. Even with Tom, intimate though they were, he always kept a certain unpassable space around him, a definite *noli me tangere** distance which gave the limit to all approach. It would have been difficult to define this reserve. Jack seemed absolutely the most open and accessible individual in the world, a perfect child. He seemed to lay himself far too open, to anybody's approach. But those who knew him better, like Mrs Ellis or his mother, knew the cold inward reserve, the savage unwillingness to be touched, which was central in him, as in a wolf-cub. There was something reserved, fierce and untouched at the very centre of him. Something, at the centre of all his openness and his seeming softness, that was cold, overbearing, and a little angry. This was the old overweening English blood in him, which would never really yield to promiscuity or to vulgar intimacy. He seemed to mix in with everybody, at random. But as a matter of fact, he had never finally mixed in with anybody, not even with his own mother and father, not even with Tom.* And certainly not with any casual girl. Essentially, he kept himself a stranger to everybody.

Aunt Matilda was in green satin with a tiara of diamonds. "The devil you know is better than the devil you don't know," was Jack's inward comment as he approached her.

Aloud he said:

"Would it be right if I asked you to let me have the pleasure of taking you in to supper later, Marm?"

"Oh you dear boy!" simpered Aunt Matilda. "So like y' dear father. But you see I'm engaged on these occasions. We have to go in in order of rank and precedence.—But you can take Mary. She says she has hurt her foot and can't dance much."

Mary took his arm, and they went out on to the terrace. There was clear moonlight, and trees against a shadowy, grey-blue sky, a dark perfume of tropical flowers. Jack felt the beauty of it, and it moved him. He waited for his soul to melt. But his soul would never melt. It was hard and clear as the moon itself.

"It is much better here!" he said, looking at the sky.

"Oh, it's beautiful!" said Mary. "I wanted so much to sit quietly and talk to you. It seems so long, and you looked so wild and different this morning. I've been so frightened, reading so much about the natives murdering people."*

Mary was different too, but Jack didn't know wherein.

"I don't believe there's much more danger in one place than in another," he said, "so long as you keep yourself in hand. Shall we sit down and have a real wongie?"*

They found a seat under the overspreading tree, and sat listening to the night-insects.

"You're not *very* glad to be back, are you?" asked Mary.

"Yes I am," he asserted, without a great deal of vigour. "What has been happening to you all this while, Mary?"

"The little things that are nothing," she said. "The only thing—" she hesitated—"is that they want me to marry. And I lie awake at night wondering about it."

"Marry who?" asked Jack, his mind running at once to Rackett.

They were sitting under a magnolia tree. Jack could make out the dark shape of a great flower against the moon, among black leaves. And the perfume was magnolia flowers.

"Do you want me to talk about it?" she said.

"I do."

Jack was glancing rather fiercely down the slope of the black-and-white moonlit garden, that sloped its lawns to the river. Mary sat very still beside him, in a cream lace dress.

"It's a Mr Boyd Blessington. He is a widower with five children, but he's an interesting man. He's got a black beard."

"Goodness!" said Jack. "Have you accepted him?"

"No. Not yet."

"Why do you think of marrying him? Do you like him?"

"For some things. He is a good man, and he wants me in a good way. He has a beautiful library. And he is a man of the world, there seems to be a big world round him. Yes, he is quite somebody. And Aunt Matilda says it is a wonderful opportunity for me. And I know it is."

Jack mused in silence.

"It may be," he said. "But I hardly fancy you kissing a widower of fifty, with a black beard and five children. Lord!"

"He's only thirty-seven. And he's a *man.*"

Jack thought about Monica. He wanted Monica. But also he

couldn't bear to let Mary go. This arrogance in him made him silent for some moments. Then he turned to Mary, his head erect, and looked down sternly on her small, sinking figure in the pale lace dress.

"Do you *want* him?" he asked, in a subtle tone of authority and passion.

Mary was silent for some moments.

"No-o!" she faltered. "Not—not—"

Her hands lay inert in her lap. They were small, soft, dusky hands. The flame went over him, over his will. By some curious destiny, she really belonged to him. And Monica? He wanted Monica too. He wanted Monica first. But Mary also was his. Hard and savage he accepted this fact.

He took her two hands and lifted them to his lips, and kissed them with strange, blind passion. When the flame went over him, he was blind. Mary gave a little cry, but did not withdraw her hands.

"I thought you cared for Rackett," he said suddenly, looking at her closely. She shook her head, and he saw she was crying.

He put his arm round her and gathered her in her lace dress to his breast. She was small, but strangely heavy. Not like that whip-wire of a Monica. But he loved her heaviness too, the heaviness of a dark, magnetic stone. He wanted that too.

And in his mind he thought, "Why can't I have her too? She is naturally mine?"

His soul was hard and unbending. "She is naturally mine!" he said to himself. And he kissed her softly, softly, kissed her face and her tears. And all the while Mary knew about Monica. And he, his soul fierce, would not yield in either direction. He wanted to marry her, and he wanted to marry Monica. Something was in Mary that would never be appeased unless he married her. And something in him would never be appeased unless he married Monica. His young, clear instinct saw both these facts. And the inward imperiousness of his nature rose to meet it.—"Why can't I have both these women?" he asked himself. And his soul, hard in its temper like a sword, answered him: "You can if you will."

Yet he was wary enough to know he must go cautiously. Meanwhile, determined that one day he would marry Mary and Monica both, he held the girl soft and fast in his arms, kissing her, wanting her, but wanting her with the slow knowledge that he must wait and travel a long way before he could take her, yet take her he would. He wanted Monica first. But he also wanted Mary: the soft, slow weight of her as she lay silent and unmoving in his arms.

They could hear the music inside.

"I must go in for the next dance," she said in a muted tone. He kissed her mouth and released her. Then he escorted her back to the ball-room. She went across to Aunt Matilda, as the dance ended. And in her lace dress, the small, heavy, dusky Mary was like a lode-stone passing among flimsy people. She had a certain magnetic heaviness* of her own, and a certain stubborn, almost ugly kind of beauty which, in its heavy quietness, seemed like a darkish, perhaps bitter flower that rose from a very deep root. You were sensible of a deep root going down into the dark.

A tall, thin, rather hollow-chested man in perfect evening suit and with orders on his breast, was speaking to her. He too had a faint air of proprietorship. He had a black beard and eyeglasses. But his face was sensitive, and delicate in its desire. It was evident he loved her with a real, though rather social, uneasy, desirous love, as if he wanted all her answer. He was really a nice man, a bit frail and sad. Jack could see that. But he seemed to belong so entirely to the same world as the General, Jack's father. He belonged to the social* world, and saw nothing really outside.

Mary too belonged almost entirely to the social world, her instinct was strongly social. But there was a wild tang in her. And this Jack depended on. Somewhere deep in himself he hated his father's social world. He stood in the doorway and watched her dancing with Blessington. And he knew that as Mrs Blessington, with a thoughtful husband and a good position in society, she would be well off. She would forfeit that bit of a wild tang.

If Jack let her. And he wasn't going to let her. He was hard and cool inside himself. He took his impetus from* the wild sap that still flows in most men's veins, though they mostly choose to act from the tame sap. He hated his father's social sap. He wanted the wild nature in people, the unfathomed nature, to break into leaf again. The real rebel, not the mere reactionary.

He hated the element of convention and slight smugness which showed in Mary's movements as she danced with the tall, thin reed of a man. Anything can become a convention, even unconventionality, even the frenzied jazzing of the modern ball-room. And then the same element of smugness, very repulsive, is evident, evident even in the most scandalous jazzers. This is curious, that as soon as any movement becomes accepted in the public consciousness,* it becomes ugly and smug, unless it be saved by a touch of the native wild individuality.

And Mary dancing with Mr Blessington was almost smug. Only the downcast look on her face showed she remembered Jack. Blessington himself danced like a man neatly and efficiently performing his duty.

The dance ended. Aunt Matilda was fluttering her fan at him like a ruffled cockatoo.* There was a group: Mary, Blessington, Mr George, Mr James Watson, Aunt Matilda's brother-in-law, and Aunt Matilda. Mr Blessington, with the quiet assurance of his class, managed to eclipse Mr George and Jim Watson entirely, though Jim Watson was a rich man.

Jack went over and was introduced. Blessington and he bowed at one another. "Stay in your class, you monkey!" thought Jack, with some of the sensual arrogance he had brought with him from the North-West.

Mr Blessington introduced him to a thin, nervous girl, his daughter. She was evidently unhappy, and Jack was sorry for her. He took her out for refreshments, and was kind to her. She made dark-grey, startled round eyes at him, and looked at him as if he were an incalculable animal that might bite. And he, in manner if not in actuality, laughed and caressed the frail young thing to cajole some life into her.

Mary danced with Tom, and then with somebody else. Jack lounged about, watching with a set face that still looked innocent and amiable, keeping a corner of his eye on Mary, but chatting with various people. He wouldn't make a fool of himself, trying to dance.

When Mary was free again—complaining of her foot—he said to her:

"Come outside a bit."

And obediently she came. They went and sat under the same magnolia tree.

"He's not a bad fellow, your Blessington," he said.

"He's not my Blessington," she replied. "Not yet, anyhow. And he never would be *really* My Blessington."

"You never know. I suppose he's quite rich."

"Don't be horrid to me."

"Why not?—I wish I was rich. I'd do as I liked.—But you'll never marry him."

"Why shan't I?"

"You just won't."

"I shall if Aunt Matilda makes me. I'm absolutely dependent on her—and do you think I don't feel it! I want to be free. I should be much freer if I did marry Mr Blessington. I'm tired of being as I am."

"What would you really like to do?"

She was silent for a time. Then she answered:

"I should like to live on a farm."

"Marry Tom," he said maliciously.

"Why are you horrid?" she said, in hurt surprise.

He too was silent for a time.

"Anyhow you won't marry Boyd Blessington."

"Why are you so sure. Aunt Matilda is going to England in April. And I won't travel with her. Travel with *her* would be unspeakable. I want to stay in Australia."

"Marry Tom," he said again, in malice.

"Why," she asked in amazement, "do you say that to me?"

But he didn't know himself.

"A farm—" he was beginning, when a figure sailed up in the moonlight. It was Aunt Matilda. The two young people rose to their feet. Jack was silent and rather angry. He wanted to curl his nose and say "It isn't done, Marm!" But he said nothing. Aunt Matilda did the talking.

"I thought it was *your* voices," she said coldly. "Why do you make yourself conspicuous, Mary? Mr Blessington is looking for you in all the rooms."

Mary was led away, Jack followed. Aunt Matilda had no sooner seen Mary led out by Mr Blessington for the Lancers, than she came full sail upon Jack, as he stood lounging in the doorway.

"Come for a little walk on the terrace, dear boy," she said.

"Can't I have the pleasure of piloting you through this set of Lancers, Marm?" he retorted.

She stood and smiled at him fixedly.

"I've heard of y'r dancing, dear boy," she said. "And your father was a beautiful dancer.—This governor is very particular. He sent his A. D. C. to stop Jimmie Short reversing, right at the beginning of the evening."—She eyed him with a shrewd eye.

"Surely worse form to hurt a gentleman's feelings, than to reverse, Marm!" retorted Jack.

"It wasn't bad form, it was bad temper. The Governor can't

reverse himself. Ha-ha-ha! Neither can I go through a set of Lancers with you. So come and take me out a minute."

They went in silence down the terrace.

"Lovely evening! Not at all too hot!" he said.

She burst into a sputter of laughter.

"Lor'! m' dear! you *are* amusin' " she said. "But y' won't get out of it like that, young man. What have y' t' say f' y'self, running off with Mary like that, *twice*!"

"You told me I could take her, Marm."

"I didn't ask you to keep her out and get her talked about, m' dear! I'm not a fool, my dear boy, and I'm not going to let her let slip the chance of a life-time. You want her y'self for *one night*!" She slapped her fan crossly. "*You* leave well alone. We don't want *another* scandal in the family. Mr Blessington is a good man, and a good man for Mary, a God-send. For she's heavy, she's heavy, she's heavy for any man to take up with." Aunt Matilda said this almost spitefully. "Mr Blessington's the very man for her, and a wonderful match. She's got her family. She's the granddaughter of Lord Haworth. And he has position. Besides, they're *suited* for one another. It's the very finger of heaven!* Don't you dare make another scandal in the family."

She had stopped under a lamp, and was leaning forward peering at him. Her large person exhaled a scent of artificial perfume—Jack hated perfume, especially in the open air. And her face, with its powder and wrinkles, in the mingled light of the lamp and the moon, made him think of a lizard.

"D' you want Mary yourself?" she snapped, like a great lizard. "It's out of the question. You've got to make your way. She'd have to go on waiting for years. And you'd compromise her."

"God forbid!" said Jack ironically.

"Then leave her alone," she said. "If you compromise her, *I'll* do no more for her, mind that."

"Just exactly what do you mean, compromise her?" he asked.

"Get her talked about—as you're trying to," she snapped.

He thought it over. He must anyhow appear to yield to circumstances.

"All right," he said. "I know what you mean."

"See you do!" she retorted. "Now take me back to the ballroom."

They returned, in a silence that was safe, if not golden. He was inwardly more set than ever. His appearance, however, was calm and innocent. She was much more ruffled. She wondered if she had said too much or too little, if he were merely stupid, or really dangerous.

He politely steered a way back to the reception room, placed her in a chair, and turned to disappear. One thing he could not stand, and that was her proximity.

But as she sat down she clutched his sleeve, cackling her unendurable laugh.

"Sit down then," she said. "We're friends now, aren't we?" And she tapped his tanned cheek, that still had a bit of the peach-look, with her feathery black fan.

"On the contrary, Marm!" he said, bowing but not taking a seat.

"Lor', but you are an amusin' boy, m' dear!" she said, and she let go his sleeve as she turned to survey the field.

In that instant he slipped away from her disagreeable presence. He slipped behind a stout judge from Melbourne, then past a plumed woman apparently of fashion, and was gone.

What he had to do was to reconnoitre his own position. He wanted Monica first. That was his fixed determination. But he was not going to let go of Mary either. Not in spite of battalions of Aunt Matildas or correct social individuals.—It was a battle.

But he had to gauge Mary's disposition. He saw how much she was a social thing: how much, even, she was Lord Haworth's grand-daughter. And how little she was that other thing.

But it was a battle, a long, slow, subtle battle. And he loved a fight, even a long, invisible one.

In the ball-room, the A. D. C. pounced on him.

When he was free again, he looked round for Mary. It was the sixteenth dance, and she was being well nursed. When the dance was over, he went calmly and sat between her and Aunt Matilda, on a red and gilt sofa. Things were a little stiff. Even Mary was stiff.

He looked at her programme. The next dance was a polka, and she was not engaged.

"You are free for this dance?" he said.

"Yes, because of my foot," she said firmly. He could see she too was on Aunt Matilda's side, at the moment.

"I can dance a polka. Come and dance it with me," he said.

"And my foot?"

He didn't answer, merely looked her in the face. And she rose.

They neither of them ever forgot that absurd, jogging little dance.

"I must speak to you, Mary," he said.

"What about?"

"Would you really like to live on a farm?"

"I *think* I should."

The conversation was rather jerky and breathless.

"In two years I can have a farm," he said.

She was silent for some time. Then she looked into his eyes, with her queer, black, humble-seeming eyes. She was thinking of all the grandeur of being Mrs Boyd Blessington. It attracted her a great deal. At the same time, something in her soul fell prostrate, when Jack looked straight into her. Something fell prostrate, and she couldn't help it. His eyes had a queer power in them.

"In two years I can have a farm—a good one," he said.

She only gazed into his eyes with her queer, black, fascinated gaze.

The dance was over. Aunt Matilda was tapping Jack's wrist with her fan, and saying:

"Yes, Mr Blessington, do be so good as to take Mary down to supper."

Supper was over. It was the twentieth dance. Jack had been introduced to a sporting girl in her late twenties. She treated him like a child, and talked quite amusingly. Tom called her a "barrack hack."*

Mr Blessington went by with Mary on his arm.

"Mary," said Jack, "do you know Miss Brackley."

Mary stopped and was smilingly introduced. Miss Brackley at once pounced amusingly on Mr Blessington.

"I want to speak to you," Jack said once more to Mary. "Behind the curtain of the third window."

He glanced at the red, ponderous plush curtain he meant. Mary looked frightened into his eyes, then glanced too. Mr Blessington, extricating himself, walked on with Mary.

Jack looked round for Tom. That young man was having a drink, at the supper extra.* Jack left the Barrack Hack for the moment.

"Tom," he said. "Will you stand by me in anything I do or say?"

"I will," said the glistening, scarlet-faced Tom, who was away on the gay high seas of exaltation.

"Get up a rubber of whist for Aunt Matilda. I know she'd like one. Will you?"

"Before you c'n say Wiggins,"* replied Tom, laughing as he always did when he was tipsy.

"And I say Tom. You care for Mary, don't you? Would you provide a home for her if she was wanting one?"

"I'd marry Mary if she'd 'ave me 'n I hadn't got a wife."

"Shut up!"

Tom broke into a laugh.

"Don't go back on me, Tom."

"Never, s'elp me bob."*

"Get a move on then, and arrange that whist."

He sent him off with the Barrack Hack. And then he watched Mary. She still was walking with Mr Blessington. They were not dancing. She knew Jack was watching her, and she was nervous. He watched her more closely.

And at the third window she fluttered, staggered a little, left go Mr Blessington's arm, and turned round to gather up her skirt behind. She pretended she had torn a hem. She pretended she couldn't move without a pin. She asked to be steered into the alcove. She sent Mr Blessington away to the ladies' dressing-room, for the pin.

And when he came back with it, she was gone.

Jack, outside in the night, was questioning her.

"Has Mr Blessington proposed to you yet?"

"No."

"Don't let him.—Would you *really* be happy on a farm—?—even if it was rather hard work?"

He had to look down on her very steadfastly as he asked this. And she was slow in answering, and the tears came into her eyes before she murmured:

"Yes."

He was touched, and the same dominating dark desire came over him again. He held her fast in his arms, fast and silent. The desire was dark and powerful and permanent in him.

"Can you wait for me, even two years?" he asked.

"Yes," she murmured faintly.

His will was steady and black. He knew he could wait.

"In two years I shall have a farm for you to live on," he said. And he kissed her again, with the same dark, permanent passion.

Then he sent her off again.

He went and found Mr George, in the cardroom. There was old Aunt Matilda, playing for her life, her diamonds twinkling but her fan laid aside.

"We're going to Wandoo tomorrow morning, sir," said Jack.

"That's right lad," said Mr George.

"I say, sir, won't you do Tom a kindness?" said Jack. "You're coming down yourself one day this week, aren't you?"

"Yes, I shall be down on Wednesday or Thursday."

"Bring Mary down with you. Make her Aunt Matilda let her come. Tom's awfully gone on her, and when he sees her with Boyd Blessington he straightway goes for a drink.—I don't think she's suited for Mr Blessington, do you, sir? He's nearly old enough to be her father. And Tom's the best fellow in the world, and Mary's the one he cares for. If nothing puts him out and sends him wrong, there's not a better fellow in the world."

Mr George blew his nose, prrhed! and bahed! and was in a funk. He feared Aunt Matilda. He was very fond of Mary, might even have married her himself, but for the ridicule. He liked Tom Ellis. He didn't care for men like Blessington. And he was an emotional old Australian.

"That needs thinking about! That requires thought!" he said.

Not the next day, but the day following that, the boys drove away from Perth in a new sulky, with a horse bought from Jimmie Short. And Mr George had promised to come on the coach the day after, with Mary.

Chapter XIX.

The Welcome at Wandoo.*

"Things change," said Jack, as he and Tom drove along in the sulky, "and they never go back to what they were before."

"Seems like they don't," said Tom uneasily.

"And men change," continued Jack. "I have changed, and I shall never go back to what I was before."

"Oh dry up!" said the nervous Tom. "You're just the blanky same."

Both boys felt a load on their spirits, now they were actually on the home road. They hated the load, too.

"We're going to make some change at Wandoo," said Tom. "I wish I could leave Ma on the place. But Mr George says she absolutely refuses to stay, and he says I've not got to try an' force her. He sortta winked at me, and told me I should want to be settlin' down myself. I wondered what 'n hell he meant. Y'aven't let on nothing about—about that Honeysuckle trip, have y'? I don't mean t' insult you by askin', but it seemed kinder funny like."

"No," said Jack. "I've not breathed Honeysuckle to a soul, and never will. You get it off your mind—it's nothing."

"Well then I dunno what 'e meant. I told him I hadn't made a bean anyhow. An' I asked him what 'n hell Ma was goin' ter live on. He seemed a bit down in the mouth about 'er himself, old George did. Fair gave me the bally hump.* Wisht I was still up north, strike me lucky I do.

"We've been gone over two years, yet I feel I've never been away, an' yet I feel the biggest stranger in the world, comin' back to what's supposed to be me own house. I hate havin' ter come, becos o' the bloomin' circumstances. Why 'n hell couldn't Ma have had the place for while she lived, an' me be comin' back to her an' the kids. Then I shouldn't feel sortta sick about it. But as it is—it fair gets me beat. Lennie'll resent me, an' Katie an' Monica'll hate havin' to get inter a smaller house, an' the twins an' Harry an' th' little ones don' matter so much, but I do worry over pore ole Ma."

There he was, with a blank face, driving the pony homewards. He hadn't worried over pore ole Ma till this very minute, on the principle "out of sight, out of mind." Now he was all strung up.

"Y' know Jack," he said, "I kinder don' want Wandoo. I kinder don' want to be like Dad, settlin' down with a heap o' responsibilities an' kids an' all that. I kinder don' want it."

"What do you want?" said Jack.

"I'd rather knock about with you for me mate, Jack. I'd a sight rather do that."

"You can't knock about for ever," said Jack.

"I don' know whether you can or you can't. I only know I never knew my own mother. I only know *she* never lived at Wandoo, *she* never raised me there. I bet she lugged me through the bush. An' when all comes to all, I'd rather do the same. I don' want Dad's property. I don' want that Ellis property. Seems ter me it's bad luck. What d' yer think?"

"I should think it depends on you," said Jack.

"I should think it does. Anyhow shall you stop on with me, an' go shares in the blinkin' thing?"

"I don't know," said Jack.

He was thinking that soon he would see Monica. He was wondering how she would be. He was wondering if she was ready for him, or if she would have a thousand obstacles around her. He was wondering if she would want him to plead and play the humble and say he wasn't good enough for her. Because he wouldn't do it. Not if he never saw her again. All that flummery of love he would not subscribe to. He would not say he adored her, because he didn't adore her. He was not the adoring sort. He would not make up to her, and play the humble to her, because it insulted his pride. He didn't feel like that, and he never would feel like that, not towards any woman on earth.—Even Mary, once he had "declared himself," would fetch up her social tricks and try to bring him to his knees. And he was not going down on his knees, not for half a second, not to any woman on earth, nor to any man either. Enough of this kneeling flummery.

He stood fast and erect on his two feet, that had travelled many wild miles. And fast and correct he would continue to stand. Almost he wished he could be clad in iron armour, inaccessible. Because the thought of women bringing him down and making him humble himself, before they would give themselves to him, this turned his soul black.

Monica! He didn't love her. He didn't feel the slightest bit of sentimental weakening towards her. Rather, when he thought of her, his muscles went stiffer and his soul haughtier. It was not he who must bow the head. It was she.

Because he wanted her. With a deep, arrowy desire, and a long, lasting dark desire, he wanted her. He wanted to take her apart from all the world, and put her under his own roof.

But he didn't want to plead with her, or weep before her, or adore her, or humbly kiss her feet. The very thought of it made his blood curdle and go black.—Something had happened to him in the Never-Never. Before he went over the border,* he might have been tricked into a surrender to this soft and hideous thing they called love. But now, he would have love in his own way, haughtily, passionately, and darkly, with dark, arrowy desire, and a strange, arrowily-submissive* woman: either this, or he would not have love at all.

He thought of Monica. And sometimes the thought of her sent him black with anger. And sometimes, as he thought of her wild, delicate, reckless, lonely little profile, a hot tenderness swept over him, and he felt he would envelop her with a fierce and sheltering tenderness, like a scarlet mantle.

So long as she would not fight against him, and strike back at him. Jeer at him, play with Easu in order to insult him. Not that, my God, not that.

As for Mary, a certain hate of her burned in him. The queer heavy stupid conceit with which she had gone off to dance with Boyd Blessington, because he was an important social figure. Mary, wanting to live on a farm, but at the same time absolutely falling before the social glamour of a Blessington, and becoming conceited on the strength of it. Inside herself, Mary thought she was very important, thought that all sorts of eternal destinies depended on *her* choice and *her* actions. Even Jack was nothing more than an instrument of *her* divine importance.

He had sensed this clearly enough. And it was this that made Aunt Matilda a bit spiteful against her, when she said Mary was "heavy" and wouldn't easily get a man.

But there was also the queer black look in Mary's eyes, that was outside her conceit and her social importance. The queer, almost animal dark glisten, that was full of fear and wonder and vulnerability. Like the look in the eyes of a caught wild animal. Or the look in the shining black eyes of one of the aborigines, especially the black woman looking askance in a sort of terror at a white man, as if a white man were a sort of devil that might possess her.

Where had Mary got that queer aboriginal look, she the granddaughter of an English earl?

"Y're real lively today, aintcher Jack? Got a hundred quid for your birthday, and my, some talk!"

"Comes to that," said Jack, rousing himself with difficulty: "We've come fifteen or twenty miles without you opening your mouth either."

Tom laughed shortly, and relapsed into silence.

"Well," he said, "let's wake up now, there's the outlying paddock." He pointed with his whip.—"And there's the house through the dip in the valley." Then suddenly, in a queer tone: "Say matey, don't it look lovely from here, with all that afternoon sun falling over it like snow... You think I've never seen snow: but I have, in my dream."

Jack's heart contracted as he jumped down to open the first gate. For him too, the strange fulness of the yellow afternoon light was always unearthly, at Wandoo. But the day was still early, just after dinner-time, for they had stayed the night half way.*

"Looks in good trim, eh?" said Jack.

"So it does! A. 1.," replied Tom. "Mr George says Ma done wonders. Made it pay hand over fist. Y' remember that fellow Pink-eye Percy, what come from Queensland and had studied agriculture an' was supposed to be a bad egg an' all that? At that 'roo hunt, you remember? Well he bought land next to Wandoo, off-side from the Reds. An' Ma sortta broke wi' the Reds over something, an' went in wi' him, an' 't seems they was able to do wonders. Anyway old George says Ma's been able to buy a little place near her own old home in Beverley, to go to.—But seems to me—"

"What?"

"Funny how little anyone *tells* you, Jack."

"How?"

"I felt I couldn't get to th' bottom of what old George was tellin' me. I took no notice then. But it seems funny now. An' I say—"

"What?"

"You'd 'a thought Monica or Katie might ha' driven to the cross-roads for us, like we used to in Dad's days."

"Yes, I thought one of them would have been there."

The boys drove on, in tense silence, through the various gates. They could see the house ahead.

"There's Timothy!" said Tom.

The old black was holding open the yard gate. He seemed to have almost forgotten Jack, but the emotion in his black, glistening eyes was strange, as he stared with strange adoration at the young master. He caught Tom's hand in his two wrinkled dark hands, and clung to it, heaving it passionately up and down, as if clinging to life itself.

The twins ran out, waved, and ran back. Katie appeared, looking bigger, heavier, more awkward than ever. Tom patted Timothy's hands again, then went across and kissed Katie, who blushed with shyness.

"Where's Ma, Katie?"

"In the parlour."

Tom broke away, leaving Katie blushing in front of Jack. Jack was thinking how queer and empty the house seemed. And he felt an outsider again. He stayed outside, sat down on the bench.

A boy much bigger than Harry, but with the same blue eyes and curly hair, appeared chewing a haystalk, and squatted on a stone near by. Then Og and Magog, a bit taller but no thinner, came and edged on to the seat. Then Ellie, a long-legged little girl, came running to his knees. And then what had been baby, but was now a fat, toddling little girl,* came racing out, fearless and inconsequential as the twins had been.

"Where's Len?" said Jack.

"He's in th' paddock seein' t' th' sheep," said Harry.

There was a queer tense silence. The children seemed to cling round Jack for male protection.

"We're goin' t' live nearer in to th' township now," said Harry, "in a little wee sortta house."

He stared with bold blue eyes, unwinking and yet not easy, straight into Jack's eyes.

"Well Harry," said Jack. "You've grown quite a man."

"I hev' so!" said Harry. "Quite the tyke!* I ken kill birds for Ma to put in th' pot. I ken skin a kangaroo. I ken—"

But Jack didn't hear what else, because Tom was calling him from the doorway. He went slowly across.

"Say mate," said Tom in a low tone. "Stand by me. Things is not all right." Aloud he said: "Ma want t' see ye, Jack."

Jack followed through the back premises, down the three steps into the parlour. It all seemed forlorn.

Ma sat with her face buried in her hands. Jack knitted his brows. Tom put his hand on her shoulder.

"What is it, Ma? What is it? I wouldn't be anything but good to yer, Ma, you knows that.—Here's Jack Grant."

"Ye were always a good boy, Tom. I'm real glad t' see ye back. And Jack," said Ma through her hands.

Tom looked at Jack in dismay. Then he stooped and kissed her hair.

"You look to me," he said. "We'll fix everything all right, for Lennie 'n everybody."

But Ma still kept her face between her hands.

"There's nothing t' worry about, Ma, sure there isn't," persisted the distracted Tom. "I want y' t' have everything you want, I do, you an' Lennie an' th' kids."

Mrs Ellis took her hands from her face. She looked pale and worn. She would not turn to the boys, but kept her face averted.

"I know you're as good a boy as ever lived," she faltered. Then she glanced quickly at Tom and at Jack, the tears began to run down her face, and she threw her apron over her head.

"God's love!" gasped the bursting Tom, sinking on a chair.

They all waited in silence. Mrs Ellis suddenly wiped her face on her apron and turned with a wan smile to the boys.

"I've saved enough to buy a little place near Beverley, which is where I belong," she said. "So me and the children are all right. And I've got my eye—at least Lennie's got *his*—on a good selection east of here, between this and my little house, for Lennie. But we want cash for that, I'm afraid.—Only—it's not that. That's not it."

"Lennie's young yet to take up land, Ma!" Tom plunged in. "Why won't he stop here and go shares wi' me?"

"He wants to get married," said the mother wanly.

"Get married! Len! Why he's only seventeen!"

At this very natural exclamation, Ma threw her apron over her head, and began to cry once more.

"He's been so good!" she sobbed. "He's been so good! And his Ruth is old enough and sensible enough for two. Better anything—" with more sobbing—"than another scandal in the family."

Tom rubbed his head. Gosh, it was no joke being the head of a family!

"Well Ma, if you wish it, what's the odds. But I'm afraid it'll have to wait a bit. Jack'll tell you I haven't any cash. Not a stiver,* Ma! Blown out! It takes it outter yer up north. We never struck it rich."

Mrs Ellis, under her apron, wept softly.

"Poor little Lennie! Poor little Lennie! He's been so good, Tom. Working day and night. And never spending a shilling. All his learning gone for nought, Tom, and him a little slave, at his years, old and wise enough to be his father, Tom. And he wants to get married. If we could start him out fair! The new place has only four rooms and an out-kitchen, and there's not enough to keep him, much less a lady wife. She's a lady earning her bread teaching. He could go to Grace's. Alec Rice would have him. But—"

She had taken her apron off her face, and was staring averted at the door leading into Gran's old room.

The two boys listened mystified and a little annoyed. Why all this about Lennie. Jack was wondering where Monica was. Why didn't she come? Why wasn't she mentioned? And why was Ma so absolutely downcast, on the afternoon of Tom's home-coming. It wasn't fair on Tom.

"Where is Monica?" asked Jack shyly at last.

But Mrs Ellis only shook her head faintly and was mute, staring across at Gran's door.

"Lennie married!" Tom was brooding. "Y'll have to put it out of y'r mind for a bit, Ma. Why it wouldn't hardly be decent."

"Let him marry if he's set on it—an' the girl's a good girl," said Mrs Ellis, her eyes swamping with tears again and her voice breaking as she rocked herself again.

"Yes if we could afford it," Tom hastily put in. And he raised his stunned eyes to Jack. Jack shrugged, and looked in the empty fireplace, and thought of the little fires Gran used to have.

Money! Money! Money! The moment you entered within four walls it was the word money, and your mouth full of ashes.

And then again something hardened in his soul. All his life he had been slipping away from the bugbear of money. It was no good. You had to turn round and get a grip on the miserable stuff. There was nothing else for it. Though money nauseated him, he now accepted the fact that he must have control over money, and not try just to slip by.

He began to repent of having judged Gran. That little old witch of a Gran, he had hated the way she had seemed to hoard money and gloat in the secret possession of it. But perhaps she knew, *somebody* must control it, somebody must keep a hand over it. Like a deadly weapon. Money! Property! Gran fighting for them, to bequeath them to the men she loved.

Perhaps she too had really hated money. She wouldn't make a will. Neither would Dad. Their secret repugnance for money and possessions. But you *had* to have property, else you were down and out. The men you loved had to have property, or they were down and out. Like Lennie!

Poor old plucky Gran, fighting for her men. It was all a terrible muddle anyhow. But he began to understand her motive.

Yes, if Lennie had got a girl into trouble and wanted to marry her, the best he could do would be to have money and buy himself a little place. Otherwise, heaven knows what would happen to him. With their profound indifference to the old values, these Australians seemed either to exaggerate the brutal importance of money, or they wanted to waste money altogether, and themselves along with it. This was what Gran feared: that her best male heirs would go and waste themselves, as Jacob had begun to waste himself. The generous ones would just waste themselves, because of their profound mistrust of the old values.

Better rescue Lennie for the little while it was still possible to rescue him. Jack's mind turned to his own money. And then, looking at that inner door, he seemed to see Gran's vehement figure, pointing almost viciously with her black stick. She had tried so hard to drive the wedge of her meaning deep into Jack's consciousness. And she had failed. He had refused to take her meaning.

But now, with a sigh that was almost a groan, he took up the money burden. The "stocking" she had talked about, and which he had left in the realms of unreality, was an actuality. That witch Gran, with her uncanny, hateful second sight, had put by a stocking for Lennie, and entrusted the secret of it to Jack. And he had refused the secret. He hated those affairs.

Now he must assume the mysterious responsibility for this money. He got up and went to the chimney, and peered into the black opening. Then he began to feel carefully along the side of the chimney-stack, inside, where there was a ledge. His hand went deep in soot and charcoal and grey ash.

He took off his coat and rolled up his sleeve.

"Gone off y'r bloomin' nut, Jack?" asked Tom, mystified.

"Gran told me she had put a stocking for Len in here," said Jack.

"Stocking be blowed!" said Tom testily. "We've heard that barm-stick* yarn before. Leave it alone, boy."

He was looking at Jack's bare, brown, sinewy arm. It reminded him of the great North-West, and the heat, and the work, and the absolute carelessness. This money and stocking business was like a mill-stone round his neck. He felt he was gradually being drowned in soot, as Jack continued to fumble up inside the chimney, and the soot poured down over the naked arm.

"Oh God's love, leave it alone, Jack!" he cried.

"Let him try," said Mrs Ellis quietly. "If Gran told him—I wonder he didn't speak before."

"I never really thought about it," said Jack.

"Don't think about it now!" shouted Tom.

Jack could feel nothing in the chimney. He looked contemplatively at the fireplace. Something drew him to the place near Gran's arm-chair. He began feeling, while the other two watched him in a state of nervous tension. Tom hated it.

"She pointed here with her stick," said Jack.

There was a piece of tin fastened over the side of the fireplace, and black-leaded.

"Mind if we try behind this?" he asked.

"Leave it alone!" cried Tom.

But Jack pulled it out, and the ash and dirt and soot poured down over the hearth. Behind the sheet of thin iron was the naked stone of the chimney piece. Various stones were loose: that was why Gran had had the tin sheet put over.

He got out of a cavity behind the stones, where the loose mortar had all crumbled, a little square dusty box that had apparently been an old tea-caddy. It was very heavy for its size, and very dirty. He put it on the table in front of Mrs Ellis. Tom got up excitedly to look in. He opened the lid. It was full to the brim of coins, gold and silver coins and dust and dirt, and a sort of spider filament. He shook his head over it.

"Isn't that Old Gran to a t!" he exclaimed, and poured out the dust and the money on the table.

Ma began eagerly to pick out the gold from the silver, saying:

"I remember when she made Dad put that iron plate up. She said insects came out and worried her."

Ma only picked out the gold pieces, the sovereigns and the

half-sovereigns. She left Tom to sort the silver crowns and half-crowns into little piles. Jack watched in silence. There was a smell of soot and old fire-dust, and everybody's hands were black.

Mrs Ellis was putting the sovereigns in piles of ten. She had a queer sort of satisfaction, but her gloom did not really lift. Jack stayed to know how much it was. Mentally he counted the piles of gold she made: the pale washy gold of Australia,[*] most of it. She counted, and counted again.

"Two hundred and fourteen pounds!" she said in a low voice.

"And ten in silver," said Tom.

"Two hundred and twenty-four pounds," she said.

"It's not the world," said Tom, "but it's worth having. It's a start, Ma. And you can't say *that* isn't Lennie's."

Jack went out and left them. He listened in all the rooms downstairs. What he wanted to know about was Monica. He hated this family and family money business, it smelled to him of death. Where was Monica? Probably, to add to the disappointment, she was away staying with Grace.

The house sounded silent. Upstairs all was silent. It *felt* as if nobody were there.

He went out and across the yard to the stable. Lucy whinnied. Jack felt she knew him. The nice, natural old thing: Tom would have to christen her afresh. At least *this* Lucy wouldn't leave a "Stocking" behind her when she was dead. She was much too clean. Ah, so much nicer than that other Lucy with her unpleasant perspiration, away in Honeysuckle.

Jack stood a long while with the sensitive old horse. Then he went round the out-buildings, looking for Lennie. He drifted back to the house, where Harry was chopping something with a small hatchet.

"Where's Monica, Harry?" he asked.

"She's not home," said Harry.

"Where's she gone?"

"Dunno."

And the resolute boy went on with his chopping.

Tom came out, calling: "I'm going over to have a word wi' th' Reds, Jack. Comin' with me?"

Tom didn't care for going anywhere alone, just now. Jack joined him.

"Where's Monica, Tom?" he asked.

"Ay, where is she?" said Tom, looking round as if he expected her to appear from the thin air.

"She's not at home, anyhow," said Jack.

"She's gone off to Grace's, or to see somebody, I expect," said Tom, as they walked across the yard. "And Len is out in the paddocks still. He don't seem in no hurry to come an' meet us, neither. The little cuss! Fancy that nipper wantin' to be spliced! Gosh, I'll bet he's old for his age, the little old wallaby! An' that bloomin' teacher woman, Ruth, why she's older 'n me. She oughtta be ashamed of herself, kidnappin' that nipper."

The two went side by side across the pasture, almost as if they were free again. They came to a stile.

"Gosh!" said Tom. "They've blocked up this gate, 'n put a stile over, see! Think o' that!"

They climbed the stile and continued their way.

"God's love, boy, didn't we land in it over our heads! Ever see Ma like that? I never! Good for you, Jack, lad, findin' that tea-caddy. That's how the Ellises are—ain't it the devil? 'Spect I take after my own mother, f'r I'm not in the tea-caddyin' line. But Ma's cheered up a bit. She'll be able to start Lennie in a bit of a way, now, 'n the twins can wait for a bit, thank goodness! My, but ain't families lively!—Here I come back to be boss of this bloomin' place, an' I feel as if I was goin' to be shot.—Say, boy, d' y' think I'm really spliced to that water-snake in Honeysuckle? Because I s'll have to have somebody to put a crease in my pants for me, if ever I'm going to continue on this outfit. Alone I will not face it.—Say, matey, promise me you won't leave me till I'm fixed up a bit. Give me your word you'll stand by me here for a time, anyhow."

"I'll stay for a time," said Jack.

"Right-O! An' then if I'm not copped by the Honeysuckle bird—'appen Mary might have me, what d' you think? I shall have to have somebody. I simply couldn't stand this place, all on my lonesome. What d' you think about Mary? D' you think she'd like it, here?"

"Ask her," said Jack grimly.

Chapter XX.

The Last of Easu.

i

They knew that Easu was married, but they were hardly prepared for the dirty baby crawling on the verandah floor. Easu had seen them come through the gate, and was striding across to meet them, after bawling something in his bullying way to someone inside the house: presumably his wife.

Outwardly, he was not much altered. Yet there was an undefinable change for the worse. He was one of those men whom marriage seems to humiliate, and to make ugly. As if he despised himself for being married.

Easu ignored the baby as if it were not there, striding past into the house, leading the newcomers into the parlour. It was darkened in there, to keep out the flies; but he pulled up the blind: "t' see their blanky fisogs."* And he called out to the missis to bring glasses.

The parlour was like most parlours. Enlarged photographs of Mr and Mrs Ellis, the Red parents, in large pine frames, on the wall. A handsome china clock under a glass case on the mantel-piece, with flanking vases to match, on fawn-and-red woolen crochet mats. An oval, rather curly table in the middle of the room, with the family bible, and the meat under a fly-proof wire cover. The parlour was the coolest place for the meat.

Easu shifted this red obnoxity, wire cover and all, to the top of a cupboard where some cups and saucers were displayed, and drew forth a demijohn of spirit from the back of the horsehair sofa, in front of the window.

Mrs Easu came in with the glasses. She was a thin, pale-faced young woman with big dark eyes and her hair in huge curling pins, and a hostile bearing. She took no notice of the visitors: only let her big, what-do-*you*-want eyes pass over them with distaste, beneath her bald forehead.* It was her fixed belief that whoever came to the house came to *get* something, if they could. And they were not going to get it out of *her*. She made an alliance with Easu so far.—But her rather protruding teeth and her vindictive mouth showed that Easu would get as many bites as kisses.[*]

She set the glasses from her hands on to the table and looked down at Easu under her pale lashes.

"What else d' yer want?" she asked rudely.

"Nothing. If I want anything I'll holloa."

They seemed to be on terms of mutual rudeness. She had been quite an heiress: brought Easu a thousand pounds. But the way she said it—a tharsand parnds!—as if it was something absolutely you couldn't get beyond, made even Easu writhe. She was common, to put it commonly. She spoke in a common way, she thought in a common way, and she acted in a common way. But she had energy, and even a vulgar *suffisance*. She thought herself as good as anybody, and a bit better, on the strength of the "tharsand parnd!"

"'S not eddication as matters, it's munney!" she said blatantly to Lennie. "At your age y' ought t'ave somethink in th' bank."

He of course hated the sight of her after that. She had looked at him with a certain superciliousness and contempt in her conceited brown eyes, because he had no money and was supposed to be clever. He never forgave her.

But what did she care! She jerked up her sharp-toothed mouth, and sailed away. She wasn't going to be put down by any penniless snobs. The Ellises! Who were the Ellises? Yes indeed! They thought themselves so superior. Could *they* show a tharsand parnd? Pah!

She felt a particularly spiteful, almost vindictive scorn of Jack. He was somebody, was he? Ha! What was he *worth*? That was the point. How much *munney* did he reckon he'd got?

"If yer want *me* ter think anythink of yer, yer mun show me yer bank-book," she said.

Easu listened, and grinned, and said nothing to all this. But she had a fiery temper of her own, and they went for one another like two devils. She wasn't going to be daunted, she wasn't.

She had her virtues too. She had no method, but she was clean. The place was for ever in a muddle, but she was always cleaning it, almost vindictively, as if the shine on the door-knob reflected some of the tharsand parnd. Even the baby was turned out and viciously cleaned once a day. But in the intervals it groped where it would. As for herself, she was a sight this morning, with her hair in huge iron waving-pins, and her forehead and her teeth both sticking out. She looked a sight to shudder at.—But wait. Wait till she was dressed up and turning out in the buggy, in a coat-and-skirt of thick brown cord silk with orange and black braiding, and a hugely feathered hat, with huge floating ostrich feathers, an orange one and a brown one. And her teeth sticking out, and a huge brooch of a lump of gold set with pearls and diamonds, and a great gold chain. And the baby, in a silk cape with pink ribbons, and a frilled silk bonnet of alternate pink-and-white ruches, mercilessly held against her chains and brooches! Wait!

Therefore, when Jack glanced at her from a strange distance, she tossed her bald forehead with the curling-irons, and thought to herself: "You can look, Master Jack Nobody. And you can look again, next Sunday, when I've got my proper things on. *Then* you'll see who's got the munney!"

She seemed to think her Sunday gorgeousness absolutely obliterated the grimness of her week of curling pins. "Six days shalt thou labour in thy curling irons. But the seventh day is the sabbath of thy bank account."[*]—She liked her curling irons. She lived in them. They kept her hair out of the way and saved her having to do it up all the time.

And it may be that Easu never really looked at her in her teeth and pins. That was not the real Sarah Ann. The real Sarah Ann swayed with ostrich feathers; brown silk, brown and orange feathers, reddish hair, brown eyes, pale skin, and a stiff, militant, vulgar bearing that wasn't going to let *anybody* put it over *her*. "They can't put *me* down, whoever they are!" she asserted. "I consider myself equal to the best, and perhaps a bit better."

This Easu heard and saw with curious gratification. This was his Sarah Ann.

None the less, he was no fool. He saw the baffled, surprised look Jack turned upon this grisly young woman in curlers and teeth, as if he could not quite enter her in the class of human beings. And Easu was enough of an Ellis to know what that look meant. It was a silent: "Good God!" And no man, when his wife enters the room, cares to hear another man's horrified ejaculation: "Good God!", at the sight of her.

Easu wanted his wife to be common. Nevertheless, with the anomalousness of human beings, it humiliated him and put acid in his blood.

"Have a jorum!" said Easu to Tom.

"I s'd think you're not goin' to set down drinkin' at this time of day," she said, in her loud, common, interfering voice.

"What's the time of the day to you?" asked Easu acidly, as he filled Tom's glass.

"We can't stop. Ma'll be expecting us back," said Tom.

Easu silently filled Jack's glass, and the wife went out, banging the door. Immediately she fell upon the baby and began to vituperate the little animal for its dirt. The men couldn't hear themselves speak.

But Easu lifted up his chin and poured the liquor down his throat. He had shaved his beard, and had only three days of yellowish stubble. He smacked his lips as he set down his glass, and looked at the two boys with a sarcastic, gloating look.

"Find a few changes, eh?" he observed.

"Just a few."

"How's the place look?"

"All right."

"Make a pile up north?"

"No."

Easu grinned slowly.

"Thought y' didn't need to, eh?" he asked maliciously.

"Didn't worry myself," said Tom.

"Jack Grant come in for a fortune?" Easu asked, looking at Jack.

"No!" said Jack coldly. There was something about Easu's vulgar, taunting eyes, which he couldn't stand.

"Oh you 'aven't!" The pleased sneer was unbearable.

"How's Ma?" asked Easu.

"All right," said Tom, surprised.

"Don't see much of her now," said Easu.

"No, I saw the gate was blocked up," said Tom.

"Looks like she blocked the wrong gate up."

"How?"

"How?—Well don't you think she'd better have blocked up the gate over to Pink-eye Percy's place?"—Easu was smiling with thin, gloating lips.

"Why?"

"Why, don't y' know?"

"What?"

"Don't y' know about Monica?"

Jack's blood stood still for a moment, and death entered his soul again, to stay.

"No. What?"

"Didn't old George say nothing to y' in Perth?"

"No!" said Tom, becoming sullen and dangerous.

"Well that's funny now! And Ant Alice said nothing?"

"No! What about?"

Easu was smiling gloatingly, in silence, as if he had something very good.

"Well that's funny now! Think of your getting right here, and not having heard a thing! I shouldn't have thought it possible."

Tom was going white under his tan.

"What's amiss, Red?" he said curtly.

"To think as you haven't heard! Why it was the talk of the place.—Ross heard all about it in Perth. Didn't you come across him there? He's been in the Force quite a while now."

"No! What was it he heard about?"

"Why, about Monica."

"What about her?"

"D' y' mean to say you don't know?"

"I tell you I don't know."

"Well!" and Easu smiled with curious, poisonous satisfaction. "I don't know as I want to be the one to tell you."

There was a moment's dead silence. The sun was setting.

"What have you got to say?" asked Tom, his face set and blank, and his mouth taking on the lipless, Australian look.

"Funny thing nobody has told you. Why it happened six or seven months* since."

This was received in dead silence.

"She went off with Percy when the baby was a month old."

Again there was nothing but dead silence.

"Mean she married Pink-eye Percy?" asked Tom, in a muffled tone.

"I dunno about marryin' him. They say he's got a wife or two already: legal and otherwise.—All I know is, they cleared out a month after the baby was born, and went down south."

Still dead silence from the other two. The room was full of golden light. Jack was looking at the fly-dirts and the lamp-black on the ceiling. He was sitting in a horse-hair arm-chair, and the broken springs were uncomfortable, and the horse-hair scratched his wrist. Otherwise he felt vacant, and in a deathly way, remote.

"You're minding what you're saying?" came Tom's empty voice.

"Minding what I'm saying!" echoed Easu cunningly. "*I* didn't want to tell ye. It was you who asked me."

"Was the baby Percy's baby?" asked Jack.

"I should say so," Easu replied, stumbling. "I never asked her, myself. They were all thick with Percy at that time, and I was married with a family of my own. Why I've not been over to Wandoo for—for—for close on two years, I should think."

"That's what was wrong with Ma!" Tom was saying, in a dull voice, to himself.

"I wonder old George or Mary didn't prepare ye," said Easu. "They both came down before the baby came. But seemingly old George couldn't do nothing, Percy confessing he was married, and trying to say he wasn't to blame. However, he's run off with Monica all right. Ma had a letter from her from Albany, to say there was no need to worry, Percy was playin' the gentleman."

"She never cared for him," Jack cried.

"I dunno about that. Seems she's been mad about him all the time. Maybe she waited for you to come back. I dunno! I tell you, I've never been over to Wandoo for nigh on two years."

Jack could not bear any more. The golden light had gone out of the room, the sun was under that ridge—that ridge——

"Let's get, Tom!" said Jack, rising to his feet.

They stumbled out of the house, and went home in silence through the dusk. Again the world had caved in, and they were walking through the ruins.

Ma was upstairs when they got home, but Katie had got the tea on the table, and Lennie was in. He was a tall, thin, silent, sensitive youth.

"Hello, you two wanderin' Jews!" he said.

"Hello Len!"

"Come an' 'ave y' teas."

Lennie was like the head of the house. They ate their meal in silence.

ii

Tom and Jack and Lennie still slept in the cubby, but Og and Magog had moved indoors. The three of them lay in the dark, without sleeping.

"Say young Len," said Tom at length, "what was you after, letting Monica get mixed up with that Pink-eye Percy."

"Me? What was I after? How could I be after 'er every minute. She snapped my 'ead off if I looked at 'er. What for did you an' Jack stop away for all that time, an' never write a word to nobody? Blame me, all right! But you go 'avin' 'igh jinks in the Never-Never, and nobody says a word to you. *You* never did nothing wrong, did you? An' *you* kep' an eye on the fam'ly, didn't you? An' it's only me to blame. 'F course! 'T would be! But what about yourselves?"

This outburst was received in silence. Then a queer, sullen snake reared its head haughtily in Jack's soul.

"I shouldn't have thought she'd have cared for Percy," said he.

"No more would nobody," replied Len. "You never knows what women's up to. Give me a steady woman, Lord, I pray. Because for the last year, Monica wasn't right in 'er mind, that's what I say. It wasn't Percy's fault. It was she made 'im. She made 'im as soft as grease about 'er. Percy's not bad, he's not. But women can make him as soft as grease. An' I knows what that means myself.—Either there shouldn't *be* no men an' women, or they should be kept apart till they're pitched into the same pen, to breed."

Tom, with Honeysuckle Lucy on his conscience, said never a word.

"Is it true that Percy's got a wife already out east?" asked Jack.

"He says he has. But he wrote to find out if she was dead.—At first he said he wasn't to blame. Then he said he was but he couldn't marry her. An' Monica like a wild cat at us all. She wouldn't let nobody write an' tell you. She went over to Reds, but Easu had just got married, an' Sarah Ann threatened to lay her out. Then she turned on Percy. I tell you, she skeered me. The phosphorus came out of her eyes like a wild cat's. She's bewitched or something. Or else possessed by a devil. That's what I think she is. Though I needn't talk, for maybe I am myself.—Oh, mates, leave me alone, I'm sick of it all. Lemme go to sleep."

"What did she go over to Easu's for?"

"God knows. She'd been nosing round with Easu, till Ma got mad an' put a stop to it. But that's a good while since. A good while afore Easu married the lovely Sarah Ann, with her rows o' cartridges on her forehead. Oh Cripes, *marriage*! Leave m' alone, I tell you."

"Funny she should go to Easu's, if she was struck on Percy," said Jack.

"Don't make me think of it, sonny!" came Len's voice. "She went round like a cat wot's* goin' t' have kittens, an' nobody knew what was amiss with her. Oh Jehosaphat!* Talk about bein' born in sin, I should think we are. But say, Jack! Do you suppose the Lord gets awful upset, whether Monica has a baby or not? I don't believe He does. An' I don't believe Jesus either turns a hair. I don't believe He turns half a hair. Yet we get into all this stew. Tell you what, makes a chap sick of bein' a humin bein'. Wish I grew feathers, an' was a emu."

"Don't you bother," said Jack.

"Not me," said Len. "I don't bother! Anyhow I know all about the parsley bed,* 'n I don't care, I'd rether know an' have done with it. 'S got to come some time. I'm a collar-horse, I am, like ol' Rackett said. All right, let me be one. Let me be one, an' pull me guts out. Might just as well do that, as be a sick outlaw like Rackett, or a softy like Percy. Leave m' alone! I've got the collar on, an' the load behind, an' I'll pull it out if I pulls me guts out. That's the past, present an' future of Lennie."

"Where is Rackett?"

"Hanged if I know. Don't matter where he is. He wanted to educate me an' make a gentleman of me. Else I'd be nothing but a cart-'oss, he said. Well I *am* nothing but a cart-'oss. But if I enjoys pullin' me guts out, let me. I enjoys it all right."

Tom lay in silence in the dark, and felt scared. He hated having to face things. He hated taking a long view. Sufficient unto the day is the evil thereof,* was his profound conviction. He hated even to look round the next corner.

"Say Jack!" came Lennie's voice again. "You always turns up like a silver lining. I got your cheques all right—fifty-seven pound. That's only a pair o' socks, that is, compared to Gran's stocking. I had to have a laugh over that stockin'. You're the angel that stood in Jacob's doorway an' looked like a man,* you are. I'd love it if you'd come an' live with me an' Ruthie."

But Jack was thinking his own thoughts. It had come over him that it was Easu who had betrayed Monica. The picture of her wandering across like a cat that is going to have kittens, to the Reds' place, and facing that fearful, common Sarah Ann, and Easu grinning and looking on, made his spirit turn to steel. Pink-eye Percy was not the father of that baby. Percy was as soft as wax. Monica would never have fallen for him. She had simply made use of him. The baby was Easu's.

"Was the baby a girl or a boy?" he asked.

"A girl."

"Did it look like Percy?"

"Not it. It didn't have any of Percy's goo-goo brown eyes or anything. Ma said it was the spitten image of Harry when he was born."

iii

Jack decided what he would do. In the morning he would take the new horse and set off south, to Albany. He would see Monica and ask her. Anyhow he would see her.

He was up at dawn, saddling his horse. He told Tom of his plan, and Tom merely remarked:

"It's up to you, mate."

Tom was relapsing at once into the stiff-faced, rather taciturn Australian he had been before. The settled life on the farm at once pulled him to earth, the various calamities had brought him down with a bump.

So Jack rode off almost unnoticed, with a blanket strapped behind his saddle, and a flat water-bottle, a pistol in his belt, and a hatchet and a little bag of food tied to the front saddle-strings. Something made him turn his horse past the place where he had fought Easu, and along the bush trail to the Reds' place.

The sun had come up hot out of a pink, dusty dawn. In an hour it would be blazing like a fiend out of the bare blue heavens. Meanwhile it was still cool, there was still a faint coolness on the parched dry earth, whose very grass was turning into yellowish dust. Jack jogged along slowly, at a slow morning jog-trot. He was glad to be in the saddle again.

As he came down the track, he saw the blue smoke rising out of the chimneys of Easu's house, and a dark movement away in one of the home paddocks. He got down for the gates, then rode on, over to the paddock fence, and sat there on his horse watching Easu and Herbert and three blacks, sorting out some steers from a bunch of about thirty cattle. They were running the steers through a gate to a smaller enclosure.

There was a good deal of yelling and shouting and running and confusion, as the bunch of young cattle, a mixed little mob of all colours, black and black-and-white and red and red-and-white, tossed and swayed, the young cows breaking away and running nimbly on light feet, excited by the deep, powerful lowing of the stock bull, which had wandered up to the outer corner of the fence under a group of ragged gum-trees, and there stood bellowing at the excitement that was going on in the next paddock.

Jack kept an eye on the bull, as he sat on his uneasy horse outside the shut gate, watching. Near by, two more horses stood saddled and waiting. One of them was Easu's big black mare with the two white forefeet. The other was a thin roan, probably Herbert's horse.

Herbert was quite a man now: tall and thin and broad, with a rather small red face and dull fairish hair that stood up straight from his brow. He was the only one of the brothers left with Easu. He was patient, and didn't pay any attention to that scorpion of a Sarah Ann. Sam and Ross had cleared out at the first sight of her.

It was Herbert who did most of the running, Easu who stood with his feet apart and did most of the bossing—he was never happy unless he was bossing, and finding fault with somebody—and the blacks who did most of the hallooing. Easu didn't move much. He seemed to have gone heavier, and where he stood, with his feet apart and his bare arm waving, he seemed stuck, as if he were inert. This was unlike him. He was always stiffish, but he used to be quick. Now he seemed slow and wooden in his movements, his body had gone inert, the life had gone out of it, and he could only shout and jeer. He used to have a certain flame of life, that made him handsome even if you hated him. A certain conceit and daring, inside all his bullying. Now the flame had gone, the conceit and daring had sunk, he was only ugly and defeated, common, and a little humiliated.* He was getting fat, and it didn't suit him at all.

He had glanced round, when Jack rode up, and it was evident he hated the intrusion. Herbert had waved his arm—Herbert still felt a certain gratitude—and the blacks had all stopped for a moment to stare. But Easu shouted them on.

At last the sorting out was done, and the bars put up. The bull went bellowing along the far fence. Herbert came striding to the gate, his smallish red face shining, and Jack got down to greet him. The two shook hands, and Herbert said:

"Glad to see you back."

He was the first to say he was glad to see Jack back. Even Len had not said it.—The two men stood exchanging awkward sentences, beside the horse.

Easu too came through the gate. He looked grudgingly at Jack and at Jack's horse. Jack thought how ugly he was, now his face had gone fatter and his mouth with its thin, jeering line looked mean. The alert bird-look was gone, he was heavy, and consumed with grudging. His very healthiness looked heavy, a bit dead. His light blue eyes stared and pretended to smile, but the smile was a grudging sneer.

"Where'd you get y'oss?"

"From Jimmie Short, in Perth."

"Bit long in the barrel.—Making a trip, are y'?"

And Easu looked with his pale blue eyes straight and sneering into Jack's eyes, and smiled with his grudging, mean mouth. Jack noticed that Easu had begun to belly, inside his slack black trousers. He was no longer the spruce straight fellow. Easu saw the glance, and was again humiliated. He himself hated his growing belly.* He looked a second time into Jack's eyes, furtively, before he said:

"Find out if it was right what I was tellin' y'?"

Jack was ready for the insult, and did not answer. He turned to Herbert asking about Joe Low, who had been a pal of Herbert's. Joe Low also was married, and had gone down Busselton way. Jack asked for his directions, saying perhaps he might be able to call on him.

"What, are y' goin' south?" put in Easu.

Jack looked at him. It was impossible not to see the slack look of defeat in Easu's face. Something had defeated him, leaving him all sneering and acid and heavy. Again Jack did not answer.

"What did you say?" Easu persisted, advancing a little, insolently.

"What about?"

"I asked y' if y' was goin' south."

"That's my business, where I'm going."

"Of course it is," said Easu with a sneer and a grin. "You don't think anyone wants to get ahead of you, do you?" He stood with a faint, sneering smile on his face, malevolent with impotence. "You'll do Percy a lot o' hurt, I'll bet. I wouldn't like to be Percy, when you turn up."—And he looked with a grin at Herbert. Herbert grinned faintly, in echo.

"I should think, whatever Percy is, he wouldn't want to be you," said Jack, going white at the gills with anger, but speaking with calm superiority, because he knew that enraged Easu most.

"What's that?" cried Easu, the grin flying off his face at once, and leaving it stiff and dangerous.

"I should think Percy wouldn't want to be you, let him be what he may in himself," said Jack, in the cold, clear, English voice which he knew infuriated Easu unbearably.

Easu searched Jack's face intently with his pale blue eyes.

"How's that?" he asked curtly.

Jack stared at the red, heavy face with the smallish eyes, and thought to himself: "You pig! You intolerable white-fat pig!" But aloud he said nothing.

Easu smiled a defeated grin, and strode away heavily to his horse. He unhitched, swung heavily into the saddle, and moved away, then at a little distance reined in to hear what Jack and Herbert were talking about. He couldn't go.

Herbert was giving Jack directions, how to find Joe Low down Busselton way. Then he sent various items of news to his old pal. But he asked Jack no questions, and was careful to avoid any hint of inquiry concerning Jack's business.

Easu sat on his black horse a little way off, listening. He had a rope, and an axe tied to his saddle. Presumably he was going into the bush.—Herbert was asking questions about the North-West, about the cattle stations* and the new mines. He talked as if he would like to talk all day. And Jack answered freely, laughing easily and making a joke of everything. They spoke of Perth, and Jack told how Tom and he had been at the Governor's ball a few nights ago, and what a change it was from the North-West, and how Tom had enjoyed himself. Herbert listened, impressed.

"Gosh! that's something to rag old Tom about!" he said.

"*When you've done gassing there*!" called Easu.

Jack turned and looked at him.

"You don't have to wait," he said easily, as if to a servant.

There was really something about Easu, now, that suggested a servant.—He went suddenly yellow with anger.

"What's that?" he said, moving his horse a few paces forward.

And Jack, also white at the gills, but affecting the same ease, repeated distinctly and easily, as if to a man-servant:

"We're talking. You don't have to wait."

There was no answer to this insult. Easu remained stock motionless on his horse for a few moments. Was he going to have to swallow it?

Jack turned laughing to Herbert, saying:

"I've got several things to tell you about old Tom."

But he glanced up quickly. Easu was kicking his horse, and it was dancing before it would take a direction. Herbert gave a loud, inarticulate cry. Jack turned quickly to his own horse, to put his foot in the stirrup. Just as quickly, he refrained, swung round, drew his pistol, and cocked it. Easu, once more a horseman, was kicking his restive horse forward, holding the small axe in his right hand, the reins in his left. His face was livid, and looked like the face of one returning from the dead. He came bearing down on Jack and Herbert, like Death returning from the dead,* the axe held back at arm's length, ready for the swing, half urging, half holding his horse, so that it danced strangely nearer. Jack stood with the pistol ready, his back to his own horse, that was tossing its head nervously.

"Look out!" cried Herbert, suddenly jumping at the bit of Jack's horse, in terror, and making it start back, with a thudding of hoofs.

But Jack did not move. He stood with his pistol ready, his eyes on Easu. Easu's horse was snaffling and jerking, twisting, trying to get round, and Easu was forcing it slowly forward. He had on his death face. He held the axe at arm's length, backward, and with his pale-blue, fixed death-eyes he watched Jack, who stood there on the ground. So he advanced, waiting the moment to swing the axe, fixing part of his will on the curvetting horse, which he forced on.

Jack, in a sort of trance, fixed Easu's death-face in the middle of the forehead. But he was watching with every pore of his body.

Suddenly he saw him begin to heave in the stirrups, and on that instant he fired at the mystic place in Easu's forehead,* under his old hat, at the same time springing back. And in that self-same instant he saw two things: part of Easu's forehead seemed to shift magically open, and the axe, followed by Easu's whole body, crashed at him as he sprang back. He went down in the universal crash, and for a moment his consciousness was dark and eternal. Then he wriggled to his feet, and ran, as Herbert was running, to the black horse, which was dancing in an agony of terror, Easu's right foot having caught in the stirrup, the body rolling horribly on the ground.

He caught the horse, which was shying off from Herbert, and raised his right hand to take the bridle. To his further horror and astonishment, he saw his hand all blood, and his fore-finger gone. But he clutched the bridle of the horse with his maimed hand, then changed to his left hand, and stood looking in chagrin and horror at the bloody stump of his finger, which was just beginning, in a distant sort of way, to hurt.

"My God, he's dead!" came the high, hysterical yell from Herbert, on the other side the horse, and Jack let go the bridle again, to look.

It was too obvious. The big, ugly, inert bulk of Easu lay crumpled on the ground, part of the forehead shot away. Jack looked twice, then looked away again. A black had caught his horse, and tied it to the fence. Another black was running up. A dog came panting excitedly up, sniffing and licking the blood. Herbert, beside himself, stood helpless, repeating: "He's dead! My God he's dead! He is."

Then he gave a yell, and swooped at the dog, as it began to lick the scattered brains.

Jack, after once more looking round, walked away. He saw his pistol lying on the ground, so he picked it up and put it in his belt, although it was bloody, and had a cut where the axe had struck it. Then he walked across to his horse, and unhitched the bridle from the fence. But before he mounted, he took his handkerchief and tied it round his bleeding hand, that was beginning to hurt with a big, aching hurt. He knew it, and yet he hardly heeded it. It was hardly noticeable.

He got into the saddle, and rode calmly away, going on his journey southward just the same. The world around him seemed faint and unimportant. Inside himself was the reality and the assurance. Easu was dead. It was a good thing.

He had one definite feeling. He felt as if there had been something damming life up, as a great clot of weeds will dam a stream and make the water spread marshily and dead over the surrounding land. He felt he had lifted this clod out of the stream, and the water was flowing on clear again.

He felt he had done a good thing. Somewhere inside himself he felt he had done a supremely good thing. Life could flow on to something beyond. Why question further!

He rode on, down the track. The sun was very hot, and his body was re-echoing with pain from his hand. But he went on calmly, monotonously, his horse travelling in a sort of sleep, easy in its single-step. He didn't think where he was going, or why; he was just going.

Chapter XXI.

Lost.☆

At evening he was still riding. But his horse lagged, and would not be spurred forward. Darkness came with swift persistence. He was looking anxiously for water, a burning thirst had made him empty his bottle.

As if directed by God, he felt the horse rousing up and pressing eagerly forward. In a few minutes it stopped. Darkness had fallen. He found the horse nosing a timber-lined Government well.

He got down, and awkwardly drew water, for the well was low. He drank, and the horse drank. Then with some difficulty he unsaddled, tied the reins round a sapling and removed the bit. The horse snorted, nosed round, and began to crop in the dark. Jack sat on the ground and looked up at the stars. Then he drank more water, and ate a piece of bread and dry cheese.

Then he began to go to sleep. He saw Easu coming at him with the axe. Ugh, how good it was Easu was dead. Dead, to go in the earth to manure the soil. Hadn't old George said it? This land wanted dead men dug into it, to manure it. Men like Easu, dead and turned to manure. And men like old Dad Ellis. Poor old Dad.

Jack thought of Monica. Monica, with her little flower-face. All messed up by that nasty dog of an Easu. He should be twice dead. Jack felt she was a little repulsive too. To let herself be pawed over and made sticky by that heavy dog of an Easu! Jack felt he could never follow where Easu had been messing. Monica was no good now. She had taken on some of Easu's repulsiveness.

Aunt Matilda had said "another scandal in the family!" Well, the death of Easu should make a good scandal.

How lonely it was in the bush! How big and weaponlike the stars were. One great star very flashing.

"I have dipped my hand in blood!" he thought to himself. And looking at his own bloody, hurting hand, in the starlight, he didn't realise whether it was Easu's blood or his own.

"I have dipped my hand in blood!"☆

"So be it. Let it be my testament."

And he lifted up his hand to the great flashing star, his wounded hand, saying aloud:

"Here! Here is my hand in blood! Take it then. There is blood between us for ever."

The blood was between him and his mysterious Lord, for ever. Like a sort of pledge, or baptism, or a sacrifice: a bond between them. He was speaking to his mysterious Lord.

"There is blood between us for ever," he said to the star.

But the sound of his own hoarse, rather deep voice reminded him of his surroundings. He looked round. He heard his horse, and called to it. It nickered in the loneliness, still cropping. He started up to see if it was all right, to stroke it and speak to it. The bush was very lonely.

"Hello you!" he said to it. "In the midst of life we are in death.* There's death in the spaces between the stars. But somehow it seems all right. I like it. I like to be lord of Death. Who do they call the Lords of Death.* I am a lord of death."

He patted the horse's neck as he talked.

"I can't bear to think of Monica messy with Easu," he said. "But I suppose it's my destiny. I suppose it means I am a lord of death. I hope if I have any children they'll have that look in their eyes, like soldiers from the dark kingdom. I don't want children that aren't warriors. I don't want little love children for my children. When I beget children I want to sow dragon's teeth, and warriors will spring up.* Easu hadn't one grain nor spark of a warrior in him. He was absolutely a groping civilian, a bully. That's why he wanted to spoil Monica. She is the wife for a fighting man. So he wanted to spoil her.... Funny, my father isn't a fighting man at all. He's an absolute civilian. So he became a general.—And I'm not a civilian. I know the spaces of death between the stars, like spaces in an Egyptian temple.* And at the end of life I see the big black door of death, and the infinite black labyrinth beyond. I like to think of going in, and being at home and one of the masters in the black halls of death, when I am dead. I hope I die fighting, and go into the black halls of death as a master: not as a scavenger servant, like Easu, or a sort of butler, like my father. I don't want to be a servant in the black house of death. I want to be a master."

He sat down again, with his back to the tree, looking at the sharp stars, and the fume of stars, and the great black gulfs between the stars. His hand and arm were aching and paining a great deal. But he watched the gulfs between the stars.

"I suppose my Lord meant me to be like this," he said. "Think if I had to be tied up* and a gentleman, like that Blessington. Or a lawyer like old George. Or a politician dropping his aitches, like that Mr Watson. Or empty and important like that A. D. C. Or anything that's successful and goes to church and sings hymns and has supper after church on the best linen table-cloth! What Lord is it that likes these people? What God can it be that likes success and Sunday dinners? Oh God! It must be a big, fat, reesty* sort of God.

"My God is dark and you can't see him. You can't even see his eyes, they are so dark. But he sits and bides his time and smiles, in the spaces between the stars. And he doesn't know himself what he thinks. But there's deep, powerful feelings inside him, and he's only waiting his time to upset this pigsty full of fat white pigs.—I like my Lord. I like his dark face, that I can't see, and his dark eyes, that are so dark you can't see them, and his dark hair that is blacker than the night on his forehead, and the dark feelings he has, which nobody will ever be able to explain. I like my Lord, my own Lord, who is not Lord of pigs."

He slept fitfully, feverishly, with dreams, and rose at daylight to drink water, and dip his head in water. His horse came, he tended it, and with great difficulty got the saddle on. Then he left it standing. And when he came again, it wasn't where he had left it.

He called, and it whinnied, so he went into the scrub for it. But it wasn't where the sound of whinnying came from. He went a few more steps forward, and called. The scrub wasn't so very thick either, yet you couldn't see that horse. He was sure it was only a couple of yards away. So he went forward, coaxing and calling. But nothing.... Queer!

He looked round. The track wasn't there. The well wasn't there. Only the silent, vindictive, scattered bush.

He couldn't be lost. That was impossible. The homestead wasn't more than twenty miles away—and the settlement.

Yet as he tramped on, through the brown, heath-like undergrowth, past the ghost-like trunks of the scattered gum-trees, over the fallen, burnt-out trunks of charred trees, past the bushes of young gum-trees, he gradually realised he *was* lost. And yet it was impossible. He would come upon a cabin, or pick up the tracks of a wood-cutter, or a 'roo hunter. He was so near to everywhere.

There is something mysterious about the Australian bush. It is so absolutely still. And yet, in the near distance it seems alive. It seems alive, and as if it hovered round you to maze you and circumvent you.

There is a strange feeling, as if invisible hostile things were hovering round you and heading you off.

Jack stood still and Coo-eed! long and loud. He fancied he heard an answer, and he hurried forward.* He felt light-headed. He wished he had eaten something. He remembered he had no water. And he was walking very fast, the sweat pouring down him. Silly this. He made himself go slower. Then he stood still, and looked around. Then he Coo-eed again, and was afraid of the ringing sound of his own cry.

The changeless bush, with scattered, slender tree-trunks everywhere. You could see between them into the distance, to more open bush: a few brown rocks: two great dead trees as white as bone: burnt trees with their core charred out: and living trees hanging their motionless clusters of brown, dagger-like leaves. And the permanent soft blue of the sky overhead.

Nothing was hidden. It was all open and fair. And yet it was haunted with a malevolent mystery. You felt yourself so small, so tiny, so absolutely insignificant in the still, eternal glade. And this again is the malevolence of the bush, that it reduces you to your own absolute insignificance, go where you will.

Jack collected his wits, and began to make a plan.

"First look at the sky, and get your bearing." Then he would go somewhere straight west from the Reds. The sun had been in his eyes as he rode last evening.

Or had he better go east, and get back? There were scores of empty miles, uninhabited, west. It was settled, he would go east. Perhaps someone would find his horse, and come to look for him.

He walked with the sun straight bang in his eyes. It was very hot, very very hot, and he was tired. He was thirsty, his arm hurt and throbbed. Why did he imagine he was hungry? He was only thirsty. And so hot! He took off his coat and threw it away. After a while, his waistcoat followed. He felt a little lighter. But he was an intolerable burden to himself.

He sat down under a bush, and went fast asleep. How long he slept he did not know. But he woke with a jerk, to find himself lying on the ground in his shirt and trousers, the sun still hot in the heavens, and the mysterious bush all around. The sun had come round and was burning his legs.

What was the matter?—Fear, that was the first thing. The great, resounding fear. Then, a second, he was terribly thirsty. For a third, his arm was aching horribly. He took off his shirt and made a sling of it, to carry his arm in.

For a fourth thing, he realised he had killed Easu, and something was gnawing at his soul.

He heard himself sob, and this surprised him very much. It even brought him to his senses.

"Well!" he thought. "I have killed Easu." It seemed years and years ago. "And the bush has got me, Australia has got me, and now it will take my life from me. Now I am going to die.—Well then, so be it. I will go out and haunt the bush, like all the other lost dead. I shall wander in the bush throughout eternity, with my bloody hand. Well then, so be it. I shall be a lord of death hovering in the bush, and let the people who come beware."

But suddenly he started to his feet in terror and horror. The fear of death had really got him this time. It was as if a second waking had come upon him, and his life, which had been sinking, suddenly flared up in a frenzy of struggle and fear. He Coo-eed! again and again, and once more plunged forward in mad pursuit of an echo.

He might certainly run into a 'roo shooter's camp, any minute. The place was alive with them, great big boomers! Their silly faces! Their silly complacency, almost asking to be shot. There were a lot of wallabies out here too. You might make a fortune hunting skins.

Christ! how one could want water.

But no matter. On and on! His soul dropped to its own sullen level. If he was to die, die he would. But he would hold out through it all.

On and on, in a persistent dogged stupor. Why give in?

Then suddenly he dropped on a log, in weariness. Suddenly he had thought of Monica. Why had she betrayed him? Why had they all betrayed him, betrayed him and the thing he wanted from life. He leaned his head down on his arms and wept hoarsely and dryly, and went silent again even as he sat, realising the futility of weeping. His heart, the heart he wept from, went utterly dark. He had no more heart of torn sympathy. That was gone. Only a black, deep male volition. And this was all there was left of him. He would carry the same into death. Young or old, death soon or late, he would carry just this one thing into the further darkness, his deep, black, undying male volition.

He must have slept. He was in great misery, his mouth like an open sepulchre, his consciousness dull. He was hardly aware that it was late afternoon, hot and motionless. The outside things were all so far away. And the blackness of death and misery was thick, but transparent, over his eyes.

He went on, still obstinately insisting that ahead there was something, perhaps even water, though hope was dead in him. It was not hope, it was heavy volition that insisted on water.

The sling dragged on his neck, he threw it away, and walked with his hand against his breast. And his braces dragged on him. He didn't want any burden at all, none at all. He stopped, took off his braces and threw them away, then his sweat-soaked undervest. He didn't want these things. He didn't want them. He walked on a bit.

He hesitated, then came for a moment to his senses. He was going to throw away his trousers too. But it came to him: "Don't be a fool, and throw away your clothes, man. You know men do it who are lost in the bush, and then they are found naked, dead."

He looked vaguely round for the vest and braces he had just thrown away. But it was half an hour since he had flung them down. His consciousness tricked him, obliterating the interval. He could not believe his eyes. They had ghostlily disappeared.

So he rolled his trousers on his naked hips, and pressed his hurt hand on his naked breast, and set off again, in a sort of fear. His hat had gone long ago. And all the time he had this strange desire to throw all his clothes away, even his boots, and be absolutely naked, as when he was born. And all the time something obstinate in him combatted the desire. He wanted to throw everything away, and go absolutely naked over the border. And at the same time, something in him deeper than himself obstinately withstood the desire. He wanted to go over the border. And something deeper even than his consciousness, refused.

So he went on, scarcely conscious at all. He himself was in the middle of a vacuum, and pressing round were visions and agonies. The vacuum was perhaps the greatest agony, like a death-tension. But the other agonies were pressing on its borders: his dry, cardboard mouth, his aching body. And the visions pressed on the border too. A great lake of ghostly white water, such as lies in the valleys where the dead are. But he walked to it, and it wasn't there. The moon was shining whitely.

And on the edge of the aching void of him, a wheel was spinning in his brain like a prayer-wheel.

"Petition me no petitions sir today;
Let other hours be set apart for business.
Today it is our pleasure to be drunk
And this our queen— — —"*

Water! Water! Water! Was water only a visionary thing of memory, something only achingly, wearyingly thought, and thought, and thought, and never substantiated?

"A Briton even in love should be
A subject not a slave— —"*

The wheel of words went round, the wheel of his brain, on the edge of the vacuum. What did that mean? What was a Briton?

"A Briton even in love should be
A subject not a slave— — —"

The words went round and round, and were absolutely meaningless to him.

And then out of the dark another wheel was pressing and turning.

"How fast—has brother followed brother
From sunshine to the sunless land."

Away on the hard dark periphery of his consciousness, the wheel of these words was turning and grinding.

His mind was turning helplessly, but his feet walked on. He realised in a weird, mournful way that he was shut groping in a dark, unfathomable cave, and that the walls of the cave was his own aching body. And he was going on and on in the cave, looking for the fountain, the water. But his body was the aching, ghastly, jutting walls of the cave. And it made this weary grind of words on the outside. And he had need to struggle on and on.

In little flickers he tried to associate his dark cave-consciousness with his grinding body. Was it night, was it day?

But before he had decided it was night, the two things had gone apart again, and he was groping and listening to the grind:

"But hushed be every thought that springs
From out the bitterness of things.
Those obstinate questionings
Of sense and outward things
Falling from us, vanishing—"*

He was so weary of the outward grind of words. He was stumbling as he walked. And waiting for the walls of the cave to crash in and bury him altogether. And the spring of water did not exist.

> "Blank misgivings of a creator moving about in a world
> not realised."

This phrase almost united his two consciousnesses. He was going to crash into this Creator who moved about unrealised. Other people had gone, and other things. Monica, Easu, Tom, Mary, mother, father, Lennie—they were all like papery, fallen leaves blowing about outside in some street. Inside here there were no people at all, none at all. Only the Creator moving around unrealised. His Lord.

He stumbled and fell, and in the white flash of falling knew he hurt himself again, and that he was falling for ever.

Chapter XXII.

The Find.

i

The subconscious self woke first, roaring in distant wave-beats, unintelligible, unmeaning, persistent, and growing in volume. It had something to do with birth. And not having died."I have not let my soul run like water out of my mouth."*

And as the roaring and beating of the wave increased in volume, tiny little words emerged like flying-fish out of the black ocean of consciousness. "Ye must be born again,"* in little silvery, twinkling spurts like flying-fish* which twinkle silver and spark into the utterly dark sea again. They were gone and forgotten before they were realised. They had merged deep in the sea again. And the roar of dark consciousness was the roar of death. The kingdom of death. And the lords of death.

"Ye must be born again."—But the twinkling words had disappeared into the lordly, powerful darkness* of death. And the baptism is the blackness of death between the eyes, that never lifts, for ever, neither in life nor death. You may be born again. But when you emerge, this time you emerge with the darkness of death between your eyes, as a lord of death.

The waves of dark consciousness surged in a huge billow, and broke. The boy's eyes were wide open, and his voice was saying:

"Is that you, Tom!"

The sound of his voice paperily rustling* these words, was so surprising to him that he instantly went dark again. He heard no answer.

But those surging dark waves pressed him again and again, and again his eyes were open. He recognised nothing. Something was being done to him on the outside of him. His own throat was moving. And life started again with a sharp pain.

"What was it?"

The question sparked suddenly out of him. Someone was putting a metal rim to his lips, there was liquid in his mouth. He put it out. He didn't want to come back. His soul sank again like a dark stone.

And at the very bottom, it took a command from the Lord of Death, and rose slowly again.

Someone was tilting his head, and pouring a little water again. He swallowed with a crackling noise and a crackling pain. One had to come back. He recognised the command from his own Lord. His Lord was the Lord of Death. And he, Jack, was dark-anointed and sent back. Returned with the dark unction between his brows.* So be it.

He saw green leaves hanging from a blue sky. It was still far off. And the dark was still better. But the dark green leaves were also like a triumphal banner. He tries to smile, but his face is stiff. The faintest irony of a smile sets in its stiffness.

He is forced to swallow again, and know pain and tearing. Ah! He suddenly realised the water was good. He had not realised it those other times. He gulped suddenly, everything forgotten. And his mind gave a sudden lurch towards consciousness.

"Is that you, Tom?"

"Yes. Feel better?"

He saw the red mistiness of Tom's face near. Tom was faithful. And this time his soul swayed, as if it too had drunk of the water of faithfulness. The deeper water of faithfulness.

He drank the water from the metal cup, because he knew it came from Tom's faithfulness.

Gradually Jack revived. But his burning, bloodshot eyes were dilated with fever, and he could not keep hold of his consciousness. He realised that Tom was there, and Mary, and somebody he didn't for a long time recognise as Lennie; and that there was a fire, and a smell of meat;* and night was again falling. Yes, he was sure night was falling. Or was it his own consciousness going dark? He didn't know. Perhaps it was the everlasting dark.

"What time is it?" he asked.

"Sundown," said Tom. "Why?"

But he was gone again. It was no good trying to keep a hold on one's consciousness. The ache, the nausea, the throbbing pain, the swollen mouth, the strange feeling of cracks in his flesh, made him let go. Tom was there, and Mary. He would leave himself to Tom's faithfulness and Mary's tenderness, and Lennie's watchful intuition. The mystery of death was in that bit of deathless faithfulness which was in Tom. And Mary's tenderness, and Lennie's intuitive care, both had a touch of the mystery and stillness of the death that surrounds us darkly all the time.

ii

They got Jack home, but he was very ill. His life would seem to come back. Then it would sink away again like a stone, and they would think he was going. The strange oscillation. Several times, Mary watched him almost die. Then from the very brink of death, he would come back again, with a strange, haunted look in his blood-shot eyes.

"What is it, Jack?" she would ask him. But the eyes only looked at her.

And Lennie, standing there silently watching, said:

"He's had about enough of life, that's what it is."

Mary, blenched with fear, went to find Tom.

"Tom," she said, "he's sinking again. Lennie says it's because he doesn't want to live."

Tom silently threw down his tool, and walked with her into the house. It was obvious he was sinking again.

"Jack!" said Tom in a queer voice, bending over him. "Mate! Mate!" He seemed to be calling him in to camp.

Jack's expressionless, fever-dilated, blood-shot eyes opened again. The whites were almost scarlet.

"Y' aren't desertin' us, are y'?" said Tom, in a gloomy, reproachful tone.—"Are y' desertin' us, mate?"

It was the Australian, lost but unbroken on the edge of the wilderness, looking with grim mouth into the void, and calling to his mate not to leave him. Man for man, they were up against the great dilemma of white men, on the edge of the white man's world, looking into the vaster, alien world of the undawned* era, and unable to enter, unable to leave their own.

Jack looked at Tom, and smiled faintly. In some subtle way, both men knew the mysterious responsibility of living. Tom was almost fatalistic-reckless. Yet it was a recklessness which knew that the only thing to do was to go ahead, meet death that way. He could see nothing but meeting death ahead. But since he was a man, he would go ahead to meet it, he would not sit and wait.

Jack smiled faintly, and the courage came back to him. He began to rally.

The next morning he turned to Mary and said:

"I still want Monica."

Mary dropped her head, and did not answer. She recognised it as one of the signs that he was going to live. And she recognised the unbending obstinacy in his voice.

"I shall come for you, too, in time," he said to her, looking at her with his terrible scarlet eyes.

She did not answer, but her hand trembled as she went for his medicine. There was something prophetic and terrible in his sallow face and burning, blood-shot eyes.

"Be still!" she murmured to him. "Only be still."

"I shan't ever really drop you," he said to her. "But I want Monica first. That's my way."

He seemed curiously victorious, making these assertions.

Chapter XXIII.

Gold.

i

The boy Jack never rose from that fever. It was a man who got up again. A man with all the boyishness cut away from him, all the childishness gone, and a certain unbending recklessness in its place.

He was thin, and pale, and the cherubic look had left his face for ever. His cheeks were longer, leaner, and when he got back his brown-faced strength again, he was handsome. But it was not the handsomeness, any more, that would make women like Aunt Matilda exclaim involuntarily: "Dear boy!" They would look at him twice, but with misgiving, and a slight recoil.

It was his eyes that had changed most. From being the warm, emotional dark blue eyes of a boy, they had become impenetrable, and had a certain fixity. There was a touch of death in them, a little of the fixity and changelessness of death. And with this, a peculiar power. As if he had lost his softness in the otherworld of death, and brought back instead some of the relentless power that belongs there. And the inevitable touch of mockery.

As soon as he began to walk about, he was aware of the change. He walked differently, he put his feet down differently, he carried himself differently. The old drifting, diffident careless bearing had left him. He felt his uprightness hard, bony. Sometimes he was aware of the skeleton of himself. He was a hard skeleton, built upon the solid bony column of the back-bone, and pitched for balance on the great bones of the hips. But the plumb-weight was in the cage of his chest. A skeleton!

But not the dead skeleton. The living bone, the living man of bone, unyielding and imperishable. And the bone of his forehead like iron against the world, and the blade of his breast like an iron wedge held forward. He was thin, and built of bone.

And inside this living, rigid man of bone, the dark heart heavy with its wisdom and passions and emotions and its correspondences. It* was living, softly and intensely living. But heavy and dark, plumb to the earth's centre.

During his convalescence, he got used to this man of bone which he had become, and accepted his own inevitable. His bones, his skeleton was isolatedly itself. It had no contact. Except that it was forged in the kingdom of death, to be durable and effectual. Some strange Lord had forged his bones in the dark smithy where the dead and the unborn came and went. And this was his only permanent contact: the contact with the Lord who had forged his bones, and put a dark heart in the midst.

But the other contacts, they were alive and quivering in his flesh. His passive but enduring affection for Tom and Lennie, and the strange quiescent hold he held over Mary. Beyond these, the determined molten stirring of his desire for Monica.

And the other desires. The desire in his heart for masterhood. Not mastery. He didn't want to master anything. But to be the dark lord of his own folk: that was a desire in his heart. And the concurrent knowledge that, to achieve this, he must be master too of gold. Not gold for the having's sake. Nor for the spending's sake. Nor for the sake of the power to hire services, which is the power of money. But the mastery of gold, so that gold should no longer be like a yellow star to which men hitched the wagon of their destinies. To be master of gold, in the name of the dark Lord who had forged his bones neither of gold nor silver nor iron, but of the white glisten of life. Masterhood, as a man forged by the Lord of Hosts,[*] in the innermost fires of life and death. Because, just as a red fire burning on a hearth is a fusion of death into what was once live leaves, so the creation of man in the dark is a fusion of life into death, with the life dominant.

The two are never separate, life and death. And in the vast dark kingdom of the afterwards, the Lord of Death is Lord of Life, and the God of Life and Creation is Lord of Death.

But Jack knew his Lord as the Lord of Death. The rich, dark mystery of death, which lies ahead, and the dark sumptuousness of the halls of death. Unless Life moves on to the beauty of the darkness of death, there is no life, there is only automatism. Unless we see the dark splendour of death ahead, and travel to be lords of darkness at last, peers in the realms of death, our life is nothing but a petulant, pitiful backing, like a frightened horse, back, back to the stable, the manger, the cradle. But onward ahead is the great porch of the entry into death, with its columns of bone-ivory. And beyond the porch is the heart of darkness, where the lords of death arrive home out of the vulgarity of life, into their own dark and silent domains, lordly, ruling the incipience of life.

ii

At the trial Jack said, in absolute truth, he shot Easu in self-defence. He had not the faintest thought of shooting him when he rode up to the paddock: nor of shooting anybody. He had called in passing, just to say Good-day. And then he had fired at Easu because he knew the axe would come down in his skull if he didn't.

Herbert gave the same deposition. The shot was entirely in self-defence.

So Jack was free again. There had been no further mention of Monica, after Jack had said he was riding south to see her, because he had always cared for her. No one hinted that Easu was the father of her child, though Mrs Ellis knew, and old George knew.

Afterwards Jack wondered why he had called at the Reds' place that morning. Why had he taken the trail past where he and Easu had fought? He had intended to see Easu, that was why. But for what unconscious purpose, who shall say?—The death was laid at the door of the old feud between Jack and Red. Only old George knew the whole, and he, subtle and unafraid, pushed justice as it should go, according to his own sense of justice, like a real Australian.

Meanwhile he had been corresponding with Monica and Percy. They were in Albany, and on the point of sailing to Melbourne, where Percy would enter some business or other, and the two would live as man and wife. Monica was expecting another child. At this news, Mr George wanted to let them go, and be damned to them. But he talked to Mary, and Mary said Jack would want Monica, no matter what happened.

"When he wants a thing really, he can't change," said Mary gloomily. "He is like that."

"An obstinate young fool that's never had enough lickings," said old George. "Devil's blood of his mother's devil of an obstinate father.—But very well then, let him have her, with a couple of babies for a dowry. Make himself the laughing-stock of the colony."

So he wrote to Monica: "If you care about seeing Jack Grant again, you'd better stop in this colony. He sticks to it he wants to see you, being more of a fool than a knave, unlike many people in Western Australia."

She, being obstinate like the rest, stayed on in Albany, though

Percy, angry and upset, sailed on to Melbourne. He said she could join him if she liked. He stayed till her baby was born, then went, because he didn't want to face Jack.

Jack arrived by sea. He was still not strong enough to travel by land. He got a vessel going to Adelaide, that touched at Albany.

Monica, thinner than ever, with a little baby in her arms, and her flower-face like a chilled flower,* was on the dock to meet him. He saw her at once, and his heart gave a queer lurch.

As he came forward to meet her, their eyes met. Her yellow eyes looked straight into his, with the same queer, panther-like scrutiny, and the eternal question. In Monica's eyes was an undying, challenging question. She was a question, and she had got to be answered.* It made her fearless, almost shameless, whatever she did.

But with Percy, the fear had nipped her, the fear that she would go for ever unanswered, as if life had rejected her.

This nipped look, and her strange yellow flare of question as she peered at him under her brows, like a panther, made Jack's cheek slowly darken, and the life-blood flow into him stronger, heavier. He knew his passion for her was the same. Thank God he met her at last.

"You're awfully thin," she said.

"So are you," he answered.

And she laughed her quick, queer, breathless little laugh, showing her pointed teeth. She had seen the death-look in his eyes, and it was her answer, a bitter answer enough. She stopped to put straight the tiny bonnet over her little baby's face, with a delicate, remote movement. He watched her in silence.

"Where do you want to go?" she asked him, without looking at him.

"With you," he said.

Then she looked at him again, with the dry-eyed question. But she saw the unapproachable death-look there in his eyes, at the back of their dark-blue, dilated emotion and passion. And her heart gave up.

She looked down the pier, as if to walk away. He carried his own bag. They set off side by side.

She lived in a tiny slab cottage in a side lane. But she called first at a neighbour's cottage, for her other child. It was a tiny, toddling thing with a defiant stare in its pale-blue eyes. Monica held her baby on one arm, and led this tottering child by the other. Jack walked at her side in silence.

The cottage had just two rooms, poorly furnished. But it was clean, and had bright cotton curtains and sofa-bed, and a pale-blue convolvulus vine* over the window.

She laid the baby down in its cradle, and began to take off the bonnet of the little girl. She had called it Jane.

Jack watched this little Jane as if fascinated. The infant had curly reddish hair, of a lovely fine texture* and a beautiful tint, something like raw silk with threads of red. Her eyes were round and light blue, and rather defiant, and she had the delicate complexion of her kind. She fingered her mother's brooch, like a little monkey touching the bit of glittering gold, as Monica stooped to her.

"Daddy gone!" she said in her chirping, bird-like, quite emotionless tone.

"Yes, Daddy gone!" replied Monica, as emotionlessly.

The child then glanced with unmoved curiosity at Jack. She kept on looking and looking at him, sideways. And he watched her just as sharply, her sharp, pale-blue eyes.

"Him more Daddy?" she asked.

"I don't know," replied Monica, who was suckling her baby.

"Yes," said Jack, in a rather hard tone, smiling with a touch of mockery. "I'm your new father."

The child smiled back at him a faint, mocking little grin, and put her finger in her mouth.

The day passed slowly in the strange place, Monica busy all the time with the children and the house. Poor Monica, she was already a drudge. She was still careless and hasty in her methods, but clean, and uncomplaining. She kept herself to herself, and did what she had to do. And Jack watched, mostly silent.

At last the lamp was lighted, the children were both in bed. Monica cooked a little supper over the fire.

Before he came to table, Jack asked:

"Is Jane Easu's child?"

"I thought you knew," she said.

"No-one has told me. Is she?"

Monica turned and faced him, with the yellow flare in her eyes as she looked into his eyes, challenging.

"Yes," she said.

But his eyes did not change. The remoteness at the back of them did not come any nearer.

"Shall you hate her?" she asked, rather breathless.

"I don't know," he said slowly.

"Don't!" she pleaded, in the same breathlessness. "Because I rather hate her."

"She's too little to hate," said Jack.

"I know," said Monica, rather doubtfully.

She put the food on the table. But she herself ate nothing.

"Aren't you well, you don't eat?" he asked.

"I can't eat just now," she said.

"If you have a child to suckle, you should," he replied.

But she only became more silent, and her hands hung dead in her lap. Then the baby began to cry, a thin, poor, frail noise, and she went to soothe it.

When she came back, Jack had left the table and was sitting in Percy's wooden arm-chair.

"Percy's child doesn't seem to have much life in it," he said.

"Not *very* much," she replied. And her hands trembled as she cleared away the dishes.

When she had finished, she moved about, afraid to sit down. He called her to him.

"Monica!" he said, with a little jerk of his head, meaning she should come to him.

She came, rather slowly, her queer, pure-seeming face looking like a hurt. She stood with her thin hands hanging in front of her apron.

"Monica!" he said, rising and taking her hands. "I should still want you if you had a hundred children. So we won't say any more about that. And you won't oppose me when there's anything I want to do, will you?"

She shook her head.

"No, I won't oppose you," she said, in a dead little voice.

"Let me come to you then," he said. "I should have to come to you, if you went to Melbourne or all round the world.—And I should be glad to come," he added whimsically, with the warmth of his old smile coming into his eyes; "I suppose I should be glad to come, if it was in hell."

"But it isn't hell, is it?" she asked, wistfully and a little defiantly.

"Not a bit," he said. "You've got too much pluck to spoil. You're as good to me as you were the first time I knew you.—Only Easu might have spoiled you."

"And you killed him," she said quickly, half in reproach.

"Would you rather he'd killed me?" he asked.

She looked a long time into his eyes, with that watchful, searching look that used to hurt him. Now it hurt him no more.

She shook her head, saying:

"I was always in love with you, really."

"Ah Monica!" he exclaimed softly, teasingly, with a little smile. And she flushed, and flashed with anger.

"If you never knew, it was your own fault!" she jerked out.

"'*Really*'," he said, quoting and echoing the word as she had said it, and smiling with a touch of raillery at her, before he added:

"You always loved me *really*—but you loved the others as well, unreally."

"Yes," she said, baffled, defiant.

"All right, that day is over. You've *had** your unreal loves. Now come and have your real one."

In the next room Easu's child was sleeping in its odd little way, a sleep that was neither innocent nor not innocent; queer and naïvely "knowing," even in its sleep. Jack watched it as he took off his things: this little inheritance he had from Easu. An odd little thing. With an odd, loveless little spirit of its own, cut off and not daunted. He wouldn't love it, because it wasn't loveable. But its odd little dauntlessness and defiance amused him, he would see it had fair play.

And he took Monica in his arms, glad to get into grips with his own fate again. And it was good. It was better, perhaps, than his passionate desirings of earlier days had imagined. Because he didn't lose and scatter himself. He gathered, like a reaper at harvest gathering.

And Monica, who woke for her baby, looked at him as he slept soundly and she sat in bed suckling her child. She saw in him the eternal stranger. There he was, the eternal stranger, lying in her bed sleeping at her side. She rocked her baby slightly as she sat up in the night, still rocking in the last throes of rebellion. The eternal stranger, she must fear him, because she could never finally know him, and never entirely possess him. He would never *belong* to her. This had made her rebel so dangerously against the thought of him. Because *she* would have to belong to *him*. Now he had arrived again before her like a doom,* a doom she still stiffened herself against, but could no longer withstand. Because the emptiness of the other men, Percy, Easu, all the men she knew, was worse than the doom of this man who would never give her his ultimate intimacy, but who would be able to hold her till the end of time. There was something enduring and changeless in him. But she would never hold *him* entirely. Never! She would have to resign herself to that.

Well, so be it. At least it relieved her of the burden of responsibility for life. It took away from her her own strange, fascinating female power, which she couldn't bear to part with. But at the same time she felt saved, because her own power frightened her, having brought her to a brink of nothingness that was like a madness. The nothingness that fronted her with Percy was worse than submitting to this man. After all, this man was magical.

She put her child in its cradle, and returning, waked the man. He put out his hand quickly for her, as if she were a new, blind discovery. She quivered and thrilled, and left it to him. It was his mystery, since he would have it so.

iii

They were married in Albany, and stayed there another month, waiting for a ship. Then they sailed away, all the family, away to the North-West. They did not go to Perth: they did not go to Wandoo. Only Jack saw Mr George in Fremantle, and waved to him Good-bye as the ship proceeded north.

Then came two months of wandering, a pretty business with a baby and a toddling infant. The second month, Percy's baby suddenly died in the heat, and Monica hardly mourned for it. As Jack looked at its pinched little dead face, he said: "*You are better dead.*" And that was true.

The little Jane, however, showed no signs of dying. The knocking about seemed to suit her. Monica remained very thin. It was a sort of hell-life to her, this struggling from place to place in the heat and dust, no water to wash in, sleeping anywhere like a lost dog, eating the food that came. Because she loved to be clean and good-looking and in graceful surroundings. What fiend of hell had ordained that she must be a sort of tramp woman in the back of beyond?

She did not know, so it was no good asking. Jack seemed to know what he wanted. And she was his woman, fated to him. There was no more to it. Through the purgatory of discomfort she had to go. And he was good to her, thoughtful for her, in material things. But at the centre of his soul he was not thoughtful for her. He just possessed her, mysteriously owned her, and went ahead with his own obsessions.

Sometimes she tried to rebel. Sometimes she wanted to refuse to go any further, to refuse to be a party to his will. But then he suddenly looked so angry, and so remote, looked at her with such far-off, cold, haughty eyes, that she was frightened. She was afraid he would abandon her, or ship her back to Perth, and put her out of his life for ever.

Above all things, she didn't want to be shipped back to Perth.—Here in the wild she could have taken up with another man. She knew that. But she knew that if she did, Jack would just put her out of his life completely. There would be no return. His passion for her would just take the form of excluding her for ever from his being. Because passion can so reverse itself, and from being a great desire, that draws the beloved towards itself, it can become an eternal revulsion,* excluding the once-beloved for ever from any contact at all.

Monica knew this. And whenever she tried to oppose him, and the deathly anger rose in him, she was pierced with a fear so acute, she had to hold on to some support, to prevent herself sinking to the ground. It was a strange fear, as if she were going to be cast out of the land of the living, among the unliving that rove like pariahs outside.

Afterwards she was puzzled. Why had he got this power over her? Why couldn't she be a free woman, to go where she chose, and be a complete thing in herself?

She caught at the idea. But it was no good. When he went away prospecting for a week or more at a time, she would struggle to regain her woman's freedom. And it would seem to her she had got it: she was free of him again. She was a free being, by herself.

But then, when he came back, tired, sunburnt, ragged, and still unsuccessful: and when he looked at her with desire in his eyes, the living desire for her; she was so glad, suddenly, as if she had forgotten, or as if she had never known what his desire of her meant to her. She was so glad, she was weak with gladness instead of fear. And if, in perversion, she still tried to oppose him, in the light of her supposedly regained freedom; and she saw the strange glow of desire for her go out of his eyes, and the strange loveliness, to her, of his wanting to have her near, in the room, giving him his meal or sitting near him outside in the shade of evening; then, when his face changed, and took on the curious look of aloofness, as if he glistened with anger looking down on her from a long way off: then, she felt all her own world turn to smoke, and her own will mysteriously evaporate, leaving her only wanting to be wanted again, back in his world.* Her freedom was worth less than nothing.

Still, often, when he was gone, leaving her alone in the little cabin, she was glad. She was free to spread her own woman's aura round her, she was free to delight in her own woman's idleness and whimsicality, free to amuse herself half-teasing, half-loving that little odd female of a Jane. And sometimes she would go to the cabins of other women, and gossip. And sometimes she would flirt with a young miner or prospector who seemed handsome. And she would get back her own young, gay liveliness and freedom.

But when the man she flirted with wanted to kiss her, or put his arm round her waist, she found it made her go cold and savagely hostile. It was not as in the old days, when it gave her a thrill to be seized and kissed, whether by Easu or Percy or Jack or whatever man it was she was flirting with. Then, there had been a spark between her and many a man. But now, alas, the spark wouldn't fly. The man might be never so good-looking and likeable, yet when he touched her, instead of the spark flying from her to him, immediately all the spark went dead in her. And this left her so angry, she could kill, or* so wretched, she couldn't even cry.

That little goggle-eyed imp of a Jane, in spite of her one solitary year of age, seemed somehow to divine what was happening inside her mother's breast, and she seemed to chuckle wickedly. Monica always felt that the brat knew, and that she took Jack's side.

Jane always wanted Jack to come back. When he was away, she would toddle about on her own little affairs, curiously complacent and impervious to outer influences. But if she heard a horse coming up to the hut, she was at the door in a flash. And Monica saw, with a pang, how steadily intent the brat was on the man's return. Somehow, from Jane, Monica knew that Jack would go with other women. Because of the spark that flashed to him from that brat of a baby of Easu's.

And at evening, Jane hated going to bed if Jack hadn't come home. She would be a real little hell-monkey. It was as if she felt the house wasn't safe, wasn't real, till he had come in.

Which annoyed Monica extremely. Why wasn't the mother enough for the child?

But she wasn't. And when Jane was in bed, Monica would take up the uneasiness of the manless house. She would sit like a cat shut up in a strange room, unable to settle, unable really to rest, and hating the night for having come and surprised her in her empty loneliness. Her loneliness might be really enjoyable during the day. But after nightfall it was empty, sterile, a mere oppression to her. She wished he would come home, if only so that she could hate him.

And she felt a flash of joy when she heard his foostep on the stones outside, even if the flash served only to kindle a great resentment against him. And he would come in, with his burnt, half-seeing face, unsuccessful, worn, silent, yet not uncheerful. And he spoke his few rather low words, from his chest, asking her something. And she knew he had come back to her. But where from, and what from, she would never know entirely.

She had always known where Percy had been, and what he had been doing. She felt she would always have known, with Easu. But with Jack she never knew. And sometimes this infuriated her. But it was no good. He would tell her anything she asked. And then she felt there was something she couldn't ask about.

The months went by. He staked his claim, and worked like a navvy. He *was* a navvy, nothing but a navvy. And she was a navvy's wife, in a hut of one room, in a desert of heat and sand and grey-coloured bush, sleeping on a piece of canvas stretched on a low trestle, eating on a tin plate, eating sand by the mouthful when the wind blew. Percy's baby was dead and buried in the sand: another sop to the avid country. And she herself was with child again, and thin as a rat. But it was his child this time, so she had a certain savage satisfaction in it.

He went on working at his claim. It was now more than a year he had spent at this game of looking for gold, and he had hardly found a cent's worth. They were very poor, in debt to the keeper of the store. But everybody had a queer respect for Jack. They dared not be very familiar with him, but they didn't resent him. He had a good aura. The other men might jeer sometimes at his frank but unapproachable aloofness, his subtle sort of delicacy, and his simple sort of pride. Yet when he was spoken to, his answer was so much in the spirit of the question, with a subtle understanding, that you couldn't resent him. In ordinary things he was gay and completely one of themselves. The self that was beyond them he never let intrude. Hence their curious respect for him.

Because there was something unordinary in him. The biggest part of himself he kept entirely to himself, and a curious sombre steadfastness inside him made shifty men uneasy with him. He could never completely mix in, in the vulgar way, with men. He would take a drink with the rest, and laugh and talk half an hour away. Even get a bit tipsy and talk rather brilliantly. But always, always at the back of his eyes was this sombre aloofness, that could never come forward and meet and mingle, but held back, apart, waiting.

They called him, after his father, the General. But never was a General with so small an army at his command. He was playing a lone hand. The mate he was working with suddenly chucked up the job, and travelled away, and the General went on alone. He moved about the camp at his ease. When he sat in the bar drinking his beer with the other men, he was really alone, and they knew it. But he had a good aura, so they felt a certain real respect for his loneliness. And when he was there, they talked and behaved as if in the aura of a certain blood-purity, although he was in rags, for Monica hated sewing and couldn't bear, simply couldn't bear to mend his old shirts and trousers. And there was no money to buy new ones. There was no money for anything.

He held on. He did not get depressed or melancholy. When he got absolutely stumped, he went away and did hired work for a spell. Then he came back to the gold-field. He was now nothing but a miner. The miner's instinct had developed in him. He had to wait for his instinct to perfect itself. He knew that. He knew he was not a man to be favoured by blind luck. Whatever he won, he must win by mystic conquest.

If he wanted gold, he must master it in the veins of the earth. He knew this. And for this reason he gave way neither to melancholy nor to impatience.—"If I can't win," he said to himself, "it is because I'm not master of the thing I'm up against."

"If I can't win, I'll die fighting," he said to himself. "But in the end I will win."

There was nothing to do but to fight, and fight on. This was his creed. And a fighter has no use for melancholy or impatience.

He saw the fight his boyhood had been, against his aunts, and school, and college. He didn't want to be made *quite* tame, and they had wanted to tame him, like all the rest. His father was a good man and a good soldier: but a tame one. He himself was not a soldier, nor even a good man. But also he was not tame. Not a tame dog, like all the rest.

For this reason he had come to Australia, away from the welter of vicious tameness. For tame dogs are far more vicious than wild ones. Only they can be brought to heel.

In Australia, a new sort of fight. A fight with tame dogs that were playing wild. Easu was a tame dog, playing the wolf in a mongrel, back-biting way. Tame dogs escaped and become licentious. That was Australia. He knew that.

But they were not all quite tame. Tom, the safe Tom, had salt of wild savour still in his blood. And Lennie had his wild streak. So had Monica. So, somewhere, had the *à terre** Mary. Some odd freakish wildness of the splendid, powerful, wild old English blood.

Jack had escaped the tamers: they couldn't touch him now. He had escaped the insidious tameness, the slight degeneracy, of Wandoo. He had learned the tricks of the escaped tame dogs who played at licentiousness. And he had mastered Monica, who had wanted to be a domestic bitch playing wild. He had captured her wildness, to mate his own wildness.

It was no good *playing* wild. If he had any real wildness in him, it was dark, and wary, and collected, self-responsible, and of unbreakable steadfastness: like the wildness of a wolf or fox, that knows it will die if it is caught.

If you had a tang of the old wildness in you, you ran with the most intense wariness, knowing that the good tame dogs are really turning into licentious, vicious tame dogs. The vicious tame dogs, pretending to be wild, hate the real clean wildness of an unbroken thing much more than do the respectable tame people.

No, if you refuse to be tamed, you have to be most wary, most subtle, on your guard all the time. You can't afford to be licentious. If you are, you will die in the trap. For the world is a great trap set wide for the unwary.

Jack had learned all these things. He refused to be tamed. He knew that the dark kingdom of death ahead had no room for tame dogs. They merely were put into earth as carrion. Only the wild, untamed souls walked on after death over the border and into the porch of death, to be lords of death and masters of the next living. This he knew.—The tame dogs were put into earth as carrion, like Easu and Percy's poor little baby, and Jacob Ellis.—He often wondered if that courageous old witch-cat of a Gran had slipped into the halls of death, to be one of the ladies of the dark. The lords of death, and the ladies of the dark! He would take his own Monica over the dark border when she died. She would sit unbroken, a quiet, fearless bride in the dark chambers of the dead, the dead who order the goings of the next living.

That was the goal of the afterwards, that he had at the back of his eyes. But meanwhile here on earth he had to win. He had to make room again on earth for those who are not unbroken, those who are not tamed to carrion. Some place for those who know the dark mystery of being royal in death, so that they can enact the shadow of their own royalty on earth.* Some place for the souls that are in themselves dark and have some of the sumptuousness of proud death, no matter what their fathers were. Jack's father was tame, as kings and dukes today are almost mongrelly tame. But Jack was not tame. And Easu's weird baby was not tame. She had some of the eternal fearlessness of the aristocrat whose bones are pure. But a weird sort of aristocrat.

Jack wanted to make a place on earth for a few aristocrats-to-the-bone. He wanted to conquer the world.

And first he must conquer gold. As things are, only the tame go out and conquer gold, to make a lucrative tameness. The untamed forfeit their gold.

"I must conquer gold!" Jack said to himself. "I must open the veins of the earth and bleed the power of gold into my own veins, for the fulfilling of the aristocrats of the bone. I must bring the great stream of gold flowing in another direction, away from the veins of the tame ones, into the veins of the lords of death. I must start the river of the wealth of the world rolling in a new course, down the sombre, quiet, proud valleys of the lords of death and the ladies of the dark, the aristocrats of the afterwards."

So he talked to himself, as he wandered alone in his search, or sat on the bench with a pot of beer, or stepped into Monica's hot little hut. And when he failed, he knew it was because he had not fought intensely enough, and subtly enough.

The bad food, the climate, the hard life gave him a sort of fever and an eczema. But it was no matter. That was only the pulp of him paying a penalty. The powerful skeleton he was was powerful as ever. The pulp of him, his belly, his heart, his muscle seemed not to be able to affect his strength, or at least his power, for more than a short time. Sometimes he broke down. Then he would think what he could do with himself, do for himself, for his flesh and blood. And what he *could* do, he would do. And when he could do no more, he would go and lie down in the mine, or hidden in some shade, lying on the earth, alone, away from anything human. Till the earth itself gave him back his power. Till the powerful living skeleton of him resumed its sway and serenity and fierce power.

He knew he was winning, winning slowly, even in his fight with the earth, his fight for gold. It was on the cards he might die before he realised his victory. Then it would be death, he would have to accept it. He would have to go into death, and leave Monica and Jane and the coming baby to fate.

Meanwhile he would fight, and fight on. The baby was near, there was no money. He had to stay and watch Monica. She, poor thing, went to bed with twins, two boys. There was nothing hardly left of her. He had to give up everything, even his thoughts, and bend his whole life to her, to help her through, and save her and the two quite healthy baby boys. For a month he was doctor and nurse and housewife and husband, and he gave himself absolutely to the work, without a moment's failing. Poor Monica, when she couldn't bear herself, he held her hips together with his arms, and she clung to his neck for life.

This time he almost gave up. He almost decided to go and hire himself out to steady work, to keep her and the babies in peace and safety. To be a hired workman the rest of his days.

And as he sat with his eyes dark and unchanging, ready to accept this fate, since this his fate must be, came a letter from Mr George with an enclosure from England and a cheque for fifty pounds, a legacy from one of the aunts who had so benevolently died at the right moment. He decided his dark Lord did not intend him to go and hire himself out for life, as a hired labourer. He decided Monica and the babies did not want the peace and safety of a hired labourer's cottage. Perhaps better die and be buried in the sand and leave their skeletons like white messages in the ground of this Australia.

So he went back to his working. And three days later struck gold, so that there was gold on his pick-point. He was alone, and he refused at first to get excited. But his trained instinct knew that it was a rich lode. He worked along the vein, and felt the rich weight of the yellow-streaked stuff he fetched out. The light-coloured, softish gold. He sat looking at it in his hand, and the glint of it in the dark earth-rock of the mine, in the light of the lamp. And his bowels leaped in him, knowing that the white gods of tameness would wilt and perish as the pale gold flowed out of their veins.

There would be a place on earth for the lords of death. His own Lord had at last spoken.

Jack sent quickly for Lennie to come and work with him. For Lennie, with a wife and child, was struggling very hard.

Len and Tom both came. Jack had not expected Tom. But Tom lifted his brown eyes to Jack's and said:

"I sortta felt I couldn't stand even Len being mates with you, an' me not there. I was your first mate, Jack. I've never been myself since I parted with you."

"All right," Jack laughed. "You're my first mate."

"That's what I am, General," said Tom.

Jack had showed Monica some of the ore, and told her the mine seemed to be turning out fairly. She was getting back her own strength, that those two monstrous young twins had almost robbed from her entirely. Jack was very careful of her. He wanted above all things that she should become really strong again.

And she, with her rare vitality, soon began to bloom once more. And as her strength came back, she was very much taken up with her babies. These were the first she had enjoyed. The other two she had never really enjoyed. But with these she was as fussy as a young cat with her kittens. She almost forgot Jack entirely. Left him to be busy with Tom and Lennie and his mine. Even the gold failed to excite her.

And she had rather a triumph. She was able to be queenly again with Tom and Lennie. As a girl, she had always been a bit queenly with the rest of them at Wandoo. And she couldn't bear to be humiliated in their eyes.

Now she needn't. She had "the General" for her husband, she had his twins. And *he* had gold in his mine. Hadn't she a perfect right to be queenly with Tom and Lennie? She even got into the habit, right at the beginning, of speaking of Jack as "the General" to them.

"Where's the General, didn't he come down with you?" she would snap at them, in her old sparky fashion.

"He's reviewing his troops," Lennie sarcastically answered.

Whereupon Jack appeared in the door, still in rags. And it was Lennie who mended his shirt for him, when it was torn on the shoulder and showed the smooth man underneath. Monica still couldn't bring herself to these fiddling jobs.

Chapter XXIV.

The Offer to Mary.*

i

They worked for months at the mine, and still it turned out richly. Though they kept as quiet as possible, the fame spread. They had a bonanza. They were all three going to be rich, and Jack was going to be very rich. In the light of his luck, he was "the General" to everybody.

And in the midst of this flow of fortune, came another, rather comical windfall. Again the news was forwarded by Mr George, along with a word of congratulation from that gentleman. The forwarded letter read:

"Dear Sir

"This come hopping to find you well as it leeves me at prisent thanks be to almity God. Your dear uncle Passed Away peaceful on satterday nite And though it be not my place to tell you of it i am Grateful to ave the oppertunity to offer my umble Respecs before the lord and Perlice I take up my pen with pleashr to inform you that He passed without Pain and even Drafts as he aloud the umberrela to be put down and the Book read

"the 24 salm and i kep the ink and paper by to rite of his sudden dismiss but he lingered long years after the bote wint so was onable to Inform you before he desist the doctor rote a butiful certicket of death saying he did of sensible decay but I don no how he brote himself to rite it as the pore master was wite as driven snow and no blemish And being his most umble and Duitful servants we could not ave brout ourself to hever ave rote as he was sensible Pecos god knows the pore sole was not. be that as it may we burried him proud under the prisent arangement of town councel the clerk who was prisent xcepts the docters will he mad up the nite you was hear* in the cimetary and pending your Return Holds It In Bond as Being rite for Us we are Yor Respectable servants to Oblige Hand Commend

Emma and Amos Lewis"

Jack and Tom roared with laughter over this epistle, that brought back so vividly the famous trip up north.

"Gloryanna, General, you've got your property at Coney Hatch* all right," said Tom.

There was a letter from Mr George saying that the defunct John Grant was the son of Jack's mother's elder sister, that he had been liable all his life to bouts of temporary insanity, but that in a period of sanity he had signed the will drawn up by Dr Rackett, when the two boys called at the place several years before, and that the will had been approved. So that Jack, as legal heir and nearest male relative, could now come down and take possession of the farm.

"I don't want that dismal place," said Jack. "Let it go to the Crown. I've no need of it now."

"Don't be a silly cuckoo!" said Tom."You saw it of a wet night with Ally Sloper* in bed under a green cart umbrella. Go an' look at it of a fine day. An' then if you don't want it, sell it or lease it, but don't let the Crown rake it in."

So in about a fortnight's time Jack rather reluctantly left the mine, with its growing heaps of refuse, and departed from the mining settlement which had become a sort of voluntary prison for him, and went west to Perth. He was already a rich man and notorious in the colony. He rode with two pistols in his belt, and that unchanging aloof look on his face. But he carried himself with pride, rode a good horse, wore well-made riding-breeches and a fine bandanna handkerchief loose round his neck, and looked, with a silver-studded band round his broad felt hat, a mixture of a gold-miner, a gentleman settler, and a bandit chief. Perhaps he felt a mixture of them all.

Mr George received him with a great welcome. And Jack was pleased to see the old man. But he refused absolutely to go to the club or to the Government House, or to meet any of the responsible people of the town.

"I don't want to see them, Mr George. I don't want to see them."

And poor old George, his nose a bit out of joint, had to submit to leaving Jack alone.

Jack had his old room in Mr George's house. The Good Plain Cook was still going. And Aunt Matilda, rather older, stouter, with more lines in her face, came to tea with Mary and Miss Blessington. Mary had not married Mr Blessington. But she had remained friends with the odd daughter, who was now a self-contained young woman, shy, thin, well-bred and delicate. Mr Blessington had not married again. In Aunt Matilda's opinion, he was still waiting for Mary. And Mary had refused Tom's rather doubtful offer. Tom was still nervous about Honeysuckle. So there they all were.

When Jack shook hands with Mary, he had a slight shock. He had forgotten her. She had gone out of his consciousness. But when she looked up at him with her dark, clear, waiting eyes, as if she had been watching and waiting for him afar off, his heart gave a queer dizzy lurch. He had forgotten her. They say the heart has a short memory. But now, as a dark hotness gathered in his heart, he realised that his blood had not forgotten her. He had only forgotten her with his head. His blood, with its strange submissiveness and its strange unawareness of time, had kept her just the same.

The blood has an eternal memory. It neither forgets nor moves on ahead. But it is quiescent and submits to the mind's oversway.

He had a certain blood-connection with Mary. He had utterly forgotten it, in the stress and rage of other things. And now, the moment she lifted her eyes to him, and he saw her dusky, quiet, heavy, permanent face, the dull heat started in his breast again, and he remembered how he had told her he would come for her again.

Since his twins were born and he had been so busy with the mine, and he had Monica, he had not given any thought to women. But the moment he saw Mary, and met her eyes, the dark thought struck home in him again: I want Mary for my other woman. He didn't want to displace Monica. Monica was Monica. But he wanted this other woman too.[*]

Aunt Matilda dear-boyed him more than ever. But now he was not a dear boy, he didn't feel a dear boy, and she was put out.

"Dear boy, and how does Monica stand that trying climate?"

"She is quite well again, Marm."

"Poor child! Poor child! I hope you will bring her into a suitable home here in Perth, and have the children suitably brought up. It is so *fortunate* for you your mine is so successful! Now you can build a home here by the river, among us all, and be charming company for us, like your dear father."[*]

Mary was watching him with black eyes, and Miss Blessington with her wide, quick, round, dark-grey eyes. There was a frail beauty about that odd young woman; frail, highly-bred, sensitive, with an uncanny intelligence.

"No Marm," said Jack cheerfully. "I shall not come and live in Perth."

"Dear boy, of course you will! You won't forsake us, and take your money and your family and your attractive self far away to England? No, don't do that. It is just what your dear father did. Robbed us of one of our sweetest girls, and never came back."

"No, I shan't go to England either," smiled Jack.

"Then what will you do?"

"Stay at the mine for the time being."

"Oh, but the mine won't last for ever. And dear boy, don't waste your talents and your charm mining, when it is no longer necessary! Oh do come down to Perth, and bring your family. Mary is pining to see your twins: and dear Monica. Of course we all are!"

Jack smiled to himself. He would no longer give in a hair's-breadth to any of these dreary world-people.

"A la bonne heure!"[*] he said, using one of his mother's well-worn tags. But then his mother could rattle bad colloquial French, and he couldn't.

Mary asked him many questions about the mine and Monica, and Hilda Blessington listened with lowered head, only occasionally fixing him with queer searching eyes, like some odd creature not quite human. Jack was something of a hero. And he was pleased. He wanted to be a hero.

But he was no hero any more for Aunt Matilda. Now that the cherub look had gone for ever, and the shy, blushing, blurting boy had turned into a hard-boned, healthy young man with a half-haughty aloofness and a little, reckless smile that made you feel uncomfortable, she was driven to venting some venom on him.

"That is the worst of the colonies," she said, from her bluish, powdered face. "Our most charming, cultured young men go out to the back of beyond, and they come home quite—quite—"

"Quite what, Marm?"

"Why I was going to say uncouth, but that's perhaps a little strong—"

"I should say, not at all," he answered. He disliked the old lady, and enjoyed baiting her. Great stout old hen, she had played cock-o'-the-walk long enough.

"How many children have you got out there?" she suddenly asked, rudely.

"We have only the twins, of our own," he answered. "But of course there is Jane."

"Jane! Jane! Which is Jane?"

"Jane is Easu Ellis' child—Monica's first."

Everybody started. It was as if a bomb had dropped in the room. Miss Blessington coloured to the roots of her fleecy brown hair. Mary studied her fingers, and Aunt Matilda sat in a Queen-Victoria-statue pose,* outraged.

"What is she like?" asked Mary softly, looking up.

"Who Jane? She's a funny little urchin. I'm fond of her. I believe she'd always stand by me."

Mary looked at him. It was a curious thing to say.

"Is that how you think of people—whether they would always stand by you or not?" she asked softly.

"I suppose it is," he laughed. "Courage is the first quality in life, don't you think?—and fidelity the next."

"Fidelity?" asked Mary.

"Oh, I don't mean automatic fidelity. I mean faithful to the living spark," he replied a little hastily.

"Don't you try to be too much of a spark, young man," snapped Aunt Matilda, arousing from her statuesque offence in order to let nothing pass by her.

"I promise you I won't try," he laughed.

Mary glanced at him quickly—then down at her fingers.

"I think fidelity is a great problem," she said softly.

"Pray why?" bounced Aunt Matilda. "You give your word, and you stick to it."

"Oh, it's not just simple word-faithfulness, Mrs Watson," said Jack.

He had Mary in mind.

"Well, I suppose I have still to live and learn," said Aunt Matilda.

"What's that you have still to live and learn, Matilda?" said Mr George, coming in again with papers.

"This young man is teaching me lessons about life.—Courage is the first quality in life, if you please."

"Well, why not?" said old George amiably. "I like spunk myself."

"Courage to do the *right thing*!" said Aunt Matilda.

"And who's going to decide which is the right thing?" asked the old man, teasing her.

"There is no question of it," said Aunt Matilda.

"Well," said the old lawyer, rubbing his head, "there often is, my dear woman, a very big question!"

"And fidelity is the second virtue," said Mary, looking up at him with trustful eyes, inquiringly.

"A man's no good unless he can keep faith," said the old man.

"But what is it that one must remain faithful to?" came the quiet cool voice of Hilda Blessington.

"Do you know what old Gran Ellis said?" asked Jack. "She said a man's own true self is god in him. She was a queer old bird."

"His *true* self," said Aunt Matilda. "His true self!—And I should say old Mrs Ellis was a doubtful guide of young people, judging from her own family."

"She made a great impression on me, Marm," said Jack politely.

Mr George had brought the papers referring to the new property. Jack read various documents, rather absently. Then the title deeds. Then he studied a fascinating little green-and-red map, "delineating and setting forth," with "easements and encumbrances," whatever they were. There was a bank-book showing a balance of four hundred pounds nineteen shillings and sixpence, in the West Australia Bank.

Jack told about his visit to Grant farm, and the man under the umbrella. They all laughed.

"The poor devil had a bad start," said Mr George. "But he was a good farmer and a good business man, in his right times. Oh, he knew who he was leaving the place to, when Rackett drew up that will."

"Gran Ellis told me about him," said Jack. "She told me about all the old people. She told me about my mother's older sister. And she told me about the father of this crazy man as well, but—"

Mr George was looking at him coldly and fiercely.

"The poor fellow's father," said the old man, "was an Englishman who thought himself a swell, but wasn't too much of a high-born gentleman to abandon a decent girl and go round to the east side and marry another woman, and flaunt round in society with women he hadn't married."

Jack remembered. It was Mary's father: seventh son of old Lord Haworth. What a mix-up! How bitter old George sounded!

"It seems to have been a mighty mix-up out here, fifty years ago, sir," he said mildly.

"It was a mix-up then—and is a mix-up now."

"I suppose," said Jack, "if the villain of a gentleman had never abandoned my aunt—I can't think of her as an aunt—he'd never have gone to Sydney, and his children that he had there would never have been born."

"I suppose not," said Mr George drily. But he started a little, and involuntarily looked at Mary.

"Do you think it would be better if they had never been born?" Jack asked pertinently.

"I don't set up to judge," said the old man.

"Does Mrs Watson?"

"I certainly think it would be better," said Mrs Watson, "if that poor half-idiot cousin of yours had never been born."

"I've got Gran Ellis on my mind," said Jack. "She was funny, what she condemned and what she didn't. I used to think she was an old terror. But I can understand her better now. She was a wise woman, seems to me."

"Indeed!" said Aunt Matilda. "I never put her and wisdom together."

"Yes, she was wise. I can see now. She knew that sins are as vital a part of life as virtues, and she stuck up for the sins that are necessary to life."*

"What's the matter with you, Jack Grant, that you go and start moralising?" said old George.

"Why, sir, it must be that my own sinful state is dawning on my mind," said Jack. "And I'm wondering whether to take Mrs Watson's advice, and repent and weep etc. etc. Or whether to follow old Gran Ellis' lead, and put a sinful feather in my cap."

"Well," said old George, smiling, "I don't know. You talk about courage and fidelity. Sin usually means doing something rather cowardly, and breaking your faith in some direction."

"Oh I don't know, sir. Tom and Lennie are faithful to me. But that doesn't mean they are not free. They are free to do just what they like, so long as they are faithful to the spark that is between us. As I am faithful to them. It seems to me, sir, one is true to one's *word* in *business*, in affairs. But in life one can only be true to the spark."

"I'm afraid there's something amiss with you, son, that's set you off arguing and splitting hairs."

"There is. Something is always amiss with most of us. Old Gran Ellis was a lesson to me, if I'd known. Something is always wrong with the lot of us—And I believe in thinking before I act."

"Let us hope so," said Mr George. "But it sounds funny sort of thinking you do."*

"But," said Hilda Blessington, with wide, haunted eyes. "What is the spark that one must be faithful to? How are we to be sure of it?"

"You just feel it. And then you act on it. That's courage.—And then you always live up to the resonsibility of your act. That's faithfulness. You have to keep faith in all kinds of ways. I have to keep faith with Monica and the babies, and young Jane, and Lennie and Tom and dead Gran Ellis: and—and more—yes, more—"

He looked with clear hard eyes at Mary, and at the young girl. They were both watching him, puzzled and perturbed. The two old people in the background were silent but hostile.

"Do you know what I am faithful to?" he said, still to the two young women, but letting the elders hear. "I am faithful to my own inside,* when something stirs in me. Gran Ellis said that was God in me. I know there's a God outside of me. But he tells me to go my own way, and never be frightened of people and the world, only be frightened of *him*. And if I felt I really wanted two wives, for example, I would have them and keep them both. If I really wanted them, it would mean it was the God outside me bidding me, and it would be up to me to obey, world or no world."*

"You describe exactly the devil driving you," said Aunt Matilda.

"Doesn't he!" laughed Mr George, who was oddly impressed. "I only hope there isn't a streak of madness in the family."

"No there's not. The world is all so tame, it's like an idiot to me. A dangerous idiot. So that if I do want two wives—or even three;——well, I *do*. Why listen to the Idiot."

"Sounds like *you'd* gone cracked, out there in that mining settlement," said Mr George.

"If I said I wanted two fortunes instead of one," said Jack with a malicious smile, "you wouldn't think it cracked."

"No, only greedy," said old George.

"Not if I could use them. And the same if I can really value two wives, and use them—or even three—" Jack glanced with a queer bright grin at Hilda Blessington—"Well, three wives would be three fortunes for my blood and spirit."

"For your wickedness," said Aunt Matilda. "You are not allowed to say such things, even in joke."

"Surely I may say them in dead earnest," persisted Jack mischievously. He was aware of Mary and Hilda Blessington listening, and he wanted to throw a sort of lasso over them.

"You'll merely find yourself in gaol for bigamy," said Mr George.

"Oh," said Jack, "I wouldn't risk that. It would really be a Scotch marriage. Monica is my legal wife. But what I pledged myself to, I'd stick to, as I stick to Monica. I'd stick to the others the same."

"I won't hear any more of this nonsense," said Aunt Matilda, rising.

"Nonsense it is," said old George testily.*

Jack laughed. Their being bothered amused him. He was a little surprised at himself for breaking out in this way. But the sight of Mary, and the sense of a new, different responsibility had struck it out of him. His nature was ethical, inclined to be emotionally mystical. Now, however, the sense of the foolish complacency and empty assurance in Aunt Matilda, and in all the dead-certain people of this world struck out of him a hard, sharp, non-emotional opposition. He felt hard and mischievous, confronting them. Who were they, to judge and go on judging? Who was Aunt Matilda, to judge the dead fantastic soul of the fierce Gran? The Ellises, the Ellises, they all had some of Gran's fierce pagan uneasiness about them, they were all a bit uncanny.* That was why he loved them so.

And Mary! Mary had another slow, heavy, mute mystery, that waited and waited for ever, like a lode-stone. And should he therefore abandon her, abandon her to society and a sort of sterility? Not he. She was his to fertilise.* His, and no other man's. She knew it herself. He knew it. Then he would fight them all. Even the good old George. For the mystery that was his and Mary's.

Let it be an end of popular goodness. Let there be another, deeper, fiercer, untamed sort of goodness, like in the days of Abraham and Samson and Saul. If Jack was to be good, he would be good with these great old men, the heroic fathers, not with the Saints. The Christian goodness had gone bad, decayed almost into poison. It needed again the old heroic goodness of untamed men, with the wild great God who was for ever too unknown to be a paragon.

Old George was a little afraid of Jack, uneasy about him. He thought him not normal. The boy had to be put in a category by himself, like a madman in a solitary cell. And at the same time, the old man was delighted. He was delighted with the young man's physical presence. Bewildered by the careless, irrational things Jack would say, the old bachelor took off his spectacles and rubbed his tired eyes again and again, as if he were going blind, and as if he were losing his old dominant will.

He had been a dominant character in the colony so long. And now this young fellow was laughing at him and stealing away his power of resistance.

"Don't make eyes at me, sir," said Jack laughing. "I know better than you what life means."

"You do, do you? Oh you do?" said the old man. And he laughed too. Somehow it made him feel warm and easy. "A fine crazy affair it would be if it were left to you." And he laughed aloud at the absurdity.*

ii

Jack persuaded Mary to go with Mr George and himself to look at Grant Farm. Mary and the old lawyer went in a buggy, Jack rode his own horse. And it seemed to him good to be out again in the bush and forest country. It was rainy season, and the smell of the earth was delicious in his nostrils.

He decided soon to leave the mine. It was running thin. He could leave it in charge of Tom. And then he must make some plan for himself. Perhaps he would come and live on the Grant farm. It was not too far from Perth, or from Wandoo, it was in the hills, the climate was balmy and almost English, after the gold-fields, and there were trees. He really rejoiced again, riding through strong, living trees.

Sometimes he would ride up beside Mary. She sat very still at Mr George's side, talking to him in her quick, secret-seeming way. Mary always looked as if the things she was saying were secrets. And her upper lip, with its down of fine black hair, would lift and show her white teeth as she smiled with her mouth. She only smiled with her mouth: her eyes remained dark and glistening and unchanged. But she talked a great deal to Mr George, almost like lovers, they were so confidential and so much in tune with one another. It was as if Mary was happy with an old man's love, that was fatherly, warm, and sensuous, and wise and talkative, without being at all dangerous.

When Jack rode up, she seemed to snap the thread of her communication with Mr George, her ready volubility failed, and she was a little nervous. Her eyes, her dark eyes, were afraid of the young man. Yet they would give him odd, bright, corner-wise looks, almost inviting. So different from the full, confident way she looked at Mr George. So different from Monica's queer yellow glare. Mary seemed almost to peep at him, while her dark face, like an animal's muzzle with its slightly heavy mouth, remained quite expressionless.

It amused him. He remembered how he had kissed her, and he wondered if she remembered. It was impossible, of course, to ask her. And when she talked, it was always so seriously. That again amused Jack. She was so voluble, especially with Mr George, on all kinds of deep and difficult subjects. She was quite excited, just now, about authoritarianism. She was being drawn to the Roman Catholic Church.

"Oh!" she was saying, "I am an authoritarian. Don't you think that the whole natural scheme is a scheme of authority, one rank having authority over another?"

Mr George couldn't quite see it. Yet it tickled his paternal male conceit of authority, so he didn't contradict her. And Jack smiled to himself. It amused him to hear her so wound up. But also it annoyed him. "She runs too much to talk!" he thought. "She runs too much in her head."—She seemed, indeed, to have forgotten quite how he kissed her. It seemed that "questions of the day" quite absorbed her.

They came through the trees in the soft afternoon sunshine. Jack remembered the place well. He remembered the jamboree, and that girl who had called him dearie! His first woman! And insignificant enough; but not bad. He thought kindly of her. She was a warm-hearted soul. But she didn't belong to his life at all. He remembered too how he had kicked Tom. The faithful Tom! Mary would never marry Tom, that was a certainty. And it was equally certain, Tom would never break his heart.

Jack was thinking to himself, that he would build a new house on this place, and ask Mary to live in the old house. That was a brilliant idea.

But as he drove up, he thought: "The first money you spend on this place, my boy, will be on a bran new five-barred white gate."

Emma and Amos came out full of joy. They too were a faithful old pair. Jack handed Mary down. She wore a dark blue dress and white silk gloves. It was so like her, to put on white silk gloves. But he liked the touch of them, as he handed her down. Her small, short, rather passive hands.

He and she walked round the place, and she was very much interested. A new place, a new farm, a new undertaking always excited her, as if it was she who was making the new move.

"Don't you think *that* will be a good place for the new house?" he was saying to her. "Down there, near that bunch of jolly old trees. And the garden south of the trees. If you dig in that flat you'll find water, sure to."

She inspected the place most carefully, and uttered her mature judgments.

"You'll have to help think it out," he said. "Monica's as indifferent as an opossum. Would you like to build yourself a house here, and tend to things? I'll build you one if you like. Or give you the old one."

She looked at him with glowing eyes.

"Wouldn't that be splendid!" she said. "Oh, wouldn't that be splendid! If I had a house and a piece of land of my own! Oh yes!"

"Well I can easily give it you," he said. "Just whatever you like."

"Isn't that lovely!" she exclaimed.

But he could tell she was thinking merely of a house and a bit of land, and herself a sort of Auntie to his and Monica's children. She was fairly jumping into old-maiddom, both feet first. Which was not what he intended. He didn't want her as an auntie for his children.

They went back to the house, and inspected there. She liked it. It was a stone one-storey house with a great kitchen and three other rooms, all rather low and homely. The dead cousin had wanted his house to be exactly like the houses of the other respectable farmers. And he had not been prevented.

The place was a bit tumble-down, but clean. Emma was baking scones, and the sweet smell of scorched flour filled the house. Mary lit the lamp in the little parlour, and set it on the highly-polished but rather ricketty rose-wood table, next the photograph album. The family bible had been moved to the bed-room. But the old man had a photograph album, like any other respectable householder.

Mary drew up one of the old green-rep chairs, and opened the book. Jack, looking over her shoulder, started a little as he saw the first photograph: an elderly lady in lace cap and voluminous silken skirts was seated reading a book, while negligently leaning with one hand on her chair was a gentleman with long white trousers and old-fashioned coat and side-whiskers, obviously having his photograph taken.

This was the identical photograph which held place of honour in Jack's mother's album; the photograph of her father and mother.

"See!" said Jack. "That's my grandmother and grandfather. And he must have been the man who took Gran Ellis' leg off. Goodness!"

Mary gazed at them closely.

"He looks a domineering man!" she said. "I hope you're not like him."

Jack didn't feel at all like him. Mary turned over, and they beheld two young ladies of the Victorian period. Somebody had marked a cross, in ink, over the head of one of the young ladies. They must be his own aunts, both of them many years older than his own mother, who was a late arrival.

"Do you think that was his mother?" said Mary, looking up at Jack, who stood at her side. "She was beautiful."

Jack studied the photograph of the young woman. She looked like nobody's mother on earth,* with her hair curiously rolled and curled, and a great crinoline flouncing round her. And her beauty was so photographic and abstract, he merely gazed seeking for it.

But Mary, looking up at him, saw his silent face in the glow of the lamp, his rather grim mouth closed ironically under his moustache, his open nostrils, and the long, steady, self-contained look of his eyes under his lashes. He was not thinking of her at all, at the moment. But his calm, rather distant, unconsciously imperious face was something quite new and startling, and rather repellant to her. She became intensely aware of his thighs standing close against her, and her heart went faint. She was afraid of him.

In agitation, she was going to turn the leaf. But he put his work-hardened hand on the page, and turned back to the first photograph.

"Look!" he said. "*He*—" pointing to his grandfather—"disowned *her*—" turning to the aunt marked with a cross—"and she died an outcast, in misery, and her son burrowed here, half crazy.—Yet their two faces are rather alike.—Gran Ellis told me about them."

Mary studied them.

"They are both a bit like yours," she said, "their faces."

"Mine!" he exclaimed. "Oh no! I look like my father's family."

He could see no resemblance at all to himself in the handsome, hard-mouthed, large man, with the clean face and the fringe of fair whiskers, and the black cravat, and the overbearing look.

"Your eyes are set in the same way," she said. "And your brows are the same. But your mouth is not so tight."

"I don't like what I heard of him, anyhow," said Jack. "A puritanical surgeon! Turn over."

She turned over, and gave a low cry. There was a photograph of a young elegant with drooping black moustachios, and mutton-chop side-whiskers, and large, languid black eyes,* leaning languidly and swinging a cane. Over the top was written, in a weird hand-writing: *The Honourable George Rath, blasted father of*  .*

This skull and crossbones was repeated on the other three sides of the photograph.*

"Oh!" said Mary, covering her face with her hands.

Jack's face was a study. Mary had evidently recognised the portrait of her father as a young man. Yet Jack could not help smiling at the skull and crossbones, in connection with the Bulwer Lytton young elegant, and the man under the green umbrella.

"My God!" he thought to himself. "All that happens in a generation! From that sniffy young dude* to that fellow here who made this farm, and Mary with her face in her hands!"

He could not help smiling to himself.

"Had you seen that photograph before?" he asked her.

She, unable to answer, kept her face in her hands.

"Don't worry," he said. "We're all more or less that way. We're none of us perfect."

Still she did not answer. Then he went on, almost without thinking, as he studied the rather fetching young gentleman with the long black hair and bold black eyes, and the impudent, handsome, languid hips:

"You're a bit like *him* too. You're a bit like him in the look of your eyes. I bet he wasn't tall, either. I bet he was rather small."

Mary took her hands from her face and looked up fierce and angry.

"You have no feeling," she said.

"I have," he replied, smiling slightly. "But life seems to me too rummy to get piqued about it. Think of him leaving a son like the fellow I saw under the umbrella! Think of it! Such a dandy! And that his son! And then having you for a daughter when he was getting quite on in years. Do you remember him?"

"How can you talk to me like that?" she cried.

"But why! It's life. It's how it was. Do you remember your father?"

"Of course I do."

"Did he dye his whiskers?"

"I won't answer you."

"Well, don't then. But this man under the umbrella here—you

should have seen him—was your half-brother and my cousin. It makes us almost related."

Mary left the room. In a few minutes Mr George came in.

"What's wrong with Mary?" he asked, suspiciously, angrily.

Jack shrugged his shoulders, and pointed to the photograph. The old man bent over and stared at it: and laughed. Then he took the photograph out of the book, and put it in his pocket.

"Well I'm damned!" he said! "Signs himself skull and cross-bones! Think of that now!"

"Was the Honourable George a smallish built man?" asked Jack.

"Eh!" The old man started. Then, startled, he began to remember back. "Ay!" he said. "He was. He was smallish built, and the biggest little dude you ever set eyes on. Something about his back-side always reminded me of a woman. But all the women were wild about him. Ay, even when he was over fifty, Mary's mother was wild in love with him. And he married her because she was going to be a big heiress. But she died a bit too soon, an' he got nothing, nor Mary neither, because she was *his* daughter."—The old man made an ironic grimace. "He only died a few years back, in Sydney," he added. "But I say, that poor lass is fair cut up about it. We'd always kept it from her. I feel bad about her."

"She may as well get used to it," said Jack, disliking the old man's protective sentimentalism.

"Eh! Get used to it! Why? How can she get used to it?"

"She's got to live her own life some time."

"How d' y' mean, live her own life? She's never going to live *that* sort of life, as long as I can see to it." He was quite huffed.

"Are you going to leave her to be an old maid?" said Jack.

"Eh? Old maid! No! She'll marry when she wants to."

"You bet," said Jack, with a slow smile.

"She's a child yet," said Mr George.

"An elderly child—poor Mary!"

"Poor Mary! Poor Mary! Why poor Mary? Why so?"

"Just poor Mary!" said Jack, slowly smiling.

"I don't see it. Why is she poor?—You're growing into a real young devil you are." And the old man glanced into the young man's eyes half in mistrust and fear, half in admiration.

They went into the kitchen, the late tea was ready. It was evident that Mary was waiting for them to come in. She had recovered her composure, but was more serious than usual. Jack laughed at her, and teased her.

"Ah Mary," he said, "do you still believe in the Age of Innocence?"

"I still believe in good feeling," she retorted.

"So do I. And when good feeling's comical, I believe in laughing at it," he replied.

"There's something wrong with you," she replied.

"Quoth Aunt Matilda," he echoed.

"Aunt Matilda is very often right," she said.

"Never, in my opinion. Aunt Matilda is a wrong number. She's one of life's false statements."

"Hark at him!" laughed old George.

As soon as the meal was over, he rose, saying he would see to his horse. Mary looked up at him as he put his hat on his head and took the lantern. She didn't want him to go.

"How long will you be?" she asked.

"Why, not long," he answered, with a slight smile.

Nevertheless he was glad to be out and with his horse. Somehow those others made a false atmosphere, Mary and old George. They made Jack's soul feel sarcastic. He lingered about the stable, in the dim light of the lantern, preparing himself a bed. There were only two bedrooms in the house. The old couple would sleep on the kitchen floor, or on the sofa. He preferred to sleep in the stable. He had grown so, that he did not like to sleep inside their fixed, shut-in houses. He did not mind a mere hut, like his at the camp. But a shut-in house with fixed furniture made him feel sick. He was sick of the whole pretence of it.

And he knew he would never come to live on this farm. He didn't want to. He didn't like the atmosphere of the place. He felt stifled. He wanted to go north, or west,* or North-West once more.

Suddenly he heard footsteps: Mary picking her way across.

"Is your horse all right?" she asked. "I was afraid something was wrong with him. And he is so beautiful. Or is it a mare?"

"No," he said. "It's a horse. I don't care for a mare, for riding."

"Why?"

"She has so many whims of her own, and wants so much attention paid to her. And then ten to one you can't trust her. I prefer a horse, to ride."

She saw the rugs spread on straw.

"Who is going to sleep here?" she said.

"I."

"Why—but—"

He cut short her expostulations.

"Oh, but do let me bring you sheets. Do let me make you a proper bed!" she cried.

But he only laughed at her.

"What's a *proper* bed?" he said. "Is this an improper one, then?"

"It's not a comfortable one," she said with dignity.

"It is for me.—I wasn't going to ask you to sleep on it too, was I now?"

She went out, and stood looking at the Southern Cross.

"Weren't you coming indoors again?" she asked.

"Don't you think it's nicer out here? Feels a bit tight in there.—I say, Mary, I don't think I shall ever come and live on this place."

"Why not?"

"I don't like it."

"Why not?"

"It feels a bit heavy—and a bit tight to me."

"What shall you do then?"

"Oh, I don't know. I'll decide when I'm back at the camp.—But I say, wouldn't *you* like this place? I'll give it you if you would. You're *really* the next of kin. If you'll have it, I'll give it you."

Mary was silent for some time.

"And what do you think you will do, if you don't live here?" she asked. "Will you stay always on the gold-fields?"

"Oh dear no.—I shall probably go up to the Never-Never, and raise cattle. Where there aren't so many people, and photo-albums, and good old Georges and Aunt Matildas and all that."

"You'll be *yourself*, wherever you are."

"Thank God for that.—But it's not quite true. I find I'm less myself down here, with all you people."

Again she was silent for a time.

"Why?" she asked.

"Oh, that's how it makes me feel, that's all."

"Are you more yourself on the gold-fields?" she asked, rather contemptuously.

"Oh yes."

"When you are getting money, you mean?"

"No. But I've got so that Aunt-Matilda-ism and old-Georgism

don't agree with me. They make me feel sarcastic, they make me feel out of sorts all over."

"And I suppose you mean Mary-ism too," she said.

"Yes, a certain sort of Mary-ism does it to me as well. But there's a Mary without the ism that I said I'd come back for.—Would you like this place?"

"Why?"

"To cultivate your Mary-ism. Or would you like to come to the North-West?"

"But why* do you trouble about me?"

"I've come back for you. I said I'd come back for you. I am here."

There was a moment of tense silence.

"You have married Monica now," said Mary in a low voice.

"Of course I have. But the leopard doesn't change his spots when he goes into a cave with a she-leopard. I said I'd come back for you as well, and I've come."

A dead silence.

"But what about Monica?" Mary asked, with a little curl of irony.

"Monica?" he said. "Yes, she's my wife, I tell you. But she's not my only wife. Why should she be? She will lose nothing."

"Did she say so? Did you tell her?" Mary asked insidiously.

Slowly an anger suffused thick in his chest, and then seemed to break in a kind of explosion. His heart seemed to be shaking with explosion. And the curious tension of his desire for Mary snapped with the explosion of his anger.

"No," he said. "I didn't tell her. I had to ask *you* first. Monica is thick with her babies now. She won't care where I am. That's how women are. They are more *creatures* than men are. They're not separated out of the earth. They're like black ore. The metal's in them, but it's still part of the earth. They're all part of the matrix, women are, with their children clinging to them."

"And men are pure gold?" said Mary sarcastically.

"Yes, in streaks. Men are the pure metal, in streaks. Women never are. For my part, I don't want them to be. They *are* the mother-rock. They *are* the matrix. Leave them at that. That's why I want more than one wife."

"But why?" she asked.

He realised that, in his clumsy fashion, he had taken the wrong tack. The one thing he should never have done, he had begun to do: explain and argue. Truly, Mary put up a permanent mental resistance. But he should have attacked elsewhere. He should have made love to her. Yet, since she had so much mental resistance, he had to make his position clear.—Now he realised he was angry and tangled.

"Shall we go in?" he said abruptly.

And she returned with him in silence back to the house. Mr George was in the parlour, looking over some papers. Jack and Mary went in to him.

"I have been thinking, sir," said Jack, "that I shall never come and live on this place. I want to go up to the North-West and raise cattle. That'll suit me better than wheat and dairy. So I offer this place to Mary. She can do as she likes with it. Really, I feel the property is naturally hers."

Now old George had secretly cherished this thought for many years, and it had riled him a little when Jack calmly stepped into the inheritance.

"Oh you can't be giving away a property like this," he said.

"Why not? I have all the money I want. I give the place to Mary. I'd much rather give it to her than sell it. But if she won't have it, I'll ask you to sell it for me."

"Why—! Why—!" said old George fussily, stirring quite delighted in his chair, and looking from one to the other of the young people, unable to understand their faces. Mary looked sulky and unhappy, Jack* looked sarcastic.

"I won't take it, anyhow!" exclaimed Mary.

"Eh? Why not? If the young millionaire wants to throw it away—"* said the old man ironically.

"I won't! I won't take it!" she repeated abruptly.

"Why what's amiss?"

"Nothing! I won't take it."

"Got a proud stomach from your aristocratic ancestors, have you?" said old George. "Well, you needn't have; the place is your father's son's place, you needn't be altogether so squeamish."

"I wouldn't take it if I was starving," she asserted.

"You're in no danger of starving, so don't talk," said the old man testily. "It's a nice little place. I should enjoy coming out here and spending a few months of the year myself. Should like nothing better."

"But I won't take it," said Mary.

Jack went grinning off to his stable. He was angry, but it was the kind of anger that made him feel sarcastic.

Damn her! She was in love with him. She had a passion for him. What did she want? Did she want him to make love to her, and run away with her, and abandon Monica and Jane and the twin babies?—No doubt she would listen to such a proposition hard enough. But he was never going to make it her. He had married Monica, and he would stick to her. She was his first and chief wife, and whatever happened, she should remain it. He detested and despised divorce; a shifty business. But it was nonsense to pretend that Monica was the beginning and end of his marriage with woman. Woman was the matrix, the red earth, and he wanted his roots in this earth. More than one root, to keep him steady and complete. Mary instinctively belonged to him. Then why not belong to him completely?

Why not? And why not make a marriage with her too? The legal marriage with Monica, his own marriage with Mary. It was a natural thing. The old heroes, the old fathers of red earth, like Abraham in the bible, like David even, they took the wives they needed for their own completeness,[*] without this nasty chop-and-change business of divorce. Then why should he not do the same?

He would have all the world against him. But what would it matter, if he were away in the Never-Never, where the world just faded out? Monica could have the chief house. But Mary should have another house, with garden and animals if she wanted them. And she should have her own children: his children. Why should she be only Auntie to Monica's children? Mary, with her black, glistening eyes and her short, dark, secret body, she was asking for children. She was asking him for his children, really. He knew it, and secretly she knew it; and Aunt Matilda, and even old George knew it, somewhere in themselves. And old George was funny. He wouldn't really have minded an affair between Jack and Mary, provided it had been kept dark. He would even have helped them to it, so long as they would let nothing be known.

But Jack was too wilful and headstrong, and too proud, for an intrigue. An intrigue meant a certain cringing before society, and this he would never do. If he took Mary, it was because he felt she instinctively belonged to him. Because, in spite of the show she kept up, her womb was asking for him. And he wanted her for himself. He wanted to have her and to answer her.[*] And he would be judged by nobody.

He rose quickly, returning to the house. Mary and the old man were in the kitchen, getting their candles to go to bed.

"Mary," said Jack, "come out and listen to the night-bird."

She started slightly, glanced at him, then at Mr George.

"Go with him a minute, if you want to," said the old man.

Rather unwillingly she went out of the door with Jack. They crossed the yard in silence, towards the stable. She hesitated outside, in the thin moonlight.

"Come and sleep in the stable with me," he said, his heart beating thick, and his voice strange and low.

"Oh Jack!" she cried, with a funny little lament; "you're married to Monica! I can't! You're Monica's."

"Am I?" he said. "Monica's mine, if you like, but why am I all hers? She's certainly not all mine. She belongs chiefly to her babies just now. Why shouldn't she? She's their red earth. But I'm not going to shut my eyes. Neither am I going to play the mild Saint Joseph.* I don't feel that way. At the present moment I'm not Monica's, any more than she is mine. So what's the good of your telling me? I shall love her again, when she is free. Everything in season,* even wives. Now I love you again, after having never thought of it for a long while. But it was always slumbering inside me, just as Monica is asleep inside me this minute. The sun goes, and the moon comes. A man isn't made up of only one thread. What's the good of keeping your virginity! It's really mine. Come and sleep with me in the stable, and then afterwards come and live in the North-West, in one of my houses, and have your children there, and animals or whatever you want."

"Oh God!" cried Mary. "You must really be mad. You don't love me, you can't, you must love Monica. Oh God, why do you torture me!"

"I don't torture you. Come and sleep in the stable with me. I love you too."

"But you love Monica."

"I shall love Monica again, another time. Now I love you. I don't change. But sometimes it's one, then the other. Why not?"

"It can't be! It can't be!" cried Mary.

"Why not? Come into the stable with me, with me and the horses."

"Oh don't torture me! I hate my animal nature. You want to make a slave of me," she cried blindly.

This struck him silent. Hate her animal nature? What did she mean? Did she mean the passion she had for him? And make a slave of her? How?

"How make a slave of you?" he asked. "What are you now? You are a sad thing as you are. I don't want to leave you as you are. You are a slave now, to Aunt Matilda and all the conventions. Come and sleep with me in the stable."

"Oh, you are cruel to me! You are wicked! I can't. You know I can't."

"Why can't you? You can. I am not wicked. To me it doesn't matter what the world is. You *really* want it. The middle of you *really* wants me, and nothing but me. It's only the outside of you that's afraid. There is nothing to be afraid of, now we have enough money. You will come with me to the North-West, and be my other wife, and have my children, and I shall depend on you as a man has to depend on a woman."

"How selfish you are! You are as selfish as my father, who betrayed your mother's sister and left this skull-and-cross-bones son," she cried. "No, it's dreadful, it's horrible. In this horrible place, too, proposing such a thing to me. It shows you have no feelings."

"I don't care about feelings. They're what people have because they feel they ought to have them. But I know my own real feeling. I don't care about your feelings."

"I know you don't," she said. "Good-night!" She turned abruptly and hurried away in the moonlight, escaping to the house.

Jack watched the empty night for some minutes. Then he turned away into the stable.

"That's that!" he said, seeing his little plans come to nought.

He went into the stable and sat down on his bed, near the horses. How good it was to be with the horses! How good animals were, with no "feelings" and no ideas. They just straight felt what they felt, without lies and complications.

Well, so be it! He was surprised. He had not expected Mary to funk the issue, since the issue was clear. What else was the right thing to do? Why, nothing else!

It seemed to him so obvious. Mary obviously wanted him, even more, perhaps, than he wanted her. Because she was only a part thing, by herself. All women were only parts of some whole, when they were by themselves: let them be as clever as they might. They were creatures of earth, and fragments, all of them. All women were only fragments; fragments of matrix at that.

No, he was not wrong, he was right. If the others didn't agree, they didn't, that was all. He still was right. He still hated the nauseous one-couple-in-one-cottage domesticity. He hated domesticity altogether. He loathed the thought of being shut up with one woman and a bunch of kids in a house. Several women, several houses, several bunches of kids: it would then be like a perpetual travelling,* a camp, not a home. He hated homes. He wanted a camp.

He wanted to pitch his camp in the wilderness: with the faithful Tom, and Lennie, and his own wives. Wives, not wife. And the horses, and the come-and-go, and the element of wildness. Not to be tamed. His men, men by themselves. And his women never to be tamed. And the wilderness still there. He wanted to go like Abraham under the wild sky, speaking to a fierce wild Lord, and having angels stand in his doorway.*

Why not? Even if the whole world said No! Even then, why not?

As for being ridiculous, what was more ridiculous than men wheeling perambulators and living among a mass of furniture in a tight house?

Anyhow it was no good talking to Mary at the moment. She wasn't a piece of the matrix of red earth. She was a piece of the upholstered world. Damn the upholstered world! He would go back to the goldfields, to Tom and Lennie and Monica, back to camp. Back to camp, away from the upholstery.

No, he *wasn't* a man who had finished when he had got one wife.

And that damned Mary, by the mystery of fate, was linked to him from her womb.

And damn her, she preferred to break that link, and turn into an upholstered old maid. Of all the hells!

Then let her marry Blessington and a houseful of furniture. Or else marry old George, and gas to him while he could hear. She loved gassing. Talk, talk, talk, Jack hated a talking woman. But Mary would rather sit gassing with old George than sleep with him, Jack, in the stable along with the horses. Of all the surprising hells!

At least Tom wasn't like that. And Monica wasn't. But Monica was wrapped up in her babies, she seemed to swim in a sea of babies, and Jack had to let her be. And she too had a hankering after furniture. He knew she'd be after it, if he didn't prevent her.

Well, it was no good preventing people, even from stuffed plush furniture and knick-knacks. But he'd keep the brake on. He would do that.

Chapter XXV.

Trot Trot Back Again.[*]

But as he rode back to Perth, with Mary rather stiff and silent, and Mr George absorbed in his own thoughts; and as they greeted people on the road, and passed by settlements; and as they saw far off the pale blue sea with a speck of a steamer smoking, and the dim fume of Perth down at sea-level: he thought to himself: "I had better be careful. I had better be wary. I know the chief fault of my nature, that I am not cold and cautious enough. The world is cold and cautious, it has cold blood, like ants and centipedes. They, all the men in the world, they hardly want one wife, let alone two. And they would take any excuse to destroy me. They would like to destroy me, because I am not cold and like an ant, as they are. Mary would like me to be killed. Look at her face. She would feel a real deep satisfaction if my horse threw me against those stones and smashed my skull in. She would feel vindicated. And old George would think it served me right. And practically everybody would be glad. Not Tom and Len. But practically everybody else. Even Monica. Even Monica, though she is my wife. Even she feels a judgment ought to descend on me. Because I'm not what she wants me to be. Because I'm not as she thinks I should be. And because she can't get beyond me. Because something inside her knows she can't get past me. Therefore, in one corner of her, she hates me, like a scorpion lurking. If I'm unaware, and put my hand unthinking in that corner, she'll sting me and hope to kill me.—How curious it is! And since I have found the gold it is more emphatic than before. As if they grudged me something. As if they grudged me my very being. Because I'm not one of them, and just like they are, they would like me destroyed. It has always been so, ever since I was born. My aunts, my own father. And my mother didn't want me destroyed, as they secretly did, but even my mother would not have tried to prevent them from destroying me. Even when they like me, as old George does, they grudge their own liking, they take it back whenever they can. He defended me over Easu, because he thought I was defending Monica and going the good way of the world. Now he scents that I am going my own way, he feels as if I were a sort of snake that should be put out of existence. That's how Mary feels too: and Mary loves me, if loving counts for anything. Tom and Len don't wish me destroyed. But if they saw the world destroying me, they'd acquiesce. Their fondness for me is only passive, not active. I believe, if I ransacked earth and heaven, there's nobody would fight for me as I am, not a soul, except that little Jane of Easu's. The others would fight like cats and dogs for me *as they want me to be*. But for me as I am, they would do nothing, they would like to see me killed. They would think it a just punishment on me, for not being as they want me to be, and as the world is. Me as I am, they think I *ought* to be destroyed.

"And I, I am a fool, talking to them, giving myself away to them. Even asking to give myself away to them, as to Mary. Why, Mary ought to go down on her knees before the honour, if I want to take her. Instead of which she puffs herself up, and spits venom in my face, like a cobra.

"Very well, very well. Soon I can go out of her sight again, for I loathe the sight of her. I can ride down Hay Street without yielding a hair's-breadth to any man or woman on earth. And I can ride out of Perth without leaving a vestige of myself behind, for them to work mischief on.

"God, but it's a queer thing, to know that they *all* want to destroy me-as-I-am, even out here in this far-off colony. I thought it was only my aunts, and my father because of his social position. But it is everybody. Even, passively, my mother, and Tom and Len. Because inside my soul I don't conform: can't conform. They would all like to kill the non-conforming me. Which is me myself.

"And at the same time, they all love me extremely the moment they think I am in line with them. The moment they think I am in line with them, and that I am only *playing* at being out of the line, they're awfully fond of me. Monica, Mary, old George, even Aunt Matilda, they're almost all of them in love with me then, and they'd give me anything. If I asked Mary to sleep with me, as a sin, as something I shouldn't but I went down on my knees and begged her, because I couldn't help myself, she'd give in to me like anything. And Monica, if I was willing to be forgiven, would forgive me with unction.

"But since I refuse the sin business, and I never go down on my knees; and since I say that my way is better than theirs, and that I should have my two wives, and both of them *know* that it is an honour for them to be taken by me, an honour for them to be put into my house and acknowledged there, they would like to kill me. It is *I* who must grovel, I who must submit to judgment. If I would but submit to their judgment, I could do all the wicked things I like, and they would only love me better. But since I will never submit to their judgment, they would like to destroy me off the face of the earth, like a rattle-snake.

"They shall not do it. But I must be wary. I must not put out my hand to ask them for anything, or they will strike my hand like vipers out of a hole. I must take great care to ask them for nothing, and to take nothing from them. Absolutely I must have nothing from them, not so much as let them carry a cup of tea for me, unpaid. I must be very careful. I should not have let that brown snake of a Mary see I wanted her. As for Monica, I married her, so that makes them all allow me certain rights, as far as she is concerned. But she has her rights too, and the moment she thinks I trespass on them, she will unsheathe her fangs.

"As for me, I refuse their social rights, they can keep them. If they will give me no rights, to the man I am, to me as I am, they shall give me nothing.

"God, what am I going to do? I feel like a man whom the snake-worshipping savages* have thrown into one of their snake-pits. All snakes. And if I touch a single one of them, it will bite me. Man or woman, wife or friend, every one of them is ready for me now, since I am rich. Daniel in the lions' den* was a comfortable man in comparison. These are all silent, damp, creeping snakes, like that yellow-faced Mary there, and that little whip-snake of a Monica, whom I have loved. 'Now they bite me where I most have sinned,' says the old Don Rodrigo, when the snakes of the Inferno bite his genitals.* So they shall not bite me. God in heaven, no, so they shall not bite me. Snakes they are, and the world is a snake-pit into which one is thrown. But still they shall not bite me. As sure as God is God, they shall not bite me. I will crush their heads rather.

"Why did I want that Mary? How unspeakably repulsive to me she is now! Why did I ever want Monica so badly? God, I shall never want her again. They shall not bite my genitals, as they bit Don Rodrigo, or Don Juan. My name is John, but I am no Don. God forbid that I should take a title from them.

"And the soft, good Tom and Lennie, they shall live their lives, but not with my life.

"Am I not a fool! Am I not a pure crystal of a fool! I thought they would love me for what I am, for the man I am, for me as I am. And they only love me for the me as they want me to be. They only love me because they get themselves glorified out of me.

"I thought at last they would give me a certain reverence, because I am myself and because I am different, in the name of the Lord. But they have all got their fangs full and surcharged with insult, to vent it on me the moment I stretch out my hand.

"I thought they would know the Lord was with me, and a certain new thing with me on the face of the earth. But if they know the Lord is with me, it is only so that they can intensify and concentrate their poison, to drive Him out again. And if they guess a new thing in me, on the face of the earth, it only makes them churn their bile and secrete their malice into a poison that would corrode the face of God.

"Lord! Lord! That I should ever have wanted them, or ever wanted to touch them! That ever I should have wanted to come near them, or to let them come near me. Lord, as the only boon, the only blessedness, leave me intact, leave me utterly isolate and out of reach of all men.

"That I should have wanted! That I should have wanted Monica so badly! Well, I got her, and she saves her fangs in silent readiness for me, for the me as I am, not the me that is hers. That I should have wanted this Mary, whom I now despise. That I should have thought of a new little world of my own!

"What a fool! To think of Abraham, and the great men in the early old days. To think that I could take up land in the North-West, a big wild stretch of land, and build my house and raise my cattle and live as Abraham lived, at the beginning of time, but myself at another, later beginning. With my wives and the children of my wives, and Tom and Lennie with their families, my right hand and my left hand, and absolutely fearless. And the men I would have to work for me, because they were fearless and hated the world. Each one having his share of the cattle and the horses, at the end of the year. Men ready to fight with me and for me, no matter against what. A little world of my own, in the North-West. And my children growing up like a new race on the face of the earth, with a new creed of courage and sensual pride, and the black wonder of the halls of death ahead, and the call to be lords of death on earth. With my Lord, as dark as death and splendid with a lustrous doom, a sort of spontaneous royalty, for the God of my little world. The spontaneous royalty of the other

Overlord, giving me earth-royalty, like Abraham or Saul, that can't be quenched, and that moves on to perfection in death. One's last and perfect lordliness in the halls of death, when slaves have sunk as carrion, and only the serene in pride are left to judge the unborn.

"A little world of my own!—As if I could make it with the people that are on earth today! No no, I can do nothing but stand alone. And then, when I die, I shall not drop as carrion on the earth's earth. I shall be a lord in death, and sway the destinies of the life to come."

Chapter XXVI.

The Rider on the Red Horse.

Jack was glad to get away from Perth, to ride out and leave no vestige of his soul behind, for them to work mischief on. He saddled his horse before dawn, and still before sun was up, he was trotting along beside the river. He loved the world, the early morning, the sense of newness. It was natural to him to like the world, the trees, the sky, the animals, and even, in a casual way, people. It was his nature to like the casual people he came across. And, casually, they all liked him. It was only when he approached nearer, into intimacy, that he had a revulsion.

In the casual way of life he was good-humored, and could get on with almost everybody. He took them all at their best, and they responded. For on the whole, people are glad to be taken at their best, on trust.

But when he went further, the thing broke down. Casually, he could get on with anybody. Intimately, he could get on with nobody. In intimate life, he was quiet and unyielding, often oppressive. In the casual way, he was most yielding and agreeable. Therefore it was his friends who suffered most from him.

He knew this. He knew that Monica and Lennie suffered from his aloofness and a certain arrogance, in intimate life. So friendly with everybody, he was. And at the centre, not really friendly even with his wife and his dearest friends. Withheld, unyielding, exacting even in his silence, he kept them in a sort of suspense.

As he rode his bright bay stallion on the soft road, he became aware of this. Perhaps his horse was the only creature with which he had the right relation. He did not love it, but he harmonised with it. As if, between them, they made a sort of centaur. It was not love. It was a sort of understanding in power and mastery and crude life. A harmony even more than an understanding. As if he himself were the breast and arms and head of the ruddy, powerful horse, and it, the flanks and hoofs. Like a centaur. It had a real joy in riding away with him to the bush again. He knew by the uneven, springy dancing. And he had perhaps a greater joy. The animal knew it in the curious pressure of his knees, and the soft rhythm of the bit. Between them, they moved in a sort of triumph.

The red stallion was always glad when Jack rode alone. It did not like company, particularly human company. When Jack rode alone, his horse had a curious bubbling, exultant movement. When he rode in company, it went in a more suppressed way. And when he stopped to talk to people, in his affable, rather loving manner, the horse became irritable, chafing to go on. He had long ago realised that the bay could not bear it when he reined in and stayed chatting. His voice, in its amiable flow, seemed to irritate the animal. And it did not like Lennie. Lucy, the old mare, loved Lennie. Most horses liked him. But Jack's stallion got a bit wicked, irritable with him.

And when Jack had made a fool of himself, as with Mary, and felt tangled, he always craved to get on his horse Adam, to be put right. He would feel the warm flow of life from the horse mount up him and wash away in its flood the human entanglements in his nerves. And sometimes he would feel guilty towards his horse Adam, as if he had betrayed the natural passion of the horse, giving way to the human travesty.

Now, in the morning before sunrise, with the red horse bubbling with exultance between his knees, his soul turned with a sudden jerk of realisation away from his fellow-men. He really didn't want his fellow-men. He didn't want that amiable casual association with them, which took up so large a part of his life. It was a habit and a bluff on his part. Also it was part of his nature. A certain real amiability in him, and a natural kindly disposition towards his fellow-men combatted inside him with a repudiation of the whole trend of modern human life, the emotional, spiritual, ethical, and intellectual trend. Deep inside himself, he fought like a wild-cat against the whole thing. And yet, because of a naturally amiably-disposed,* even benevolent nature in himself, he took any casual individual into his warmth, and was bosom friends for the moment. Until, inevitably, after a short time the individual betrayed himself a unit of the universal human trend, and then Jack recoiled in anger and revulsion again.

This was a sort of dilemma. Monica, and Tom, and Lennie, who knew him intimately, knew the absoluteness of his repudiation of mankind and mankind's direction in general. They knew it to their cost, having suffered from it. Therefore the anomaly of his casual intimacies and his casual bosom-friendships was considerably puzzling and annoying to them. He seemed to them false to himself, false to the other thing he was trying to put across. Above all, it seemed false to *them*, his real, old friends, towards whom he was so silently exacting and overbearing.

This morning, after his fiasco with Mary, he vaguely realised himself.* He vaguely realised that he had to make a change. The casual intimacies were really a self-betrayal. But they made his life easy. It was the easiest way for him to encounter people. To suppress for the time being his deepest self, his thoughts, his feelings, his vital repudiation of the way of human life now, and to play at being really pleasant and ordinary. He liked to think that most people, casually and superficially, were nice. He hated having to withdraw.

But now, after the fiasco with Mary, he realised again his necessity to withdraw. To pass people by. They were all going in the opposite direction to his own. Then he was wrong to rein up and pretend a bosom-friendship for half an hour. As he did so, he was only being borne down-stream, in the old, deadly direction, against himself.

Even his horse knew it: even old Adam. He pressed the animal's sides with his legs, and made a silent pact with him: not to make this compromise of amiability and casual friendship, not for ever to be reining up and allowing himself to be carried backwards in the weary flood of the old human direction. To forfeit the casual amiabilities, and go his way in silence. To have the courage to turn his face right away from mankind. His soul and his spirit had already turned away. Now he must turn away his face, and see them all no more.

"I never want to see their faces any more," he said aloud to himself. And his horse between his thighs danced and began to canter, as the sun came sparkling up over the horizon. Jack looked into the sun, and knew that he must turn his own face aside for ever from the people of his world, not look at them or communicate with them again, not any more. Cover his own face with shadow, and let the world pass on its own way, unseen and unseeing.

And he must know as he knew his horse, not face to face, never any more face to face, but communicating as he did with his stallion Adam, from a pressure of the thighs and knees. The arrows of the Archer, who is also a centaur.*

Vision is no good. It is no good seeing any more. And words are no good. It is useless to talk. We must communicate with the arrows of sightless, wordless knowledge, as Jack communicated with his horse, by a pressure of the thighs and knees.

The sun had risen gold above the far-off ridge of the bush. Jack drew up at an inn by the side of the road, to eat breakfast. He left his horse at the hitching-post near the door, and went into the bar parlour. There was a smell of mutton chops frying, and he was hungry.

As he sat eating, he heard his horse neighing fiercely. He pricked his ears. Again Adam's powerful neigh, and far off, a high answering call of a mare.* He went out quickly to the door of the inn. Adam stood by the post, his feet apart, his ears erect, his head high up, looking with flashing eyes back down the road. How beautiful he was! in the newly-risen sun shining bright almost as fire, every fibre of him on the alert, tall and overweening. And down the road, a grey horse, cloud colour, running eagerly forwards, its rider, a young lady, flushing scarlet and trying to hold up her mare. It was no good. The mare's shrill, wild neigh came answering the stallion's, and the lady rider was powerless to hold her creature back. Strong, like bells in his deep chest, came the stallion's call once more. And lifting her head as she ran on swift, light feet, the mare sang back.

The girl was Hilda Blessingon. Jack took his horse and quickly ran him, rearing and flaming, round to the stable. There he shut him up, though his feet were thudding madly on the wooden floor, and his powerful neighing shook the place with a sound like fire.

The grey mare came running straight to the stable, carrying its helpless, scarlet-flushing rider. Jack lifted the girl down, and held the mare. There was a terrific thudding from the stable.

"I'll put her in the paddock, shall I?" said Jack.

"I think you'd better," she said.

He looked uneasily at the stable, whence came a sound of something going smash. The shut-up stallion sounded like an enclosed thunder-storm.

"Shall I put them both in the paddock?" said Jack. "It seems the simplest thing to do."

"Yes," she murmured in confusion. "Perhaps you'd better."

She was rather frightened. The duet of neighing was terrific, like the bells of some wild cathedral going at full clash. The landlord of the inn came running up. Jack was just slipping the mare's saddle off.

"Steady! Steady!" he said. Then to the landlord: "Take her to the paddock and turn her loose. I'm going to turn the horse loose with her."

The landlord dragged the frantic grey animal away, while she screamed and reared and pranced.

Jack ran to the stable door, calling to his horse. He opened carefully. The first thing he saw was the blazing eyes of the stallion. The horse had broken the halter, and had his nose and his wild eyes at the door, prepared to charge. Jack called to him again, and managed to get in front of him and close the door behind him. The animal was listening to two things at once, thinking two things at once. He was quivering in every fibre, in a state almost of madness. Yet he stood quite still while Jack slipped off the loosened saddle.

Then again he began to jump. Already he had smashed in one side of the stall, and had a bleeding fetlock. Jack got hold of the broken halter, and opened the door. The horse, like a great ruddy thunderbolt sprang out of the stable, jerking Jack with him. The man, with a flying jump, got on the bright, brilliant bare back of the stallion, and clung there as the creature, swerving on powerful haunches past the terrified Hilda, ran with a terrific, splendid neighing towards the paddock, moving rhythmic and handsome.

There was the grey mare at the gate, inside, neighing back, and the landlord keeping guard. The men had to be very quick, the one to open the gate, the other to slip down.

Jack left the broken halter-rope dangling from his horse's head—it was broken quite short—and went back into the yard.

"What a commotion!" he said laughingly, to the flushed, deeply embarrassed girl. "But you won't mind if your grey mare gets a foal to my horse?"

"Oh no," she said. "I shall like it."

"Why not!", said he. "They'll be all right. There's the landlord and another fellow there with them. Will you come in? Have you had breakfast? Come and eat something."

She went with him into the bar parlour, where he sat down again to eat his half-cold mutton chops. She was silent and embarrassed, but not afraid. The colour still was high in her young, delicate cheeks, but her odd, bright, round, dark-grey eyes were fearless above her fear. She had really a great dread of everything, especially of the social world in which she had been brought up. But her dread had made her fearless. There was something slightly uncanny about her, her quick, rabbit-like alertness and her quick, open defiance, like some unyielding animal. She was more like a hare than a rabbit: like a she-hare that will fight all the cats that are after her young. And she had a great capacity for remaining silent and remote, like a quiet rabbit unmoving in a corner.

"Were you riding this way by accident?" he asked her.

"No," she said quickly. "I hoped I might see you. Mary said you were leaving early in the morning."

"Why did you want to see me?" he asked, amused.

"I don't know. But I did."

"Well, it was a bit of a hubbub," he laughed.

She glanced at him sharply, warily, on the defensive, and then laughed as well, with a funny little chuckle.

"Why did you leave so suddenly?" she asked.

"No, it wasn't sudden. I'd had enough."

"Enough of what?"

"Everything."

"Even of Mary?"

"Chiefly of Mary."

She eyed him again sharply, wonderingly, searchingly, then again gave her odd little chuckle of a laugh.

"Why 'chiefly of Mary'?", she asked. "I think she's so nice. She'd make me such a good step-mother."

"Do you want one?" he asked.

"Yes, I do rather. Then my father would want to get rid of me. I should be in the way."

"And do you want to be got rid of?"

"Yes, I do rather."

"What for?"

"I want to go right away."

"Back to England."

"No. Not that. Never there again. Right away from Perth. Into the unoccupied country. Into the North-West."

"What for?"

"To get away."

"What from?"

"Everything. Just everything."

"But what would you find when you'd got away?"

"I don't know. I want to try. I want to try."

She had such an odd, definite decisiveness and self-confidence, he was very much amused. She seemed the queerest, oddest, most isolated bird* he had ever come across. Exceedingly well-bred, with all the charm of pure breeding. By nature, timorous like a hare. But now, in her queer state of rebellion, like a hare that is perfectly fearless, and will go its own way in determined singleness.

"You must come and see Monica and me when we move to the North-West. Would you like to?"

"Very much. When will that be?"

"Soon. Before the year is out. Shall I tell Monica you're coming? She'd be glad of another woman."

"Are you sure you want me?"

"Quite."

"Are you sure everybody will want me? I shan't be in the way? Tell me quite frankly."

"I'm sure everybody will want you. And you can't be in the way, you are much too wary."

"I only seem it."

"Do come, though."

"I should love to."

"Well, do. When could you come?"

"Any time. Tomorrow if you wish. I am quite independent. I have a certain amount of money, from my mother. Not much, but enough for all I want. And I am of age. I am quite free.—And I think if I went, father would marry Mary. I wish he would."

"Why?"

"Then I should be free."

"But free what for?"

"Anything. Free to breathe. Free to live. Free not to marry. I know they want to get me married. They've got their minds fixed on it. And I'm afraid they'll force me to do it, and I don't want it."

"Marry who?"

"Oh, nobody in particular. Just somebody, don't you know."

"And don't you want to marry?" asked Jack, amused.

"No. No, I don't. Not any of the people I meet. No! Not that sort of man. No. Never!"

He burst into a laugh, and she, glancing in surprise at his amusement, suddenly chuckled.

"Don't you like men?" he asked, still laughing.

"No. I don't. I dislike them very much."

Her quick, cool, alert manner of statement amused him more than anything.

"Not any men at all?"

"No. Not yet. And I dislike the idea of marriage. I just hate it. I don't think I'd mind men so much, if it weren't for marriage in the background. I can't do with marriage."

"Might you like men without marriage?" he asked, laughing.

"I don't know," she said, with her odd precision. "So far it's all just impossible. I can't stand it. All that sort of thing is impossible to me. No, I don't care for men at all."

"What sort of thing is just impossible?" he asked.

"Men! Particularly *a* man. Impossible!"*

Jack roared with laughter at her. She seemed rather to like being laughed at. And her odd, cool, precise intensity tickled him to death.

"You want to be virgin in the virgin bush?" he asked.

She glanced at him quickly.

"Something like that," she said, with her little chuckle. "I think, later on, not now, not now—" she shook her head—"I might like to be a man's second or third wife: if the other two were living. I would never be the first. Never.—You remember you talked about it."

She looked at him with her round, bright, odd eyes, like an elf or some creature of the border-land, and as he roared with laughter, she smiled quickly and with an odd, mischievous response.

"What you said the other night, when Aunt Matilda was so angry, made me think of it.—She hates you," she added.

"Who, Aunt Matilda? Good job."

"Yes, *very* good job! Don't you think she's *terrible*?"

"I do," said Jack.

"I'm glad you do. I can't stand her. I like Mr George. But I don't care for it when he seems to like *me*."

Jack roared with laughter again, and again, from some odd corner of herself, she smiled.

"Why do you laugh?" she said. But the infection of laughter made her give a little chuckle.

"It's all such a real joke," he said.

"It is," she answered. "Rather a bad joke."

Slowly he formed a dim idea of her precise life, with a rather tyrannous father who was fond of her in the wrong way, and brothers who had bullied her and jeered at her for her odd ways and appearance, and her slight deafness. The governess who had mis-educated her, the loneliness of the life in London, the aristocratic but rather vindictive society in England, which had persecuted her in a small way, because she was one of the odd, border-line people who don't, and *can't*, really belong. She kept an odd, bright, amusing spark of revenge twinkling in her all the time. She felt that with Jack she could kindle her spark of revenge into a natural sun.* And without any compunction, she came to tell him.

He was tremendously amused. She was a new thing to him. She was one who knew the world, and society, better than he did, and her hatred of it was purer, more twinkling, more relentless in a quiet way. Her way was absolutely relentless, and absolutely quiet. She had gone further along that line than himself. And her fearlessness was of a queer, uncanny quality, hardly human. She was a real border-line being.

"All right," he said, making a pact with her. "By Christmas we'll ask you to come and see us in the North-West."

"By Christmas! It's a settled thing?" she said, holding up her forefinger with an odd, warning, alert gesture.

"It's a settled thing," he replied.

"Splendid!" she answered. "I believe you'll keep your word."

"You'll see I shall."

She rose. The horses, quieted down, were caught and saddled and brought round. She glanced from her blue-grey mare to his red stallion, and gave her odd, squirrel-like chuckle.

"What a *contretemps*!" she said. "It's like the sun mating with the moon." She gave him a quick, bright, odd glance: some of the coolness of a fairy.*

"Is it!" he exclaimed, as he lifted her into the saddle. She was slim and light, with an odd, remote reserve.

He mounted his horse.

"We go different ways for the moment," she said.

"Till Christmas," he answered. "Then the moon will come to the sun, eh? Bring the mare with you. She'll probably be in foal."

"I certainly will. Goodbye, till Christmas. Don't forget. I shall expect you to keep your word."

"I will keep my word," he said. "Goodbye till Christmas."

He rode away, laughing and chuckling to himself. If Mary had been a fiasco, this was a real joke. A real, unexpected joke.

His horse travelled with a quick, strong, rhythmic movement, inland, away from the sea. At the last ridge he turned and saw the pale blue ocean full of light. Then he rode over the crest and down the silent grey bush, in which he had once been lost.

APPENDIX I

Chronology of *The Boy in the Bush*

Chronology of *The Boy in the Bush*

The following table, based on indications of season and some exact dates, points to a degree of chronological organisation in the novel. (Reference is by page and line number; where none is provided, the date has been deduced from the preceding entry.)

Most dates are rough approximations, and the possibility of unseasonal weather is ignored. In the last seven chapters there are only two clear seasonal references (277:21–2, 320:13), and they are about two-and-a-half years apart. Resolution of the dates of the intervening events depends on some assumptions, open to question, as to likely periods of time elapsed, and the Explanatory note on 229:29 records a chronological inconsistency.

1864	Jack Grant is born (7:32, 9:37)
June 1882	Jack arrives in Fremantle (15:13), then Perth and, soon after, Wandoo
c. July or August 1882	Tom and Lennie Ellis leave to fetch the girls (59:4), and Jack rides Stampede; Herbert Ellis is injured (69:10)
August 1882	Jack goes to the camp at Gum Tree Valley (93:6) and visits the Greenlows occasionally to help with mustering and shearing
c. October 1882	The kangaroo hunt (96:12)
by Christmas 1882	Jack returns to Wandoo (108:4)
31 December 1882	New Year's Eve at Wandoo (111:10)
c. late February or March 1883	Jack fetches the Greenlows to Wandoo (150:23–4)
c. March 1883	Jack and Easu Ellis fight (156:24); Jack recuperates 'soon' (171:4)
c. April or May 1883	Dad Ellis and Gran die (the 'first rains had set in' – 171:18 – but the rainy season has not yet begun in earnest – June/July – because the Avon river near Wandoo is not flowing, 183:38–9)
c. May or June 1883	Jack sickens again and is sent to the Greenlows to recuperate (186:36) for a time involving, apparently, only one Sunday (187:7); he returns to Wandoo for an unspecified period (in seeming ignorance of Mr George's recommen-

	dation that they catch the next boat n. from Geraldton 'about a month from now', 188:20)
June 1883	Jack and Tom leave Wandoo for Geraldton via Paddy's Crossing and Uncle John Grant's farm (209:8)
24 July 1883	Jack and Tom sail n. from Geraldton (see Explanatory note on 188:20)
between December 1886 and February 1887	Jack and Tom return from the North-West, attend the ball (229:28–9 and 246:7 suggest late 1886) and travel to Wandoo. A few days later (280:19) Jack kills Easu, becomes lost in the bush and is found (but it is already mid- to late-summer [January–February]: 277:21–2, 282:28, 286:28–9). His recovery and trial occupy, say, three months
?between March and May 1887	Jack sails to Albany and marries Monica Ellis, and they stay there 'another month' (302:15)
?between April and June 1887	Jack and Monica sail to the North-West; 'two months of wandering' follow (302:20)
?between June and August 1887	Percy Stockley's baby dies (302:21–2); Monica becomes pregnant after some months (305:23) – say, six – while Jack digs unsuccessfully for gold for 'more than a year' (305:26)
?between September and November 1888	Monica has twins; Jack discovers gold, and Tom and Lennie arrive and work 'for months' – say, six – in the mine (311:4)
?between March and May 1889	Uncle John Grant dies; a fortnight later Jack travels to Perth (312:18)
June or July 1889	No time is recorded as passing before Jack, Mary Rath and Mr George visit the Grant farm (320:13); Jack returns to Perth and then leaves for an undisclosed destination. Hilda Blessington catches up with him at the inn; Jack arranges for her to join him and Monica in the North-West at Christmas (347:13)

APPENDIX II

Jack Grant's family tree

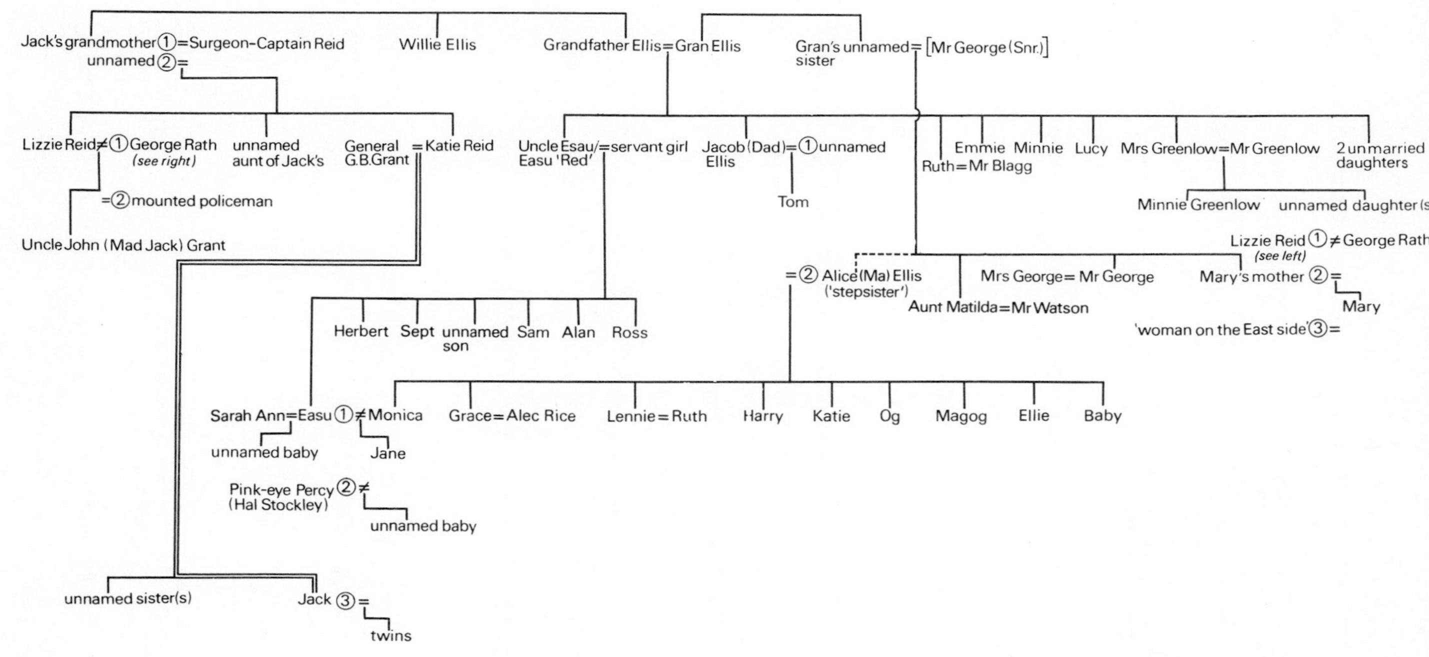
Jack's grandmother ① = Surgeon-Captain Reid
unnamed ② =
Willie Ellis
Grandfather Ellis = Gran Ellis
Gran's unnamed sister = [Mr George (Snr.)]
Lizzie Reid ≠ ① George Rath
(see right)
=② mounted policeman
Uncle John (Mad Jack) Grant
unnamed aunt of Jack's
General G.B.Grant = Katie Reid
Uncle Esau/Easu 'Red' = servant girl
Jacob (Dad) Ellis = ① unnamed
Tom
Ruth = Mr Blagg
Emmie
Minnie
Lucy
Mrs Greenlow = Mr Greenlow
2 unmarried daughters
Minnie Greenlow
unnamed daughter(s)
Lizzie Reid ① ≠ George Rath
(see left)
= ② Alice (Ma) Ellis ('stepsister')
Aunt Matilda = Mr Watson
Mrs George = Mr George
Mary's mother ② =
Mary
'woman on the East side' ③ =
Herbert
Sept
unnamed son
Sam
Alan
Ross
Sarah Ann = Easu ① ≠ Monica
unnamed baby
Jane
Pink-eye Percy (Hal Stockley) ② ≠
unnamed baby
Grace = Alec Rice
Lennie = Ruth
Harry
Katie
Og
Magog
Ellie
Baby
unnamed sister(s)
Jack ③ =
twins

APPENDIX III

Maps

Western Australia
Perth to Beverley (inset: Fremantle)
Perth, *c.* 1882

AUSTRALIA
WESTERN AUSTRALIA
Moreton Bay
NEW SOUTH WALES
Adelaide
Sydney
Thirroul
Melbourne
N
THE KIMBERLEYS
King R.
Hall's Creek
Cossack
Roebourne
Marble Bar
Nullagine
THE
NORTHWEST
WESTERN AUSTRALIA
INDIAN OCEAN
Shark Bay
Geraldton
Walkaway
Jurien Bay
Southern Cross
Kalgoorlie
Coolgardie
Gingin
Perth
York
Beverley
Fremantle
Darling Range
Bunbury
Wagin
Katanning
Busselton
Blackwood R.
Stirling Range
Cape Leeuwin
Albany
Eucla
SOUTHERN OCEAN
0
500 km
0
300 miles

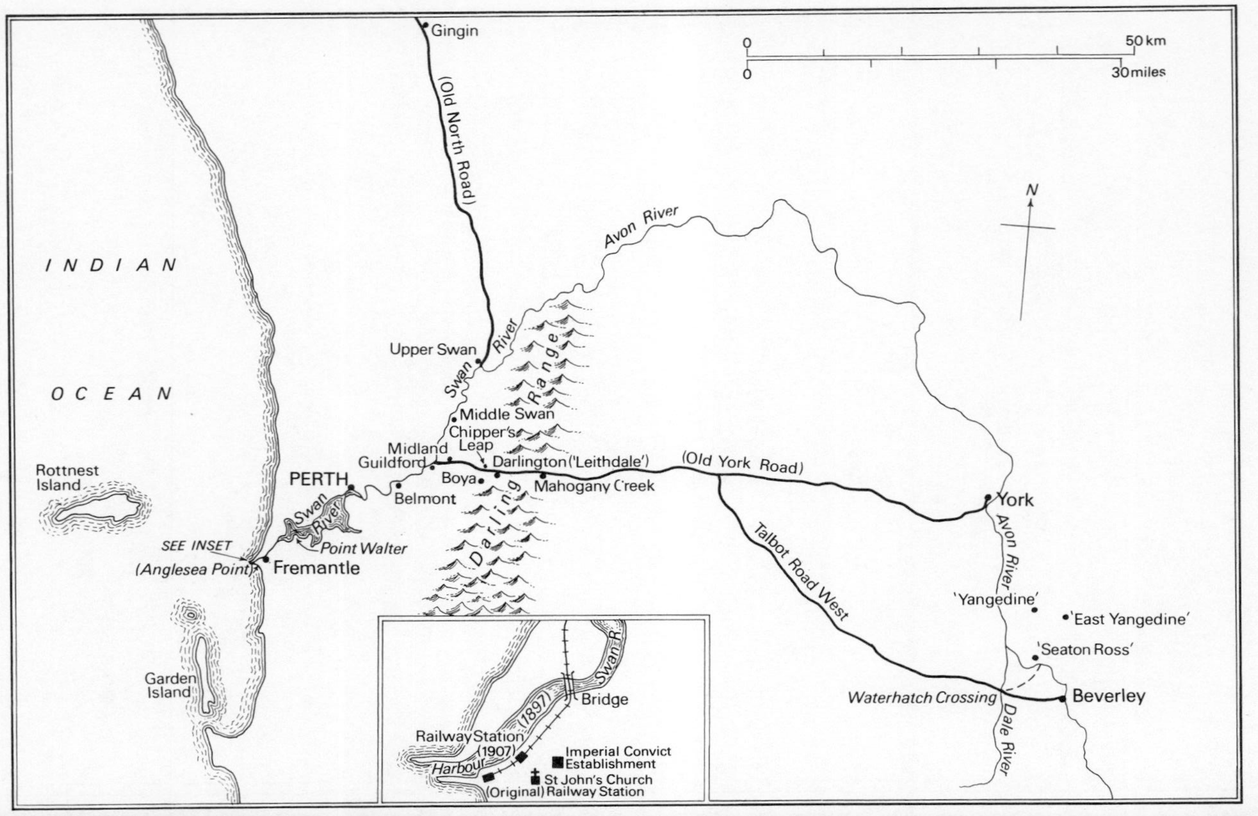
Gingin
0
50 km
0
30 miles
(Old North Road)
N
Avon River
INDIAN
OCEAN
Upper Swan
Swan River
Range
Middle Swan
Chipper's Leap
Midland
Guildford
Darlington ('Leithdale')
(Old York Road)
Rottnest Island
PERTH
Boya
Mahogany Creek
Belmont
Darling
Swan River
Point Walter
SEE INSET
(Anglesea Point)
Fremantle
York
Avon River
Talbot Road West
'Yangedine'
'East Yangedine'
'Seaton Ross'
Garden Island
Swan R.
Bridge
(1897)
Railway Station (1907)
Harbour
Imperial Convict Establishment
St John's Church
(Original) Railway Station
Waterhatch Crossing
Beverley
Dale River

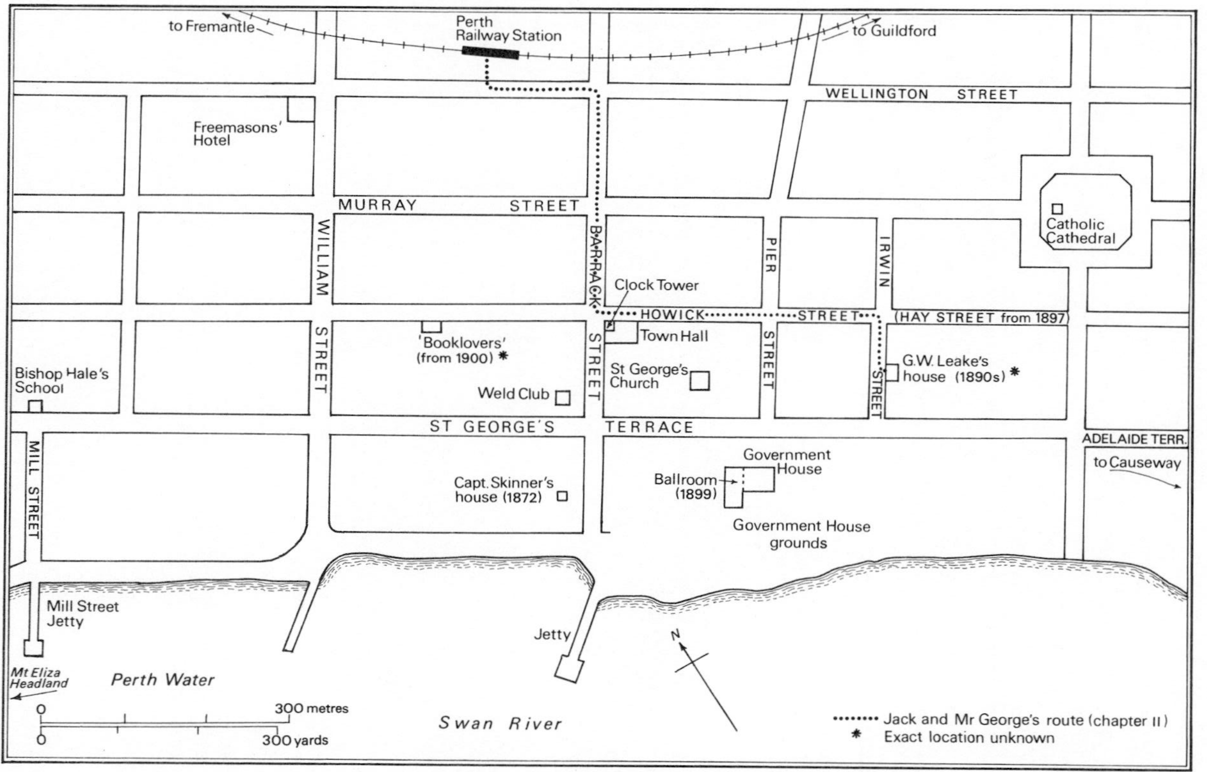
to Fremantle
Perth Railway Station
to Guildford
WELLINGTON STREET
Freemasons' Hotel
MURRAY STREET
WILLIAM STREET
BARRACK STREET
PIER STREET
IRWIN STREET
Catholic Cathedral
Clock Tower
HOWICK STREET
(HAY STREET from 1897)
Town Hall
'Booklovers' (from 1900) *
St George's Church
G.W. Leake's house (1890s) *
Bishop Hale's School
Weld Club
ST GEORGE'S TERRACE
ADELAIDE TERR.
MILL STREET
Government House
Ballroom (1899)
to Causeway
Capt. Skinner's house (1872)
Government House grounds
Mill Street Jetty
Jetty
N
Mt Eliza Headland
Perth Water
0
300 metres
300 yards
Swan River
Jack and Mr George's route (chapter II)
* Exact location unknown

APPENDIX IV

A historical background to the setting of *The Boy in the Bush*

A historical background to the setting of *The Boy in the Bush*

In June 1829 James Stirling arrived at the south-western shore of New Holland to found what was designated in enabling legislation by the British Parliament as the Colony of Western Australia; this was the first Parliamentary sanction of the term Australia – which had been in circulation for some time. Until the late 1870s the colony would be generally known, however, as the Swan River Colony or Settlement. A determined and zealous man, Stirling had secured the Government's (half-hearted) agreement to subsidise a largely private-enterprise colonising scheme, with Thomas Peel (cousin of the Home Secretary, Sir Thomas Peel) as principal investor. Since 1826 there had been a garrison at present-day Albany, intended to do little more than show the flag to passing ships; the Settlement would give credibility to a simultaneous claim of annexation of the western third of the continent.

Almost nothing was known of WA (Western Australia). For the previous three centuries Dutch, French and English explorers had consistently returned adverse reports about the natives and the fertility of the land. But on his earlier trip to the Swan River in 1827, Stirling had reported over-optimistically, falsely generalising from the fertile alluvial ground his party found along the banks of the Swan. His conclusions, reinforced by those of Colonial Botanist Charles Fraser, were selectively and enthusiastically disseminated in the British press. At a time when Australia's white population was only 62,000 and only two sizeable towns, Sydney and Hobart (both convict headquarters), existed, sufficient public interest was whipped up to convince 1,800 people to emigrate to WA – to attempt to settle an area of a million square miles, ten times the size of the British Isles. It was the first colony in Australia intended purely for private settlement. Workmen, farmers, tradesmen and officers on half-pay after the end of the Napoleonic Wars, most of them from urban backgrounds in London and the south-eastern counties, found the lure of substantial land-ownership irresistible; expectations were high.

Fresh reports of French interest in settling the region made the preparations very hurried: the first colonists arrived in early winter 1829 to find disembarkation on the mainland impossible, and they were forced to spend June and July on Garden Island. Land was then allotted before there was time to survey it properly and with insufficient knowledge of the countryside. The size was liberally calculated on the value of material goods and the number of labourers, if any, introduced into the colony, so that the best land on either side of the Swan above Perth was rapidly allocated, thus forcing newcomers to take up land in unfavourable locations. Because money was not a basis for land allocation, it was in the colonists' interests to convert what they had into goods and equipment, thus initiating what was to be a perennial problem for the colony – a shortage of currency needed to pay for imports for diversification and development, and for the wages of workmen.

The colony did not in fact have good wheat and pasture lands near Perth and Fremantle (which were almost immediately laid out as the principal village and port). The best regions turned out to be across the Darling Range in the Avon valley (developed from the mid-1830s), and north around Geraldton (from the 1850s). Discovery, and experiment with land use and farming methods required time, transport facilities to and from the suitable areas were non-existent, and capital funds to develop them rapidly, impossible to obtain. Inevitably speculators' hopes were dashed, many early colonists left and the bad news discouraged further emigration – for which the British Government was, in any case, unprepared to pay. There were shortages of food in the early years and exports were very slow to develop; the outlook was discouraging. Nevertheless, by 1837 steady progress had begun to be made, so that, by the end of the decade and in spite of a subsequent recession in 1843–4, a measure of economic success began to be felt – as Mr George recalls in chapter 1. The first full ship-load of the colony's exports was despatched in 1840, the exporting of horses to India started in 1844, and sandalwood to China the following year. By 1849 over 7,000 acres were under cultivation, but the wheat, liable to outbreaks of rust, was not always sufficient to supply the growing local market (immigration had resumed). The land regulations had been emended in 1832 to allow purchase of land at auction, and a system devised in 1837 to facilitate part-exchange of land provided under the original grants, thus encouraging farmers and pastoralists (mainly, sheep farmers) to take up land further afield. Despite local poison grasses, diseases and high sheep mortality in the early years, the wool industry had become established; wool was to be the colony's most profitable export until the 1890s. Agricultural societies were set up, and a number of churches, schools and roads constructed. But the backwardness and isolation of the still radically under-capitalised colony remained palpable: Perth was 2,400 miles by sea from Sydney, 9,800 from London; it was not on the main route from England to India or New South Wales; and in any case it lacked a safe harbour, Fremantle having proved unsuitable because of a rock bar at the mouth of the Swan. (This was not remedied until 1897, most overseas cargo and passenger ships calling instead at Albany, and mail being brought overland by coach to Perth.)

One uncounted cost of this moderate success was the dispossession of the Aborigines. The early settlers, who at first saw no obvious evidence of permanent native settlement and met with no organised resistance, were unaware that the Aborigines required extensive and specific lands (to which they had a spiritual link) if they were to maintain their hunting–gathering culture. The misunderstandings which resulted could not be solved by treaty, since Aboriginal society had no structure of authority capable of agreeing to and enforcing one. Conflict was inevitable as attitudes hardened, and a punitive expedition was led against a tribe south of Fremantle in 1834. As traditional food harvest areas were surveyed, allocated and fenced, and rights of entry denied, the Aboriginal population of the settled areas dwindled, the situation gravely exacerbated by European diseases and their own habit of inter-tribal vendetta. Some were trained for domestic and farm work, and by 1881 there were 2,346 in employment (as at Wandoo and the Red Ellises'). But in 1854 there were only 233: the introduction of convicts in 1850, many with tickets-of-leave enabling them to work virtually as free men within a designated district, had eased one of the colony's principal problems – the chronic labour shortage. In desperation at the deficiency of investment and labour and with their population only 5,886, the colonists, although divided on the issue, had successfully petitioned the British Government to establish a convict system.

Transportation lasted until 1868. The £2 million expended within the colony in supporting it, and the labour force thus introduced, allowed a very significant increase in public works, particularly in the 1860s. This included the building of the Town Hall and Government House in Perth, and a new Causeway across the Swan; the Imperial Convict Establishment (prison) and the first bridge across the Swan in Fremantle; and elsewhere police stations, court houses, administrative offices, roads, bridges and jetties. As all the convicts were men (9,688 were sent), the already high proportion of males in the population was further accentuated – despite substantial Government-assisted immigration designed to counteract the potential moral evils of the convict system. (WA was the only British colony to which convicts were being sent in the 1860s.) By 1864 the ratio of males to females was almost two to one; thereafter, until the goldrushes of the 1880s and 90s, it began slowly to even out. But the inevitable result was that, by 1881 (when the population had reached 30,156), only three per cent of women aged 45–9 had never married; for men of the same age, it was 43.5 per cent.

During the convict period the pastoral industry greatly expanded, partly because of the opening up of the newly-explored North-West in the 1860s: in 1850, official figures put the number of sheep at 128,111; by 1869 there were 648,683. But in the North-West – and more acutely further north in the Kimberleys when that region was opened for pastoral selection in the early 1880s, again following exploration – the Aborigines presented a more organised and violent resistance than they had in the south-west. It was quelled, but with greater brutality and often by second-generation colonists who no longer felt constrained by the consideration (so much more obviously the case in the early years) that they were invading someone else's land. By the 1880s, as police and itinerant magistrates began to enforce a new system of labour contracts which detained workmen within the limits of the assigned station, Aborigines became the principal work force of the North-West, and their tribal life was broken up. In the south-west it had virtually disappeared, a measles epidemic in 1883 delivering the final blow; but a half-caste population, unable to return to tribal life and unwelcome in colonial society, survived and increased throughout WA.

Despite the expansion in the North-West, economic growth had slowed down in other areas after 1868, and WA continued to lag behind the eastern colonies, making it less attractive to immigrants. The area under crop did not increase and red rust remained a serious problem, making the colony a net importer of wheat. However the land regulations were revised every few years to take into account changing circumstances; they had the effect of making land available (by licence or leasehold) at low rents. And transport improved with the establishment, in the 1870s, of municipal councils and roads boards throughout the colony, a regular coastal shipping service from Albany to the North-West, and, in the 1880s, a railway link between Fremantle, Perth, York and Albany. Domestic gas became available in Perth in 1882, and electricity in the 1890s.

The financing of such developments (most of which the novel reflects) derived from the colony's newly won ability to float loans overseas. Once transportation had ended, the colony was considered suitable to receive a measure of control over its own affairs through an elected (but essentially advisory) Legislative Council; this grant was extended to nearly complete representative government in 1890, John Forrest becoming the first Premier. Prior to 1870 the Governor, assisted by appointed advisers, had exercised power on behalf of (and sometimes countermanded by) the British Government; political pressure was exerted through the operations of agricultural societies, newspapers and public meetings, and by direct lobbying in London. In the 1870s, elections were frequently uncontested; neither party politics nor trade unionism became significant till the 1890s; and the only potentially explosive political issue – state aid to church schools – was resolved by restoring the aid impartially when state elementary education was put on a firm footing in 1871. Political disagreements tended to revolve instead around either the land regulations, tariffs and public works, or personality. But in a society where nearly everyone at the upper levels (including the Skinners and Leakes) was related to everyone else in a way that crossed divides between agriculture, pastoralism and commerce, most problems were able to be resolved in social rather than political currency.

The colony's legislators and many businessmen belonged to the exclusive Weld Club (1871), and met one another at social functions at Government House, at the racecourse, regattas and at performances sponsored by the Perth Musical Union. At the time of the colony's Jubilee in 1879, celebrating 50 years of settlement, about 5,000 of the colony's 29,000 inhabitants lived in Perth which had about 1,000 buildings, from imposing public edifices to makeshift shanties. The fashionable residential area was the south side of Adelaide Terrace; and architecture, and styles of furnishing and dress were predominantly British.

Although continuing to cling to the rhetoric and sentimental affiliations of 'Home' (including the ideals of home and hearth with the woman as moral cornerstone of the family), the early colonists could not hope to duplicate the society they remembered. The rich found servants hard to come by and difficult to keep; WA society was not classless, but the upper and lower extremes of its British model did not develop. By force of circumstances, masters and servants worked together and often their children played and went to school together. A gentleman-farmer in WA had a social freedom his English counterpart lacked: there was no shame in getting his hands dirty since it could hardly be avoided. There was a great deal of hard, physical work to be done – clearing, fencing and building – over and above the normal duties of a farm.

To be successful, the farming family needed to be as self-sufficient in food as possible, which meant much work for women and children. The average family had eight children, and (in 1881) 70 per cent of houses had four rooms or less – which must have made privacy almost unobtainable. A woman could expect a child-bearing period of about 20 years, and mortality figures suggest that the Ellises' case was typical: few families would have avoided the experience of death, whether a parent's or a child's.

Sunday visits, shooting excursions, riding parties, musical evenings and picnics filled out what little time for leisure remained. Neither before nor after the convict era was crime a problem, apart from the long drunken sprees indulged in by bushworkers (as in chapter XVII) disposing of their accumulated earnings.

The discoveries of gold from the mid-1880s, and in particular those of the early 1890s around Kalgoorlie, were to lead to spectacular increases in population and economic activity, and to contribute to a ferment in politics in the run-up to statehood within the new Commonwealth of Australia in 1901. The advisability of incorporation was a very real question in a colony so distant from its eastern counterparts, but although many rural areas in the south-west (including York and Beverley) voted solidly against the proposal in a referendum in 1900, the overall result was decisively in favour.

Principal sources for this note: J. S. Battye, *Western Australia: A History from its Discovery to the Inauguration of the Commonwealth* (Oxford, 1924); F. K. Crowley, *Australia's Western Third: A History of Western Australia from the First Settlements to Modern Times* (1960); and *A New History of Western Australia*, ed. C. T. Stannage (Perth, 1981).

APPENDIX V

Note on Miss M. L. Skinner

Note on the text

The text is taken from the autograph manuscript (MS owned by Frederick Jeffrey) written on the verso of two photographs (depicting Mexican scenes) which DHL sent to his mother-in-law for Frieda's sister, Else Jaffe, on 22 November 1924 (*Letters*, v. 178 and n. 2) to serve as a preface to her German translation of *The Boy in the Bush* (H. D. Lawrence and M. L. Skinner, *Jack im Buschland*, Stuttgart: Deutsche Verlagsanstalt, 1925); the 'Note', translated and abridged, appears on pp. 5–6). This is the first publication of the 'Note' in English. DHL's ampersands are silently expanded, the title is presented without his underlining and the opening paragraph is not indented (MS indents); other editorial emendations of MS are noted in the Textual apparatus.

Note on Miss M. L. Skinner

When a friend motored us out from Perth, Western Australia, about thirty miles, to the hills, we came to a tiny little summer place, with bungalows scattered among the gum trees, on the edge of the wild bush—the bush wild all round. There we went to a bungalow, where convalescents could stay—and were introduced to Miss Skinner, who was in nurse's dress, all white. She was a woman about forty, with hair already greying. She and a strong Scotchwoman, her friend, ran the house—and we stayed there a couple of weeks. When she knew I was a writer, Molly Skinner lent me a book she had written: *Letters from a V. A. D.**—a V. A. D. being a volunteer nurse, during the war. Miss Skinner served in Burma, but writes as if in France. The book interested me, so then she confessed to a MS. I read the MS.—it began interestingly, but trailed off into impossible adventures.* I said to her, write something you really know.—And so, a year later, wandered in the MS. of what is now *The Boy*: she had called it *The House of Ellis*. We were in Chapala, in Mexico: and *The House of Ellis*, full of good stuff, was so confused as to make one despair. I left it, not knowing what to do. Showed it to publishers in New York—they said it was hopeless.* So in the autumn, in Los Angeles and Guadalajara, I wrote it all out again, altering freely. Some of the chapters, and the whole of the end, after the return to Perth, are mine*—the rest is Miss Skinner's material.

Miss Skinner is the daughter of an English general.* Near the bungalow in Darlington, W. A., across a hollow in the bush, were two little cabins. We went to visit. In one cabin was Mrs Skinner, the mother, a big, rosy, handsome woman in black silk, kind and warm. There she was, in the two room log cabin, with fine Persian rugs on the floor: the general's widow, still in camp.*—A few months after we saw her, she died.—In the next cabin was the son, the brother whom Molly Skinner has loved so much: a tall, thin fellow going grey, real Australian careless, looking like a laborer. He had had a bullet in his throat, a great bullet as big as my finger end, for months, in Egypt, during the war: and they sent him to Gallipoli with it, brutally telling him, time after time, he was malingering. Till at last the bullet rolled into his throat and he got it up. But his health is shattered.—Mrs Skinner, the general's widow, belonged to one of the very oldest families in W. A. But after the father died, the son lost money all the time, on sheep farms etc.—Miss Skinner came to London last July, with an MS. *Black Swans*—the first MS. re-written according to suggestion. This novel is being considered now by the publishers. Miss S. set off *steerage* from Perth but managed luckily to get a patient to nurse.* People were not very nice to her in London and she has been unhappy. She is staying now with another retired general, a cousin, till her companion is ready to go back to W. A.—to the bungalow.*

APPENDIX VI

Preface to *Black Swans*

Note on the Text

The text, written in Oaxaca, Mexico before 3 January 1925 (*Letters*, v. 190) and probably on 24 December 1924 (see 379:28), is taken from the four-page autograph manuscript (MS; Roberts E49.5) in a notebook at UT. The 'Preface' was not used for Mollie Skinner's *Black Swans* (1925) as DHL had initially intended; it was first published in 1968 in *Phoenix II* 294–6 (E1). (See Introduction, p. xlviii and footnote 111.)

Variant readings in E1 are recorded in the Textual apparatus, as are editorial emendations. Deleted and added readings in MS are recorded in the text thus: < > and ⌜ ⌝. Except at 377:4 DHL puts a stop after 'MS' (E1 does not), he fails to underline *Black Swans* on five of nine occasions (including in the title; E1 italicises in each case), and he indents the opening paragraph; this edition silently supplies the stop, italicises, but does not indent.

Preface to *Black Swans*

Difficult to write about *Black Swans*, when I have barely seen so much <of> as the egg of the book. Yet I suppose the MS. I did see in Western Australia may be considered the egg. It was a wild MS., climbing the mountain of impossibilities and improbabilities by leaps and bounds: a real rolling stone of an egg, no doubt.

There was Miss Skinner, in the house on the hills at the edge of the bush, in Western Australia, darting about rather vaguely in her white nurse's dress, with the nurse's white band over her head, looking after her convalescents who, mercifully, didn't need much looking after. Miss Skinner darting about on the brink of all the balances, and her partner, a wise, strong woman, sitting plumb at the centre of equilibrium.

Oh, and the ponderous manuscript, tangled, and simply crepitating with type-writer's mistakes, which I read with despair in that house in Western Australia. Such possibilities! And such impossibilities.

But the possibilities touched with magic. Always hovering over the borderline where probability merges into magic: then tumbling, like a bird gone too far out to sea, flopping and splashing into the wrong element, to drown soggily.

"Write," said I, like an old hand giving advice, "an Australian book about things you *actually* know, which you don't have to invent out of the ink-bottle."

Eighteen months later, when I was in Mexico and Miss Skinner in Australia, wandered in to me the MS. called *The House of Ellis*. It was better than the first *Black Swans*, because it was pretty well about happenings in Australia. But tangled, gasping, and forever going under in the sea of incoherence. Such a queer, magical bird of imagination, always drowning itself.

What's to be done! One has a terrible feeling, in front of a MS. that glimmers with imagination and chokes with incoherence. The authoress away in Australia, putting her hopes high. Myself in Mexico, too old a hand to put many hopes on the public or the critics or ⌜on⌝ anything mortal at all. Still, unwilling to play the hand-washing part.*

I am not good at suggesting and criticising. I did the only thing I knew well how to do: that is, I wrote the whole book over again, from start to finish, putting in and leaving out, yet keeping the main substance of Miss Skinner's work. Yet let me here make the confession that the last chapters and anything in the slightest bit "shocking," are, of course, my fault: not Molly Skinner's.

Miss Skinner had quite another conclusion. In her *House of Ellis*, which I turned into the *Boy in the Bush*, Monica went to the bad and disappeared, among the tears of the family. Jack set off to find her: got <found> ⌜lost⌝: and "came to" with Mary gazing lovingly upon him. In that instant, he knew he loved Mary far, far more than Monica. In fact, his love for Monica was a dead bluebottle. Mary and Jack happy ever after, virtue rewarded, *finale*!

Now I have my own ideas of morality. A young man who is supposed to love a young girl through years, with passion, and whose love just goes pop when she gets in a mess, bores me. He has no real integrity: and that, to my mind, is immorality.

At the same time, this Jack had always had a second "feeling" for Mary. Australia is a land which believes not at all in externally imposed authority. There is no limit to love. All right, there is no limit to love. The popular method would be for a hero, having got his Monica, and not having got his Mary, for whom he had a latent feeling all the time, suddenly to realise that he no longer "loved" Monica, but only Mary: then an "affair," Monica left in the lurch, sympathy streaming towards the virtuous, long-neglected Mary.

Public, popular morality seems to me a pig's business. If a man has ever cared for a woman enough to marry her, he always cares for her. And divorce is all bunk.* Forgetting, as Miss Skinner's Jack forgot Monica, is all bunk. Once you care, and the connection is made, you keep the connection, if you are half a man.

But the further question, as to whether this one connection is final and exclusive, is up to us to settle.* Largely a question of discipline. And since Australia is the most undisciplined country I have met, discipline won't settle the question there. Fall back on evasion and sentimentalism.

Discipline is a very good thing. Evasion and sentimentalism very bad.

I wonder very much how *Black Swans* has wound up. When I saw it, it was about a girl, and a convict, and a Peter: Lettie, I think her name was, poised between the entirely praiseworthy Peter, and the fascinating convict. But then the tale tumbled away into a sort of pirate-castaway-Swiss-Family-Robinson-Crusoe-Treasure-Island in the North West. This "adventure" part was rather pointless. I suggested to Miss Skinner that she work out the Peter-Lettie-Convict combine on ordinary terra-firma.*

I believe she has done so in *Black Swans*.

She sailed off penniless, with a steerage ticket from Fremantle to England, the MS. of *Black Swans* in her bag, and hopes, heaven high!

Ay-ay! anticipations! The *Boy in the Bush* was not yet out.

She arrived in London to be snubbed* and treated as if she did not exist, and certainly *ought not* to exist, by the same-as-ever London literairy <lot> ⌜people⌝. Those that esteemed me, literairily, decided that *Mr.* Skinner* was probably a myth, and didn't matter anyhow. Those that didn't esteem me declared that *Mr.* Skinner, if he existed, couldn't amount to anything, or he would never have made such a connection. Certainly I am a safe mark for the popular moralists to aim their slosh at. "Mr. Skinner" was buried before he went any further.

Of course Miss Skinner felt badly. But if Stafford put not his trust in Princes*—or realised that he shouldn't have done—the first business of anybody who picks up a pen, even so unassuming a pen as Miss Skinner's, ⌜now,⌝ is to put <not> no trust in the literairy rabble, nor in the rabble of the critics, nor in the vast rabble of the people. A writer should steer his aristocratic course through all the shoals and sewerage outlets of popular criticism, on to the high and empty seas where <the Morning Star shines alone> ⌜he finds his own way into the distance⌝.

Poor Molly Skinner, she had a bad time. But two sorts of bad time. The first sort, of being informed she ought not to exist, and of having her *Black Swans* turned down. The second sort, when old Edward Garnett tackled her. He saw her *Black Swans* floundering and flopping about, and went for them tooth and nail, like a rough-haired Yorkshire terrier. Poor old Molly Skinner, she saw the feathers of her birds flying like black snow, and the swans squawked as if they were at their last gasp. But old Edward towsled at them till they knew what's what.

I am dying to see *Black Swans* now, since <Garnett> ⌜Edward⌝ put their mistress through her paces.* She is fleeing breathless back to Australia. I am laughing in the hot Mexican sun. Tonight is Christmas Eve, and who knows what sort of a child* the Virgin is going to bring forth, this time!

Oaxaca. 1924. D. H. Lawrence

EXPLANATORY NOTES

EXPLANATORY NOTES

7:4 **He** Jack Grant is based on John Russell ('Jack') Skinner (1881–1925); DHL confirmed this (*Letters*, v. 114). See also Introduction, p. xlv, and cf. *Letters*, v. 292.

7:16 **port was Fremantle,** Named after Captain (later Admiral Sir) Charles Howe Fremantle (1800–69) who arrived in H. M. S. *Challenger* on 25 April 1829, in advance of the first settlers, to take formal possession of Western Australia (hereafter WA) in the name of King George IV. (See maps in Appendix III for this and other Australian place names.) See Appendix IV: the novel opens in 1882 (9:37), making the reference to 'the harbour mouth' at 8:9 an anachronism and Jack's ship's arrival at Fremantle (rather than Albany) improbable.

7:21 **were a few ... certain excited** DHL's revision of the original reading in MS (pp. 1–2), 'he had certain ... certain romantic', illustrates the tendency of about half the revisions in MS: that of expunging repetitions or redundancies, and of sharpening the definition of a state of mind or feeling by a small change. Some may represent changes to readings DHL had adopted from 'The House of Ellis'.

7:29 **gold and pearl findings ... bush-ranging,** Pearlers had been operating since the 1860s in the North-West – a term which refers loosely, as at 280:15, to the northern half of WA (i.e. the n.w. of Australia), but, strictly, excludes the Kimberleys district.

While major gold discoveries had been made in the eastern colonies from the 1850s, by 1882 no significant gold discoveries had been made in WA (cf. 21:40). The first goldfield (largely unsuccessful), near Hall's Creek, was proclaimed in 1886; and in 1888 more successful fields in the North-West (Marble Bar, Nullagine) and at Southern Cross were operating, but the more significant fields at Coolgardie and Kalgoorlie were not producing until the 1890s. Jack discovers gold in the North-West (302:17) in late 1888. (For a chronology of the novel, see Appendix I.) However there is a confusion, for at 312:21 Jack returns 'west to Perth' from his mine and, in a superseded passage in MS, Jack had mined in Kalgoorlie (see Textual apparatus for 318:26)...

Joseph Bolitho Johns ('Moondyne Joe', *c.* 1827–1900) is the only widely known WA bushranger (cf. 37:32–3; he was active during the 1860s), but WA has many tales about bushrangers from the convict era (1850–68; see Appendix IV) – although they were not as prevalent as in the eastern colonies. For 'bush', see note on 17:38.

7:30 **the back of beyond,** The 'outback', or 'back country' as it was called in the 1880s, was remote, sparsely inhabited country far from the principal towns (*AND* gives first printed source of 'back of beyond' as 1888; other possible linguistic anachronisms are indicated thus: '1888, *AND*'); see note on 115:27.

7:33 **And Jack . . . his surroundings.** MS (p. 2) originally read 'Jack didn't pay much attention to landscape.'

8:2 **pure sky . . . unbreathed by man.** Cf. *Letters*, iv. 238: 'The land is here: sky high and blue and new, as if no one had ever taken a breath from it; and the air is new, strong, fresh as silver'. MLS recorded her return to WA from England in 1900 thus: 'the air was indescribably pure and sparkling with colour as if reflecting hidden jewels. It was air that healed sick lungs, brought joy to saddened hearts, lifted care from burdened minds' (*Fifth Sparrow* 22).

8:6 **bible-language . . . came to his aid.** In *Apocalypse* (1929–30) DHL described how 'Long before one could think or even vaguely understand, this Bible language . . . became an influence which affected all the processes of emotion and thought' (*Apocalpyse and the Writings on Revelation*, ed. Mara Kalnins, Cambridge, 1980, p. 59). The biblical rhythms of the Authorised Version in DHL's prose are often noted in commentaries as are his frequent borrowings and adaptations of biblical phrasings: e.g. see notes on 173:36, 247:8, 276:29. MLS's response was more orthodox: 'Those old hymns so easily parodied and mocked, had a lasting influence on me. They soaked into my mind so that later in life the phrases served as ejaculatory prayers in dire danger, soothed me in anxious night watches with the sick, stood forth like swords against temptation' (*Fifth Sparrow* 16). Cf. 141:16–23.

8:8 **"There shall be a new heaven and a new earth."** Revelation xxi. 1 ['And I saw a new . . . earth for the first heaven and the first earth were passed away; and there was no more sea']. (Biblical quotations and references are to the Authorised Version unless otherwise indicated.)

8:18 **among the sand** [8:9] . . . **church with a turret:** Until the boom of the 1890s gold rush era, buildings in Fremantle were mostly unornamented box-like constructions made of whitewashed local limestone, and with shingle roofs; the dominant style was a simple colonial Georgian ('Royal Engineer Georgian'). With the importation of convict labour more elaborate Gothic Revival buildings appeared. The first settlers had removed the trees and bushes for makeshift houses; this exposed the shifting white sand and necessitated the construction of limestone boundary walls to contain it . . . The late Georgian stone prison was built by convict labour 1850–8 on an elevated position behind the town . . . A photograph of the original (roofed) railway station, built 1866–7, suggests it was a large timber building able partially to accommodate two trains . . . St John's (Anglican) Church, built 1879–82, is Victorian Gothic of (substantial) limestone and brick; it occupies a central position in the town and replaced the original church of 1843. The stone bell turret was added in 1907.

8:34 **Bedford College.** Cf. 63:12: Public (i.e. exclusive private) schools commonly prepared boys for admission to university, military academies (Woolwich and Sandhurst) or the Civil Service (see note on 20:8); but it cannot be established that Jack Skinner attended one of the Public schools in Bedford. None was an agricultural college (cf. 19:17, 59:13), and 18 or 19 was the maximum age for scholars (cf. 20:5).

9:5 **rumbustical** I.e. rumbustious (boisterous): possibly DHL's coinage.

9:15 **"terrific memory,"** [9:5] . . . **a seat on the bench,** Similar anecdotes appear in early drafts of *Fifth Sparrow* (all MLS's papers are at Battye) concerning

George Walpole Leake (1825–95), MLS's maternal grandfather; the published version has: 'I scarcely remember him but I grew up with his legend. They say he bore no trace of colonial background [cf. 9:13–14] but [had] ... a sophisticated, often too caustic wit, and a prodigious memory for facts, faces, names and apt quotations ... He could never resist the sarcastic rejoinder, the ironical turn of phrase that came so readily to his tongue. His quips and stories – often unfortunately rather coarse and locally known as "Leakiana" – were quoted around Perth for many years after his death' (p. 2).

Born in England, Leake came to Australia on the *Cygnet* in 1833 (cf. 22:28), his father Luke Leake (1784–1838) having arrived in WA in October 1829, several months after the first settlement. Sent to England for education he returned to study law in Adelaide, subsequently practising in Perth as a barrister. In 1852 he was admitted to practise as a notary public (22:34) and at various times acted as Chief Justice and Attorney-General. However his principal appointment was that of Police Magistrate – a judge of the Local Court where, unassisted by a jury, he was able to develop a personal style of rough and ready justice, for which he was generally respected (cf. 297:19–21).

A Mr George appears in other (unpublished) writings by MLS including '"Noise of Swans." A Saga of the West' (*c.*1932–3; see Introduction footnote 103). In the typescript of a radio broadcast, 'The Old Mill' (p. 1), MLS reports some of her grandfather's stories about the early decades of the colony – which MLS presumably got from her mother (cf. 9:13–14), Leake having died five years before MLS's return to WA in 1900. Thus Leake family lore is a probable source of some of the 'historical' vignettes in the novel (e.g. see notes on 195:19 and 226:18, and cf. 95:3–5).

9:21 **hard.** The rejected TSIa (and b) reading (see Textual apparatus) is probably due to the typist's duplication of the previous, more usual phrasing (l. 19).

9:26 **baggy trousers** Referred to frequently in the novel; MLS's original phrasing may have been neutral, as in 'Noise of Swans': 'a bunch of Colonial gentlemen in wide white breeches' (p. 21). The climate had made such concessions to comfort necessary.

9:30 **lumpers** Wharf workers.

9:38 **official report** *The Handbook of Western Australia* (Perth, 1880), by C. G. Nicolay best fits the description; it was not official, as the *Year-Book*s were to be (see Introduction, p. xxiii; the first *Year-Book* appeared in 1887), but was nevertheless published and sold by the Government Printer and dedicated to Governor C. F. Robinson 'In fulfilment of the trust which I had the honour to receive from you' (p. [v]).

10:6 **fiftieth anniversary** [9:39] ... **"Establishment"** See Appendix IV ... The Imperial Convict Establishment was the name of the Fremantle prison.

10:14 **a sinner, a Cain.** See Genesis iv. 1–16, and cf. 193:29–30.

10:25 **father was an officer in Her Majesty's Army.** Jack (and Mollie) Skinner's father, Colonel James Tierney Skinner (d. 1902), served in the 18th Royal Irish Regiment; in the 1870s he served in WA where, in July 1872, he married Jessie Leake (1853–1923; see next note). Jack Grant's father is referred to as a colonel and general (11:9, 11); DHL mistakenly thought Skinner was a general (see Appendix V).

11:22 **his mother ... went off ... to ... Khartoum,** Based on Jessie Skinner accompanying her husband on his postings to Khartoum (for the Relief-of-Gordon campaign) and Egypt (cf. 39:30–2), and leaving her children behind (*Fifth Sparrow* 9, 13). Cf. 11:26, 34–6, and 12:26 to DHL's description of her in Appendix V; and also *Letters*, iv. 467.

13:19 **kangaroo dog.** Dog bred for kangaroo hunting (Australianism).

13:28 **Woolamooloo Station."** Probably a misspelling of Wooloomooloo, an inner Sydney dockside suburb which is pronounced as DHL spelled it; 'station' is an extensive rural establishment for raising sheep or cattle (Australianism).

13:37 **"Mercy and truth have met ... each other."** Psalms lxxxv. 10 ['... truth are met ...'].

14:9 **New chum,** Newly arrived British immigrant (Australianism); see also 221:20.

14:31 **wood-eating little engine** [14:27] **... open carriages ... to York,** The first (wood-burning) locomotives were unable to carry enough timber to cover the distance between fuelling stations, so there was a necessity to 'chop a new supply' (14:32–3) along the way ... Photographs of the first passenger trains show small, four-wheeled, enclosed carriages (cf. 236:28–38), but the source of the text's 'open carriages' may be a frequently reproduced photograph taken in Fremantle on 31 August 1880, prior to the official opening of the line, which shows town councillors standing to be photographed in open rail-trucks ... In 1882 the railway (opened 1881) ran from Fremantle through Perth to Guildford (cf. 23:4–6), but did not extend to York till 1885; however this extension is ignored after chap. XVII (summer 1886–7), e.g. at 257:20.

After each extension of the railway line there was a corresponding shortening of the horse-drawn coach service which had originally run from Perth via York to Albany (Mr George's route at 37:4–6). Jack, Mr George and Dad Ellis leave by coach for Wandoo in chap. III, but, in 1882, this was only possible from Guildford, not Perth (the Causeway the coach traverses is in Perth: 37:19; see note on 16:3), and at 9 a.m. not in 'the chilly dark' before dawn (37:7). However, prior to the opening of the Perth–Guildford railway the coach did leave very early in the morning.

15:6 **landed with Captain Fremantle ... when that** DHL originally wrote in MS: 'seen the arrival of the first settlers, when Captain Stirling arrived' (p. 16 [17]: DHL misnumbered MS from p. 12; in these notes, actual page numbers follow in square brackets). This is probably a case of DHL's initially skipping, and then restoring, information in 'The House of Ellis': that Reid would have to have come with Captain Fremantle to see Lieutenant-Governor James Stirling (1791–1865) arrive on 1 June 1829 with the first settlers in the *Parmelia*. Because the stormy winter weather made mainland disembarkation difficult, the first tents and huts were erected on Garden Island (15:10) – where the first winter was spent, miserably.

15:17 **in midwinter, June** [15:12] ... **dull look of the bushes.** In the 1880s in WA winter was reckoned (in almanacs) to start on 21 June (the shortest day) which is the same day as the traditional (Northern) midsummer's day (cf. *Letters*, iv. 263). Winters in the Perth region are mild by northern European standards: frosts are infrequent (see 39:9–10), and the mean minimum winter temperature in Perth is 9°C (48°F). Australian native flora is not deciduous, so the appearance of the trees and bushes, except when they are in bloom, remains relatively unchanged.

16:3 **Causeway ...** ***Convict Labour*** **... the bridge** The original Causeway, near Perth, was opened in 1843, washed away by floods in 1862 (cf. 18:26) and re-built by convict labour ... The controversial introduction of convicts into the colony in 1850 went contrary to an original understanding that WA, unlike New South Wales (hereafter NSW), would be for free men only ... The bridge spanned the Swan at Fremantle and was built by convicts in 1866; detachments of (British Army) Sappers and Miners were stationed in WA.

16:6 **looked eagerly for the black swans.** Native Australian swans, famous because of their oppositeness of colour to European swans, were first discovered by Europeans in 1697 when the Dutch navigator Willem de Vlamingh led an expedition to what he named the Black Swan River (hence its subsequent name, 'Swan River').

16:11 **"It must have been here that the Carpenter wept—"** From a poem in *Alice Through the Looking Glass* (1871) by Lewis Carroll:

> The Walrus and the Carpenter
> Were walking close at hand:
> They wept like anything to see
> Such quantities of sand:
> 'If this were only cleared away,'
> They said, 'it would be grand!'

Perhaps only a personal association on MLS's part rather than a widely known 'Westralian' joke (16:18): cf. 'Fremantle ... reminded me of the scene depicted by Lewis Carroll' (*Fifth Sparrow* 22). As Jack's mother has been absent from the colony since before Jack was born (1864), i.e. before the poem first appeared, the joke is unlikely to have been 'handed on to Jack by his mother' (16:19). ('Westralian' is a common contraction of Western Australian, its currency, from *c.* 1890, reflecting the attempt to find an identity unassociated with the Swan River, i.e. convict, Colony.)

16:23 **A gentleman without it** Stirling was without 'discernment': cf. note on 18:24.

16:27 **"Sorrow, Sin, and Sand,"** 'The prison surgeon's reports [1853] showed that ophthalmia [caused, it was believed, by the sand and its glare] was by far the most prevalent disease among convicts, and no doubt this gave rise to the saying, that Western Australia was "A Land of Sand, Sin, Sorrow and Sore Eyes"' (Alexandra Hasluck, *Unwilling Emigrants: A Study of the Convict Period in Western Australia*, Melbourne, 1959, p. 61).

16:35 **way ... nodding** When DHL substituted 'they had of nodding' in MS (p. 20 [21]) for 'they nodded' he accidentally deleted 'way' as well.

16:40 **Groperland,** 'Sandgropers' (1896, *AND*) is a disparaging Australianism for Western Australians (cf. 16:24–5 and 23:7–8): hence 'Groperland' (1900, *AND*). Until the streets of Perth were macadamised in the mid- to late-1890s, pedestrians had to traverse ('grope' through) sandy streets and open spaces (see 26:10–12, and cf. *Fifth Sparrow* 4). Paths made of oyster shells dredged from the Swan (see 26:12–13) were constructed to palliate the problem, and water carts were used to settle the sand-dust.

17:13 **horses ... to supply the army in India—"** After low wheat prices in the 1870s many settlers turned to breeding horses to be sold to the British Army in India, but the breeding schemes had mixed results and overall did not realise the income expected (see also 18:36–8).

17:38 **bush humpy:** Bush is wild country, covered with forest or bushy vegetation, but the term often also refers to the countryside in general, away from the towns; a humpy is a temporary bush shelter or hut (Australianisms).

18:5 **bob."** Slang for shilling: see Note on pounds, shillings and pence.

18:6 **"By the waters of Babylon there we sat down—"** Psalms cxxxvii. 1: 'By the rivers of ... down, yea, we wept, when we remembered Zion' – for the early settlers, the easier life of England.

18:15 **'indented' servants,** I.e. indentured servants: early settlers received a grant of 200 acres of land for every labourer or servant whose passage to the colony they paid.

18:24 **Our flocks prospered ... On milk and honey—"** Cf. 'I will send grass in thy fields, for thy cattle, that thou mayest eat and be full' (Deuteronomy xi. 15) ... Refers to God's pledge of prosperity for the Israelites in a Promised Land 'that floweth with milk and honey' (xi. 9).

The irony of the phrase, 'On milk and honey', derives from its use by colonists, contemporary commentators (and, later, historians) as a measure of the disappointed expectations of the early settlers who had been deceived by the reports of Stirling and Charles Fraser (Colonial Botanist of NSW; *c.* 1788–1831) describing the region as beautiful, rich and abundant; they had wrongly interpreted the prolific native flora as evidence of well-watered, fertile soil. The colonial surgeon Thomas Braidwood Wilson, in *Narrative of a Voyage Round the World* (1835), wrote that the settlers 'expected to be immediately inducted into a land, if not "flowing – easily capable of being made to flow – with milk and honey"' (p. 225).

Stirling reported to Sir Ralph Darling (1775–1858), Governor of NSW 1825–31: Swan River 'appears to hold out every attraction that a Country in a State of nature can possess' (18 April 1827), and enclosed Fraser's 'Observations on the Soil, etc., etc., of the Banks of Swan River' (*Historical Records of Australia*, ed. Frederick Watson, Sydney, 1923, ser. III, vi. 576).

18:27 **floods of '62 ... '72 ruined *you.*** Serious flooding and extensive property damage occurred in many areas of the colony in both years, the 1872 flood being the worse.

18:36 **Rust destroys fourteen thousand acres ... Dingoes ... Cattle run wild ... Horses** During the convict period – which helped the colony get 'on its feet' (l. 35) – the area under cultivation increased more than sixfold; and in 1868, despite the failure of large areas of wheat because of red rust (13,895 acres in the Victoria district: *Year-Book* 40), 13,000 bushels of wheat and 1,163 tons of flour were exported ... Dingoes – the Australian wild dog – were a constant threat to sheep, and the Government offered money for each one killed (90:16) ... Even up to the 1870s many freehold properties were inadequately fenced so that stock strayed, and hundreds of wild horses roamed the northern coastal plains (cf. 103:27–9).

18:39 **"Moth and rust!** A play on Matthew vi. 19–20 ['Lay not up ... treasures upon earth, where moth and rust doth corrupt'] and the actual moth-blight and rust diseases (see previous note). The popular novelist Anthony Trollope (1815–82) visited WA in 1872 and reported reading 'constantly of rust and moth, and of the insufficiency of the grain produced' (*Australia and New Zealand*, 1873, ii. 102).

19:7 **joke at the "Establishment" identity's expense.** The joke is probably an anachronism: being an 'Establishment' identity (in the sense of a convict transported to WA and subsequently become prosperous) was a painful matter in the 1870s and 1880s, when many people with convict origins were striving to live down their past.

19:17 **calmly**. Revised in MS from 'defiantly' (p. 26 [27]).

20:1 **chivoo** 'Chivoo' or 'shivoo' (also spelled '*shiveau*', 'shevoo', 'shivaroo' in the nineteenth century) means a celebration or spree in Australian English (e.g. at 112:11). However here and at 20:11 Jack means a riot, and is probably invoking the (British) nautical slang for a drunken bout or free-fight: see Eric Partridge, *A Dictionary of Slang and Unconventional English*, ed. Paul Beale, 8th edn (1984), p. 1046, where like spellings are given (e.g. 'sheevo').

20:8 **chaps were** [20:4] ... **exams for the Indian Civil, or the Naval or Military,** A report to the British Parliament by Sir Charles Trevelyan and Sir Stafford Northcote in 1853 led to the replacement of patronage in recruitment to the Civil (and Indian Civil) Service by open, competitive examination (held in London). The Report had recommended, for the upper division of the Service, that examinees be aged 21–5; however Departments were able to prescribe their own age limits (the Indian, for instance, lowered the age of entry in 1876 from 23 to 19). The new system did not apply to Naval officer cadets; for the Army, see note on 8:34.

21:12 **"When to sow and when to reap ... Latin motto attached?"** I.e. when to sow his wild oats: Mr George implies Jack's being expelled was his reaping ... The ability to provide Latin tags in conversation was associated (as a sneer) with having a gentleman's education.

22:35 **here since '31** [22:27] ... **Grammar School** Most of these details are provided within a convenient compass in the *Year-Book*, the probable source; but the following, either explicitly or by their placement, are chronologically inaccurate (possibly the result of DHL's condensation of a longer passage in 'The House of Ellis'): the wreck of the *Rockingham* (carrying immigrants who came as part of Thomas Peel's settlement scheme: see Appendix IV) occurred in May 1830 (not 1831); the *Shepherd* sailed for London in January 1840 (not 1841), the first outgoing vessel to be 'laden wholly with colonial produce' (*Year-Book* 35); the Mill

Street Jetty in Perth was opened in 1842, and the Grammar school (before Mr George left for London) in 1840.

22:36 **lot of exploration done. Eyre had legged it from Adelaide** Various explorations were made in the s.w. corner of WA (1831–6), the extreme n.w. (1837–8) and the country n. of Perth to Shark Bay (1839), before Edward John Eyre (1815–1901) travelled by horse and foot from Adelaide along the barren southern coast to Albany in 1841 – the first European to arrive in WA other than by ship.

23:8 **wooden houses with wooden platforms** Perth townhouses in the 1870s typically had two stories with a verandah and balcony across the street front; however many were of brick (cf. 28:8).

23:13 **Mature—manure ... in the ground.** Cf. 'Fifth Sparrow' Draft: 'The Early Settlers had produced about seven daughters apiece, and but few sons. As Grandfather [G. W. Leake] ... had been wont to say, "It's nature adjusting herself to conditions. Men come out in scores, and it's up to us to provide wives for 'em." And he would mutter, "It's manure that's wanted, manure"' (p. 36). See also 283:17–19.

DHL had evolved a similar idea: cf. 'Study of Thomas Hardy' (written 1914): 'Three people die and are taken back into the Heath [Egdon Heath in Hardy's *The Return of the Native*], they mingle their strong earth again with its powerful soil ... It is very good. Not Egdon is futile, sending forth life on the powerful heave of passion' (*Study of Thomas Hardy and Other Essays*, ed. Bruce Steele, Cambridge, 1985, p. 25), and *Kangaroo* (1923), chap. V: 'somebody will have to water Australia with their blood before it's a real man's country. The soil, the very plants seem to be waiting for it'; and cf. 22:17–21 with *Letters*, iv. 273.

24:5 **saw as through a glass, darkly.** Cf. 1 Corinthians xiii. 12 ['For now we see through a glass, darkly; but then face to face']; see also 341:35–6.

24:11 **already backing** On both typescripts 'already' is written interlinearly by the same unknown hand but in different positions (see Textual apparatus). This hand appears only in pp. 1–167 and the last chap. (see Introduction, pp. xxxiv–xxxv and footnote 55). Except here and at 93:18 where the correction is entered only in TSIa, the MS readings are restored on both copies and thus must have been checked against the original typescript and the MS of the last chap.; other corrections are evidently the work of copy-editors.

25:2 **pound a week for your board.** Cf. *Fifth Sparrow* 31: 'Father had paid the usual fee for him [Jack Skinner] to learn farming with Uncle Tom Lodge ... at Beverley' (see note on 37:4).

25:7 **We're all related ... in this colony.** In *Fifth Sparrow* MLS wrote of her return to WA in 1900: 'I found myself in a maze of relationships, our Australian cousins numbering ten Parkers and ten Cliftons, three Lodges, four Parrys, four Kelsalls, four Leakes – some grown up, some little ones. And there were *their* cousins, and mother's cousins and *their* relations spread over most of the settled parts of Western Australia' (p. 23); cf. 223:16–21 and note on 223:29.

25:37 **Rath,** DHL was still sorting out this detail of the complex family relationships on the proofs, having altered it in MS and at typescript revision stage (see Textual apparatus, and Introduction footnote 35). Cf. 'You might have thought she [Mary] had native blood' (30:34–5); she does not – see Appendix II.

26:1 **Wandoo,** See note on 37:4.

26:8 **a rare jorum** Drinking bowl; but Mr George may be punning on the biblical Joram who 'brought with him vessels of silver, and vessels of gold, and vessels of brass' (2 Samuel viii. 10): cf. Jack's baggage (7:11).

26:21 **the pretentious buildings** [26:15] **... were married.** For the walk, see map of Perth. The limestone nave of the Catholic Cathedral of the Immaculate Conception can be seen from the intersection of Barrack and Murray Streets. It was completed in 1863 (Jack was born in 1864; cf. ll. 18–19) but later extended in darker stone. Directly ahead is the Town Hall (Tudor Revival, brick decorated with stone, 1867–70), with its striking 125 foot four-faced clock tower ... St George's Church of England (consecrated 1848, demolished 1889) is almost certainly where MLS's parents were married (in a double wedding ceremony, hence requiring 'more muslin and red jackets than would stock a shop', ll. 21–2). It was classical Georgian with a tower above a columned entrance porch, and was replaced on an adjacent site by the present St George's Cathedral, consecrated in 1888, but used for services from 1885. Looking right at Pier Street the 'turrets and gables' (28:5) of Government House can be picked out. (Built 1859–64 in brickwork of a chequered pattern, with pointed arched arcades, towers and cupolas, and with gardens in the English Landscape style enclosed by a long and low brick wall: 245:3–4.) G. W. Leake lived in Irwin Street (28:7) in his latter years.

26:31 **football eleven.** A 'football team' is confused here with a 'cricket eleven'; cf. note on 113:2. At a Public school in the 1880s Jack is unlikely to have been playing Association football ('Soccer') – which has a team of eleven – but Rugby, with fifteen. (Rugby was firmly established throughout England by 1870, having started at Rugby School in 1823.) Moreover Jack lost a tooth in a (Rugby) football scrum (241:10–11). '[I]n front of the sticks' (27:4) means at the wicket (i.e. as a batsman, in cricket) and is *OED*'s earliest example of the phrase (but 'sticks' meaning wicket is given as 1840).

27:8 **in front of him like Balaam's ass,** Originally in MS: 'in front of the youth' (p. 41 [42]). The biblical allusion, a common one with DHL, is here reversed since the angel stood in the way of Balaam and his ass (Numbers xxii. 23–35).

27:28 **bush-whacker** Someone who lives in the 'bush' and is lacking in social graces or acumen (1896, *AND*).

28:25 ***beau*!"** French word usually meaning handsome (when applied to a man), but Grace could be implying its feminine form 'belle' – a thrust at Jack's feminine complexion (7:7) and uncolonial elegance of attire.

29:9 **a forehead ... like the plaster-cast of Minerva ... under her brows,** The particular statue of the Roman goddess of intelligence, the handicrafts and arts and, later, war, is unidentified, but taking plaster casts of classical statues (and colouring them to resemble bronze) was common in the nineteenth century. The sculptures of Athena (Greek counterpart of Minerva) by Phidias (fl.

c. 490–30 B.C.), known only through marble copies, are the most famous; the strong, overarching forehead is smooth and calm, even serene.

29:10 **Funny pair of lambs, these.** Monica's 'queer yellow-grey eyes,' 'shy, wild' nature (28:33–4), tawny hair, her 'slinking about like a lean young panther ... as if she was going to pounce on him' (30:8–10) and MS revisions ('these frightful "lambs."' at 32:5–6 had read 'these devilish sirens.', and 'There stood ... on him' at 28:23–4 replaced: 'They were evidently the twins, girls of sixteen or seventeen'; MS, pp. 44 [45] and 31 [52]) suggest DHL is drawing on the polarity of the tiger and the lamb (cf. 7:4) which he had developed at length in 'The Crown' (1915; see *Reflections on the Death of a Porcupine and Other Essays*, ed. Michael Herbert, Cambridge, 1988, pp. 253–306) and *Twilight in Italy* (1916). The metaphor is ultimately biblical (Isaiah xi. 6); DHL continued to experiment with it in MS. Monica's eyes are the same colour as Frieda's were (and Ciccio's in *The Lost Girl*), and her facial appearance is similar (e.g. 78:33–6).

30:3 **"Ancien, beau ... adjectives which precede,"** The beginning of an alphabetical list of common French adjectives (old, handsome, good, dear) which precede the noun, learned by rote.

31:3 **put in Mr** Jacob Ellis is visiting Perth without his wife. When revising the original typescript DHL must have changed the two preceding words and may also, in error, have changed the MS reading 'Mr' to 'Mrs' (see Textual apparatus). The error was not picked up till the correction of the E1 proofs (see note on 67:30), but since 'Mr' was not transmitted to A1 it may not have been DHL who noticed it.

31:25 **six-thousand-mile voyage,** Jack's voyage via Colombo (95:21) was closer to 10,000 nautical miles: London–Suez–Colombo–Fremantle, is about 9,800; Suez–Colombo–Fremantle is about 6,500.

32:31 **satisfactorily,** I.e. satisfying or answering a possible charge of indiscretion.

33:33 **pot ... Malachite,"** Earthenware or stoneware (here, glazed green) ... Bright-green mineral (hydrated copper carbonate) which takes high polish.

34:7 **benefit concert ... Town Hall,** Changed in MS (p. 35 [56]) from 'sacred concert ... Episcopalian Church'.

34:10 **"Angels Ever Bright And Fair," ... "home" solos,** From Handel's oratorio 'Theodora', first performed in 1750 ... Sentimental songs of the 'mother country': 'Home' used to refer to Britain.

34:24 **riding over ... lady dear.** This parody contains elements of Tennyson's 'Lady of Shalott' (1832; set to music in 1884 by Wilfred Bendall and by others later) where Sir Lancelot rides 'down to Camelot' (l. 86), and 'Elsa's Dream' in Wagner's opera, *Lohengrin* (1850), where Elsa has a vision of a knight 'in splendour shining ... of glorious mien' whom 'Heaven has sent to save me'; he arrives – in a boat drawn by a swan – and claims her as his wife.

34:31 **"And it's ... my ain folk."** 'My Ain Folk', Scottish song by Canadian-born Laura G. Lemon (1866–1924), published in 1904.

35:2 **a smouldering desire ... in him.** MS originally read (p. 37 [58]): 'he *hated* it all.'

35:5 **Dirty cads, to sing ... got you.** See Textual apparatus: the question mark after 'you' in MS derives from the cancelled reading: 'He left *them* alone. Why should they want to sing ... got you?' (p. 37 [58]).

35:21 **always homesick for somewhere else ... hated where he was ... deeply.** A frequent topic in DHL's letters: see *Letters*, iv. 250, 254 (cf. 35:19–21), and 239: 'I love trying things and discovering how I hate them'. Somers' response to Sydney in *Kangaroo*, chap. I, is similar: 'He was not happy, there was no pretending he was. He longed for Europe with hungry longing ... He felt he would have given anything on earth to be in England'.

37:4 **Wandoo.** The commonly used Aboriginal name for *Eucalyptus wandoo* or 'white gum', found mainly on the eastern slopes of the Darling Range. The Ellis farm is based on 'Seaton Ross', purchased by 16 March 1899 (*Eastern Districts Chronicle*, 1 April 1899, p. 3) by MLS's uncle, Thomas Soutter Lodge (1852–1938) and maternal aunt, Constance Sarah (1860–1939), née Leake, and also on 'Yangedine', a thriving nearby property (cf. 111:12 and see map) where Lodge had been manager. In 1897 Thomas's cousin, Frank Lodge (1876–*c.* 1960), purchased 'East Yangedine', an inferior property adjoining and formerly part of 'Yangedine': the properties parallel the proximity (and origin) of the Red Ellises' farm and Wandoo (64:35–6).

Thomas's daughter, Joan Martin (1892–), recalled Jack Skinner being jackeroo at 'Seaton Ross' (transcript of 'Interview with Mrs Joan Soutter Martin [born Lodge, 1892], 1986', conducted by Michael Adams, pp. 17–18; Battye), and his name appears in the *Eastern Districts Chronicle* as a batsman (of moderate success: cf. 113:11–38) for the Beverley side in cricket matches reported in the issues of 30 December 1899 and 21 April 1900. MLS says her brother went n. soon after the 'Seaton Ross' homestead (which she probably never saw) burnt down about 1 March 1900 (*Chronicle*, 10 March 1900, p. 3); he had spent a year working with his uncle (*Fifth Sparrow* 31).

Neither the original, 1850s house at 'Yangedine' nor 'Seaton Ross' was two-storeyed (which would have been unusual), and the first description of Wandoo at 51:33 implies it is one-storey and of stone; and the haphazard evolution of its ground floor (59:31–60:8) is typical of the period. 'Seaton Ross' was a three-roomed, mud-brick dwelling (see note on 45:3) with a thatched roof of native black-boy bush, a front verandah and two lean-to rooms on the side verandahs, and with a permanent pool nearby (111:14–16) – a valuable asset as the Avon River flows for only part of the year.

37:7 **he decided ... staying behind.** MS had read 'he determined to carry the boy along before Mr Ellis and the twins got a start' (p. 40 [61]). In cancelling this reading (and thus keeping Grace and Monica in Perth), and in adding 'and Mr Ellis both sleepily' (p. 52 [73]) when the passengers emerge from the coach at Guildford (43:18–19), DHL may have been departing from 'The House of Ellis'.

37:15 **today's prison.** This reading replaces '*what is*' in MS (p. 40 [61]).

37:29 **I drives ... relays fifteen or twenty miles,** Thomas Horton (the son of Henry Horton who won the contract for the York run in 1876) drove the coach from Guildford to York and Albany and back. According to Trollope, who travelled from Albany to Perth, the journey of 260 miles took four days and was done in fifteen mile sections (*Australia and New Zealand*, ii. 126–8). At 37:27 'years without end amen' is an adaptation of the standard doxology in *The Book of Common Prayer*.

38:18 **office in Victoria Street . . . passages to Australia.'** The consular offices of some of the Australasian colonies were situated in Victoria Street, London in the 1880s, but those of the steamship companies were in or near Leadenhall Street.

38:23 **a pearl beyond price,** Cf. Matthew xiii. 46.

38:24 **in double 'arness collar-proud."** Restive and resentful at being in the harness of her obligations (literally, like a horse chafed at the neck through being put in harness after a period of rest from work).

39:2 **booming of the frogs.** Trollope remarked that the 'commonest noise' on the journey from Albany to Perth was that of the bullfrog (*Limnodynastes dorsalis*): 'very loud, and altogether unlike the sound of frogs in Europe' (*Australia and New Zealand*, ii. 127).

39:21 **six A.1. families in Perth . . . seven daughters.** Cf. the local belief (e.g. *Fifth Sparrow* 3) that the colony had been settled by gentry and respectable farmers whose descendants were related and formed a kind of colonial aristocracy. An oligarchy of ruling families developed (cf. 232:5 and note), exercising considerable economic and political power (the source-expression, 'the Six Hungry Families', first gained currency in the late 1880s as part of a WA election campaign); they were 'reputed to be the Burts, Leakes, Lefroys, Lee Steeres, Shentons and Stones, though other lists were frequently compiled' (F. K. Crowley, *Australia's Western Third*, 1960, p. 143; Annie Jenkins – see Introduction, p. xxii – was born a Burt, MLS's mother a Leake). Tensions developed with the flood of immigrants to the WA goldfields in the 1890s. MLS felt that 'few of the newcomers were our social equals' (*Fifth Sparrow* 36), and refers (p. 3) to 'jumped-up t'other siders [people from the eastern states]' (cf. 226:35) – the antonym of 'sandgropers' (see Appendix IV) . . . MLS's mother was one of seven daughters (cf. note on 23:13). There had always been more men than women (as high a ratio as 2 to 1 at times; in 1882 there were 17,551 males to 13,215 females). The coach driver's wish for more young men (ll. 17–18) excludes the many ex-convicts, servants and labourers. (Hence also Mr George's remark at 22:21–4.)

40:37 **threatened him** [40:3] **. . . fank you."** For this episode cf. *Fifth Sparrow* 12–13:

> Jack [Skinner] . . . had grown into a strange, rebellious boy . . . Annie the maid often threatened to give him to a policeman . . . He was given to screaming fits, during which Annie would lock him in the attic . . . he would shout: 'Annie, Annie, I'm goin' ter be good.' But when she got up to let him out he'd say, 'I'm *not* goin' ter be good,' and start to yell again. Tired of his tantrums, Annie one day popped him over the garden wall into the shrubbery of Sir Austin Blake's estate, where he was found by the gardener, brushed down and taken to her ladyship . . . in the grand drawing-room. Suddenly Jack decided to turn on the charm . . . Mother heard afterwards that Jack had said he had been told never to ask for cake, but that if it was offered him he didn't have to refuse it.

'She stepped . . . window-doors' (40:26–7) is found in TSIb, not in MS (p. 46 [67]) or TSIa (p. 50 – a page of original typescript): for the marginal note which caused it to be added, see Introduction footnote 66 and also Textual apparatus for 40:14.

41:17 **baby 'roos joeys,** I.e. baby kangaroos; 'joey' was used as early as 1839 (*AND*).

41:29 **parrots flew shrieking "Twenty-eight!** The parrot from s.w. Australia, *Barnardius zonarius semitorquatus*, has a three-syllable call, the last note being higher in pitch than the first two.

41:32 **black-and-white handsome birds, that they call magpies,** The Western magpie (*Gymnorhina tibicen dorsalis*) is a large bird, about 17 inches long, unrelated to the English or American magpie; cf. *Kangaroo*, chap. v: 'In West Australia Somers could sit in the bush and talk to the flocks of big, handsome, black-and-white birds that they call magpies'.

42:10 **their 'claims' ... nobody else can touch it."** Cf. *Year-Book* 27: 'Numerous persons, indeed, left the Colony in disgust, but retained possession of the immense tracts of land granted to them; so that those who arrived afterwards were unable to obtain land in favourable localities ... the best of the land being unprofitably locked up'; in addition, much land fell into the hands of speculators. See also notes on 44:23 and 32.

42:20 **another, mute world,** The omission of this phrase in TSIa and b is probably not an authorial revision of the original typescript but the result of typist's eye-skip (as also at 110:10). The typesetters of A1 and E1 similarly skipped phrases and sentences: see apparatus for 73:5 and 178:27 where an eye-skip in E1 was transferred to A1 (p. 195 which has, rather than the usual 38 lines of type, only 37 – suggesting a deletion).

42:38 **"There *are* policemen ... mounted police,** There being little crime in the colony and a military force available to deal with Aboriginal disturbances, a part-time constabulary sufficed until 1840 when the first full-time policeman was appointed. In 1851 a police force was established which, by 1877, consisted of 20 officers, and 137 mounted and foot constables; cf. 226:32. Cf. 'Force' at 273:13, and 114:33.

43:5 **nobody to hold up the coach,"** Jack is failing to distinguish between ordinary criminals and bushrangers.

43:15 **Guildford where the roses grow."** 'Guildford was always a pretty place, right from the early times' (Jesse E. Hammond [b. *c.* 1856], *Western Pioneers: The Battle Well Fought*, Perth, 1936, p. 131).

44:4 **the coach came alongside ... He did not mount, but walked on up the hill.** In MS the coach had originally 'picked him up', and the sentence was added interlinearly (p. 53 [74]).

44:9 **the steep Darling Ranges** [44:5] ... **unknown sea.** Named after Governor Darling by Stirling during the latter's original exploration of Swan River in 1827, the range runs n.–s. for 300 miles, about 18–20 miles from and parallel with the Indian Ocean coast; and the highest peak is *c.* 1,910 feet. In 1869 Governor Weld (see note on 246:5) described the 'easy ascent' to the summit and the 'fine view': 'had the sun not been too low, we should have seen Perth and the sea beyond it. The forest stretched far below us. Here and there a break of lighter green denoting patches of cultivation [cf. 44:19–20] and we slept at a neat little roadside inn at a place called Mahogany Creek [cf. 45:11–14]' (Trevor Tuckfield, *The Old York Road*, Perth, 1975, p. 22).

44:23 **land of promise ... I bid £1080 for 2,700 acres ... Hammersley** Free land grants (the size based on the amount of capital introduced into the colony by a settler) came to an end in 1830 ... After 1832 unoccupied Crown Lands were sold at auction for a set minimum price of 5s an acre; in 1838 it rose to 12s, and in 1842 to £1, being reduced to 10s in 1859. (Mr George was bidding 8s; if this was the 1840s or 50s – G. W. Leake was in WA 1843–8 and from 1852 – he was underbidding) ... Edward Hamersley (1810–74) arrived in 1837, subsequently accumulated at least eight properties, mostly in the Avon valley, became a director of the Western Australian Bank in 1841 (see 316:15–16, opened in 1841, incorporated 1879) and was a member of the Legislative Assembly, 1857–65.

44:32 **he can jump it** [44:28] ... **Land Acts, Grants, Holdings, Claims,** 'The history of the Colony is at first principally that of the Land Regulations and their consequences' (Nicolay, *Handbook*, p. 68). After free land grants (see previous note) were discontinued a system of either outright or conditional purchase evolved. The regulations were detailed, couched in legalistic phrasing and altered from time to time, generating continuing discussion of the relative advantages; cf. 105:24–5.

The (WA) Commissioner of Crown Lands issued copies, and they were reproduced in WA almanacs and official handbooks. The paraphrased version at 105:27–106:2 is inaccurate in some details. The rules prevailing in 1882 allowed Crown land to be sold at 10s an acre for a minimum of 40 acres or licensed in 100–500 acre holdings for a fee of 1s an acre per annum for ten years (cf. 219:15–16). If the required improvements were made (the land 'enclose[d] ... with a good and substantial fence, and ... at least one-fourth of the whole area' cleared and cropped; regulations quoted in Nicolay, *Handbook*, p. 159 and cf. 48:6), the occupation licence would become a land grant, or after three years, it could be exchanged for a grant on payment of the remaining 7s an acre. If the improvements were not carried out (e.g. often only productive parts of the holding were fenced – see 213:26–7), the licensee could obtain successive seven-year leases at the same annual fee, with the Crown reserving the right to resume the land in cases of non-payment. In anticipation of abandoned holdings becoming available for re-selection, they could, with some risk, be 'jumped'. See note on 212:38.

45:1 **Jarrah ... likes this barren ironstone formation.** *Eucalyptus marginata*, a hard and durable timber, attains heights of 90–120 feet, with trunks 3–5 feet in diameter and 50–60 feet to the first branch; it grows principally along the Darling Range. Cf. *Year-Book* 146: 'this tree delights in an ironstone formation, and it would almost appear as though the rougher and more the site is composed of ironstone rocks and barren of almost any other vegetation, the better the tree will grow'.

45:3 **mud-brick buildings** Simple early colonial mode of construction, especially in remote areas: mud-bricks are made by compacting mud (or mud and straw) into frames and then drying them in the sun until hard.

45:7 **One of the convicts . . . wanderin' yet.** A 'convict, named Peacock, escaped from a road gang when working close to the inn [at Mahogany Creek: see 45:11] . . . Whether he became lost, or whether he was murdered, is not known, but his ghost, it is said, still haunts the inn' (Tuckfield, *Old York Road*, p. 16).

45:9 **Darlington.** The name given (in 1884) to the new railway siding, and thus the locality – after 'Darlington' vineyard (est. 1882). The story about Governor Darling is apocryphal (ll. 9–10): he did not visit the area. There may be a confusion with nearby Chipper's Leap, named after John Chipper (1805–71) who, in 1832, escaped attacking Aborigines by leaping down this large rock outcrop.

45:26 **a little by-road,** Talbot Road West.

46:3 **baby girl . . . an Ellis,"** In fact, Ellie (see 57:4 and note). There has been no mention of the child's being Mr Ellis's; when Jack was waiting at 44:13, he saw at first in MS (p. 54 [75]) 'the face of the woman with the floss-haired child' (cf. 44:16–17).

46:14 **slip-rail,** Moveable rail(s) allowing a fence to serve as a gateway (Australianism).

46:22 **sweet scent . . . million acres."** Derives from *Year-Book* 151: 'The vernacular name is derived from the peculiar scent of the wood, which is wonderfully similar to that of raspberries . . . The wood is very dense, and is largely used for fencing, survey posts, etc. . . . It is a beautiful wood . . . sometimes turned into pipes and walking sticks. A large quantity is now [i.e. 1902] being yearly cut down and burned in clearing the land'. It is a small tree (with a trunk up to one foot in diameter) – which is why Tom makes quick work of removing it (46:17–23).

46:25 **a "ginger-bread" house,** The alluring house in the woods in the children's story 'Hansel and Gretel' by Hans Christian Andersen (1805–75).

47:5 **the cross roads . . . another twenty miles yet."** The meeting of the York Road and Talbot Road West . . . The distance to Beverley is about 28 miles; the road bridges the Dale River at Waterhatch Crossing (48:28). Some way along there was a shortcut direct to 'Seaton Ross' (shown on a WA Lands and Surveys Department map of 1893); it was still in use in the 1920s.

47:7 **dree,** Tiresome, dreary (dialect).

47:33 **Berkshire** Variety of pig (bred near Faringdon, Berkshire).

47:36 **Og an' Magog . . . wopped** Named (ironically) after Gog and Magog, legendary giants, statues of which, dating from 1708, are at the Guildhall, London. Gogmagog is the giant killed by Jack in an old version of the fairy story, 'Jack and the Beanstalk' . . . 'Whopped' means whacked soundly (colloquialism).

48:37 **Ghostly and weird . . . like skeletons.** Cf. Somers' experience of 'the Westralian bush' in *Kangaroo*, chap. I: 'It was so phantom-like, so ghostly, with its tall pale trees . . . like corpses'.

49:32 **sidey** [49:26] **. . . puttin' on jam . . . Macaroni. Cockadoodle . . . dickey-toffs . . . flash sparks** Conceited, pretentious (usually 'sidy') . . . adopting an affected speech or manner (cf. *Fifth Sparrow* 28) . . . fop, dandy ('Cockadoodle' may be Lennie's coinage, implying vain strutting – cf. 112:32) . . . fashionably dressed people, 'swells' with superior airs ... cf. 'bright sparks'; 'flash' means fashionably smart (slang).

49:34 **"Not enough ... with me."** MS (p. 65 [86]) originally read: '"I'm not good enough for 'em at home, neither flash enough nor nosey enough. They think me too much of a hard-fist."'

49:39 **stow the haw-haw gab!** 'Stop your bragging' (colloquial). Jack's shaping up (i.e. assuming a fighting stance, l. 37) is, to Tom, a form of laughable ('haw-haw') boast ('gab').

51:16 ***veni ... vidi ... vici,*** Usually taken as Julius Caesar's comment on his (partly successful) expedition to Britain in 55 B.C.: 'I came, I saw, I conquered' (Latin); in fact, he was describing his victory over Pharnaces at Zela in Pontus (47 B.C.).

51:25 **Look slippy** Be quick; 'Look slippery' – i.e. lively (dialect).

51:31 **smell of flowering shrubs: silver wattle, spirea, daphne and syringa** Mr Ellis's gardening has involved some effort (cf. 57:17 and notes on 60:14 and 82:18) for only the silver wattle is native; it and the fragrant daphne bloom in June, the novel's present (15:13). Spirea (common name 'May'; many varieties) is cultivated for foliage and flowers; syringa, properly shrubs of the genus *Philadelphus* (especially the mock-orange, but the name is often used for lilac), has creamy white, strongly sweet-scented flowers blooming October–November.

52:32 **"The blue ... blue below—"** From 'The Sea' by Barry Cornwall (pseud. for Bryan Waller Procter, 1787–1874), ll. 2 and 8–9; ll. 19–20 are quoted at ll. 35–6.

53:5 **"And wherever [52:34] ... childhood's *our* ... I never loved ... loved me ... it was sure to die."** Misremembered from 'The Fire-Worshippers' in *Lalla Rookh* (1817) by Thomas Moore (1779–1852): 'Oh! ever thus, from childhood's hour, / I've seen my fondest hopes decay; / I never loved a tree or flower, / But 't was the first to fade away. / I never nurs'd a dear gazelle, / ... But when ... love me, it was sure to die!' (ll. 279–86).

53:15 **under the peppermint tree** WA native (*Agonis flexuosa*) with dense, drooping foliage, good for shelter, shade and ornamental purposes; its crushed leaves give off a strong peppermint smell.

53:32 **Tom came [53:23] ... naked look.** Cf. a fragment of an early, draft chap. of *Fifth Sparrow*. MLS had 'lately' attended 'a maternity case on a farm'; she described to DHL the children she saw: 'So wild in the country. Naked to the elements. Pants and vests, bloomers and frocks. Little girls sometimes minus the bloomers the boys never without pants'. Cf. Lennie Ellis's cleverness and his later refusal to go to England for schooling (190:6–23) with 'Lennie bright as a jackass [cf. note on 66:14] – a know-all, [at] eleven the cleverest imp ever at a State school ... He didn't want to go ['to one of these higher educational places we have in the principal towns'], not he! Not off the farm'; and cf. Tom at 63:30–1 with Austey, one of the eldest boys, 'dull as a wombat'. This family also had twins, but further details of the original children could not be ascertained because of restrictions on general access to files at the Registrar-General's office, Perth.

54:37 **"Obey an' ... aid ye—"** Probably Lennie's own adaptation of an unidentified hymn; cf. 'his rhyme' (l. 39), and MLS's description in an interview of 'that dear, loyal, imp of a rhyming Lennie' (*Sunday Times*, Perth, 15 February 1925, p. 29). 'Lord Tom Noddy' was evidently a popular name for a foolish or very simple-minded aristocrat (not in *OED*); it has this meaning as 'LORD TOM N*DD*' in Charles Henry Ross, *"Stage Whispers," and "Shouts Without": A Book About Plays and Players, Actors and Actresses*, 1882, p. 26.

54:40 **the fiends of air** The evil or bad angels of popular reference, e.g. William Blake's 'fiend ... in a cloud' ('Infant Sorrow', 1794, l. 4).

55:18 **double-gees:** WA term for *Emex australis*, a weed with many angular, spiny seeds at ground level found in pasture land – hence Lennie's fear.

56:20 **bell-topper?"** Silk (top) hat (Australianism).

57:5 **even** The sentences describing Harry and 'the baby' were inserted interlinearly in MS (p. 78 [99]), but the omission of 'even' in TSIa is unlikely to be DHL's. 'Ellie' at first read 'baby' (as she was at 45:31), and at 88:6 DHL mistakenly calls her 'Effie' (MS, p. 138 [159]); the error appears in E1 and A1.

Another interlinear reference to Harry, whom DHL had at first forgotten, is added at 59:21–2: 'Then there <were>⌜was Harry, whom Jack didn't like, and⌝ the little girls' (MS, p. 83 [104]). (In these notes original and second readings cancelled by DHL are shown within angle brackets: < > and ≪ ≫; added readings (first and second) by half brackets: ⌜ ⌝ and ⌜⌜ ⌝⌝.) See Textual apparatus for 60:2.

57:21 **look** There is a general change in MS into the present tense for this scene – which, at its first occurrence, a typist (and DHL, when correcting) would naturally overlook (see Textual apparatus); two later inconsistencies (at 57:29 and 30) are changed; and cf. entries for 98:20, 99:8 and 104:12.

59:19 **the silent, unobtrusive pillars of the house.** Cf. Anna's newfound peace as a child, in *The Rainbow* (1915), when Tom and Lydia's marriage becomes settled: 'She played between the pillar of fire and the pillar of cloud in confidence' (ed. Mark Kinkead-Weekes, Cambridge, 1989, p. 91 and note). And cf. Jack's 'passionate love for the family' (58:20) and ll. 16–18 with the first long alteration suggested by DHL (Introduction, pp. xl–xli) and Paul Morel's attachment to the Leivers family in *Sons and Lovers* (1913).

60:14 **a pepper ... pittosporum ... Norfolk pine** The pepper (or peppercorn, *Schinus molle* – native of Peru) and the pine of Norfolk Island (off the e. coast of Australia), *Araucaria heterophylla.* In her unpublished essay 'D. H. Lawrence and M. L. Skinner' (Battye; p. 10), MLS describes 'Leithdale's' 'great Pitostrium tree covered with sweet smelling blossom' (probably *Pittosporum tobira*); cf. Textual apparatus for 60:13.

60:21 **all their names," he declared.** See Textual apparatus; MS (p. 84 [105]) read after revision: '⌜all⌝ their names," <he>⌜all⌝ declared.' Cf. MS reading (p. 93 [114]) 'That's all there ⟨is⟩⌜we know⌝ about me.' at 65:1–2 and apparatus.

60:23 **a tuppenny** I.e. 'a tuppenny [i.e. twopenny] damn', Australianism meaning 'virtually nothing'.

62:17 **sukey** Softie, crybaby (Australianism; 1933, but as an adjective – usually 'sooky' or 'sookie' – 1901, *AND*). DHL's misspelling may derive from his having confused the word with 'Sukey' (meaning 'Susan').

62:22 **huckaback** Towel (from the name of a rough linen fabric formerly used for towelling).

62:25 **damper,** Simple form of bread, often unleavened, baked in the ashes of a fire and (formerly) widely used in outback Australia (Australianism).

62:38 **dif . . . nips** Different . . . nippers (colloquialism for young children – as at l. 28).

63:2 **Aunt's school in th' settlement, till Dr Rackett came.** Children aged 6–14 were required to attend government schools, unless being tutored elsewhere; in 1882, there were two such one-teacher schools in Beverley and three in York, and four of the teachers were women.

63:14 **Tears came . . . from a rock.** Cf. Exodus xvii. 6.

64:8 **East India business.** Trade with India was opened to private merchants after 1813 when the East India Company lost its monopoly, and there were bank failures there in 1830 and 1834.

64:16 **A'nts** I.e. aunts (see 101:38–102:1 and 237:4), but not pronounced in Australian English with a short 'a'. The pronounciation is Irish and therefore historically possible in WA (Easu also uses it at 273:3; cf. note on 204:4), but DHL may simply have assumed the standard Australian pronunciation to be the same as in the USA. And cf. his mistaken use of ''oss' (instead of ''orse') for 'horse' (e.g. at 65:35, 243:11).

64:20 **Uncle Easu's family the Reds . . . the eldest.** Easu is a transposed spelling of Esau (68:25), the son of Isaac and Rebekah and twin brother of Jacob (Dad Ellis's name, but originally he was 'Frank': see Textual apparatus for 31:28); cf. Genesis xxv. 25: 'And the first came out red, all over like an hairy garment: and they called his name Esau [Hebrew for shaggy, hairy]'. Rebekah prefers Jacob (xxv. 28), and they deceive the dying Isaac into blessing Jacob with his land and flocks (xxvii. 6–29); cf. 64:14–15, 18–20. Jacob is sent away to find a wife, but marries two (xxix. 18–30); cf. 64:12–13, 39, 65:2–3. He names his second (and last) child by Rachel, Benjamin (meaning son of his right hand; cf. 141:5).

65:1 **was his servant, and** MS originally read: 'he was my nurse' (p. 93 [114]). It was an immediate revision, for the role is re-assigned in the next clause.

65:30 **and reddish beard** This is an interlinear addition in MS (p. 95 [116]), and other descriptions of Easu were revised: e.g. at 114:34 'tall, thin' was cancelled for 'tall, broad' (p. 187 [211]). DHL made more changes at typescript revision stage: see Textual apparatus entries for 66:18, 79:30, 114:31 and 114:37; in the last there were two layers of revision: 'his blue, <quick> ≪ ⌜rather prominent⌝ ≫ ⌜⌜rivet⌝⌝ eyes' (p. 169).

66:1 **Hyde Park costume** Well-groomed riding attire suited to public recreation. Hyde Park in central London, popular for riding since the seventeenth century (especially for the aristocracy), was a place in which to be seen.

66:14 **grinning jackasses.** Adaptation of 'laughing jackasses' – an Australian colloquialism referring to the (Australian) bird, the kookaburra *Dacelo gigas*, known for its raucous, laughing call.

66:27 **Jackeroo ... blankey thing to.** Young man of 'good family' working on a station to gain experience of station management (Australianism); cf. its etymology ('Jack' plus 'roo' from 'kangaroo') with the likely significance of Jack Grant's surname (see note on 117:14) ... 'Blankey' (or 'blankety') is a colloquial euphemism for damned, accursed or bloody: see also 269:16. (The dash after 'to.' in MS – see Textual apparatus – originally linked to a cancelled sentence: 'They all seemed to have a horror of being "taught" anything', p. 97 [118].)

67:30 **made him tremble** See Textual apparatus. This is probably an example of DHL revising differently the proofs he sent to Seltzer and Secker. In other cases (31:3 and note, 43:23, 54:34, 97:40, 273:40), DHL failed to transcribe the correction, or it was overlooked by Seltzer's office (or printer) when the A1 proofs were checked against the duplicate E1 proofs. E1 readings are preferred (see Introduction, p. lxii), but exceptions occur at 67:35 (second entry), 295:34 (see notes) and 112:5.

67:36 **corkscrew bucks,** The E1 reading, 'corkscrew buck,' is suspect: DHL's usage could well have been corrected by the typesetter. Cf. Textual apparatus for 112:5, 265:13 and 300:31. However, at 87:32, 98:20, 106:25 (first entry), 114:13, 116:13 and 145:4, the (predictable) A1 readings are probably compositorial.

68:21 **Inwardly he ... and defied.** Inserted interlinearly in MS, and further revised in proofs (see Textual apparatus); at ll. 10–16 there are revisions in MS also on the subject of English-colonial tensions: "⌜hostile⌝ ... <cruel> ⌜retrogressive⌝ ... <cruel> ⌜brute of a⌝ ... country <⌜that lay⌝> behind ... <he was never going> ⌜he would never go⌝". And 'yield his manliness before' (l. 17) read in MS 'accept the <slight degradation> ⌜deterioration⌝ of' (p. 100 [121]).

69:8 **suddenly appeared ... like the Lord in Judgment.** Cf. Malachi iii. 1: 'the Lord, whom ye seek [i.e. 'the God of judgement'; ii. 17], shall suddenly come to his temple'.

69:10 **rainy season,** Although there is no true rainy season in the districts around Perth (for the climate is not tropical: see note on 15:17), average rainfall June–August can be up to twenty times higher than December–February, and its onset can be quite pronounced. However, the term has been used since at latest the 1880s.

69:33 **"Poor Tom!" thought Jack.** The redundant comma in MS (see Textual apparatus) was part of a cancelled reading, '"In the dying room," thought Jack', which is his response to Gran's original offer (ll. 31–2): '... Tom could have slept <in my room> ⌜here on the sofa⌝' (p. 103 [124]).

69:35 **sawneys!** Simpletons (colloquialism).

70:8 **a Bluebeard's chamber.** From the fairy tale based on French popular tradition by Charles Perrault (1628–1703) in *Histoires et contes du temps passé, avec des moralités. Contes de ma mère l'Oye* (Paris, 1697). The character gets his name from the colour of his beard; his chamber was a locked turret, in which hung the bodies of his murdered wives.

71:8 **As usual Dad did nothing ... Jack was by no means one too many.** When revising the original typescript DHL may have meant to change 'As usual' to 'Usually' when he added 'also' to the end of the previous sentence (a distinction between Dad's efforts is presumably intended). Although 'Yangedine' had thriven under the 'popular and enterprising' Thomas Lodge (*Eastern Districts Chronicle*, 10 March 1900, p. 3), and although while at 'Seaton Ross' he served on the Beverley Roads Board, Lodge's daughter described him as having 'never worked as far as I can remember. He overseed. Mother was the worker in our family ... Father had no go ... no push or go' (Adams, 'Interview with Mrs Joan Soutter Martin', pp. 17, 124). But the healthy Lodge can only have been part of the inspiration behind the ailing Dad Ellis (177:26–178:37); cf. *Fifth Sparrow* 30: MLS's father kept his imminent death – in 1902 – a secret. As there were only three Lodge children and one farm labourer at 'Seaton Ross', Jack Skinner's assistance as jackeroo would have been useful.

71:13 **"tea"** Tea, in Australian and regional English usage, commonly means the main meal of the day, taken in the early evening.

75:4 **virtue gone out of him.** See Mark v. 30: 'virtue' here in the sense of potency or efficacy. Cf. Rawdon Lilly's ministering to the sick Aaron Sisson in *Aaron's Rod*, ed. Mara Kalnins (Cambridge, 1988), p. 96; and *The Trespasser*, ed. Elizabeth Mansfield (Cambridge, 1981), p. 155.

75:22 **"Out of the mouths ... and sucklings——"** Psalms viii. 2 ['... mouth ...'] continues: 'hast thou ordained strength because of thine enemies, that thou mightest still the enemy and the avenger'.

75:26 **He cut off my leg.** In MLS's *Black Swans* (1925), set in the 1850s, a young Mr and Mrs Ellis of Wandoo appear briefly, and she also has a wooden leg (see 69:37). The novel includes a long adventure in the North-West followed by a return to what is felt as the confines of civilisation, a mysterious grandmother figure and a servant, Tim, who 'only wanted to serve' (p. 338; cf. Tom's loyalty to Jack). MLS's 'The Hand' (see Introduction, p. lii and footnote 122) and a radio play of the same name (unpublished) recycle the story of a man lost in the bush; in *Letters of a V.A.D.* there is a comically misspelled letter which starts 'This comes opping to find you well as it leaves me at precnt thank God but not so the missus ...' (p. 262); cf. 234:32–3; and see Introduction footnote 103.

76:13 **disapproving of Gran's language** DHL's revision in typescript of 'devil' to 'man' in the previous sentence has given Jack less of which to disapprove; and see note on 144:15. (DHL elsewhere removed 'devil' and 'Lucifer': see Textual apparatus entries for 72:37 and 114:31.)

76:14 **Had two daughters** The novel is inconsistent: cf. 323:7 and 312:6. At 77:39–40 Gran says she is aunt to Mary's mother, so she is also the aunt of Mr George, Aunt Matilda and possibly Alice (Ma) Ellis (25:9), but they refer to her as 'Gran'. (A necessary Mr George Snr, unmentioned in the novel, is added to the Family tree in Appendix II.)

76:17 **bowels of compassion.** 1 John iii. 17.

77:26 **y'rself is God ... the glow inside you."** Cf. *Kangaroo*, chap. VI: 'the fire that is in my heart is God'.

79:3 **his face,** MS gives Jack a 'wet face' (p. 122 [143]), whereas it is Monica who has just come in out of the rain: hence the revision in TSIa.

82:15 **bombilation** Normally means humming or buzzing but seems intended here to mean a continuous banging or thudding.

82:18 **Moreton Bay fig** Very large tree (*Ficus macrophylla* or *platypoda*), native to the area surrounding Moreton Bay, Queensland but widely planted in Australia; it produces fig-like, inedible fruit which drop with some force (also called 'Bay Fig', as at 115:35).

83:15 **without father ... or people.** Cf. Luke xviii. 29.

85:2 **[not]** Lennie is not trying to trap Jack but warn him (given his 'dangerous nod of the head' it is unlikely he is being ironic). DHL also omitted a word in the next sentence in MS (p. 132 [153]) – see Textual apparatus – which he or a typist noticed.

85:8 **"God is a Higher Law than the Constitution."** From a speech by Senator W. H. Seward (1801–72) in the US Senate, 11 March 1850 ['But there is a Higher...'].

85:15 **'Self is ... and joy.'"** Apart from the addition of 'Self is' and 'And selves', a conflation of two passages from Milton's *Paradise Lost* (1667): 'Their glittering tents he passed, and now is come/ Into the blissful field, through groves of myrrh,/ And flow'ring odours, cassia, nard, and balm,/ A wilderness of sweets' (Book V, ll. 291–4); and, describing the angels: 'On flow'rs reposed, and with fresh flow'rets crowned,/ They eat, they drink, and in communion sweet/ Quaff immortality and joy' (ll. 636–8).

85:20 **bingy** Belly (Australianism, from the Aboriginal).

85:28 **spot,"** Alcoholic drink; cf. 236:17 (colloquialism).

85:36 **success comes to those that work and don't drink.** Adaptation of the proverb that success 'is the reward of toil' (originally, Sophocles, *Electra*, l. 945).

86:26 **billy-can.** Can with a wire handle used most often to boil water for making tea (as at 93:9–13) – also called 'billy', 209:23 (Australianism).

86:30 **Garn ... David skirmishing before Goliath.** Colloquial elision of 'go on' in broad Australian and regional English ... See 1 Samuel xvii. 32–51.

86:35 **spoonin'** Wooing in a silly or sentimental way (colloquialism); cf. note on 15:2 in *Mr Noon*, ed. Lindeth Vasey (Cambridge, 1984), p. 297.

88:10 **a knot instead of a bow,** In MS (p. 139 [160]), DHL tried to improve Lennie's joke: the cancelled reading is 'tied in a knot'.

88:14 **clearing gang** The felling of trees, clearing away of undergrowth and burning off (88:20) was a constant activity in the colony.

88:39 **Moses' sister watching over events.** See Exodus ii. 4.

89:34 **weer's** [89:29] **... y're a bloke at it ... dinkey** Where is ... i.e. you do it well and without unnecessary fussing as a man ('bloke') would (coinage) ... dainty, usually 'dinky' (colloquialism).

90:12 **swag** Blanket with a few belongings wrapped up inside (also called 'bluey', 130:14, 'drum' or 'Matilda', 225:13–14) carried by a swagman or 'swaggy' (i.e. country tramp [1891,*AND*], 225:11–12; see also 221:3 and note): Australianisms.

90:32 **a whale, on the wrong side."** Perhaps a joke (the saddle being as small as a whale is large), or DHL may have misunderstood and changed a slang reference in 'The House of Ellis' to 'a whale of a saddle' well-adapted for 'putting on side' (i.e. pretention: see note on 49:32).

90:38 **assam silk** A coarse silk, exported from the eastern (British) India province, Assam.

91:10 **'tree mounted** I.e. mounted on a saddle-tree, the framework which forms the foundation of a saddle; 208:34 refers to the saddle-bow, the arched front of the saddle-tree.

92:8 **Tom was the growing trunk of the tree.** Cf. 'Study of Thomas Hardy' where DHL contrasts the state of being 'like a palpitating leading-shoot of life' with 'mov[ing] as it were in the trunk of the tree ... Such is a man at work, safe within the proven, deposited experience, thrilling as he traverses the fixed channels and courses of life ... he has only made himself one with what has been, travelling the old, fixed courses, through which life still passes, but which are not in themselves living' (*Study of Thomas Hardy*, ed. Steele, pp. 34–5).

92:29 **kangaroos calling to one another** Cf. MLS's recalling when DHL asked her 'Do you hear the kangaroos calling softly when everything is still? Roo! Roo! Roo!'; she replied she did but that 'People say it's my imagination' (*Fifth Sparrow* 112); see also 227:27–8. The Western Grey kangaroo subspecies found in WA, *Macropus fuliginosus ocydromus*, is not, strictly, mute: when alarmed, both sexes (and males when aggressive) emit a guttural cough, and mother and young communicate via a series of chucking sounds; and, as Jack discovers at 101:26, this kangaroo has an objectionably strong smell.

93:6 **spring in** [92:18] **... the month of August.** Although there are some factual errors here – crickets 'birr' in summer, not winter (92:29); the red gum (*Eucalyptus calophylla*, 92:34–93:1) flowers February–March, but other eucalypts do blossom in spring (92:23–4); and cf. MLS's report of her describing to DHL the blooming of the wildflowers 'in September after the winter rains' (*Fifth Sparrow* 113) – the beauty of WA wildflowers in spring is renowned (cf. note on 93:32).

The red gum, widely distributed in s.w. Australia, exudes during summer a thick gum which gives it the appearance of being spattered with blood (93:4). See *Fifth Sparrow* 112 where DHL is reported as saying: 'This tree seems to sweat blood'; and *Year-Book* 153 which describes the tree's 'giving the leaves and herbage under ... the appearance of being bestrewed with blood', its flowers as 'large, white, prolific and full of honey', and the bark as 'hard, rough, and [of an] irregularly-furrowed or broken appearance' (cf. 92:33–93:1). Varieties of banksia and wattle do flower in August (93:27–30) but the banksia described (probably *Banksia ashbyi*), a native of WA, flowers in spring (i.e. from September).

When Jack and Tom leave Wandoo to ride to Geraldton (194:35), the 'bush was now full of sparks of the beautiful, uncanny flowers of Western Australia' (i.e. September, 195:9–10), and near Paddy's Crossing wattle and crimson-flowering gum are in bloom (July/August and January/March respectively; 196:27, 198:4) though it is *early* winter (i.e. June, see 209:8).

93:21 **camp oven . . . built,** Cast-iron pot on three short legs with a lid for holding hot ashes (Australianism) . . . set up.

93:32 **Jack never forgot . . . mimosa,** Probably based on DHL's first seeing wattle in bloom (near Thirroul in late July 1922); see *Kangaroo*, chap. XVIII ('Nothing is lovelier than to drive into the Australian bush in spring . . .'); and *Letters*, iv. 280 where he refers to wattle as mimosa: wattle (the common name; many varieties) belongs to the mimosaceous genus *Acacia*.

93:34 **not the region for these giants.** The camp is about 7 miles s. of the Greenlow homestead (150:39–40), which itself is 40 miles n.e. of the Stirling Range (102:20) and thus 150 miles from Beverley, so ruling out a morning's round trip on horseback and buggy from Wandoo (150:21–2, 151:1–2; cf. note on 195:19). Sandalwood (*Santalum cygnorum*, 93:31) is found there, but not the tallest karri (*Eucalyptus diversicolor*, 93:33) which grow – to 250 feet high – in the s.w. of the state.

94:2 **Strongly the . . . motionless aloofness.** Cf. *Fifth Sparrow* 112: MLS advised DHL not to venture too far into the bush at night; she reports him as replying: 'It frightens me – all the bush out beyond stretching away over these hills frightens me, as if dark gods possessed the place'.

94:26 **jinkers,** Wheeled conveyances for carrying logs; see 225:7–8 (Australianism: 1889, *AND*).

94:31 **bandicoots . . . bungarras . . . boodie rats;** Small insectivorous Australian marsupial . . . monitor lizard (*Varanus gouldii*) . . . burrowing rat-kangaroo. The preceding passages are full of the local detail with which DHL is unlikely to have been familiar and which he almost certainly adapted from 'The House of Ellis': cf. Textual apparatus for 94:31 and 99:6.

95:9 **about two . . . always four . . . several months,** These readings in MS (p. 151 [173]) replace: '⌜two or⌝ three . . . six . . . six months'. The mail to England did take two months, and the charge for letters until the early 1890s was sixpence (95:5–6).

95:38 **variolettes . . . cockles pill** Proprietary medicines: 'Varalettes', taken for gout, available in 1909 and probably earlier . . . '[James] Cockle's Anti-Bilious Pills', available in WA in the 1880s.

96:14 **boomers,** Large male kangaroos (Australianism).

96:22 **Pink-eye . . . "Cornseed"** Form of conjunctivitis: see note on 16:27; advertisements for a lotion for 'Colonial Ophthalmia' appear in the 1880s WA press. . . . Probably a mistake for 'hayseed', an ignorant bush dweller (see especially 189:39, colloquial; 1889, *OED*), rather than a conjoining of 'hayseed' and 'cornstalk' (obsolete Australianism meaning a native-born Australian, or, still current, a New South Welshman in particular – as being generally taller and thinner than the immigrant).

96:37 **sang out** The proximity of the next typescript revision (l. 38) suggests DHL changed this reading (see Textual apparatus) from the colloquial Australian usage which he may have originally taken from 'The House of Ellis'.

97:39 **quarters** I.e. hind-quarters (as at 98:34).

99:5 **salty paper-bark country** Native trees (*Melaleuca leucadendron*) so named because of their layers of paper-like bark; the *Year-Book* gives their habitat as 'in swamps, on river banks, and in the moist alluvial flats bordering the rivers, and all chiefly upon the sea-coast' (p. 159).

99:16 **shrub,** See Textual apparatus: the typist typed 'c' over 'h', and so may have been correcting to match 99:2 and the context ('undergrowth').

101:13 **doubled its queer front paws** [101:1] ... **the toe claw.** Herbivorous and not usually aggressive, the kangaroo can spar vigorously, but is more effective when grasping its enemy with its fore-paws, rocking back on its powerful tail and ripping with its large, clawed hind feet; kangaroo hunting was a colonial sport. (The female usually carries only one joey, 103:21–2.)

101:27 **back up the stream-bed,** A revision in MS for 'over the edge of the pit,' (p. 164 [186]); the kangaroo hunt is otherwise very little revised.

102:10 **the Lost Sheep ... cursing him when you find him.** Cf. the parable of the Lost Sheep in Luke xv. 4–6; there is 'rejoicing' when the sheep is found.

102:24 **at a long shot ... swobbed** Recklessly ... i.e. swabbed – slopped (the intransitive usage here may be a coinage).

103:8 **tucker ... keeping a bit of land warm** (Daily) rations or supply of food (see also 195:36), and food generally; cf. 'to get your tucker's-worth out of you' (104:9–10), meaning being made to work very hard merely for one's keep (Australianisms) ... Occupying the land so that the owner satisfies a requirement in the Land Regulations.

104:16 **Jinks,** Mild expletive (as an alternative to 'Jesus' in Australian usage).

105:11 **select.** I.e. select land for occupation – as at 150:40.

106:2 **1. Any** [105:27] ... **with rights.** For the regulations, see note on 44:32. At 105:40 'purchase' originally read 'purpose' in MS (p. 172 [194]) – a nonsense, and 'substantial' (105:34) read 'good stout'.

108:17 **holiday—*pinki*,** Aboriginal word spelled 'pinkeye', 'pinkhi', or 'pinki' (1899, *AND*).

108:29 **native cats** Spotted-bodied marsupials (genus *Dasyurinae*) with slender bodies, short legs, long hairy tails and sharp muzzles.

109:2 **more-porks** [108:30] ... **blue-birds** Native birds (except the pigeon, introduced in the late nineteenth century) with species found in s. of WA. The more-pork (usually mopoke or boobook owl, *Ninox novaeseelandiae*) is named after its call (cf. 138:11) ... The timeline is the only untraced common name, but one of the family *Timaliidae* – the white-browed babbler, *Pomatostomus superciliosus* – is native to the Avon River ... The willy-wagtail flits about restlessly, darts after prey, rides on livestock and is particularly aggressive when breeding ... The banded wren (usually, splendid wren, *Malurus splendens*) has brilliant blue plumage; the blue-bird (*Coracina novaehollandiae*) is light grey, with black forehead, face and throat.

110:38 **blue: like an ancient Briton,** Ancient Britons stained themselves with the blue dye, woad, in ceremonial animal patterns; the Picts (painted people) tattooed themselves with it.

111:13 **so-called Avon river,** The Avon is in fact the upper reaches of the Swan but had already been discovered and named before this was established in 1834 (and see note on 37:4).

111:32 **outdid Solomon ... in glory.** Cf. Matthew vi. 29: 'Solomon in all his glory was not arrayed like one of these.'

112:1 **sporting dog's yank** Rhyming slang for 'swank', i.e. in the style of the dedicated sportsman.

112:24 **riding breeches made India fashion,** I.e. jodhpurs (originally Indian), popular in the Western world from the 1920s.

112:32 **parson from York ... handle a bat.** York's cricket team was described as 'at the top of the tree as regards Cricketing in this Colony' (*Eastern Districts Chronicle*, 20 December 1879, n. p.).

113:2 **Ross Ellis ... getting the wicket of the best man from York,** Frank Lodge remembered practising 'cricket sometimes on Sundays' at 'Yangedine' in the 1890s and that Thomas Lodge was an 'enthusiastic' cricketer ('Frank Lodge's Journal', 13 weekly parts from 29 June 1962, *Beverley Times*, xii, 14 September 1962, p. 8). MLS played cricket (*Fifth Sparrow* 85), but DHL can have been only partially familiar with it (this is his only account of a match).

Readers unfamiliar with the complexities of cricket are advised to consult a standard encyclopædia such as Maurice Golesworthy, *The Encyclopædia of Cricket* (1962) to follow this scene in detail. Those familiar with cricket will nevertheless find difficulties in comprehending the match as described. Presumably MLS's account has been overlaid by DHL's additions and changes in terminology. Points at which his language and understanding of cricket are at fault include: 'twenty-six rounds' (113:8) instead of 'runs'; 'get the loose end on Ross' (113:9) when the suggestion appears to be that Jack should try to bat against Ross's loose bowling and score from it; 'Nine wickets had fallen to Easu' (113:20) when Tom's side would be out if Easu had taken nine wickets and Ross one; 'a sulky grubber which Jack naturally skied' (113:29–30) when it is unlikely Jack could loft a ball which bounces more than once; and 'a terrific full pitch came down crash over his head on to the middle wicket' (113:39–40) when a full toss from a fast bowler (which Easu presumably is) could hit the middle stump only by deflecting off Jack's head, not passing 'over' it.

A melodramatically exciting but possible match may be conjecturally reconstructed if these points are corrected. Jack goes in to bat at number ten, after Easu's side have taken eight wickets. When Jack has scored, Joe Low loses his wicket to Easu in the last ball of the over, but Jack reaches the opposite end during the dismissal. As the last man in to bat, the parson forgets his own match plan and hits three runs off the first ball of Ross's over; Jack hits three off the second; the parson a four off the third and then an (unreported) single, allowing Jack to make a single off the last ball, dropped by Herbert. He then faces Easu with increased confidence and goes on to score fifty runs, before being dismissed by Easu's uncontrolled or unsportsmanlike full toss. The second innings is a virtual impossibility in a half-day match.

113:3 **paddock,** A likely authorial correction on the original typescript: the parson calls and then talks to Jack, which would be impossible across more than one paddock: see Textual apparatus.

113:16 **If a gentleman . . . it. He . . . Finds good . . . to flame** Untraced, but such moral precepts often provided subject matter for handwriting drill in schools.

113:23 **another three,** The last page of the re-typed section (p. 166) ends mid-page with a typed full stop after 'another' (see Textual apparatus), and in both typescripts the words 'run on' have been added in pencil, while the first words on p. 167 of TSIa and b – 'three, and got in.' – have been deleted in pencil, all probably by DHL. He paginated in pencil (see Introduction footnote 54) and would probably have joined the two parts at the same time, not bothering to check the MS reading – which is restored (see Introduction footnote 30).

115:10 **cockeys** Impoverished farmers (Australianism), usually spelled 'cocky' (plural 'cockies').

115:27 **Waybacks** People of the outback or 'away back' (130:19) – (1899, *AND*).

115:30 **googlies and sneaks an' leg-breaks,** Types of bowling in cricket: a googly is a deceptive but very skilful, and a leg-break a standard, spin ball; a sneak is a (dishonourable) bowling of the ball along the ground.

116:32 **muff.** Foolish, silly person (slang).

117:14 **Pommy Grant,"** 'Pommy', Australian slang for an Englishman (1912, *AND* – but it may have been in colloquial use during the later nineteenth century); no etymological source has been authenticated but the one DHL recorded in *Kangaroo*, chap. VII (rhyming slang: immigrant–pomegranate), probably explains the choice of Jack's surname. And cf. his middle name, Hector (the famous Trojan warrior), with 307:1–2 and 309:1–3.

118:37 **sod!"** Omitted in E1 (see Textual apparatus), and almost certainly censorship by Secker or his printer. See also apparatus for 162:7 and 8; but cf. 158:13.

120:37 **a living** This had read 'sympathetic' in MS (p. 199 [223]); cf. DHL's conception of the sympathetic plexuses in *Fantasia of the Unconscious* (1922), chap. III, and his account of the horse's psyche, chap. V.

122:32 **animal force** MS originally read 'assertive power' (p. 202 [226]).

123:7 **jump in your stomach,** Untraced, but cf. the colloquialism 'to jump down your throat', meaning to interrupt violently.

123:10 **bean-feast.** Celebration or party.

123:20 **Foot . . . a half-caste Huck** Infantry ('foot') regiment . . . Part-Aboriginal – either hump ('huck')-backed (dialect, *OED*) or a reference to Huckleberry Finn's only partly civilised condition in Mark Twain's novel of the same name (1884).

123:33 **shouted** The 'ed' in 'shouted' is tilted in E1 (p. 126), evidence of a correction in proofs (see Textual apparatus); cf. the misaligned 's' in 'hires' and tilted 't' in 'this' in A1 (134:24, 144:36).

123:34 **Grand March."** Procession of couples round the room, popular in Australia in the 1880s as a formal start to a ball program (cf. ll. 35–6) and usually leading directly (without, as here, allowing the couples to disperse – 124:20–1) into a quadrille (126:12–128:28). The Master of Ceremonies organises sets of four couples in a square facing inwards (125:30–126:5). Each man's partner is beside him on his right; the woman opposite is his 'vis-a-vis' (125:29), and the one to his left is his 'corner' (125:28). The sequence of figures (cf. 127:5) commences – here those of the Lancers (128:17–19 describes its 'grand chaining', and 'playing soldiers' at 128:24 is an antic often indulged in during its fifth figure by the four men who are then in a line). In WA this quadrille frequently replaced the First Set, more common in the eastern colonies. Cf. DHL's 'Making Love to Music' (written 1927): 'Our mothers' mothers danced quadrilles and sets of Lancers ... Our mothers' mothers' mothers danced minuets and Roger de Coverleys' (*Phoenix: The Posthumous Papers of D. H. Lawrence*, ed. Edward D. McDonald, New York: Viking, 1936, p. 162); see also 251: 31–2.

125:35 **Alice?** Here and at 126:4 Mrs Ellis is called 'Jane' in all states (see Textual apparatus), but elsewhere her name is given as Alice (145:17, 189:13).

128:11 **innocent and cherubic.** Cf. Somers who in *Kangaroo* is described as having, when humiliated – as DHL was – by war-time medical examiners, 'the faculty of becoming quite deaf to anything that might disturb his equanimity' (chap. VII). Like Somers who undergoes 'a volcanic eruption in his consciousness' (chap. XII), Jack's anger is only temporarily repressed (see chap. XX).

129:5 **top sawyer.** The one in control (literally, the sawyer who works the upper handle of a pit-saw).

129:26 **Bushies ... Scotch marriage,** Uncomplicated bush-dwellers (1887, *AND*) ... Marriage by mutual declaration before witnesses.

130:10 **Missioner half-castes!** Half-caste Aborigines from a Christian mission station.

130:14 **Hump** Carry – her blanket, i.e. she is as poor as a swagman.

130:38 ***museau.*** Muzzle, often used by DHL of a woman's face (French); cf. 81:18 ('muzzle') and 321:1.

132:10 **bad enough ... a woman** Cf. 'The Crown': 'The sensitive man ... seeking a woman, knows the destruction of some basic self in him ... So that a woman becomes repulsive to him, in the thought of connection with her' (1915 version, in *Reflections on the Death*, ed. Herbert, p. 472).

132:38 **Governor General.** The Australian colonies had Governors; the first Governor-General was appointed at the Federation of the colonies into the Commonwealth of Australia in 1901.

134:10 **just the ticket** Exactly what is needed (slang).

134:21 **wonderful pictures ... Blessed Son."** Mary was probably the heroine in 'The House of Ellis': see Introduction, p. xlix. MLS, a former High Anglican on the road to Quakerism, may have wished to muffle her dalliance with Roman Catholicism in a character partly based on herself; see her requested deletions (in Introduction, p. xl). At 321:8–9 Mary is described as 'being drawn to the Roman Catholic Church' – as is the central character in *Letters of a V.A.D.* (passim; see also *Fifth Sparrow* 79). Mary is 'so self-sacrificing' (177:7); MLS referred to herself as 'the fifth sparrow' (Luke xii. 6), and her writings contain abundant evidence of self-denigration used defensively (see Paul Eggert, 'Lawrence in Western Australia: Mollie Skinner and *The Boy in the Bush*', *Journal of the D. H. Lawrence Society*, iv, 1987–8, 26–7). Boyd Blessington's interest in Mary may be based on a similar episode (*c.* 1907) in MLS's life: when an 'honoured citizen' with 'grown-up children' proposed to her she was 'appalled at the thought of taking on a man I did not love' (*Fifth Sparrow* 69; cf. 248:15–249:8).

134:38 **lass of his own sort ... find ... ugly harness,** MS had read: 'simpleton ... land ... ghastly harness,' (p. 223 [248]).

135:2 **like a young witch, in a whirlwind.** May be a confused reference to L. Frank Baum's popular *The Wonderful Wizard of Oz* (Chicago, 1900) in which Dorothy is carried off by a cyclone to the land of Oz where she has dealings with witches.

136:2 **"Cheer Boys Cheer!" ... "God Bless the Prince of Wales," ... "John Brown's Body," ... "Britons Never Never Never."** Air of farewell to a regiment going abroad, by Henry Russell (1812–1900) ... Song (1862), by Welsh pianist and composer (Henry) Brinley Richards (1819–85), and words by J. Ceiriog Hughes ... 'Say brothers will you meet us' is an old song with additional words by C. S. Hall and arranged by William Steffe (l. 1: 'John Brown's body lies a mouldering in the grave') ... 'Rule, Britannia' (l. 2 of the chorus: 'Britons never never never shall be slaves'), by Thomas Arne (1710–78) and words probably by James Thomson (1700–48), is from the masque *Alfred* (1740) by Thomson and David Mallett (1705?–65).

139:28 **sweating his soul away ... in the tropics,** As DHL had in Ceylon, in 1922: cf. *Letters*, iv. 226.

140:18 **obstropulous** I.e. obstreperous (probably Lennie's coinage).

141:29 **Almighty God, Maker of Heaven and Earth ... always Jehovah ... or Isaiah,** From the Creed in *The Book of Common Prayer*: 'I believe in one God the Father Almighty, Maker of Heaven and earth...' ... Jack's preference (which strengthens – e.g. 167:23–4, 319:24–31 – and develops into Patriarchal ambitions by chap. XXIV; see note on 330:18) is for the Old Testament God, Jehovah, who communed directly with and gave protection and power to his servants: David (2 Samuel ii. 1; who also – scandalously, vi. 20 – danced naked before Him; cf. 141:28), Jacob (Genesis xxviii. 12–15), Abraham (ibid. xvii. 1), Moses (Exodus iii. 4–iv. 17), Joshua (Joshua i. 1–9) and Isaiah (Isaiah vii. 3–9); and cf. 'Do what ... the Lord' (141:23–4) with Hoshea, David's son, who 'did that which was right in the sight of the Lord' (2 Kings xviii. 3), including destroying the shrines and images of other gods. The Lord's blessing is generally recognised and respected by these men's people – which explains Jack's surprise and resentment at 337:5–10.

142:20 **"Ha-a-appy Ho-ome ... with Thee!"** Possibly from a forgotten 'revival' hymn, or a parodic composite: cf. 'Jerusalem, my happy home', a famous medieval anonymous hymn, and the ending of 'The saints of God, their conflict past' by William Dalrymple Maclagan (1826–1910): 'That with all saints our rest may be/ In that bright paradise with Thee'.

143:35 **allus** Always.

144:15 **hard-hearted grandfather.** MS (p. 240 [265]) originally read 'old devil of a grandfather', and Gran had been at first a 'witch' rather than a 'cat' (144:5).

144:22 **Annie Brockman died the other day.** The Brockman family became part of the landed pseudo-aristocracy of WA; Anne Francis Brockman died in 1876 (which could be 'the other day' to Gran).

146:25 **"A blue [146:19] ... dawn O'."** American Negro song, 'Clear [or 'Clare'] the kitchen' or 'De Kentucky Screamer', *c.* 1835; words and music anonymous.

147:2 **Daniel-like,** In Daniel iii. 14–25 three men are cast into a furnace for refusing to bow down to Nebuchadnezzar's image of gold; God saves them. DHL may be referring to the fourth figure seen in the flames (iii. 25), but he is conventionally interpreted as an angel.

148:2 **"Oh Jane ... the rye—"** '(When the) Bloom is on the Rye' or 'My Pretty Jane' (1832), words by Edward Fitzball, music by Henry Rowley Bishop (1786–1855).

150:8 **go hence and be no more seen.** Cf. Psalm xxxix. 13 ['go hence, and be no more'].

150:18 **ol' Nelson ... 'Kiss me 'Ardy' ... 'Ardy kissed him,** Words uttered by the dying Lord (Horatio) Nelson (1758–1805) to Flag-Captain Thomas Masterman Hardy (1769–1839) in the moment of victory at the Battle of Trafalgar; Hardy knelt and kissed Nelson's cheek.

151:6 **sulkies** Light, two-wheeled one-horse carriages; cf. 'shay', of similar meaning, at 185:7: both terms are used in Australia in preference to 'buggy', which occurs more frequently in the text (e.g. 150:29, 195:34; and cf. *Letters*, iv. 263).

152:37 **the foolish virgins** See Matthew xxv. 1–3.

153:12 **skeered** Scared.

154:40 **aged female Time,** I.e. a female version of Old Father Time.

157:6 **queer evening noise of the magpies,** Cf. *Kangaroo*, chap. v: 'they would gurgle little answers in their throats, and cock their heads on one side'.

157:18 **Sunday black reach-me-downs ... cricketing boots,** MS originally had Easu dressed in 'riding breeches and white shirt and cartridge belt' (p. 262 [287]). 'Reach-me-downs' are cheap ready-made or second-hand clothes (here, trousers).

158:2 **Jack the Giant-killer.** English folk-tale also known as 'The History of Jack and the Giants'; Jack's fearlessness and ingenuity enable him to kill many giants including Cormilan, Blunderboar and the two-headed Thunderdel.

161:33 **floor.** I.e. ground: a colloquialism DHL uses elsewhere (e.g. *Aaron's Rod*, ed. Kalnins, p. 33 and note).

162:6 **to talk wide.** I.e. to talk wide of the truth, to mislead.

162:22 **agony that . . . a strange** MS (p. 270 [296]) originally began: 'infinity of pain that it cleared all the mists from his head in the sheer scream of'. Another MS revision of the fight was 'Easu stared . . . Dr Rackett' (163:9–11) which had read: 'But neither hero rose. Time was up, and he went anxiously to Jack, followed by Tom and Len.' (p. 272 [298]).

162:28 **Man is . . . higher level.** Reflects DHL's 1917 reading of *Apocalypse Unsealed* (New York, 1910) by James M. Pryse (see *The Letters of D. H. Lawrence*, ed. James T. Boulton and Andrew Robertson, Cambridge, 1984, iii. 150 n. 3). The yoga theory of 'chakras' or 'plexuses' – nerve centres in the spine which are said to correspond to ascending levels of consciousness – had continuing currency in DHL's writings: e.g. in *Apocalypse*, ed. Kalnins, pp. 5–6. See also note on 120:37.

164:28 **diminishing slit, Hun-like.** I.e. the appearance of Huns, the Asiatic race of warlike nomads who invaded Europe in 375. According to DHL in *Movements in European History* (1921), the men 'were dreadful to look at . . . Tiny black eyes sparkled deep in the flesh of the flat face', ed. Philip Crumpton (Cambridge, 1989), pp. 66–7.

165:17 **the one now.** I.e. the one to be concerned about now (colloquialism).

166:19 **"And when . . . awful pains."** One of Charles Wesley's hymns, 'And am I only born to die' (1763), is similar; it continues: 'What after death for me remains?/ Celestial joys or hellish pains/ To all eternity'.

167:1 **Love your enemies.** Matthew v. 44.

167:26 ***This is my Body***, Christ's words at the Last Supper (Luke xxii. 19–20), used in the consecration of the bread and wine ('Blood', l. 27).

170:27 **their hands cut off, in the old days,"** Cf. Exodus xxi. 23–4: 'Thou shalt give life for life . . . hand for hand'; and cf. 169:27–8.

171:2 **The Great Passing.** The original title in MS was 'The Great Change' (p. 286 [312]).

171:31 **he could not read** [171:24] **. . . peculiar Sundayness** Cf. *Kangaroo*, chap. x, where Somers says: 'I don't wonder they can't read English books . . . All the scruples and the emotions and the regrets in English novels do seem waste of time out here' . . . And chap. ii: 'This was Sunday afternoon [in NSW], but with none of the surfeited dreariness of English Sunday afternoons.'

172:16 **"Who shall ... sworn deceitfully."** Psalm xxiv. 3–4 ['... not lifted up his soul unto ...'].

172:30 **to pluck them out.** Cf. Matthew xviii. 9: 'if thine eye offend thee, pluck it out'.

172:35 **the cup.** I.e. his fate (see Matthew xxvi. 42).

173:8 **Seraphim ... a dark side.** The Seraphim stand above God's throne ('each one had six wings; with twain he covered his face'; Isaiah vi. 2–6) and the Cherubim are on either side (xxxvii. 16). DHL's description was different in 1914 (commenting on Mrs Henry Jenner's *Christian Symbolism*, 1910): 'I cannot forget that the Cherubim who are nearest God and palpitate with his brightness are *absorbed in praise*' (*Letters*, ii. 250).

173:14 **"Forsake me ... to come."** Psalm lxxi. 18 ['Now also when I am old and gray-headed, O God, forsake me not; until I have shewed thy strength unto this ... to every one that is to come'].

173:19 **great everlasting wind ... of the Lord,** Cf. the 'rushing mighty wind' of God at Pentecost (Acts ii. 2), and 'woman ... can only find Him as the ... Wind', *Study of Thomas Hardy*, ed. Steele, p. 85.

173:36 **"There is ... stars— — —There is ... and a spiritual body— —"** Cf. 174:34–5: DHL is adapting and arguing with 1 Corinthians xv. 40–4: 'There are also celestial bodies, and bodies terrestrial: but the glory of the celestial is one, and the glory of the terrestrial is another. There is ... stars: for one star differeth from another star in glory. So also is the resurrection of the dead. It is sown in corruption; it is raised in incorruption: It is sown in dishonour; it is raised in glory: it is sown in weakness; it is raised in power: It is sown a natural body: it is raised a spiritual body. There is ... and there is a spiritual body.'

174:18 **full moon had followed him** [174:12] **... destroy him,** Cf. *Kangaroo*, chap. 1: 'one night at the time of the full moon he walked alone into the bush. A huge electric moon ... He felt it was watching, and waiting. Following with certainty, just behind his back ... Richard S. had never quite got over that glimpse of terror in the Westralian bush.'

174:20 **destroy ... consume** See Textual apparatus (and at 305:34): neither first edition prints the revised reading. DHL's revision was in TSIa only, and A1 reverted to the original reading given in the E1 proofs. Since two undoubtedly authorial proof revisions nearby were incorporated into A1 (174:17 and 174:21), 'not' at 174:12 is probably authorial too.

174:26 **"The sun is thy right hand ... in the two hands of the Lord.** Adaptation of 1 Corinthians xv. 41 (see note on 173:36) and Revelation i. 16 ['he had in his right hand seven stars'].

175:8 **roaring yellow ... following him,** See Textual apparatus: DHL had already revised this in MS: '<burning> ⌜roaring⌝ of the ⌜yellow⌝ ... ⌜following him.⌝' (p. 293 [319]).

175:16 **the moon "raises her lamp above ... stars are "candles" in heaven.** Both metaphors are Shakespearean but not usually infused with such unproblematic innocence (e.g. *Macbeth* II. iv. 7 and i. 5); the closest in feeling are in *All's Well That Ends Well* II. i. 164) ('Moist Hesperus hath quenched her sleepy lamp') and *Romeo and Juliet* III. v. 9 ('Night's candles are burnt out').

175:28 **a natural dislike of Shelley and vegetarians and socialists ... Blake's pictures ... of underwater.** Percy Bysshe Shelley's poetry, in particular his ode 'To a Skylark' (written 1820), was for DHL a reference point for excessive spirituality and denial of the body: see *Study of Thomas Hardy*, ed. Steele, pp. 71, 126, and 'The Theatre' in *Twilight in Italy* (1916). The Goddards in *Mr Noon* (see especially chap. I) are 'socialists and vegetarians' (ed. Vasey, p. 5), and cf. *Letters*, v. 355. After 1917 DHL dabbled with radical leftist politics (*The Letters of D. H. Lawrence*, ed. Boulton and Robertson, iii. 4–8) but by March 1920 he admitted his 'remaining belief ... in Socialism' was dying 'more and more as the time goes by' (ibid., p. 486). See his 'Epilogue' (written September 1924) to *Movements in European History* (ed. Crumpton, pp. 261–3) for a retrospective account of his disenchantment ... *The Book of Urizen* (1794), plate 15, shows three men leaning from the sky with an arm and beards waving downwards, and numbers of Blake's designs show people in fire or water (but Blake reproductions were rare in the 1870s and 80s).

175:32 **this Hindu Nirvana business.** Buddhist theology, not Hindu. Cf. *Letters*, iv. 218: '[the] high-flownness of Buddhism ... exists mostly on paper ... its denial of the soul makes it always rather barren'; and 'Things' (written 1927 and collected in *The Lovely Lady*, 1933).

177:2 **the body of straight fire.** The metaphor is an adaptation of Exodus xiii. 21: 'And the Lord went before them ... in a pillar of fire'.

178:7 **was!** In transcribing his correction to TSIb (see Textual apparatus for 178:7 and 8), DHL chose a different place for the punctuation, whereas at 214:14 and 261:14 he appears to have mistranscribed.

178:13 **"There is a quiet ... Was that scripture?** The last two sentences are biblical; the first is an adaptation: see note on 173:36.

179:19 **tantalus,** A decanter stand secured by a hidden lock (1898, *OED*).

180:11 **brick Church of England ... wooden Presbyterian Church ... slab Meeting House of the Methodists.** The (implied) relative prosperity of the congregations is only partially right: in 1882 in York there were 333 practising Wesleyan Methodists and five times as many Anglicans, but there was no Presbyterian church (in 1882, the only one in the colony was in Perth). The Church of England (reddish brick, 1858) is the most substantial of the churches in York; and before the present Methodist church was built (stone, 1888), a smaller church was used (brick, 1852–4).

180:32 **dark, strange Australian night ... aboriginal bush again.** Cf. *Kangaroo*, chap. II: 'the bush had gone dark and spectral again ... As soon as night came, all the raggle-taggle of amorphous white settlements disappeared, and the continent ... reassumed its strange, unvisited glamour'.

184:37 **pinch.** Steep incline (as at 185:13): *OED* gives this as dialect but it is also an Australianism.

185:11 **Easu's horses ... afraid they** The A1 compositor or DHL evidently attempted to make sense of defective copy: see Textual apparatus for 185:10 and 11.

186:2 **Hymn Number 225** [185:35] ... **hearts expect——"** Hymn 225 in *Hymns Ancient and Modern*, 'Brief life is here our portion' (trans. J. M. Neale from Latin), ll. 29–32; ll. 31–6 are quoted at 186:21–6.

186:5 **Blagg** See Textual apparatus (and for 190:7). Previously the name had been typed 'Blogg'; DHL fell into line, changing 'Blagg' to 'Blogg'.

188:20 **Rob-Roy sails from Geraldton about a month from now;** The *Government Gazette of Western Australia* for 1883 announced that the S. S. *Rob Roy* sailed from Fremantle to Cossack (near Roebourne, l. 18) approximately once a month, stopping at ports, including Geraldton, along the way. Predicted departure dates from Geraldton for winter 1883 (see Appendix I) were: 12 June, 15 delayed to 24 July, 24 August.

188:22 **Midland country.** I.e. the region between Perth and Geraldton. Mr George's estimate (188:27–8) of the distance from Beverley (Wandoo) to Geraldton is fairly accurate.

190:15 **go to England.** While in the 1880s there were government-funded elementary schools throughout the colony (Len is now about 14 years, 51:10), there was only one (government) high school – Perth Boys'.

190:37 **'Here rests ... a friend.'** From 'Elegy Written in a Country Church-yard' (1751) by Thomas Gray (1716–71), ll. 117–24.

194:8 **eyes of the aborigines ... Great Serpent** Cf. *Kangaroo*, chap. v: 'aborigines with his wonderful dark eyes that have such a incomprehensible ancient shine in them, across gulfs of unbridged centuries' ... A reference to the Rainbow Snake (cf. 'eternal, brilliant', l. 4) of Aboriginal legend, but its life-giving capacity (cf. l. 9) is associated with water, not anger (l. 8).

195:19 **travelling due west from York ... Paddy's Crossing.** Tom and Jack go w. over the Darling Range (196:5) and then down to near Midland or Guildford; the next day, leaving Paddy's Crossing, they go n. (perhaps via Upper Swan, towards Gingin) to Uncle John Grant's farm (more likely to be on the coastal plain than 'in the hills', 320:18), but their route is hazily defined. If MLS's mother's great uncle, George Leake's substantial farm at Upper Swan is the model for the Grant farm, Tom and Jack's taking a full day to ride 10 miles sits oddly beside their previous day's 60 (if Guildford was their destination). Gran locates the farm 'beyond Atherton' (77:35–6) – not a WA place name; cf. note on 93:34.

But MLS, apparently drawing on family stories, had a Paddy O'Toole (cf. his initials with 201:28–32) operating a ferry crossing prior to the construction of the Causeway in 1843 and running a wayside inn, called Halfway House, at Point Walter (typescripts of radio broadcasts, 'The Causeway', dated in an unknown hand, 1955, and 'The Old Mill'; Battye).

195:27 **the ridge ... huge karri trees ... ended here with a jerk.** Karri does not grow along the ridge of the Darling Range w. of York; jarrah predominates, giving way to the tuart (*Eucalyptus gomphocephala*) of the coastal plain.

196:8 **Whenever man drives his tent-pegs deep ... waters of sorrow.** Cf. Isaiah xxxiii. 20 (RV): 'Jerusalem ... an immovable tent, whose stakes will never be plucked up' (and xxii. 23 for the term '[tent-]peg') ... Echo of (or confusion with) 'man of sorrows' (liii. 3).

196:36 **He grows grapes, and makes wine** Formerly a common practice for keepers of wayside inns in WA.

197:9 **Tom Coo-eed!** Originally in MS 'Tom Halloo'd!' – which seems more appropriate in the circumstances (p. 329 [355]).

197:14 **P. O. T.?"** I.e. a pot – a measure of beer.

197:40 **oleographs of the Queen and the Prince Consort ... wire things with coloured beads** Reproductions printed in oil colours of paintings of Queen Victoria (1819–1901) and her husband Prince Albert (1819–61) ... Possibly an abacus, a school toy.

198:11 **Madame Tussaud's ... Last Trump.** Waxworks (est. 1802) of Marie Tussaud, née Grosholtz (1760–1850), in London ... The trumpet that will signal the end of the world when the dead shall be raised (1 Corinthians xv. 52).

199:12 **mole trousers,** I.e. mole-skin trousers.

200:4 **foine** I.e. fine.

201:26 **wet the baby's eye.** Cf. the colloquial usages: 'to wet the baby's head', meaning to celebrate a child's birth; and 'to wet the other eye', meaning to drink one glass after the other.

202:7 ***The Stranger within our gates!*" ... whether the baby was meant, or himself.** Cf. 'Welcome, little stranger!' printed or embroidered on articles for nursery use in the early nineteenth century (*OED*), and 'thy stranger that is within thy gates' (Exodus xx. 10).

202:10 **that black limb o' salvation!"** Ironic play on the traditional 'limb [agent or functionary] of Satan' (see 199:19); in 'Noise of Swans', MLS describes Steve as 'that smart young limb of Satan' (p. 28).

202:16 **Westminster chimes** Clock chimes on four bells or gongs playing the tune of the chimes on the House of Parliament clock in London.

203:16 **splother** Onomatopoeiac combination of 'splatter' and 'bother' (coinage); cf. 'splosh'.

204:1 **Good on y'!** Colloquial Australian expression of approval (1907, *AND*).

204:4 **whure** Obsolete spelling of 'whore' (*OED*): a non-standard – Celtic, or dialect – pronunciation in this melting pot of nationalities.

205:19 **mostly ... half** In MS originally: 'all ... all' (p. 342 [368]).

205:26 **The dim-lighted ... figures moved.** Cf. the rustic dance at Chaseborough in chap. x of Hardy's *Tess of the d'Urbervilles* (1891), first included in the 1912 Wessex edition – probably the edition DHL read in 1914 (*Study of Thomas*

Hardy, ed. Steele, p. xx n. 7): 'on drawing nearer [Tess] perceived that it was a cloud of dust, lit by candles within the outhouse ... When she came close and looked in she beheld indistinct forms racing up and down to the figure of the dance'. Added interlinearly to MS (p. 342 [368]) were 'The air ... in the barn.' (205:29–30), and 'in a haze of dust' (205:33); and cf. the routine of Angel Clare's life at Talbothays dairy with 109:22–5.

205:36 **costermonger outfit ... pearl buttons,** Traditional Cockney costume for roadside fruiterers (originally, apples – costards).

206:3 **Sandy and Taffy ... *British Grenadiers* or *Campbells Are Comin'*** Nicknames for a Scotsman and a Welshman ... Traditional songs patriotic, respectively, to England (late seventeenth century and of unknown origin) and Scotland (['The Campbells Are Coming'], eighteenth century).

206:34 **"Shan't I ... flore space—"** These lines replaced '"Shan't I though! She's comin'! She's comin'!"' in MS; at 207:2 'Cockroaches' replaced 'Crickets' (pp. 344–5 [370–1]).

211:15 **that they ... his last.** MS (p. 339 [377]) originally read: 'you know, when he dies.' See note on 212:38.

211:25 **"Bush mad!"** Deranged by the isolation and privations of living in the bush (this is *AND*'s earliest printed usage).

212:38 **I died when I left my mother's husband's house."** Uncle John Grant, the illegitimate son of Lizzie Reid (therefore, Jack's cousin; cf. 213:13–15, 34–6), was banished by his step-father (76:29–36); this is the 'scandal' of 253:13. Tom's pleasantries suggest Uncle John assumed his maternal aunt's married name (219:14–18) so as to register his farm in Jack's name and avoid forfeiture to the Crown on his death (211:14–15, 213:30–1). But even if the registration preceded Jack's birth, legality is assured by the will: see 312:5–11. Land held by occupation licence could be transferred, but Jack had to be alerted to his inheritance so he could fulfil his obligations as licensee. (When Rackett assured Jack that his welcome at the farm was a 'Case of mistaken identity' and inquired as to the owner's name, 212:5, 20, he was dissimulating; see 210:31–2.)

213:20 **baldachino** I.e. baldachin (DHL uses the Italian): a canopy above an altar or throne used in a cathedral or religious procession; cf. Frieda's usage, 'baldachino hats' (*The Letters of D. H. Lawrence*, ed. James T. Boulton, Cambridge, 1979, i. 449).

213:27 **dog-leg fences,** Fence formed of bare branches of the gum tree laid obliquely, several side by side, with the ends overlapping and an upright stick at intervals, with a fork at the top, on which some of the cross-branches rest.

214:38 **kill a fowl ... make ink with ... gall.** A confusion between gall (from the liver) and the gall (a vegetable excrescence formed on plants and trees) used to make ink – needed, here, to write the will.

216:10 **their corroborees.** MLS described a corroboree (Aboriginal gathering of sacred, festive or warlike character) in *Black Swans* (chap. XI, 'Corroboree', pp. 125–32), a version of which DHL may have read (see Introduction, p. xxiv).

216:30 **Moloch.** The god of the Ammonites to whom children were sacrificed; thus anything requiring terrible sacrifice.

217:9 **Death has** [216:40] ... **road. Let** MS has several revisions (pp. 348–9 [386–7]): '⌜Death has ... And ever-recurring.⌝ ... <careless> ⌜reckless⌝ ... <lilt> ⌜will⌝ ... ⌜splendidly⌝ ... [217:6] <to death> ⌜the same⌝ ... <hearse> ⌜slow⌝ ... gallantly, <let> ⌜let me have the black joy of the road. Let⌝'.

219:29 **Something somebody had told him.** See Gran's remarks at 76:14–36, 77:34–40 and 144:10–11.

220:7 **tiny bushman's flowers sparking** Possibly 'bushman's torch' (*Sarcocaulon burmanii*) which grows (in Australia) to a height of one foot but is a native of South Africa.

220:16 **high road merely a bush-track** The Old North Road was mostly a rough, often muddy track through the bush and meandered from one homestead to another. It 'came down to the sea' near Jurien Bay (228:19) and then 'went inland again' (228:31).

220:40 **enormous hollow tree** [220:33] ... **sandal wood.** MLS's 'Noise of Swans' reads 'one day they came to the camp of a grey bearded man who lived in the bole of a great tree with a black wife and a dozen children' (p. 33) ... Sandalwood (used for ornamental carving and burnt as incense) was collected in many parts of the colony for export.

221:3 **sundowner** Swagman so called because he arrives at a homestead at sundown in time to eat but not to work; this one is showing unusual industry (Australianism).

223:5 **putting over his horse and drawing to the girl's side** I.e. moving his horse so as to be closer to the girl on horseback: in MS (p. 358 [396]) 'drawing to' replaced 'riding at'.

223:29 **Tom's or Jack's relations** [223:16] ... **huge tracts of land** In the 1850s many York-based pastoralists took part in the opening up of the n. – hence the web of relationships. The Gales moved n. from York; Major John Logue, a substantial landowner at Walkaway, married the daughter of Lockyer Burges, owner of much land in the n. (and the Avon valley) and of a cattle company; and there were Brockmans near Gingin.

224:23 **kangaroo and 'possum snarers ... sugar ... bark for export, and manna-gum.** Hunting supplemented the income of farmers and itinerant workers along the Old North Road and elsewhere: opossum skins were used for rugs, coats and carpets; kangaroo skins for harness, upholstery and footwear ... Slang for money (see 225:15) ... Wattle and redgum bark were used for tanning but manna-gum trees are not native to WA.

224:26 **fifty-three ... jinkers ... swabs,** Poker ('Poker with the bug' or 'Joker Poker') played with the fifty-two card pack plus a wild card ... men working with jinkers (see 225:7–8) ... contemptible, useless people (colloquialism).

225:14 **Waltzing Matilda."** Written in 1895 (published 1917) by Australian poet A. B. ('Banjo') Paterson (1864–1941); it is about the life of a swagman; the poem (and subsequently, song) gave the expression currency. 'Billy' (l. 13) does not mean swag: see notes on 86:26 and 90:12.

225:20 **Clink is . . . Chow . . . ticketer . . . Child's Guide to Knowledge** In MS, DHL twice wrote 'Chink' for 'Clink' (see Textual apparatus for 225:17; but in *Kangaroo*, chap. IV, he uses 'Chink' correctly). Chink and Chow both mean Chinese (Australian English); clink means prison: DHL may either have miscopied 'The House of Ellis', or copied its typing error . . . A 'ticketer' is a convict ('lag') with a 'ticket-of-leave' giving conditional freedom within a district of the colony for the term of his sentence . . . Fanny Ward's *The Child's Guide to Knowledge; being a collection of useful and familiar questions and answers on every-day subjects, adapted for young persons, and arranged in the most simple and easy language*; by 1880 it was in its 53rd edition (Simpkin, Marshall and Co.).

225:23 **dog is . . . bully—tinned meat . . . *stouch*?"** Canned meat in general (here, bully beef) was referred to as 'tinned dog' (Australianism) . . . DHL's revisions of 'stouch' (see Textual apparatus) indicate he did not know this Australianism meaning fighting or violence, usually spelled 'stoush' (1893, *AND*). 'Landin' him one' (l. 24) is slang for 'punching him'.

225:28 **remittance man . . . the line,** Tom's contempt for a man's reliance on a regular remittance from his family in England was widely shared . . . the equator.

226:5 **on the high fiddle,** Pretentiously; cf. 'to play first fiddle' (coinage).

226:18 **One youth . . . Australia's leading lights.** Cf. MLS's recording that John Forrest had walked, 'when he reached teen-age' (i.e. *c.* 1860), 110 miles to Perth through bushland from near Bunbury, to go to Bishop Hale's school (typescript of a radio broadcast, 'We Called Him "Jarrah Jack"', *c.* 1955, p. 2; Battye). See Introduction footnote 5.

226:25 **Never-Never,** Unsettled or unexplored regions remote from civilisation, here northern WA.

226:28 **earnings . . . coast-town** MS originally read: 'savings . . . later'; 'trailers' at 226:20 had read 'men' (p. 364 [402]).

226:35 **dago boat "from the other side."** Foreign boat from the (Australian) eastern colonies. *OED* records the first usage of 'Dago' ('of the Latin races'; an Americanism) as 1888.

226:39 **in Colombo,** DHL arrived in Colombo, the port of Ceylon, on 13 March 1922, and he stayed in the hills at Kandy.

227:9 **what Gingin means?"** Probably derives from an Aboriginal word meaning 'footprint' (but it may come from 'janjin', meaning pear tree).

227:29 **wild, brown, aboriginal honey.** Darker honey of native bees; 'aboriginal' originally read 'passionate' in MS (p. 366 [404]).

228:10 **experience . . . reserve vitality,** Replaced in MS: 'human beings . . . unknown life,' (p. 367 [405]); and 'indigo ocean . . . the nearness,' (228:32–3) superseded 'indigo ⌜ocean⌝, with' (p. 368 [406]).

229:19 **schooner "Venus";** A licensed cargo (sailing) boat, *Venus*, took part in a regatta on Perth Water in 1870 (*Perth Gazette and W. A. Times*, 22 April 1870, p. 3).

229:26 **greasy dirty dungarees ... disreputable outcasts.** Jack Skinner returned to Perth in 'a disreputable ulster flapping over his dungarees and vest', having worked his passage from the North-West to Fremantle on a steamer transporting sheep, and 'stayed in the stinking hold with them' (*Fifth Sparrow* 32; cf. ll. 16, 20).

229:29 **Two years, nearer three ... more than four years since Jack landed** Jack and Tom left Wandoo in June 1883; if it is 'more than four years' since June 1882, Tom and Jack must have been away longer than three years (cf. chap. title and 258:26).

232:5 **squatters** Influential holders of very substantial amounts of grazing land (Australianism: in the eastern colonies land had often originally been held – 'squatted on' – without government permission).

232:38 **Circe.** Sorceress in Homer's *Odyssey* who turns Ulysses' companions into swine when they taste her liquor; but he resists her spells, eventually forcing her to restore his men (cf. 233:39–234:2).

233:7 **the eastern "swim"** Social life in the eastern colonies – settled earlier and much more populous.

233:11 **Provident concern,** Provident (or Friendly) society which provides for the relief or maintenance of its members in sickness or need.

233:33 **She was** [233:23] **... way-back Circe.** Except for 'Poor Tom ... silent disgust.' (ll. 25–6) this passage is crossed through in pencil on TSIb (p. 366), and 'Run on' is written in an unidentified hand in the margin. There are authorial corrections on this page (see Textual apparatus entries for 233:5, 6 and 7), and since the passage is intact in TSIa, the censorship in TSIb must be the responsibility of Secker's office (see Introduction, p. xlii). The deletions must have been transmitted to A1 via the duplicate E1 proofs, but the two paragraphs (see entry for 233:26) were not run together as A1 was already typeset. For the deletion at 233:38, see Introduction, p. xliii; Secker neglected to delete a later, linked reference to Lucy's perspiration at 267:25.

234:3 **"Honeysuckle"** Not an actual place name in WA.

234:12 **By** From here to 235:28 is deleted in pencil in TSIb, and there are authorial corrections within the passage; see note on 233:33. The omission is again almost certainly the responsibility of Secker's office, and was transmitted to A1 via the duplicate E1 proofs (in its absence 268:23–4 makes little sense). DHL's only correction which does not fall into a silent emendation category (at 234:17), and two editorial corrections, are recorded in the Textual apparatus, but variants between MS and TSIa and b, being of no textual significance, are not. A later passage of 19 words (at 245:33–4) which refers to the omitted letter was deleted in A1 only; see Textual apparatus.

234:15 **"Mr Harry Smith/ West Australia"** In *Fifth Sparrow* 53–4, MLS reported letters in outback regions being addressed vaguely: 'Harry or Ikey Smith,/ Taken up land by a lake,/ Dumbell or some such (meaning Dumbleyung),/ Wagin'.

234:37 **the futre King of England ... broke his por mother's heart once more.** Prince Albert Victor Christian Edward (b. 1864), known as Prince Edward, was heir presumptive to the throne, being the eldest son of Albert Edward, Prince of Wales (1841–1910), later Edward VII. He died in January 1892 at Sandringham ('his palace', l. 34) of pneumonia, only six weeks after his betrothal – which helps explain the extensive mourning. He was the first of Princess Alexandra's children to die, but 'his por mother's heart' probably means that of his grandmother, Queen Victoria, who referred to the death of 'my dear grandson, whom I loved as a son' as an 'occasion more sad and tragical than any but one [her husband's death]' ('The Queen to Her People' in Charles Bullock, *"Ich Dien: I Serve": Prince Edward: A Memory*, n. d. [1892], pp. 14, 13). In December 1892 Prince Edward's brother George had had typhoid (cf. 'fevvers', l. 36).

236:18 **dry it up ... My shout ... Shout it back** Be quiet (258:8 has the more usual form, 'dry up') ... My turn to buy drinks ... I'll return the shout (Australianisms).

236:21 **Best an' bitter's mine."** I.e. 'I'll have "best and bitter"': a mixture of kinds of beer.

236:26 **posted a** Originally read in MS: 'kept one cheque, even if not a big one' (p. 388 [420]).

236:30 **out of the Hotel and down the platform,** The present Fremantle railway station (built 1907) contained a bar (although not a hotel) giving on to the main platform.

237:5 **Turns me right over."** Makes me feel sick (slang); MS originally began: 'Makes me feel fair' (p. 388 [420]).

237:22 **sweeps!"** Scoundrels (colloquialism).

238:8 **stand y' a fiver apiece** Give you each a five-pound note (slang).

238:23 **Stow it,** Shut up (slang).

238:27 **Miners Refuge,** Probably an ironic reference to a hotel (playing on the notion of an institution, based on philanthropic principles, providing accommodation for workmen); no contemporary mention of a Miners Refuge has been found – gold mining had only just begun. The Freemasons' Hotel (238:37), located (in the 1880s) at the corner of William and Wellington Streets, was, by the 1890s, one of the most popular for miners.

238:32 **the long principal street** Hay Street; at 239:6 'Hay' originally read 'Market' in MS (p. 392 [424]).

239:6 ***in puris naturalibus.*** Stark naked (Latin).

239:24 ***The Booklovers Latest!*** DHL visited a Perth bookshop, 'The Booklovers,' opened in 1900 (*Letters*, iv. 237).

240:30 **ponies.** A pony is colloquial either for a small glass of beer or for £25. DHL probably intended the latter but was unsure of the amount: cf. 244:1 where it refers to Mr George's offer of £5 each (238:8).

240:36 **stop one on me,** Have a beer at my expense (Australian slang; this is *AND*'s earliest citation).

240:39 **'arf a mo'!"** Just (half) a moment (slang; 1903, *OED*).

241:25 **pecos y' amuth me."** Because you amuse me.

242:9 **a dead cert f' Belmont** A horse certain to win a race at Headquarters Course of the Western Australian Turf Club (est. 1852) at Belmont, Perth (slang).

242:12 **lettin' me inter th' know,"** Passing on inside information (colloquial).

242:30 **on the divvy with a book** I.e. on to a dividend (payout from a bet) with a bookmaker ('div': 1891, *AND*). To 'get twenties' (242:34) is to place a bet at odds of twenty to one, but 'a safe forty [pounds]' (242:36) would be accurate if Tom and Jack had a pound each, whereas they have only 'about a quid atween [them]' (242:35).

242:37 **"Bob on!"** Let's anxiously await the result (of the race), then (slang; 1925, *OED*).

242:40 **tip it y'** Give you private or secret information (colloquial; 1891, *OED*).

243:15 **cramblin'** Shaky, tottering; figuratively, lame (dialect).

243:19 **"Bon soir, as Frenchy used to say?"** Literally, 'Good evening', i.e. 'I'm a wake-up now – I understand the "language" [the conman's tricks] now'.

243:23 **"Fireproof!"** I.e. so fortified by alcohol as not to feel it if one were on fire.

243:34 **Ned Kelly.** Famous (eastern) Australian bushranger and popular hero (1854–80).

246:5 **Weld Club ... Private Secretary.** Gentlemen's club named after Frederick Aloysius Weld (1823–91, Governor of WA 1869–74), opened in 1871 and patronised by political and business leaders ... I.e. the Governor's private secretary (this read 'Governor' at first in MS, p. 402 [434]); Frederick Napier Broome (1842–96) was Governor, 1883–9.

246:17 **Representative.** I.e. the Governor, the representative of the British Crown (see preceding note).

246:27 **bill-head ... an owl of a dancer.** List of dancing partners, programme [literally, printed account form] ... Grave (like an owl) – uncarefree, anxious – when dancing.

246:29 **"Don't desert me, you swine."** MS originally read: '"Go on! I'm not your keeper' (p. 403 [435]).

247:8 **space around him ... *noli me tangere*** MS (p. 404 [436]) read 'space between them' at first, and 'a perfect child' at l. 11 is an interlinear addition ... 'Touch me not', John xx. 17 (Vulgate): the resurrected Christ's words to Mary Magdalene – which DHL frequently used, e.g. Somers in *Kangaroo*, chap. VI, and the Christ figure in *The Escaped Cock* (Paris, 1929), Part II.

247:22 **his seeming** [247:17] ... **with Tom.** Revisions in MS (p. 404 [436]) were: 'his <complete> ⌜seeming⌝ ... <haughty> ⌜cold⌝ ... <sullen> ⌜angry⌝ ... [247:21] <would not really mix> ⌜had never finally mixed⌝ ... even ⌜with⌝ his ... even ⌜with⌝ Tom.'

248:4 **the natives murdering people."** With the influx of gold miners to the Kimberleys in 1886 conflict occurred with Aborigines. Two diggers were murdered in May and June (cf. Appendix IV), and another in 1888; and there were a series of punitive expeditions against the Aborigines.

248:8 **wongie?"** Chat, usually 'wongi' (Aboriginal word; 1903, *AND*).

250:9 **heaviness** Originally 'quietness' in MS (p. 409 [441]).

250:20 **though rather ... the social** The portrait of Blessington was revised in MS: '<but> ⌜though rather social,⌝ ... <But he> ⌜He was⌝ really ... ⌜frail and⌝ sad ... <fixed> social' (p. 409 [441]).

250:30 **cool ... impetus from** Original MS reading was: 'fierce ... stand on' (p. 410 [442]).

251:2 **frenzied jazzing ... public consciousness,** Cf. 'Making Love to Music' in *Phoenix* (ed. McDonald, pp. 160–6).

251:9 **a ruffled cockatoo.** The sulphur-crested cockatoo *Cacatua galerita*, common in the eastern Australian states, opens its forward-curving yellow crest when landing or alarmed (also described in *Kangaroo*, chap. XI).

253:20 **the very finger of heaven!** What Heaven intends or points to (like a fingerpost). The next sentence and 'We don't ... the family' at ll. 13–14 were added in MS (p. 412 [446]). See also 283:27–8.

255:22 **"barrack hack."** A play on the first syllable of Miss Brackley's surname; it means prostitute or slut ('hack' or 'hackney' being a horse for hire, and barracks, on a station, being the quarters intermediate in the social scale between the proprietor's house and the ordinary working men's hut).

255:33 **Tom. That young ... supper extra.** See Textual apparatus: an interlinear addition in MS (p. 416 [450]) is responsible for the confusion: 'Tom. ⌜That young ... extra. Jack⌝ He left'. The Government House ballroom, built in 1899 and the only one MLS would have seen as an adult (replacing a temporary timber building of 1869), has two storeys, the ground floor being the supper room (247:30). On one side of the ballroom upstairs, an area about 12 feet wide between curtained arches and the side windows had a table left spread with food and drinks after supper was served – presumably the 'supper extra'. The arches on the other side make possible a private meeting behind curtains (255:27–8), and provide access to the gardens, which originally extended to the Swan River (248:24).

255:39 **Wiggins,"** Mr Wiggins is '"Any mannerist of small brains and showy feather"' (Partridge, *Dictionary of Slang*, p. 1338).

256:7 **s'elp me bob."** Euphemism for 'so help me God'.

258:2 **The Welcome at Wandoo.** The title was originally 'The Break-up of "Wandoo."' (MS p. 420 [454]).

258:24 **hump.** Fit of bad humour (colloquial).

260:11 **adore her, or humbly kiss her feet . . . he went over the border,** As the Earl does his wife, Lady Daphne, in 'The Ladybird' (1923; finished December 1921) . . . She imagines what it would be like 'actually to cross the border and be gone . . . To be gone from this herself' (cf. note on 308:5). The expression is here meant metaphorically – not in relation to colonial borders: cf. 307:30–40 with 'The Border-Line' (short story, written March 1924), and cf. related descriptions of Hilda at 346:20, 347:1–2, 11–12. The term had come from DHL's reading Emil Lucka's *Grenzen der Seele* (1916) in October 1921: see *Letters*, iv. 99 and cf. 288:26–7.

260:15 **arrowy desire . . . arrowily-submissive** 'Arrowy', meaning piercing or keen, is used from the late eighteenth century, but 'arrowily' is probably a coinage. Cf. 'ghostlily' (1879, *OED*) at 288:20, and 'paperily' (also a coinage) at 291:25.

261:21 **For him . . . half way.** Revised in MS (p. 425 [459]): '<⌜They had spent the night on the way, so they were arriving in⌝> For him . . . ⌜⌜But the . . . half way.⌝⌝'

262:24 **girl,** The initial reading in MS was 'boy,' (p. 427 [461]).

262:35 **tyke!** Here a nick-name for a Yorkshireman, with the implication of capable or cunning. At l. 32, 'easy, straight' originally read 'reassured,' in MS (p. 428 [462]).

264:2 **Not a stiver,** Nothing.

266:3 **barm-stick** Feeble-minded person.

267:7 **gold of Australia,** Gold from the eastern states was minted locally from 1855; from 1867 it was identical to British coinage except for the mint mark.

269:16 **fisogs."** Faces (physiognomies); DHL probably added the inverted commas around 't' see . . . fisogs.' in the typescripts to indicate the transition to Easu's vernacular (see Textual apparatus).

269:32 **pale-faced** [269:28] **. . . bald forehead.** Sarah-Ann's description was altered in MS: '<red-haired> ⌜pale-faced young⌝ . . . ⌜and her hair in huge curling pins,⌝ . . . distaste<.>⌜, beneath her bald forehead.⌝' Also at 270:13, '<common> ⌜vulgar⌝ *suffisance* [conceit, French] . . . [271:1] <for the gods> ⌜to shudder at⌝ . . . [271:24] <conceit> ⌜bearing⌝' (pp. 440–4 [474–7]).

270:2 **as many bites as kisses.** An uncompleted correction in MS (p. 440 [474]) explains the adoption of the TSIa reading (see Textual apparatus): '<more> ⌜as many⌝ bites than kisses.'

271:18 **Six days . . . bank account."** Parody of Exodus xx. 9–10 ['. . . thou labour, and do all thy work: But the . . . sabbath of the Lord thy God'].

273:25 **six or seven months** Deleted MS reading was 'nearly a year' (p. 446 [480]).

275:39 **wot's** The reading in TSIa and b (p. 425) – 'wot's' typed over 'who's' – is the likely cause of the A1 and E1 reading (see Textual apparatus).

275:40 **Jehoshaphat!** Euphemism for Jesus (2 Chronicles xvii. 1); and similarly 'Cripes' (Christ) at l. 35.

276:9 **the parsley bed,** The female genitals (as in 'to take a turn in the parsley-bed'; Partridge, *Dictionary of Slang*).

276:23 **Sufficient unto . . . evil thereof,** Matthew vi. 34.

276:29 **the angel that stood in Jacob's doorway an' looked like a man,** A confusion of Jacob's vision, 'And Jacob was left alone; and there wrestled a man [angel] with him' (Genesis xxxii. 24), with Abraham's of the 'three men [angels]' whom he saw as he 'sat in the tent door in the heat of the day' (xviii. 1–2), but cf. 333:11–13.

278:25 **certain conceit . . . conceit . . . defeated, common, and a little humiliated.** MS originally read 'certain pride . . . pride . . . common, a nasty piece of clay.'; 'slack' (279:9) and 'but speaking . . . Easu most' (279:34–5) are additions in MS (pp. 455–7 [489–91]).

279:11 **belly.** The reading exclusive to E1 ('bulk') may be a case of Secker's interference: DHL's other publishers were reluctant to print 'belly' (see *The Rainbow*, ed. Kinkead-Weekes, p. lxvi); but cf. l. 9 where, used as a verb, it was not changed.

280:16 **cattle stations** A vast area in the Kimberleys had been made available for pastoral selection from 1880.

281:5 **a horseman . . . like Death returning from the dead,** In Revelation vi. 8 the rider of the pale horse is called Death, and cf. ll. 1299–1369 of 'Gareth and Lynette' (1872) in Tennyson's *Idylls of the King* where Gareth fights the knight on horseback dressed as Death.

281:21 **the mystic place in Easu's forehead,** In yoga philosophy, the position of the third eye and the ultimate level of consciousness and power: see *Apocalypse*, ed. Kalnins, p. 107.

283:2 **Lost.** Newspaper reports in the 1880s and 90s of people becoming lost in the bush were fairly frequent, and on 2 November 1922 (about the time MLS began 'The House of Ellis': *Fifth Sparrow* 117) the Perth *Western Mail* reported a man 'lost in the bush for five days and rescued . . . when he was nearly dead' (p. 29).

283:34 **"I have dipped my hand in blood!"** Cf. Psalm lxviii. 22–3: 'The Lord said . . . thy foot may be dipped in the blood of thine enemies, and the tongue of thy dogs in the same'. See also 282:3–4.

284:14 **In the midst . . . in death.** From 'The Burial of the Dead' in *The Book of Common Prayer*.

284:17 **I like to be lord of Death. Who do they call the Lords of Death.** Cf. 'he is not a God of the dead, but of the living' (Luke xx. 38); Jack is implicitly rejecting the God of the New Testament (see 141:26–7). The ancient Egyptians believed in the prolongation of life after death similar in kind to earthly existence and contingent upon the conservation of the body (hence mummification). Harry R. Hall in *The Ancient History of the Near East: from the Earliest Times to the Battle of Salamis* (1913 – DHL may have read it in 1916: *Letters*, ii. 528) described the Egyptian god Osiris as having, during the period of the Middle Kingdom, 'advanced to the position of "Universal Lord" . . . of the world of the dead' (p. 169). He presides over the judgment of the dead, but there were other gods associated with the dead. See note on 284:31.

Given his readings in Mexican history in 1923 (see *Letters*, iv. 527 and *The*

Plumed Serpent, ed. L. D. Clark, Cambridge, 1987, p. xxv n. 49), DHL may also have had in mind Mictlantecuhtli, Aztec lord of the dead; in one creation myth involving him, blood and bone are mixed to fashion a new humanity (ibid., Appendix I, p. 554). Cf. the idea of an aristocracy of the blood and bone which DHL introduced at typescript revision stage (e.g. see Textual apparatus for 306:13, 308:10, 12 and 19) – having already, in MS, developed Jack's (initiated) awareness of being a 'man of bone' (295:33) and related to a 'strange Lord [who] had forged his bones' (296:7); see also *The Plumed Serpent*, p. 248 and note.

284:25 **sow dragon's teeth, and warriors will spring up.** Cadmus, sowing the dragon's teeth as ordered by Athene, saw armies of warriors spring up from them; they immediately began to fight, until only a few were left (Ovid, *Metamorphoses*, iii. 95 ff.).

284:31 **like spaces in an Egyptian temple.** The image of Egyptian darkness appears in DHL's writings at latest by 1912 (in 'A Hay Hut Among the Mountains', *Phoenix II* 38) but its association with power and potency followed his visit to the British Museum in 1914 (see *Letters*, ii. 218, 293 and 521 n. 3; and *Women in Love*, ed. Farmer, Vasey and Worthen, p. 318 and notes); cf. 308:3–5 and note.

285:2 **tied up** Replaces 'hideous' in MS (p. 466 [500]).

285:8 **reesty** Rancid (dialect).

286:4 **Jack stood ... hurried forward.** Added in MS; 'Then he ... own cry.' (ll. 7–9) is a related addition (p. 468 [502]).

289:4 **"Petition me ... our queen— — — "** From the play *Tom Thumb the Great* (1730), by Henry Fielding, which continues 'shall be as drunk as we' (I. ii. 15–18).

289:9 **"A Briton ... a slave— —"** From 'Ere with cold beads of midnight dew' (1827) by William Wordsworth (ll. 19–20). 'How fast ... sunless land' at 289:17–18 is from his 'Extempore Effusion upon the Death of James Hogg' (1835), ll. 22–3.

289:36 **"But hushed ... us, vanishing—"** First two lines are from Wordsworth's 'Elegiac Stanzas (Addressed to Sir G. H. B. Upon the Death of his Sister-in-Law)' (1827), ll. 37–8. The remaining lines are from 'Ode: Intimations of Immortality' (1807), ll. 142–4 ['... Fallings from us, vanishings']; and ll. 145–6 are misquoted at 290:1–2 ['... Creature/ Moving about in worlds ...'].

291:7 **"I have ... of my mouth."** Cf. Proverbs xiii. 3.

291:10 **"Ye must be born again,"** John iii. 7.

291:11 **little silvery, twinkling spurts like flying-fish** DHL revised this passage in typescript (see Textual apparatus) in January 1924 after having seen flying-fish on his return journey from Mexico in November–December 1923: see Catherine Carswell, *The Savage Pilgrimage: A Narrative of D. H. Lawrence* (1932, reprinted Cambridge, 1981), p. 196. Cf. 'The Flying-Fish' (written March 1925), in *St. Mawr and Other Stories*, ed. Brian Finney (Cambridge, 1983), pp. 212, 219–20.

291:17 **But the . . . powerful darkness** MS originally began: '≪But out of the lordly, <surgica> ⌜powerful⌝≫' (p. 475 [510]).

291:25 **paperily rustling** Deleted MS reading was 'saying hoarsely' (p. 476 [511]); see note on 260:15.

292:9 **dark-anointed and sent back . . . dark unction between his brows.** Cf. the Old Testament ritual of royal anointing (to indicate divine warrant: e.g. for Saul and David, 1 Samuel x. 1 and xvi. 12–13; see also Psalm cxxxiii. 2) and the anointing of the sick with oil in the last rites (including a prayer that the person should be spared – 'sent back'). Cf. James v. 14–15.

292:30 **burning . . . of meat;** Revised in MS: '⌜burning, bloodshot⌝ . . . <recognise but who was> ⌜for a long time recognise as⌝ Lennie . . . of <food> ⌜meat⌝;' (p. 477 [512]).

293:29 **gloomy, reproachful tone.—** [293:23] . . . **wilderness . . . great . . . undawned** These MS readings replaced 'kind of reproach—. . . great void . . . edge of . . . next'. At 294:3–4 DHL added: 'And she recognised <that> the . . . his voice' (pp. 479–80 [514–15]).

295:34 **It** DHL may have decided to delete 'too' (see Textual apparatus) when transcribing the proof revisions at 295:33 and 296:1 to the proofs for A1 but did not alter the set for E1 (or his alteration was not carried out).

296:25 **Lord of Hosts,** Old Testament title of Jehovah ('God of armies').

298:7 **like a chilled flower,** MS read originally 'just as flowery,' (p. 486 [521]).

298:13 **She was a question . . . to be answered.** Cf. 'Bei Hennef' in *Love Poems and Others* (1913): 'You are the call and I am the answer' (l. 14); *Fantasia of the Unconscious*, chap. IX: 'Man must . . . have the courage to go home to his woman and become a perfect answer to her deep sexual call'; and *Kangaroo*, chap. XIII: 'Life makes no absolute statement. It is all Call and Answer'.

299:2 **passion vine** I.e. the passion-fruit vine (*Passiflora edulis*), common in Australia.

299:6 **reddish hair, of a lovely fine texture** In MS DHL started to describe Jane's hair as 'yellow hair that was already going' (p. 488 [523]); cf. note on 65:30.

301:13 **baffled, defiant . . . You've *had*** See Textual apparatus: while it is possible that DHL cut this in proof to accommodate expansion at l. 4 (see Introduction, p. xxxix), he may have decided to delete the accountancy metaphor which he had already changed in MS from 'to play off against' to 'as an offset for' (p. 492 [527]); the deletion is therefore accepted.

301:36 **She saw** [301:28] . . . **like a doom,** In his strengthening in the typescripts of Jack's character and its effects (e.g. see Textual apparatus for 301:28 and 305:36), DHL was probably influenced by Joseph Conrad's *The Rover* (1923), which he read in December 1923 'with astonishing intentness', according to Catherine Carswell (*Savage Pilgrimage*, p. 197). The taciturn sailor, Peyrol, is 'a born leader' who 'has received a sign from death' (pp. 196, 195); to the young woman, Arlette, he was 'like a messenger from the unknown . . . something immensely strong . . . unaffected by familiarity and remaining invincible' (p. 244).

See Introduction, pp. lx–lxi, for the preference of the TSIb reading for 301:28–302:9.

303:14 **passion can so reverse itself ... a great desire ... can become an eternal revulsion,** An adaptation of Empedocles' conception of life as an eternally opposed dynamic of Strife and Love, one principle making for complete differentiation and the other for reconciliation and togetherness. After reading John Burnet's *Early Greek Philosophy* (2nd edn, 1908), DHL developed the idea in 'The Lemon Gardens' (expanded version written August 1915 and published in *Twilight in Italy*) and almost immediately thereafter in 'The Crown' (in *Reflections on the Death*, ed. Herbert, e.g. pp. 256–9 and 469); it subsequently merged with his long-standing interest in polarities.

304:2 **curious look ... his world.** This reading (see Textual apparatus) is the only case where there is no firm basis for choosing between variant typescript revisions; however evidence from earlier and later in the chap. counsels preference of TSIbR (p. 471): see Introduction, pp. lx–lxi and footnote 140.

304:19 **left her ... kill, or** See Textual apparatus and previous note; also, 'herself' may have been added by a typesetter to E1 proofs, and then transmitted to A1.

307:7 ***à terre*** Conventional, down-to-earth (literally, 'at the level of the earth'; French).

308:5 **dark mystery of being royal in death ... royalty on earth.** Jack's vision parallels Count Dionys's in 'The Ladybird': cf. his drawing strength from darkness, his feeling himself destined to be a 'master of the after-life' and his being compared to 'an Egyptian King-god in the statues'. (See also Textual apparatus for 308:4 and 5: the typist inserted an omission interlinearly, with parentheses, and A1 included them.)

311:2 **The Offer to Mary.** MS titles read: '⌜The Grant Farm⌝/ <Bonanza>' (p. 506 [543]).

311:30 **dismiss** [311:22] **... bote ... did of sensible decay** [311:24] **... burried him proud under ... was hear** Demise ... bottle [i.e. of ink] ... died of a [protracted] decay of the nervous system [not the Lewises' interpretation – physical decay] ... buried him with some pride [i.e. in the funeral arrangements]. Under the present [legal] provisions of town council, the clerk who was present accepts the doctor's will which he [Rackett] made up the night you were here.

312:3 **Coney Hatch** Lunatic asylum – after Colney Hatch, a Middlesex village with a mental hospital, est. 1852 (figuratively: 1890, *OED*).

312:15 **Ally Sloper** Cartoon caricature (mentioned also in *Kangaroo*, chap. VI) created by the popular humourist-buffoon, Charles Henry Ross (1842?–97), e.g. in his *Ally Sloper's Comic Kalendar* (1875–87). A large, battered umbrella was Ally's hallmark: cf. 213:5–6.

313:27 **woman too.** Originally followed in MS (p. 510 [547]) by 'He was a good deal disturbed.'

313:36 **home here ... like your dear father."** In 1872 Jack Skinner's father lived in Barrack Street, near the well-to-do area on the s. side of Adelaide Terrace.

314:16 **"A la bonne heure!"** Sarcastic French colloquialism meaning 'That's right!' or 'Well done!'; Jack intends the literal meaning, 'At the right time!'

315:6 **a Queen-Victoria-statue pose,** Statues of Queen Victoria were erected throughout the Empire especially towards the end of, and shortly after, her reign (1837–1901).

317:17 **"I've got Gran** [317:9] ... **to life."** MS from here to 319:5 (pp. 516–18 [553–5]) and TSIa and b (see Textual apparatus, and note on 319:5) are extensively revised. The original MS reading was:

> "I'll tell you what Gran Ellis made me see," said Jack. "She made me see that sins are as mysterious and vital as virtues. She made me see that the world is at least half made up of sins."
>
> "Some people's world." (p. 516 [553])

Other revisions are '<I am just becoming acutely aware of my own sinful state> ⌜it must . . . my mind⌝ [317:20–1] . . . [317:22] <for forgiveness> ⌜etc. etc.⌝ . . . [317:29] <my true me> ⌜between us⌝'. At 316:5, '<told me many things> ⌜was a queer old bird⌝' (p. 514 [551]).

317:38 **amiss with** [317:32] ... **amiss with most ... was a ... known. Something ... of us—... thinking you do."** MS originally read:

> wrong with you, my boy, if you've taken to arguing and splitting hairs."
>
> "Of course. Something is always wrong with most . . . was the lesson of my life. Something . . . of us—"
>
> "You are right there." (p. 517 [554])

318:11 **yes, more—"** [318:5] ... **hard eyes ... puzzled and perturbed ... own inside,** At first MS read: 'to my own God." . . . wide eyes . . . deeply perturbed . . . own soul,' (p. 517 [554]). Other revisions in MS (see Textual apparatus for final MS reading) were, at 318:11, '<my own burning soul is> ⌜I take it for⌝'; and, at 318:12, '<It comes from my own God> ⌜I've got . . . own⌝'.

319:5 **something stirs** [318:11] ... **George testily.** MS revisions (see Textual apparatus for final MS readings) were: '"<Why so?> ⌜Not I!⌝ Why . . . cracked <that> ⌜than⌝ Paul was? <Have I no God that I can know?"> ⌜Why is . . . smiling wickedly.⌝ *P* "You . . . haven't. <You may have. I should never dispute it. But Paul saw a new god. And I see my own god. I don't say he is your god. But he is mine. He is behind me, and he looks with dark eyes over my shoulder."> ⌜I'm sorry . . . should ≪[?]he≫ I . . . you look."⌝ *P* "If . . . have <understood.> ⌜known like . . . laughed Jack⌝ *P* "She . . . except <on matters of business. And I suppose you're the same"> ⌜where money . . . an antimacassar"⌝' (p. 518 [555]; '*P*' indicates a new paragraph).

The passage was almost entirely rewritten at typescript revision stage (TSIa and b, pp. 495–6). Until the revision starts towards the bottom of p. 495, evidence suggests that DHL was using TSIb (carbon throughout the chap.) as his correction copy and transcribing to TSIa: e.g. on p. 484 of TSIb DHL first corrected 'borabza' by changing letters and then by writing 'bonanza'; on TSIa he simply rewrote (311:6); and backwards-sloping corrections suggest he leaned to his left to transcribe in TSIa (pp. 494–5) – e.g. 'better' and 'the lot' (317:11, 36). Thus the preference for TSIaR (p. 493) at 316:27.

However DHL then reversed the direction: in TSIa, 'a God' (318:12) is written 'god' before being changed to 'God'; TSIb has only 'a God' – and similarly

'Scotch' at 318:40. Compositional evidence confirms the shift: as DHL transcribed the rewritten passage from TSIa into TSIb, he continued to revise (see examples below). He then read over TSIb and made three fully or partly interlinear additions, transcribing one back into TSIa exactly ('for example,'; 318:14), omitting one ('value ... and use them' – see below) and altering one to fit TSIa (318:21–3):

> The world is all so tame, it's a bit imbecile, in my opinion. ⌜Really a dangerous idiot.—⌝ If I do want two wives—or even three— —I *do*.<”> ⌜Why should I mind what the Idiot says.”⌝ (TSIaR)
>
> The world ... tame, it's like an idiot to me. ⌜A dangerous idiot.⌝ So that if I ... even three;— —well, I *do*.<”> ⌜Why listen to the Idiot.”⌝ (TSIbR)

In this case there is no single final reading; TSIbR is preferred because it witnesses the last of an unbroken line of authorial revision, whereas TSIaR is a mixture of earlier and late, reflecting scribal haste as much as creative revision.

In other transcriptions DHL stuck to his habit of adding and amplifying rather than deleting or condensing: e.g. TSIaR reads 'I have real use for two wives', and TSIbR: 'I can really <use> ⌜value⌝ two wives⌜, and use them⌝' (318:29–30). And at 319:2 TSIaR has 'stick to.”', but TSIbR reads: 'stick to,<”> ⌜as I stick to Monica.<<”>>⌝⌜⌜I'd stick to the others the same.”⌝⌝'

319:17 **bothered amused** [319:6] **... a bit uncanny.** In MS this read '<annoyed> ⌜bothered⌝ amused ... <powerful> ⌜different⌝ responsibility ... [319:15] fierce <old> Gran ... <mystery> ⌜uneasiness⌝ ... <canny> ⌜a bit uncanny⌝' (pp. 518–19 [555–6]).

319:21 **to fertilise.** The ommission of these words from A1 was very likely censorship by Seltzer. For further examples, see Textual apparatus for 331:7, 22 and 29, 332:3, 333:25 and 31 (second and third entries), 335:34, and 336:29 and 36.

320:8 **absurdity.** DHL deleted almost two pages worth of typescript from here to section ii by crossing out text on pp. 498 and 499 and discarding a page (not extant) that originally came in between: '“Your money's ... old bones' (see Textual apparatus). DHL had already revised the passage in MS (p. 520 [557]: for final readings see apparatus): 'absurdity ... give <new direction> ⌜next shove⌝ to ... Sir?” *P* <Because you> ⌜Why not? You⌝ are ... are <?an> ⌜the⌝ old <hero> ⌜leader⌝ who ... fought <to make a way for us that come after> ⌜all the way so far, to get ahead⌝ ... of delight.'

323:12 **studied the ... on earth,** Original MS reading (pp. 527–8 (564–5]) was 'looked at the young woman. She looked like any other young woman,'; and, at 323:14, '<looking> ⌜seeking⌝ ... [323:16] <handsome closed mouth> ⌜rather grim ... closed ironically⌝ ... [323:20] <utterly new and beautiful and terrible to her> ⌜quite new ... to her⌝.'

324:1 **black moustachios ... black eyes,** In MS this replaced: 'moustachios in the Bulwer Lytton style' (p. 528 [565]).

324:3  . See Textual apparatus: DHL also drew the skull-and-crossbones in TSIa and b. Someone redrew it for E1, and the professional version in A1 is enlarged, centred and set off.

324:5 **three sides of the photograph.** The A1 reading (see Textual apparatus) is probably a typesetter's attempt to clarify a confusing expression in TSIa, but if it is authorial it is a response to defective copy.

324:12 **Bulwer Lytton young elegant ... dude** A dandy of the genteel kind found in the novels of Edward Bulwer-Lytton, first Baron Lytton (1803–73) ... a swell, fop (US colloquialism, *c.* 1883; Partridge, *Dictionary of Slang*).

326:31 **wanted to go ... west,** Since the Grant farm is near the Old North Road (see note on 195:19; also 210:27–8, 220:9, 221:4), Jack cannot go west very far (see map).

328:10 **"But why** From here to the end of the chap. are the pages in TSIa and b (513–21) typed by DHL; see Introduction, pp. xxxv–xxxvi. From 330:1 where DHL departs completely from MS, authorial corrections on TSIa and b are only distinguished in the Textual apparatus (as *TSIaR* or *TSIbR*) when they result in variant readings. When DHL typed, he often incorporated the original typist's mistakes and made new ones, particularly with punctuation; accordingly, MS punctuation is preferred. At 328:23 (see Textual apparatus), a MS (substantive) reading is restored because of the strong possibility of eye-skip on the part of the professional typist or DHL.

329:23 **unhappy, Jack** See Textual apparatus: the TSIa punctuation is preferred because of the proximity of DHL's deletion of 'a little' and the possibility that the two changes were linked.

329:25 **not? If ... it away—"** The accepted variants in TSIa are the result of DHL's re-typing p. 515 (329:24–330:13) after a carbon reversal. MS punctuation is overruled here because its context has been re-worked.

330:18 **like Abraham ... David ... the wives they needed for their own completeness,** Many Old Testament Patriarchs were polygynous, including Abraham (Genesis xvi. 1–10) and David (2 Samuel ii. 2; v. 13); this is usually explained as an economic or political necessity reinforcing the cultural (and natural) value of having sons. For 'nasty ... business of divorce' (330:18–19), see note on 378:22.

330:38 **to have her and to answer her.** Adapts the phrasing of the marriage vow, 'To have and to hold from this day forward ...' ('Solemnization of Matrimony' in *The Book of Common Prayer*); and cf. 298:12–13 and note.

331:14 **mild Saint Joseph.** I.e. Joseph, husband of Christ's (virgin) mother – implying, on his part, control or absence of sexual desire. Cf. Joseph as 'grey with waiting', in 'Ballad of a Wilful Woman' (Part v, l. 1) in *Look! We Have Come Through!* (1917).

331:17 **Everything in season,** See Ecclesiastes iii. 1: 'To every thing there is a season'.

333:5 **a perpetual travelling,** Cf. *The Letters of D. H. Lawrence*, ed. Boulton and Robertson, iii. 224: 'my ideal now is to have a caravan and a horse, and move on for ever, and never have a neighbour'.

333:13 **like Abraham under the wild sky ... angels stand in his doorway.** See note on 276:29, and cf. 'The Song of a Man Who has Come Through' in *Look! We Have Come Through!*

334:2 **Trot Trot Back Again.** Source unidentified, but may derive from new dances involving trotting popular after World War I (e.g. Fox-Trot, Turkey-Trot) – cf. 250:37–8. See Textual apparatus: this is the third version of this chap. title, DHL having cancelled 'The Rider on the Last Horse.' in MS (p. 540 [577]). Thereafter, the chap. is almost entirely free of revision in MS.

336:22 **snake-worshipping savages** Snake worshipping cults have existed in various countries including Mexico, to which DHL is probably referring.

336:25 **Daniel . . . lions' den** Daniel vi. 16–23.

336:30 **'Now they bite . . . bite his genitals.** From 'The Penitence of Don Roderick', trans. John Gibson Lockhart, *The Spanish Ballads* (1873; published Edinburgh, 1823 as *Ancient Spanish Ballads Historical and Romantic*). For penance after a sexual affair, Roderick has to make his bed in a tomb that holds a two-headed serpent which eats his genitals with one head and his heart with the other: 'He eats me now, he eats me now, I feel the adder's bite,/ The part that was most sinning my bedfellow doth rend . . .' (ll. 50–1).

340:31 **amiably-disposed,** Typist's and copy-editor's corrections (in pencil) resume in this chap. (See Textual apparatus: DHL habitually misspelled 'amiable', and the TSIa copy-editor corrected it, but it was evidently the typist who restored the hyphen in TSIa and b.) The only ink corrections in TSIb are two misspellings of 'amiable' and one of 'amiability' (pp. 530–1; see Textual apparatus for 340:10, 23 and 26) – and they appear to be in the same ink as used for the pagination, which is in a hand probably DHL's. Thus it is possible that he gave the typing a cursory inspection. In TSIa there are also in ink a word-count on four pages (arriving at an estimation of the novel's total on the verso of p. 533; the hand appears to be DHL's); a rough (unidentified) street map on the verso of p. 531, and a new paragraph symbol at 344:11 which restores MS (but is unlikely to be DHL's).

341:6 **himself.** MS read at first 'this.' (Roberts E55b, p. 3 [583]).

341:38 **the Archer . . . a centaur.** I.e. Sagittarius (in the Zodiac).

342:10 **fiercely. He . . . a mare.** DHL altered MS: '<shrilly> ⌜fiercely⌝. He . . . Adam's <shrill> ⌜powerful⌝ neigh<.>⌜, and far . . . a mare.⌝' In this chap. two stages of MS revision can be distinguished because DHL used darker ink when reviewing the chap.; the earlier corrections were evidently made during the original writing. (Here, only 'fiercely' is in the darker ink.) Other MS alterations are on this page (Roberts E55b, p. 4 [584]): at 342:18 'was powerless to hold her' read 'could not hold the'; 'whence came . . . of something' at 342:30–1 read 'where something seemed to be'; and 'like an enclosed' at 342:31–2 read 'as if he were bringing the place down, like a'. The second and fourth are in the darker ink – as are 'and close the door behind him' at 343:9 (which replaced 'without opening the door') and 'moving rhythmic and handsome' (which is added at 343:20; p. 5 [585]). There are 28 second-stage revisions or additions of substantives in this chap.

345:1 **queerest, oddest . . . bird** Hilda is based on Dorothy Brett; see Introduction, p. xxxii and footnote 46. Cf. Hilda's early life (346:35–347:1) with Sean Hignett's *Brett: From Bloomsbury to New Mexico, A Biography* (1984), chaps. I–VII, especially pp. 12–14, 30.

346:10 **All that . . . a man. Impossible!"** Cf. *Women in Love*, ed. Farmer, Vasey and Worthen, p. 9, where Gudrun says 'The man makes it impossible.' But DHL may have been adapting something Brett told him: cf. 'For years I would never let a man come near me' (from her unpublished autobiographical essay, 'Adolescence', quoted in Hignett, *Brett*, p. 31).

347:4 **a natural sun.** Cf. 173:34–7 and note.

347:25 **the coolness of a fairy.** Cf. the 'mysterious woman from the faery' in DHL's sketch of a novel (probably written *c.* 26 December 1923) as a proposal for a collaboration with Catherine Carswell (see her *Savage Pilgrimage*, pp. 202–4); DHL's 'The Princess' was the result (in *St. Mawr*, ed. Finney, pp. 159–96).

Note on Miss M. L. Skinner

373:10 ***Letters from a V. A. D.*** The title is *Letters of a V.A.D.*: see Introduction, p. xxii and footnote 5.

373:14 **the MS. . . . trailed off into impossible adventures.** An early version of *Black Swans*: see below and Appendix VI.

373:19 **We were in Chapala . . . publishers in New York . . . said it was hopeless.** DHL misremembers the chain of events: see Introduction, pp. xxv–xxvii and footnote 26.

373:21 **Some of . . . are mine** See Introduction, pp. xlvi–xlvii and xlix, and 377:34–378:7.

373:23 **general.** See note on 10:25.

373:28 **fine Persian . . . in camp.** Cf. *Fifth Sparrow* 30: 'the beautiful drawing-room [of the Skinner family home in Perth, *c.* 1902] with its furnishing of Egyptian rugs, divans, brass trays and miniature mummies that he and Mother had procured in Egypt'.

374:1 **set off *steerage* . . . patient to nurse.** See *Fifth Sparrow* 134–7.

374:4 **People were not very nice . . . her companion . . . the bungalow.** See note on 379:2 . . . Nellie Beakbane, MLS's partner in 'Leithdale' (see Introduction, p. xxii; 377:11–12; and *Fifth Sparrow* 148, 152).

Preface to *Black Swans*

377:33 **the hand-washing part.** I.e. Pilate's washing his hands of responsibility for Christ's crucifixion (Matthew xxvii. 24).

378:22 **If a man has ever cared . . . marry her . . . divorce is all bunk.** Cf. 'let none be faithless to the wife of his youth. "For I hate divorce" says the Lord . . . So . . . do not be faithless' (Malachi ii. 15–16, RV).

378:26 **whether this . . . to settle.** In 'The Novel' (of June 1925) DHL added: 'if a character in a novel wants two wives—or three—or thirty: well, that is true of that man, at that time, in that circumstance . . . But to infer that all men at all times want two, three, or thirty wives; or that the novelist himself is advocating furious polygamy; is just imbecility' (in *Study of Thomas Hardy*, ed. Steele, p. 185).

378:37 **how *Black Swans* has wound up** [378:30] **. . . pirate-castaway-Swiss-Family-Robinson-Crusoe-Treasure-Island . . . ordinary terra-firma.** DHL suggests a composite background source for *Black Swans*: *The Swiss Family Robinson*

(1812–13), the romance of a family wrecked on a desert island, by Johann David Wyss, Swiss novelist and pastor (1743–1818), which was modelled on *Robinson Crusoe* (1719) by Daniel Defoe (1660–1731); and the Robert Louis Stevenson (1850–94) pirate adventure story, *Treasure Island* (1883). The published version of *Black Swans* retains romance elements. Letty, an irresponsible and wilful child, convinces Tim, a convict assigned to work her father's garden in Fremantle, to escape and to hide nearby 'like Robinson Crusoe' (p. 31) with her procuring food for him. After his capture she escapes with him and a friend, Peter, on a small boat; they are picked up by an illegal Malay fishing vessel, subjected to rough usage and danger, shipwrecked and taken by Aborigines. Tim is their saviour throughout; after his repairing the wreck they return to civilisation. The second half of the novel is set first in England where an older Letty becomes engaged to a Mr Percy, whom she does not love, elopes with Peter back to WA and thereafter, because of her continuing attachment to Tim, hesitates about accepting Peter as husband – until near the end when she realises she loves him.

MLS rewrote *Black Swans* once after DHL left Perth and again (probably twice) after travelling to England (*c.* May 1924) – with the benefit of Edward Garnett's advice and detailed notes (Battye; see Introduction, p. xxiv and footnote 12).

379:2 **She arrived in London to be snubbed** In *Fifth Sparrow* (138, 148–51) MLS mentions being snubbed by Curtis Brown's secretary, gaining the impression that Martin Secker would not read her manuscript and being told to take it herself to Jonathan Cape. However Secker did read it, thought it 'quite hopeless as it stands' (letter to DHL, 13 August 1924, Secker Letter-Book, UIll; cf. 379:18–20) and raised with DHL the possibility of his rewriting it. He toyed with the idea (letter from Secker to Curtis Brown, 20 February 1925; ibid.), but decided against it (*Letters*, v. 114). In a letter to MLS on 17 November 1924 DHL wrote: 'I'm glad Jonathan Cape is going to do *Black Swans*, and even that Edward Garnett roars at you to make you do it better' (ibid., v. 171; cf. 379:20–7 and note).

379:4 ***Mr.* Skinner** See Introduction, p. liv.

379:11 **if Stafford put not his trust in Princes** Cf. Psalm cxlvi. 3. Edward Stafford, 3rd Duke of Buckingham (1478–1521) and a powerful courtier, was viewed suspiciously by Henry VIII; he was accused, probably falsely, of treasonable practices, tried and executed.

379:27 **I am dying to see *Black Swans* ... her paces.** He was to be disappointed: 'I've just finished *Black Swans.* It irritates me, by its foolish facility. She herself knows life isn't like that – conceited slipshod nonsense – so why does she write it?' (*Letters*, v. 351). Garnett, when reader for Gerald Duckworth, had put DHL through *his* paces with *Sons and Lovers*: see *Letters of D. H. Lawrence*, ed. Boulton, i. 423, 426–7, 476–8 and 481–2; and Paul Eggert, 'Edward Garnett's *Sons and Lovers*', *Critical Quarterly*, xxvii (1986), 51–62.

379:29 **hot Mexican sun ... a child** Probably, as Ross Parmenter suggests (*Lawrence in Oaxaca: A Quest for the Novelist in Mexico*, Salt Lake City, 1984, pp. 157–8), a play on two births: Christ's and that of the flint knife which, in the Aztec creation myth, Star Skirt delivers: DHL was concurrently working on *The Plumed Serpent* (ed. Clark, p. 555).

TEXTUAL APPARATUS

TEXTUAL APPARATUS

The Boy in the Bush

The following symbols are used to distinguish states of the text:

MS = Autograph manuscript
TSIa= Composite typescript, setting-copy for first American edition
TSIb= Composite typescript, setting-copy for first English edition
E1 = First English edition
A1 = First American edition

Alterations in *TSIa* or *TSIb* are indicated by:

R = Revision by DHL; see also Explanatory note on 328:10
C = Corrections by another person; see notes on 24:11 and 340:31

Wherever the base-text (*MS*) reading is adopted, it appears within the square bracket with no symbol. Variant readings follow in sequence, with only the first state in which they appear denoted. When a reading from a state subsequent to *MS* has been preferred or coincides with it, it appears with its symbol within the square bracket; the *MS* reading and other variants follow in sequence. This sequence, designed for precision in recording and not strictly chronological, is: *TSIa* follows *MS*; *TSIb* and its authorial revisions (*TSIbR*) follow, respectively, *TSIa* and its authorial revisions (*TSIaR*); *A1* follows, where they exist, the revisions and corrections of *TSIa*, otherwise *TSIa* itself; and similarly *E1* with *TSIb*. Where DHL revised only *TSIa*, the *TSIb* reading is noted (e.g. 175:7), and there is no sequence in '*C*' corrections from *TSIa* to *TSIb*. Subsequent Secker (English) impressions till DHL's death follow *E1* (except at 333:35: see Introduction footnote 97).

With the exception of pp. 15, 27, 31–3, 37 and 50 of *TSIa* (corresponding to 16:23–17:7, 24:27–25:18, 27:15–29:17, 31:17–32:3, 40:24–41:8), the first 166 pages (to 113:23) of both *TSIa* and *TSIb* are a copy of the original typescript which DHL corrected; when *TSIa* or *TSIb* is the source of a preferred reading up to 113:23, this is because it is deemed to have incorporated an authorial revision or corrected an obvious error, or because it witnesses a majority practice in *MS*.

Some long entries have short variants recorded in braces within the reading of another state with which the variant state is otherwise identical; and the entry for 330:1 has, for clarity, been broken down into several entries.

The following symbols are used editorially:

Ed. = Editor
Om. = Omitted
P = New paragraph
~ = Repeated word in recording a punctuation variant

/ = Line or page break associated with an error
[...] = Illegible
[ ] = Editorially supplied word
{ } = Partial variant reading

List of variant authorial revisions in the typescripts and of authorial revisions occurring in only one typescript (see Introduction, pp. lviii–lxii)

The *TSIaR* reading is adopted as chronologically superseding the *TSIbR* reading at: 159:22, 314:21 and 316:27 (see Explanatory note on 319:5); at 159:21 an editorial reading is preferred, partly based on the (later) *TSIaR* reading. (For the preference of *TSIaR* at 214:14 see note on 178:7.)

The *TSIbR* reading is adopted as chronologically superseding the *TSIaR* reading at: 147:21, 172:33 (third entry), 202:4 (third entry), 301:28 (see Introduction, pp. lx–lxi), 302:4, 303:38 (see note on 304:2), 304:19, 305:32 (first entry), 318:12 (see note on 319:5), 318:19 (see ibid.), 322:39, 328:4, 335:35 (see Introduction, p. lxi footnote 141), 336:9 (see ibid.) and 337:40; at 318:26 an editorial reading (and at 328:8 a first edition reading) is preferred, based on the (later) *TSIbR* reading. (At 128:36, 150:18 (second entry), 174:17 (second entry), 189:39 and 227:36 neither *TSIaR* nor *TSIbR* readings are adopted, and at 158:1 *TSIbR* is preferred because it witnesses a majority practice.)

Cases where a *TSIaR* reading is adopted in the absence of an authorial revision in *TSIb* (if the *TSIaR* reading restores the *MS* reading an asterisk follows): 174:20, 175:7, 189:38, 205:16, 261:13 (see note on 178:7), 305:34, 318:24 (second entry), 319:16,* 323:20, 328:3, 336:29 (second entry; see Introduction, p. lxi), 336:33 (see ibid.) and 338:4*; the *TSIaR* reading is rejected at 178:8 (see note on 178:7), 204:22 and 276:26.

Cases where a *TSIbR* reading is adopted in the absence of an authorial revision in *TSIa* (if the *TSIbR* reading restores the reading in *MS* an asterisk follows): 133:10,* 162:14, 178:7 (first entry; see notes), 183:24, 190:5, 206:32 (second entry),* 306:1, 340:10, 23 and 26 (see note on 340:31); the *TSIbR* reading is rejected at 166:33, 197:35 and 261:14 (first entry; see note on 178:7).

7:6 dark-blue] dark blue *TSIa*
7:7 girl] ~, *E1*
7:9 on] in *TSIa*
7:12 bran-new] brand-new *TSIa*
7:16 nondescript *TSIa*] non-descript *MS*
7:16 Australia:] ~; *TSIa*
7:18 which ... aware, *TSIa*] which *MS*
7:19 bank. *TSIa*] bank: that he knew. *MS*
7:20 five-pound *MS*, *TSIaC*] five pound *TSIa*
7:23 free," *Ed.*] ~;" *MS* ~" *TSIa*
7:27 a long] ~ ~, *A1*, *E1*
7:29 were *TSIa*] was *MS*
7:30 beyond,] ~ *TSIa*
7:30 misery] ~, *A1*, *E1*
7:30 too, *TSIa*] too, but this was *MS*
7:33 surroundings. Yet] ~, yet *TSIa*
8:3 scripture] Scripture *TSIa*
8:4 bible-language *Ed.*] Bible-language *MS* Bible language *TSIa*
8:5 bible *Ed.*] Bible *MS*
8:6 scripture] Scripture *TSIa*
8:10 stone,] ~ *TSIa*
8:11 windows,] ~ *TSIa*
8:11 whitewashed] white-/ washed *A1* white-washed *E1*
8:13 whitewashed] white-washed *E1*

8:15 railway-station] railway station *TSIa*
8:17 church *MS, A1*] Church *TSIa*
8:25 lost,] ~ *E1*
8:27 sand-hills] sand hills *TSIa*
8:38 deck:] ~; *E1*
9:5 memory," *MS, A1*] ~" *TSIa*
9:6 quotations,"] ~" *TSIa*
9:10 and delivering *TSIa*] with *MS*
9:10 "a tongue] ~ "~ *TSIa*
9:11 razor,"] ~" *TSIa*
9:12 stout,] ~ *TSIa*
9:17 wife-beating] ~, *TSIa*
9:18 Not Guilty] not guilty *TSIa*
9:19 years] ~' *E1*
9:21 years] ~' *E1*
9:21 hard] hard labour *TSIa see notes*
9:26 seemed *TSIa*] looked *MS*
9:27 sort of trousers *TSIa*] look *MS*
9:29 trancelike *TSIa*] trance-/ like *MS, E1*
9:36 horsey *TSIa*] stable *MS*
10:1 boatload *TSIa*] boat-/ load *MS*
10:17 sin." *A1, E1*] sin." In fact he knew he wouldn't. *MS* sin." *TSIa*
10:24 recoil *TSIa*] re-coil *MS*
10:26 reason,] ~ *E1*
10:28 officer,] ~ *E1*
10:35 handsome,] ~ *TSIa*
10:35 why oh why] ~, ~ ~ *TSIa* ~, ~, ~ *TSIaC* ~, ~ ~, *E1*
11:3 Oh] ~, *TSIa*
11:8 man." *MS, A1*] ~". *TSIa* ~" *E1*
11:9 colonel your father] ~, ~ ~, *TSIa*
11:10 him."] ~" *E1*
11:11 General *Ed.*] general *MS*
11:15 General *Ed.*] general *MS*
11:16 amiable *TSIa*] aimiable *MS*
11:17 Punch-and-Judy] Punch and Judy *E1*
11:26 ripe *TSIa*] vivid *MS*
11:34 quarreling] quarrelling *TSIa*
11:36 persian] Persian *TSIa*
11:39 Of] of *TSIa*
12:1 really was] was really *TSIa*
12:8 claim, and] ~. And *E1*
12:10 Oh] ~, *A1, E1*
12:12 settlements] settlement *A1*
12:16 good." *P* That] ~." That *A1*
12:19 wild,] ~ *TSIa*
12:24 rail fences] rail-fences *TSIa*
12:32 world,] world, and *TSIa*
12:37 child: he] ~. He *TSIa*
13:4 say:] ~ *TSIa*
13:7 realising] realizing *TSIa*
13:13 fact] ~, *TSIa*
13:13 kissing;] ~: *TSIa*
13:18 grey-hound] greyhound *TSIaC*
13:22 without *TSIa*] with out *MS*
13:22 Prrh] Prh *TSIa*
13:26 '59.—] '59— *E1*
13:29 gentlemen] gentleman *TSIa*
13:31 say] ~, *TSIa*
13:31 Thank you *TSIa*] Thankyou *MS*
13:32 mine!"— *MS, E1*] ~!" *TSIa*
13:40 openly,] ~ *TSIa*
14:5 Swallow,] ~ *E1*
14:9 you." *P* They] ~."—They *TSIa* ~." They *E1*
14:14 Wolf,] ~ *TSIa*
14:22 together,' ha! ha! *A1, E1*] ~, ~! ~!' *MS* ~', ~! ~! *TSIa*
14:23 everything,] ~ *E1*
14:23 me—] ~—— *E1*
14:33 there!] ~? *TSIa*
14:35 men, all wearing *TSIa*] men with their *MS*
14:35 whiskers, *TSIa*] ~ *MS*
15:5 River *MS, TSIaC*] river *TSIa*
15:6 H.M.S.] H. M. S. *A1*
15:12 June 1827:] ~, ~; *E1*
15:12 grandfather!] ~. *E1*
15:13 June] ~, *E1*
15:19 long:] ~; *TSIa*
15:25 education,] ~ *A1*
15:28 W.A.] Western Australia *A1, E1*
15:30 convicts, . . . convicts,] ~ . . . ~ *TSIa*
15:31 outfit:] ~, *E1*
15:35 speaks.] ~! *TSIa*
15:36 lean,] ~ *A1*

15:37 pipe-stem] pipe stem *TSIa*
15:37 window:] ~. *TSIa*
15:38 sir *TSIa*] Sir *MS*
16:2 Sappers . . . Miners] sappers . . . miners *TSIa*
16:2 *Convict Labour*] *convict labour TSIa*
16:2 sir *TSIaC*] Sir *MS*
16:2 Yes, *MS*, *E1*] ~ *TSIa*
16:3 *Convict* Labour] *convict* labour *TSIa*
16:7 state,] ~ *TSIa*
16:9 sand] ~, *A1*
16:11 wept—] ~, *E1*
16:11 Jack *TSIa*] he *MS*
16:12 voice,] ~ *TSIa*
16:16 sand." *P* Then *Ed.*] ~."/ Then *MS* ~." Then *TSIa*
16:18 recognised] recognized *A1*
16:24 ago, *MS*, *E1*] ~ *TSIa*
16:28 free and easy] free-and-easy *TSIb*
16:31 Cockney *MS*, *TSIaC*] cockney *TSIa*
16:31 grammar] ~, *E1*
16:32 you"—] ~", *TSIa* ~," *E1*, *A1*
16:32 y'." *Ed.*] y'". *MS* y'" *TSIa*
16:34 clothes,] ~ *TSIa*
16:35 way *TSIa*] *Om. MS see notes*
16:37 Bell;] ~, *TSIa*
16:38 him.—] ~— *TSIa*
17:2 three-quid's-worth] three quid's worth *TSIa*
17:3 apiece—] ~—— *E1*
17:4 George. *P* "—and *MS*, *TSIb*] ~. *P* "And *TSIa* ~./ "—and *TSIaC* ~. *P* "——and *E1*
17:5 Bell,] ~ *TSIa*
17:7 property—] ~—— *E1*
17:10 —came] ——~ *E1*
17:11 of cotton . . . of . . . of] Of ~ . . . Of . . . Of *TSIa*
17:11 —and] And *TSIa*
17:13 India—] ~—— *E1*
17:15 —the] ——~ *E1*
17:16 sand—] ~—— *E1*
17:19 —along] ——~ *E1*
17:21 paisley] Paisley *TSIa*
17:21 shawl,] ~ *TSIa*
17:22 guineas—] ~. *TSIa*
17:25 unborn? *MS*, *A1*] ~. *TSIa*
17:27 sir *TSIa*] Sir *MS*
17:29 Harps. Paisley shawls. *TSIa*] ~, paisley ~, *MS*
17:29 Ornamental glass *TSIa*] *Om. MS*
17:30 for the mantelpiece; *TSIa*] *Om. MS*
17:30 bibles, *Ed.*] Bibles, *MS* Bibles *TSIa*
17:38 humpy:] ~, *TSIa*
17:39 after—] ~—— *E1*
18:1 years—] ~—— *E1*
18:6 down—] ~—— *E1*
18:20 wheat—] ~—— *E1*
18:23 flourished—] ~—— *E1*
18:24 honey—] ~—— *E1*
18:30 per-cent—] per cent— *TSIa* per cent; *E1*
18:31 per-cent,] per cent, *TSIa* per cent., *E1*
18:32 fifty:] ~; *E1*
18:33 per-cent] per cent *TSIa*
18:35 cent,] ~., *E1*
18:37 'em, and *MS*, *E1*] ~ ~ *TSIa*
18:38 market—] ~. *TSIa*
19:5 Well] ~, *TSIa*
19:6 identity's *TSIa*] identities' *MS*
19:7 But unfortunately] ~, ~, *E1*
19:12 upside down *TSIa*] upside-down *MS*
19:14 sir—] ~. *TSIa* ~, *TSIaC*, *E1*
19:16 dark. *MS*, *E1*] ~, *TSIa*
19:19 anyway. *Ed.*] any way. *MS* anyway— *TSIa* anyway—— *E1*
19:37 say. *P* "You] ~. "You *TSIa*
19:38 College? Oh] ~. ~, *E1*
19:38 Well] ~, *A1*
19:39 harness-cleaner] ~, *E1*
20:1 —you] You *TSIa*
20:4 —most] Most *TSIa*
20:5 twenty, as] ~. As *TSIa*
20:5 twenty three] twenty-three *TSIa*
20:7 exams] ~. *E1*
20:8 big] ~, *TSIa*

20:9 bet—] ~—— *E1*
20:12 Principal's *MS*, *TSIaC*] principal's *TSIa*
20:21 door—] ~—— *E1*
20:23 so—] ~—— *E1*
20:24 Principal *MS*, *TSIaC*] principal *TSIa*
20:25 had,] ~ *TSIa*
20:34 the] *Om. TSIa*
20:36 Jack. "He] ~, "he *E1*
20:37 because,] ~ *TSIa*
20:38 said *MS*, *E1*] ~, *TSIa*
21:3 again,] ~ *E1*
21:10 ha'porth,] ~ *TSIa*
21:11 well!] ~. *E1*
21:12 reap,] ~ *TSIa*
21:12 Latin] latin *A1*
21:12 attached?] ~! *TSIa*
21:14 Vet?] ~.? *E1*
21:15 Well] ~, *E1*
21:16 surgeon,] ~ *TSIa*
21:17 attacks,] ~ *E1*
21:18 the pub] a pub *TSIa*
21:23 Well,] ~— *TSIa*
21:26 windows] ~, *TSIa*
21:29 enough:] ~— *TSIa*
21:30 lot *TSIa*] objects *MS*
21:33 god] God *TSIaC*
21:38 country. And] ~, and *A1*
21:40 gold fields] goldfields *TSIaC*
22:7 yourself,] ~ *TSIa*
22:13 "the] "The *TSIa*
22:17 y',] y' *TSIa*
22:17 offspring, and] ~. And *TSIa*
22:19 son's] sons' *A1*
22:20 drowsy. No *MS*, *TSIaC*] ~, ~ *TSIa* ~, no *E1*
22:23 ne'er-do-wells *Ed.*] neer-do-wells *MS* neer-do-wells, *TSIa* ne'er-do-wells, *TSIaC*, *E1*
22:24 bone—] ~—— *E1*
22:28 sailing-ship] ~, *TSIa*
22:30 '41—] '41, *E1*
22:30 sailing-vessel,] ~ *TSIa*
22:33 advancement.—Wonderful *MS*, *TSIaC*] ~—~ *TSIa* ~—wonderful *E1*
22:33 colony] ~, *E1*
22:37 time—] ~—— *E1*
23:3 platform] ~, *TSIa*
23:5 yelled *MS*, *E1*] ~, *TSIa*
23:10 manure—] ~, *TSIa*
23:13 fertiliser] fertilizer *TSIa*
23:14 in—] ~—— *E1*
24:11 already backing] backing already *TSIb see notes*
24:13 etherealised *TSIaC*, *E1*] etherialised *MS* etherealized *A1*
24:15 again,] ~ *TSIa*
24:21 inquire *A1*] enquire *MS*
24:24 say— —] ~— *TSIa* ~—— *E1*
24:32 cuckoo *TSIb*] fossil *MS*
24:32 too.] ~.— *A1*
25:1 or a] or *A1*
25:2 know—] ~—— *E1*
25:3 Yes.—] ~— *TSIa*
25:4 yourself.—] ~— *TSIa*
25:5 Ellis' *MS*, *TSIaC*] Elli's *TSIa* Ellis's *TSIb*
25:6 mine] ~, *TSIa*
25:8 Well now,] ~, ~. *TSIa*
25:8 Ellis'] Ellis's *E1*
25:11 to *MS*, *TSIb*] *Om. TSIa*
25:13 why—] ~—. *TSIaC*, *TSIb* ~—— *E1*
25:13 silence—But] ~.—~ *A1* ~—but *E1*
25:17 said] ~, *E1*
25:17 colourless *TSIaC*, *E1*] colorless *MS*
25:26 cat's-paw *Ed.*] cats'-paw *MS* cat's paw *TSIa*
25:32 sir *TSIa*] Sir *MS*
25:33 But] ~, *E1*
25:36 niece] ~, *TSIa*
25:37 Rath *A1*, *E1*] Bradley *MS* Stopford *TSIa see notes*
25:39 Good Plain Cook] good, plain cook *TSIa* good plain cook *E1*
25:40 now:] ~; *E1*
26:3 goat *TSIa*] goose *MS*
26:4 goats *TSIa*] geese *MS*
26:6 clothing—] ~—. *TSIa* ~—— *E1*
26:10 They *TSIa*] So they *MS*
26:21 Slap-dash] ~, *TSIa*

26:30 scripture *Ed.*] Scripture *MS*
26:30 Shakspeare] Shakespeare *TSIa*
26:33 said: *P* "You'd *MS, A1*] ~, *P* "You'd *TSIa* ~, "You'd *E1*
26:34 Australia—] ~; *E1*
27:3 said,] ~ *TSIa*
27:4 voice. "And *MS, E1*] ~, "~ *TSIa* ~, "and *A1*
27:10 glaring,] ~ *TSIa*
27:11 saying: *P* "You'll] ~, "You'll *TSIa*
27:18 Man *MS, E1*] man *A1*
27:23 say,] ~ *TSIa*
27:26 born—] ~.— *TSIa* ~. *E1*
27:30 himself, *MS, TSIb*] ~ *TSIa*
27:33 girls,] ~ *E1*
27:34 you, then, *MS, TSIb*] ~, ~ *TSIa* ~ ~, *A1*
27:36 boy:] ~, *TSIb*
27:37 advice,] ~ *A1*
28:11 brass knocker *A1, E1*] brass-knocker *MS*
28:12 into *A1, E1*] in to *MS*
28:21 toilet,] ~ *E1*
28:25 Oh] ~, *TSIa*
28:32 crisp-curly *Ed.*] crisp curly *MS* crisp, curly *TSIa*
28:36 said:] ~, *TSIa*
29:2 one] ~, *TSIaC*
29:7 crisp] ~, *E1*
29:18 side] sides *TSIaC, E1*
29:20 at home *A1, E1*] usual *MS*
29:21 woman] ~, *E1*
29:21 hair] ~, *E1*
29:21 frock] ~, *E1*
29:22 Watson *TSIa*] Hawkins *MS*
29:24 shoulders,] ~ *TSIa*
29:24 repellant] repellent *TSIaC*
29:28 woman *TSIa*] widow *MS*
29:29 well] ~, *TSIa*
29:29 Jack;] ~: *A1* ~, *E1*
29:37 Bow *TSIa*] Beau *MS*
30:8 Jack,] ~ *TSIa*
30:9 panther] ~, *E1*
30:13 shabby,] ~ *TSIa*
30:14 baggy,] ~ *E1*
30:19 room,] ~ *TSIa*
30:21 the carvers *A1, E1*] carvers *MS*
30:28 niece] ~, *E1*
30:32 young pig roasted *TSIa*] sucking pig *MS*
31:3 put in *TSIa*] said *MS*
31:3 Mr *MS, E1*] Mrs. *TSIa see notes*
31:9 George. *P* "Matilda] ~. "Matilda *A1*
31:17 hustle] bustle *E1*
31:21 George.] ~, *TSIa*
31:25 six-thousand-mile] six thousand mile *TSIa*
31:28 Jacob *TSIb, A1*] Frank *MS*
31:31 Jack,] ~ *A1*
31:32 gaze *TSIb*] moons *MS*
31:37 him, *MS, TSIb*] ~ *TSIa*
31:40 had *TSIb*] *Om. MS*
32:8 place *TSIa*] country *MS*
32:15 Oh . . . Oh] ~, . . . ~, *A1, E1*
32:28 Matilda's *TSIa*] Mary's *MS*
32:28 voice] voice was *E1*
32:28 time!] ~. *TSIa*
32:34 doorway] ~, *E1*
32:39 no!] ~, *E1*
33:6 her] the *TSIa*
33:15 pretty,] ~ *TSIa*
33:23 nobody,] ~ *TSIa*
33:25 eyelashes," *MS, E1*] ~", *TSIa* ~?" *TSIaC*
33:32 cuff-links!"] ~", *TSIa* ~," *A1, E1*
33:37 Oh] ~, *A1, E1*
34:7 episcopalian choir] Episcopalian Choir *TSIa*
34:8 singing:] ~, *TSIa* ~ *E1*
34:8 And] and *TSIaC, E1*
34:11 book-end:] ~; *E1*
34:17 noise] ~, *E1*
34:17 long,] ~ *TSIa*
34:18 next. Which,] ~, which *TSIa* ~, which, *E1*
34:23 towards] toward *TSIa*
34:27 O-O-O-h] o-o-oh *TSIa* o—o—oh *A1*
34:28 the-e-e-ey] the-e-ey *TSIa* the—e—ey *A1*
34:30 beee-e-e] beee-ee *TSIa* be-e-e-e-e *A1* bee-ee *E1*
34:31 folk.] ~, *TSIaC*

34:32 Scotland. And] ~ and *TSIa*
35:4 cads, *MS, E1*] ~ *TSIa*
35:5 you. *TSIaC, E1*] ~? *MS see notes*
35:6 with possible *TSIa*] and possibly *MS*
35:11 out,] ~ *A1, E1*
35:14 awful] ~, *E1*
35:17 home-sickness] homesickness *TSIa*
35:24 Monica! *TSIa*] Mona. *MS*
35:25 Mary! *TSIa*] ~. *MS*
35:31 hard, as] ~ ~ *TSIa*
36:1 gymnast] ~, *A1*
36:7 night-shirt] nightshirt *A1*
36:9 about,] ~ *TSIa*
37:10 away"—] away", as *TSIa* away," as *A1, E1*
37:11 consider:] ~, *TSIa*
37:14 or] of *E1*
37:26 back'ards] backards *TSIa*
37:27 end] ~, *E1*
38:4 Drive,] ~ *A1*
38:5 th'osses] the 'osses *TSIa*
38:8 But] ~, *E1*
38:9 'what's] 'What's *TSIa*
38:10 lady?'] ~!' *TSIa* ~'! *E1*
38:10 days,] ~ *E1*
38:11 do!] ~? *TSIa*
38:16 grocer'—] ~,' *TSIa*
38:17 life—] ~, *E1*
38:19 me,] ~ *E1*
38:21 said. 'We're] ~, '~ *TSIa* ~, 'we're *A1, E1*
38:22 says:] ~, *TSIa*
38:22 Miss] miss *E1*
38:24 'arness] ~, *TSIa*
38:32 man!] ~? *A1, E1*
38:36 saying: *P* "Frogs] ~, "~, *TSIa*
38:38 came,] ~ *E1*
38:39 frogs: couldn't *Ed.*] ~: Couldn't *MS* ~. Couldn't *E1*
39:1 alongside,] ~ *TSIa*
39:10 It's] it's *TSIa*
39:11 Country. Poor] ~, poor *TSIa*
39:12 place,] place, as if *TSIa*
39:16 Oh] ~, *A1, E1*
39:18 Why] ~, *E1*
39:19 A.1. *MS, E1*] A.I. *TSIa* A1 *A1*
39:21 daughters— — —] ~—— *A1* ~ . . . *E1*
39:23 question: *P* "I'm] ~, "I'm *TSIa*
39:25 Contrairy," *MS, TSIaC*] ~", *TSIa* ~" *E1*
39:26 Insubordinate.] ~, *TSIa*
39:26 Untrustworthy] untrustworthy *TSIaC, E1*
39:27 prickled] pricked *TSIa*
39:37 sorry.] ~? *TSIaC*
40:10 wasn't sorry . . . therefore he *TSIa*] *Om. MS*
40:11 "say it"; *TSIa*] ~ ~, *MS*
40:12 field,] ~ *TSIa*
40:13 off. *P* To] ~, to *TSIa*
40:14 somehow *TSIa*] *Om. MS*
40:14 kitchen-garden *TSIa*] drawing-room *MS*
40:18 pause.] ~— *E1*
40:23 Come] ~, *A1*
40:23 you.] ~? *A1, E1*
40:26 lady. She . . . window-doors. He *TSIb*] lady. *P* He *MS* lady. He *TSIa see note on* 40:37
40:37 some,] ~ *E1*
40:37 no] No *TSIa*
40:39 wandering] Wandering *TSIaC*
41:4 garden?] ~. *A1*
41:7 Well] ~, *TSIa*
41:9 walkin' *TSIa*] walkin *MS*
41:9 me—] ~—— *TSIaC, E1*
41:10 —"And] — —"~ *TSIa* ——"~ *TSIaC* "——~ *E1*
41:10 as] *Om. A1*
41:11 shack—] ~. *TSIaC* ~—— *E1*
41:13 there's] There's *TSIa*
41:15 looked,] ~ *E1*
41:17 'roos *MS, E1*] ~, *TSIa*
41:21 brownish-pale] brownish pale *TSIa*
41:27 gum-trees] gum trees *TSIa*
41:27 colourless *TSIa*] colorless *MS*
41:27 in a *TSIa*] there was *MS*
41:28 and a *TSIa*] where a *MS*
41:29 shrieking] ~, *TSIaC*
41:32 magpies *TSIa*] mag-pies *MS*
41:37 country] ~, *E1*

42:4 parrots,] ~ *TSIa*
42:4 man *TSIa*] men *MS*
42:5 saying:] ~. *A1*
42:9 ever lock] ~, ~ *TSIa* ~, ~, *E1*
42:11 hopes *TSIa*] hope *MS*
42:11 you *TSIaC, E1*] you'll *MS*
42:11 settles ... makes *TSIa*] settle ... make *MS*
42:12 marries ... has *TSIa*] marry ... have *MS*
42:12 sir *TSIa*] Sir *MS*
42:14 Pontesbeach *TSIa*] Wigston *MS*
42:14 Hall—] ~—— *A1, E1*
42:17 coach driver] coachdriver *TSIa* coach-driver *E1*
42:19 another, mute world,] *Om. TSIa see notes*
42:20 himself, apart] ~. Apart *TSIa*
42:22 Australia,] ~ *TSIa*
42:29 "good-for-nothings." ... "good-for-nothings" *TSIa*] street-arabs ... street-arabs *MS*
42:30 ones *TSIa*] souls *MS*
42:31 Not altogether tamed *TSIa*] Unharnessed daring *MS*
42:23 tameness *TSIa*] harness *MS*
43:1 me] ~, *TSIa*
43:3 bush—] ~—— *A1, E1*
43:4 "Need protecting ... himself, cynically. *TSIa*] *Om. MS*
43:6 scrub *TSIa*] and scrubby bushes *MS*
43:11 with] with a *TSIaC*
43:19 BAR] Bar *E1*
43:23 Oh] ~, *TSIa*
43:23 Gwey! Mr *E1*] Gwey! Oh Mr *MS* Gwey! Oh Mr. *TSIa* Gwey! Oh, Mr. *A1*
43:29 for,] ~ *TSIa*
44:22 promise!"] ~," *TSIa*
44:26 Ellis,] ~ *E1*
44:35 it.] ~? *TSIa*
44:37 timber,"] ~" *TSIa*
44:39 Jack] ~, *E1*
44:40 Jarrah] jarrah *A1*
45:1 likes] like *TSIa*
45:7 wanderin'] wandering *E1*
45:9 there—] ~, *TSIa*
45:13 spuds,—] ~— *E1*
45:18 Well] ~, *TSIa*
45:28 'Ere *A1, E1*] Ere *MS*
45:29 well. *P* "Here *MS, E1*] ~./ "Here *TSIa*
45:39 Goodbye] Goodby *TSIa* Good-bye, *TSIaC, E1*
46:2 trouser-legs] trouser legs *TSIa*
46:12 gum-trees] gum trees *A1*
46:16 bush] ~, *TSIaC*
46:18 cart,] ~ *TSIa*
46:21 walking-sticks—] ~. *TSIa*
46:33 each *TSIa*] either *MS*
46:37 in] ~, *TSIaC*
47:1 more,] ~ *E1*
47:11 conversation:] ~. *TSIa*
47:22 alright] all right, *TSIa*
47:31 smiled *TSIa*] laughed *MS*
47:33 beauty] ~, *TSIaC*
47:34 come] came *TSIa*
47:36 bitch] ~, *TSIaC*
47:40 wif *TSIaC, E1*] wif' *MS*
48:4 sometime] some time *TSIa*
48:6 Well] ~, *TSIaC, E1*
48:14 's long] s' long *TSIa*
48:17 fool.] ~? *TSIa*
48:27 jingle] jangle *TSIa*
48:28 something," *MS, TSIaC*] ~", *TSIa* ~" *E1*
48:32 Stop—hope—] ~! —~!— *TSIa*
48:38 hand, there] ~. There *TSIa*
49:2 Alright] All right, *TSIa*
49:3 right] ~, *TSIaC, E1*
49:3 dear!] ~, *E1*
49:4 voice ...] ~--------- *TSIa* ~—— *A1* ~ ... *E1*
49:5 Well] ~, *TSIaC, E1*
49:5 were,] ~ *E1*
49:7 hand,] ~ *TSIa*
49:18 cubby-hole] cubby hole *TSIa*
49:19 fresh *TSIa*] sweet *MS*
49:20 It wasn't ... and remote. *TSIa*] *Om. MS*
49:21 nightshirt *MS, A1*] night-/ shirt *TSIa*

49:26 an' *E1*] an *MS*
49:29 Jam] ~, *TSIaC*
49:30 jam.] ~, *TSIa*
49:30 Macaroni.] macaroni, *TSIa*
49:30 Cockadoodle] cockadoodle *TSIa*
49:30 hereaways] here-aways *TSIa*
49:31 mantel-ornaments] mantel ornaments *TSIa*
49:32 see.] ~? *TSIa*
49:34 toff] ~, *TSIa*
50:1 sharply. "Out] ~, "out *E1*
50:2 inter] into *TSIa*
50:15 naïve *MS*, *TSIaC*] naive *TSIa*
50:16 wearily] ~, *TSIa*
50:17 Amen!] ~. *TSIa*
51:6 with his *TSIa*] with *MS*
51:9 cubby-hole] cubby hole *TSIa*
51:14 undervests] under-vests *TSIa*
51:15 *O veni,*] *Oveni!*, *TSIa* *Veni!*, *TSIaC*, *TSIbC* *Veni!* *A1* *Veni*, *E1*
51:15 smartly,—] ~— *E1*
51:15 *vidi*, *MS*, *E1*] ~! *A1*
51:16 horizontal;—] ~, — *TSIa* ~— *E1*
51:16 *vici*,] ~! *A1*
51:22 Jack] ~, *A1*
51:23 th'osses] th' osses *TSIa* th' 'osses *E1*
52:6 milk-bottle] milk bottle *A1*, *E1*
52:9 dumb-bells] dumb-bell *TSIa*
52:13 random. *P* "Hey] ~. "Hey *A1* ~. *P* "Hey, *E1*
52:14 impatiently.] ~, *TSIa*
52:15 cart-'oss] cart 'oss *TSIa*
52:18 amiability *TSIa*] aimiability *MS*
52:19 cart-'oss] cart 'oss *TSIa*
52:20 naïve *MS*, *TSIaC*] naive *TSIa*
52:22 lost people *TSIa*] street-arabs *MS*
52:32 below—"/ Then] ~—" *P* Then *A1* ~——"/ Then *E1*
52:34 childhood's *'our"*/ The] ~ *our"*/ The *TSIaC* ~ *our—"* *P* The *A1* childhood *s'our"*/ The *E1*
52:35 twins: "I] ~:/ "I *TSIa*
52:36 more—"/ Again] ~—" *P* Again *A1* ~"/ Again *E1*
52:37 Lennie.] ~: *E1*
53:4 me—"/ Here] ~—" *P* Here *A1* ~——"/ Here *E1*
53:5 hypnotised] hypnotized *A1*
53:5 out—"it] ~—/ "it *TSIa* ~—/ "—it *TSIaC* ~:/ "It *E1*
53:6 new,] ~ *E1*
53:26 barelegged] bare-/ legged *A1* bare-legged *E1*
53:28 undervest:] ~, *E1*
53:28 last *TSIa*] latter *MS*
53:35 d' ye *MS*, *TSIaC*] d'e *TSIa*
53:36 cos] 'cos *TSIaC*
54:4 un] 'un *TSIaC*, *E1*
54:10 Risin',] Risin,' *E1*
54:12 Now] ~, *A1*, *E1*
54:18 I s'll] I'll *TSIa*
54:21 lonely] lovely *TSIa*
54:23 odd] ~, *TSIa*
54:24 lonely] lovely *TSIa*
54:24 pathos:] ~, *TSIa*
54:31 him] ~, *TSIa*
54:34 here, goes— *E1*] here— *MS*
54:36 "Obey an' ... Noddy ... aid ye—" said] "~ ~ ... ~, ... ~ ~—"/ ~ *TSIa* *"Obey an' ... Noddy, ... aid ye——"* ~ *A1* "~ ~' ... ~, ... ~ ~——"/ ~ *E1*
55:1 Aw] ~, *TSIaC*, *E1*
55:15 k'n *TSIa*] kn *MS*
55:17 heap] ~, *TSIa*
55:17 boots] ~, *TSIaC*
55:23 side] ~, *E1*
55:29 stock horse] stock-horse *TSIa*
55:31 draught horses] draft horses *TSIa* draft-horses *TSIaC*
55:34 halter-ropes] halter ropes *TSIa*
55:36 walkin', *MS*, *E1*] walkin[...] *TSIa* ~; *A1*
55:36 an'] and *TSIa*
55:37 an' *MS*, *E1*] an *TSIa*
55:37 pillion *Ed.*] pinion *MS*
56:3 "Let ... go!" *TSIa*] ~ ... ~! *MS*
56:4 gate *MS*, *E1*] ~, *TSIa*
56:8 haven't] haven' *TSIa*

56:9 doc] dock *TSIa*
56:9 is] ~, *TSIa*
56:14 Well] ~, *E1*
56:14 corpse—] ~, *TSIa*
56:27 ventured:] ~. *TSIa*
56:28 Doctor] Dr. *A1*
57:4 floss-haired *TSIa*] floss haired *MS*
57:5 even] *Om. TSIa see notes*
57:16 baby *E1*] Baby *MS*
57:17 What my] ~, ~ *TSIaC* ~! My *E1*
57:17 bulbs,] ~ *E1*
57:17 Why] ~, *A1*, *E1*
57:18 Dickens] dickens *TSIaC*, *E1*
57:19 An' besides—] ~, ~, *E1*
57:21 look] looked *TSIa see notes*
57:22 evil] ~, *E1*
57:26 says] ~, *TSIa*
57:26 gosh!",] Gosh!", *TSIaC* Gosh!" *A1* gosh!" *E1*
57:29 continues *TSIa*] continued *MS*
57:30 toddles *TSIa*] toddled *MS*
57:34 they] ~, *TSIa*
57:35 mornin'] ~, *E1*
57:37 Narcissi *TSIa*] Narcisii *MS* narcissi *E1*
57:37 Narcissuses] narcissuses *E1*
58:2 Everybody *TSIa*] Every body *MS*
58:12 old old] ~, ~ *TSIa*
58:12 immovable] ~, *TSIa*
58:18 meal-times] meal times *TSIa*
59:7 woolen] woollen *TSIa*
59:8 advice] ~, *E1*
59:12 riding-breeches] riding breeches *TSIa*
59:25 into *TSIa*] in to *MS*
59:25 individuality, *MS*, *TSIaC*] ~ *TSIa*
60:1 purpose,] ~ *A1*
60:2 brother *TSIa*] son *MS*
60:7 the *TSIaC*, *E1*] The *MS*
60:8 sitting-room] sitting room *TSIa*
60:13 pittosporum *Ed.*] phetosphorum *MS* photosporum *A1*, *E1*
60:16 Why] ~, *TSIaC*
60:17 Uncle *TSIa*] uncle *MS*
60:21 he *TSIa*] all *MS see notes*
60:22 try"] ~", *TSIa* ~," *A1*, *E1*
60:24 lady] ~, *E1*
60:27 sitting-room] sitting room *A1*
60:27 Jack] ~, *TSIa*
60:31 floss hair,] floss-hair *TSIa* floss-/ hair *A1* floss-/ hair, *E1*
60:40 baby. ... baby] Baby. ... Baby *TSIaC*
61:4 baby] Baby *TSIaC*
61:6 dear!] ~. *TSIa*
61:9 Ya—some] ~.—Some *TSIa* ~! Some *E1*
61:10 Oh] ~, *A1*, *E1*
61:10 quiet] ~, *TSIaC*, *E1*
61:10 do———] ~—— *A1* ~ . . . *E1*
61:11 baby *Ed.*] Baby *MS*
61:16 baby *Ed.*] Baby *MS*
61:19 ecstasy *MS*, *E1*] ecstacy *TSIa*
61:22 porridge!] ~. *E1*
61:24 And] ~, *E1*
61:37 stable] ~, *TSIa*
62:1 favourite *TSIaC*, *E1*] favorite *MS*, *A1*
62:5 dust] ~, *TSIa*
62:5 possible...] ~. ... *TSIa*, *E1* ~ *A1*
62:11 —And] —and *TSIa* And *E1*
62:16 one.] ~! *TSIa*
62:21 pump,] ~ *TSIa*
62:23 else. *TSIa*] ~? *MS*
62:27 Tom: *MS*, *E1*] ~. *TSIa*
62:29 Well] ~, *TSIa*
62:37 Xactly] 'Xactly *TSIaC*, *E1*
62:38 and] an' *E1*
63:4 rattle-snake] rattlesnake *TSIa*
63:5 cos] 'cos *TSIaC*
63:7 son.—] ~— *E1*
63:7 Doc *MS*, *TSIaC*] Dock *TSIa*
63:8 not] ~, *TSIa*
63:9 And—"] ~"— *E1*
63:12 public *MS*, *E1*] Public *TSIa*
63:17 grown-up *MS*, *A1*] grown up *TSIa*
63:37 strange,] ~ *A1*
64:2 away,] ~ *E1*

64:2 all activity *A1*, *E1*] the house *MS*
64:8 merchant,] ~ *TSIa*
64:9 Gran *TSIa*] gran *MS*
64:10 Granpa *MS*, *E1*] Grampa *TSIa*
64:11 will;] ~: *TSIa*
64:13 years, *MS*, *E1*] ~ *TSIa*
64:13 no-one] no one *TSIa*
64:17 Reds' *Ed.*] Reds *MS* Red's *TSIa*
64:20 Anyhow] ~, *E1*
64:21 twins—] ~.— *TSIa* ~. *E1*
64:22 Easus *TSIaC*] Easu's *MS*, *A1*
64:26 family] ~, *TSIa*
64:29 colony] ~, *E1*
64:31 Oh,] ~. *A1*
64:31 alright] all right *TSIa*
64:38 Anyhow] ~, *E1*
65:1 servant, *MS*, *E1*] ~ *TSIa*
65:2 all *Ed.*] all there *MS* all there is *TSIa see note on* 60:21
65:13 Anyhow] ~, *E1*
65:24 dead. A *TSIa*] ~, a *MS*
65:25 the Reds *TSIa*] they *MS*
65:29 thirty *TSIa*] twenty-seven *MS*
65:30 beard] ~, *E1*
65:32 over *TSIa*] out *MS*
65:32 This was . . . at Wandoo. *TSIa*] *Om. MS*
66:4 trousers.] ~? *TSIaC*, *E1*
66:6 n' lively *MS*, *E1*] n'lively *TSIa* 'n'lively *A1*
66:6 n' y' socks] n' y'socks *TSIa* 'n' y'socks *A1*
66:9 black-boys] black boys *E1*
66:11 Well] ~, *TSIa*
66:12 hear.—] ~?— *TSIaC* ~. *E1*
66:14 jackasses.] ~? *A1*
66:16 Oh] ~, *A1*, *E1*
66:17 Easu *TSIa*] He *MS*
66:18 tall *TSIa*] big *MS*
66:23 view,] ~ *E1*
66:27 to. *TSIa*] ~.— *MS see notes*
66:30 'im *MS*, *TSIaC*] 'em *TSIa*
66:31 time—] ~. *E1*
66:34 stables] stable *TSIa*
66:40 Easu. But *Ed.*] Esau. But *MS* Easu, but *TSIa*
67:4 backward] backwards *A1*, *E1*
67:5 gate.] ~! *TSIaC*
67:6 Meanwhile] ~, *E1*
67:7 Steady] ~, *E1*
67:18 vise *MS*, *A1*] vice *TSIa*
67:19 jerked *A1*, *E1*] thrown *MS*
67:21 Easu *TSIa*] Esau *MS*
67:24 whilst] while *TSIa*
67:27 trembling *A1*, *E1*] hard power *MS*
67:28 exertion *A1*, *E1*] pleasure *MS*
67:30 made him tremble with . . . not relax *E1*] was like love. A sort of wild love, not bullying *MS* made him tremble strangely with . . . not relax *A1 see notes*
67:33 really:] ~; *E1*
67:33 keyed up *A1*, *E1*] exultant *MS*
67:35 tossed body *A1*, *E1*] fierce legs *MS*
67:35 corkscrew bucks *A1*] sudden stops *MS* corkscrew buck *E1 see notes*
67:38 times,] ~ *E1*
67:38 Up he . . . about by . . . [68:1] beneath him *E1*] With his thighs, with his knees, with his calves, with his feet, with his hands he held on and balanced, as galloping, sidling, jumping, shying and bucking, the horse made a tortured way across the open, with intervals of tossing and kicking *MS* Up he . . . about, by . . . beneath him *A1*
68:4 black-boys *MS*, *TSIaC*] black boys *TSIa*
68:12 was barely . . . Yet he *A1*, *E1*] knew what he was about. He *MS*
68:15 own old] ~, ~ *TSIa*
68:17 yield his . . . before *E1*] accept the deterioration of *MS* yield in . . . before *A1*
68:18 give in to *A1*, *E1*] accept *MS*
68:20 loved. There] ~. *P* There *TSIa*
68:21 refused and defied *A1*, *E1*] just repudiated *MS*

68:24 unconscious] ~, *E1*

68:26 black] ~, *TSIa*

69:13 cortège *MS*, *TSIaC*] cortege *TSIa*

69:28 O' me] o'me *TSIa*

69:29 so!—] ~:— *TSIa* ~?— *TSIaC* ~. *E1*

69:29 Well then—] ~, ~, *E1*

69:30 in *TSIa*] in' *MS*

69:33 Tom! *Ed.*] ~!, *MS* ~, *TSIaC*, *E1* ~. *TSIa*

69:34 Don't—!"] ~"— *TSIa*

69:39 doctor," *MS*, *E1*] ~", *TSIa* ~!" *TSIaC*

70:1 Halloed!] halloed *TSIa*

70:6 Halloed!] halloed *TSIa*

70:11 Doctor] doctor *E1*

70:11 "So … that!" *TSIa*] ~ … ~! *MS*

70:15 drawing-room] drawing room *TSIa*

70:15 there] ~, *E1*

70:15 dying-room] dying room *TSIa*

70:18 Lucy] ~, *E1*

70:18 saddle-horse;] ~, *E1*

70:19 around] round *TSIa*

70:26 blues *TSIa*] blue *MS*

70:34 watch-chain] watchchain *TSIa*

70:38 baby *MS*, *E1*] Baby *A1*

71:4 also *TSIa*] *Om. MS see note on* 71:8

71:4 usual] ~, *E1*

71:5 family,] ~ *A1*

71:6 said.—] ~, *TSIa*

71:7 Dad] dad *E1*

71:17 Usually,] ~ *E1*

71:18 today,] to-day *E1*

71:21 baby] Baby *A1*

71:23 crumbs] ~, *E1*

71:27 Harry,] ~ *E1*

71:28 Ah] ~, *A1*, *E1*

71:28 family! the] ~! The *A1*

71:32 *one*] one *A1*

72:2 sitting-room *MS*, *E1*] sitting room *TSIa*

72:9 living-room] living room *TSIa*

72:11 here.] ~? *TSIa*

72:13 horse,] ~*TSIa*

72:15 vise] vice *TSIa*

72:26 section *TSIa*] section beyond *MS*

72:27 attention *TSIa*] attention, however, *MS*

72:36 Easu] ~, *E1*

72:37 reddish *TSIa*] red *MS*

72:37 demon *TSIa*] devil *MS* demon, *E1*

72:38 experience,] ~ *TSIa*

73:1 first:] ~ *E1*

73:5 Every time, he … the bed.] *Om. A1* Every time he … bed. *E1 see note on* 42:20

73:12 said;] asked, *TSIa*

73:20 Katie's *TSIa*] katies' *MS*

73:22 pulled: *MS*, *E1*] ~, *TSIa*

73:22 hurt,] ~ *E1*

73:26 hands] hand *TSIa*

73:27 great] ~, *TSIa*

73:39 silence] ~, *TSIa*

73:39 done,] ~ *E1*

74:1 brothers:] ~, *TSIa*

74:13 help *TSIa*] quiet *MS*

74:14 creature's] creatures' *TSIa*

74:38 worry] ~, *TSIa*

75:6 some one] someone *TSIa*

75:13 again—] ~. *TSIa*

75:22 suckling — —] ~— *A1* ~. … *E1*

76:9 y're *Ed.*] y'r *MS*

76:9 stocky] ~, *TSIa*

76:11 man *TSIa*] devil *MS*

76:16 Regular *A1*, *E1*] Absolute *MS*

76:23 then I *TSIa*] *Om. MS*

76:24 things] ~, *TSIa*

77:6 your] you're *TSIa*

77:11 son] ~, *E1*

77:17 heart-disease] heart disease *TSIa*

77:35 back,] ~ *TSIa*

78:1 But] ~, *E1*

78:11 deary-me] dreary-me *E1*

78:11 done?—] ~. *TSIa*

78:27 saying: *P* "Hello] ~: "Hello, *A1* ~: *P* "Hello, *E1*

78:28 Bow!" *P* Queer] ~!" Queer *A1*

78:29 the] this *TSIa*

78:30 soft: *P* "Hello] ~, "Hello *TSIa* ~ "Hello, *A1* ~, "Hello, *E1*
78:32 they *A1*, *E1*] they both *MS*
78:32 rain,] ~. *TSIa*
78:33 tight-crisp *Ed.*] tight crisp *MS*
78:38 sleeve. *MS*, *E1*] ~, *TSIa*
78:39 back." *P* And] ~." And *TSIa*
79:3 face *TSIa*] wet face *MS*
79:6 smells] Smells *TSIa*
79:17 doorway *TSIa*] doorway too *MS*
79:21 Easu *TSIa*] Esau *MS*
79:21 uncouth] ~, *TSIa*
79:22 side] side of *A1*, *E1*
79:29 show *TSIa*] feel *MS*
79:30 submissiveness to *TSIa*] kindliness for *MS*
79:30 Jack,] ~ *E1*
79:31 Gran. *MS*, *E1*] ~, *TSIa*
79:31 you. *MS*, *E1*] ~, *TSIa*
80:15 soul!—] ~— *TSIa*
80:15 pillow-frills] pillow frills *TSIa*
80:24 fire,] ~ *TSIa*
80:24 arm chair] arm-chair *TSIa*
80:26 itself, and] ~. And *TSIa*
80:27 "What . . . done?" *Ed.*] ~ . . . ~? *MS*
80:28 "Conquered . . . world." *Ed.*] ~ . . . ~. *MS*
80:32 ticked!] ~. *E1*
80:33 boxing-gloves] boxing gloves *A1*
80:34 couldn't *Ed.*] couldnt *MS* could *TSIa*
80:35 down,] ~; *TSIa* ~: *E1*
80:37 counting *TSIa*] Counting *MS*
80:40 minute] ~, *TSIa*
81:2 it] ~, *TSIaC*, *E1*
81:2 man!] ~. *TSIa* ~? *TSIaC*
81:3 "There . . . fire." *TSIa*] ~ . . . ~. *MS*
81:6 half past] half-past *A1*, *E1*
81:17 know.—But] ~—but *E1*
81:20 She—"] ~"— *TSIa*
82:15 opossums] oppossums *TSIa*
82:17 shatteringly] ~, *E1*
82:20 immense,] ~ *E1*
82:24 dense,] ~ *E1*
82:25 out—] ~. *TSIa*
83:1 own,] ~ *TSIa*
83:4 the other *TSIa*] he *MS*
83:6 Oh] ~, *A1*, *E1*
83:7 Oh] ~, *A1*, *E1*
83:8 die.] ~? *TSIa*
83:11 "Yourself is God." It . . . than this. *A1*, *E1*] *Om. MS* "Yourself is God". It . . . than this. *TSIa*
83:16 doom of *A1*, *E1*] *Om. MS* doom *TSIa*
83:16 Somewhere outside . . . who decreed. *TSIa*] *Om. MS*
83:18 life] ~, *TSIa*
83:23 his *TSIa*] a *MS*
84:4 telling,] ~ *TSIa*
84:20 pump-spout] pump spout *TSIa*
84:20 Oh] ~, *A1*, *E1*
84:20 'twas *TSIa*] 't was *MS*
84:29 undervest] under-vest *E1*
84:31 riddle] ~, *TSIa*
85:2 [not] *Ed.*] *Om. MS see notes*
85:4 but I *TSIa*] but *MS*
85:10 left him cold *TSIa*] pleased him *MS*
85:12 stop] Stop *TSIa*
85:12 It 'ud *MS*, *A1*] It'ud *TSIa*
85:13 is. 'Self] ~. *P* 'Self *TSIa* ~. *P* "Self *A1* ~. *P* "'Self *E1*
85:15 joy.'"] ~." *A1*
85:18 Og?" *MS*, *TSIaC*] ~? *TSIa*, *A1*
85:19 Why] ~, *A1*, *E1*
85:19 success—] ~—— *E1*
85:25 one.] ~! *TSIa*
85:25 one Jack.] ~, ~! *TSIa*
85:27 supportin'] supporting *E1*
85:27 y' pants] y'r pants *TSIa*
85:28 th'] the' *A1*
85:37 But—" and he] ~"—he *TSIa*
85:37 y've] ye've *TSIa*
86:1 holding] holdin' *TSIa*
86:4 stoopin' *TSIa*] stoopin *MS*
86:11 Oh] ~, *A1*, *E1*
86:11 one-two-three-four] one—two—three—four *E1*
86:15 floor."] ~?" *TSIaC*, *E1*
86:18 Oh] ~, *TSIa*

86:19 prize-fightin'] prize fightin' *TSIa*
86:23 sense.] ~! *TSIa*
86:24 doin' *A1*, *E1*] doin *MS*
86:32 morning. *P* Len's] ~. Len's *TSIa*
86:34 yes,—] ~— *TSIa*
86:34 y' like!— *MS*, *A1*] y'like!— *TSIa* y'like. *E1*
86:35 nights—] ~. *TSIa*
86:39 d' y' *Ed.*] d' y *MS* d'y *TSIa*
87:5 again,] ~ *E1*
87:10 filled:] ~, *TSIa*
87:13 sitting-room] sitting room *TSIa*
87:15 untied, Bow. Do] ~. ~, do *TSIa*
87:17 Gran's *TSIa*] gran's *MS*
87:25 nodded,] ~ *TSIa*
87:29 come. *TSIa*] come, will you. *MS*
87:32 him] *Om. A1 see note on* 67:36
88:6 pittosporum *Ed.*] photosporum *MS*
88:6 Ellie *Ed.*] Effie *MS see note on* 57:5
88:10 bow,] ~ *TSIa*
88:17 Christmas,] ~ *E1*
88:20 clearing,] ~ *E1*
88:22 Besides—"] ~"— *A1*, *E1*
88:23 in *MS*, *E1*] in' *TSIa*
88:26 quietly. "He] ~, "he *TSIa*
88:32 slowly;] ~, *TSIa*
88:40 queer *TSIa*] queer and warm *MS*
89:11 Monica *TSIa*] Mona *MS* Monica, *E1*
89:13 dead] a dead *E1*
89:17 Doctor] Dr. *A1*
89:18 And] ~, *E1*
89:18 Doctor] Dr. *A1*
89:18 Mallett.] ~? *TSIa*
89:19 Course] 'Course *A1*
89:23 Well] ~, *TSIa*
89:29 horse-shoes *MS*, *E1*] horse-/ shoes *TSIa* horseshoes *A1*
89:30 on—] ~. *E1*
89:31 Oh] ~, *A1*, *E1*
89:31 Monica! *TSIa*] Mona! *MS* Monica; *E1*
89:31 y' are.] y'are! *TSIa*
89:31 fer] for *TSIa*
89:31 do, y're] ~! Y're *TSIa*
89:32 good. — —] ~.— — — *TSIa* ~.— *A1* ~. . . . *E1*
89:32 Git] Gitt *TSIa*
89:33 feet?—] ~!— *TSIa* ~? *E1*
89:34 come] Come *E1*
89:34 stuff.— —] ~.— *A1* ~. . . . *E1*
89:35 There] ~, *A1*, *E1*
89:35 Ocha] Ooha *TSIa*
89:36 don'] don't *A1*, *E1*
89:37 Lennie] ~, *E1*
89:38 Ma—] ~. *TSIa*
89:38 didn't y',—] did y' *TSIa*
90:1 arm. *MS*, *E1*] ~, *TSIa*
90:3 submitted,] ~ *TSIa*
90:4 stocking-feet] stocking feet *TSIa*
90:7 him,] ~? *E1*
90:17 box.] ~? *TSIaC*
90:22 neck, *MS*, *A1*] ~ *TSIa*
90:30 asked] said *TSIa*
90:31 saddle-bags *MS*, *E1*] saddle bags *TSIa*
90:31 strap-holder *MS*, *E1*] strap holder *TSIa*
90:36 saddle-cloths] saddle cloths *TSIa*
90:37 tissue-paper] tissue paper *TSIa*
90:38 assam] Assam *TSIaC*
91:7 him;] ~: *A1*, *E1*
91:8 tittering *TSIa*] dithering *MS*
91:9 Oh] ~, *A1*, *E1*
91:10 1. grade] 1 Grade *TSIa*, *E1*
91:10 'tree] tree *TSIaC*, *E1*
91:10 mounted] ~, *A1*, *E1*
91:12 ornamented] ~, *TSIa*
91:12 An' oh] ~ ~, *A1* ~, ~, *E1*
91:16 Oh] ~, *TSIa*, *E1*
91:16 Lor' *TSIa*] Lor *MS*
91:16 oh] ~, *E1*
91:16 My—] my— *TSIa* my—— *A1*, *E1*
91:18 barn. *P* "Now] ~. "Now *TSIa* ~. "Now, *E1*
91:20 stirrup-leathers] sti[. . .]

leathers *TSIa* stirrup leathers *TSIb*, *A1*
91:22 it's *TSIa*] it *MS*
91:23 Now] ~, *A1*, *E1*
91:24 yours, you're] ~. You're *TSIa*
91:26 Camp] camp *TSIa*
92:2 Back,] ~ *TSIa* BACK *A1* BACK *E1*
92:5 strange] ~, *TSIa*
92:11 life-long *MS*, *E1*] life-/ long *TSIa* lifelong *A1*
92:15 Camping] camping *TSIa*
92:21 paradise, *Ed.*] Paradise, *MS* Paradise *TSIa*
92:24 sticks,] ~ *E1*
92:25 rain] the rain *TSIa*
92:26 timber—] ~. *TSIa*
92:32 coming *TSIa*] Coming *MS*
93:8 stood] ~, *E1*
93:13 handle] ~, *A1*
93:17 partition poles] partition-poles *TSIa*
93:18 the shape *TSIaC*] shape *MS* *see note on* 24:11
93:18 looking glasses] looking-glasses *A1*, *E1*
93:19 etc.—] ~. *TSIa* ~., *A1*, *E1*
93:22 well:] ~, *TSIa*
93:25 around] ~, *E1*
93:28 cone-shaped] ~, *E1*
93:30 pale-gold] pale gold *TSIa*
93:35 rock-face] ~, *E1*
93:39 the gang *TSIa*] they *MS*
94:7 horse:] ~; *E1*
94:8 Coo—ee!,] Coo-ee! *TSIa*, *E1* "Coo-ee!" *A1*
94:15 in *TSIa*] it *MS*
94:16 cross-bar *MS*, *A1*] cross bar *TSIa*
94:17 brush-wood] brushwood *TSIa*
94:17 long] ~, *TSIa*
94:19 —savage—] ~ *TSIa*
94:21 frying pans] frying-pans *E1*
94:24 saw-mill] sawmill *E1*
94:24 outlying *MS*, *A1*] out-/ lying *TSIa* out-lying *E1*
94:31 boodie rats *Ed.*] bloody-rats *MS* blood-rats *TSIa* boody-rats *E1* *see notes*
95:3 pitying-admonishing] pitying admonishing *TSIa*
95:6 sixpence. And the *Ed.*] six'pence. And the *MS* sixpence, and a *TSIa*
95:9 months,] ~ *TSIa*
95:9 her] the *TSIa*
95:10 money] ~, *A1*
95:20 Saw-mill] saw-mill *TSIa*
95:21 letter—"You] ~.—"You *TSIa* ~. *P* "You *A1* ~. "You *E1*
95:24 back *TSIa*] stationed *MS*
95:25 course] ~, *TSIa*
95:25 molly coddle] mollycoddle *TSIa*
95:29 downpours—] ~—— *A1*, *E1*
95:34 Mother,] ~: *A1*
95:40 Tim the half-caste] ~, ~ ~, *TSIa*
96:4 paraffin *E1*] parafin *MS*
96:7 sisters] sister *TSIa*
96:8 well—] ~—— *A1*, *E1*
96:14 old-man] old man *TSIa* Old Man *A1*
96:15 hoof-marks] ~, *E1*
96:17 the *TSIa*] a *MS*
96:18 greyhounds] ~, *E1*
96:20 unmanageable,] ~ *TSIa*
96:22 Cornseed *TSIa*] cornseed *MS*
96:24 again;] ~, *TSIa*
96:24 stallion,] ~; *E1*
96:24 riding-breeches] riding breeches *TSIa*
96:37 sang *TSIa*] sung *MS* *see notes*
96:38 with the reins *TSIa*] at the same time *MS*
97:3 zig-zag] zigzag *TSIa*
97:3 north *TSIaC*, *E1*] North *MS*
97:4 gentleman—] ~—— *A1*, *E1*
97:9 However] ~, *TSIa*
97:15 ye— *TSIa*] ye see—*MS* ye—— *A1*, *E1*
97:23 Lennie, "because] ~. "Because *TSIa*
97:24 heel] heels *A1*
97:34 burning,] ~ *TSIa*

97:35 supper,] ~ *TSIa*
97:35 directions] ~, *TSIa*
97:36 towards] toward *TSIa*
97:40 projectile *E1*] catapult *MS*
98:2 vise] vice *TSIaC*
98:4 Coo—ee] Coo-ee *TSIa*
98:5 Coo—ee! Coo—ee! Coo—ee] Coo-ee! Coo-ee! Coo-ee *TSIa*
98:7 Coo—ee! Coo—ee! Coo—ee] Coo-ee! Coo-ee! Coo-ee *TSIa*
98:8 Jack,] ~ *E1*
98:11 coo," *A1*] ~;" *MS* ~" *TSIa* ~", *TSIaC*
98:12 then] *Om. TSIa*
98:12 eee!] ~. *TSIa*
98:13 and the] and then the *TSIa*
98:14 Coo—eee! Coo—eee! Coo—eee] Coo-eee! Coo-eee! Coo-eee *TSIa*
98:18 Indian's] Indians *TSIa* Indians' *TSIaC*, *E1*
98:20 are] were *TSIa*
98:20 and] to *A1*
98:22 taken,] ~. *TSIa*
98:28 fly,] ~! *TSIa*
98:28 crash!— —] *Crash*!— *TSIa* *Crash!*— *A1*, *E1*
98:29 all] All *TSIa*
98:29 a dream] A ~ *TSIaC*
98:32 "Look *TSIa*] ~ *MS*
98:33 head." *Ed.*] ~. *MS* ~!" *TSIa*
98:34 hind-quarters] hind quarters *TSIa*
98:37 wind,] ~. *E1*
99:2 Scrub,] scrub, *TSIa* scrub *E1*
99:2 than *TSIa*] that *MS*
99:6 boodie rat *Ed.*] bloody-rat *MS* blood-rat *A1* boody-rat *E1*
99:6 holes,] ~ *TSIa*
99:7 rocks,] ~ *TSIa*
99:8 are] were *TSIa*
99:13 Up!",] ~!" *A1*
99:16 shrub] scrub *TSIa*, *E1* scrubs *A1 see notes*
99:20 mother-doe] mother doe *TSIa*
99:22 springs—] ~ *TSIa*
100:8 gully *TSIa*] gulley *MS*
100:9 dogs.] ~, *TSIa*
100:9 boulder,] ~ *TSIa*
100:17 Cooe-eed] coo-eed *TSIa*
100:23 stanched] staunched *TSIa*
100:38 were all] all *A1*
101:12 flail-like *TSIa*] flail like *MS*
101:15 him. The *TSIa*] him, and the *MS*
101:26 consciousness! Its overpowering smell! *TSIa*] consciousness!— — *MS*
101:34 vet] ~. *E1*
102:11 first hand] first-hand *E1*
102:16 by,] ~ *TSIa*
102:19 Darling.—And] ~—~ *TSIa* ~—and *A1*, *E1*
102:28 Tom,] ~: *E1*
102:28 you] ye *TSIa*
102:29 Sure.' And] ~.' and *TSIa* ~.'—and *E1*
102:36 dirt—] ~. *E1*
102:37 him—'] ~.— *TSIa* ~.'— *TSIaC* ~;'— *TSIbC* ~.' *E1*
102:38 talking] ~, *E1*
102:39 stranger, *MS*, *E1*] ~ *TSIa*
103:2 said] ~, *TSIa* ~: *E1*
103:3 long,] ~! *TSIa*
103:14 miles,] ~ *TSIa*
103:23 Old Man *TSIa*] old man *MS*
103:28 lot *TSIa*] fine lot *MS*
103:32 Jack."] "JACK." *E1*
103:34 friend] ~, *TSIa*
103:34 wrote] ~: *A1*, *E1*
103:35 "Dear *TSIa*] ~ *MS*
103:35 Pug] ~: *TSIa* ~, *E1*
104:4 brute] brutes *TSIa*
104:8 devil] Devil *TSIa*
104:9 tucker's-worth] tucker's worth *TSIa*
104:10 Today] To-day, *E1*
104:10 Sabbath] ~, *E1*
104:12 fetches] fetched *TSIa*
104:14 horror!] ~. *TSIa*
104:14 sons] ~, *E1*
104:17 up,] ~. *TSIa*
104:24 to] a *TSIa*
104:28 pray] pray that *TSIa*

104:34 friend] ~, *E1*
104:35 Jack." *TSIa*] ~. *MS* "JACK." *E1*
105:6 into *E1*] in to *MS*
105:17 axe-handling] axe handling *TSIa*
105:23 Government *TSIa*] government *MS*
105:27 50] fifty *E1*
105:29 25] twenty-five *E1*
105:31 death] ~, *TSIa*
105:38 10/-] 10s. *E1*
105:39 1/-] 1s. *E1*
105:40 2/-] 2s. *E1*
106:1 presumptive *TSIa*] pre-emptive *MS*
106:5 Government *TSIa*] government *MS*
106:7 things:] ~; *TSIa*
106:11 had] *Om. A1*
106:11 taking-up-land] taking-up land *TSIa*
106:15 purpose] ~, *E1*
106:20 present. *MS, E1*] ~ *TSIa*
106:21 affec] ~. *TSIa*
106:22 Jack."] "JACK." *E1*
106:25 this] his *A1*
106:25 answer.] ~: *A1*
106:26 Terrace] ~, *TSIa*
106:27 Bournemouth] ~. *TSIa* ~, *E1*
106:28 2. 2. '83] 2/2/'83 *E1*
106:29 Jack, *MS, E1*] ~: *TSIa*
106:37 death—] ~.— *A1* ~. *E1*
107:1 which ... me] ~, ... ~, *E1*
107:1 £1.] £1 *E1*
107:3 felicitations] ~. *E1*
107:4 father] ~, *E1*
107:5 G.] "~. *E1*
107:5 Grant." *P* But] ~."/ But *TSIa* GRANT."/ But *E1*
107:6 this is running ahead *TSIa*] we anticipate *MS*
108:5 Sundown *MS, A1*] Sun-/ down *TSIa* Sun-down *E1*
108:7 Then] ~, *E1*
108:12 with a] with *TSIa*
108:13 glossy,] ~ *E1*
108:17 *pinki*] *pinkie TSIa*
108:17 midsummer] mid-/ summer *TSIa* mid-summer *E1*
108:24 paper-bark] paper-back *TSIa*
108:24 gum-trees] gum trees *TSIa*
108:33 noise] noises *TSIa*
109:8 food-stuff] food-stuffs *A1*
109:19 that of course] ~, ~ ~, *TSIa*
109:20 cocky *TSIa*] very cocky *MS*
109:30 afar,] ~ *E1*
109:30 smoking] Smoking *TSIa*
109:34 OOh!"] Oooh" *TSIa* Oooh!" *A1* Oooh," *E1*
109:34 suddenly. "Ooh] ~, "Oooh *TSIa*
109:36 chips—,] ~— *TSIa*
110:9 chinaman's] Chinaman's *TSIa*
110:10 never] *Om. TSIa see note on* 42:20.
110:13 eyes:] ~; *E1*
110:15 chinaman's-hat *Ed.*] Chinaman's-hat *MS* Chinaman's hat *E1*
110:16 meatsafe] meat-safe *TSIa*
110:19 now,] ~ *TSIa*
110:28 cool] ~, *E1*
110:29 bliss.] ~, *TSIa*
111:2 round] ~, *A1*
111:3 head!" *P* Monica *Ed.*] ~!" *P* Mona *MS* ~!" Monica *TSIa*
111:13 river] River *TSIa*
111:18 Jack,] ~ *E1*
111:24 venomously. "Because] ~, "because *E1*
111:27 Oo—er] Oo-er *TSIa*
111:28 half-way *Ed.*] half-/ way *MS* halfway *E1*
111:31 outdid *MS, TSIaC*] out did *TSIa* out-did *A1, E1*
111:33 Tom,] ~ *E1*
111:33 jacket *MS, TSIaC, E1*] Jacket *TSIa* jacket, *A1*
111:35 exclaimed: *MS, E1*] ~, *TSIa*
112:1 'em] 'm *TSIa*
112:4 it] ~, *A1*
112:5 from round the country *A1*] *Om. MS* from ... country, *E1*
112:7 Hallelujah] ~, *E1*
112:8 dyin'-room] dyin' room *TSIa*

112:9 cubby!] ~. *E1*
112:11 shivoo] chivoo *TSIa*
112:13 feed bags] feed-bags *A1*
112:15 ties,] ~; *E1*
112:17 young] ~, *E1*
112:20 concertina-playing] concertina playing *E1*
112:26 set—] ~. *TSIa*
112:30 Aw] ~, *A1*, *E1*
112:34 twenty five] twenty-five *TSIa*
112:35 Rossy *Ed.*] Rosy *MS* Ross *A1*
112:35 bowling. *MS*, *E1*] ~, *TSIa*
113:3 paddock *TSIa*] paddocks *MS* *see notes*
113:5 excited,] ~ *E1*
113:6 couldn't *E1*] could n't *MS* Couldn't *TSIa*
113:10 the] th' *TSIa*
113:12 eyes. But] ~, but *TSIa*
113:13 He——] ~—— *A1*, *E1*
113:14 "Here . . . Easu!" *Ed.*] ~ . . . ~! *MS*
113:15 "How's that!" *Ed.*] ~ . . . ~! *MS*
113:16 to—] ~—— *A1*
113:17 stripling] ~, *TSIa*
113:22 Jack hitched *TSIa*] "~ ~ *MS*
113:23 another three, and got 'em.] another. three, and got in *TSIa* another. *TSIaC*, *E1* *see notes*
113:25 —no] ~ *TSIa* No *E1*
113:25 boundary. *P* Lennie's] ~. Lennie's *TSIa*
113:31 missed—.] ~. *TSIa*
114:1 half century] half-century *E1*
114:3 Nevertheless] ~, *A1*
114:3 runs, *TSIaR*] ~ *MS*, *A1*
114:13 all older] older *A1*
114:18 to get through *TSIaR*] effective *MS*
114:22 had quick] ~ ~, *TSIa*
114:24 the] a *TSIa*
114:27 small-headed demons out *TSIaR*] hammers *MS*
114:31 malevolent *TSIaR*] destructive *MS*
114:31 venom *TSIaR*] Lucifer *MS*
114:37 blonde] blond *A1*
114:37 rivet *TSIaR*] quick *MS*
115:8 sportsmen—] ~. *TSIa*
115:9 Why] ~, *A1*
115:10 cockeys *TSIaR*] poor cockeys *MS*
115:13 jumps] the jumps *TSIa*
115:17 anyfin] anyfin' *TSIaC*
115:18 you] ~, *TSIa*
115:20 teeth] ~, *TSIa*
115:26 Well] ~, *A1*, *E1*
115:26 nipper] Nipper *TSIa*
115:30 O. K. *MS*, *A1*] O.K. *TSIa*
115:35 a rest] to rest *TSIa*
116:2 tense,] ~ *TSIa*
116:13 and his] and *A1*
116:18 eyes] ~, *TSIa*
116:32 miffed *Ed.*] niffed *MS*
117:6 finishing *TSIaR*] closing *MS*
117:7 but *TSIaR*] but with *MS*
117:12 Coast] coast *TSIa*
117:14 you] ~, *E1*
117:20 small, *MS*, *E1*] ~ *TSIa*
117:32 jeering *TSIaR*] bully-ragging *MS*
117:34 butter-cup] buttercup *TSIa*
117:36 doing!] ~? *E1*
118:7 —and] ~ *TSIa*
118:8 Joe, and] ~, ~, *E1*
118:10 pistol-shot] pistol shot *TSIa*
118:11 you!] ~; *A1*
118:14 parts . . .] ~. *TSIa*
118:21 Oh] ~, *A1*, *E1*
118:23 Oh] ~, *TSIa*
118:26 I!] ~, *TSIa*
118:30 a fortnight *TSIaR*] five days *MS*
118:31 Yah] Zah *TSIa*
118:31 o'] of *TSIa*
118:32 blacks] ~, *A1*
118:32 durstn't—.] ~. *TSIa*
118:34 An' *TSIa*] An *MS*
118:35 round—] ~. *TSIa*
118:36 Oh] ~, *E1*
118:36 well—] ~, *TSIa*
118:37 The sod!] The ——! *E1* *see notes*
119:5 them] the *TSIa*
119:14 chestnut, and with *TSIaR*] chestnut and *MS*

119:17 an'] and *TSIa*
119:19 Low *A1*, *E1*] Loe *MS*
119:25 don't!] ~, *TSIa*
119:36 Say] ~, *A1*, *E1*
120:21 see] see if *TSIa*
120:26 it; *TSIaR*] ~, *MS*, *E1*
120:34 its *MS*, *TSIaC*] it's *TSIa*
120:34 all,] ~ *A1*
120:40 For] ~, *E1*
121:1 master] Master *TSIaC*, *E1*
121:5 strange] ~, *TSIa*
121:9 fixed *A1*, *E1*] cruel *MS*
122:10 delapidated] dilapidated *TSIaC*, *E1*
122:11 demoralised] ~, *E1*
122:11 baby *Ed.*] Baby *MS*
122:19 candle-ends] candle ends *TSIa*
122:19 on to] on *A1*
122:23 They too] ~, ~, *E1*
123:1 their] *Om A1*
123:4 also] *Om. TSIa*
123:9 Ceremonies:] ~, *TSIa*
123:9 we *TSIaR*] you *MS*
123:11 hectoring *TSIaR*] bullying *MS*
123:17 Sunday *TSIa*] sunday *MS*
123:33 shouted *A1*, *E1*] shouting *TSIa* *see notes*
123:37 straight away] straight-/ away *A1*
123:40 And] ~, *E1*
124:2 blushed] ~, *A1*
124:2 bridled] ~, *A1*
124:20 Mamas *TSIa*] Mama's *MS* mammas *E1*
124:21 and] ~, *E1*
124:21 following *TSIaR*] after *MS*
124:26 oration] ovation *TSIa*
124:36 unchosen. He] ~. *P* He *E1*
124:38 done.] ~? *TSIa*
125:5 packing-case *MS*, *E1*] packing case *TSIa*
125:10 "Oh] "~, *A1*, *E1*
135:20 Marm *Ed.*] marm *MS*
125:23 enjoyment! *TSIaR*] ~. *MS*
125:29 vis-a-vis] vis-à-vis *TSIaC*
125:34 said,] ~ *TSIa*
125:34 You] You're *TSIa*
125:35 Alice *Ed.*] Jane *MS*
125:38 there—] ~, *TSIa*
126:3 bawled] howled *TSIa*
126:3 centre—] ~. *TSIa*
126:4 Alice *Ed.*] Jane *MS*
126:5 left—] ~. *TSIa*
126:11 M.C.] M. C. *A1*
126:21 Oh] ~, *A1*, *E1*
126:22 go,] ~ *TSIa*
126:25 Why oh] ~, ~, *A1*, *E1*
126:26 half pleased] half-pleased *TSIa*
126:30 Was Easu trying to bully him?] *Om. TSIa*
127:1 Oh] ~, *A1*, *E1*
127:11 clinging] clinged *E1*
127:17 And why oh why] ~ ~, ~, ~ *A1* ~, ~, ~, ~, *E1*
127:23 to her] *Om. TSIa*
127:24 answered] asked *TSIa*
127:30 Steady] ~, *A1*
127:37 boy—] ~, *TSIa*
127:38 it, *TSIaR*] ~ *MS*
128:4 vise *Ed.*] vice *MS*
128:7 Oh] ~, *A1*, *E1*
128:12 nice] ~, *E1*
128:13 boy!—] ~! *TSIa*
128:14 herself,] ~ *E1*
128:17 You've done] You're doing *TSIa*
128:18 ring] ~, *E1*
128:24 Oh] ~, *A1*, *E1*
128:34 involved *TSIaC*] envolved *MS*
128:36 mêlée *TSIaC*, *A1*] mélée *MS*, *TSIaR* melee *TSIa* mélèe *TSIbR*
129:3 "games."] ~. *TSIa*
129:3 was of course] ~, ~ ~, *E1*
129:7 "original"] ~ *TSIa*
129:13 me] ~, *TSIa*
129:16 Unanimously] unanimously *A1*
129:28 expressions] expression *TSIa*
129:31 P. *MS*, *A1*] ~ *TSIa* ~., *E1*
129:35 got] *Om. TSIa*
129:38 geese,] ~ *A1*
129:38 an' *TSIa*] an *MS*
129:38 no-one] no one *TSIa*
130:1 mornin'] ~, *E1*
130:1 sharp] ~, *E1*
130:4 pink, *MS*, *E1*] ~ *TSIa*

130:4 the wide] a wide *E1*
130:5 mother'll] Mother'll *TSIa*
130:6 coal barge] coal-barge *TSIa*
130:8 bony] long *TSIa*
130:9 Oh] ~, *A1*, *E1*
130:14 Hump *TSIa*] ~, *MS*
130:18 arrivals:] ~. *TSIa*
130:18 come] came *TSIa* had come *TSIaR*
130:20 doctor too] ~, ~, *E1*
130:30 supper-room] supper room *TSIa*
130:33 again] ~, *TSIa*
130:33 close:] ~; *TSIa*
130:35 queer,] ~ *TSIa*
130:36 And of course] ~, ~ ~, *E1*
131:2 also, *TSIaR*] though, *MS* also *A1*
131:4 against *TSIaR*] in *MS*
131:7 further] farther *E1*
131:12 big] ~, *TSIa*
131:15 hand] head *E1*
131:31 for—] ~, *TSIa*
132:1 dim,] ~ *TSIa*
132:4 with] *Om. TSIa*
132:7 intense. He] ~. *P* He *TSIa*
132:10 race:] ~; *E1*
132:14 sweeps *TSIaR*] sweep *MS*
132:16 Yet] ~, *TSIa*
132:23 —free] ...~ *TSIa*
132:28 I don't *TSIaR*] But I don't *MS* But I didn't *TSIa*
132:32 grand-daughter] granddaughter *A1*
132:32 earl—] ~. *TSIa*
132:33 further] farther *A1*
132:35 Though of course] ~, ~ ~, *E1*
132:37 A. D. C.] A.D.C. *TSIa*
132:38 Governor General] Governor-General *A1*, *E1*
132:39 mother] Mother *TSIa*
133:5 subtle] a subtle *TSIaC*
133:10 pipe-stem *MS*, *TSIbR*] pipe stem *TSIa*
133:21 England, *MS*, *E1*] ~ *TSIa*
133:25 barefoot,] ~ *TSIa*
133:34 me] ~, *TSIaC*, *E1*
133:36 myself.] ~? *TSIa*
133:38 *men TSIaR*] men *MS*
134:6 *choose," Ed.*] ~;" *MS* ~:" *TSIa* ~!" *A1*, *E1*
134:7 Jack,] ~ *TSIa*
134:7 ear,] ~ *TSIa*
134:8 persisting:] ~. *A1*
134:10 just the ticket *TSIaR*] perfect *MS*
134:18 up too:] ~ ~. *TSIa* ~, ~. *E1*
134:20 thirteen] nineteen *TSIa*
134:20 of Our ... Blessed Son] *Om. A1* with very noble subjects *E1*
134:23 Yet—"] ~——" *A1* ~"— *E1*
134:23 laughed—] ~, *A1*
134:24 hires *A1*, *E1*] hired *MS see note on* 123:33
134:27 Best] But *TSIa* And *A1* Then *E1*
134:27 But] *Om. TSIaR*
134:33 servant-lasses *MS*, *TSIaC*] servant lasses *TSIa*
134:35 cocky *TSIaC*] cooky *MS*
135:3 Hello ... Hello] Hullo ... H[...]llo *TSIa* Hullo ... Hello *TSIb* Hullo ... Hullo *TSIaC* Hullo, ... Hullo, *A1* Hello, ... Hello, *E1*
135:3 She had] And she *TSIa*
135:6 right] ~, *TSIa*
135:9 Oh] ~, *TSIa*
135:13 arm *TSIa*] arms *MS*
135:19 ring—] ~. *TSIa*
135:20 hand—and ... Mary's other] *Om. TSIa*
135:27 There] ~, *E1*
135:33 good-humour] good humour *TSIa*
135:35 hostile *TSIaR*] brutal *MS*
135:39 Cheer] ~, *A1*, *E1*
135:39 Boys] boys, *TSIa* Boys, *A1*
136:1 Cheer *MS*, *A1*] cheer *TSIa*
136:2 Britons Never Never] ~, ~, ~, *A1*
136:5 jew's] Jew's *TSIa*
136:7 sing,] ~ *E1*
136:8 forgot] ~, *TSIa*
136:11 the] *Om. TSIaC*
136:12 For] "~ *A1*

136:12 dear] ~, *TSIaC, E1*
136:15 the] *Om. TSIaC*
136:18 acquaintance] ~, *TSIa*
136:20 Rackett,] Rackett and *TSIa* Rackett, and *E1*
136:23 fact,] ~ *TSIa*
136:23 *wanted*] wanted *TSIa*
136:29 half-audible *MS, TSIaC*] half audible *TSIa*
136:31 Lang Syne] lang syne *TSIa*
136:35 half past] half-past *TSIaC, E1*
137:1 handkerchiefs *A1, E1*] with handkerchiefs *MS*
137:4 step] steps *E1*
137:7 aimlessly *TSIaR*] a little aimlessly *MS*
137:19 pale-pink] pale pink *TSIa*
137:22 naïve *MS, TSIaC*] naive *TSIa*
137:27 and young] the young *TSIa*
137:35 a gum tree] the gum tree *TSIa* the gum-tree *A1*
137:36 eucalyptus *TSIaC, E1*] Eucalyptus *MS*
137:36 away—] ~. *TSIa*
137:39 when] where *TSIa*
138:3 And] ~, *E1*
138:4 were *MS, A1*] was *TSIa*
138:4 Tom,] ~ *TSIa*
138:7 possible,] ~ *A1*
138:11 morepork] more-pork *TSIaC*
138:12 *now*] now *TSIa*
138:15 family, to any one of the] *Om. TSIa*
138:19 that.] ~? *TSIa*
138:20 pittosporum *Ed.*] pitosperum *MS* photosporum *A1*
138:34 bad, *MS, E1*] ~ *TSIa*
138:35 all matter] matter *E1*
139:4 morning,] ~ *TSIa*
139:8 while,] ~ *TSIa*
139:11 almost blithe *TSIaR*] abiding *MS*
139:11 that,] ~ *TSIa*
139:12 cover them with *TSIaR*] almost an *MS*
139:15 hot hot] ~, ~ *TSIa*
139:16 over him] ~ ~, *E1*
139:29 and] and his *TSIa*
139:30 poles] people *TSIa*
139:30 Now] ~, *E1*
140:4 working,] ~ *TSIa*
140:7 heat-preoccupied] heat-occupied *TSIa* heat-oppressed *TSIaR*
140:16 limit!] ~, *TSIa*
140:19 sniff;] ~: *TSIa*
140:32 chignon *TSIaC*] chinon *MS*
141:2 woolen] woollen *TSIaC, E1*
141:3 else] *Om. TSIa*
141:11 Church] church *TSIa*
141:14 Tick-tock] Tick, tock *TSIa*
141:17 contrary, *MS, E1*] ~ *TSIa*
141:20 with christianity] ~ Christianity *TSIa*
141:21 christianity of] Christianity ~ *A1, E1*
141:22 christianity] Christianity *TSIaC, E1*
141:27 side issue] side-issue *TSIaC*
141:34 mouthpiece *TSIa*] mouth-/ piece *MS, E1*
141:35 scripture *Ed.*] Scripture *MS*
141:39 her,] ~ *TSIa* ~: *TSIaR*
141:39 him] ~, *E1*
142:1 fine sharpened] fine shaped *TSIa* fine-shaped *TSIaR*
142:2 subtly-arched] subtly arched *TSIa*
142:3 dead-looking *MS, TSIaC*] dead looking *TSIa*
142:7 dim,] ~ *TSIa*
142:9 half-painful *MS, TSIaC*] half painful *TSIa*
142:10 yards] ~, *TSIa*
142:19 O . . . O] Oh . . . Oh *TSIa* Oh, . . . Oh, *E1*
142:20 Thee] thee *TSIa*
142:22 these . . . hymns] these . . . hymn *TSIa* this . . . hymn *TSIaR*
142:24 *Paradise*] Paradise *TSIa*
142:25 *coffin*] coffin *TSIa*
142:25 he too] ~, ~, *E1*
142:29 draught-horses] draft-horses *A1*
142:37 thin, *MS, A1*] ~ *TSIa*

142:37 voice. *P* He] ~. He *TSIa*
143:3 will,] ~ *E1*
143:5 Marm *Ed.*] marm *MS*
143:6 Well] ~, *A1*, *E1*
143:8 driving,) ~ *E1*
143:10 grandfather] ~, *A1*
143:25 cat-look] cat look *TSIa*
143:26 it'll] it will *TSIa*
143:27 Ellis—] ~, *TSIa*
143:28 won't do] do *TSIa* do know *TSIaR*
143:29 dying-room] dying room *TSIa*
143:29 his] this *E1*
143:30 it,] ~. *TSIa*
143:32 himself] ~, *A1*
143:32 it! *MS*, *TSIaR*] ~' *TSIa* ~. *A1*
143:39 it,] ~? *E1*
144:1 lady,] ~ *TSIa*
144:1 England, *MS*, *A1*] ~ *TSIa*, *E1*
144:2 woman] ~, *A1*
144:3 charm] ~, *A1*
144:3 fifty-odd *TSIa*] fifty odd *MS*
144:4 But then] ~, ~, *E1*
144:6 *Did* you] Did *you E1*
144:6 eyeing *MS*, *E1*] eying *TSIa*
144:6 know,] ~ *TSIa*
144:17 in] in a *TSIa*
144:19 But] ~, *E1*
144:21 old,] ~. *TSIa*
144:24 this,] ~ *TSIa*
144:25 What . . . awfully old.] "~ . . . ~ ~." *TSIa*
144:27 school girls] school-girls *E1*
144:28 ball-room] ball room *TSIa*
144:29 beards,] ~ *TSIa*
144:34 Marm! *Ed.*] marm! *MS* marm, *TSIa*
144:35 Marm!' *Ed.*] marm!' *MS*, *A1* marm! *TSIa* marm' *E1*
144:36 this *A1*, *E1*] his *MS* *see note on* 123:33
144:36 Marm *Ed.*] marm *MS*
144:39 here—] ~. *TSIa*
145:1 Listen!] ~, *TSIa*
145:1 said,] ~ *TSIa*
145:4 And] *Om. A1 see note on* 67:36
145:14 *I'm*] I'm *TSIa*
145:14 Jacob *MS*, *E1*] Jack *TSIa*
145:18 woman] ~, *TSIa*
145:20 Lennie,] ~ *TSIa*
145:24 portentousness *TSIaR*] mysteriousness *MS*
145:26 queer aged] ~, ~, *A1*
145:28 half ghoulish] half-ghoulish *TSIa*
145:34 soot] ~, *A1*
145:41 Marm! *Ed.*] marm! *MS* marm, *TSIa*
146:4 drawing-room *MS*, *E1*] drawing room *TSIa*
146:5 ever] even *TSIa*
146:8 Mary!] ~, *TSIa*
146:9 you.] ~? *TSIa*
146:11 cat's-cradle, *Ed.*] cats'-cradle *MS* cats'-cradle, *TSIaR*
146:19 limb] ~, *TSIa*
146:21 stone] ~, *TSIa*
146:22 nigger] Nigger *TSIa*
146:25 O'."/ Harry *Ed.*] 'O."/ ~ *MS* O". *P* ~ *TSIa* O." *P* ~ *A1*, *E1*
146:26 words *TSIaR*] American words *MS*
146:26 loud,] ~ *TSIa*
146:29 low] slow *TSIa*
146:32 gum trees] gum-trees *A1*
146:36 the vast] a vast *TSIa*
147:3 welter *TSIaR*] vast welter *MS*
147:13 west *TSIaR*] glory *MS* West *A1*
147:17 Though after all] ~, ~ ~, *E1*
147:20 liquid] ~, *A1*
147:21 molten, wavering long ridge towards *TSIbR*] yellow, low-lying land of *MS* wavering long ridge towards *TSIaR* molten, wavering, long . . . towards *A1*
147:28 swaggering] staggering *TSIa*
147:33 meal-times] meal times *TSIa*
147:36 hymn.] ~, *TSIa*
147:39 Jane my] ~, ~ *TSIa*
147:39 Jane/ Ah] ~, / ~ *A1*
148:1 moon-light] moonlight *TSIa*
148:2 rye—"/ Someone] ~." *P* Someone *TSIa*
148:8 Then at last] ~, ~ ~, *E1*
148:11 hands] hand *TSIa*
148:19 back door] back-door *TSIa*

148:25 shame,] ~ *TSIa*
148:35 in the dark *TSIaR*] lost *MS*
149:2 caressive] caressing *TSIa*
149:23 love-making,] ~ *TSIa*
149:23 again] ~, *A1*
150:2 room] ~, *A1*
150:6 you] ~, *A1*, *E1*
150:7 Sooner] ~, *A1*
150:10 But] ~, *E1*
150:12 Anyway] ~, *TSIa*
150:18 me] ~, *TSIa*
150:18 'Ardy'] ' ~ *TSIa* '~'; *TSIaR* '~,' *TSIbR*
150:18 grimy] *Om. TSIa*
150:30 the seat] his seat *TSIa*
150:30 neck rope] neck-rope *TSIaC*
150:30 his horse] the horse *TSIa*
150:36 "showing sorrow." *TSIa*] '~ ~.' *MS*
150:37 the] this *TSIa*
150:38 Book. *P* The] ~. The *TSIa*
150:40 selection] Selection *TSIa*
151:1 midday] mid-day *TSIa*
151:6 odd] ~, *A1*
151:10 cyclamen] cyclamens *TSIa*
151:13 kitchen,] ~ *TSIa*
151:16 Oh] ~, *A1*, *E1*
151:16 poor] Poor *A1*, *E1*
151:17 a form] the floor *TSIa*
151:20 Oh . . . Oh] ~, . . . ~, *A1*, *E1*
151:27 "everlasting" *TSIa*] '~' *MS*
151:28 bars. . . .] ~ . . . *A1* ~. . . . *E1*
151:40 baby] Baby *A1*
152:6 were *TSIaR*] *Om. MS*
152:9 methodist *Ed.*] Methodist *MS*
152:15 want.] ~? *TSIa*
152:16 Come—"] ~"— *E1*
152:16 hesitated— "to *MS*, *E1*] ~. "—~ *TSIa* ~ "—~ *A1*
152:18 me,] ~ *TSIa*
152:18 got. But] ~, but *E1*
152:26 Well] ~, *A1*, *E1*
152:26 you? *MS*, *TSIaC*, *E1*] ~ *TSIa* ~! *A1*
152:26 voice,] ~ *A1*
152:28 mother *Ed.*] Mother *MS*
152:33 Upstairs] ~, *TSIaC*, *E1*
152:33 mother] Mother *E1*
152:38 mother] Mother *E1*
153:1 brother-in-laws] brothers-in-law *TSIaC*, *E1*
153:2 poor] the poor *TSIa*
153:4 the ghost] a ghost *TSIa*
153:7 till] until *TSIa*
153:8 sipped, *MS*, *A1*] ~ *TSIa*, *E1*
153:12 Lennie, *TSIaR*] ~ *MS*
153:17 pressure,] ~ *A1*
153:18 dark] ~, *A1*
153:23 you—] ~ *TSIa*
153:24 word] words *TSIa*
153:29 it, *MS*, *A1*] ~ *TSIa*
153:29 methodist *Ed.*] Methodist *MS*
153:29 sunk] sank *TSIaC*, *E1*
153:31 Amen!] Amen *TSIa* *Amen TSIaR*
153:32 it,] ~ *TSIa*
153:37 son-in-laws] sons-in-law *TSIaC*, *E1*
154:3 son-in-laws] sons-in-law *TSIaC*, *E1*
154:12 will.—] ~— *TSIa*
154:12 marriage.—Children] ~ ~ *TSIa* ~. ~ *TSIaC*, *E1* ~—children *A1*
154:13 claim—Stocking—] ~—stocking— *A1* ~. Stocking—— *E1*
154:14 plainly,] ~ *TSIa*
154:17 minded:] ~ *TSIa* ~, *TSIaR*
154:30 shop *TSIaR*] store *MS*
154:35 in] on *TSIa*
154:37 open:] ~. *TSIa*
154:38 round,] ~ *TSIa*
155:1 preoccupied] pre-/ occupied *A1* pre-occupied *E1*
155:3 female! *P* He *Ed.*] ~. *P* He *MS* ~. He *TSIa* ~! He *TSIaR*
156:5 starling *TSIaR*] black-bird *MS*
156:13 really] *Om TSIa*
156:18 pool] ~, *A1*
156:19 luke-warm *TSIa*] luke-/ warm *MS* lukewarm *TSIaC*
156:21 bathing,] ~ *TSIa*
156:32 those] the *TSIa*
156:32 full,] ~ *TSIa*
156:33 evenings] ~, *E1*

157:7 So . . . intuition] ~, . . . ~, *E1*
157:22 She, *MS, A1*] ~ *TSIa*
157:22 riding-dress *TSIaR*] riding dress *MS*
157:23 absurd] ~, *A1*
157:30 dismay *TSIaR*] hate *MS*
157:31 Easu,] ~ *TSIa*
157:33 passion *TSIa*] kind of passion *MS*
157:33 desire *TSIaR*] love *MS*
157:38 bearded *A1, E1*] bully's *MS*
157:39 skirts] skirt *TSIa*
158:1 "Quite . . . picture!" *TSIbR*] ~ . . . ~! *MS* "~ . . . ~! *TSIaR* ~ . . . ~! *TSIaC, A1*
158:2 calmly] *Om. TSIa*
158:2 Giant-killer *TSIaR*] giant-killer *MS*
158:7 Easu,] ~ *TSIa*
158:7 black] *Om. TSIa*
158:9 himself,] ~ *TSIa*
158:13 Why] ~, *A1, E1*
158:13 sod!] ~? *E1*
158:14 feet] ~, *A1*
158:18 queer] ~, *A1*
158:21 "Ah] "~, *E1*
158:21 Ah! ha-ha-ha-ha!—ha! ha! ha!] ha-ha-ha! *TSIa* Ha-ha-ha! *E1*
158:22 Ah!! ha-ha-ha-ha!] ~!! Ha-ha-ha-ha-ha! *TSIa* ~! ! Ha-ha-ha-ha-ha! *A1*
158:22 ha-ha-ha!] Ha-ha-ha *E1*
158:22 Ah!!! ha-ha-ha-ha-ha-ha-ha] ~! ! ! ha-ha-ha-ha-ha-ha-ha *A1* ~!!! Ha-ha-ha-ha-ha-ha-ha *E1*
158:23 Ah!—ha-ha] ~! ha-ha *TSIa* ~! Ha-ha *E1*
158:25 ha-ha-ha-ha-ha! Ah! ha-ha-ha] Ha-ha-ha-ha-ha! ~! Ha-ha-ha *E1*
158:27 strange] ~, *A1*
158:30 Monica, *MS, A1*] ~ *TSIa*
158:31 mouth] ~, *A1*
158:33 queer] strange *TSIa*
159:2 trail] track *TSIa*
159:5 light-blue] light blue *TSIa*
159:9 how] How *TSIa*
159:10 was *TSIaR*] is *MS*
159:12 eyes, *TSIaR*] eyes, is *MS*
159:18 shirt cuffs] shirt-cuffs *TSIaC*
159:20 reddish *TSIaR*] yellow *MS*
159:21 reddish-haired, *Ed.*] yellow-haired, *MS* yellow-haired *TSIa* reddish-haired *TSIaR* red-haired *TSIbR*
159:22 brown-red *MS, TSIaR*] brown red *TSIa* bright red *TSIbR*
159:38 queer, *MS, E1*] ~ *TSIa*
160:1 round,] ~ *TSIa*
160:6 hearts' *Ed.*] heart's *MS*
160:23 himself *TSIaR*] that he was *MS*
160:24 strike,] ~ *TSIa*
160:36 more: Bang! Bang] ~. ~! bang *E1*
160:36 in] of *TSIa*
161:1 Ellis] Easu *TSIa*
161:2 —pong . . . pong] Pong . . . Pong *TSIa*
161:5 deadly] ~, *TSIa*
161:6 Ellis] Easu *TSIa*
161:7 fist] *Om. A1*
161:7 fell *TSIaR*] went down *MS*
161:8 posed] poised *E1*
161:9 he *TSIaR*] Jack *MS*
161:12 Ellis] Easu *TSIa*
161:12 then . . . feet] ~, . . . ~, *E1*
161:17 and *TSIaR*] but *MS*
161:21 wofully] woefully *E1*
161:21 only. . .] ~... *TSIa* ~ . . . *A1, E1*
161:38 Ellis] Easu *TSIa*
162:3 fear. He *MS, A1*] ~. *P* He *TSIa*
162:7 little sod] little —— *E1*
162:7 jaw] ~, *A1*
162:8 meself] myself *TSIa*
162:8 little sod] little —— *E1*
162:14 crowin' *TSIbR*] crowin' from England, *MS*
162:14 over *TSIbC*] crowin' over *MS*
162:20 home] ~, *A1*
162:28 entirety] ~, *A1*
162:30 clair-audient *MS, A1*] clair-/audient *TSIa* clairaudient *E1*

162:36 hand *TSIaR*] *Om. MS*
162:36 and of] and *TSIa*
162:37 Meanwhile] ~, *E1*
163:8 crashed,] ~ *E1*
163:9 Doctor] Dr. *TSIaC*
163:16 horse] ~, *A1*
163:20 said. *P* And] ~. And *TSIa*
163:22 a] the *TSIa*
163:24 face] his face *TSIaC*
163:25 disfigured *TSIaR*] very ugly *MS*
163:29 shirt-cuffs] shirt cuffs *TSIa*
163:29 shirt-collar] shirt collar *E1*
163:32 chin,] ~ *E1*
163:33 large] huge *TSIa*
163:37 still] ~, *A1*
163:38 skin,] ~ *TSIa*
164:2 else] else's *TSIa*
164:18 derision,] ~ *E1*
164:21 and] ~, *E1*
164:28 diminishing] diminished *A1*
164:40 No, you] ~. You *E1*
165:17 now. You] ~, you *TSIa*
165:19 Grace] ~, *E1*
165:24 nightshirt *MS, TSIaC*] night-shirt *TSIa*
165:27 awoke,] ~ *E1*
165:29 big,] ~ *E1*
165:30 Oh] ~, *A1, E1*
165:33 relief *MS, E1*] ~, *TSIa*
165:35 nightshirts] night-shirts *E1*
165:36 a-matter] ~, *A1, E1*
165:37 couldn't] wouldn't *A1*
166:1 Aw, go] ~! ~ *TSIa* ~! Go *E1*
166:4 enormous. He] ~. *P* He *TSIa*
166:6 Tain't] 'Taint *E1*
166:12 stiff, *MS, E1*] ~ *TSIa*
166:16 "And *MS, TSIaC*] ~ *TSIa*
166:17 hell *MS, A1*] Hell *TSIa*
166:19 pains." *MS, TSIaC*] ~. *TSIa*
166:20 at] to *TSIa*
166:23 "In hell . . . pains." *MS, TSIaC*] ~ ~ . . . ~. *TSIa* ~ Hell . . . ~. *E1*
166:31 boy,] ~ *A1*
166:32 Then] '~ *A1*
166:33 lie—" etc.] ~— —~. *TSIa* ~"— —~. *TSIaC* ~— —~." *TSIbR* ~'—~. *A1* ~——~. *E1*
167:5 "Lord!] "~, *TSIa*
167:20 said,] ~ *E1*
167:23 lose his] lose *TSIa*
167:26 sacrament:] Sacrament: *TSIa* Sacrament, *A1, E1*
167:26 *This is my Body* . . . Blood *Ed.*] This is my Body . . . Blood *MS* This is my body . . . Blood *TSIa* *This is my body* . . . Blood *TSIaR* something in his soul stood cold, and he knew this was no Sacrament to him *A1* something . . . stood still and cold. He knew that Sacrament was no . . . him *E1*
167:28 communication,] ~ *TSIa*
167:34 won't,] ~. *E1*
167:34 won't bother *Ed.*] wont bother *MS* won't, I won't bother *TSIa* won't. I won't bother *E1*
167:35 pledge,] ~ *TSIa*
167:35 submission,] ~ *A1*
168:2 And] ~, *E1*
168:11 power;] ~, *A1*
168:13 Then the *MS, E1*] The the *TSIa* The *A1*
168:14 Only] ~, *TSIa*
168:29 extreme *TSIaR*] honest *MS*
168:35 connection] connections *TSIa*
169:1 came,] ~ *TSIa*
169:8 heart, she] ~. She *TSIa*
169:17 it!] ~? *E1*
169:17 crueler] crueller *TSIaC*
169:23 nicer. *P* This] ~. This *TSIa*
169:34 Somehow,] ~ *TSIa*
170:5 eyes,] ~ *TSIa*
170:7 day,] ~ *A1, E1*
170:12 Why] ~, *A1, E1*
170:17 *never*] never *E1*
170:20 be!] ~? *E1*
170:23 gleam. *P* "He] ~. "He *A1*
170:27 off,] ~ *A1*
170:27 fierceness. "How] ~. *P* "How *TSIa*
170:28 face!] ~? *E1*

170:28 he! *MS*, *TSIaC*] ~[...] *TSIa* ~? *E1*
170:32 brute!] ~, *TSIa*
170:36 fierceness, "to me." *A1*, *E1*] fierceness. *MS* fierceness *TSIb*
171:19 if the *TSIa*] if the/ the *MS*
171:33 Grace] ~, *E1*
171:34 boy-twins] boy twins *TSIa*
172:10 for ever *TSIa*] forever *MS*, *A1*, *E1*
172:12 "Who shall ... sworn deceitfully." *TSIaC*] ~ ~ ... ~ ~. *MS*
172:23 Easu's,] ~ *TSIa*
172:33 *Lord TSIaR*] Lord *MS*
172:33 *if ... Easu TSIaR*] if ... Easu *MS*
172:33 *I won't ... to, I will TSIbR*] I won't ... to, I will *MS I won't ... to, I will TSIaR*
173:5 his] His *TSIa*
173:9 and] to *TSIa*
173:10 coals,] ~ *TSIa*
173:12 not] ~, *TSIa*
173:12 God] ~, *TSIaR*
173:13 shown] sown *A1*
173:13 thy] Thy *TSIa*
173:20 not] ~, *A1*, *E1*
173:20 Oh] ~, *A1*
173:20 God] ~, *A1*, *E1*
173:25 thy] Thy *TSIa*
173:27 own] *Om. TSIa*
173:34 moon,] ~ *A1*
173:35 stars———] ~ ... *TSIa* ~.... *A1* ~ ... *E1*
173:36 body— —] ~ ... *TSIa* ~. ... *A1* ~ ... *E1*
173:37 sun—" But] ~——" *P* But *A1* ~." But *E1*
173:37 realise all] all realise *TSIa*
174:6 consideration] considerations *TSIa*
174:9 sun ..." And] ~—" ~ *TSIa* ~——" *P* And *A1* ~." ~ *E1*
174:9 vast and ... who is *TSIaR*] of the vast fierce God who is Lord of *MS*
174:11 moon—" That] ~——" *P* That *A1* ~." ~ *E1*
174:12 not *A1*, *E1*] never *MS see note on* 174:20
174:13 immense] ~, *A1*
174:15 vast] ~, *A1*
174:15 white] ~, *TSIa*
174:17 broad *TSIaR*] great *MS* broad, *A1*
174:17 capture him, ... white demon ... its prey *A1*, *E1*] dissolve him, dissolve him right away, as in some transcendent, pure, white-shining acid *MS* capture him, ... white tiger ... prey *TSIaR* capture him, ... white panther ... prey *TSIbR*
174:20 destroy ... consume *TSIaR*] dissolve ... dissolve *MS*, *TSIb*, *A1 see notes*
174:21 liquid, gleaming] gleaming, liquid *TSIa*
174:21 lusting *A1*, *E1*] smiling *MS*
174:21 following] following him *E1*
174:23 moon— —" And] ~—" ~ *TSIa* ~——" *P* And *A1* ~." ~ *E1*
174:24 hand—] ~. *TSIa*
174:27 stars—" The] ~——" *P* The *A1* ~." ~ *E1*
174:28 drooping *A1*, *E1*] dropping *MS*
174:30 them] ~, *A1*
174:34 body—] ~. *TSIa*
174:38 clothes] ~, *TSIa*
175:3 *had*] had *TSIa*
175:4 really *A1*, *E1*] had *MS*
175:5 aunts] Aunts *TSIaC* Aunts, *A1*
175:5 parsons] parson *TSIa* parson, *A1*
175:5 by] by the *TSIa*
175:7 power of the roaring *TSIaR*] great god in the roaring of the *MS* Great God in the ... the *TSIa*, *TSIb*, *A1*
175:8 smile *TSIaR*] god *MS* God *TSIa*
175:8 full moon] full-moon *TSIa*

175:9 weapon-threat] weapon-thrust *A1*
175:16 "candles" *TSIaR*] ~ *MS*
175:24 pure"] ~," *A1*
175:25 Shelley and vegetarians and socialists] ~, ~ ~, ~ ~, *A1*
175:26 Spirit] spirit *TSIa*
175:27 sort] kind *TSIa*
175:27 sea-weed] sea weed, *TSIa* sea-weed, *TSIaR*
175:28 underwater] under water *TSIaC*
175:33 food ... sheep ... money] ~, ... ~, ... ~, *A1*
175:35 setting] ~, *A1*
176:3 seen] *Om. TSIa*
176:7 fear] ~, *A1*
176:15 Antichrist *A1*, *E1*] Beast *MS* Snake *TSIaR*
176:16 that *A1*, *E1*] this *MS*
176:18 distant] ~, *A1*
176:19 this too] ~, ~, *E1*
176:25 drank] ~, *A1*
176:34 horse too] ~, ~, *E1*
176:38 angel,] ~ *E1*
177:1 Monica too] ~, ~, *E1*
177:2 she too] ~, ~, *E1*
177:3 will;] ~: *E1*
177:13 shovelfuls *TSIaR*] sheer dust-fuel *MS*
177:14 would] ~, *A1*
177:14 them] ~, *A1*
177:28 But] And *TSIa*
177:32 was! *TSIaR*] ~. *MS*
177:37 breathing] ~, *A1*
178:3 waistcoat,] ~ *TSIa*
178:4 watch-chain *MS*, *TSIaC*, *E1*] wach-chain *TSIa* watchchain *A1*
178:6 have *TSIaR*] almost have *MS*
178:7 was! *TSIbR*] ~. *MS see notes*
178:7 chair,] ~ *E1*
178:8 realise. *MS*, *TSIb*] ~! *TSIaR*
178:9 baby] Baby *A1*
178:9 There is] There's *TSIa*
178:9 sun, *MS*, *A1*] ~ *TSIa*
178:12 body.— —] ~. *TSIa*
178:13 scripture] Scripture *TSIaC*, *E1*
178:13 Or *MS*, *E1*] or *TSIa*
178:14 cold] ~, *A1*
178:17 strange] ~, *TSIa*
178:17 quietnesses] quietness *TSIa*
178:19 Oh] ~, *A1*, *E1*
178:26 started] ~, *A1*
178:27 Jack did ... his ear.] *Om. A1*, *E1 see note on* 42:20
178:30 Uncle *Ed.*] uncle *MS*
178:35 across] ~, *A1*
178:38 said] ~, *TSIa*
179:2 goodness] ~, *A1*, *E1*
179:2 him] ~, *A1*
179:3 dying-room] dying room *TSIa*
179:5 dying-room] dying room *TSIa*
179:7 inquiringly] enquiringly *TSIa*
179:12 dying-room] dying room *TSIa*
179:13 methodist] Methodist *TSIa*
179:16 methodist] Methodist *TSIa*
179:16 black] ~, *A1*
179:18 Ruth of course] ~, ~ ~, *E1*
179:18 The] Her *TSIa*
179:22 minutes:] ~; *TSIa*
179:24 Blagg] Blogg *TSIa* Blogg, *E1*
179:24 course] ~, *E1*
179:27 things...] ~ ... *TSIa* ~ ... *A1*, *E1*
179:27 property] ~, *A1*, *E1*
179:27 too—] ~. *TSIa*
179:30 Blagg] Blogg *TSIa*
179:31 see—] ~. *TSIa*
179:33 Jack,] ~ *E1*
179:36 half-past *TSIaR*] half past *MS*
180:3 sunset, *MS*, *A1*] ~ *TSIa*
180:4 last, cracked ping-ping] last ping! ping *TSIa*
180:13 within, *MS*, *E1*] ~ *TSIa*
180:17 queer,] ~ *E1*
180:18 make-belief] make-believe *TSIa* make believe *E1*
180:20 make-belief] make-believe *A1*
180:28 very sure] very sure, very sure *A1*
180:33 Jenkins] ~, *E1*
180:35 Well] ~, *A1*, *E1*
180:37 Well] ~, *A1*, *E1*
180:37 an'] and *TSIa*
180:38 dogs,] ~ *E1*

180:38 see—"] ~"— *E1*
180:40 But] ~, *E1*
180:40 done,] ~; *E1*
180:40 oh] ~, *A1*, *E1*
180:40 I s'll] I's'll *TSIa*
181:2 mind] ~, *E1*
181:4 Let's see! She] She *E1*
181:5 three] ~, *E1*
181:6 coffin?" *P* He] ~?" He *TSIa*
181:9 sewing-machine] sewing-machines *E1*
181:10 J.P.] J. P. *A1* J.P., *E1*
181:11 well] ~, *E1*
181:19 wild,] ~ *TSIa*
181:20 in to] into *TSIa*
181:22 left] felt *TSIa*
181:26 caring,] ~ *TSIa*
181:31 and *TSIaR*] but *MS*
181:33 him. The ... over Jack,] him, *TSIa*
182:3 Len,] '~,' *A1*, *E1*
182:3 says"—] ~," *TSIa* ~,"— *TSIaC*
182:4 "y' father's ... gone,] "'y' ~ ... ~,' *A1*, *E1*
182:5 blub! "Be] ~!—"~ *TSIaC* ~—"'~ *A1* ~. "'~ *E1*
182:6 onst—] ~'— *A1*, *E1*
182:14 *not*] not *TSIa*
182:15 *her— Ed.*] her— *MS* her. *TSIa* *her. TSIaR*
182:16 then] and then *TSIa*
182:19 in the dark *TSIaR*] there *MS*
182:25 Oh ... Oh] ~, ... ~, *A1*, *E1*
182:26 Ma, your] ~! Your *TSIa*
182:29 Aunt] aunts *TSIa* Aunts *TSIaC*
182:30 asked,] ~ *TSIa*
182:31 buggy-light] buggy light *TSIa*
182:32 Whooo!",] ~'.", *TSIa* ~," *A1*, *E1*
182:36 in] *Om. TSIa*
182:36 mother] Mother *TSIa*
182:39 Tom." *P* Tom] ~." Tom *TSIa*
182:40 short] ~, *TSIa*
183:2 mother] Mother *TSIa*
183:12 some] a *TSIa*
183:17 it,] ~? *TSIa*
183:20 me!] ~? *TSIa*
183:23 hands *TSIaR*] hands with me *MS* hands, *A1*
183:23 alive—] ~, *TSIa*
183:24 on it. *TSIbR*] with me then. *MS* on it, then. *A1*
183:25 hand,] ~ *TSIa*
183:30 unrestrained] unrestrainedly *TSIa*
183:35 day. The *TSIaR*] ~: ~ *MS*
184:13 t'] to *TSIa*
184:14 sir *TSIaC*, *E1*] Sir *MS*
184:15 gotta"—and] ~." ~ *TSIa* ~." And *TSIaR*
184:28 Granfather] grandfather *TSIa*
184:30 Grandfather] grandfather *TSIa*
184:38 cortège *MS*, *TSIaC*] cortege *TSIa*
185:2 black] ~, *E1*
185:3 floor-boards *TSIa*] floor-/ boards *MS*
185:4 wofully] woefully *E1*
185:10 horses] horse *TSIa*
185:11 they] the horses *A1* *see notes*
185:13 house *TSIaR*] remains *MS*
185:14 cortège *MS*, *TSIaC*, *A1*] cortege *TSIa* cortége *TSIaR*
185:32 side] side of *TSIa*
185:35 Hymn Number] hymn number *TSIa*
185:36 Jack *TSIaR*] People *MS*
185:36 mourners *TSIaR*] people *MS*
185:38 overture.] ~: *TSIa*
186:2 expect— —] ~ .. *TSIa* ~ ... *A1*, *E1*
186:5 Blagg] Blogg *TSIaR* *see notes*
186:6 methodist] Methodist *TSIaC*, *E1*
186:10 Tom, *MS*, *E1*] ~ *TSIa*
186:21 "—Oh] "~ *TSIa*
186:26 blest] blessed *TSIa*
186:27 voice] ~, *TSIa*
186:28 die] ~, *E1*
186:32 Greenlows' *A1*] Greenlow's *MS*
187:18 clearing-up] clearing up *TSIa*
187:19 died *TSIaR*] died itself *MS*
187:20 meantime,] ~ *E1*
187:23 Jack *TSIaR*] He *MS*

187:29 had left] left *TSIa*
187:31 Meanwhile] ~, *E1*
187:39 Ma, *TSIaR*] ~. *MS*
188:7 regret] repent *TSIa*
188:15 oats] ~, *E1*
188:15 you've] you've got *E1*
188:18 Well-Well] Well. Well *TSIa* Well *TSIaR*
188:19 stay your] stay a *TSIa*
188:20 year. The] ~. *P* The *TSIa* ~. *P* "The *TSIaC*, *E1*
188:20 Rob-Roy] 'Rob Roy' *A1*
188:22 Midland] midland *TSIa*
188:26 colony] ~, *A1*
188:29 Now] ~, *A1*, *E1*
188:34 will—] ~. *TSIa*
188:39 plan:] ~, *TSIa*
189:1 dream,] ~ *TSIa*
189:5 Prrrh] Prrh *TSIa*
189:6 permission] ~, *A1*
189:11 Prrrh] Prrh *TSIa*
189:12 d' y'] d'ye *TSIa*
189:18 No] ~, *TSIaC*, *E1*
189:20 eye-glasses] eyeglasses *TSIa*
189:22 never—!] ~! *TSIa*
189:29 never—] ~, *E1*
189:29 said. "You] ~, "you *E1*
189:32 dead, your] ~. Your *TSIa*
189:35 well educated] well-educated *TSIaC*
189:38 as *TSIaR*] all *MS*, *TSIb*
189:39 as any … Cornseed's *Ed.*] and uneasy *MS* as any … cornseeds *TSIaR* as any … cornseed's *TSIbR*, *A1*
189:41 quarter-educated bush-whacker *TSIaR*] quarter educated Australian *MS*
190:4 "But—] ~— *TSIa* ~"—— *E1*
190:5 face *TSIaC*, *TSIbR*] face all *MS*
190:6 educated!] ~? *TSIaC*
190:7 don'] don't *E1*
190:7 Blagg] Blogg *TSIaR*
190:7 wantta] wantter *TSIa*
190:8 even—" *Ed.*] ~"— *MS* ~." *TSIa*
190:8 don'] don't *E1*
190:8 wantta] wantter *TSIa*
190:9 Grant] ~, *E1*
190:9 wantta. I tell] ~ […] ~ ~ *TSIa* ~, ~ ~ *TSIaR*
190:11 want] would want *TSIa*
190:14 b'lieve] believe *TSIa*
190:15 an'] and *TSIa*
190:19 plough *MS*, *E1*] ~, *TSIa*
190:20 th'] the *TSIa*
190:21 git] get *TSIa*
190:29 naïve, *Ed.*] naive, *MS* naïve *TSIaC*
190:29 actor] ~, *TSIa*
190:30 "'Here *MS*, *A1*] "~ *TSIa*
190:31 to fortune] of fortune *A1*
190:34 Large] "'~ *A1*
190:37 friend.'/ There! *Ed.*] ~'/ ~! *MS* ~." *P* "There, *TSIa* ~.' *P* "There, *A1*
190:39 fool!] ~, *TSIa*
191:1 Misery] misery *TSIaC*
191:2 idiotic *TSIaR*] farthing *MS*
192:3 in] to *TSIa*
192:18 still,] ~ *TSIa*
192:30 *her*] her *E1*
192:31 as] *Om.* *A1*
192:32 Indeed] ~, *E1*
192:33 *his*] his *TSIa*
193:9 silent] silver *TSIa*
193:19 the] *Om.* *TSIa*
193:23 limits] ~, *A1*
193:25 hostility *TSIaR*] indignation *MS*
193:27 it. And] ~ and *TSIa* ~, and *TSIaR*
193:31 which] that *TSIa*
193:31 the] *Om.* *TSIa*
193:32 him, *MS*, *A1*] ~ *TSIa*
193:35 young gipsy-woman] gipsy woman *TSIa*
193:39 old *TSIaR*] deep *MS*
194:2 Australia] ~, *E1*
194:6 *aware*] aware *TSIa*
194:8 same *TSIaR*] *Om.* *MS*
194:8 Great *MS*, *TSIaR*] […]reat *TSIa* great *A1*, *E1*
194:11 he] ~, *E1*
194:12 Greenlows' *A1*] Greenlow's *MS*, *E1*

194:17 would both] both would *TSIa*
194:19 But] ~, *E1*
194:19 Always] always *TSIa*
194:23 Well]~, *TSIa*
194:23 goodbye] good-bye *TSIa* good-bye, *TSIaC*, *E1*
194:26 Goodbye!] Good-bye. *TSIa*
194:33 *I*] I *TSIa*
195:3 And anyhow] ~, ~, *E1*
195:5 karri] Rarri *TSIa* Karri *TSIaR*
195:5 Wandoo, *Ed.*] "~," *MS* "~" *TSIa* ~ *TSIaR*
195:7 Goodbye] Good-bye! *TSIa*
195:7 it!] ~. *TSIa*
195:8 else] *Om. TSIa*
195:12 sharp,] ~ *TSIa*
195:19 towards] toward *TSIa*
195:20 went,] ~ *TSIa*
195:26 karri *MS*, *A1*] Karri *TSIa*
195:27 karri *MS*, *A1*] Karri *TSIa*
195:28 slopes] ~, *A1*
195:30 at *TSIaR*] at the *MS*
196:2 driving-seat] driving seat *TSIa*
196:5 ridge,] ~ *TSIa*
196:7 waters] water *TSIa*
196:8 tent-less] tentless *TSIa*
196:10 place-where ... private-jamboree. What *MS*, *A1*] ~. *P* What *TSIa* placewheremenw entwhentheywantedaprivatej amboree. *P* What *E1*
196:12 gentleman,] ~— *E1*
196:12 is, *MS*, *E1*] ~ *TSIa*
196:12 lady,] ~— *E1*
196:14 soft *TSIaR*] ~, *MS*
196:20 Fording,] Fording *TSIa* Fording it *TSIaC*
196:23 chimneyless] chimney-less *TSIa*
196:26 in a] in the *TSIa*
196:33 this,] ~ *TSIa*
196:34 with] with a *TSIa*
196:35 whitewashed] white-washed *TSIa*
196:38 wine] ~, *A1*
197:9 Coo-eed *Ed.*] Coo-eeed *MS* coo-eeed *A1*
197:12 down,] ~ *TSIa*
197:13 "Gone] "'~ *A1*
197:14 T"] ~." *TSIa* ~.'" *A1*
197:18 clatter] canter *TSIa*
197:21 ontta] outta *TSIa* on *A1* onta *E1*
197:22 elst] else *A1*
197:24 jist] just *TSIa*
197:25 th'] the *TSIa*
197:29 half past] half-past *TSIaC*
197:32 appearance,] ~ *TSIa*
197:34 But] ~, *E1*
197:35 half-past-one] half past one *TSIa* half-past one *TSIaC*, *E1*
197:37 slab building—] slab-building, *TSIa*, *E1* slab building, *TSIbR* slab-building— *A1*
197:39 Robes] robes *E1*
197:39 black-board *MS*, *E1*] black board *TSIa* black[...]board *TSIaR* blackboard *A1*
197:40 wire things] wire-things *E1*
197:40 coloured *TSIa*] colored *MS*
198:2 entirely by ... boughs. *TSIaR*] by ... boughs entirely. *MS*
198:5 Prince *TSIaR*] *Om. MS*
198:9 figure in] creature in *TSIa*
198:10 waist-coat] waistcoat *TSIaC*, *E1*
198:11 waiting, apparently,] ~ ~ *TSIa*
198:14 "I ... in boots." *TSIaC*, *E1*] ~ ... ~ ~. *MS*
198:16 staring] ~, *A1*
198:22 saints,] ~ *TSIa*
198:23 wi'] with *TSIa*
198:23 turmagants] termagants *A1*
198:24 making] makin *TSIa* makin' *TSIaR*
198:24 For] ~, *E1*
198:29 Denny] Danny *E1*
198:31 matrimony, may] ~, May *TSIa* ~. May *TSIaR*
198:33 Denny] Danny *E1*
198:37 side] side of *TSIa*
199:2 man] ~, *A1*
199:4 broad] ~, *A1*
199:5 would] ~, *E1*
199:5 time,] ~ *E1*
199:8 improperly-dressed *MS*, E1] improperly dressed *TSIa*

199:10 this] the *TSIa*
199:11 well-set-up] well set-up *TSIa*
199:16 ye're] yer *TSIa*
199:16 Prendy, *TSIaR*] ~ *MS*
199:20 o'] of *TSIa*
199:22 marryin' *MS*, *E1*] marrin' *TSIa*
199:23 Denny *Ed.*] Danny *MS*
199:23 wedding-breakfast] wedding breakfast *TSIa*
199:24 Paddy] ~, *A1*, *E1*
199:25 enough,] ~ *TSIa*
199:31 Wheer's] Where's *TSIa*
199:32 to] *Om. A1*
199:37 behind-hand *MS*, *E1*] behindhand *TSIaC*
199:39 sakes] sake *TSIa*
199:39 Grand-dad] grand-dad *TSIa* granddad *A1*
200:1 y'] Y8 *TSIa* ye *TSIaR*
200:2 seat] ~, *A1*
200:2 utmost] the utmost *TSIaC*
200:5 an'] and *TSIa*
201:3 "Let's] i/ "Let's *TSIbC* "LET's *A1* i/ "LET's *E1*
201:3 uncomfortably] ~, *A1*
201:5 fun,] ~ *TSIa*
201:6 Oh] ~, *A1*, *E1*
201:9 wedding *MS*, *TSIb*] ~, *TSIaC*
201:15 major] Major *TSIa*
201:16 explain,] ~ *A1*, *E1*
201:16 his circumstances, *TSIaR*] all *MS*
201:18 major *Ed.*] Major *MS*
201:19 was] was in *TSIa*
201:22 cakes,] ~ *TSIa*
201:24 in! Come] ~, come *TSIa*
201:24 major] Major *TSIa*
201:26 Sure] ~, *A1*
201:27 man an' a baby] baby an' a man *TSIa*
201:30 ye] yer *TSIa*
201:32 P.O.T,] P.O.T. *TSIa* P. O. T. *A1* P. O. T., *E1*
201:34 yourself] yerself *TSIa*
201:34 sir *TSIaC*, *E1*] Sir *MS*
202:1 down,] ~ *TSIa*
202:2 the] *Om. TSIa*
202:4 *The TSIaR*] The *MS*
202:4 *Stranger Ed.*] Stranger *MS* stranger *TSIa stranger TSIaR*
202:4 *within our gates! TSIbR*, *A1*] within our gates! *MS within our gates*! *TSIaR*
202:7 minute,] moment *TSIa*
202:9 Bride!": *Ed.*] ~!:" *MS* ~!." *TSIa* ~!" *A1* ~!", *E1*
202:9 Groom!": *Ed.*] ~!:" *MS* ~", *TSIa* ~!" *A1* ~!", *E1*
202:10 Priest,] ~! *TSIa*
202:12 laughed] ~, *A1*
202:12 present: at least,] ~, ~ ~ *TSIa*
202:14 waiting. *P* One] ~. One *TSIa*
202:16 grandfather's *MS*, *E1*] Grandfather's *TSIa*
202:17 lamps] lights *TSIa*
202:30 swimmingly] ~, *A1*
202:31 in. He] ~. *P* He *TSIa*
202:37 here] Here *TSIa*
203:3 me] ~, *E1*
203:7 no] ~, *TSIaC*
203:11 square] ~, *TSIa*
203:11 oldish, *TSIaR*] old, *MS* oldish; *E1*
203:18 man *TSIaR*] old man *MS*
203:19 shadow] ~, *A1*
203:19 languishingly] laughingly *TSIa*
203:24 cow:] ~. *TSIa*
203:30 branch] bunch *TSIa*
203:32 Jake *TSIaR*] Jack *MS*
203:34 sayin'!] ~? *TSIa*
203:36 His girl!] Take his girl? *TSIa*
203:38 an' *TSIa*] an *MS*
203:40 Jake *TSIaR*] Jack *MS*
204:1 y'! Good] ye'! Good *E1*
204:1 Jake *TSIaR*] Jack *MS*
204:1 cock bird] cock-bird *TSIaC*
204:3 Jake *TSIaR*] Jack *MS*
204:3 cock bird] cock-bird *TSIaC*
204:5 amiable *A1*, *E1*] aimiable *MS*
204:8 swaggering— — —] ~ . . . *A1*, *E1*
204:11 'osses!] ~? *TSIaC*
204:12 'em!] ~? *TSIaC*
204:22 moonlit] moon lit *TSIa*, *TSIb* moon-lit *TSIaR*, *E1*

204:24 it] *Om. TSIa*
204:29 ye *TSIa*] ye' *MS*
204:35 ventured] ~, *TSIa*
204:37 wild-animal's] wild-animal *TSIa*
204:37 that] the *TSIa*
205:11 the] a *TSIa*
205:16 you, *TSIaR, E1*] ~ *MS, TSIb*
205:18 of] of the *TSIa*
205:19 half dark. *MS, E1*] ~ ~.. *TSIa* ~ ~ . . *A1*
205:27 always *TSIaR*] still *MS*
205:32 Scotchman] Scotsman *E1*
206:3 *British Grenadiers*] "British Grenadiers" *TSIbC*
206:3 *Campbells Are Comin'*] *Campbells [. . .]re Coming TSIa Campbells Are Coming TSIaC Campbells are Coming TSIbR* "Campbells are Coming" *TSIbC* "Campbells are Coming," *E1*
206:6 Australia] Australian *TSIa*
206:8 I'm an . . . when I'm] I am *TSIa*
206:11 could. *MS, E1*] ~.. *TSIa* ~ . . *A1*
205:21 laughed,] ~ *TSIa*
206:24 thought.] ~, *E1*
206:29 bed] ~, *TSIa*
206:30 waitin'] waiting *E1*
206:32 get—] ~—— *E1*
206:32 shall . . . shall *MS, TSIbR*] shal . . . shal *TSIa*
206:34 space—] ~. *TSIa*
207:1 floor-space] floor space *TSIa*
207:3 directions;] ~: *TSIa*
207:4 bellies] ~, *A1*
207:5 Jack *TSIa*] Tom *MS*
207:12 forward,] ~ *TSIa*
207:14 at? *TSIaR*] ~! *MS*
207:17 Hopeless, *MS, E1*] ~ *TSIa*
207:17 beanfeast] breakfast *TSIa*
207:18 bench *TSIaR*] form *MS*
207:20 figures] ~, *A1*
208:3 It] i/ It *TSIbC* IT *A1* i/ IT *E1*
208:4 sleeping] asleep *TSIa* sleep *A1*
208:5 red] ~, *TSIa*
208:5 face,] face and *TSIa* face was *TSIaR*
208:6 b'fore] before *TSIa*
208:10 bags, *MS, A1*] ~ *TSIa*
208:11 paddock] paddock there *TSIa*
208:12 'n *E1*] n' *MS*
208:12 splash-board] splash board *TSIa*
208:12 th'osses] th' osses *TSIa* th' 'osses *A1, E1*
208:18 half-way *MS, E1*] half way *TSIa*
208:21 in] of *TSIa*
208:33 pack-horse, . . . socket,] ~ . . . ~ *E1*
209:1 jamboree *A1*] Jamboree *MS*
209:2 not of] not *TSIa*
209:6 who] that *TSIa*
209:7 real] a real *TSIa*
209:14 half-savage] half savage *TSIa*
209:17 God] ~, *E1*
209:21 jamboree *A1*] Jamboree *MS*
209:21 Why in heaven] ~, ~ ~, *E1*
209:22 jamborees *MS, A1*] Jamborees *TSIa*
209:33 rain] ~, *TSIa*
209:37 so] *Om. TSIa*
209:38 much] *Om. A1*
209:39 rain. *P* Tom *MS, E1*] ~./ Tom *TSIa* ~. Tom *A1*
210:9 on the grey] on the *TSIa*
210:9 bush,] ~[. . .] *TSIa* ~; *TSIaR*
210:9 evening,] ~ *E1*
210:26 *are*] are *TSIa*
210:28 Anyhow] ~, *E1*
210:34 hereabouts] hereabout *E1*
211:1 last,] ~ *TSIa*
211:7 barn] ~, *TSIa*
211:13 Ellis! *TSIaR*] Elliott! *MS* Elliot *TSIa* Ellis: *E1*
211:13 I've] I *TSIa*
211:13 heered] heared *A1, E1*
211:15 breathes *TSIaR*] breathe *MS*
211:16 Oh] ~, *TSIaC, E1*
211:16 o't *MS, E1*] o' t *TSIa*
211:18 which . . . Lord] ~, . . . ~, *E1*
211:23 govenment] Government *TSIa*
211:24 sakes] sake *TSIa*

211:24 aside. "The] ~, "the *E1*
211:25 mad!] ~, *TSIa*
211:31 Doctor] Dr *TSIa* Dr. *TSIaC*
211:35 other,] ~! *TSIa*
211:38 Oh] ~, *A1*, *E1*
211:38 Glory-Glory] Glory, Glory *TSIa*
211:38 in, come] ~. Come *TSIa*
212:7 delapidated, low] dilapidated, *TSIa* dilapidated *TSIaR*
212:9 last,] ~. *TSIa*
212:20 master's *MS*, *E1*] Master's *TSIa*
212:22 y're] ye're *TSIa*
212:22 lookin'] looking *TSIa*
212:23 room! *TSIaR*] ~. *MS*
212:31 into *TSIa*] in to *MS*
212:37 died *TSIaR*] *Om. MS*
213:4 in a] in *A1*
213:5 with *TSIaR*] and *MS*
213:7 colourless *TSIa*] colorless *MS*
213:8 cunning] ~, *A1*
213:15 y're] ye're *TSIa*
213:20 cart umbrella] cart-umbrella *TSIa*
213:21 murmured *MS*, *E1*] ~, *TSIa*
213:23 Cousin] cousin *E1*
213:27 fences, *TSIaR*] ~ *MS*
213:27 in] up *TSIa*
213:28 more,] ~ *E1*
213:29 Well] ~, *TSIa*
213:31 *determined*] determined *TSIa*
213:34 John] ~, *E1*
213:35 say] ~, *TSIa*
213:35 Right-you-are, Uncle John] Right you are, Uncle John *TSIa* *Right you are, Uncle John TSIaR*
214:3 eyes, *MS*, *E1*] ~ *TSIa*
214:5 said] said Dr *TSIa* said Dr. *TSIaC*, *E1*
214:5 Rackett.] ~, *A1*, *E1*
214:7 right. Let] ~, let *TSIa*
214:14 Jack, because *TSIaR*, *E1*] ~[...] ~ *MS* ~ ~ *TSIa* ~ ~, *TSIbR see note on* 178:7
214:19 urged] said *TSIa*
214:26 Amos] ~, *TSIa*
214:35 shoulder. *P* "It's] ~. "It's *TSIa*
214:37 ink,] ~ *TSIa*
214:38 him] to him *TSIa*
215:1 surely!] ~. *E1*
215:6 Now] ~, *E1*
215:11 but] but to *TSIa*
215:14 sight] ~, *TSIa*
215:21 centre-pin] centre pin *TSIa*
215:23 unhinged. *A1*, *E1*] ~, *MS*
215:27 here? You] ~ you *TSIa*
215:29 strangers] ~, *A1*
216:2 Monica,] ~ *TSIa*
216:2 seemed *MS*, *A1*] seemed as *TSIa*
216:9 skeletons, *TSIaR*] ~ *MS* skepetons *TSIa*
216:9 night like] night, light *A1*
216:10 corroborees *Ed.*] corrobees *MS*
216:11 clicketty] clickety *E1*
216:12 death! *TSIaR*] ~. *MS*
216:18 Death] ~, *A1*
216:25 black] ~, *TSIa*
216:27 vast] ~, *A1*
216:31 twins] ~, *A1*
216:37 he *MS*, *A1*] He *TSIa*
217:1 handsomeness] ~, *A1*
217:1 fatality] ~, *A1*
217:2 Oh] ~, *A1*, *E1*
217:4 into] unto *TSIa* towards *TSIaR*
217:9 courage] ~, *A1*
217:22 Mary!] —~! *TSIa*
217:25 Brief.] ~! *TSIa*
217:35 him.] ~? *E1*
217:39 he'd] he had *TSIa*
218:3 now,] ~ *TSIa*
218:10 children—] ~.— *A1* ~. *E1*
218:14 up] ~, *A1*
218:14 open] ~, *A1*
218:22 defiant, unsubmissive *TSIaR*] passionate, violent *MS*
219:4 Nephew] nephew *TSIa*
219:10 would] should *TSIa*
219:12 speechless, *TSIaR*] ~ *MS*
219:16 So ... shilling] ~, ... ~, *E1*
219:17 grant] ~, *E1*
219:21 care— —] ~. *TSIa*
219:22 In this vein Tom ranted *TSIaR*] This was how Tom went *MS*
219:22 the *TSIa*] *Om. MS*

219:23 dawn *TSIaR*] morning *MS*
219:26 crazy] ~, *A1*, *E1*
219:27 felt *TSIaR*] knew *MS*
220:1 darkness;] ~, *TSIa*
220:2 sorrow,] ~ *TSIa*
220:3 into *TSIaR*] in *MS*
220:9 midday] mid-day *TSIa*
220:16 high road] high-road *TSIaC*
220:17 settlement, *TSIaR*] ~ *MS*
220:18 But] ~, *E1*
220:22 back] ~, *E1*
220:30 But] ~, *E1*
220:32 wild *TSIaR*] bush *MS*
220:40 sandal wood] sandal-wood *A1*
221:9 mate!] ~? *E1*
221:10 Good-O] Good O *TSIa*
221:10 said] asked *TSIa*
221:12 hopeful—] ~. *TSIa*
221:13 How's *MS*, *A1*] [...]ow's *TSIa* 'Ow's *E1*
221:13 y'r] y' *TSIa*
221:17 bacca!] ~. *TSIa*
221:18 you!] ~? *TSIa*
221:18 pleasantly. And] ~, and *TSIa*
221:19 baby, *MS*, *A1*] ~ *TSIa*
221:21 gi'e] gi[...]e *TSIa* give *TSIaR*
221:25 we] ~, *TSIaC*, *E1*
221:26 villainous,] ~ *TSIa*
221:27 dirty] ~, *E1*
221:31 fire, and] ~ ~, *E1*
221:34 ye] you *TSIa*
222:9 fell too] ~, ~ *E1*
222:13 which] of which *TSIaC*
222:17 of— — — —.] ~—— *A1* ~ ... *E1*
222:18 arm of his] wrist of the *TSIa*
222:19 then he *TSIaR*] *Om. MS*
222:21 wastrels *TSIaR*] wastrel *MS*
222:32 staring.] ~, *E1*
222:36 explained;] ~, *TSIa*
222:37 so] So *E1*
223:1 school,] ~. *TSIa*
223:5 side] ~, *A1*
223:7 Oh] ~, *A1*, *E1*
223:10 But] ~, *E1*
223:17 grand *TSIaR*] Grand *MS*
223:18 relations they] ~, ~ *A1*
223:19 Gales] the Gales *E1*
223:20 Edgars,] ~ *TSIa*
223:22 other:] ~; *TSIa*
223:26 reappeared] re-appeared *E1*
223:26 *Brackman*] Brackman *TSIa*
223:33 queer,] ~ *TSIa*
223:35 you *TSIaR*] anyone *MS*
223:36 matriarchy] Matriarchy *TSIa*
224:3 question; ... off; ... grub; ... fit; ... right; ... fast;] ~: ... ~: ... ~: ... ~: ... ~: ... ~: *E1*
224:7 bugs] bed-bugs *E1*
224:8 greasy-whiskered] grassy-whiskered *TSIa*
224:9 glasses,] ~ *TSIa*
224:12 Jack. "Wherever] ~. wherever *TSIa* ~, "wherever *TSIaR*
224:14 the] *Om. TSIa*
224:14 labourers *TSIa*] laborers *MS*
224:17 the] *Om. TSIa*
224:20 skin-hunter *TSIaR*] skin hunter *MS*, *E1* skin-/ hunter *A1*
224:25 jinkers] junkers *TSIa*
224:26 swabs *TSIaR*] swobs *MS*
224:30 loaf] ~, *A1*
224:33 He too] ~, ~, *E1*
224:34 face] ~, *A1*
224:38 sinewy *TSIaR*] powerful *MS*
225:7 jinker] junker *TSIa*
225:8 low] ~, *TSIa*
225:8 log-hauler] log hauler *TSIa*
225:9 swab *TSIaR*] swob *MS*
225:14 Waltzing *TSIaR*] waltzing *MS*
225:16 Right-O!] ~, *E1*
225:17 Clink ... Clink *Ed.*] Chink ... Chink *MS see note on* 225:20
225:19 Now] ~, *E1*
225:19 Guide to Knowledge *TSIaR*] guide to knowledge *MS*
225:22 bully—] ~ *A1*, *E1*
225:23 what's *stouch Ed.*] *'s touch MS* what's *touch TSIaR* what's *stosh A1*, *E1 see notes*
225:28 on] to *TSIa*
225:30 stead] 'stead *A1*, *E1*
225:35 an'] and *TSIa*
225:38 body, *TSIaR*] ~ *MS*

226:1 I dunno] dunno *TSIa* Dunno *TSIaR*
226:8 Rackett! *TSIaR*] ~. *MS*
226:9 hail-fellow-well-met *TSIaR*] hail fellow well met *MS* hail-fellow well-met *E1*
226:12 far—!"] ~" *TSIa*
226:13 all *TSIaR*] *Om. MS*
226:14 goin'?— — —] ~? . . . *A1* ~?" . . . *E1*
226:25 Never-Never *TSIaR*] Never Never *MS*
226:25 degeneration] degradation *TSIa*
226:36 minister] Minister *TSIa*
226:36 gospel] Gospel *TSIaC, E1*
227:5 milestones *MS, A1*] mile-/stones *TSIa* mile-stones *E1*
227:11 *gin TSIaR*] gin *MS*
227:15 was glad *TSIaR*] loved it *MS*
227:17 it,] ~— *TSIa*
227:20 man] Man *TSIa*
227:23 They'll never find *TSIaR*] Never *MS*
227:27 strange,] ~ *TSIa*
227:30 early for the boat, *TSIaR*] early, *MS* early *TSIa*
227:31 evening,] ~ *TSIa*
227:35 desire,] desires *TSIa*
227:36 Or . . . other God. *E1*] *Om. MS* [. . .]r . . . ~ ~. *TSIaR* or . . . ~ ~. *TSIbR* Or . . . ~ god. *A1*
227:39 Yes *TSIaR*] Yet *MS*
227:39 god *MS, A1*] God *TSIa*
227:40 god] God *TSIaC, E1*
228:1 god] God *E1*
228:2 god.] God. *E1*
228:2 god, *MS, A1*] God, *TSIa*
228:4 dusky-grey, *Ed.*] dusky-gray, *MS* dusky, gray *TSIa* dusky, grey *E1*
228:6 potency] ~, *TSIa*
228:8 strange] ~, *TSIa*
228:8 gum-smelling] gun-smelling *A1*
228:11 dim] ~, *TSIa*
228:18 had had] had *E1*
228:20 strange,] ~ *E1*
228:20 shores, *MS, E1*] ~ *TSIa*
228:25 home,] ~ *TSIa*
228:29 wing-feathers] wing feathers *E1*
228:32 sun] the sun *TSIa*
228:34 emerald-green *TSIaR*] emerald green *MS*
229:2 After Two Years. *Ed.*] Back in Perth. *MS BACK IN PERTH. TSIa AFTER TWO YEARS. TSIaR* AFTER TWO YEARS. *TSIaC* AFTER TWO YEARS *A1* AFTER TWO YEARS *E1*
229:10 Further] Farther *E1*
229:12 North-West *Ed.*] north-west *MS*
229:13 into *TSIa*] in to *MS*
229:13 oyster, *MS, E1*] oysters *TSIa*
229:16 Nor' West] Nor'-West *TSIaC*
229:18 into *Ed.*] in to *MS* to *TSIa*
229:19 Venus"; *A1, E1*] ~;" *MS*
229:21 manœuvring *TSIaC, E1*] manoeuvring *MS*
229:21 to] *Om. TSIa*
229:25 stubbly] stubby *TSIa*
229:29 four] three *TSIa*
230:15 sister—] ~, *TSIa*
230:37 you you] ~, ~ *TSIa*
231:6 back. And] ~, and *TSIa*
231:10 enemy] ~, *TSIa*
231:11 Camp . . . Camp] camp . . . camp *TSIa*
231:16 civilisation *MS, TSIaC*] civilization *TSIa*
231:17 civilised *MS, TSIaC*] civilized *TSIa*
231:25 Oh] ~, *TSIa*
231:25 hotels,] ~ *TSIa*
231:26 rum,] ~ *TSIa*
231:26 whiskey] whisky *E1*
231:28 brutal,] ~ *TSIa*
231:36 cattle] cable *TSIa*
231:38 then] and *TSIa*
232:4 them;] ~, *TSIa*
232:5 squatters] ~, *A1*
232:8 civilisation *MS, TSIaC*] civilization *TSIa*

232:10 mission-stations] mission stations *TSIa*
232:11 mining-camps] mining camps *TSIa*
232:14 feared] thought *TSIa*
232:20 stood,] ~ *TSIa*
232:28 wall-less. And] ~, and *TSIa*
232:29 around] round *TSIa*
232:29 bar;] ~, *TSIa*
232:34 boss, or husband,] ~ ~ ~ *TSIa*
232:35 team,] ~ *TSIa*
232:37 turns] turn *A1*
232:37 mamma] mama *A1*
233:1 familiarised *MS*, *TSIaC*] familiarized *TSIa*
233:2 boarding-house, *Ed.*] boarding house, *MS* boarding house *TSIa* boarding-house *TSIaR*
233:5 boarding-house] boarding house, *TSIa* boarding-house, *TSIaR*
233:6 high-born *TSIaR*] noble-born *MS*
233:7 "swim" *TSIaR*] aristocracy *MS*
233:11 y' understand] y'understand, *TSIa*
233:12 We] We're *TSIa*
233:15 Boss'] Boss's *E1*
233:16 paradise] Paradise *TSIaC*, *E1*
233:23 She was ... sort ... of perspiration.] She ... type ... perspiration. *TSIa Om. TSIbC*, *A1 see note on* 233:33
233:26 disgust. Because ... chair, in ... [233:31] Circied ... stupefied ... [233:33] Circe. *P* There *Ed.*] disgust. Because ... chair, in ... Circied ... stupified ... Circe. *P* There *MS* disgust. Because ... chair in ... circied ... Circe. *P* There *TSIa* disgust. Because ... chair in ... circied ... stupefied ... Circe. *P* There *TSIaC* disgust. There *TSIbC* disgust. *P* There *A1 see note on* 233:33
233:38 But Tom ... swine. He] Tom *E1 see note on* 233:33
234:8 tracks,] ~ *TSIa*
234:12 By the ... [234:17] patent-medicine ... [234:31] "Dear ... "This ... [235:28] we remain." *Ed.*] By the ... patent-medicine ... Dear ... This ... we remain." *MS* By the ... patent medecine {patent medicine *TSIaR*} ... Dear ... This ... we remain." *TSIa Om. TSIbC*, *A1 see notes*
235:30 letter] ~, *E1*
235:31 qualms] qualm *E1*
235:36 you] ~, *A1*, *E1*
235:39 Jack. *MS*, *E1*] ~— *TSIa* ~—— *A1*
236:16 mates] mater *TSIa* mate *TSIaR*
236:24 Jack, *MS*, *E1*] ~ *TSIa*
236:24 a] *Om. TSIa*
236:27 this,] ~ *TSIa*
236:30 Hotel] hotel *E1*
236:33 as *TSIa*] have *MS*
236:36 in] into *TSIa*
236:37 refrained,] ~ *TSIa*
236:38 further] farther *E1*
237:3 musk] mush *TSIa Om. TSIaR*
237:4 ant] aunt *TSIa*
237:8 civilisation] civilization *E1*
237:32 pale grey] pale-grey *A1*
237:32 glanced *Ed.*] glancd *MS* glared *TSIa*
237:34 then] ~, *TSIaC*, *E1*
237:35 Why—] ~—— *A1*
237:35 sheepishly—] ~. *TSIa*
237:36 —mate] Mate *E1*
237:36 —want] Want *E1*
237:39 Why—] ~—— *A1*
238:1 Well] ~, *A1*, *E1*
238:4 *little*] little *TSIa*
238:15 six thirty] six-thirty *TSIa*
238:23 me.] ~? *TSIa*
238:24 lappels] lapels *A1*
238:26 'F *MS*, *E1*] 'f *TSIa*
238:27 Miners] ~' *A1*, *E1*
238:28 Come] ~, *TSIaC*, *E1*
238:28 matey—"] ~"— *TSIa*
238:36 river-side] riverside *TSIaC*

238:37 Freemasons'] Freemason's *TSIa*
239:1 with] with a *TSIa*
239:4 North-West *A1*] North West *MS*
239:15 Well] ~, *A1*, *E1*
239:16 it's *MS*, *E1*] its *TSIa*
239:17 Watson *TSIa*] Watkins *MS*
239:17 book-shop] bookshop *A1*
239:21 ne'er-do-wells *TSIa*] neer-do-wells *MS*
239:24 book-shop,] bookshop, *A1* book-shop *E1*
239:24 *The*] "The *TSIbC*
239:24 *Booklovers*] *Book-/ lovers TSIa* Book-/ lovers *TSIbC* Book-lovers' *E1*
239:24 *Latest*!] Latest!" *TSIbC Latest! A1*
239:32 black-kid-gloved] black kid-gloved *TSIa*
239:34 half a quid] half-a-quid *TSIaC*
240:5 Tomorrow] ~, *TSIaC* To-morrow, *E1*
240:5 O. K.] O.K. *TSIa*
240:10 the] *Om. TSIa*
240:10 half-a-quid *MS*, *TSIaC*] half a quid *TSIa*
240:14 disgraceful—] ~—— *A1*, *E1*
240:23 old *Ed.*] Old *MS*
240:23 tonight,] ~? *TSIa* to-night? *E1*
240:24 still-careless] still careless *E1*
240:25 ter] to *TSIa*
240:25 sport.] ~? *TSIa*
240:26 relations'll] relations 'll *TSIa*
240:27 lest] that *TSIa*
240:31 River] river *E1*
240:33 St.] Street *A1*, *E1*
240:37 Right-O *Ed.*] Right o' *MS* Righto *TSIa*
240:39 him.—But *MS*, *A1*] ~,—~ *TSIa* ~—but, *E1*
240:40 pawnbrokers] pawnbroker's *A1*, *E1*
241:3 Now] ~ *E1*
241:3 then] ~, *TSIaC*, *E1*
241:13 gentleman,] ~ *TSIa*
241:13 friend, *MS*, *E1*] ~ *TSIa*
241:15 first-class] ~, *E1*
241:16 gents] ~' *TSIaC*, *E1*
241:18 him] me *TSIa*
241:21 deposit:] ~, *E1*
241:22 they'd] they would *TSIa*
241:26 Alright] All right, *TSIaC* Alright, *E1*
241:29 Miners] Miners' *TSIaC*, *E1*
241:31 Say] ~, *A1*
241:32 local?" *P* The *TSIa*] ~?"/ The *MS*
242:4 Scottie] ~, *E1*
242:10 tomorrer."—He ... face. *P* "Y'] tomorrer." *P* "Y' *TSIa* tomorrer. *P* "Y' *TSIaR* tomorrer. Y' *A1* to-morrer. *P* "Y' *E1*
242:15 tomorrer] to-morrer *E1*
242:18 north *Ed.*] North *MS*
242:19 fiver.] ~? *A1*, *E1*
242:20 O. K."] O.K.," *A1* O.K.", *E1*
242:21 Well] ~, *E1*
242:22 wot's *TSIaC*] wots' *MS* wots *E1*
242:29 th'oss *Ed.*] th ' oss *MS* the 'oss *TSIa*
242:29 said—"But] ~,"—but *E1*
242:33 north *Ed.*] North *MS*
242:35 about] *Om. TSIa*
242:37 book-shop] bookshop *A1*
243:5 Tom] ~, *E1*
243:7 counter. *MS*, *A1*] ~, *TSIa*
243:17 The fellow *TSIaR*] He *MS*
243:26 boys.] ~? *E1*
243:29 Right-O] Right-o *TSIa* Righto *A1*
243:29 Gold dust] gold ~ *TSIa* golddust *A1*
243:32 curiously, *MS*, *E1*] ~ *TSIa*
243:34 Jimmy] Jimmie *TSIa*
243:36 Why] ~, *A1*, *E1*
244:1 "We've *MS*, *E1*] ~ *TSIa*
244:1 old *Ed.*] Old *MS*
244:2 Jimmie *TSIa*] Jimmy *MS*
245:17 Anyhow] ~, *E1*
245:22 General *Ed.*] general *MS*
245:24 of: My] ~ "~ *TSIa*
245:27 something, *MS*, *A1*] ~ *TSIa*
245:28 do.] ~." *TSIa*
245:29 General's *TSIa*] general's *MS*

245:33 doting ... 'Appy ... Cossack way."] doting ... 'appy ... Cossack way." *TSIa* doting. *A1* *see note on* 234:12
246:2 still] *Om. TSIa*
246:12 wait,] ~ *TSIa*
246:13 ladies,] ~ *TSIa*
246:13 and] *Om. A1, E1*
246:17 Representative] Representation *TSIa*
246:22 straws] straw *TSIa*
246:30 Go-on ... Go-on] Go on ... Go on *E1*
246:31 ter] to *TSIa*
246:32 face] ~, *A1*
246:35 A. D. C.] A.D.C. *TSIa*
247:3 distance] ~, *TSIa*
247:12 open,] ~ *TSIa*
247:19 promiscuity] ~, *TSIa*
247:20 everybody,] ~ *TSIa*
247:20 random. But] ~, but, *E1*
247:21 fact, *MS, E1*] ~ *TSIa*
247:22 mother and father] father and mother *TSIa*
247:27 inward *TSIa*] inward/ inward *MS*
247:31 Oh] ~, *TSIa*
247:31 Matilda. *MS, A1*] ~, *TSIa*
247:32 But you see] ~, ~ ~, *E1*
247:36 grey-blue] green-blue *E1*
247:36 a dark] and a dark *TSIa*
247:37 it,] ~ *TSIa*
247:40 here!] ~, *TSIa*
248:5 different] ~, *E1*
248:7 said, "so] ~. "So *E1*
248:12 asserted] assented *TSIa*
248:13 while] time *TSIa*
248:14 thing—"] ~"— *TSIa*
248:24 moonlit] *Om. TSIa*
248:27 he's] he is *TSIa*
248:32 And] And as *A1, E1*
248:37 said. "But *MS, A1*] ~, "~ *TSIa* ~, "but *E1*
248:40 also he] he also *TSIa*
249:3 small, *MS, E1*] ~ *TSIa*
249:5 asked,] ~ *E1*
249:8 not—] ~—— *A1, E1*
249:11 destiny,] ~ *E1*
249:12 Monica] ~, *E1*
249:21 her heaviness] ~ ~, *E1*
249:21 too, the] ~. The *TSIa*
249:22 dark,] ~ *TSIa*
249:22 that] ~, *E1*
249:23 thought, "Why *TSIaR*] ~: ~ *MS* ~. ~ *TSIa*
249:23 her] ~, *E1*
249:24 mine?" *TSIaR*] ~? *MS* ~." *A1, E1*
249:37 Mary and Monica] Monica and Mary *TSIa*
250:1 Mary: the] ~. The *TSIa*
250:6 ball-room] ballroom *A1*
250:10 which,] ~ *TSIa*
250:13 in] in a *TSIaC*
250:14 He too] ~, ~, *E1*
250:17 uneasy, *Ed.*] delicate, *MS* delicate *TSIa* uneasy *TSIaR*
250:20 General *A1*] general *MS*
250:22 Mary too] ~, ~, *E1*
250:37 even] even a n *TSIa* even an *TSIaR*
250:37 unconventionality *MS, A1*] unconventiality *TSIa*
250:38 ball-room] ball-/ room *TSIa* ballroom *A1, E1*
251:3 native] *Om. TSIa*
251:5 she] that she *TSIa*
251:15 Jack,] ~ *A1*
251:17 North-West *A1*] north-west *MS* North-west *TSIa, E1*
251:21 dark-grey, startled round *TSIaR*] big, forget-me-not blue *MS*
251:21 looked at ... might bite *TSIaR*] thought him a hero from the unknown *MS*
251:22 manner] ~, *TSIa*
251:23 laughed *TSIaR*] kissed *MS*
251:23 cajole some *TSIaR*] caress the *MS*
251:27 amiable *A1, E1*] aimiable *MS*
251:35 replied. *MS, E1*] ~, *TSIa*
251:35 yet, *MS, E1*] ~ *TSIa*
251:36 My] my *TSIa*
251:39 not?—] ~— *E1*
252:4 it!] ~? *TSIa*

252:5 did marry] married *TSIa*
252:10 horrid] so horrid *TSIa*
252:11 too] *Om. TSIa*
252:12 Anyhow] ~, *E1*
252:13 sure.] ~? *A1*
252:19 farm—"] ~"— *E1*
252:22 say] ~: *TSIa*
252:27 away,] ~. *TSIa*
252:32 Lancers *MS, E1*] lancers *TSIa*
252:34 said. "And] ~, "and *TSIa*
252:35 governor] Governor *TSIaC*
252:36 A. D. C. *MS, A1*] A.D.C. *TSIa*
252:36 Jimmie *A1*] Jimmy *MS*
252:37 —She *TSIaR*] ~ *MS*
253:4 hot!] ~. *TSIa* ~, *A1, E1*
253:6 Lor' *Ed.*] Lor *MS*
253:6 m' dear!] m'dear. *TSIa*
253:6 *are*] are *TSIa*
253:6 amusin'"] ~!" *TSIa*
253:6 y'] you *TSIa*
253:8 that,] ~ *A1*
253:11 let slip] slip *TSIa* lose *TSIaR*
253:13 *You TSIaR*] You *MS*
253:13 well] well enough *A1*
253:13 alone. We] ~, we *TSIa*
253:14 man, and a good] *Om. TSIa*
253:15 heavy, she's heavy, she's] heavy, she's *E1*
253:19 Besides, *MS, E1*] ~ *TSIa*
253:20 heaven!] Heaven. *TSIa*
253:21 had] *Om. TSIa*
253:22 perfume—] ~. *TSIa*
253:26 yourself?] ~, *A1*
253:29 ironically *TSIaR*] involuntarily *MS*
253:33 to] to do *E1*
253:34 must anyhow] ~, ~, *E1*
253:37 do!] ~, *TSIa*
253:37 ball-room] ball-/ room *TSIa* ballroom *A1, E1*
254:4 chair,] ~ *TSIa*
254:6 down] ~, *TSIa*
254:8 down] ~, *A1*
254:11 Marm!] ~, *TSIa*
254:14 presence. He] ~. *P* He *TSIa*
254:15 judge *MS, E1*] Judge *TSIa*
254:16 woman] ~, *TSIa*
254:19 Matildas] ~, *TSIa*
254:23 grand-daughter *MS, E1*] grand-/ daughter *TSIa* granddaughter *A1*
254:24 slow,] ~ *A1*
254:26 ball-room,] ball-room *TSIa* ballroom *A1*
254:26 A. D. C.] A.D.C. *TSIa*
254:29 Matilda,] ~ *A1*
254:30 and] *Om. TSIa*
254:35 at] for *TSIa*
255:16 fan,] ~ *TSIa*
255:24 Brackley.] ~? *TSIaC*
255:26 on] upon *TSIa*
255:33 Jack *TSIa*] Jack He *MS see notes*
255:33 for the] for a *TSIa*
255:34 do or say] say or do *TSIa*
256:1 say] ~, *TSIaC, E1*
256:1 Tom. You] ~," you *TSIa* ~, you *TSIaC*
256:11 she *TSIaR*] *Om. MS*
256:13 left] let *A1*
256:17 to] into *TSIa*
256:17 the pin] a pin *TSIa*
256:22 *really*] really *TSIa*
256:22 farm—?—even] ~?" ~ *TSIa* ~?—~ *TSIaR* ~,—~ *TSIaC, A1* ~? Even *E1*
256:37 cardroom] card room *TSIa*
256:40 sir *E1*] Sir *MS*
257:1 right] ~, *TSIaC, E1*
257:2 sir *E1*] Sir *MS*
257:8 Blessington,] ~; *E1*
257:8 sir *MS, E1*] Sir *TSIa*
257:12 his] *Om. A1*
257:12 and bahed *TSIa*] & bahed *MS*
257:17 requires] needs *TSIa*
257:19 Jimmie *A1*] Jimmy *MS*
258:8 up!] ~, *TSIa*
258:11 home road] road home *TSIa*
258:11 load,] ~ *TSIa*
258:17 —about] *Om. TSIa*
258:17 t'] to *TSIa*
258:21 Well] ~, *A1, E1*
258:21 then] ~, *TSIaC*
258:21 'e] he *TSIa*
258:24 north,] ~; *E1*
258:25 lucky] ~, *E1*

258:28 becos] because *TSIa*
258:30 an' the] and the *TSIa*
258:30 kids.] ~? *A1*
258:32 to] ter *TSIa*
258:33 th'] the *TSIa*
258:34 ole] ol' *TSIa*
258:35 was,] ~ *TSIa*
259:1 ole] ol' *TSIa*
259:2 "out *A1*] '~ *MS*
259:2 mind." *A1*] ~.' *MS*, *E1* ~'. *TSIa*
259:3 know] ~, *A1*, *E1*
259:7 Jack.] ~, *TSIa* ~; *E1*
259:11 Wandoo, *she Ed.*] '~', ~ *MS* ~. *She TSIa*
259:14 it's] *Om. TSIa*
259:17 Anyhow] ~, *E1*
259:17 on] *Om. A1*
259:30 "declared himself,"] ~ ~," *TSIa* ~ ~, *TSIaR*
259:36 correct] erect *A1*, *E1*
260:2 Rather,] ~ *TSIa*
260:2 her,] ~ *TSIa*
260:11 border,] ~ *A1*
260:15 arrowily-submissive] arrowly-submissive *TSIaC*
260:17 Monica. And] ~ and *TSIa* ~, and *E1*
260:33 *her*] her *TSIa*
260:35 said] said that *A1*
260:39 wonder] ~, *TSIa*
261:3 were] was *TSIa*
261:4 grand-daughter *MS*, *E1*] grand-/ daughter *TSIa* granddaughter *A1*
261:6 aintcher] ~, *A1*, *E1*
261:8 difficulty: "We've] ~. "~ *TSIa* ~, "we've *E1*
261:11 shortly,] ~ *TSIa*
261:12 now, *TSIaR*] ~ *MS*
261:13 whip.— *TSIaR*] ~. *MS*, *TSIb*
261:14 valley." *MS*, *E1*] ~". *TSIa* ~":— *TSIbR* ~!" *A1* *see note on* 178:7
261:14 suddenly,] ~ *TSIa*
261:14 Say] ~, *A1*, *E1*
261:16 snow ...] ~ ... *A1*, *E1*
261:19 him] ~, *E1*
261:23 A. 1.,] A.I!, *TSIa* A1! *A1* A.1.! *E1*
261:24 fellow] ~, *TSIa*
261:25 come] came *E1*
261:25 Queensland] ~, *A1*
261:27 Well] ~, *TSIa*
261:29 an'] and *E1*
261:29 't *Ed.*] t' *MS*
261:29 Anyway] ~, *E1*
261:30 old *TSIaC*] Old *MS*, *A1*
261:31 me—] ~—— *E1*
261:35 old *TSIaC*] Old *MS*
261:36 say—] ~—— *E1*
261:39 cross-roads] Cross Roads *TSIa*
261:39 to *TSIaR*] to do *MS*
261:40 Yes,] ~ *E1*
262:3 Timothy!] ~, *TSIa*
262:7 and clung ... and down,] *Om. TSIa*
262:16 Jack *TSIaR*] He *MS*
262:21 taller] ~, *TSIa*
262:23 baby *TSIa*] Baby *MS*, *A1*
262:27 in th'] in the *TSIa*
262:27 t'] to *TSIa*
262:30 t'] to' *A1*
262:32 bold] ~, *E1*
262:34 Well] ~, *E1*
262:34 Jack. "You've] ~, "~ *TSIa* ~, "you've *E1*
262:35 hev'] hev *TSIa*
262:35 Harry. "Quite] ~: "~ *TSIa* ~, "quite *E1*
262:36 ken—] ~—— *E1*
262:39 Say] ~, *A1*, *E1*
262:39 tone. "Stand] ~, "stand *E1*
262:40 want] wants *A1*, *E1*
263:6 you knows] ye know *TSIa*
263:8 Ma] ~, *E1*
263:12 Lennie] ~, *E1*
263:16 th'] the *TSIa*
263:20 at Jack] Jack *TSIa*
263:27 eye—] ~, *TSIa*
263:27 *his*—] ~ *TSIa*
263:29 Only—] ~, *TSIa* ~ *A1*, *E1*
263:31 wi'] with *TSIa*
263:33 Why] ~, *E1*
263:33 only *TSIaR*] not *MS*
263:36 good!"] ~," *TSIa*

263:37 anything—"] ~"— *E1*
263:39 Gosh, it] ~! ~ *TSIa* ~! It *A1*
264:1 Well] ~, *TSIa*
264:1 odds.] ~? *A1*
264:2 Ma! Blown out! *TSIaR*] ~. ~ ~. *MS*
264:3 north *Ed.*] North *MS*
264:5 Tom. Working] ~, working *TSIa*
264:12 But—] ~—— *E1*
264:16 Lennie.] ~? *TSIaC, E1*
264:18 home-coming.] ~? *TSIaC, E1*
264:24 Why] ~, *A1, E1*
264:26 again] ~, *A1*
265:4 men] man *TSIa*
265:10 men] man *A1*
265:12 Lennie *MS, E1*] Len *TSIa*
265:13 best] best thing *E1 see note on* 67:36
265:23 And] ~, *E1*
265:26 deep] *Om. TSIa*
265:28 now,] ~ *TSIa*
265:37 chimney-stack,] chimney-/ stack *TSIa* chimney stack *E1*
266:10 Oh] ~, *A1, E1*
266:11 him—] ~. *TSIa* ~, *E1*
266:17 arm-chair. *MS, E1*] ~... *TSIa* ~ ... *A1*
266:20 fireplace] fire-/ place *TSIa* fire-place *E1*
266:26 chimney piece] chimney-piece *A1, E1*
266:28 a] the *TSIa*
266:29 dusty *TSIaR*] chinese *MS*
266:32 gold] gold coins *TSIa*
266:35 Old] old *TSIa*
266:35 t] 't' *TSIaC* T *A1, E1*
266:40 and the] and *TSIa*
267:1 half-sovereigns] half sovereigns *TSIa* half-/ sovereigns *A1*
267:7 pale] ~, *E1*
267:8 counted,] ~ *TSIa*
267:15 What he ... know *TSIaR*] All he cared *MS*
267:18 away] ~, *TSIa*
267:20 were] was *TSIa*
267:23 "Stocking"] stocking *TSIa*
267:36 calling: *MS, E1*] ~. *TSIa*
268:7 spliced!] ~. *A1*
268:8 Gosh,] ~,' *TSIa* ~,! *TSIaR* ~, *A1*
268:8 wallaby!] ~ *TSIb* ~. *E1*
268:9 why] ~, *E1*
268:9 older 'n *Ed.*] older'n *MS*
268:14 that! *TSIaR*] ~. *MS*
268:17 never!] ~. *E1*
268:18 devil?] ~! *TSIa*
268:19 But] *Om. TSIa*
268:20 way,] ~ *E1*
268:23 d' y'] d'ye *TSIa*
268:25 to put ... to continue] *Om. TSIa*
268:30 Right-O *Ed.*] Right' O *MS* Right O *TSIa* Righto *A1*
268:30 An'] an' *TSIa*
268:32 place,] ~ *E1*
268:32 on] by *TSIa*
269:2 The Last of Easu./ i *Ed.*] i/ The Last of Easu. *MS The Last of Easu./* I. *TSIa* THE LAST OF EASU/ I *TSIaC* THE LAST OF EASU/ i *E1*
269:15 "t' see *Ed.*] t' see *MS* t'see *TSIa* "t'see *TSIaR*
269:16 fisogs." *TSIaR*] ~. *MS*
269:16 missis] missus *TSIa*
269:19 mantel-piece] mantel-/ piece *TSIa* mantelpiece *A1, E1*
269:20 woolen] woollen *TSIaC, E1*
269:21 curly] curvy *TSIa*
269:24 this] the *TSIa*
269:31 big,] ~ *TSIa*
269:31 eyes] eye *A1*
269:31 distaste,] ~ *TSIa*
270:2 as kisses *TSIa*] than kisses *MS see notes*
270:3 table] ~, *A1*
270:5 d' yer] d'ye *TSIa*
270:9 parnds!] ~ *E1*
270:14 "tharsand parnd!" *Ed.*] '~ parnd!' *MS* ~ parnds! *TSIa*
270:21 care!] ~? *E1*
270:24 show] draw *TSIa*
270:26 vindictive] ~, *A1*
270:28 got? *P* "If *Ed.*] ~? "If *MS*

270:29 *me*] me *TSIa*
270:31 listened,] ~ *TSIa*
270:33 going] *Om. E1*
270:33 wasn't. *P* She] ~. She *TSIa*
270:35 for ever *Ed.*] forever *MS*
271:2 coat-and-skirt] coat and skirt *TSIa*
271:5 out,] ~ *TSIa*
271:8 pink-and-white] pink and white *TSIa*
271:10 Therefore,] ~ *A1*
271:11 curling-irons *MS, A1*] curling irons *TSIa*
271:15 think] think that *TSIa*
271:16 shalt] shall *A1*
271:17 curling irons.] ~ ~." *TSIaR* curling-irons." *A1*
271:17 But the ... curling irons.] *Om. TSIa*
271:25 *anybody*] anybody *A1*
271:27 bit] little *TSIa*
271:29 Sarah Ann *TSIa*] Sarah-Ann *MS*
271:33 silent:] ~ *TSIa*
271:35 God!",] ~!" *TSIa*
271:37 Easu *TSIaR*] But Easu *MS*
272:17 north] North *TSIa*
272:20 y'] you *TSIa*
272:23 No!] ~, *TSIa*
272:25 Oh you] ~ ~ *TSIa* ~, ~ *TSIaR*
272:32 Well] ~, *E1*
272:36 Why, don't] ~? Don't *TSIa*
272:36 y'] ye *TSIa*
273:1 old *Ed.*] Old *MS*
273:3 Well] ~, *TSIa*
273:3 Ant] Aunt *TSIa*
273:7 Well] ~, *E1*
273:19 with] with a *E1*
273:24 Why] ~, *E1*
273:32 is,] ~ *TSIa*
273:38 and] ~, *E1*
273:40 cunningly *E1*] rejoicingly *MS*
273:40 *I*] I *A1*
273:41 ye] you *TSIa*
274:4 Why] ~, *E1*
274:8 old *Ed.*] Old *MS*
274:9 old *MS, TSIaC*] Old *TSIa, A1*
274:10 nothing,] ~. *A1*
274:19 under that] under the *A1*
274:19 ridge—— *MS, A1*] ~— *TSIa*
174:20 Jack,] ~ *TSIa*
274:21 silence] ~, *TSIa*
274:27 Hello *MS, E1*] Hullo *TSIa*
274:36 Say] ~, *TSIa*
274:36 what *MS, A1*] What *TSIa*
274:37 Percy.] ~? *TSIa*
275:2 for] *Om. TSIa*
275:4 *You ... you TSIaR*] You ... you *MS*
275:6 'T would *Ed.*] 'Twould *MS*
275:10 knows] know *TSIa*
275:12 year,] ~ *TSIa*
275:16 *be*] be *TSIa*
275:21 says] say *A1*
275:22 was] ~, *A1*
275:23 wouldn't] would *TSIa*
275:27 wild cat's] wildcat's *A1*
275:28 by] of *TSIa*
275:33 an'] and *TSIa*
275:39 wot's *TSIa*] wots' *MS* who's *A1, E1 see notes*
275:40 sin,] ~. *TSIa*
276:3 He *MS, TSIaC*] he *TSIa*
276:5 a emu] an emu *TSIa*
276:8 Anyhow] ~, *E1*
276:9 rether] rather *TSIa*
276:10 collar-horse *MS, A1*] collar horse *TSIa*
276:19 Well] ~, *TSIa*
276:19 *am*] am *TSIa*
276:25 Say] ~, *TSIaC, E1*
276:25 Jack!] ~, *TSIa*
276:26 right—fifty-seven] ~. fifty-seven *TSIa, TSIb* ~. Fifty-seven *TSIaR, E1*
276:27 stocking] store *TSIa*
276:28 stockin'. You're] ~, you're *TSIa*
277:8 Anyhow] ~, *E1*
277:18 saddle-strings] saddle strings *TSIa* saddle-/ strings *A1*
277:30 horse] ~, *TSIa*
277:36 black] blacks *TSIa*
278:11 patient,] ~ *TSIa*

278:13 running, Easu] ~. ~ *TSIa* ~. ~, *TSIaR*
278:14 apart and] apart, *TSIaR*
278:15 fault *TSIaR*] sneering fault *MS*
278:16 who] *Om. TSIaR*
278:16 hallooing] holloaing *TSIa* halloaing *A1*
278:19 stiffish *TSIaR*] cumbersome *MS*
278:22 handsome] ~, *TSIa*
278:27 he] that he *TSIa*
278:28 arm—] ~. *TSIa*
278:35 back." *P* He *TSIa*] ~."/ He *MS*
278:37 sentences,] ~ *TSIa*
278:39 Easu too] ~, ~, *E1*
279:1 was gone] had gone *TSIa*
279:4 y'oss] y' oss *TSIa* y' 'oss *A1*, *E1*
279:5 Jimmie *A1*] Jimmy *MS*
279:7 pale blue] pale-blue *A1*
279:8 mouth. Jack] ~./ Jack *TSIa* ~. *P* Jack *E1*
279:10 spruce] ~, *TSIa*
279:11 belly] bulk *E1 see notes*
279:12 time] ~, *TSIa*
279:15 Herbert] ~, *E1*
279:23 little,] ~ *TSIa*
279:25 y' if] if *TSIa*
279:30 Percy,] ~ *E1*
279:32 faintly,] ~ *TSIa*
279:36 off] out of *TSIa*
279:41 pale blue] pale-blue *A1*
280:2 eyes,] ~ *E1*
280:3 white-fat] white fat *TSIaC*
280:11 hint] kind *TSIa*
280:12 inquiry] enquiry *TSIa*
280:14 rope,] ~ *TSIa*
280:19 nights] night *E1*
280:20 North-West *TSIa*] North West *MS*
280:20 had] *Om. A1*
280:22 that's] That's *TSIa*
280:26 Easu, now,] ~ ~ *TSIa*
280:30 man-servant *MS*, *TSIaC*] man servant *TSIa*
280:31 talking. You] ~, you *TSIa*
280:40 quickly,] ~ *TSIa*
281:13 death face] death-face *A1*
281:15 death-eyes *MS*, *A1*] death eyes *TSIa*
281:16 waiting] waiting for *A1*, *E1*
281:23 magically] mystically *TSIa*
281:32 fore-finger] fore finger *E1*
281:38 side] side of *TSIa*
282:5 dead! My] dead! He's dead! My *TSIa*
282:5 God] ~, *TSIa*
282:7 scattered brains] blood *A1*, *E1*
282:8 after *TSIaR*] *Om. MS*
282:13 that] which *TSIa*
282:13 big,] ~ *TSIa*
282:17 around] about *TSIa*
282:21 damming] damning *E1*
282:27 further!] ~? *TSIa*
282:29 with] with the *TSIa*
283:10 down,] ~ *TSIa*
283:11 drank,] ~ *TSIa*
283:11 Then … difficulty] ~, … ~, *E1*
283:18 old *MS*] Old *A1*, *E1*
283:18 This] The *TSIa*
283:21 Monica. Monica,] ~, ~ *TSIa* ~. ~ *E1*
283:23 repulsive] ~, *E1*
283:27 said "another] ~, "Another *TSIa*
283:29 weaponlike] weapon-like *TSIa* weapon-/ like *E1*
283:34 blood!" *P* "So] ~! So *A1*
284:3 it] ~, *E1*
284:4 for ever] forever *TSIa*
284:8 blood *TSIaR*] a bond of blood *MS*
284:9 voice] ~, *TSIa*
284:16 lord] Lord *E1*
284:17 Lords] lords *A1*
284:17 Death.] ~? *TSIaC*
284:17 lord of death] Lord ~ Death *TSIa* lord ~ Death *TSIaC*
284:28 her....] ~ ..... *TSIa* ~.... *A1*, *E1*
285:3 old *TSIaC*] Old *MS*, *A1*
285:4 A. D. C.] A.D.C. *TSIa*
285:6 table-cloth *MS*, *E1*] table cloth *TSIa*
285:8 dinners?] ~. *E1*

285:8 Oh] ~, *E1*
285:8 reesty *MS, E1*] rusty *TSIa*
285:13 fat white] white fat *TSIa*
285:15 hair] ~, *E1*
285:16 night] ~, *E1*
285:20 it, *MS, E1*] ~ *TSIa*
285:21 standing. And] ~, and *TSIa*
285:25 thick] ~, *E1*
285:27 and] *Om. TSIa*
285:28 nothing....] ~ .... *TSIa* ~ . . . *A1, E1*
285:33 Yet] ~, *TSIa*
285:37 tracks] track *TSIa*
285:38 wood-cutter] wood cutter *TSIa* woodcutter *A1*
285:40 distance] ~, *TSIa*
286:1 invisible] ~, *TSIa*
286:3 Coo-eed] coo-eed *TSIa*
286:4 light-headed *TSIaR*] light headed *MS* light-/ headed *A1, E1*
286:7 still,] ~ *TSIa*
286:8 Coo-eed] coo-eed *TSIaC, E1* coo-eed! *A1*
286:10 tree-trunks *TSIaR*] tree trunks *MS*
286:14 leaves] leave *A1*
286:18 insignificant] ~, *TSIa*
286:21 wits,] ~ *TSIa*
286:29 very very hot,] *Om. TSIa*
286:30 hungry? *MS, A1*] ~. *TSIa*
286:31 while,] ~ *TSIa*
286:34 bush,] ~ *TSIa*
286:38 legs. *P* What] ~. What *A1*
287:9 Well] ~, *TSIa*
287:9 then,] ~ *E1*
287:12 Well] ~, *A1, E1*
287:14 fear] face *TSIa*
287:15 waking] wakening *TSIa*
287:17 Coo-eed *Ed.*] coo-eeed *MS* coo-eed *E1*
287:19 shooter's *Ed.*] shooters *MS* hunters *TSIa* hunter's *TSIaR* hunters' *E1*
287:19 camp,] ~ *E1*
287:22 here] ~, *E1*
287:27 on,] ~ *TSIa*
287:34 deep] ~, *E1*
287:36 soon or late] sooner or later *TSIa*
288:10 undervest *MS, A1*] under-/ vest *TSIa* under-vest *E1*
288:14 trousers] ~, *E1*
288:20 eyes] eye *A1*
288:22 again,] ~ *TSIa*
288:26 combatted] combated *A1*
288:27 And] ~, *E1*
288:30 consciousness,] ~ *E1*
288:34 borders] border *TSIa*
288:36 border] ~, *E1*
289:1 petitions] ~, *TSIaC, E1*
289:1 sir] Sir *TSIa* Sir, *TSIaC* sir, *E1*
289:4 queen— — —] ~ ... *TSIa*
289:6 wearyingly thought, and thought,] ~, ~ ~ ~ *TSIa*
289:9 slave— —] ~ ... *TSIa*
289:13 slave— — —"/ The] ~." *P* The *TSIa* ~ . . ." *P* The *E1*
289:14 round,] ~ *TSIa*
289:17 fast—] ~ *TSIa*
289:19 periphery *A1*] periphera *MS*
289:19 consciousness,] ~ *E1*
289:22 dark, *MS, E1*] ~ *TSIa*
289:23 was] were *TSIa*
289:25 was the *MS, A1*] was *TSIa*
289:30 decided] decided that *TSIa*
289:31 grind:] ~. *TSIa*
289:36 vanishing—] ~. *TSIa*
290:4 Creator] creator *TSIa*
290:5 mother, father] Mother, Father *TSIa*
290:6 Lennie—they] ~. They *TSIa*
291:4 wave-beats, *TSIaC*] wave-/ beats, *MS, A1* wave-beats *TSIa*
291:8 wave] waves *TSIa*
291:10 little *TSIa*] ~, *MS, E1*
291:10 silvery, *TSIa*] ~ *MS*
291:11 spurts *TSIaR*] *Om. MS* spurts, *E1*
291:17 into *TSIaR*] again into *MS*
291:17 lordly,] ~ *TSIa*
291:20 this time *TSIaR*] *Om. MS*
291:25 words,] ~ *A1*
291:29 He] The *TSIa* They *TSIaR*
292:3 bottom,] ~ *TSIa*

292:8 dark-anointed *TSIaR*] dark anointed *MS*
292:14 stiffness. *P* He] ~. He *TSIa*
292:15 pain] the pain *TSIa*
292:16 those] the *TSIa*
292:19 Tom? *MS, TSIaC*] ~ *TSIa* ~. *E1*
292:23 The deeper … faithfulness.] *Om. TSIa*
292:26 burning,] ~ *TSIa*
292:30 meat;] ~, *TSIa*
292:38 go. Tom] ~. *P* Tom *TSIa*
292:38 there,] ~ *TSIa*
293:7 Then] ~, *E1*
293:14 blenched] blanched *A1*
293:20 in to] into *TSIa*
293:22 scarlet. *TSIaR*] scarlet, so blood-shot. *MS*
293:24 mate *MS, TSIaC*] Mate *TSIa*
293:31 Tom,] ~ *TSIa*
293:32 responsibility] responsibilities *TSIa*
293:39 morning] ~, *TSIaC*
294:2 head,] ~ *TSIa*
294:5 you, too, *MS, E1*] ~ ~ *TSIa*
294:10 still!] ~, *TSIa*
294:11 drop *TSIaR*] forsake *MS*
294:12 way *TSIaR*] fate *MS*
294:13 victorious *TSIaR*] peaceful *MS*
295:6 childishness gone … its place. *TSIaR*] carelessness and rashness and playfulness gone. *MS*
295:8 for ever] forever *A1, E1*
295:15 dark blue] dark-blue *A1*
295:18 otherworld] other world *E1*
295:20 And the … of mockery. *TSIaR*] *Om. MS*
295:23 diffident] ~, *A1*
295:27 But the … A skeleton! *A1, E1*] As a hard, powerful skeleton he felt himself moving. *MS*
295:30 And the] Ad *TSIa* The *TSIaR*
295:33 dark heart … its wisdom *A1, E1*] soft flesh stirring with its desires *MS*
295:34 It *A1*] It two *MS* It too *TSIa* It, too, *E1* *see notes*
296:1 heavy and … earth's centre *E1*] subordinate to the man of bone *MS* heavy … center *A1*
296:8 went. And] ~. *P* And *TSIa*
296:9 bones, and … the midst. *A1, E1*] bones. *MS*
296:14 determined *TSIaR*] strange, *MS*
296:15 heart *A1, E1*] bones *MS*
296:17 heart *A1, E1*] bones *MS*
296:18 master too] ~, ~, *E1*
296:19 having's sake. Nor] having's sake. Not *TSIa*
296:22 master] Master *TSIa*
296:23 gold] Gold *TSIa*
296:24 life *MS, E1*] kife *TSIa* knife *A1*
296:26 Because, *TSIaR*] ~ *MS*
296:26 on a] on the *TSIa*
296:30 of the] of *TSIa*
296:31 Life *MS, E1*] life *TSIa*
296:31 Creation] creation *TSIa*
296:41 heart of darkness *A1, E1*] mystery *MS*
297:6 paddock:] ~; *E1*
297:7 Good-day] good-day *A1, E1*
297:14 knew,] ~ *A1*
297:14 old *TSIaR*] Old *MS, A1, E1*
297:15 Afterwards] ~, *E1*
297:18 purpose,] ~ *E1*
297:19 old George *TSIaC*] Old ~ *MS, A1*
297:32 old *TSIaC*] Old *MS, A1*
297:34 laughing-stock] laughing stock *TSIa*
297:39 She, *MS, E1*] ~ *TSIa*
298:2 went,] ~ *TSIa*
298:8 once,] ~ *E1*
298:11 In Monica's … challenging question.] *Om. TSIa*
298:14 would] sould *TSIa* should *TSIaR*
298:15 for ever *Ed.*] forever *MS*
298:16 look,] *Om. TSIa* look *TSIaR*
298:17 cheek] cheeks *TSIa*
298:23 eyes,] ~ *TSIa*
298:32 up. *P* She] ~. She *TSIa*
298:36 cottage] house *TSIa*
299:1 sofa-bed] a sofa-bed *TSIaC*

299:5 this] the *TSIa*
299:7 raw silk *TSIaR*] terra-cotta *MS* terra cotta *TSIa*
299:7 red *TSIaR*] gold *MS*
299:7 light] bright *TSIa*
299:9 the] a *TSIa*
299:16 sharp, *MS, A1*] ~ *TSIa*
299:19 Jack,] ~ *TSIa*
299:19 tone, smiling ... of mockery. *TSIaR*] voice. *MS* tone. *TSIa*
299:21 back *TSIaR*] *Om. MS*
299:21 him] ~, *E1*
299:25 She was ... and uncomplaining *TSIaR*] But there was no slackness or complaining about her *MS*
299:30 to] to the *TSIa*
299:33 No-one] No one *TSIa*
299:34 eyes] ~, *TSIa*
299:39 breathless] breathlessly *TSIa*
300:4 Monica,] ~ *TSIa*
300:6 well, you] ~? You *TSIa*
300:6 eat?] ~. *TSIa* ~, *A1, E1*
300:19 said, *MS, E1*] ~ *TSIa*
300:21 came,] ~ *TSIa*
300:30 you] ~, *TSIa*
300:31 you,] ~ *TSIa*
300:31 went] had gone *E1 see note on* 67:36
300:33 eyes;] ~. *A1*
300:36 pluck] pluck in you *TSIa*
300:37 Only] ~, *E1*
301:4 "I] "I'm glad you killed him. I couldn't bear to think of him living on, and sneering—sneering!—I *A1* "I'm glad ... sneering,—sneering.—I *E1 see note on* 301:13
301:5 Ah] ~, *TSIa*
301:8 '*Really*'," *Ed.*] '~'", *MS* ~," *TSIa*
301:9 with a ... raillery *TSIaR*] teasingly *MS*
301:10 *really*—] ~, *TSIa*
301:10 but you ... as well, *A1, E1*] and the others you loved *MS* an the others you loved *TSIa* but you hankered after the others a good deal, *TSIaR*
301:12 baffled, defiant ... You've *had A1, E1*] baffled. *P* "What will you do," he said, "if you can't have any unreal loves as an offset for your real ones?" *P* "Now you're horrid!" she {horrid," she *TSIa*} said. *P* "All right, I won't be. You've had *MS* baffled, defiant. *P* "What will ... horrid," she ... right, your day is over. You've *had TSIaR*
301:16 innocent;] ~, *TSIa*
301:20 loveable] lovable *TSIaC*
301:28 saw ... side. She ... [301:32] stranger, she must fear him, because ... finally know him, and never entirely possess him. He ... so dangerously against ... [301:36] still stiffened herself against ... men, Percy, Easu, all ... [302:2] to that. *TSIbR*] would never be able to get really near to him: that she knew. She would never be able to get from him that delicious but deadly intimacy which she craved, but which she knew was a sort of calamity. He had been willing to give it, before. {it before. *TSIa*} So she had taunted him with Easu. And now he had turned away, to something that belonged to his own male self, alone. {self alone. *TSIa*} He had turned to his own male god, and would never give final intimacy to any human being whatsoever. He had given his ultimate intimacy to his own male God, and she was powerless. *MS* saw ... side; She ... stranger, whom she feared, because ... finally possess him, and never finally know him! He ... so terribly against ... still fought against ... men, Easu, Percy, all ... to this. *TSIaR see note on* 301:36.

302:4 from her ... strange, fascinating ... like a madness ... man. After ... [302:9] was magical. *TSIbR*] her own strange, fascinating, but distracting responsibility. She was free of her own responsibility, even if she had lost her dangerous power. *MS* from her ... strange and fascinating ... like madness ... man beside her. After ... was magical. *TSIaR* *see note on* 301:36

302:10 returning,] ~ *TSIa*

302:11 blind *TSIaR*] tremendous *MS*

302:12 quivered and thrilled *TSIaR*] laughed to herself *MS*

302:12 mystery, since *TSIaR*] affair, if *MS*

302:15 month,] ~ *TSIa*

302:17 North-West *MS*, *TSIaC*] North West *TSIa*

302:17 Perth:] ~; *E1*

302:19 Good-bye] good-bye *E1*

302:19 proceeded *TSIaR*] went on *MS*

302:19 north *MS*, *E1*] North *TSIa*

302:20 Then came *TSIaR*] It was *MS*

302:23 "*You are better dead.*" *E1*] You are better dead. *MS* *You are better dead. TSIaR*

302:31 tramp woman] tramp-woman *TSIaC*

302:33 woman, fated to him. *TSIaR*] woman. *MS*

303:3 looked *TSIaR*] went *MS*

303:6 for ever] forever *TSIa*

303:10 completely] altogether *TSIa*

303:11 for ever] forever *A1*, *E1*

303:12 desire,] ~ *TSIa*

303:14 for ever *Ed.*] forever *MS*

303:14 at all *TSIaR*] whatsoever *MS*

303:17 acute,] ~ *TSIa*

303:20 rove] rave *TSIa* slink *TSIaR*

303:26 she] as if she *TSIa*

303:33 perversion] perverseness *TSIa*

303:37 of] of the *TSIa*

303:38 changed, *TSIa*] changed, and his eyes changed, and his whole bearing changed, *MS*

303:38 curious look ... off: then, she ... evaporate, leaving her only wanting to be wanted ... again, back in his world. Her *TSIbR*] deathly cold look like a landscape when the sun sets; then she felt all the world turn to ashes, and life turn to ashes, and death turn to ashes the same. And her *MS* curious look ... off; then she ... evaporated, she only wanted to be wanted ... again, in his world. Her *TSIaR* curious look ... off; then {then, *E1*} she ... evaporated, {evaporate, *E1*} leaving her only wanting to be wanted again, back in his world. Her *A1* *see note on* 304:2.

304:3 Still,] ~ *TSIa*

304:6 herself] ~, *E1*

304:6 half-teasing *MS*, *E1*] half teasing *TSIa*

304:6 half-loving *MS*, *E1*] half loving *TSIa*

304:10 own] *Om. TSIa*

304:12 savagely hostile *TSIaR*] wretched *MS*

304:14 seized and kissed *TSIa*] seized/kissed *MS*

304:14 Easu or] Easu by *TSIa* Easu, by *A1*, *E1*

304:14 Jack] ~, *A1*

304:17 never] ever *A1*

304:17 yet *TSIaR*] *Om. MS*

304:19 left her so ... kill, or *TSIbR*] made her *MS* left her either so ... kill, or *TSIaR* left her so ... kill herself, or *A1*, *E1* *see notes*

304:28 saw,] ~ *TSIa*

304:36 extremely] exceedingly *TSIa*

305:20 grey-coloured *TSIa*] grey-colored *MS*

305:26 he had spent *TSIaR*] that he had been *MS*

305:31 frank but *TSIaR*] *Om. MS*

305:32 his subtle sort of delicacy, *TSIbR*] *Om. MS* his subtle delicacy, *TSIaR*

305:32 simple *TSIaR*] dark *MS*
305:34 with a subtle understanding *TSIaR*] so frank *MS*, *TSIb*, *A1* *see note on* 174:20
305:35 gay and completely *TSIaR*] just a man like *MS*
305:36 themselves. The ... him. *P* Because *TSIaR*] themselves. *P* But *MS*
305:40 shifty *TSIaR*] ordinary *MS*
305:40 could never completely *TSIaR*] now refused entirely *MS*
306:1 mix *TSIaC*, *TSIbR*] to mix *MS*
306:5 but *TSIaR*] but which *MS*
306:7 playing a lone hand *TSIaR*] absolutely alone *MS*
306:8 was working with *TSIaR*] had *MS*
306:9 job,] ~ *E1*
306:10 at his ease *TSIaR*] alone *MS*
306:11 But he ... they felt *TSIaR*] They had *MS*
306:13 there,] ~ *E1*
306:13 aura ... blood-purity *TSIaR*] presence of a superior *MS*
306:15 bear] ~, *A1*
306:16 to buy ... for anything.] for anything. *TSIa* to buy new. *TSIaR*
306:19 spell *TSIaR*] while *MS*
306:20 gold-field] gold field *TSIa* goldfield *A1*
306:21 had developed *TSIaR*] began to develop *MS*
306:23 favoured *TSIaC*, *E1*] favored *MS*
306:24 mystic *TSIaR*] *Om. MS*
306:25 gold,] ~ *TSIa*
306:25 master *TSIaR*] conquer *MS*
306:32 or] and *TSIa*
306:34 school,] ~ *TSIa*
307:3 become] became *TSIa*
307:7 somewhere,] ~ *TSIa*
307:8 wild] ~, *E1*
307:12 had wanted to be *TSIaR*] also was *MS*
307:13 He had ... own wildness. *TSIaR*] *Om. MS*
307:15 he ... him *TSIaR*] you ... you *MS*
307:17 fox] a fox *TSIa*
307:20 turning into *TSIaR*] less dangerous than the *MS*
307:30 earth] the earth *A1*
307:30 wild *TSIaR*] royal *MS*
307:31 and] *Om. TSIa*
307:33 earth] the earth *TSIa*
307:35 into *TSIa*] in to *MS*
307:38 dark] *Om. TSIa*
308:1 win *TSIaR*] conquer *MS*
308:4 death, so *MS*, *E1*] ~. (~ *TSIa* ~, (~ *TSIaR* ~ (~ *A1* *see notes*
308:5 their own *TSIaR*] *Om. MS* the *TSIa*
308:5 earth. *MS*, *E1*] ~.) *TSIa* ~). *A1*
308:10 whose bones are pure *TSIaR*] to the death *MS*
308:12 aristocrats-to-the-bone *TSIaR*] aristocrats to the death *MS* artistocrats-to-the-bone *A1*
308:15 to] and *TSIa*
308:15 lucrative *TSIaR*] golden *MS*
308:17 Jack said] said Jack *TSIa*
308:19 aristocrats of the bone *TSIaR*] aristocrats to the death *MS* aristocrats-of-the-bone *TSIaC*
308:27 failed,] ~ *TSIa*
308:31 a] the *TSIa*
308:36 *could* do, *TSIaR*] could ~ *MS*
308:37 hidden] hide *A1*
309:2 he realised] *Om. TSIa*
309:6 Meanwhile] ~, *E1*
309:18 workman] workman for *TSIa*
309:21 England] ~, *A1*
309:22 aunts] Aunts *TSIaC* Aunts, *A1*
309:22 died at the right moment *TSIaR*] oppressed his childhood *MS*
309:24 labourer *TSIaC*, *E1*] laborer *MS*
309:25 labourer's *TSIaC*, *E1*] laborer's *MS*
309:26 sand] ~, *A1*
309:27 messages] messengers *TSIa*
309:32 light-coloured,] light colored

TSIa light-colored *TSIaR* light-coloured *A1*, *E1*
309:33 gold] stuff *TSIa*
309:40 child] a child *TSIa*
310:2 Jack's] Jack *TSIa*
310:6 Jack laughed] laughed Jack *TSIa*
310:14 back,] ~ *TSIa*
310:21 girl,] ~ *E1*
310:21 a bit *TSIaR*] rather *MS*
310:24 "the General" *Ed.*] '~ ~' *MS* ~ ~ *TSIa*
310:28 General, didn't] ~? Didn't *TSIa*
310:29 old] ~, *E1*
310:34 jobs *E1*] bothering jobs *MS*
311:2 The Offer to Mary *TSIaR*] The Grant Farm *MS* *The Grant Farm* *TSIa* THE OFFER TO MARY *TSIaC*, *A1* THE OFFER TO MARY *E1*
311:7 General *TSIa*] general *MS*
311:13 Sir] ~, *TSIa*
311:14 "This *Ed.*] ~ *MS*
311:14 leeves] leaves *TSIa*
311:15 Your *MS*, *E1*] You *TSIa*
311:16 satterday] Satterday *TSIa*
311:17 ave] have *TSIa*
311:20 read] ~. *TSIa*
311:21 "the *Ed.*] the *MS* The *TSIa* "The *E1*
311:26 blemish] ~. *TSIa*
311:26 Duitful] Dutiful *TSIa*
311:29 arangement] arrangements *TSIa*
311:29 councel] council *E1*
311:29 who] *Om.* *E1*
311:30 xcepts] xpects *TSIa*
311:30 docters] doctors *E1*
311:32 Us] us *TSIa*
311:33 Emma ... Amos Lewis"] ~ ... ~ ~. *TSIa* ~ ... ~ ~." *A1* EMMA ... AMOS LEWIS." *E1*
312:2 north] North *A1*
312:6 elder] eldest *A1*
312:8 Dr] Doctor *TSIa* Dr. *E1*
312:15 cart umbrella] cart-umbrella *E1*
312:24 riding-breeches] riding breeches *TSIa*
312:25 silver-studded] silver studded *TSIa*
312:26 a gold-miner] gold miner *TSIa*
312:34 old] Old *A1*
312:40 odd *TSIaR*] poor thin *MS*
312:40 self-contained *TSIaR*] grown-up *MS*
313:1 well-bred] ~, *TSIa*
313:5 Mary,] ~ *E1*
313:8 queer] ~, *E1*
313:12 His *TSIaR*] But his *MS* But is *TSIa*
313:19 heavy, *MS*, *E1*] ~ *TSIa*
313:22 his *TSIaR*] the *MS*
313:24 Mary,] ~ *TSIa*
313:27 woman] ~, *E1*
313:28 dear-boyed] "~" *E1*
313:30 boy,] ~! *TSIa*
313:30 trying] drying *A1*
313:34 successful!] ~. *TSIa*
313:38 quick, round, dark-grey *TSIaR*] delicate, light-blue *MS*
313:39 odd *TSIaR*] plain *MS*
314:1 Marm *TSIa*] marm *MS*
314:3 will!] ~. *E1*
314:3 us,] ~ *TSIa*
314:7 England] ~, *E1*
314:10 And] ~, *E1*
314:12 Oh] ~, *TSIaC*, *E1*
314:13 are!] ~. *TSIa*
314:14 hair's-breadth] hair's breadth *TSIa*
314:21 fixing ... queer searching ... human *TSIaR*] stealing a glance at him *MS* fixing ... queer, searching ... human *TSIbR*
314:26 man] ~, *A1*
314:26 half-haughty] half haughty *TSIa*
314:27 little,] ~ *TSIa*
314:27 reckless *TSIaR*] annoying *MS*
314:29 said,] ~ *TSIa*
314:29 bluish,] ~ *TSIa*
314:31 quite—"] ~——" *E1*
314:33 Why] ~, *E1*

314:34 strong—] ~. *TSIa*
314:35 say,] ~ *TSIa*
314:37 cock-o'-the-walk *TSIa*] cock-o-the-walk *MS*
314:40 twins,] ~ *TSIa*
314:40 our] my *TSIa*
314:40 But of course] ~, ~ ~, *E1*
315:2 Easu Ellis'] Easu's *TSIa*
315:2 child—] ~. *TSIa*
315:3 had] had been *TSIa*
315:4 fleecy brown *TSIaR*] honey-pale *MS*
315:5 Queen-Victoria-statue] Queen Victoria statue *TSIa*
315:8 Who] ~, *TSIa*
315:14 —and] ~ *TSIa* And *TSIaC*
315:24 Pray *MS*, *E1*] ~, *A1*
315:24 why?] ~, *E1*
315:27 Jack. *P* He] ~. He *TSIa*
315:34 old *Ed.*] Old *MS*
315:34 amiably *A1*, *E1*] aimiably *MS*
315:35 *right thing*] right thing *E1*
315:38 There is] There's *TSIa*
315:39 lawyer, *MS*, *A1*] ~ *TSIa*
315:42 inquiringly *Ed.*] enquiringly *MS*
316:2 that] *Om. TSIa*
316:2 quiet *TSIaR*] silvery *MS* quiet, *E1*
316:5 god] God *TSIa*
316:7 of] to *TSIa*
316:12 green-and-red *TSIaR*] green and red *MS*
316:16 Australia] Australian *TSIa*
316:17 farm] Farm *A1*
316:19 devil] fellow *TSIa*
316:24 older] old *TSIa*
316:25 but—] ~—— *E1*
316:27 said the old man, *TSIaR*] he said, *MS* the old man said, *TSIbR see note on* 319:5
316:30 woman, *TSIa*] ~," *MS*
316:33 mix-up *MS*, *TSIaC*] mix up *TSIa*
316:33 old *TSIa*] Old *MS*, *A1*
316:35 sir *TSIa*] Sir *MS*
317:1 little,] ~ *TSIa*
317:3 be] have been *TSIa*
317:11 better *TSIaR*] *Om. MS*
317:19 old *MS*, *TSIaC*] Old *TSIa*, *A1*
317:20 Why, *MS*, *E1*] ~ *TSIa*
317:21 Jack. "And] ~, "and *TSIa*
317:22 advice,] ~ *TSIa*
317:22 weep etc.] ~, ~., *A1*, *E1*
317:24 old *MS*, *TSIaC*] Old *TSIa*, *A1*
317:24 smiling, *TSIaR*] ~. *MS*
317:27 sir *TSIa*] Sir *MS*
317:30 sir *E1*] Sir *MS*
317:31 *business TSIaR*] business *MS*
317:34 most *TSIaR*] all *MS*
317:36 the lot *TSIaR*] all *MS*
317:36 us—] ~. *TSIa*
317:39 eyes. "What] ~, "what *A1*, *E1*
318:1 on] upon *TSIa*
318:4 Monica] ~, *E1*
318:4 Lennie and Tom] ~, ~ ~, *E1*
318:5 more—"] ~." *TSIa*
318:6 clear] ~, *E1*
318:11 something stirs *TSIaR*] it burns *MS*
318:11 Gran Ellis said that was *TSIaR*] And I take it for *MS*
318:12 I know . . . *him.* And . . . outside me bidding . . . [318:17] no world *TSIbR*] I've got a God of my own, who stands behind me. I've got a God who stands behind me, and his eyes are black and shining, and he pushes me. But my own eyes are wide open, I see where I am going. My God with the dark-burning {dark burning *TSIa*} eyes pushes me, and then I look with my day-eyes to see the way. And then I go *MS* I know . . . *him.*" And {*Him.* And *A1*} . . . outside of me bidding . . . no world *TSIaR* I know . . . him. And . . . outside me bidding . . . no world *E1 see note on* 319:5
318:19 impressed. "I only hope . . . No there's . . . it's like an idiot to me. A dangerous idiot. So that if I . . . three;— —well, I . . . [318:23] Why listen to the Idiot

TSIbR] impressed. *P* "No, {"No *TSIa*} it's not the devil. It is {It's *TSIa*} my own God, because he's got a hot heart, not a cold heart. It's my own God with a hot heart, and fierce {got a hot heart, and fierce *TSIa*} dark eyes just behind my shoulder {shoulders *TSIa*} *MS* impressed. "I hope No there's {No, there's *A1*} it's a bit imbecile, in my opinion. Really a dangerous idiot.—If I {idiot. If I *A1*} ... three— —I {three—I *A1*} ... Why should I mind what the Idiot says *TSIaR* impressed. "I only hope ... to me, a dangerous ... three—well ... the Idiot *E1 see note on* 319:5

318:24 *you'd TSIaR*] you'd *MS*

318:24 cracked, *TSIaR*] ~ *MS*, *TSIb*

318:26 If I ... of one," said Jack with ... it cracked." *P* "No, ... greedy," said old ... if I can really ... three—" Jack ... [318:30] queer bright ... Blessington—"Well, ... spirit." *P* "For ... in joke." *P* "Surely I may say ... Mr George. *P* "Oh," ... Scotch marriage. Monica is ... Monica. I'd ... the same." *P* "I won't ... [319:5] said old George testily. *Ed.*] Not I! {I. *TSIa*} Why am I any more cracked than Paul was? Why is it cracked to say I've got a god {God *TSIa*} of my own?" said Jack, smiling wickedly. *P* "You have the Lord Jesus Christ," said Aunt Matilda coldly. *P* "No {"No, *TSIa*} I haven't. I'm sorry, but I haven't. Of course you have. That {have, that *TSIa*} I should never dispute. But if Paul went to Damascus, I went to Kalgoorlie. Why should I not have seen my own god? {God? *TSIa*} I have seen him, {him. *TSIa*} I do see him. I don't say he is your god. {God. *TSIa*} I would never presume so far. But he is mine. And he is behind me. And you may see his dark eyes over my shoulder if you look." *P* "If you go on, boy, we shall have to put you down *non compos*", {*non-compos*," *TSIa*} said Mr George, {George *TSIa*} laughing uneasily. *P* "Old Gran Ellis would have known like a shot," laughed Jack {Jack. *TSIa*} *P* "She was crazy herself: except {herself—except *TSIa*} where money came in; {in, *TSIa*} or the man she wanted—But {wanted. But *TSIa*} perhaps it was the man she was crazy about.—Anyhow {about. Anyhow *TSIa*} I can see nothing over your shoulder except an antimacassar." {anti-/macassar." *TSIa*} *MS* If I ... of one, you wouldn't think it cracked," said Jack, with a malicious smile. *P* "No, ... greedy", said old ... if I have real use for two wives—or even three—" said Jack, grinning, but with a queer bright intention, at Hilda Blessington—"well, ... spirit." *P* "You are not allowed to say such things, even as a joke," said Aunt Matilda, with ponderous disapproval. "It is no joke to *me*." *P* "Surely I may say ... Scotch marriage. But what I pledged myself to, I'd stick to." *P* "I won't ... added old George. *TSIaR* If I ... "Oh," ... testily. *TSIbR* If I ... of one, you wouldn't ... cracked," said ... greedy," said Old ... Blessington. "Well ... Surely I say ... Scotch marriage. Monica is my legal wife. But what I pledged myself to, I'd stick to, as I stick to Monica, I'd stick to the others the same." *P* "I won't ... Mr. George ... said Old George testily. *A1* If I ... of one," said Jack, with ... greedy," said Old ... three"—Jack ... queer, bright ... said Old George testily. *E1 see note on* 319:5

319:7 for] *Om. TSIa*

319:8 responsibility] ~, *TSIa*

319:10 of the] of *TSIa*

319:10 complacency] ~, *E1*

310:11 in Aunt Matilda, and in *TSIaR*] of Aunt Matilda and *MS* in Aunt Matilda' and *TSIa*

319:13 mischievous *TSIaR*] cold *MS*

319:16 Ellises, *MS*, *TSIaR*] ~ *TSIb*
319:18 mystery,] ~ *TSIa*
319:19 for ever *E1*] forever *MS*
319:19 lode-stone] lode stone *E1*
319:20 to *MS*, *A1*] *Om. TSIa*
319:21 to fertilise] *Om. A1 see notes*
319:22 old] Old *A1*
319:23 his and Mary's *TSIaR*] in Mary *MS*
319:24 another,] ~ *TSIa*
319:26 good,] ~ *TSIa*
319:28 Saints] saints *TSIa*
319:28 Christian *MS*, *A1*] christian *TSIa*
319:30 for ever *E1*] forever *MS*
320:3 sir *TSIaC*, *E1*] Sir *MS*
320:3 Jack] ~, *A1*
320:7 aloud] loud *TSIa*
320:8 absurdity. *TSIaR*] absurdity. *P* "Oh {"Ah *TSIa*} no! Besides it will be left to me. It is I who will give the next shove to life, Sir, and not you." *P* "Then why do you call me Sir?" *P* "Why not? You {you *TSIa*} are old, and you are the old leader who has fought all the way so far, to get ahead. So you are Sir to me, Sir.—But {Sir. But *TSIa*} I shan't carry on your old road, nevertheless. No!" *P* "Why!" {"Why?" *TSIa*} said the old lawyer with a burst of laughter. "Your money's made a real fighting-cock of you. I should never have believed it—never! A real Indian game-bird. Only your head's gone." *P* And he chuckled with odd, youthful amusement. *P* "No, my head hasn't gone. It's only just coming," said Jack. "Only wait, and you'll see. I've got my own idea of a life that is a life. But it doesn't matter to anybody but me and a few people concerned—and we're just apart. I wouldn't disturb Aunt Matilda's own show, not for anything. But *my* show'll be a different one." *P* "Well, tell us what sort of show it will be." *P* "Nay, you might shoot me." *P* "Might shoot you!"—The old man gave another burst of laughter. "What, is it as bad as that! Might shoot you! Might shoot you! Why should *I* want to shoot y', d' y' think?" *P* "Because you disapproved." *P* "What, am I going to disapprove?" And Mr George eyed Jack in an odd way. *P* "Oh yes," said Jack laughing. *P* "What makes you so sure of what I'm going to approve of and disapprove of?" *P* "Oh—all that's gone before. Your antecedents." *P* "My antecedents!" said the old man, ruminating as he polished his glasses. "Why when you get to my age you'll realise that my antecedents as you call 'em, are about as far-off and senseless to me as they are to you. Antecedents! They're like the old bones that the old dog has buried and forgotten—buried and forgotten. {has buried and forgotten. *TSIa*} I've got no more antecedents than you have." *P* "I've got lots," said Jack. "A whole curiosity-shop {curiosity shop *TSIa*} full." *P* "About like me that," laughed the old man. "Nothing but curiosities. Why, now I've got as old as I am, I've been wondering and wondering if there *was* anybody {anybidy *TSIa*} as young as myself left." He gave Jack a sudden quick nudge. "That's what I've been wondering." {wondering" *TSIa*} *P* "And I thought you {You *TSIa*} were as fixed as a church," said Jack. *P* "Thought I was! Prrh! {was, prrh! *TSIa*} You should have seen me twenty, twenty-five years ago for that. Then I *was* as fixed as a church. Now I'm about as fixed as an emu chicken three days hatched." *P* And the old man went off into a long chuckle of delight. *MS see notes*
320:12 good] to be good *TSIa*
320:16 plan] plans *TSIa*
320:17 farm] Farm *A1*
320:19 gold-fields] gold-/ fields *TSIa* goldfields *A1*
320:24 secrets. And] ~. *P* And *TSIa*
320:25 lip,] ~ *TSIa*
320:25 black] dark *TSIa*

320:30 warm,] ~ *E1*
320:32 up,] ~ *E1*
321:7 excited,] ~ *E1*
321:7 now,] ~ *TSIa*
321:8 to] by *TSIa*
321:10 Oh!] ~. *TSIa*
321:15 It amused ... annoyed him.] *Om. TSIa*
321:16 talk!] ~, *TSIa*
321:21 jamboree *Ed.*] Jamboree *MS*
321:22 dearie] Dearie *TSIaR*
321:23 enough;] ~: *E1*
321:24 remembered too] ~, ~, *E1*
321:26 certain,] ~ *E1*
321:28 himself,] ~ *A1*, *E1*
321:31 up,] ~ *E1*
321:32 bran *Ed.*] brand *MS*
321:33 They too] ~, ~, *E1*
321:34 dark blue] dark-blue *A1*
321:35 her,] ~ *E1*
322:1 house? *MS*, *E1*] ~, *TSIa*
322:2 bunch of jolly] jolly bunch of *TSIa*
322:7 indifferent] different *TSIa*
322:14 Well] ~, *E1*
322:16 a house and a] the house and the *TSIa*
322:18 old-maiddom] old-maidom *A1*
322:19 auntie] Auntie *TSIa*
322:23 of the] of *A1*
322:28 rose-wood] rosewood *A1*
322:29 moved] removed *TSIa*
322:29 bed-room] bedroom *A1*
322:31 old] *Om. TSIa*
322:35 gentleman] ~, *A1*
322:36 old-fashioned] old fashioned *E1*
322:36 side-whiskers] side-/ whiskers *A1* side whiskers *E1*
322:39 the photograph of *TSIbR*] being *MS* being the photograph of *TSIaR*
322:40 grandmother and grandfather] grandfather and grandmother *TSIa* grandfather and grand-/ mother *A1*
322:40 And *MS*, *E1*] "~ *TSIa*
323:13 crinoline] *Om. TSIa* dress *TSIaR*
323:20 repellant *TSIaR*] frightening *MS*, *TSIb*, *A1* repellent *TSIaC*
323:23 agitation,] ~ *E1*
323:26 *He*—"] ~——" *A1* ~"— *E1*
323:26 grandfather— *MS*, *E1*] ~. *TSIa* ~, *TSIaR*
323:27 *her*—"] her—" *TSIa* her——" *A1* her"— *E1*
323:27 cross—"and *MS*, *E1*] ~."—~ *TSIa* ~, "——~ *A1*
323:40 over,] ~ *TSIa*
324:1 side-whiskers] side whiskers *TSIa*
324:1 languid] ~, *TSIa*
324:2 handwriting: *The ... father of A1*] handwriting: The ... father of *MS* hand-/ writing: *The ... father of TSIaR* handwriting:/ *The ... father of E1*
324:3  .]  *A1* *E1 see notes*
324:4 crossbones] cross bones *TSIa* cross-bones *TSIaR*
324:4 three sides] sides *TSIa* margins *A1 see notes*
324:7 portrait] photograph *TSIa*
324:9 crossbones] cross bones *TSIa* cross-bones *TSIaR*
324:20 fetching *TSIaR*] Byronic *MS*
324:22 hips] lips *TSIa*
324:23 *him Ed.*] him *MS* him, *TSIa* *him*, *TSIaR*
324:24 tall,] ~ *TSIa*
324:33 cried] said *TSIa*
324:34 why!] ~? *TSIa*
325:8 Well] ~, *TSIa*
325:9 that] ~, *E1*
325:10 Honourable *TSIa*] Honorable *MS*
325:10 smallish built] smallish-built *TSIaC*
325:12 Eh!] ~? *E1*
325:12 Then,] ~ *TSIa*

325:13 smallish built] smallish-built *TSIaC*
325:19 *his A1, E1*] his *MS*
325:24 protective *TSIaR*] *Om. MS*
325:25 Eh!] ~? *E1*
325:28 life] a life *TSIa*
325:28 it"? *MS, E1*] ~"? *TSIa* ~!" *A1*
325:30 maid!] ~? *TSIa*
325:31 Jack,] ~ *TSIa*
325:35 Mary!] ~, *TSIa*
325:35 Jack, *MS, A1*] ~ *TSIa*
325:37 devil] ~, *TSIaC, E1*
325:38 half in mistrust and fear, half] half in mistrust, and fear, half *TSIa* in mistrust, and fear, and also *TSIaR*
326:3 Ah] ~, *TSIaC, E1*
326:13 old *TSIaC*] Old *MS, A1*
326:20 old] Old *A1, E1*
326:21 stable,] ~ *TSIa*
326:25 so,] ~ *TSIa*
326:31 north *Ed.*] North *MS*
326:31 west] West *TSIa*
326:31 North-West *TSIaC*] north-west *MS* North-west *TSIa*
326:35 It's] It is *TSIa*
326:38 horse,] ~ *TSIa*
326:40 straw] the straw *TSIa*
327:1 said] asked *TSIa*
327:3 but—] ~—— *A1*
327:10 it] ~, *E1*
327:10 was I] ~ ~, *TSIaC*
327:12 out,] ~ *TSIa*
327:23 *really* . . . kin.] next of kin *really*. *TSIa*
327:25 you will do,] you'll do *TSIa*
327:26 gold-fields] gold fields *TSIa* goldfields *A1*
327:27 no.] ~! *TSIa*
327:28 photo-albums] photo-/ albums *TSIa* photo albums *A1*
327:29 old *TSIa*] Old *MS, E1*
327:31 that.—But] ~, but *TSIa*
327:36 gold-fields] goldfields *TSIaC* gold fields *TSIa*
327:36 asked,] ~ *TSIa*
327:40 Aunt-Matilda-ism] Aunt Matilda-ism *TSIa*
327:40 old-Georgism *Ed.*] Old-Georgism *MS* Old Georgism *TSIa* old Georgism *TSIaC* Old George-ism *E1*
328:1 sarcastic, *TSIaR*] at outs, *MS* sarcastic! *E1*
328:1 they] They *E1*
328:3 said *TSIaR*] said acidly *MS, TSIb*
328:4 But there's . . . without the ism that . . . for.—Would . . . this place? *TSIbR, A1*] That's why I think you'd better {betrer *TSIa*} have this place. *MS* But there's . . . with no ism, that . . . this place? *TSIaR* But there's . . . without the ism that . . . for. Would . . . this place? *E1*
328:8 Mary-ism. Or . . . the North-West? *A1, E1*] Mary-ism, so that I needn't be there to see it. *MS* Mary-ism.—Or . . . the North-West? *TSIaR* Mary-ism. Or . . . the North West? *TSIbR*
328:10 why do . . . am here." *TSIa*] what does it matter to you?" *P* "Oh, it matters to me. There's a certain sort of Mary without the ism that matters to me." *MS see notes*
328:13 Monica *MS, E1*] ~, *TSIa*
328:13 Mary] ~, *E1*
328:14 Of course . . . I've come. *TSIa*] I know it," said he. "But I'm capable of having two wives. So why shouldn't I? *MS*
328:18 But what . . . [328:21] asked insidiously. *TSIa*] Because the law won't let you," said Mary with a little pouf of laughter—half ridicule. *P* "Bah! the law! I am my own law!" *P* "Be it, for yourself. But don't try to be it for other people." *MS*
328:23 of *TSIa*] of an *MS*
328:23 His heart . . . with explosion.] *Om. TSIa see note on* 328:10

328:26 "No," he ... [328:32] Mary sarcastically ... [329:3] tangled. *P* "Shall *TSIa*] "That's why I offer you this place," he said. "So that you can cultivate your old-maidism in exactly your own way." *P* Curious, how the desire that had lain dormant for years, and awakened again dark and heavy at the sight of her again, seemed now suddenly to have snapped, along with that suffocating explosion of anger in his chest, leaving him quite cold towards her, and a little acid, and rather shaken. *P* "Thank you," she said. "I don't want the place." *P* "Think it over," he replied. "Shall *MS* "No," he ... Mary, sarcastically ... tangled. *P* "Shall *E1*

329:4 in?" he ... she returned *TSIa*] we go in?" *P* She went *MS*

329:5 house *TSIa*] old people *MS*

329:8 sir *TSIa*] Sir *MS*, *TSIaC*

329:9 North-West *MS*, *A1*] North-west *TSIa* North-west, *E1*

329:10 wheat *TSIa*] bothering with wheat *MS*

329:10 this *TSIa*] the *MS*

329:11 Really, *TSIa*] Somehow *MS*

329:13 old] Old *A1*

329:13 many *TSIa*] *Om. MS*

329:14 into *TSIa*] in to *MS*

329:16 Oh] ~, *TSIa*

329:16 property *TSIa*] place *MS*

329:18 to *TSIa*] *Om. MS*

329:20 Why—! Why—!] ~! ~! *TSIa*

329:20 old] Old *A1*

329:20 George fussily, stirring quite delighted *TSIa*] George, stirring fussily, quite delighted, *MS*

329:23 unhappy, *TSIa*] ~. *MS* *see notes*

329:23 sarcastic *TSIa*] a little sarcastic *MS*

329:24 anyhow!] ~, *TSIa*

329:25 not? If ... it away— *TSIa*] not, if ... it away? *MS* not, if the young millionaire wants to give it to you? If he wants to throw it away— {away—— *E1*} *TSIb* not? If ... it away—— *A1* *see notes*

329:28 Why] ~— *TSIa*

329:31 old] Old *A1*

329:31 Well, you needn't have; *TSIa*] Well *MS* Well, you needn't have, *TSIb*

329:34 You're in ... don't talk, *TSIa*] Well you're not starving, nor likely to be starving, so that's no reason for not taking it, *MS*

329:34 man *MS*, *TSIb*] ~, *TSIa*

329:35 place. *TSIa*] place, I tell you. *MS*, *TSIb*

330:1 Damn her ... Jane and the twin babies?—No ... would listen to such a proposition hard enough ... make it her ... [330:8] divorce; a ... [330:12] Then why not belong to him ... [333:39] do that. *TSIa*] After all, if she was a narrow fool, the loss was hers. *P* Why shouldn't he have two wives, if he wanted them? Or even more. Why not? The men in the bible had had them. And it was natural to a man—at least to a man like himself. When Mary was there, and he wanted her again, and when she let her underneath passion flow to him, then he felt splendid, riding his horse, and there was a splendour in the world, for her and him. Because, underneath all her clock-work head with its endless ticking thoughts and its self-importance, she had a steady, enduring passion for him too. Of course she had. But it was way down in her and subject to the loud ticking of her clock-work head. And she always talked and acted from her clock-work head. *P* He didn't want her just to flirt with. He hated flirting. He didn't want an "affair" with her. He loathed affairs. He wanted her for his wife. He had one wife. He had

Monica. Monica was his first wife, and she would always remain so. Monica was his first and his chief wife. *P* But why was she his only wife? He had other things inside himself, he had other currents of desire and fulfilment, that did not go to Monica. That asked for other wives. Other men had mistresses. He hated the thought of mistresses. He wanted wives. *P* And he was rich enough. He could give Mary her own house and things to attend to if she wished it. The chief house would be Monica's. But Mary's house would be there too. And she could teach his children. He would need somebody to teach his children, up in the Never-Never. *P* But most of all, she would be his wife, and he would know a certain greatness in the world, as Abraham had been great. Why not? Why not? When a man had a woman who was naturally his own, it made him feel great. And he wanted to feel great. Was it then unnatural for a man to feel great, the greater for the woman that was permanently his? *P* Monica made him feel great. Monica was his principal wife. And Monica was part of his greatness. Monica wasn't great by herself. Flirting with Easu, floating round with Percy, there was no greatness to her. She might feel *free*, and self-consciously important. But hell, what was a woman's self-conscious importance worth? Not a rotten egg. It was an addled rottenness anyhow, a woman's self-importance. *P* And this was what ailed Mary. Her blasted self-important, and her social water-tight compartment ideas. Damn her. He offered her a certain greatness, and she turned on the Aunt Matilda tap. He offered her a certain greatness in life, and she thought of her self-importance and her barren egoistic virginity. To hell with her. *P* Let her remain an old maid, or marry a Blessington. Let her marry old George if she liked. Anyhow a man like himself, Jack, was not offered twice. God no! Anything rather than give another blow to his pride. 'I am my pride, and my pride is me!' he said to himself. 'My male pride, that is me.' *P* He didn't consider he was offering something dubious, when he wanted Mary for his wife as well as Monica. He was offering Mary more than she would get from any other man. Because the first flame of her passion was towards him, and would ever be so. And Mary was not in reality one of the sentimental love-birds that can turn on the tap of their sentiments. Deep inside herself, she was not sentimental at all. She was passionate. And a really passionate nature *can't* be sentimental, and turn on taps of feeling—only ideas. *P* But she had that clock-work head of hers, and all her Aunt Matilda shell. She lived in an Aunt Matilda shell, with a tick-tack of a serious mind inside it. Damn her. And underneath, the slow, deep passion of her nature, the only part of her that was godly, was slowly wasting and silting up. *P* It wasn't, he repeated to himself as he twisted with rage and frustration on the straw, as if he wanted to have an amorous affair with her. Amorous affairs made him sick. It wasn't as if he wanted to lie with her and then clear out, as her father had betrayed Jack's aunt. That made him sick. That sort of cowardice. That running away to get pennies from society. Jack wanted nothing from society. He was himself his own pillar of society. A solitary pillar of society. And he wanted his own wives, and his own faithful adherents like Tom and Lennie. Tom and Lennie would not be shocked. They would say: I suppose the General knows what he's after. *P* Damn Mary. Let her stay where she was, niggling her days away. As for him, he would take Monica and his children and Lennie and Tom up to the Never-Never, and make a new camp in the world, like Abraham. And if Mary was not one of his wives, there would come other women over the horizon. Mary could spend herself in words, gassing to Old George. *P* As for Monica, she would get mad, but then she would have to get mad. He would take from her nothing that was hers. She was his first wife, his chief wife, and this she would always be. If she wished. But he *wasn't* a man who was finished when he'd got one wife. His nature and his character and his very soul wanted more. Wanted the bigger richness and the bigger greatness in life. Not this nauseous one-couple-in-one-cottage domesticity. He loathed domesticity. He loathed being shut up with one woman and a bunch of kids, in one house. He would rather be a tramp on the roads. *P* No, he wanted his other wives. What would Monica lose, except her dog-in-the-manger rights over things that weren't really hers. She would say she would want other men. But it was a lie. She didn't want other men. To say she did was a physical lie. *P* Whereas, for himself to say he didn't want other women—Mary for example—*that* was a physical lie. Reason as you like, he physically wanted her, and permanently; and wanting her made life seem bigger, wilder, richer, and gave it greatness. He insisted on a certain greatness in his life: like in the days of Abraham. It needed faithful men like Tom and Lennie. It needed passionate women like Monica and Mary. But above all, it needed himself, the solitary pillar in the wilderness. *P* Because he loathed the shut-in stuffiness of civilisation. He simply loathed it. He wanted to erect the solitary pillar of himself in the wilderness, and have the tents of other men around. *P* He didn't want anything the world could offer: nothing. His gold he had got out of the ground. His men were men by themselves. His women were women never to be tamed. And the wilderness was still there. He wanted to go like Abraham under the wild sky, speaking to a fierce wild Lord, and having angels stand in his doorway. *P* Why not? Even if the whole world said No, even then, Why not? *P* As for being ridiculous, all he wanted was his own way. And if his own way seemed ridiculous, hurray for ridicule. *P* Anyhow, he would go back at once to the gold-fields, and get ready for his next move. Mary could stay where she was, and be damned to her. He didn't want to speak another word to her. *MS* Damn her . . . Jane? And the babies?—No . . . would have listened close enough to this proposition . . . put it to her . . . divorce: a . . . Then why not . . . do that. *TSIb see note on* 328:10 *and also following entries to* 333:35

330:4 babies?— *TSIa*] ~? *E1*
330:12 completely? *P* Why *TSIa*] ~? Why *A1*
330:14 her *TSIa*] ~, *E1*
330:17 bible *Ed.*] Bible *TSIa*
330:28 old . . . old *TSIa*] Old . . . Old *A1*, *E1*
331:1 Mary," said Jack, *TSIb*, *A1*] ~" ~ ~/ *TSIa*
331:2 Mr *E1*] ~. *TSIa*
331:7 and sleep in *TSIa*] to *A1*
331:9 Oh *TSIa*] ~, *E1*
331:10 Monica's." *A1*] ~". *TSIa* ~!" *E1*
331:12 hers *TSIaC*] her's *TSIa*
331:15 Monica's, *TSIa*] ~ *E1*
331:22 virginity! *TSIa*, *A1*] ~? *TSIaC*
331:22 and sleep with me in *TSIa*] with me to *A1*
331:23 North-West *A1*, *E1*] North-west *TSIa*
331:26 Oh *TSIa*] ~, *E1*
331:27 Oh God, *TSIa*] ~, ~! *E1*
331:28 me! *TSIa*] ~? *E1*
331:29 and sleep in *TSIa*] to *A1*
331:30 you *TSIa*] ~, *E1*
331:32 Now *TSIa*] ~, *E1*
331:36 horses." *A1*, *E1*] ~:" *TSIa*

331:37 Oh *TSIa*] ~, *E1*
331:38 me," *A1*, *E1*] ~;" *TSIa*
332:3 and sleep with me in *TSIa*] with me into *A1*
332:4 stable." *A1*] ~:" *TSIa* ~?" *E1*
332:8 it. The ... *really* wants *TSIa*] *Om. A1*
332:12 to *TSIa*, *E1*] [...] *TSIb*
332:18 feelings." *A1*, *E1*] ~" *TSIa* ~:" *TSIaC*
332:20 feeling *TSIa*] feelings *TSIaC*
332:21 feelings." *A1*, *E1*] ~:" *TSIa*
333:9 come-and-go *TSIa*] come-an-go *E1*
333:12 fierce *TSIa*] ~, *E1*
333:18 Anyhow *TSIa*] ~, *E1*
333:21 camp. Back *TSIa*] ~, back *E1*
333:25 from her womb *TSIa*] *Om. A1*
333:29 old *TSIa*] Old *A1*, *E1*
333:31 old *TSIa*] Old *A1*, *E1*
333:31 sleep *TSIa*] be *A1*
333:31 Jack, in ... the horses. *TSIa*] Jack. *A1*
333:35 she too *TSIa*] ~, ~, *E1*
334:2 Trot Trot Back Again. *Ed.*] The Last Ride Together. *MS* *The Last Ride Together. TSIa* TROT TROT BACK AGAIN. *TSIaR* TROT TROT BACK AGAIN. *TSIaC* TROT, TROT BACK AGAIN *A1* TROT, TROT, BACK AGAIN *E1*
334:5 settlements;] ~, *E1*
334:6 pale blue] pale-blue *A1*
334:7 sea-level: *TSIa*] sea-/ level: *MS* sea-/ level, *A1*
334:8 I know ... cautious enough.] *Om. TSIa*
334:16 old *MS*, *TSIaC*] Old *TSIa*, *A1*
334:18 Even Monica.] *Om. TSIa*
334:20 on] upon *TSIa*
334:21 should] ought to *TSIa*
334:23 her,] ~ *TSIa*
334:29 so,] ~ *TSIa*
334:30 destroyed,] ~ *TSIa*
334:32 old *MS*, *TSIaC*] Old *TSIa*, *A1*
334:34 Easu,] ~ *TSIa*
334:35 Monica] ~, *TSIa*
335:2 feels] ~, *E1*
335:4 me,] ~ *TSIa*
335:9 would do ... am, they] *Om. TSIa*
335:11 *ought*] ought *TSIa*
335:13 them. Even ... away to] *Om. TSIa*
335:17 face,] ~ *TSIa*
335:20 hair's-breadth *Ed.*] hairs-breadth *MS* hair's breadth *TSIa*
335:23 *all*] all *TSIa*
335:24 me-as-I-am] me as I am *TSIa*
335:26 Because] ~, *E1*
335:29 time,] ~ *TSIa*
335:29 extremely] exceedingly *TSIa*
335:31 and that ... the line,] *Om. TSIa*
335:32 old *MS*, *TSIaC*] Old *TSIa*, *A1*
335:34 sleep with ... a sin,] sin with me *A1*
335:35 shouldn't but ... knees and begged her ... help myself, *TSIbR*] shouldn't do, *MS* shouldn't do, but ... knees and asked for it, unable to help myself, *TSIaR* shouldn't, but ... help myself, *E1*
335:38 business, and ... knees; and *TSIaR*] business. And *MS* business, and *TSIa* business, and ... knees, and *E1*
335:40 wives, and *TSIaR*] wives *MS*
335:40 *know*] know *TSIa*
336:2 *I*] I *TSIa*
336:5 their judgment] them *TSIa*
336:7 rattle-snake] rattlesnake *A1*
336:9 vipers out of a hole *TSIbR*, *A1*] a cobra-snake *MS* a viper out of a hole *TSIaR*
336:12 as] as to *TSIa*
336:12 a] the *TSIa*
336:16 rights] ~, *E1*
336:17 unsheathe *Ed.*] unsheath *MS*
336:22 snake-pits] snake pits *TSIa* snake-/ pits *A1*
336:23 snakes. And] ~, and *TSIa*
336:24 now,] *Om. TSIa*

336:25 lions' den *Ed.*] lions den *MS* den of lions *TSIa*
336:29 the old] old *TSIa*
336:29 Rodrigo, *TSIaR*] ~ *MS*, *TSIb*
336:29 his genitals] him *A1*
336:31 snake-pit *MS*, *TSIaC*] snake pit *TSIa*
336:31 into *TSIaR*] in *MS*
336:33 I *TSIaR*] But I *MS*, *TSIb*
336:34 to me she is] she is to me *TSIa*
336:36 my genitals,] my genitals *TSIa* me *A1*
337:2 for me as I am. And] and *TSIa*
337:5 last] least *TSIa*
337:12 Him *TSIaR*] him *MS*
337:14 God] the Lord *TSIa*
337:15 or ever] or even *TSIa*
337:18 reach] the reach *TSIa*
337:26 old] *Om. TSIa*
337:26 North-West *Ed.*] North-west *MS* North *TSIa*
337:29 later] late *TSIa*
337:30 Lennie] ~, *E1*
337:32 fearless . . . world *TSIaR*] brave and loyal *MS*
337:33 cattle] ~, *TSIa*
337:34 with . . . for] for . . . with *TSIa*
337:34 world *TSIaR*] land *MS*
337:35 North-West *TSIaC*, *E1*] North-west *MS*
337:36 sensual . . . black *TSIaR*] faithfulness, and the pride and *MS*
337:37 call *TSIaR*] duty *MS*
337:38 death on] ~, ~ *TSIa*
337:39 a lustrous] the lustrous *TSIa* lustrous *TSIaR*
337:40 the other *TSIbR*] my great *MS* the dark *TSIaR*
338:1 me *TSIaR*] us *MS*
338:2 quenched,] ~ *TSIa*
338:4 judge *MS*, *TSIaR*] ~. *TSIa*, *TSIb* ~, *E1*
338:6 And] ~, *E1*
338:7 as] like *TSIa*
338:8 in] of *TSIa*
339:12 good-humored *MS*, *A1*] good-humoured *TSIa*
339:14 For] ~, *E1*
339:18 life,] ~ *E1*
339:19 way,] ~ *E1*
339:23 centre,] ~ *E1*
340:4 alone,] ~ *E1*
340:6 company,] ~ *E1*
340:10 amiable *TSIaC*, *TSIbR*] aimiable *MS* *see note on* 340:31
340:23 amiable *TSIaC*, *TSIbR*] aimiable *MS*
340:26 amiability *TSIaC*, *TSIbR*] aimiability *MS*
340:27 combatted] combated *A1*
340:30 amiably-disposed *TSIaC*, *E1*] aimiably-disposed *MS*, *TSIbC* aimiably disposed *TSIa* amiably disposed *A1*
340:32 bosom friends] bosom-friends *TSIaC*
341:3 *them*] them *E1*
341:18 down-stream] down stream *A1* downstream *E1*
341:22 amiability *TSIaC*, *E1*] aimiability *MS*
341:22 for ever *Ed.*] forever *MS*
341:24 amiabilities *TSIaC*, *E1*] aimiabilities *MS*
341:34 own] *Om. TSIa*
342:8 eating,] ~ *E1*
342:9 off,] ~ *TSIa*
342:32 thunder-storm] thunderstorm *A1*
342:40 landlord: "Take] ~: *P* "Take *E1*
343:15 thunderbolt] ~, *A1*, *E1*
343:26 said] ~, *E1*
343:30 not!", *Ed.*] ~!," *MS* ~!" *TSIa* ~?" *A1*
344:3 quiet] quaint *TSIa*
344:10 laughed. *P* She *TSIaC*] ~./ She *MS*
344:21 Mary'?", *Ed.*] ~',?" *MS* ~'?" *TSIa*
344:27 do] ~, *E1*
344:30 England.] ~? *A1*, *E1*
344:32 North-West *TSIaC*, *E1*] North-west *MS*
345:6 North-West *TSIaC*, *E1*] North-west *MS*

345:15 wary *A1*, *E1*] self-sufficient *MS*
345:22 And I think] ~, ~ ~, *E1*
346:15 think,] ~ *TSIa*
346:16 now—"] ~"— *E1*
346:18 it.] ~? *E1*
346:25 *very*] very *TSIa*
347:1 odd,] ~ *TSIa*
347:2 don't,] ~ *A1*
347:5 compunction,] ~ *E1*
347:14 North-West *TSIaC*, *E1*] North-west *MS*
347:23 *contretemps*!] ~.' *TSIa* ~, *A1*, *E1*
347:34 Goodbye *MS*, *A1*] Good bye *TSIa* Good-bye, *E1*
347:37 a] *Om. TSIa*
347:39 pale blue] pale-blue *A1*
347:40 lost.] lost./THE END *A1*

Note on Miss M. L. Skinner

MS = Autograph manuscript
373:15 *The Boy Ed.*] The Boy *MS*
373:35 general's *Ed.*] Generals *MS*
373:36 W. A. *Ed.*] W.A. *MS*

Preface to *Black Swans*

MS = Autograph manuscript (Roberts E49.5)
E1 = *Phoenix II*
377:34 criticising] criticizing *E1*
377:38 shocking," *E1*] ~;" *MS*
378:16 realise] realize *E1*
378:28 evasion] evasions *E1*
378:29 Evasion] Evasions *E1*
378:31 girl, and] girl, *E1*
378:32 Peter,] ~ *E1*
378:33 then] there *E1*
378:36 terra-firma] terra firma *E1*
378:39 Fremantle] Tremanitlo *E1*
379:8 Mr. *E1*] ~ *MS*
379:11 realised] realized *E1*
379:12 Skinner's,] ~ *E1*
379:20 old] Old *E1*

Of the compound words which are hyphenated at the end of a line in this edition, only the following hyphenated forms should be retained in quotation:

8:27 sand-hills
15:1 self-conscious
22:30 sailing-vessel
28:14 four-poster
40:14 manor-house
40:26 window-doors
41:29 Twenty-eight
41:31 black-and-white
42:29 good-for-nothings
86:19 prize-fightin'
86:30 street-arab
104:9 tucker's-worth
110:15 chinaman's-hat
113:5 red-faced
118:2 skin-hunter
121:17 blood-knowledge
123:2 self-assertion
128:7 giddy-go-rounding
140:37 button-sewing
152:8 shirt-sleeves
153:1 brother-in-laws
157:17 reach-me-downs
158:21 ha-ha-ha-ha
158:22 ha-ha-ha-ha-ha-ha-ha
173:12 grey-headed
173:20 grey-headed
196:10 ...-went-when-...
199:39 Grand-dad
204:6 good-natured
205:40 bell-bottom
206:35 black-eyed
207:1 floor-space
209:40 pack-horse
226:9 hail-fellow-well-met
228:4 eucalyptus-smelling
229:24 fellow-passengers

232:10 mission-stations
232:11 mining-camps
246:14 self-consciously
248:23 black-and-white
253:37 ball-room
261:4 grand-daughter
267:1 half-crowns
308:12 aristocrats-to-the-bone
314:14 hair's-breadth
314:26 half-haughty
315:5 Queen-Victoria-statue
321:23 warm-hearted
325:8 cross-bones
340:30 amiably-disposed
346:38 mis-educated
347:11 border-line
378:33 ...-castaway-Swiss-...
378:36 terra-firma

Pounds, shillings and pence

British currency was in circulation in Western Australia in the 1880s. Before decimalisation in 1971, the pound sterling (£) was the equivalent of 20 shillings (20/- or 20s). The shilling was the equivalent of 12 pence (12d).

A price could therefore have three elements: pounds, shillings and pence (£., s., d.). (The apparently anomalous d. is an abbreviation of the Latin *denarius*; but the other two terms were also originally Latin; the pound was *Libra*; the shilling *solidus*.) Such a price might be written as £1. 2s. 6d. or £1/2/6; which was spoken as 'one pound two-and-six', or 'twenty-two and six'.

Prices below a pound were written as (for instance) 19s. 6d. or 19/6, and spoken as 'nineteen and six'. Prices up to £5 were sometimes spoken in terms of shillings: so 'ninety-nine and six' was £4/19/6.

The penny was divided into two half-pence and further into four farthings, but the farthing had minimal value and was mainly a tradesman's device for indicating a price fractionally below a shilling or a pound. So 19/11¾ (nineteen and elevenpence three farthings) produced a farthing's change from a pound, this change often given as a tiny item of trade, such as a packet of pins.

The guinea was £1/1/– (one pound, one shilling) and was a professional man's unit for fees. A doctor would charge in guineas (so £5/5/– = 5 gns). Half a guinea was 10s. 6d. or 10/6 (ten and six).

The coins used were originally of silver (later cupro-nickel) and copper, though gold coins for £1 (sovereign) and 10s. (half-sovereign) were still in use in Lawrence's time. The largest silver coin in common use was the half-crown (two shillings and sixpence, or 2/6); but the novel refers to a crown (a silver coin) which was five shillings. A two-shilling piece was called a florin. Shillings, sixpences and (in Lawrence's time) threepences were the smaller sizes. The copper coins were pennies, half-pence (ha'penny) and farthings. ('Ha'porth' meant a half-pence-worth.)

Common slang terms for money were 'quid' for pound, 'half a crown', 'two bob' for a florin, 'bob' for a shilling, 'tanner' for sixpence, 'threepenny-bit', 'copper' for a penny or half-penny. Australian slang shared some of these, and others are used in the novel: 'dollar' (five shillings), 'fiver' (five pounds), 'pony' (twenty-five pounds).